ETHICS & VALUES
BASIC READINGS IN THEORY AND PRACTICE

The Philosophy Department of Utah Valley State College

USED

Managing Editor, David Keller

Philosophy Department of Utah Valley State College

Pearson
Custom
Publishing

Cover Art: "Death of Socrates," 1786, by Jacques-Louis David.
Courtesy of the Metropolitan Museum of Art, New York, NY.

Printed in the United States of America

10 9 8 7 6 5 4 3 2 1

Please visit our web site at www.pearsoncustom.com

ISBN 0–536–63283–9

BA 993167

PEARSON CUSTOM PUBLISHING
75 Arlington Street, Suite 300, Boston, MA 02116
A Pearson Education Company

Copyright Acknowledgments

Dedicated to Our Students
Past, Present, and Future

CONTENTS

II   *Part Two: Ethics in Practice*

Wealth, Poverty, and Social Injustice

Abortion

(From *Introduction to Ethics: Personal and Social Responsibility in a Diverse World*. Edited by Gary Percesepe. Englewood Cliffs, New Jersey: Prentice Hall, 1995, 528–530.)

Acknowledgments

The completion of this reader resulted from a concerted team effort of the Department of Philosophy at Utah Valley State College. Kudos to Sharon Staples for having the idea, and David Keller for directing the project. Elaine Englehardt and David Keller wrote the Preface. Editors included Brian Birch, Jeffrey Bulger, Elaine Englehardt, David Keller, Karen Mizell, and Sharon Staples. Also thanks to Barbara Sherry at Prentice-Hall Publishing, Mary Brown, Jeanille Gooch, Larry Harper, Eberhard Lehnardt, Vicki Ridgway, Joe Wixom, and Joan Richan. We'll miss you!

Preface

This book arose out of a specific set of circumstances. The Philosophy faculty at Utah Valley State College faced the challenge of protecting and promoting the academic freedom of each individual instructor, while at the same time ensuring coherence, unity and rigor in the numerous sections of the core Ethics and Values course, which is integral to UVSC's interdisciplinary mission of applying ethics across the curriculum. The Ethics and Values course fosters this mission by instructing students in both the theoretical and practical aspects of ethics. Students study basic philosophical ethics, and apply these theories to contemporary moral dilemmas.

Ethics and Values: Basic Readings in Theory and Practice was designed to meet the challenges of the Ethics and Values course in particular, and UVSC's interdisciplinary mission in general. *Ethics and Values: Basic Readings* offers a solid grounding in Western (Occidental) ethical theory, as well as seminal discussions of contemporary controversial moral topics. This combination of readings is designed to provide an in-depth survey of ethics, and to help students evaluate the numerous moral complications of everyday life.

The Ethics and Values course and reader are aimed at reflecting several national trends:

- the study of ethics
- an interdisciplinary approach
- emphasis on student writing
- self-confrontation
- critical thinking

The study of ethics is timely. Technology and the complexities of modern life have precipitated moral dilemmas that humankind has never before confronted—complexities that are only likely to increase. It is important to have a forum to make public the many aspects of various moral issues, and consequently be exposed to a wide variety of value-systems, assumptions, and worldviews. Well-educated people should know the classical works in ethics and understand the various approaches to current moral dilemmas.

Understanding and appreciating a subject increases as one struggles to express thoughts in written form. Written communication is fundamental to all course work, and especially in a course on ethics and values. In analyzing and expressing personal viewpoints on involved ethical issues, you will not only gain a better grasp of the issues themselves, but also a better awareness of your personal beliefs as well as the moral outlook of others.

The ethical theories presented in this reader are all foundational to the Western intellectual tradition. Yet the theories—and the worldviews they are tacitly founded on—will be found to be in conflict with each other! Critical thinking and analysis should be applied as you work through the readings. Why does one author or philosopher appeal to you more than another? Does one ethical system seem to fit better with your own personal ethical system? Are your beliefs and feelings reflective of your own introspection, or are they reflective of your family, community, or culture? Can you publicly justify your moral positions? A person trained in critical thinking will not only think carefully, but also will have the tools to base one's actions on carefully-crafted moral precepts or guidelines. The Ethics and Values course and text will challenge each student to examine and reexamine deeply-held moral beliefs, as well as one's place in the world. This is how we become good citizens.

Note to Instructors: Every instructor of an introductory course faces the quandary of presenting the subject historically or thematically; either the subject-matter can be studied in chronological order, or studied by any one of a variety of themes.

Although Part 1, Ethics in Theory, is organized chronologically (according to the birth date of the author), *Ethics and Values: Basic Readings* can be taught from by either method depending on the unique goals of the instructor and students. For example, as an alternative to the historical approach, the instructor may present the theories in terms of categories and dichotomies, such as relativism/objectivism, character ethics/rule ethics, naturalism/ supernaturalism, egoism/anti-egoism, and so forth. Some heuristic possibilities are as follows (authors in brackets are supplemental):

Relativism—Thrasymachus (in the *Republic*), Hobbes, Hume, Nietzsche, [Russell], Ayer, [Sartre], [Foucault]

Objectivism—Plato, Aristotle, Augustine, Aquinas, Kant, Mill, [Rachels]

Egoism—Cicero, Hobbes, Nietzsche

Anti-Egoism—Plato, Augustine, Butler

Hedonism—Cicero, Hobbes, [Bentham], Mill

Supernaturalist Ethics—Plato, Augustine, Aquinas, [Malebranche], Henry

Christian Ethics—Augustine, Aquinas, Henry, Kierkegaard

Existentialism—Kierkegaard, Nietzsche, [Sartre], [Camus]

Naturalist (Materialist) Ethics—Aristotle, Cicero, Marcus Aurelius, Hobbes, Hume, Mill, Marx, Nietzsche, Russell, Ayer, Sartre

Character (Virtue) Ethics—Plato, Aristotle, Cicero, Marcus Aurelius, Augustine, Hume, Nietzsche, [Sartre], [Foucault]

Rule Ethics—[Bentham], Kant, Mill, Ross

Justice—Plato, Aristotle, Augustine, Aquinas, Hobbes, Hume, Kant, Mill, [Rawls]

Social Contract Theory—Hobbes, [Rousseau], [Locke], [Rawls]

Utilitarianism—[Bentham], Mill, [Sidgwick]

Emotivism—Hume, [Russell], Ayer

Gender Ethics—Kant, Mill, [Kohlberg], [Foucault], Gilligan, Friedman

Sociobiology—Hume, [Darwin], [Leopold], [Wilson]

The emphasis on primary texts in Part I makes supplemental ethics texts ideal complements to *Ethics and Values: Basic Readings*. Secondary sources can be gleaned from periodicals or book-length exegeses like William Frankena's classic *Ethics*, James Rachels' useful *The Elements of Moral Philosophy*, or Alasdair Mcintyre's erudite *A Short History of Ethics*, to name a few. The selection of readings covers basic moral theory and application, yet allows for a wide latitude of pedagogical style and technique.

Part One

ETHICS IN THEORY

Plato, *The Republic*, H. Spens, D.D. (trans.), 1906

Justice of the Soul and State
Plato

BOOK I

Characters:

Socrates (first person)

Thrasymachus

. . . This, said he, is the wisdom of Socrates: unwilling himself to teach, he goes about learning from others, and gives no thanks for it.

That indeed I learn from others, said I, Thrasymachus, is true; but in saying that I do not give thanks for it you are mistaken. I pay as much as I am able; and I am only able to commend them, for money I have not. And how readily I do this, when any one appears to me to speak well, you shall perfectly know this moment, when you make an answer: for I imagine you are to speak well.

Hear, then, said he, for I say that what is just is nothing else but the advantage of the more powerful. But why do not you commend? You are unwilling.

Let me learn first, said I, what you say, for as yet I do not understand it. The advantage of the more powerful, you say, is what is just. What at all is this you say now, Thrasymachus? For you certainly do not mean such a thing as this: If Polydamus, the wrestler, be more powerful than we, and if beef be beneficial for his body, that this food is likewise both just and advantageous for us who are weaker than he.

You are most impudent, Socrates, and lay hold of my speech on that side where you may do it the greatest hurt.

By no means, most excellent Thrasymachus, said I: but tell more plainly what is your meaning.

Do not you then know, said he, that with reference to states, some are tyrannical, others democratical, and others aristocratical?

Why are they not?

And is not the governing part in each state the more powerful?

Certainly.

And every government makes laws for its own advantage: a democracy, democratic laws; a tyranny, tyrannic; and others the same way. And when they have made them, they give out that to be just for the governed which is advantageous for themselves; and they punish the transgressor of this as one acting contrary both to law and justice. This, then, most excellent Socrates, is what I say, that, in all states, what is just and what is advantageous for the established government are the same; it hath the power. So that it appears to him who reasons rightly that, in all cases, what is the advantage of the more powerful, the same is just.

Now I have learned, said I, what you say; but whether it be true or not, I shall endeavour to learn. What is advantageous, then, Thrasymachus, you yourself have affirmed to be likewise just, though you forbid me to give this answer; but, indeed, you have added to it that of the more powerful.

Probably, said he, but a small addition.

It is not yet manifest whether it is small or great; but it is manifest that this is to be considered, whether you speak the truth, since I too acknowledge that what is just is somewhat that is advantageous: but you add to it, and say that it is that of the more powerful. This I do not know, but it is to be considered.

Consider then, said he.

That, said I, shall be done. And, tell me, do not you say that it is just to obey governours?

I say so.

Whether are the governours in the several states infallible, or are they capable of erring?

Certainly, said he, they are liable to err.

Do they not, then, when they attempt to make laws, make some of them right, and some of them not right?

I imagine so.

To make them right is it not to make them advantageous for themselves; and to make them not right, disadvantageous? Or what is it you mean?

Entirely so.

And what they enact is to be observed by the governed, and this is what is just?

Why not?

It is, then, according to your reasoning, not only just to do what is advantageous for the more powerful, but also to do the contrary, what is not advantageous.

What do you say, reply'd he?

The same, I imagine, that you say yourself. But let us consider better. Have we not acknowledged that governours, in enjoining the governed to do certain things, may sometimes mistake what is best for themselves; and that what the governours enjoin is just for the governed to do? Have not these things been acknowledged?

I think so, said he.

Think, also, then, said I, that you have acknowledged that it is just to do what is disadvantageous to governours and the more powerful, since governours unwillingly enjoin what is ill for themselves, and you say that it is just for the others to do what these enjoin. Must it not then, most wise Thrasymachus, necessarily happen that, by this means, it may be just to do the contrary of what you say? For that which is the disadvantage of the more powerful is sometimes enjoined the inferiors to do? . . .

You must thus consider it, most simple Socrates, that, on all occasions, the just man gets less than the unjust. First, in co-partnerships with one another, where the one joins in company with the other, you never can find, on the dissolving of the company, the just man gets more than the unjust, but less. Then, in civil affairs, where there are taxes to be paid from equal substance, the just man pays more, the other less; but when there is any thing to be gained, the one gains nothing, the other a great deal, for when each of them governs in any public magistracy, this, if no other loss, befals the just man, that his domestic affairs, at least, are in worse situation through his neglect, and that he gains nothing from the public, because he is just; add to this, that he comes to be hated by his domestics and acquaintance, when at no time he will serve them beyond what is just. But all these things are quite otherwise with the unjust, such an one, I mean, as I now mentioned, one who has it greatly in his power to become rich. Consider him, then, if you would judge, how much more it is for his private advantage to be unjust than just, and you will most easily understand it if you come to the most finished injustice, such as renders the unjust man most happy, but the injured, and those who are unwilling to do injustice, most wretched; and that is tyranny, which takes away the goods of others, both by secret fraud and by open violence, both things sacred and holy, both private and public, and these not by degrees, but all at once. In all particular cases of such crimes, when one committing injustice is not concealed, he is punished, and suffers the greatest ignominy; for according to the several kinds of the wickedness they commit, they are called sacrilegious, robbers, housebreakers, pilferers, thieves. But when any one, besides these thefts of the substance of his citizens, shall steal and enslave the citizens themselves, instead of those ugly names he is called happy and blest, not by his citizens alone, but likewise by others, as many as are informed that he hath committed the most consummate wickedness. For such as revile wickedness revile it not because they are afraid of doing, but because they are afraid of suffering, unjust things. And thus, Socrates, injustice, when in sufficient measure, is both more powerful, more free, and hath more absolute command than justice: and (as I said at the beginning) the advantage of the more powerful is justice; but injustice is the profit and advantage of one's self. . . .

Book IV

Characters:

Socrates (first person)

Glauco

I fancy, Glauco, we shall say that a man is just in the same way as we said a city was so?

This likewise is quite necessary.

But have we not somehow forgot this, that the city was just, when every one of the three species in it did each its own work?

We do not appear to me, said he, to have forgot it.

We must remember likewise, that each one of us will be just, and do his own work, when he doth his own affairs within himself.

We must, said he, carefully remember it.

Is it not then proper that the rational part should govern, as it is wise, and hath the care of the whole soul? and that the irascible part should be obedient and an auxiliary of the other?

Certainly.

Shall not then the mixture, as we observed, of music and exercise make these two harmonious, raising and nourishing the one with worthy reasonings and learning, and unbending the other, soothing and sweetening it by harmony and measure?

Most perfectly, said he.

And when those two are in this manner nourished, and have been truly taught and instructed in their own affairs, let them be set over the concupiscible part, which in every one is the greater part of the soul, and in its nature most insatiably desirous of being gratified: they are to take care of this part, lest being filled with these bodily pleasures, as they are called, it become great and vigorous, and do not its own work, but attempt to enslave and rule over those it ought not, and overturn the whole life of all in general.

Entirely so, said he.

And might he not, said I, by this principle guard likewise in the best manner against enemies from without, by its influence both over the whole soul and body likewise, the one deliberating, and the other fighting in obedience to its leader, and executing with fortitude the things deliberated.

It is so.

And I imagine that we call one brave when, through all the pains and pleasures of life, the irascible part preserves the opinion dictated by reason concerning what is terrible and what is not.

Right, said he.

And we call him wise, from that small part which governs in him, and dictates these things, having in it the knowledge of what is advantageous for each one, and for the whole community of the three themselves.

Perfectly so.

But what, do we not call him temperate, moreover, from the friendship and harmony of these very things, when the governing and governed agree in one, that reason ought to govern, and when they do not raise sedition?

Temperance, said he, is no other than this, both as to the city and the individual.

But as we have often said, he shall be just by these things and in this manner.

It is quite necessary.

What then, said I, hath any thing blunted us, that we should fancy justice to be anything else than what it hath appeared to be in a city?

Nothing appears to me at least, said he, to have done it.

But in this manner, let us by all means confirm ourselves, if there yet remains any doubt in the soul that can be an objection to this principle, by bringing the man into difficult circumstances.

As what?

Such as this: if we were obliged to declare concerning such a city, and concerning a man born and educated conformably to it, whether we thought such a one, when entrusted with gold or silver, would embezzle it, do you imagine that anyone would think such a one would do it sooner than those who are not of such a kind?

No one, said he.

Will not such a one then be free of sacrileges, thefts, treacheries, against companions in private, or the city in public?

He will be free.

Nor will he ever, in any shape, be faithless, either as to his oaths or other declarations?

How can he?

Adulteries, and neglect of parents, impiety against the Gods, will belong to every one else sooner than to such a one.

They will belong to every one else truly, said he.

And is not this the cause of all these things, that of all within him, each one thing doth its own work as to governing and being governed?

This is it, and nothing else.

Do you desire justice to be any thing else but such a power as produces such men and cities?

Not I truly, said he, for my part.

Our dream, then, which we conjectured is at last accomplished: that when we first began to build our city, we seemed by some God's assistance to have got to a beginning and pattern of justice.

Entirely so.

And that, Glauco, was a certain image of justice, according to which it behoved the man who was fitted by nature for the office of a shoemaker to perform properly that office, and to do nothing else, and he who is a carpenter to perform that office, and all others in the same way.

It appears so.

And of such a kind truly was justice, as it appeared to us, I do not mean as to external action, but concerning that which is really internal, relating to the man himself and those things which are properly his own; not allowing any principle in himself to attempt to do what belongs to others, nor the principles to be pragmatical, engaging in one another's affairs; but having well established his own proper affairs, and holding the government of himself, adorning himself, and becoming his own friend, and attuning those three principles in the most natural manner, as three musical strings, base, tenor, and treble, or whatever others may chance to intervene—to combine all these together, and become of many an entire one, temperate and attuned, and in that manner to perform whatever is—done either in the way of acquiring wealth, or concerning the management of the body, or any public affair or private bargain; and in all these cases to account and call that action just and handsome which always sustains and promotes this habit; and to call the knowledge which presides over this action, wisdom, but to call that an unjust action which dissolveth this habit, and the opinion which presides over this folly.

You say perfectly true, Socrates, said he.

Be it so, said I. If then we should say that we have found out a just man and city, and what justice is in them, I don't imagine we should seem to be altogether telling a lye.

No truly, said he.

May we say so?

We may say it.

Be it so, said I. But we were next, I think, to consider injustice.

That is plain.

Must it not then be some sedition among the three principles, some pragmaticalness and intermeddling in things foreign to their proper business, and an insurrection of some one principle against the whole soul, to govern in it when it does not belong to it, but which is of such a nature, as what really ought to be in subjection to the governing principle? I imagine then we shall call their tumult and mistake by such names as these, injustice, intemperance, cowardice and folly, and, in general, all vice.

These things, said he, are quite so.

To do injustice then, said I, and to be injurious, and likewise to do justly, all these must be very manifest if, to wit, injustice and justice are so.

As how?

Because they are no way different from what is salutary or noxious: as these are in the body, so are the others in the soul.

How? said he.

Such things as are healthy constitute health, and such as are noxious produce disease.

Yes.

And must not the doing justly produce justice, and doing unjustly produce injustice?

Of necessity . . .

BOOK IX

Let us not then be perswaded that pure pleasure is the removal of pain, or pain the removal of pleasure.

Let us not.

But yet, said I, these which reach the soul, by means of the body, and which are called pleasures, the greatest part of them almost, and the most considerable, are of this species, certain cessations of pain.

They are so.

And are not the pre-conceptions of pleasure and pain, which arise in the mind from the foresight of these things, of the same kind?

Of the same.

Do you know then, said I, what kind they are of, and what they chiefly resemble?

What? said he.

Do you reckon, said I, there is any such thing in nature as this, the above, the below, and the middle?

I do.

Do you imagine then, that any one when he is brought from the below to the middle, imagines any thing else than that he is brought to the above, and when he stands in the middle, and looks down whence he was brought, will he imagine he is any where else but in the above, whilst yet he hath not seen the true above?

Truly, said he, I do not think that such an one will imagine otherwise.

But if he should again, said I, be carried to the below, he would imagine he was carried to the below, and would imagine according to truth.

Why would he not?

Would he not be affected in all these respects, from his not having experience in what is really above, and in the middle, and below?

It is plain.

Should you wonder then that whilst men are inexperienced in the truth, they have unsound opinions about many other things, and that as to pleasure and pain, and what is between these, they are likewise affected in this same manner? So that even when they are brought to what is painful, they imagine truly, and are truly pained; but when from pain they are brought to the middle, they strongly imagine that they are arrived at fulness of pleasure. In the same manner as these who along with the black colour look at the grey, through inexperience of the white, are deceived; so those who consider pain along with a freedom from pain, are deceived through inexperience of pleasure.

Truly, said he, I should not wonder, but much rather if it were not so.

But consider it at least, said I, in this manner. Are not hunger and thirst, and such like, certain emptinesses in the bodily habit?

What else?

And is not ignorance and folly an emptiness in the habit of the soul?

Extremely so.

And is not the one filled when it receiveth food, and the other when it hath intelligence?

Why not?

But which is the more real repletion, that of the less, or that of the more real existence?

It is plain that of the more real.

Which species, then, do you imagine participates most of a more pure substance; whether these which participate of bread and drink, and meat, and all such sort of nourishment; or that species which participates of true opinion, and knowledge, and intelligence, and in general, of all virtue? And judge of it in this manner. That which resides in that which is always alike, and immortal, and true, and is so itself, and ariseth in what is such, does it appear to you to exist more really than that which resides in what is never alike, and mortal, is so itself, and ariseth in what is such?

This, said he, differs much from that which is always alike.

Does then the essence of that which is always alike participate any more of essence than of science?

By no means.

But what with relation to truth?

Nor of this neither.

If it participate less of truth, doth it not likewise do so of essence?

Of necessity.

In general then, do not the species relating to the care of the body participate less of truth and essence than the species relating to the care of the soul?

By far.

And the body less than the soul; do you not think so?

I do.

Is not that which is filled with more real beings, and is itself a more real being, in reality more truly filled than that which is filled with less real beings, and is itself a less real being?

Why not?

If there it be pleasant to be filled with what is suitable to nature, that which is in reality filled, and with more real being, must be made both more really and more truly to enjoy true pleasure; but that which participates of less real being must be less truly and solidly filled, and participateth of a more uncertain and less genuine pleasure.

Most necessarily, said he.

Such then as are unacquainted with wisdom and virtue, and are always conversant in feastings and such like, are carried as it appears to the below, and back again to the middle, and there they wander for life. But never at all, getting beyond this, do they look towards the true above, nor are carried to it, nor are they ever really filled with real being, nor have they ever tasted solid and pure pleasure, but after the manner of brutes looking always downwards, and bowed towards earth and their tables, they live feeding and coupling, and from a lust of these things, kicking and pushing at one another with iron horns and hoofs, they perish through their unsatiableness, as those who are filling with unreal being that which is no real being, nor friendly to themselves.

You pronounce most perfectly, Socrates, as from an oracle, said Glauco, the life of the multitude.

Must they not then, of necessity, be conversant in pleasures mixed with pains, images of the true pleasure, painted over, and coloured by their position beside one another, hence both their pleasures and pains appear vehement, and engender their mad passions in the foolish. Hence also they must fight about these things, as Stesichorus says those at Troy fought about the image of Helen, through ignorance of the true one.

Of necessity, said he, the matter must be something of this kind.

And what as to the irascible part of the soul? Must not other such like things happen wherever any one gratifies it, either in the way of envy through ambition, or in the way of violence through contentiousness, or in the way of anger through moroseness, pursuing after a glut of honour, of conquest, and of anger, both without reason and without intelligence?

Such things as these, said he, must necessarily happen with reference to this part of the mind.

What then, said I, shall we boldly say concerning all the pleasures, both respecting the avaricious and the ambitious part, that such of them as are obedient to intelligence and reason, and along with these follow after and obtain the pleasures to which wisdom points, shall obtain the truest pleasures, as far as it is possible for them to attain true pleasure, and in as much as they follow truth, pleasures which are properly their own, if indeed what is best for every one be most properly his own?

But surely it is most properly, said he, his own at least.

When then the whole soul is obedient to the philosophic part and there is no sedition in it, then every part in other respects does its proper business and is just, and also reaps its own pleasures, and such as are the best and as far as is possible the most true.

Certainly, indeed.

But when any of the others governs, it happens that it neither attains its own pleasures, and it obliges the other parts to pursue a pleasure foreign to them, and not at all true.

It does so, said he.

Do not then the parts which are the most remote from philosophy and reason most especially effectuate such things?

Extremely.

And is not that which is most remote from law and order, likewise most remote from reason?

It plainly is.

And have not the amorous and the tyrannical desires appeared to be most remote from law and order?

Extremely.

And the royal and the moderate ones, the least remote?

Yes.

The tyrant then, I imagine, shall be the most remote from true pleasure, and such as is most properly his own, and the other shall be the least.

Of necessity.

And the tyrant, said I, shall lead a life the most unpleasant, and the king the most pleasant one.

Of great necessity.

Do you know then, said I, how much more unpleasant a life the tyrant leads than the king?

If you tell me, said he.

As there are three pleasures, as it appears, one genuine, and two illegitimate, the Tyrant in carrying the illegitimate to extremity, and flying from law and reason, dwells with slavish pleasure as his life-guards, and how far he is inferior, is not easily to be told, unless it may be done in this manner.

How? said he.

The Tyrant is somehow the third remote from the Oligarchic; for the Democratic was in the middle between them.

Yes.

Does he not then dwell with the third image of pleasure, distant from him with reference to truth, if our former reasonings be true?

Just so.

But the Oligarchic is the third again from the Royal, if we suppose the Aristocratic and the Royal the same.

He is the third.

The Tyrant then, said I, is remote from true pleasure, the third from the third.

It appears so.

A plain surface then, said I, may be the image of tyrannical pleasure, as to the computation of length.

Certainly.

But as to power, and the third augment, it is manifest, by how great a distance it is remote.

It is manifest, said he, to the computer at least.

If now, conversely, one shall say the King is distant from the Tyrant as to truth of pleasure, as much as 729 and 70 are distant from 9, shall he not, on compleating the multiplication, find him leading the more pleasant life, and the Tyrant the more wretched one by this same distance?

You have heaped up, said he, a prodigious account of the difference between these two men, the just and the unjust, with reference to pleasure and pain.

Yet the numbers are true, said I, and corresponding to their lives, if indeed days, and nights, and months, and years, correspond to them.

But these said he, do correspond to them.

If then the good and just man surpasseth so far the evil and unjust man in pleasure, in what a prodigious degree further shall he surpass him in decorum of life, in beauty and in virtue?

In a prodigious degree, truly, said he.

Be it so, said I. Since now we are come to this part of our argument, let us recapitulate what we first said, on account of which we have come hither: and it was somewhere said that it was advantageous to do injustice, if one were compleatly unjust but were reputed just. Was it not so said?

It was indeed.

Now then, said I, let us settle this point, since we have now settled the other with reference to acting justly and unjustly, what power each of these hath in itself.

How? said he.

Let us in our reasoning make a resemblance of the soul, that the man who said those things may know what he said.

What kind of resemblance? said he.

One of those creatures, said I, which are fabled to have been of old, as that of Chimaera, of Scylla, of Cerberus, and many others are spoken of, where many particular natures existed together in one.

They are spoken of indeed, said he.

Form now one figure of a creature, various and many-headed, having all around heads of tame creatures and of wild, and having power in itself of changing all these heads, and of breeding them out of itself.

This is the work, said he, of a curious former; however, as the formation is easier in reasoning than in wax and such like, let it be formed.

Let there be now one other figure of a lyon, and one of a man, but let the first be by far the greatest, and the second be the second in bulk.

These are easy, said he, and they are formed.

Conjoin now these three in one, so as to exist somehow with one another.

They are conjoined, said he.

Form now around them the external appearance of one of them, that of the man, so that to one who is not able to see what is within, but who perceives only the external covering the man may appear one creature.

This is formed around, said he.

Let us now tell him who saith that it is profitable to this man to do injustice, but to do justice is unprofitable, that he saith nothing else than that it is profitable for him to feast the multiform creature, and to make it strong; and likewise the lyon, and what respecteth the lyon, whilst the man he kills with famine, and renders weak, so as to be dragged whichever way either of those drag him, and never accustom the one to live in harmony with the other, nor to make them friends, but to suffer them to be biting one another, and to fight and devour one another.

He [viz. Thrasymachus], said he, who commendeth the doing injustice saith undoubtedly these things.

Plato, *Euthyphro, Apology, Crito, Phaedo*, F.J. Church (trans.), 1948

Discussion of Divine Command Ethics
Plato

Characters:

Socrates (first person)

Euthyphro

Euth. I do not understand you, Socrates.

Socr. I will try to explain myself: we speak of a thing being carried and carrying, and being led and leading, and being seen and seeing; and you understand that all such expressions mean different things, and what the difference is.

Euth. Yes, I think I understand.

Socr. And we talk of a thing being loved, of a thing loving, and the two are different?

Euth. Of course.

Socr. Now tell me, is a thing which is being carried in a state of being carried because it is carried, or for some other reason?

Euth. No, because it is carried.

Socr. And a thing is in a state of being led because it is led, and of being seen because it is seen?

Euth. Certainly.

Socr. Then a thing is not seen because it is in a state of being seen: it is in a state of being seen because it is seen; and a thing is not led because it is in a state of being led: it is in a state of being led because it is led; and a thing is not carried because it is in a state of being carried: it is in a state of being carried because it is carried. Is my meaning clear now, Euthyphro? I mean this: if anything becomes or is affected, it does not become because it is in a state of becoming: it is in a state of becoming because it becomes; and it is not affected because it is in a state of being affected: it is in a state of being affected because it is affected. Do you not agree?

14

Euth. I do.

Socr. Is not that which is being loved in a state either of becoming or of being affected in some way by something?

Euth. Certainly.

Socr. Then the same is true here as in the former cases. A thing is not loved by those who love it because it is in a state of being loved; it is in a state of being loved because they love it.

Euth. Necessarily.

Socr. Well, then, Euthyphro, what do we say about piety? Is it not loved by all the gods, according to your definition?

Euth. Yes.

Socr. Because it is pious, or for some other reason?

Euth. No, because it is pious.

Socr. Then it is loved by the gods because it is pious; it is not pious because it is loved by them?

Euth. It seems so.

Socr. But, then, what is pleasing to the gods is pleasing to them, and is in a state of being loved by them, because they love it?

Euth. Of course.

Socr. Then piety is not what is pleasing to the gods, and what is pleasing to the gods is not pious, as you say, Euthyphro. They are different things.

Euth. And why, Socrates?

Socr. Because we are agreed that the gods love piety because it is pious, and that it is not pious because they love it. Is not this so?

Euth. Yes.

Socr. And that what is pleasing to the gods because they love it, is pleasing to them by reason of this same love, and that they do not love it because it is pleasing to them.

Euth. True.

Socr. Then, my dear Euthyphro, piety and what is pleasing to the gods are different things. If the gods had loved piety because it is pious, they would also have loved what is pleasing to them because it is pleasing to them; but if what is pleasing to them had been pleasing to them because they loved it, then piety, too, would have been piety because they loved it. But now you see that they are opposite things, and wholly different from each other. For the one is of a sort to be loved because it is loved, while the other is loved because it is of a sort to be loved. My question, Euthyphro, was, What is piety? But it turns out that you have not explained to me the essential character of piety; you have been content to mention an effect which belongs to it—namely, that all the gods love it. You have not yet told me what its essential character is. Do not, if you please, keep from me what piety is; begin again and tell me that. Never mind whether the gods love it, or whether it has other effects: we shall not differ on that point. Do your best to make clear to me what is piety and what is impiety.

Euth. But, Socrates, I really don't know how to explain to you what is in my mind. Whatever statement we put forward always somehow moves round in a circle, and will not stay where we put it.

Aristotle, *Nichomachean Ethics*, Martin Oswald (trans.), 1962

Moral Character and the Good Life
Aristotle

BOOK I

1. The good as the aim of action

Every art or applied science and every systematic investigation, and similarly every action and choice, seem to aim at some good; the good, therefore, has been well defined as that at which all things aim. But it is clear that there is a difference in the ends at which they aim: in some cases the activity is the end, in others the end is some product beyond the activity. In cases where the end lies beyond the action the product is naturally superior to the activity.

Since there are many activities, arts, and sciences, the number of ends is correspondingly large: of medicine the end is health, of shipbuilding a vessel, of strategy, victory, and of household management, wealth. In many instances several such pursuits are grouped together under a single capacity: the art of bridle-making, for example, and everything else pertaining to the equipment of a horse are grouped together under horsemanship; horsemanship in turn, along with every other military action, is grouped together under strategy; and other pursuits are grouped together under other capacities. In all these cases the ends of the master sciences are preferable to the ends of the subordinate sciences, since the latter are pursued for the sake of the former. This is true whether the ends of the actions lie in the activities themselves or, as is the case in the disciplines just mentioned, in something beyond the activities.

2. Politics as the master science of the good

Now, if there exists an end in the realm of action which we desire for its own sake, an end which determines all our other desires; if, in other words, we do not make all our choices for the sake of something else—for in this way the process will go on infinitely so that our desire

16

would be futile and pointless—then obviously this end will be the good, that is, the highest good. Will not the knowledge of this good, consequently, be very important to our lives? Would it not better equip us, like archers who have a target to aim at, to hit the proper mark? If so, we must try to comprehend in outline at least what this good is and to which branch of knowledge or to which capacity it belongs.

This good, one should think, belongs to the most sovereign and most comprehensive master science, and politics clearly fits this description. For it determines which sciences ought to exist in states, what kind of sciences each group of citizens must learn, and what degree of proficiency each must attain. We observe further that the most honored capacities, such as strategy, household management, and oratory, are contained in politics. Since this science uses the rest of the sciences, and since, moreover, it legislates what people are to do and what they are not to do, its end seems to embrace the ends of the other sciences. Thus it follows that the end of politics is the good for man. For even if the good is the same for the individual and the state, the good of the state clearly is the greater and more perfect thing to attain and to safeguard. The attainment of the good for one man alone is, to be sure, a source of satisfaction; yet to secure it for a nation and for states is nobler and more divine. In short, these are the aims of our investigation, which is in a sense an investigation of social and political matters.

3. *The limitations of ethics and politics*

Our discussion will be adequate if it achieves clarity within the limits of the subject matter. For precision cannot be expected in the treatment of all subjects alike, any more than it can be expected in all manufactured articles. Problems of what is noble and just, which politics examines, present so much variety and irregularity that some people believe that they exist only by convention and not by nature. The problem of the good, too, presents a similar kind of irregularity, because in many cases good things bring harmful results. There are instances of men ruined by wealth, and others by courage. Therefore, in a discussion of such subjects, which has to start from a basis of this kind, we must be satisfied to indicate the truth with a rough and general sketch: when the subject and the basis of a discussion consist of matters that hold good only as a general rule, but not always, the conclusions reached must be of the same order. The various points that are made must be received in the same spirit. For a well-schooled man is one who searches for that degree of precision in each kind of study which the nature of the subject at hand admits: it is obviously just as foolish to accept arguments of probability from a mathematician as to demand strict demonstrations from an orator.

Each man can judge competently the things he knows, and of these he is a good judge. Accordingly, a good judge in each particular field is one who has been trained in it, and a good judge in general, a man who has received an all-round schooling. For that reason, a young man is not equipped to be a student of politics; for he has no experience in the actions which life demands of him, and these actions form the basis and subject matter of the discussion. Moreover, since he follows his emotions, his study will be pointless and unprofitable, for the end of this kind of study is not knowledge but action. Whether he is young in years or immature in character makes no difference; for his deficiency is not a matter of time but of living and of pursuing all his interests under the influence of his emotions. Knowledge brings no benefit to this kind of person, just as it brings none to the morally weak. But those who regulate their desires and actions by a rational principle will greatly benefit from a knowledge of this subject. So much by way of a preface about the student, the limitations which have to be accepted, and the objective before us.

4. Happiness is the good, but many views are held about it

To resume the discussion: since all knowledge and every choice is directed toward some good, let us discuss what is in our view the aim of politics, i.e., the highest good attainable by action. As far as its name is concerned, most people would probably agree: for both the common run of people and cultivated men call it happiness, and understand by "being happy" the same as "living well" and "doing well." But when it comes to defining what happiness is, they disagree, and the account given by the common run differs from that of the philosophers. The former say it is some clear and obvious good, such as pleasure, wealth, or honor; some say it is one thing and others another, and often the very same person identifies it with different things at different times: when he is sick he thinks it is health, and when he is poor he says it is wealth; and when people are conscious of their own ignorance, they admire those who talk above their heads in accents of greatness. Some thinkers used to believe that there exists over and above these many goods another good, good in itself and by itself, which also is the cause of good in all these things. An examination of all the different opinions would perhaps be a little pointless, and it is sufficient to concentrate on those which are most in evidence or which seem to make some sort of sense.

Nor must we overlook the fact that arguments which proceed from fundamental principles are different from arguments that lead up to them. Plato, too, rightly recognized this as a problem and used to ask whether the discussion was proceeding from or leading up to fundamental principles, just as in a race course there is a difference between running from the judges to the far end of the track and running back again. Now, we must start with the known. But this term has two connotations: "what is known to us" and "what is known" pure and simple. Therefore, we should start perhaps from what is known to us. For that reason, to be a competent student of what is right and just, and of politics generally, one must first have received a proper upbringing in moral conduct. The acceptance of a fact as a fact is the starting point, and if this is sufficiently clear, there will be no further need to ask why it is so. A man with this kind of background has or can easily acquire the foundations from which he must start. But if he neither has nor can acquire them, let him lend an ear to Hesiod's words:

That man is all-best who himself works out every problem. . . .

That man, too, is admirable who follows one who speaks well.

He who cannot see the truth for himself, nor, hearing it from others,

store it away in his mind, that man is utterly useless.

5. Various views on the highest good

But to return to the point from which we digressed. It is not unreasonable that men should derive their concept of the good and of happiness from the lives which they lead. The common run of people and the most vulgar identify it with pleasure, and for that reason are satisfied with a life of enjoyment. For the most notable kinds of life are three: the life just mentioned, the political life, and the contemplative life.

The common run of people, as we saw, betray their utter slavishness in their preference for a life suitable to cattle: but their views seem plausible because many people in high places share the feelings of Sardanapallus. Cultivated and active men, on the other hand, believe the good to be honor, for honor, one might say, is the end of the political life. But this is clearly too superficial an answer: for honor seems to depend on those who confer it rather than on him who receives it, whereas our guess is that the good is a man's own possession which cannot easily be taken away from him. Furthermore, men seem to pursue honor to assure themselves of their own worth; at any rate, they seek to be honored by sensible men and by those who know them, and they want to be honored on the basis of their virtue or excellence. Obviously, then, excellence, as far as they are concerned, is better than honor. One might perhaps even go so far as to consider excellence rather than honor as the end of political life. However, even excellence proves to be imperfect as an end: for a man might possibly possess it while asleep or while being inactive all his life, and while, in addition, undergoing the greatest suffering and misfortune. Nobody would call the life of such a man happy, except for the sake of maintaining an argument. But enough of this: the subject has been sufficiently treated in our publications addressed to a wider audience. In the third place there is the contemplative life, which we shall examine later on. As for the money-maker, his life is led under some kind of constraint: clearly, wealth is not the good which we are trying to find, for it is only useful, i.e., it is a means to something else. Hence one might rather regard the aforementioned objects as ends, since they are valued for their own sake. But even they prove not to be the good, though many words have been wasted to show that they are. Accordingly, we may dismiss them.

BOOK II

1. Moral virtue as the result of habits

Virtue, as we have seen, consists of two kinds, intellectual virtue and moral virtue. Intellectual virtue or excellence owes its origin and development chiefly to teaching, and for that reason requires experience and time. Moral virtue, on the other hand, is formed by habit, *ethos*, and its name, *ēthikē*, is therefore derived, by a slight variation, from *ethos*. This shows, too, that none of the moral virtues is implanted in us by nature, for nothing which exists by nature can be changed by habit. For example, it is impossible for a stone, which has a natural downward movement, to become habituated to moving upward, even if one should try ten thousand times to inculcate the habit by throwing it in the air; nor can fire be made to move downward, nor can the direction of any nature-given tendency be changed by habituation. Thus, the virtues are implanted in us neither by nature nor contrary to nature: we are by nature equipped with the ability to receive them, and habit brings this ability to completion and fulfillment.

Furthermore, of all the qualities with which we are endowed by nature, we are provided with the capacity first, and display the activity afterward. That this is true is shown by the senses: it is not by frequent seeing or frequent hearing that we acquired our senses, but on the contrary we first possess and then use them; we do not acquire them by use. The virtues, on the other hand, we acquire by first having put them into action, and the same is also true of the arts. For the things which we have to learn before we can do them we learn by doing: men become builders by building houses, and harpists by playing the harp. Similarly, we become just by the practice of just actions, self-controlled by exercising self-control, and courageous by performing acts of courage.

This is corroborated by what happens in states. Lawgivers make the citizens good by inculcating (good) habits in them, and this is the aim of every lawgiver; if he does not succeed in doing that, his legislation is a failure. It is in this that a good constitution differs from a bad one.

Moreover, the same causes and the same means that produce any excellence or virtue can also destroy it, and this is also true of every art. It is by playing the harp that men become both good and bad harpists, and correspondingly with builders and all the other craftsmen: a man who builds well will be a good builder, one who builds badly a bad one. For if this were not so, there would be no need for an instructor, but everybody would be born as a good or a bad craftsman. The same holds true of the virtues: in our transactions with other men it is by action that some become just and others unjust, and it is by acting in the face of danger and by developing the habit of feeling fear or confidence that some become brave men and others cowards. The same applies to the appetites and feelings of anger: by reacting in one way or in another to given circumstances some people become self-controlled and gentle, and others self-indulgent and short-tempered. In a word, characteristics develop from corresponding activities. For that reason, we must see to it that our activities are of a certain kind, since any variations in them will be reflected in our characteristics. Hence it is no small matter whether one habit or another is inculcated in us from early childhood; on the contrary, it makes a considerable difference, or, rather, all the difference.

5. Virtue defined: the genus

The next point to consider is the definition of virtue or excellence. As there are three kinds of things found in the soul: (1) emotions, (2) capacities, and (3) characteristics, virtue must be one of these. By "emotions" I mean appetite, anger, fear, confidence, envy, joy, affection, hatred, longing, emulation, pity, and in general anything that is followed by pleasure or pain; by "capacities" I mean that by virtue of which we are said to be affected by these emotions, for example, the capacity which enables us to feel anger, pain, or pity; and by "characteristics" I mean the condition, either good or bad, in which we are, in relation to the emotions: for example, our condition in relation to anger is bad, if our anger is too violent or not violent enough, but if it is moderate, our condition is good; and similarly with our condition in relation to the other emotions.

Now the virtues and vices cannot be emotions, because we are not called good or bad on the basis of our emotions, but on the basis of our virtues and vices. Also, we are neither praised nor blamed for our emotions: a man does not receive praise for being frightened or angry, nor blame for being angry pure and simple, but for being angry in a certain way. Yet we are praised or blamed for our virtues and vices. Furthermore, no choice is involved when we experience anger or fear, while the virtues are some kind of choice or at least involve choice. Moreover, with regard to our emotions we are said to be "moved," but with regard to our virtues and vices we are not said to be "moved" but to be "disposed" in a certain way.

For the same reason, the virtues cannot be capacities, either, for we are neither called good or bad nor praised or blamed simply because we are capable of being affected. Further, our capacities have been given to us by nature, but we do not by nature develop into good or bad men. We have discussed this subject before. Thus, if the virtues are neither emotions nor capacities, the only remaining alternative is that they are characteristics. So much for the genus of virtue.

6. Virtue defined: the differentia

It is not sufficient, however, merely to define virtue in general terms as a characteristic: we must also specify what kind of characteristic it is. It must, then, be remarked that every virtue or excellence (1) renders good the thing itself of which it is the excellence. and (2) causes it to perform its function well. For example, the excellence of the eye makes both the eye and its function good, for good sight is due to the excellence of the eye. Likewise, the excellence of a horse makes it both good as a horse and good at running, at carrying its rider, and at facing the enemy. Now, if this is true of all things, the virtue or excellence of man, too, will be a characteristic which makes him a good man, and which causes him to perform his own function well. To some extent we have already stated how this will be true; the rest will become clear if we study what the nature of virtue is.

Of every continuous entity that is divisible into parts it is possible to take the larger, the smaller, or an equal part, and these parts may be larger, smaller, or equal either in relation to the entity itself, or in relation to us. The "equal" part is something median between excess and deficiency. By the median of an entity I understand a point equidistant from both extremes, and this point is one and the same for everybody. By the median relative to us I understand an amount neither too large nor too small, and this is neither one nor the same for everybody. To take an example: if ten is many and two is few, six is taken as the median in relation to the entity, for it exceeds and is exceeded by the same amount, and is thus the median in terms of arithmetical proportion. But the median relative to us cannot be determined in this manner: if ten pounds of food is much for a man to eat and two pounds little, it does not follow that the trainer will prescribe six pounds, for this may in turn be much or little for him to eat; it may be little for Milo and much for someone who has just begun to take up athletics. The same applies to running and wrestling. Thus we see that an expert in any held avoids excess and deficiency, but seeks the median and chooses it—not the median of the object but the median relative to us.

If this, then, is the way in which every science perfects its work, by looking to the median and by bringing its work up to that point—and this is the reason why it is usually said of a successful piece of work that it is impossible to detract from it or to add to it, the implication being that excess and deficiency destroy success while the mean safeguards it (good craftsmen, we say, look toward this standard in the performance of their work)—and if virtue, like nature, is more precise and better than any art, we must conclude that virtue aims at the median. I am referring to moral virtue: for it is moral virtue that is concerned with emotions and actions, and it is in emotions and actions that excess, deficiency, and the median are found. Thus we can experience fear, confidence, desire, anger, pity, and generally any kind of pleasure and pain either too much or too little, and in either case not properly. But to experience all this at the right time, toward the right objects, toward the right people, for the right reason, and in the right manner—that is the median and the best course, the course that is a mark of virtue.

Similarly, excess, deficiency, and the median can also be found in actions. Now virtue is concerned with emotions and actions; and in emotions and actions excess and deficiency miss the mark, whereas the median is praised and constitutes success. But both praise and success are signs of virtue or excellence. Consequently, virtue is a mean in the sense that it aims at the median. This is corroborated by the fact that there are many ways of going wrong, but only one way which is right—for evil belongs to the indeterminate, as the Pythagoreans imagined, but good to the determinate. This, by the way, is also the reason why the one is easy and the other hard: it is easy to miss the target but hard to hit it. Here, then, is an additional proof that excess and deficiency characterize vice, while the mean characterizes virtue: for "bad men have many ways, good men but one."

We may thus conclude that virtue or excellence is a characteristic involving choice, and that it consists in observing the mean relative to us, a mean which is defined by a rational principle, such as a man of practical wisdom would use to determine it. It is the mean by reference to two vices: the one of excess and the other of deficiency. It is, moreover, a mean because some vices exceed and others fall short of what is required in emotion and in action, whereas virtue finds and chooses the median. Hence, in respect of its essence and the definition of its essential nature virtue is a mean, but in regard to goodness and excellence it is an extreme.

Not every action nor every emotion admits of a mean. There are some actions and emotions whose very names connote baseness, e.g., spite, shamelessness, envy; and among actions, adultery, theft, and murder. These and similar emotions and actions imply by their very names that they are bad; it is not their excess nor their deficiency which is called bad. It is, therefore, impossible ever to do right in performing them: to perform them is always to do wrong. In cases of this sort, let us say adultery, rightness and wrongness do not depend on committing it with the right woman at the right time and in the right manner, but the mere fact of committing such action at all is to do wrong. It would be just as absurd to suppose that there is a mean, an excess, and a deficiency in an unjust or a cowardly or a self-indulgent act. For if there were, we would have a mean of excess and a mean of deficiency, and an excess of excess and a deficiency of deficiency. Just as there cannot be an excess and a deficiency of self-control and courage—because the intermediate is, in a sense, an extreme—so there cannot be a mean, excess, and deficiency in their respective opposites: their opposites are wrong regardless of how they are performed; for, in general, there is no such thing as the mean of an excess or a deficiency, or the excess and deficiency of a mean.

7. Examples of the mean in particular virtues

However, this general statement is not enough; we must also show that it fits particular instances. For in a discussion of moral actions, although general statements have a wider range of application, statements on particular points have more truth in them: actions are concerned with particulars and our statements must harmonize with them. Let us now take particular virtues and vices from the following table.

In feelings of fear and confidence courage is the mean. As for the excesses, there is no name that describes a man who exceeds in fearlessness—many virtues and vices have no name; but a man who exceeds in confidence is reckless, and a man who exceeds in fear and is deficient in confidence is cowardly.

In regard to pleasures and pains—not all of them and to a lesser degree in the case of pains—the mean is self-control and the excess self-indulgence. Men deficient in regard to pleasure are not often found, and there is therefore no name for them, but let us call them "insensitive."

8. The relation between the mean and its extremes

There are, then, three kinds of disposition: two are vices (one marked by excess and one by deficiency), and one, virtue, the mean. Now, each of these dispositions is, in a sense, opposed to both the others: the extremes are opposites to the middle as well as to one another, and the middle is opposed to the extremes. Just as an equal amount is larger in relation to a smaller and smaller in relation to a larger amount, so, in the case both of emotions and of actions, the middle characteristics exceed in relation to the deficiencies and are deficient in relation to the excesses. For example, a brave man seems reckless in relation to a coward, but in relation to a reckless man he seems cowardly. Similarly, a self-controlled man seems self-indulgent in relation to an insensitive man and insensitive in relation to a self-indulgent man, and a generous man extravagant in relation to a stingy man and stingy in relation to an extravagant man. This is the reason why people at the extremes each push the man in the middle over to the other extreme: a coward calls a brave man reckless and a reckless man calls a brave man a coward, and similarly with the other qualities.

However, while these three dispositions are thus opposed to one another, the extremes are more opposed to one another than each is to the median; for they are further apart from one another than each is from the median, just as the large is further removed from the small and the small from the large than either one is from the equal. Moreover, there appears to be a certain similarity between some extremes and their median, e.g., recklessness resembles courage and extravagance generosity; but there is a very great dissimilarity between the extremes. But things that are furthest removed from, one another are defined as opposites, and that means that the further things are removed from one another the more opposite they are.

In some cases it is the deficiency and in others the excess that is more opposed to the median. For example, it is not the excess, recklessness, which is more opposed to courage, but the deficiency, cowardice; while in the case of self-control it is not the defect, insensitivity, but the excess, self-indulgence which is more opposite. There are two causes for this. One arises from the nature of the thing itself: when one of the extremes is closer and more similar to the median, we do not treat it but rather the other extreme as the opposite of the median. For instance, since recklessness is believed to be more similar and closer to courage, and cowardice less similar, it is cowardice rather than recklessness which we treat as the opposite of courage. For what is further removed from the middle is regarded as being more opposite. So much for the first cause which arises from the thing itself. The second reason is found in ourselves: the more we are naturally attracted to anything, the more opposed to the median does this thing appear to be. For example, since we are naturally more attracted to pleasure we incline more easily to self-indulgence than to a disciplined kind of life. We describe as more opposed to the mean those things toward which our tendency is stronger; and for that reason the excess, self-indulgence, is more opposed to self-control than is its corresponding deficiency.

9. How to attain the mean

Our discussion has sufficiently established (1) that moral virtue is a mean and in what sense it is a mean; (2) that it is a mean between two vices, one of which is marked by excess and the other by deficiency; and (3) that it is a mean in the sense that it aims at the median in the emotions and in actions. That is why it is a hard task to be good; in every case it is a task to find the median: for instance, not everyone can find the middle of a circle, but only a man who has the proper knowledge. Similarly, anyone can get angry—that is easy—or can give away money or spend it; but to do all this to the right person, to the right extent, at the right time, for the right reason, and in the right way is no longer something easy that anyone can do. It is for this reason that good conduct is rare, praiseworthy, and noble.

The first concern of a man who aims at the median should, therefore, be to avoid the extreme which is more opposed to it, as Calypso advises: "Keep clear your ship of yonder spray and surf." For one of the two extremes is more in error than the other, and since it is extremely difficult to hit the mean, we must, as the saying has it, sail in the second best way and take the lesser evil; and we can best do that in the manner we have described.

Moreover, we must watch the errors which have the greatest attraction for us personally. For the natural inclination of one man differs from that of another, and we each come to recognize our own by observing the pleasure and pain produced in us (by the different extremes). We must then draw ourselves away in the opposite direction, for by pulling away from error we shall reach the middle, as men do when they straighten warped timber. In every case we must be especially on our guard against pleasure and what is pleasant, for when it comes to pleasure we cannot act as unbiased judges. Our attitude toward pleasure should be the same as that of the Trojan elders was toward Helen, and we should repeat on every occasion the words they addressed to her. For if we dismiss pleasure as they dismissed her, we shall make fewer mistakes.

In summary, then, it is by acting in this way that we shall best be able to hit the median. But this is no doubt difficult, especially when particular cases are concerned. For it is not easy to determine in what manner, with what person, on what occasion, and for how long a time one ought to be angry. There are times when we praise those who are deficient in anger and call them gentle, and other times when we praise violently angry persons and call them manly. However, we do not blame a man for slightly deviating from the course of goodness, whether he strays toward excess or toward deficiency, but we do blame him if his deviation is great and cannot pass unnoticed. It is not easy to determine by a formula at what point and for how great a divergence a man deserves blame; but this difficulty is, after all, true of all objects of sense perception: determinations of this kind depend upon particular circumstances, and the decision rests with our moral sense.

This much, at any rate, is clear: that the median characteristic is in all fields the one that deserves praise, and that it sometimes necessary to incline toward the excess and sometimes toward the deficiency. For it is in this way that we will most easily hit upon the median, which is the point of excellence.

Marcus Tullius Cicero, *De Finibus Bonorum et Malorum*, C.D. Yonge (trans.), 1878

Egoism
Cicero

IX.   We are inquiring what is the final and ultimate good . . . This Epicurus places in pleasure, which he argues is the chief good, and that pain is the chief evil; and he proceeds to prove his assertion thus. He says that every animal the moment that it is born seeks for pleasure, and rejoices in it as the chief good; and rejects pain as the chief evil, and wards it off from itself as far as it can; and that it acts in this manner, without having been corrupted by anything, under the promptings of nature herself, who forms this uncorrupt and upright judgment. Therefore, he affirms that there is no need of argument or of discussion as to why pleasure is to be sought for, and pain to be avoided. This he thinks a matter of sense, just as much as that fire is hot, snow white, honey sweet; none of which propositions he thinks require to be confirmed by laboriously sought reasons, but that it is sufficient merely to state them. For that there is a difference between arguments and conclusions arrived at by ratiocination, and ordinary observations and statements:—by the first, secret and obscure principles are explained; by the second, matters which are plain and easy are brought to decision. For since, if you take away sense from a man, there is nothing left to him, it follows of necessity that what is contrary to nature, or what agrees with it, must be left to nature herself to decide. Now what does she perceive, or what does she determine on as her guide to seek or to avoid anything, except pleasure and pain? But there are some of our school who seek to carry out this doctrine with more acuteness, and who will not allow that it is sufficient that it should be decided by sense what is good and what is bad, but who assert that these points can be ascertained by intellect and reason also, and that pleasure is to be sought for on its own account, and that pain also is to be avoided for the same reason.

Therefore, they say that this notion is implanted in our minds naturally and instinctively, as it were; so that we *feel* that one is to be sought for, and the other to be avoided. Others, however, (and this is my own opinion too,) assert that, as many reasons are alleged by many philosophers why pleasure ought not to be reckoned among goods, nor pain among evils, we ought not to rely too much on the goodness of our cause, but that we should use arguments, and discuss the point with precision, and argue, by the help of carefully collected reasons, about pleasure and about pain.

X.   But that you may come to an accurate perception of the source whence all this error originated of those people who attack pleasure and extol pain, I will unfold the whole matter; and I will lay before you the very statements which have been made by that discoverer of the truth, and architect, as it were, of a happy life. For no one either despises, or hates, or avoids pleasure itself merely because it is pleasure, but because great pains overtake those men who do not understand how to pursue pleasure in a reasonable manner. Nor is there any one who loves, or pursues, or wishes to acquire pain because it is pain, but because sometimes such occasions arise that a man attains to some great pleasure through labor and pain. For, to descend to trifles, who of us ever undertakes any laborious exertion of body except in order to gain some advantage by so doing? and who is there who could fairly blame a man who should wish to be in that state of pleasure which no annoyance can interrupt, or one who shuns that pain by which no subsequent pleasure is procured? But we do accuse those men, and think them entirely worthy of the greatest hatred, who, being made effeminate and corrupted by the allurements of present pleasure, are so blinded by passion that they do not foresee what pains and annoyances they will hereafter be subject to; and who are equally guilty with those who, through weakness of mind, that is to say, from eagerness to avoid labor and pain, desert their duty.

And the distinction between these things is quick and easy. For at a time when we are free, when the option of choice is in our own power, and when there is nothing to prevent our being able to do whatever we choose, then every pleasure may be enjoyed, and every pain repelled. But on particular occasions it will often happen, owing either to the obligations of duty or the necessities of business, that pleasures must be declined and annoyances must not be shirked. Therefore the wise man holds to this principle of choice in those matters, that he rejects some pleasures, so as, by the rejection, to obtain others which are greater, and encounters some pains, so as by that means to escape others which are more formidable.

Now, as these are my sentiments, what reason can I have for fearing that I may not be able to accommodate our Torquati to them—men whose examples you just now quoted from memory, with a kind and friendly feeling toward us? However, you have not bribed me by praising my ancestors, nor made me less prompt in replying to you. But I should like to know from you how you interpret their actions? Do you think that they attacked the enemy with such feelings, or that they were so severe to their children and to their own blood as to have no thought of their own advantage, or of what might be useful to themselves? But even wild beasts do not do that, and do not rush about and cause confusion in such a way that we cannot understand what is the object of their motions. And do you think that such illustrious men performed such great actions without a reason? What their reason was I will examine presently; in the meantime I will lay down this rule,—If there was any reason which instigated them to do those things which are undoubtedly splendid exploits, then virtue by herself was not the sole cause of their conduct. One man tore a chain from off his enemy, and at the same time he defended himself from being slain; but he encountered great danger. Yes, but it was before the eyes of the whole army. What did he get by that? Glory, and the affection of his countrymen, which are the surest bulwarks to enable a man to pass his life without fear. He put his son to death by the hand of the executioner. If he did so without any reason, then I should be sorry to be descended from so inhuman and merciless a man. But if his object was to establish military discipline and obedience to command, at the price of his own anguish, and at a time of a most formidable war to restrain his army by the fear of punishment, then he was providing for the safety of his fellow-citizens, which he was well aware embraced his own. And this principle is one of extensive application. For the very point respecting which your whole school, and yourself most especially, who are such a diligent investigator of ancient instances, are in the habit of vaunting yourself and using high-flown language, namely, the mention of brave and illustrious men, and the extolling of their actions, as proceeding not from any regard to advantage, but from pure principles of honor and a love of glory, is entirely upset, when once that rule in the choice of things is established which I mentioned just now,—namely, that pleasures are passed over for the sake of obtaining other greater pleasures, or that pains are encountered with a view to escape greater pains . . . .

XII. . . . Moreover, the beginnings of desiring and avoiding, and indeed altogether of everything which we do, take their rise either in pleasure or pain. And as this is the case, it is plain that everything which is right and laudable has reference to this one object of living with pleasure. And since that is the highest, or extreme, or greatest good, which the Greeks call Τέλος [telos], because it is referred to nothing else itself, but everything is referred to it, we must confess that the highest good is to live agreeably.

XIII. And those who place this in virtue alone, and, being caught by the splendor of a name, do not understand what nature requires, will be delivered from the greatest blunder imaginable if they will listen to Epicurus. For unless those excellent and beautiful virtues which your school talks about produced pleasure, who would think them either praiseworthy or desirable? For as we esteem the skill of physicians not for the sake of the art itself, but from our desire for good health,—and as the skill of the pilot, who has the knowledge how to navigate a vessel well, is praised with reference to its utility, and not to his ability,—so wisdom, which should be considered the art of living, would not be sought after if it effected nothing; but at present it is sought after because it is, as it were, the efficient cause of pleasure, which is a legitimate object of desire and acquisition. And now you understand what pleasure I mean, so that what I say may not be brought into odium from my using an unpopular word. For as the chief annoyances to human life proceed from ignorance of what things are good and what bad, and as by reason of that mistake men are often deprived of the greatest pleasures, and tortured by the most bitter grief of mind, we have need to exercise wisdom, which, by removing groundless alarms and vain desires, and by banishing the rashness of all erroneous opinions, offers herself to us as the surest guide to pleasure. For it is wisdom alone which expels sorrow from our minds, and prevents our shuddering with fear: she is the instructress who enables us to live in tranquillity, by extinguishing in us all vehemence of desire. For desires are insatiable, and ruin not only individuals but entire families, and often overturn the whole state. From desires arise hatred, dissensions, quarrels, seditions, wars. Nor is it only out of doors that these passions vent themselves, nor is it only against others that they run with blind violence; but they are often shut up, as it were, in the mind, and throw that into confusion with their disagreements.

And the consequence of this is, to make life thoroughly wretched; so that the wise man is the only one who, having cut away all vanity and error, and removed it from him, can live contented within the boundaries of nature, without melancholy and without fear. For what diversion can be either more useful or more adapted for human life than that which Epicurus employed? For he laid it down that there were three kinds of desires; the first such as were natural and necessary; the second, such as were natural but not necessary; the third, such as were neither natural nor necessary. And these are all such, that those which are necessary are satisfied without much trouble or expense: even those which are natural and not necessary, do not require a great deal, because nature itself makes the riches, which are sufficient to content it, easy of acquisition and of limited quantity: but as for vain desires, it is impossible to find any limit to, or any moderation in them.

XIV. But if we see that the whole life of man is thrown into disorder by error and ignorance; and that wisdom is the only thing which can relieve us from the way of the passions and the fear of danger, and which can teach us to bear the injuries of fortune itself with moderation, and which shows us all the ways which lead to tranquillity and peace; what reason is there that we should hesitate to say that wisdom is to be sought for the sake of pleasure, and that folly is to be avoided on account of its annoyances? And on the same principle we shall say that even temperance is not to be sought for its own sake, but because it brings peace to the mind, and soothes and tranquilizes them by what I may call a kind of concord. For temperance is that which warns us to follow reason in desiring or avoiding anything. Nor is it sufficient to decide what ought to be done, and what ought not; but we must adhere to what has been decided. But many men, because they are enfeebled and subdued the moment pleasure comes in sight, and so are unable to keep and adhere to the determination they have formed, give themselves up to be bound hand and foot by their lusts, and do not foresee, what will happen to them; and in that way, on account of some pleasure which is trivial and unnecessary, and which might be procured in some other manner, and which they could dispense with without annoyance, incur terrible diseases, and injuries, and disgrace, and are often even involved in the penalties of the legal tribunals of their country.

But these men who wish to enjoy pleasure in such a way that no grief shall ever overtake them in consequence, and who retain their judgment so as never to be overcome by pleasure as to do what they feel ought not to be done; these men, I say, obtain the greatest pleasure by passing pleasure by. They often even endure pain, in order to avoid encountering greater pain hereafter by their shunning it at present. From which consideration it is perceived that intemperance is not to be avoided for its own sake; and that temperance is to be sought for, not because it avoids pleasures, but because it attains to greater ones.

XV. The same principle will be found to hold good with respect to courage. For the discharge of labors and the endurance of pain are neither of them intrinsically tempting; nor is patience, nor diligence, nor watchfulness, nor industry which is so much extolled, nor even courage itself: but we cultivate these habits in order that we may live without care and fear, and may be able, as far as is in our power, to release our minds and bodies from annoyance. For as the whole condition of tranquil life is thrown into confusion by the fear of death, and as it is a miserable thing to yield to pain and to bear it with a humble and imbecile mind; and as on account of that weakness of mind many men have ruined their parents, many men their friends, some their country, and very many indeed have utterly undone themselves; so a vigorous and lofty mind is free from all care and pain, since it despises death, which only places those who encounter it in the same condition as that in which they were before they were born; and it is so prepared for pain that it recollects that the very greatest are terminated by death, and that slight pains have many intervals of rest, and that we can master moderate ones, so as to bear them if they are tolerable, and if not, we can depart with equanimity out of life, just as out of a theater, when it no longer pleases us. By all which considerations it is understood that cowardice and idleness are not blamed, and that courage and patience are not praised, for their own sakes; but that the one line of conduct is rejected as the parent of pain, and the other desired as the author of pleasure.

XVI. Justice remains to be mentioned, that I may not omit any virtue whatever; but nearly the same things may be said respecting that. For, as I have already shown that wisdom, temperance, and fortitude are connected with pleasure in such a way that they cannot possibly be separated or divided from it, so also we must consider that it is the case with justice. Which not only never injures any one; but on the contrary always nourishes something which tranquilizes the mind, partly by its own power and nature, and partly by the hopes that nothing will be wanting of those things which a nature not depraved may fairly derive.

Since rashness and lust and idleness always torture the mind, always make it anxious, and are of a turbulent character, so too, wherever injustice settles in any man's mind, it is turbulent from the mere fact of its existence and presence there; and if it forms any plan, although it executes it even so secretly, still it never believes that what has been done will be concealed for ever. For generally, when wicked men do anything, first of all suspicion overtakes their actions; then the common conversation and report of men; then the prosecutor and the judge; and many even, as was the case when you were consul, have given information against themselves. But if any men appear to themselves to be sufficiently fenced round and protected from the consciousness of men, still they dread the knowledge of the Gods, and think that those very anxieties by which their minds are eaten up night and day, are inflicted upon them by the immortal Gods for the sake of punishment. And how is it possible that wicked actions can ever have as much influence towards alleviating the annoyances of life, as they must have towards increasing them from the consciousness of our actions, and also from the punishments inflicted by the laws and the hatred of the citizens? And yet, in some people, there is no moderation in their passion for money and for honor and for command, or in their lusts and greediness and other desires; which acquisitions, however wickedly made, do not at all diminish, but rather inflame, so that it seems we ought rather to restrain such men than to think that we can teach them better. Therefore sound wisdom invites sensible men to justice, equity, and good faith. And unjust actions are not advantageous even to that man who has no abilities or resources; inasmuch as he cannot easily do what he endeavors to do, nor obtain his objects if he does succeed in his endeavors. And the gifts of fortune and of genius are better suited to liberality; and those who practice this virtue gain themselves goodwill, and affection, which is the most powerful of all things to enable a man to live with tranquility; especially when he has absolutely no motive at all for doing wrong.

For those desires which proceed from nature are easily satisfied without any injustice; but those which are vain ought not to be complied with. For they desire nothing which is really desirable; and there is more disadvantage in the mere fact of injustice than there is advantage in what is acquired by the injustice. Therefore a person would not be right who should pronounce even justice intrinsically desirable for its own sake; but because it brings the greatest amount of what is agreeable. For to be loved and to be dear to others is agreeable because it makes life safer, and pleasure more abundant. Therefore we think dishonesty should be avoided, not only on account of those disadvantages which befall the wicked, but even much more because it never permits the man in whose mind it abides to breathe freely, and never lets him rest.

But if the praise of those identical virtues in which the discourse of all other philosophers so especially exults, cannot find any end unless it be directed towards pleasure, and if pleasure be the only thing which calls and allures us to itself by its own nature; then it cannot be doubtful that that is the highest and greatest of all goods, and that to live happily is nothing else except to live with pleasure.

Marcus Aurelius, *Meditations,* George Long (trans.), 1882

Stoic Ethics: Rationality and Self-Discipline
Marcus Aurelius

Meditation IV

[1.] That which rules within, when it is according to nature, is so affected with respect to the events which happen, that it always easily adapts itself to that which is possible and is presented to it. For it requires no definite material, but it moves towards its purpose, under certain conditions however; and it makes a material for itself out of that which opposes it, as fire lays hold of what falls into it, by which a small light would have been extinguished: but when the fire is strong, it soon appropriates to itself the matter which is heaped on it, and consumes it, and rises higher by means of this very material.

2. Let no act be done without a purpose, not otherwise than according to the perfect principles of art.

3. Men seek retreats for themselves, houses in the country, seashores, and mountains; and thou too art wont to desire such things very much. But this is altogether a mark of the most common sort of men, for it is in thy power whenever thou shalt choose to retire into thyself. For nowhere either with more quiet or more freedom from trouble does a man retire than into his own soul, particularly when he has within him such thoughts that by looking into them he is immediately in perfect tranquillity; and I affirm that tranquillity is nothing else than the good ordering of the mind. Constantly then give to thyself this retreat, and renew thyself; and let thy principles be brief and fundamental, which, as soon as thou shalt recur to them, will be sufficient to cleanse the soul completely, and to send thee back free from all discontent with the things to which thou returnest. For with what art thou discontented? With the badness of men? Recall to thy mind this conclusion, that rational animals exist for one another, and that to endure is a part of justice, and that men do wrong involuntarily; and consider how many already, after mutual enmity, suspicion, hatred, and fighting, have been

stretched dead, reduced to ashes; and be quiet at last.—But perhaps thou art dissatisfied with that which is assigned to thee out of the universe.—Recall to thy recollection this alternative; either there is providence or atoms [fortuitous concurrence of things]; or remember the arguments by which it has been proved that the world is a kind of political community [and be quiet at last].—But perhaps corporeal things will still fasten upon thee.—Consider then further that the mind mingles not with the breath, whether moving gently or violently, when it has once drawn itself apart and discovered its own power, and think also of all that thou hast heard and assented to about pain and pleasure [and be quiet at last].—But perhaps the desire of the thing called fame will torment thee—See how soon everything is forgotten, and look at the chaos of infinite time on each side of [the present], and the emptiness of applause, and the changeableness and want of judgment in those who pretend to give praise, and the narrowness of the space within which it is circumscribed [and be quiet at last]. For the whole earth is a point, and how small a nook in it is this thy dwelling, and how few are there in it, and what kind of people are they who will praise thee.

This then remains: Remember to retire into this little territory of thy own, and above all do not distract or strain thyself, but be free, and look at things as a man, as a human being, as a citizen, as a mortal. But among the things readiest to thy hand, to which thou shalt turn, let there be these, which are two. One is that things do not touch the soul, for they are external and remain immovable; but our perturbations come only from the opinion, which is within. The other is that all these things which thou seest change immediately and will no longer be; and constantly bear in mind how many of these changes thou hast already witnessed. The universe is transformation: life is opinion.

4. If our intellectual part is common, the reason also, in respect of which we are rational beings, is common: if this is so, common also is the reason which commands us what to do, and what not to do; if this is so, there is a common law also; if this is so, we are fellow-citizens; if this is so, we are members of some political community; if this is so, the world is in a manner a state. For of what other common political community will any one say that the whole human race are members? And from thence, from this common political community comes also our very intellectual faculty and reasoning faculty and our capacity for law; or whence do they come? For as my earthly part is a portion given to me from certain earth, and that which is watery from another element, and that which is hot and fiery from some peculiar source (for nothing comes out of that which is nothing, as nothing also returns to nonexistence), so also the intellectual part comes from some source.

5. Death is such as generation is, a mystery of nature; a composition out of the same elements, and a decomposition into the same; and altogether not a thing of which any man should be ashamed, for it is conformable to [the nature of] a reasonable animal, and not contrary to the reason of our constitution.

6. It is natural that these things should be done by such persons, it is a matter of necessity; and if a man will not have it so, he will not allow the fig tree to have juice. But by all means bear this in mind that within a very short time both thou and he will be dead; and soon not even your names will be left behind.

7. Take away thy opinion, and then there is taken away the complaint, "I have been harmed." Take away the complaint, "I have been harmed," and the harm is taken away.

8. That which does not make a man worse than he was, also does not make his life worse, nor does it harm him either from without or from within.

9. The nature of that which is [universally] useful has been compelled to do this.

10. Consider that everything which happens, happens justly, and if thou observest carefully, thou wilt find it to be so. I do not say only with respect to the continuity of the series of things, but with respect to what is just, and as if it were done by one who assigns to each thing its value. Observe then as thou hast begun; and whatever thou doest, do it in conjunction with this, the being good, and in the sense in which a man is properly understood to be good. Keep to this in every action.

11. Do not have such an opinion of things as he has who does thee wrong, or such as he wishes thee to have, but look at them as they are in truth.

12. A man should always have these two rules in readiness; the one, to do only whatever the reason of the ruling and legislating faculty may suggest for the use of men; the other, to change thy opinion, if there is any one at hand who sets thee right and moves thee from any opinion. But this change of opinion must proceed only from a certain persuasion, as of what is just or of common advantage, and the like, not because if appears pleasant or brings reputation.

13. Hast thou reason? I have.—Why then dost not thou use it? For if this does its own work, what else dost thou wish?

14. Thou existest as a part. Thou shalt disappear in that which produced thee; but rather thou shalt be received back into its seminal principle by transmutation.

15. Many grains of frankincense on the same altar: one falls before, another falls after; but it makes no difference.

16. Within ten days thou wilt seem a god to those to whom thou art now a beast and an ape, if thou wilt return to thy principles and the worship of reason.

17. Do not act as if thou wert going to live ten thousand years. Death hangs over thee. While thou livest, while it is in thy power, be good.

18. How much trouble he avoids who does not look to see what his neighbor says or does or thinks, but only to what he does himself, that it may be just and pure; or as Agathon says, look not round at the depraved morals of others, but run straight along the line without deviating from it.

19. He who has a vehement desire for posthumous fame does not consider that every one of those who remember him will himself also die very soon; then again also they who have succeeded them, until the whole remembrance shall have been extinguished as it is transmitted through men who foolishly admire and perish. But suppose that those who will remember are even immortal, and that the remembrance will be immortal, what then is this to thee? And I say not what is it to the dead, but what is it to the living. What is praise, except indeed so far as it has a certain utility? For thou now rejectest unseasonably the gift of nature, clinging to something else. . . .

20. Everything, which is in any way beautiful, is beautiful in itself, and terminates in itself, not having praise as part of itself. Neither worse then nor better is a thing made by being praised. I affirm this also of the things which are called beautiful by the vulgar, for example, material things and works of art. That which is really beautiful has no need of anything; not more than law, not more than truth, not more than benevolence or modesty. Which of these things is beautiful because it is praised, or

spoiled by being blamed? Is such a thing as an emerald made worse than it was, if it is not praised? Or gold, ivory, purple, a lyre, a little knife, a flower, and a shrub?

21. If souls continue to exist, how does the air contain them from eternity?—But how does the earth contain the bodies of those who have been buried from time so remote? For as here the mutation of these bodies after a certain continuance, whatever it may be, and their dissolution make room for other dead bodies; so the souls which are removed into the air after subsisting for some time are transmuted, and diffused, and assume a fiery nature by being received into the seminal intelligence of the universe, and in this way make room for the fresh souls which come to dwell there. And this is the answer which a man might give on the hypothesis of souls continuing to exist. But we must not only think of the number of animals which are daily eaten by us and the other animals. For what a number is consumed, and thus in a manner buried in the bodies of those who feed on them? And nevertheless this earth receives them by reason of the changes [of these bodies] into blood, and the transformations into the aerial or the fiery element.

What is the investigation into the truth in this matter? The division into that which is material and that which is the cause of form [the formal] (VII. 29.)

22. Do not be whirled about, but in every movement have respect to justice, and on the occasion of every impression maintain the faculty of comprehension [or understanding].

23. Everything harmonizes with me, which is harmonious to thee, O Universe. Nothing for me is too early nor too late, which is in due time for thee. Everything is fruit to me, which thy seasons bring, O Nature: from thee are all things, in thee are all things, to thee all things return. The poet says, Dear city of Cecrops; and wilt not thou say, Dear city of Zeus?

24. Occupy thyself with few things, says the philosopher, if thou wouldst be tranquil.—But consider if it would not be better to say, Do what is necessary, and whatever the reason of the animal which is naturally social requires, and as it requires. For this brings not only the tranquillity which comes from doing well, but also that which comes from doing few things. For the greatest part of what we say and do being unnecessary, if a man takes this away, he will have more leisure and less uneasiness. Accordingly on every occasion a man should ask himself, Is this one of the unnecessary things? Now a man should take away not only unnecessary acts, but also unnecessary thoughts, for thus superfluous acts will not follow after.

25. Try how the life of the good man suits thee, the life of him who is satisfied with his portion out of the whole, and satisfied with his own just acts and benevolent disposition.

26. Hast thou seen those things? Look also at these. Do not disturb thyself. Make thyself all simplicity. Does any one do wrong? It is to himself that he does the wrong. Has anything happened to thee? Well; out of the universe from the beginning everything which happens has been apportioned and spun out to thee. In a word, thy life is short. Thou must turn to profit the present by the aid of reason and justice. Be sober in thy relaxation.

27. Either it is a well arranged universe or a chaos huddled together, but still a universe. But can a certain order subsist in thee, and disorder in the All? And this too when all things are so separated and diffused and sympathetic.

28. A black character, a womanish character, a stubborn character, bestial, childish, animal, stupid, counterfeit, scurrilous, fraudulent, tyrannical.

29. If he is a stranger to the universe who does not know what is in it, no less is he a stranger who does not know what is going on in it. He is a runaway, who flies from social reason; he is blind, who shuts the eyes of the understanding; he is poor, who has need of another, and has not from himself all things which are useful for life. He is an abscess on the universe who withdraws and separates himself from the reason of our common nature through being displeased with the things which happen, for the same nature produces this, and has produced thee too: he is a piece rent asunder from the state, who tears his own soul from that of reasonable animals, which is one.

30. The one is a philosopher without a tunic, and the other without a book: here is another half-naked: Bread I have not, he says, and I abide by reason—And I do not get the means of living out of my learning, and I abide [by my reason].

31. Love the art, poor as it may be, which thou hast learned, and be content with it; and pass through the rest of life like one who has intrusted to the gods with his whole soul all that he has, making thyself neither the tyrant nor the slave of any man.

32. Consider, for example, the times of Vespasian. Thou wilt see all these things, people marrying, bringing up children, sick, dying, warring, feasting, trafficking, cultivating the ground, flattering, obstinately arrogant, suspecting, plotting, wishing for some to die, grumbling about the present, loving, heaping up treasure, desiring consulship, kingly power. Well then, that life of these people no longer exists at all. Again, remove to the times of Trajan. Again, all is the same. Their life too is gone. In like manner view also the other epochs of time and of whole nations, and see how many after great efforts soon fell and were resolved into the elements. But chiefly thou shouldst think of those whom thou hast thyself known distracting themselves about idle things, neglecting to do what was in accordance with their proper constitution, and to hold firmly to this and to be content with it. And herein it is necessary to remember that the attention given to everything has its proper value and proportion. For thus thou wilt not be dissatisfied, if thou appliest thyself to smaller matters no further than is fit.

33. The words which were formerly familiar are now antiquated: so also the names of those who were famed of old, are now in a manner antiquated, Camillus, Caeso, Volesus, Leonnatus, and a little after also Scipio and Cato, then Augustus, then also Hadrianus and Antoninus. For all things soon pass away and become a mere tale, and complete oblivion soon buries them. And I say this of those who have shone in a wondrous way. For the rest, as soon as they have breathed out their breath, they are gone, and no man speaks of them. And, to conclude the matter, what is even an eternal remembrance? A mere nothing. What then is that about which we ought to employ our serious pains? This one thing, thoughts just, and acts social, and words which never lie, and a disposition which gladly accepts all that happens, as necessary, as usual, as flowing from a principle and source of the same kind.

34. Willingly give thyself up to Clotho [one of the fates], allowing her to spin thy thread into whatever things she pleases.

35. Everything is only for a day, both that which remembers and that which is remembered.

36. Observe constantly that all things take place by change, and accustom thyself to consider that the nature of the Universe loves nothing so much as to change the things

which are and to make new things like them. For everything that exists is in a manner the seed of that which will be. But thou art thinking only of seeds, which are cast into the earth or into a womb: but this is a very vulgar notion.

37. Thou wilt soon die, and thou art not yet simple, nor free from perturbations, nor without suspicion of being hurt by external things, not kindly disposed towards all; nor dost thou yet place wisdom only in acting justly.

38. Examine men's ruling principles, even those of the wise, what kind of things they avoid, and what kind they pursue.

39. What is evil to thee does not subsist in the ruling principle of another; nor yet in any turning and mutation of thy corporeal covering. Where is it then? It is in that part of thee in which subsists the power of forming opinions about evils. Let this power then not form [such] opinions, and all is well. And if that which is nearest to it, the poor body, is cut, burnt, filled with matter and rottenness, nevertheless let the part which forms opinions about these things be quiet, that is, let it judge that nothing is either bad or good which can happen equally to the bad man and the good. For that which happens equally to him who lives contrary to nature and to him who lives according to nature, is neither according to nature nor contrary to nature.

40. Constantly regard the universe as one living being, having one substance and one soul; and observe how all things have reference to one perception, the perception of this one living being; and how all things act with one movement; and how all things are the co-operating causes of all things which exist; observe too the continuous spinning of the thread and the contexture of the web.

41. Thou art a little soul bearing about a corpse, as Epictetus used to say.

42. It is no evil for things to undergo change, and no good for things to subsist in consequence of change.

43. Time is like a river made up of the events which happen, and a violent stream; for as soon as a thing has been seen, it is carried away, and another comes in its place, and this will be carried away too.

44. Everything which happens is as familiar and well known as the rose in spring and the fruit in summer; for such is disease, and death, and calumny, and treachery, and whatever else delights fools or vexes them.

45. In the series of things those which follow are always aptly fitted to those which have gone before; for this series is not like a mere enumeration of disjointed things, which has only a necessary sequence, but it is a rational connection: and as all existing things are arranged together harmoniously, so the things which come into existence exhibit no mere succession, but a certain wonderful relationship. (VI. 38. VII. 9.)

46. Always remember the saying of Heraclitus, that the death of earth is to become water, and the death of water is to become air, and the death of air is to become fire, and reversely. And think too of him who forgets whither the way leads, and that men quarrel with that with which they are most constantly in communion, the reason which governs the universe; and the things which they daily meet with seem to them strange: and consider that we ought not to act and speak as if we were asleep, for even in sleep we seem to act speak; and that we ought not, like children who learn from their parents, simply to act and speak as we have been taught.

47. If any god told thee that thou shalt die tomorrow or certainly on the day after

tomorrow, thou wouldst not care much whether it was on the third day or on the morrow, unless thou wast in the highest degree mean-spirited,—for how small is the difference?—so think it no great thing to die after as many years as thou canst name rather than tomorrow.

48. Think continually how many physicians are dead after often contracting their eyebrows over the sick; and how many astrologers after predicting with great pretensions the deaths of others; and how many philosophers after endless discourses on death or immortality; how many heroes after killing thousands; and how many tyrants who have used their power over men's lives with terrible insolence as if they were immortal; and how many cities are entirely dead, so to speak, Helice and Pompeii and Herclanum, and others innumerable. Add to the reckoning all whom thou has known, one after another. One man after burying another has been laid out dead, and another buries him; and all this in a short time. To conclude, always observe how ephemeral and worthless human things are, and what was yesterday a little mucus, tomorrow will be a mummy or ashes. Pass then through this little space of time conformably to nature, and end thy journey in content, just as an olive falls off when it is ripe, blessing nature who produced it, and thanking the tree on which it grew.

49. Be like the promontory against which the waves continually break, but it stands firm and tames the fury of the water around it.

Unhappy am I, because this has happened to me.—Not so, but Happy am I, though this has happened to me, because I continue free from pain, neither crushed by the present nor fearing the future. For such a thing as this might have happened to every man; but every man would not have continued free from pain on such an occasion. Why then is that rather a misfortune than this a good fortune? And dost thou in all cases call that a man's misfortune, which is not a deviation from man's nature? And does a thing seem to thee to be a deviation from man's nature, when it is not contrary to the will of man's nature? Well, thou knowest the will of nature. Will then this which has happened prevent thee from being just, magnanimous, temperate, prudent, secure against inconsiderate opinions and falsehood; will it prevent thee from having modesty, freedom, and everything else, by the presence of which man's nature obtains all that is its own? Remember too on every occasion which leads thee to vexation to apply this principle: that this is not a misfortune, but that to bear it nobly is good fortune.

Augustine, *The City of God*, Marcus Dods, D. D. (trans.), 1948

Morality and the Love of God
Augustine

If there is free will, all things do not happen according to fate; if all things do not happen according to fate, there not a certain order of causes; and if there is not a certain order of causes, neither is there a certain order of things foreknown by God,—for things cannot come to pass except they are preceded by efficient causes,—but, if there is no fixed and certain order of causes foreknown by God, all things cannot be said to happen according as He foreknew that they would happen. And further, if it is not true that all things happen just as they have been foreknown by Him, there is not, says he, in God any foreknowledge of future events.

Now, against the sacrilegious and impious darings of reason, we assert both that God knows all things before they come to pass, and that we do by our free will whatsoever we know and feel to be done by us only because we will it. But that all things come to pass by fate, we do not say; nay we affirm that nothing comes to pass by fate; for we demonstrate that the name of fate, as it is wont to be used by those who speak of fate, meaning thereby the position of the stars at the time of each one's conception or birth, is an unmeaning word, for astrology itself is a delusion. But an order of causes in which the highest efficiency is attributed to the will of God, we neither deny nor do we designate it by the name of fate, unless, perhaps, we may understand fate to mean that which is spoken, deriving it from *fari*, to speak; for we cannot deny that it is written in the sacred Scriptures, "God hath spoken once; these two things have I heard, that power belongeth unto God. Also unto Thee, O God, belongeth mercy: for Thou wilt render unto every man according to his works."[1] Now the expression, "Once hath He spoken," is to be understood as meaning *"immovably,"* that is, unchangeably hath He spoken, inasmuch as He knows unchangeably all things which shall be, and all things which He will do. We might, then, use the word fate in the sense it bears when derived from *fari*, to speak, had it not already come to be understood in another sense, into which I am unwilling that the hearts of men should unconsciously slide. But it does not follow that, though there is for God a certain order of all causes, there must therefore be nothing depending on the free exercise of our own wills, for our wills themselves are included in that order of causes which is certain to God, and is embraced by His foreknowledge, for human wills are also causes of human actions; and He who foreknew all the causes of things would certainly among those causes not have been ignorant of our wills. . . .

[I]t has come to pass, that though there are very many and great nations all over the earth, whose rites and customs, speech, arms, and dress, are distinguished by marked differences, yet there are no more than two kinds of human society, which we may justly call two cities, according to the language of our Scriptures. ⟨The one consists of those who wish to live after the flesh, the other of those who wish to live after the spirit; and when they severally achieve what they wish, they live in peace, each after their kind.⟩ . .

[I]f we are to ascertain what it is to live after the flesh (which is certainly evil, though the nature of flesh is not itself evil), we must carefully examine that passage of the epistle which the Apostle Paul wrote to the Galatians, in which he says, "Now the works of the flesh are manifest, which are these: adultery, fornication, uncleanness, lasciviousness, idolatry, witchcraft, hatred, variance, emulations, wrath, strife, seditions, heresies, envyings, murders, drunkenness, revellings, and such like: of the which I tell you before, as I have also told you in time past, that they which do such things shall not inherit the kingdom of God."[2] This whole passage of the apostolic epistle being considered, so far as it bears on the matter in hand, will be sufficient to answer the question, what it is to live after the flesh. For among the works of the flesh which he said were manifest, and which he cited for condemnation, we find not only those which concern the pleasure of the flesh, as fornications, uncleanness, lasciviousness, drunkenness, revellings, but also those which, though they be remote from fleshly pleasure, reveal the vices of the soul. For who does not see that idolatries, witchcrafts, hatreds, variance, emulations, wrath, strife, heresies, envyings, are vices rather of the soul than of the flesh? For it is quite possible for a man to abstain from fleshly pleasures for the sake of idolatry or some heretical error; and yet, even when he does so, he is proved by this apostolic authority to be living after the flesh; and in abstaining from fleshly pleasure, he is proved to be practising, damnable works of the flesh. Who that has enmity has it not in his soul? or who would say to his enemy, or to the man he thinks his enemy, You have a bad flesh towards me, and not rather, You have a bad spirit towards me? In fine, if any one heard of what I may call "carnalities," he would not fail to attribute them to the carnal part of man; so no one doubts that "animosities" belong to the soul of man. . . .

If, then, we be asked what the city of God has to say upon these points, and, in the first place, what its opinion regarding the supreme good and evil is, it will reply that life eternal is the supreme good, death eternal the supreme evil, and that to obtain the one and escape the other we must live rightly. And thus it is written, "The just lives by faith,"[3] for we do not as yet see our good, and must therefore live by faith; neither have we in ourselves power to live rightly, but can do so only if He who has given us faith to believe in His help do help us when we believe and pray. As for those who have supposed that the sovereign good and evil are to be found in this life, and have placed it either in the soul or the body, or in both, or, to speak more explicitly, either in pleasure or in virtue, or in both; in repose or in virtue, or in both; in pleasure and repose, or in virtue, or in all combined; in the primary objects of nature, or in virtue, or in both,—all these have, with a marvellous shallowness, sought to find their blessedness in this life and in themselves. . . .

The whole use, then, of things temporal has a reference to this result of earthly peace in the earthly community, while in the city of God it is connected with eternal peace. And therefore, if we were irrational animals, we should desire nothing beyond the proper arrangement of the parts of the body and the satisfaction of the appetites,—nothing, therefore, but bodily comfort and abundance of pleasures, that the peace of the body might contribute to the peace of the soul. For if bodily peace be awanting, a bar is put to the peace even of the irrational soul, since it cannot obtain the gratification of its appetites. And these two together help out the mutual peace of soul and body, the peace of harmonious life and health. For as animals, by shunning pain, show that they love bodily peace, and, by pursuing pleasure to gratify their appetites, show that they love peace of soul, so their shrinking from death is a sufficient indication of their intense love of that peace which binds soul and body in close alliance. But, as man has a rational soul, he subordinates all this which he has in common with the beasts to the peace of his rational soul, that his intellect may have free play and may regulate his actions, and that he may thus enjoy the well-ordered harmony of knowledge and action which constitutes, as we have said, the peace of the rational soul. And for this purpose he must desire to be neither molested by pain, nor disturbed by desire, nor extinguished by death, that he may arrive at some useful knowledge by which he may regulate his life and manners. But, owing to the liability of the human mind to fall into mistakes, this very pursuit of knowledge may be a snare to him unless he has a divine Master, whom be may obey without misgiving, and who may at the same time give him such help as to preserve his own freedom. And because, so long as he is in this mortal body, he is a stranger to God, he walks by faith, not by sight; and he therefore refers all peace, bodily or spiritual or both, to that peace which mortal man has with the immortal God, so that he exhibits the well-ordered obedience of faith to eternal law. But as this divine Master inculcates two precepts,—the love of God and the love of our neighbour,—and as in these precepts a man finds three things he has to love,— God, himself, and his neighbour, —and that he who loves God loves himself thereby, it follows that he must endeavour to get his neighbour to love God, since he is ordered to love his neighbour as himself. He ought to make this endeavour in behalf of his wife, his children, his household, all within his reach, even as he would wish his neighbour to do the same for him if he needed it; and consequently he will be at peace, or in well-ordered concord, with all men, as far as in him lies. And this is the order of this concord, that a man, in the first place, injure no one, and, in the second, do good to every one he can reach.

Notes

1.   Ps. lxii, 11, 12.

2.   Gal. v. 19–21.

3.   Hab. ii. 4.

Thomas Aquinas, *Summa Theologica*, Literally translated by Fathers of the English Dominican Province, 1915

Divine, Natural, and Human Law
Thomas Aquinas

QUESTION XCI. OF THE VARIOUS KINDS OF LAW

We must now consider the various kinds of law: under which head there are six points of inquiry: (1) Whether there is an eternal law? (2) Whether there is a natural law? (3) Whether there is a human law? (4) Whether there is a Divine law? (5) Whether there is one Divine law, or several? (6) Whether there is a law of sin?

First Article

Whether There Is an Eternal Law?
We proceed thus to the First Article:—

Objection 1. It would seem that there is no eternal law. Because every law is imposed on someone. But there was not someone from eternity on whom a law could be imposed: since God alone was from eternity. Therefore no law is eternal.

Obj. 2. Further, promulgation is essential to law. But promulgation could not be from eternity: because there was no one to whom it could be promulgated from eternity. Therefore no law can be eternal.

Obj. 3. Further, a law implies order to an end. But nothing ordained to an end is eternal: for the last end alone is eternal. Therefore no law is eternal.

On the contrary, Augustine says (*De Lib. Arb.* i. 6): *That Law which is the Supreme Reason cannot be understood to be otherwise than unchangeable and eternal.*

I answer that, As stated above (*Q. XC., A.1 ad 2; AA. 3, 4*), a law is nothing else but a dictate of practical reason emanating from the ruler who governs a perfect community. Now it is evident, granted that the world is ruled by Divine Providence, as was stated in the First Part (*Q. XXII., AA. 1, 2*), that the whole community of the universe is governed by Divine Reason. Wherefore the very Idea of the government of things in God the Ruler of the universe has the nature of a law. And since the Divine Reason's conception of things is not subject to time but is eternal, according to Prov. viii. 23, therefore it is that this kind of law must be called eternal.

Reply Obj. 1. Those things that are not in themselves, exist with God, inasmuch as they are foreknown and preordained by Him, according to Rom. iv. 17: *Who calls those things that are not, as those that are.* Accordingly the eternal concept of the Divine law bears the character of an eternal law, in so far as it is ordained by God to the government of things foreknown by Him.

Reply Obj. 2. Promulgation is made by word of mouth or writing; and in both ways the eternal law is promulgated: because both the Divine Word and the writing of the Book of Life are eternal. But the promulgation cannot be from eternity on the part of the creature that hears or reads.

Reply Obj. 3. The law implies order to the end actively, in so far as it directs certain things to the end; but not passively,—that is to say, the law itself is not ordained to the end,—except accidentally, in a governor whose end is extrinsic to him, and to which end his law must needs be ordained. But the end of the Divine government is God Himself, and His law is not distinct from Himself. Wherefore the eternal law is not ordained to another end.

Second Article

Whether There Is in Us a Natural Law?
We proceed thus to the Second Article:—

Objection 1. It would seem that there is no natural law in us. Because man is governed sufficiently by the eternal law: for Augustine says (*De Lib. Arb. i.*) that *the eternal law is that by which it is right that all things should be most orderly.* But nature does not abound in superfluities as neither does she fail in necessaries. Therefore no law is natural to man.

Obj. 2. Further, by the law man is directed, in his acts, to the end, as stated above (Q.XC., A. 2). But the directing of human acts to their end is not a function of nature, as is the case in irrational creatures, which act for an end solely by their natural appetite; whereas man acts for an end by his reason and will. Therefore no law is natural to man.

Obj. 3. Further, the more a man is free, the less is he under the law. But man is freer than all the animals, on account of his free will, with which he is endowed above all other animals. Since therefore other animals are not subject to a natural law, neither is man subject to a natural law.

On the contrary, A gloss on Rom. ii. 14: *When the Gentiles, who have not the law, do by nature those things that are of the law,* comments as follows: *Although they have no written law, yet they have the natural law, whereby each one knows, and is conscious of, what is good and what is evil.*

I answer that, As stated above (Q. XC., A. *1 ad 1*), law, being a rule and measure, can be in a person in two ways: in one way, as in him that rules and measures; in another way, as in that which is ruled and measured, since a thing is ruled and measured, in so far as it partakes of the rule or measure. Wherefore, since all things subject to Divine providence are ruled and measured by the eternal law, as was stated above (A. 1); it is evident that all things partake somewhat of the eternal law, in so far as, namely, from its being imprinted on them, they derive their respective inclinations to their proper acts and ends. Now among all others, the rational creature is subject to Divine providence in the most excellent way, in so far as it partakes of a share of providence, by being provident both for itself and for others. Wherefore it has a share of the Eternal Reason, whereby it has a natural inclination to its proper act and end: and this participation of the eternal law in the rational creature is called the natural law. Hence the Psalmist after saying (Ps. iv. 6): *Offer up the sacrifice of justice,* as though someone asked what the works of justice are, adds: *Many say, Who showeth us good things?* In answer to which question he says: *The light of Thy countenance, O Lord, is signed upon us:* thus implying that the light of natural reason, whereby we discern what is good and what is evil, which is the function of the natural law, is nothing else than an imprint on us of the Divine light. It is therefore evident that the natural law is nothing else than the rational creature's participation of the eternal law.

Reply Obj. 1. This argument would hold, if the natural law were something different from the eternal law: whereas it is nothing but a participation thereof, as stated above.

Reply Obj. 2. Every act of reason and will in us is based on that which is according to nature, as stated above (Q. X., A. *1*): for every act of reasoning is based on principles that are known naturally, and every act of appetite in respect of the means is derived from the natural appetite in respect of the last end. Accordingly the first direction of our acts to their end must needs be in virtue of the natural law.

Reply Obj. 3. Even irrational animals partake in their own way of the Eternal Reason, just as the rational creature does. But because the rational creature partakes thereof in an intellectual and rational manner, therefore the participation of the eternal law in the rational creature is properly called a law, since a law is something pertaining to reason, as stated above (Q. XC., A. *1*). Irrational creatures, however, do not partake thereof in a rational manner, wherefore there is no participation of the eternal law in them, except by way of similitude.

Third Article

Whether There Is a Human Law?
We proceed thus to the Third Article:—

Objection 1. It would seem that there is not a human law. For the natural law is a participation of the eternal law, as stated above (A.2). Now through the eternal law *all things are most orderly,* as Augustine states (*De Lib. Arb. i. 6*). Therefore the natural law suffices for the ordering of all human affairs. Consequently there is no need for a human law.

Obj. 2. Further, a law bears the character of a measure, as stated above (Q. XC., A. 1). But human reason is not a measure of things, but vice versa, as stated in *Metaph.* x., text. 5. Therefore no law can emanate from human reason.

Obj. 3. Further, a measure should be most certain, as stated in *Metaph.* x., text. 3. But the dictates of human reason in matters of conduct are uncertain, according to Wis. ix. 14: *The thoughts of mortal men are fearful, and our counsels uncertain.* Therefore no law can emanate from human reason.

On the contrary, Augustine (*De Lib. Arb. i. 6*) distinguishes two kinds of law, the one eternal, the other temporal, which he calls human.

I answer that, As stated above (Q. XC., A. *1, ad 2*), a law is a dictate of the practical reason. Now it is to be observed that the same procedure takes place in the practical and in the speculative reason: for each proceeds from principles to conclusions, as stated above (*ibid.*). Accordingly we conclude that just as, in the speculative reason, from naturally known indemonstrable principles, we draw the conclusions of the various sciences, the knowledge of which is not imparted to us by nature, but acquired by the efforts of reason, so too it is from the precepts of the natural law, as from general and indemonstrable principles, that the human reason needs to proceed to the more particular determination of certain matters. These particular determinations, devised by human reason, are called human laws, provided the other essential conditions of law be observed, as stated above (Q. XC., AA. 2, 3, 4). Wherefore Tully says in his *Rhetoric* (*De Invent. Rhet.* ii.) that *justice has its source in nature; thence certain things came into custom by reason of their utility; afterwards these things which emanated from nature and were approved by custom, were sanctioned by fear and reverence for the law.*

Reply Obj. 1. The human reason cannot have a full participation of the dictate of the Divine Reason, but according to its own mode, and imperfectly. Consequently, as on the part of the speculative reason, by a natural participation of Divine Wisdom, there is in us the knowledge of certain general principles, but not proper knowledge of each single truth, such as that contained in the Divine Wisdom; so too, on the part of the practical reason, man has a natural participation of the eternal law, according to certain general principles, but not as regards the particular determinations of individual cases, which are, however, contained in the eternal law. Hence the need for human reason to proceed further to sanction them by law.

Reply Obj. 2. Human reason is not, of itself, the rule of things: but the principles impressed on it by nature, are general rules and measures of all things relating to human conduct, whereof the natural reason is the rule and measure, although it is not the measure of things that are from nature.

Reply Obj. 3. The practical reason is concerned with practical matters, which are singular and contingent: but not with necessary things, with which the speculative reason is concerned. Wherefore human laws cannot have that inerrancy that belongs to the demonstrated conclusions of sciences. Nor is it necessary for every measure to be altogether unerring and certain, but according as it is possible in its own particular genus.

Fourth Article

Whether There Was Any Need for a Divine Law?
We proceed thus to the Fourth Article:—

Objection 1. Because, as stated above (A. 2), the natural law is a participation in us of the eternal law. But the eternal law is a Divine law, as stated above (A. 1). Therefore there is no need for a Divine law in addition to the natural law, and human laws derived therefrom.

Obj. 2. Further, it is written (Ecclus. xv. 14) that *God left man in the hand of his own counsel.* Now counsel is an act of reason, as stated above (Q. XIV., A. 1). Therefore man was left to the direction of his reason. But a dictate of human reason is a human law, as stated above (A. 3). Therefore there is no need for man to be governed also by a Divine law.

Obj. 3. Further, human nature is more self-sufficing than irrational creatures. But irrational creatures have no Divine law besides the natural inclination impressed on them. Much less, therefore, should the rational creature have a Divine law in addition to the natural law?

On the contrary, David prayed God to set His law before him, saying (Ps. cxviii. 33): *Set before me for a law the way of Thy justifications, O Lord.*

I answer that, Besides the natural and the human law it was necessary for the directing of human conduct to have a Divine law. And this for four reasons. First, because it is by law that man is directed how to perform his proper acts in view of his last end. And indeed if man were ordained to no other end than that which is proportionate to his natural faculty, there would be no need for man to have any further direction on the part of his reason, besides the natural law and human law which is derived from it. But since man is ordained to an end of eternal happiness which is inproportionate to man's natural faculty, as stated above (Q. V., A. 5), therefore it was necessary that, besides the natural and the human law, man should be directed to his end by a law given by God.

Secondly, because, on account of the uncertainty of human judgment, especially on contingent and particular matters, different people form different judgments on human acts; whence also different and contrary laws result. In order, therefore, that man may know without any doubt what he ought to do and what he ought to avoid, it was necessary for man to be directed in his proper acts by a law given by God, for it is certain that such a law cannot err.

Thirdly, because man can make laws in those matters of which he is competent to judge. But man is not competent to judge of interior movements, that are hidden, but only of exterior acts which appear: and yet for the perfection of virtue it is necessary for man to conduct himself aright in both kinds of acts. Consequently human law could not sufficiently curb and direct interior acts; and it was necessary for this purpose that a Divine law should supervene.

Fourthly, because, as Augustine say (*De Lib. Arb. i. 5,6*), human law cannot punish or forbid all evil deeds: since while aiming at doing away with all evils, it would do away with many good things, and would hinder the advance of the common good, which is necessary for human intercourse. In order, therefore, that no evil might remain unforbidden and unpunished, it was necessary for the Divine law to supervene, whereby all sins are forbidden.

And these four causes are touched upon in Ps. cxviii. 8, where it is said: *The law of the Lord is unspotted, i.e.,* allowing no foulness of sin; *converting souls,* because it directs not only exterior, but also interior acts; *the testimony of the Lord is faithful,* certainty of what is true and right; *giving wisdom to little ones,* by directing man to an end supernatural and Divine.

Reply Obj. 1. By the natural law the eternal law is participated proportionately to the capacity of human nature. But to his supernatural end man needs to be directed in a yet higher way. Hence the additional law given by God, whereby man shares more perfectly in the eternal law.

Reply Obj. 2. Counsel is a kind of inquiry: hence it must proceed from some principles. Nor is it enough for it to proceed from principles imparted by nature, which are the precepts of the natural law, for the reasons given above: but there is need for certain additional principles, namely, the precepts of the Divine law.

Reply Obj. 3. Irrational creatures are not ordained to an end higher than that which is proportionate to their natural powers: consequently the comparison fails.

QUESTION XCIII. OF THE ETERNAL LAW

We must now consider each law by itself; and (1) The eternal law: (2) The natural law: (3) The human law: (4) The old law: (5) The new law, which is the law of the Gospel. Of the sixth law, which is the law of the 'fomes,' suffice what we have said when treating of original sin.

Concerning the first there are six points of inquiry: (1) What is the eternal law? (2) Whether it is known to all? (3) Whether every law is derived from it? (4) Whether necessary things are subject to the eternal law? (5) Whether natural contingencies are subject to the eternal law? (6) Whether all human things are subject to it?

First Article

Whether the Eternal Law Is a Sovereign Type Existing in God?
We proceed thus to the First Article:—

Objection 1. It would seem that the eternal law is not a sovereign type existing in God. For there is only one eternal law. But there are many types of things in the Divine mind; for Augustine says (*Q. lxxxiii., qu. 46*) that God *made each thing according to its type.* Therefore the eternal law does not seem to be a type existing in the Divine mind.

Obj. 2. Further, it is essential to a law that it be promulgated by word, as stated above (Q. XC., A. 4). But Word is a Personal name in God, as stated in the First Part (Q. XXXIV., A. 1): whereas type refers to the Essence. Therefore the eternal law is not the same as a Divine type.

Obj. 3. Further, Augustine says (*De Vera Relig. xxx.*): *We see a law above our minds, which is called truth.* But the law, which is above our minds, is the eternal law. Therefore truth is the eternal law. But the idea of truth is not the same as the idea of a type. Therefore the eternal law is not the same as the sovereign type.

On the contrary, Augustine says (*De Lib. Arb. i. 6*) that *the eternal law is the sovereign type, to which we must always conform.*

I answer that, Just as in every artificer there pre-exists a type of the things that are made by his art, so too in every governor there must pre-exist the type of the order of those things that are to be done by those who are subject to his government. And just as the type of the things yet to be made by an art is called the art or exemplar of the products of that art, so too the type in him who governs the acts of his subjects, bears the character of a law, provided the other conditions be present which we have mentioned above (Q. XC.). Now God, by His wisdom, is the Creator of all things, in relation to which He stands as the artificer to the products of his art, as stated in the First Part (Q. XIV., A. 8). Moreover He governs all the acts and movements that are to be found in each single creature, as was also stated in the First Part (Q. CIII., A. 5). Wherefore as the type of the Divine Wisdom, inasmuch as by It all things are created, has the character of art, exemplar or idea; so the type of Divine Wisdom, as moving all things to their due end, bears the character of law. Accordingly the eternal law is nothing else than the type of Divine Wisdom, as directing all actions and movements.

Reply Obj. 1. Augustine is speaking in that passage of the ideal types which regard the proper nature of each single thing; and consequently in them there is a certain distinction and plurality, according to their different relations to things, as stated in the First Part (Q. XV., A. 2). But law is said to direct human acts by ordaining them to the common good, as stated above (Q. XC., A. 2). And things, which are in themselves different, may be considered as one, according as they are ordained to one common thing. Wherefore the eternal law is one since it is the type of this order.

Reply Obj. 2. With regard to any sort of word, two points may be considered: viz., the word itself, and that which is expressed by the word. For the spoken word is something uttered by the mouth of man, and expresses that which is signified by the human word. The same applies to the human mental word, which is nothing else than something conceived by the mind, by which man expresses his thoughts mentally. So then in God the Word conceived by the intellect of the Father is the name of a Person: but all things that are in the Father's knowledge, whether they refer to the Essence or to the Persons, or to the works of God, are expressed by this Word, as Augustine declares (*De Trin. xv. 14*). And among other things expressed by this Word, the eternal law itself is expressed thereby. Nor does it follow that the eternal law is a Personal name in God: yet it is appropriated to the Son, on account of the kinship between type and word.

Reply Obj. 3. The types of the Divine intellect do not stand in the same relation to things, as the types of the human intellect. For the human intellect is measured by things, so that a human concept is not true by reason of itself, but by reason of its being consonant with things, since *an opinion is true or false according as it answers to the reality.* But the Divine intellect is the measure of things: since each thing has so far truth in it, as it represents the Divine intellect, as was stated in the First Part (Q. XVI., A. *1*). Consequently the Divine intellect is true in itself; and its type is truth itself.

Second Article

Whether the Eternal Law Is Known to All?
We proceed thus to the Second Article:—

Objection 1. It would seem that the eternal law is not known to all. Because, as the Apostle says (I Cor. ii. 11), *the things that are of God no man knoweth, but the Spirit of God.* But the eternal law is a type existing in the Divine mind. Therefore it is unknown to all save God alone.

Obj. 2. Further, as Augustine says (*De Lib. Arb.* i. 6) *the eternal law is that by which it is right that all things should be most orderly.* But all do not know how all things are most orderly. Therefore all do not know the eternal law.

Obj. 3. Further, Augustine says (*De Vera Relig.* xxxi.) that *the eternal law is not subject to the judgment of man.* But according to *Ethic.* i. Any man can judge well of what he knows. Therefore the eternal law is not known to us.

On the contrary, Augustine says (*De Lib. Arb.* i. 6) that *knowledge of the eternal law is imprinted on us.*

I answer that, A thing may be known in two ways: first, in itself; secondly, in its effect, wherein some likeness of that thing is found: thus someone not seeing the sun in its substance, may know it by its rays. So then no one can know the eternal law, as it is in itself, except the blessed who see God in His Essence. But every rational creature knows it in its reflection, greater or less. For every knowledge of truth is a kind of reflection and participation of the eternal law, which is the unchangeable truth, as Augustine says (*De Vera Relig.* xxxi.). Now all men know the truth to a certain extent, at least as to the common principles of the natural law: and as to the others, they partake of the knowledge of truth, some more, some less; and in this respect are more or less cognizant of the eternal law.

Reply Obj. 1. We cannot know the things that are of God, as they are in themselves; but they are made known to us in their effects, according to Rom. i. 20: *The invisible things of God . . . are clearly seen, being understood by the things that are made.*

Reply Obj. 2. Although each one knows the eternal law according to his own capacity, in the way explained above, yet none can comprehend it: for it cannot be made perfectly known by its effects. Therefore it does not follow that anyone who knows the eternal law in the way aforesaid, knows also the whole order of things, whereby they are most orderly.

Reply Obj. 3. To judge of a thing may be understood in two ways. First, as when a cognitive power judges of its proper object, according to Job. xii. *11: Doth not the ear discern words, and the palate of him that eateth, the taste?* It is to this kind of judgment that the Philosopher alludes when he says that *anyone can judge well of what he knows,* by judging, namely, whether what is put forward is true. In another way we speak of a superior judging of a subordinate by a kind of practical judgment, as to whether he should be such and such or not. And thus none can judge of the eternal law.

QUESTION XCIV. OF THE NATURAL LAW

Fourth Article

Whether the Natural Law Is the Same in All Men?
We proceed thus to the Fourth Article:—

Objection 1. It would seem that the natural law is not the same in all. For it is stated in the Decretals (*Dist.* i.) that *the natural law is that which is contained in the Law and the Gospel.* But this is not common to all men; because, as it is written (Rom. x. 16), *all do not obey the gospel.* Therefore the natural law is not the same in all men.

Obj. 2. Further, *Things which are according to the law are said to be just,* as stated in *Ethic.* v. But it is stated in the same book that nothing is so universally just as not to be subject to change in regard to some men. Therefore even the natural law is not the same in all men.

Obj. 3. Further, as stated above (AA. 2, 3), to the natural law belongs everything to which a man is inclined according to his nature. Now different men are naturally inclined to different things; some to the desire of pleasures, others to the desire of honours, and other men to other things. Therefore there is not one natural law for all.

On the contrary, Isidore says (*Etym.* v. 4): *The natural law is common to all nations.*

I answer that, As stated above (AA. 2, 3), to the natural law belongs those things to which a man is inclined to act according to reason. Now the process of reason is from the common to the proper, as stated in *Phys.* i. The speculative reason, however, is differently situated in this matter, from the practical reason. For, since the speculative reason is busied chiefly with necessary things, which cannot be otherwise than they are, its proper conclusions, like the universal principles, contain the truth without fail. The practical reason, on the other hand, is busied with contingent matters, about which human actions are concerned: and consequently, although there is necessity in the general principles, the more we descend to matters of detail, the more frequently we encounter defects. Accordingly then in speculative matter truth is the same in all men, both as to principles and as to conclusions: although the truth is not known to all as regards the conclusions, but only as regards the principles which are called common notions. But in matters of action, truth or practical rectitude is not the same for all, as to matters of detail, but only as to the general principles: and where there is the same rectitude in matters of detail, it is not equally known to all.

It is therefore evident that, as regards the general principles whether of speculative or of practical reason, truth or rectitude is the same for all, and is equally known by all. As to the proper conclusions of the speculative reason, the truth is the same for all, but is not equally know to all: thus it is true for all that the three angles of a triangle are together equal to two right angles, although it is not known to all. But as to the proper conclusions of the practical reason, neither is the truth or rectitude the same for all, nor, where it is the same, is it equally known by all. Thus it is right and true for all to act according to reason: and from this principle it follows as a proper conclusion, that goods entrusted to another should be restored to their owner. Now this is true for the majority of cases: but it may happen in a particular case that it would be injurious, and therefore unreasonable, to restore goods held in trust; for instance if they are claimed for the purpose of fighting against one's country. And this principle will be found to fail the more, according as we descend further into detail, *e.g.*, if one were to say that goods held in trust should be restored with such and such a guarantee, or in such and such a way; because the greater the number of conditions added, the greater the number of ways in which the principle may fail, so that it be not right to restore or not to restore.

Consequently we must say that the natural law, as to general principles, is the same for all, both as to rectitude and as to knowledge. But as to certain matters of detail, which are conclusions, as it were, of those general principles, it is the same for all in the majority of cases, both as to rectitude and as to knowledge; and yet in some few cases it may fail, both as to rectitude, by reason of certain obstacles (just as natures subject to generation and corruption fail in some few cases on account of some obstacle), and as to knowledge, since in some the reason is perverted by passion, or evil habit, or an evil disposition of nature; thus formerly, theft, although it is expressly contrary to the natural law, was not considered wrong among the Germans, as Julius Cæsar relates (*De Bello Gall.* vi.).

Reply Obj. 1. The meaning of the sentence quoted is not that whatever is contained in the Law and the Gospel belongs to the natural law, since they contain many things that are above nature; but that whatever belongs to the natural law is fully contained in them. Wherefore Gratian, after saying that *the natural law is what is contained in the Law and the Gospel,* adds at once, by way of example, *by which everyone is commanded to do to others as he would be done by.*

Reply Obj. 2. The saying of the Philosopher is to be understood of things that are naturally just, not as general principles, but as conclusions drawn from them, having rectitude in the majority of cases, but failing in a few.

Reply Obj. 3. As, in man, reason rules and commands the other powers, so all the natural inclinations belonging to the other powers must needs be directed according to reason. Wherefore it is universally right for all men, that all their inclinations should be directed according to reason.

QUESTION XCVI. OF THE POWER OF HUMAN LAW

We must now consider the power of human law. Under this head there are six points of inquiry: (1) Whether human law should be framed for the community? (2) Whether human law should repress all vices? (3) Whether human law is competent to direct all acts of virtue? (4) Whether it binds man in conscience? (5) Whether all men are subject to human law? (6) Whether those who are under the law may act beside the letter of the law?

First Article

Whether Human Law Should Be Framed for the Community Rather Than for the Individual?
We proceed thus to the First Article:—

Objection 1. It would seem that human law should be framed not for the community, but rather for the individual. For the Philosopher says (*Ethic.* v. 7) that *the legal just . . . includes all particular acts of legislation . . . and all those matters which are the subject of decrees,* which are also individual matters, since decrees are framed about individual actions. Therefore law is framed not only for the community, but also for the individual.

Obj. 2. Further, law is the director of human acts, as stated above (Q. XC., AA. *1, 2*). But human acts are about individual matters. Therefore human laws should be framed, not for the community, but rather for the individual.

Obj. 3. Further, law is a rule and measure of human acts, as stated above (Q. XC., AA. *1, 2*). But a measure should be most certain, as stated in *Metaph.* x. Since therefore in human acts no general proposition can be so certain as not to fail in some individual cases, it seems that laws should be framed not in general but for individual cases.

On the contrary, The jurist says (*Pandect. Justin.* Lib. i. tit. iii., art. ii., *De legibus,* etc.) that *laws should be made to suit the majority of instances; and they are not framed according to what may possibly happen in an individual case.*

I answer that, Whatever is for an end should be proportionate to that end. Now the end of law is the common good; because, Isidore says (*Etym.* v. 21) that *law should be framed, not for any private benefit, but for the common good of all the citizens.* Hence human laws should be proportionate to the common good. Now the common good comprises many things. Wherefore law should take account of many things, as to persons, as to matters, and as to times. Because the community of the state is composed of many persons; and its good is procured by many actions; nor is it established to endure for only a short time, but to last for all time by the citizens succeeding one another, as Augustine says (*De Civ. Dei* ii. 21; xxii. 6).

Reply Obj. 1. The Philosopher (*Ethic.* v. 7) divides the legal just, i.e., positive law, into three parts. For some things are laid down simply in a general way: and these are the general laws. Of these he says that *the legal is that which originally was a matter of indifference, but which, when enacted, is so no longer:* as the fixing of the ransom of a captive.—Some things affect the community in one respect, and individuals in another. These are called *privileges,* i.e., *private laws,* as it were, because they regard private persons, although their power extends to many matters; and in regard to these, he adds, *and further, all particular acts of legislation.*—Other matters are legal, not through being laws, but through being applications of general laws to particular cases: such are decrees which have the force of law; and in regard to these, he adds *all matters subject to decrees.*

Reply Obj. 2. A principle of direction should be applicable to many; wherefore (*Metaph.* x., text. 4) the Philosopher says that all things belonging to one genus, are measured by one, which is the principle in that genus. For if there were as many rules or measures as there are things measured or ruled, they would cease to be of use, since their use consists in being applicable to many things. Hence law would be of no use, if it did not extend further than to one single act. Because the decrees of prudent men are made for the purpose of directing individual actions; whereas law is a general precept, as stated above (Q. XCII., A. 2, Obj. 2).

Reply Obj. 3. We must not seek the same degree of certainty in all things (*Ethic.* i. 3). Consequently in contingent matters, such as natural and human things, it is enough for a thing to be certain, as being true in the greater number of instances, though at times and less frequently it fail.

Thomas Hobbes, *Leviathan*, 1651

Social Contract Ethics
Thomas Hobbes

CHAPTER SIX

Of the Interior Beginnings of Voluntary Motions Commonly Called the Passions, and the Speeches by Which They Are Expressed

There be in animals two sorts of *motions* peculiar to them: one called *vital*, begun in generation and continued without interruption through their whole life—such as are the *course* of the *blood*, the *pulse*, the *breathing*, the *concoction*, *nutrition*, *excretion*, etc.—to which motions there needs no help of imagination; the other is *animal motion*, otherwise called *voluntary motion*—as to *go*, to *speak*, to *move* any of our limbs in such manner as is first fancied in our minds. That sense is motion in the organs and interior parts of man's body caused by the action of the things we see, hear, etc., and that fancy is but the relics of the same motion remaining after sense, has been already said in the first and second chapters. And because *going*, *speaking*, and the like voluntary motions depend always upon a precedent thought of *whither*, *which way*, and *what*, it is evident that the imagination is the first internal beginning of all voluntary motion. And although unstudied men do not conceive any motion at all to be there where the thing moved is invisible or the space it is moved in is, for the shortness of it, insensible, yet that does not hinder but that such motions are. For let a space be never so little, that which is moved over a greater space, whereof that little one is part, must first be moved over that. These small beginnings of motion within the body of man, before they appear in walking, speaking, striking, and other visible actions, are commonly called ENDEAVOR.

This endeavor, when it is toward something which causes it, is called APPETITE or DESIRE, the latter being the general name and the other oftentimes restrained to signify the desire of food, namely *hunger* and *thirst*. And when the endeavor is fromward something, it is generally called AVERSION. These words, *appetite* and *aversion*, we have from the Latins; and they both of them signify the motions, one of approaching, the other of retiring. So also do the Greek words for the same, which are ορμη and αφορμη. For nature itself does often press upon men those

50

truths which afterwards, when they look for somewhat beyond nature, they stumble at. For the Schools find in mere appetite to go or move no actual motion at all; but because some motion they must acknowledge, they call it metaphorical motion, which is but an absurd speech, for though words may be called metaphorical, bodies and motions cannot.

That which men desire they are also said to LOVE, and to HATE those things for which they have aversion. So that desire and love are the same thing, save that by desire we always signify the absence of the object, by love most commonly the presence of the same. So also by aversion we signify the absence, and by hate the presence of the object.

Of appetites and aversions, some are born with men, as appetite of food, appetite of excretion, and exoneration, which may also and more properly be called aversions from somewhat they feel in their bodies; and some other appetites, not many. The rest, which are appetites of particular things, proceed from experience and trial of their effects upon themselves or other men. For of things we know not at all, or believe not to be, we can have no further desire than to taste and try. But aversion we have for things, not only which we know have hurt us, but also that we do not know whether they will hurt us or not.

Those things which we neither desire nor hate we are said to *contemn*, CONTEMPT being nothing else but an immobility or contumacy of the heart in resisting the action of certain things; and proceeding from that the heart is already moved otherwise by other more potent objects or from want of experience of them.

And because the constitution of a man's body is in continual mutation, it is impossible that all the same things should always cause in him the same appetites and aversions; much less can all men consent in the desire of almost any one and the same object.

But whatsoever is the object of any man's appetite or desire, that is it which he for his part calls *good*; and the object of his hate and aversion, *evil*; and of his contempt, *vile* and *inconsiderable*. For these words of good, evil, and contemptible are ever used with relation to the person that uses them, there being nothing simply and absolutely so, nor any common rule of good and evil to be taken from the nature of the objects themselves—but from the person of the man, where there is no commonwealth, or, in a commonwealth, from the person that represents it, or from an arbitrator or judge whom men disagreeing shall by consent set up and make his sentence the rule thereof.

CHAPTER THIRTEEN

Of the Natural Condition of Mankind as Concerning Their Felicity and Misery

Nature has made men so equal in the faculties of the body and mind as that, though there be found one man sometimes manifestly stronger in body or of quicker mind than another, yet, when all is reckoned together, the difference between man and man is not so considerable as that one man can thereupon claim to himself any benefit to which another may not pretend as well as he. For as to the strength of body, the weakest has strength enough to kill the strongest, either by secret machination or by confederacy with others that are in the same danger with himself.

And as to the faculties of the mind, setting aside the arts grounded upon words, and especially that skill of proceeding upon general and infallible rules called science—which very few have and but in few things, as being not a native faculty born with us, nor attained, as prudence, while we look after somewhat else—I find yet a greater equality among men than that of strength. For prudence is but experience, which equal time equally bestows on all men in those things they equally apply themselves unto. That which may perhaps make such equality incredible is but a vain conceit of one's own wisdom, which almost all men think they have in a greater degree than the vulgar—that is, than all men but themselves and a few others whom, by fame or for concurring with themselves, they approve. For such is the nature of men that howsoever they may acknowledge many others to be more witty or more eloquent or more learned, yet they will hardly believe there be many so wise as themselves; for they see their own wit at hand and other men's at a distance. But this proves rather that men are in that point equal than unequal. For there is not ordinarily a greater sign of the equal distribution of anything than that every man is contented with his share.

From this equality of ability arises equality of hope in the attaining of our ends. And therefore if any two men desire the same thing, which nevertheless they cannot both enjoy, they become enemies; and in the way to their end, which is principally their own conservation, and sometimes their delectation only, endeavor to destroy or subdue one another. And from hence it comes to pass that where an invader has no more to fear than another man's single power, if one plant, sow, build, or possess a convenient seat, others may probably be expected to come prepared with forces united to dispossess and deprive him, not only of the fruit of his labor, but also of his life or liberty. And the invader again is in the like danger of another.

And from this diffidence of one another there is no way for any man to secure himself so reasonable as anticipation—that is, by force or wiles to master the persons of all men he can, so long till he see no other power great enough to endanger him; and this is no more than his own conservation requires, and is generally allowed. Also, because there be some that take pleasure in contemplating their own power in the acts of conquest, which they pursue farther than their security requires, if others that otherwise would be glad to be at ease within modest bounds should not by invasion increase their power, they would not be able, long time, by standing only on their defense, to subsist. And by consequence, such augmentation of dominion over men being necessary to a man's conservation, it ought to be allowed him.

Again, men have no pleasure, but on the contrary a great deal of grief, in keeping company where there is no power able to overawe them all. For every man looks that his companion should value him at the same rate he sets upon himself; and upon all signs of contempt or undervaluing naturally endeavors, as far as he dares (which among them that have no common power to keep them in quiet is far enough to make them destroy each other), to extort a greater value from his contemners by damage and from others by the example.

So that in the nature of man we find three principal causes of quarrel: first, competition; secondly, diffidence; thirdly, glory.

The first makes men invade for gain, the second for safety, and the third for reputation. The first use violence to make themselves masters of other men's persons, wives, children, and cattle; the second, to defend them; the third, for trifles, as a word, a smile, a different opinion, and any other sign of undervalue, either direct in their persons or by reflection in their kindred, their friends, their nation, their profession, or their name.

Hereby it is manifest that, during the time, men live without a common power to keep them all in awe, they are in that condition which is called war, and such a war as is of every man against every man. For war consists not in battle only, or the act of fighting, but in a tract of time wherein the will to contend by battle is sufficiently known; and therefore the notion of *time* is to be considered in the nature of war as it is in the nature of weather. For as the nature of foul weather lies not in a shower or two of rain but in an inclination thereto of many days together, so the nature of war consists not in actual fighting but in the known disposition thereto during all the time there is no assurance to the contrary. All other time is PEACE.

Whatsoever, therefore, is consequent to a time of war where every man is enemy to every man, the same is consequent to the time wherein men live without other security than what their own strength and their own invention shall furnish them withal. In such condition there is no place for industry, because the fruit thereof is uncertain: and consequently no culture of the earth; no navigation nor use of the commodities that may be imported by sea; no commodious building; no instruments of moving and removing such things as require much force; no knowledge of the face of the earth; no account of time; no arts; no letters; no society; and, which is worst of all, continual fear and danger of violent death; and the life of man solitary, poor, nasty, brutish, and short.

It may seem strange to some man that has not well weighed these things that nature should thus dissociate and render men apt to invade and destroy one another; and he may therefore, not trusting to this inference made from the passions, desire perhaps to have the same confirmed by experience. Let him therefore consider with himself—when taking a journey he arms himself and seeks to go well accompanied, when going to sleep he locks his doors, when even in his house he locks his chests, and this when he knows there be laws and public officers, armed, to revenge all injuries shall be done him—what opinion he has of his fellow subjects when he rides armed, of his fellow citizens when he locks his doors, and of his children and servants when he locks his chests. Does he not there as much accuse mankind by his actions as I do by my words? But neither of us accuse man's nature in it. The desires and other passions of man are in themselves no sin. No more are the actions that proceed from those passions till they know a law that forbids them, which, till laws be made, they cannot know, nor can any law be made till they have agreed upon the person that shall make it.

It may peradventure be thought there was never such a time nor condition of war as this, and I believe it was never generally so over all the world; but there are many places where they live so now. For the savage people in many places of America, except the government of small families, the concord whereof depends on natural lust, have no government at all and live at this day in that brutish manner as I said before. Howsoever, it may be perceived what manner of life there would be where there were no common power to fear by the manner of life which men that have formerly lived under a peaceful government use to degenerate into in a civil war.

But though there had never been any time wherein particular men were in a condition of war one against another, yet in all times kings and persons of sovereign authority, because of their independency, are in continual jealousies and in the state and posture of gladiators, having their weapons pointing and their eyes fixed on one another—that is, their forts, garrisons, and guns upon the frontiers of their kingdoms, and continual spies upon their neighbors—which is a posture of war. But because they uphold thereby the industry of their subjects, there does not follow from it that misery which accompanies the liberty of particular men.

To this war of every man against every man, this also is consequent: that nothing can be unjust. The notions of right and wrong, justice and injustice, have there no place. Where there is no common power, there is no law; where no law, no injustice. Force and fraud are in war the two cardinal virtues. Justice and injustice are none of the faculties neither of the body nor mind. If they were, they might be in a man that were alone in the world, as well as his senses and passions. They are qualities that relate to men in society, not in solitude. It is consequent also to the same condition that there be no propriety, no dominion, no mine and thine distinct; but only that to be every man's that he can get, and for so long as he can keep it. And thus much for the ill condition which man by mere nature is actually placed in, though with a possibility to come out of it consisting partly in the passions, partly in his reason.

The passions that incline men to peace are fear of death, desire of such things as are necessary to commodious living, and a hope by their industry to obtain them. And reason suggests convenient articles of peace, upon which men may be drawn to agreement. These articles are they which otherwise are called the Laws of Nature, whereof I shall speak more particularly in the two following chapters.

CHAPTER FOURTEEN

Of the First and Second Natural Laws, and of Contracts

The RIGHT OF NATURE, which writers commonly call *jus naturale*, is the liberty each man has to use his own power, as he will himself, for the preservation of his own nature—that is to say, of his own life—and consequently of doing anything which, in his own judgment and reason, he shall conceive to be the aptest means thereunto.

By LIBERTY is understood, according to the proper signification of the word, the absence of external impediments; which impediments may oft take away part of a man's power to do what he would, but cannot hinder him from using the power left him according as his judgment and reason shall dictate to him.

A LAW OF NATURE, *lex naturalis*, is a precept or general rule, found out by reason, by which a man is forbidden to do that which is destructive to his life or takes away the means of preserving the same and to omit that by which he thinks it may be best preserved. For though they that speak of this subject use to confound *jus* and *lex*, *right* and *law*, yet they ought to be distinguished; because RIGHT consists in liberty to do or to forbear, whereas LAW determines and binds to one of them; so that law and right differ as much as obligation and liberty, which in one and the same matter are inconsistent.

And because the condition of man, as has been declared in the precedent chapter, is a condition of war of every one against every one—in which case everyone is governed by his own reason and there is nothing he can make use of that may not be a help unto him in preserving his life against his enemies—it follows that in such a condition every man has a right to everything, even to one another's body. And therefore, as long as this natural right of every man to everything endures, there can be no security to any man, how strong or wise soever he be, of living out the time which nature ordinarily allows men to live. And consequently it is a precept or general rule of reason *that every man ought to endeavor peace, as far as he has hope of obtaining it; and when he cannot obtain it, that he may seek and use all helps and advantages of war.* The first branch of which rule contains the first and fundamental law of nature, which is *to seek peace and follow it.* The second, the sum of the right of nature, which is, *by all means we can to defend ourselves.*

From this fundamental law of nature, by which men are commanded to endeavor peace, is derived this second law: *that a man be willing, when others are so too, as far forth as for peace and defense of himself he shall think it necessary, to lay down this right to all things, and be contented with so much liberty against other men as he would allow other men against himself.* For as long as every man holds this right of doing anything he likes, so long are all men in the condition of war. But if other men will not lay down their right as well as he, then there is no reason for anyone to divest himself of his, for that were to expose himself to prey, which no man is bound to, rather than to dispose himself to peace. This is that law of the gospel: *whatsoever you require that others should do to you, that do ye to them. And that law of all men, quod tibi fieri non vis, alteri ne feceris.*

To *lay down* a man's *right* to anything is to *divest* himself of the *liberty* of hindering another of the benefit of his own right to the same. For he that renounces or passes away his right gives not to any other man a right which he had not before—because there is nothing to which every man had not right by nature—but only stands out of his way, that he may enjoy his own original right without hindrance from him, not without hindrance from another. So that the effect which redounds to one man by another man's defect of right is but so much diminution of impediments to the use of his own right original. Right is laid aside either by simply renouncing it or by transferring it to another. By *simply* RENOUNCING, when he cares not to whom the benefit thereof redounds. By TRANSFERRING, when he intends the benefit thereof to some certain person or persons. And when a man has in either manner abandoned or granted away his right, then he is said to be OBLIGED OR BOUND not to hinder those to whom such right is granted or abandoned from the benefit of it; and that he *ought*, and it is his DUTY, not to make void that voluntary act of his own; and that such hindrance is INJUSTICE and INJURY as being *sine jure*, the right being before renounced or transferred. So that *injury* or *injustice* in the controversies of the world is somewhat like to that which in the disputations of scholars is called *absurdity*. For as it is there called an absurdity to contradict what one maintained in the beginning, so in the world it is called injustice and injury voluntarily to undo that which from the beginning he had voluntarily done. The way by which a man either simply renounces or transfers his right is a declaration or signification by some voluntary and sufficient sign or signs that he does so renounce or transfer, or has so renounced or transferred, the same to him that accepts it. And these signs are either words only or actions only; or as it happens most often, both words and actions. And the same are the BONDS by which men are bound and obliged—bonds that have their strength, not from their own nature, for nothing is more easily broken than a man's word, but from fear of some evil consequence upon the rupture.

Whensoever a man transfers his right or renounces it, it is either in consideration of some right reciprocally transferred to himself or for some other good he hopes for thereby. For it is a voluntary act; and of the voluntary acts of every man, the object is some *good to himself*. And therefore there be some rights which no man can be understood by any words or other signs to have abandoned or transferred. As, first, a man cannot lay down the right of resisting them that assault him by force to take away his life, because he cannot be understood to aim thereby at any good to himself. The same may be said of wounds and chains and imprisonment, both because there is no benefit consequent to such patience as there is to the patience of suffering another to be wounded or imprisoned, as also because a man cannot tell, when he sees men proceed against him by violence, whether they intend his death or not. And, lastly, the motive and end for which this renouncing and transferring of right is introduced is nothing else but the security of a man's person in his life and in the means of so preserving life as not to be weary of it. And therefore if a man by words or other signs seem to despoil himself of the end for which those signs were intended, he is not to be understood as if he meant it or that it was his will, but that he was ignorant of how such words and actions were to be interpreted.

The mutual transferring of right is that which men call CONTRACT.

There is difference between transferring of right to the thing and transferring, or tradition—that is, delivery—of the thing itself. For the thing may be delivered together with the translation of the right, as in buying and selling with ready money or exchange of goods or lands, and it may be delivered some time after.

Again, one of the contractors may deliver the thing contracted for on his part and leave the other to perform his part at some determinate time after and in the meantime be trusted, and then the contract on his part is called PACT or COVENANT; or both parts may contract now to perform hereafter, in which cases he that is to perform in time to come, being trusted, his performance is called *keeping of promise* or faith, and the failing of performance, if it be voluntary, *violation of faith*.

CHAPTER FIFTEEN

Of Other Laws of Nature

From that law of nature by which we are obliged to transfer to another such rights as, being retained, hinder the peace of mankind, there follows a third, which is this: *that men perform their covenants made;* without which covenants are in vain and but empty words, and, the right of all men to all things remaining, we are still in the condition of war.

And in this law of nature consists the fountain and original of JUSTICE. For where no covenant has preceded there has no right been transferred, and every man has right to every thing; and consequently no action can be unjust. But when a covenant is made, then to break it is *unjust;* and the definition of INJUSTICE is no other than *the not performance of covenant.* And whatsoever is not unjust is just.

But because covenants of mutual trust, where there is a fear of not performance on either part, as has been said in the former chapter, are invalid, though the original of justice be the making of covenants, yet injustice actually there can be none till the cause of such fear be taken away, which, while men are in the natural condition of war, cannot be done. Therefore, before the names of just and unjust can have place, there must be some coercive power to compel men equally to the performance of their covenants by the terror of some punishment greater than the benefit they expect by the breach of their covenant, and to make good that propriety which by mutual contract men acquire in recompense of the universal right they abandon; and such power there is none before the erection of a commonwealth.

CHAPTER THIRTY

Of the Office of the Sovereign Representative

The office of the sovereign, be it a monarch or an assembly, consists in the end for which he was trusted with the sovereign power, namely, the procuration of the *safety of the people;* to which he is obliged by the law of nature, and to render an account thereof to God, the author of that law, and to none but him. But by safety here is not meant a bare preservation but also all other contentments of life which every man by lawful industry, without danger or hurt to the commonwealth, shall acquire to himself.

And this is intended should be done, not by care applied to individuals further than their protection from injuries when they shall complain, but by a general providence contained in public instruction, both of doctrine and example, and in the making and executing of good laws, to which individual persons may apply their own cases.

And because, if the essential rights of sovereignty, specified before in the eighteenth chapter, be taken away, the commonwealth is thereby dissolved and every man returns into the condition and calamity of a war with every other man, which is the greatest evil that can happen in this life, it is the office of the sovereign to maintain those rights entire, and consequently against his duty, first, to transfer to another or to lay from himself any of them. For he that deserts the means deserts the ends; and he deserts the means that, being the sovereign, acknowledges himself subject to the civil laws and renounces the power of supreme judicature, or of making war or peace by his own authority, or of judging of the necessities of the commonwealth, or of levying money and soldiers when and as much as in his own conscience he shall judge necessary, or of making officers and ministers both of war and peace, or of appointing teachers and examining what doctrines are conformable or contrary to the defense, peace, and good of the people.

Joseph Butler, *Fifteen Sermons Preached at the Rolls Chapel,* 1726

Against Egoism
Joseph Butler

Preface

[I]t is not a true representation of mankind to affirm that they are wholly governed by self-love, the love of power and sensual appetites; since, as on the one hand, they are often actuated by these, without any regard to right or wrong, so, on the other, it is manifest fact that the same persons, the generality, are frequently influenced by friendship, compassion, gratitude; and even a general abhorrence of what is base, and liking of what is fair and just, takes its turn amongst the other motives of action. . . . There is a strange affection in many people of explaining away all particular affections, and representing the whole life as nothing but one continued exercise of self-love. Hence arises that surprising confusion and perplexity in the Epicureans of old, Hobbes, the author [the Duke de la Rochefoucauld (1613–80] of *Reflexions, Sentences, et Maximes Morales,* and this whole set of writers—the confusion of calling actions interested which are done in contradiction to the most manifest known interest, merely for the gratification of a present passion. Now all this confusion might easily be avoided, by stating to ourselves wherein the idea of self-love in general consists, as distinguished from all particular movements toward particular external objects—the appetites of sense, resentment, compassion, curiosity, ambition, and the rest. When this is done, if the words "selfish" and "interested" cannot be parted with but must be applied to everything, yet, to avoid such total confusion of all language, let the distinction be made by epithets: and the first may be called cool or settled selfishness, and the other passionate or sensual selfishness. But the most natural way of speaking plainly is to call the first only "self-love" and the actions proceeding from it "interested"; and to say of the latter that they are not love to ourselves, but movements toward somewhat external: honor, power, the harm or good of another; and that the pursuit of these external objects, so far as it proceeds from these movements (for it may proceed from self-love), is no otherwise interested than as every action of every creature must, from the nature of the thing, be; for no one can act but from a desire or choice or preference of his own.

Self-love and any particular passion may be joined together; and from this complication it becomes impossible in numberless instances to determine precisely how far an action, perhaps even of one's own, has for its principle general self-love or some particular passion. But this need create no confusion in the ideas themselves of self-love and particular passions. We distinctly discern what one is and what the others are, though we may be uncertain how far one or the other influences us. And though, from this uncertainty, it cannot but be that there will be different opinions concerning mankind as more or less governed by interest, and some will ascribe actions to self-love, which others will ascribe to particular passions; yet it is absurd to say that mankind are wholly actuated by either, since it is manifest that both have their influence. For as, on the one hand, men form a general notion of interest, some placing it in one thing, and some in another, and have a considerable regard to it throughout the course of their life, which is owing to self-love; so, on the other hand, they are often set on work by the particular passions themselves, and a considerable part of life is spent in the actual gratification of them, that is, is employed, not by self-love, but by the passions.

Besides, the very idea of an interested pursuit necessarily presupposes particular passions or appetites, since the very idea of interest or happiness consists in this that an appetite or affection enjoys its object. It is not because we love ourselves that we find delight in such and such objects, but because we have particular affections toward them. Take away these affections and you leave self-love absolutely nothing at all to employ itself about, no end or object for it to pursue except only that of avoiding pain. Indeed, the Epicureans, who maintained that absence of pain was the highest happiness, might, consistently with themselves, deny all affection and, if they had so pleased, every sensual appetite, too; but the very idea of interest or happiness other than absence of pain implies particular appetites or passions, these being necessary to constitute that interest or happiness.

The observation that benevolence is no more disinterested than any of the common particular passions, seems in itself worth being taken notice of; but is insisted upon to obviate that scorn which one sees rising upon the faces of people who are said to know the world, when mention is made of a disinterested, generous, or public-spirited action. The truth of that observation might be made appear in a more formal manner of proof; for whoever will consider all the possible respects and relations which any particular affection can have to self-love and private interest, will, I think, see demonstrably that benevolence is not in any respect more at variance with self-love than any other particular affection whatever, but that it is in every respect, at least, as friendly to it. . . .

Neither does there appear any reason to wish self-love were weaker in the generality of the world than it is. The influence which it has seems plainly owing to its being constant and habitual, which it cannot but be, and not to the degree or strength of it. Every caprice of the imagination, every curiosity of the understanding, every affection of the heart is perpetually showing its weakness, by prevailing over it. Men daily, hourly sacrifice the greatest known interest to fancy, inquisitiveness, love, or hatred, any vagrant inclination. The thing to be lamented is not that men have so great regard to their own good or interest in the present world, for they have not enough; but that they have so little to the good of others. And this seems plainly owing to their being so much engaged in the gratification of particular passions unfriendly to benevolence, and which happen to be most prevalent in them, much more than to self-love. . . .

Upon the whole, if the generality of mankind were to cultivate within themselves the principle of self-love, if they were to accustom themselves often to set down and consider what was the greatest happiness they were capable of attaining for themselves in this life, and if self-love were so strong and prevalent as that they would uniformly pursue this their supposed chief temporal good, without being diverted from it by any particular passion, it would manifestly prevent numberless follies and vices. This was in a great measure the Epicurean system of philosophy. It is indeed by no means the religious or even moral institution of life. Yet, with all the mistakes men would fall into about interest, it would be less mischievous than the extravagances of mere appetite, will, and pleasure; for certainly self-love, though confined to the interest of this life, is, of the two, a much better guide than passion, which has absolutely no bound nor measure but what is set to it by this self-love or moral considerations. . . .

Sermon 7

. . . . there is a natural principle of *benevolence* in man, which is in some degree to *society* what *self-love* is to the *individual*. And if there be in mankind any disposition to friendship; if there be any such thing as compassion, for compassion is momentary love; if there be any such thing as the paternal or filial affections; if there be any affection in human nature the object and end of which is the good of another—this is itself benevolence or the love of another.

[The following two paragraphs appeared as footnotes to Sermon I.] . . . If any person can in earnest doubt whether there be such a thing as goodwill in one man toward another (for the question is not concerning either the degree or extensiveness of it, but concerning the affection itself), let it be observed that whether man be thus or otherwise constituted, what is the inward frame in this particular, is a mere question of fact or natural history, not provable immediately by reason. It is therefore to be judged of and determined in the same way other facts or matters of natural history are: by appealing to the external senses or inward perceptions respectively, as the matter under consideration is cognizable by one or the other; by arguing from acknowledged facts and actions; for a great number of actions in the same kind, in different circumstances, and respecting different objects, will prove, to a certainty, what principles they do not, and, to the greatest probability, what principles they do proceed from; and lastly, by the testimony of mankind. Now that there is some degree of benevolence amongst men may be as strongly and plainly proved in all these ways, as it could possibly be proved, supposing there was this affection in our nature. And should anyone think fit to assert that resentment in the mind of man was absolutely nothing but reasonable concern for our own safety, the falsity of this, and what is the real nature of that passion, could be shown in no other ways than those in which it may be shown, that there is such a thing in some degree as real goodwill in man toward man. It is sufficient that the seeds of it be implanted in our nature by God. There is, it is owned, much left for us to do upon our own heart and temper; to cultivate, to improve, to call it forth, to exercise it in a steady, uniform manner. This is our work; this is virtue and religion.

Everybody makes a distinction between self-love and the several particular passions, appetites, and affections; and yet they are often confounded again. That they are totally different, will be seen by any one who will distinguish between the passions and appetites themselves, and endeavoring after the means of their gratification. Consider the appetite of hunger, and the desire of esteem; these being the occasion both of pleasure and pain, the coolest self-love, as well as the appetites and passions themselves, may put us upon making use of the proper methods of obtaining that pleasure, and avoiding that pain; but the feelings themselves, the pain of hunger and shame, and the delight from esteem, are no more self-love than they are anything in the world. Though a man hated himself, he would as much feel the pain of hunger as he would that of the gout; and it is plainly supposable there may be creatures with self-love in them to the highest degree, who may be quite insensible and indifferent (as men in some cases are) to the contempt and esteem of those upon whom their happiness does not in some further respects depend. And as self-love and the several particular passions and appetites are in themselves totally different, so that some actions proceed from one, and some from the other, will be manifest to any who will observe the two following very supposable cases. One man rushes upon certain ruin for the gratification of a present desire; nobody will call the principle of this action self-love. Suppose another man to go through some laborious work upon promise of a great reward, without any distinct knowledge what the reward will be; this course of action cannot be ascribed to any particular passion. The former of these actions is plainly to be imputed to some particular passion or affection, the latter as plainly to the general affection or principle of self-love. That there are some particular pursuits or actions concerning which we cannot determine how far they are owing to one, and how far to the other, proceeds from this that the two principles are frequently mixed together, and run up into each other. This distinction is further explained in the eleventh sermon.

Sermon XI

. . . Every man hath a general desire of his own happiness, and likewise a variety of particular affections, passions, and appetites to particular external objects. The former proceeds from or is self-love, and seems inseparable from all sensible creatures who can reflect upon themselves and their own interest or happiness, so as to have that interest an object to their minds; what is to be said of the latter is that they proceed from, or together make up, that particular nature according to which man is made. The object the former pursues is somewhat internal—our own happiness, enjoyment, satisfaction; whether we have or have not a distinct particular perception what it is or wherein it consists, the objects of the latter are this or that particular external thing which the affections tend towards, and of which it hath always a particular idea or perception. The principle we call "self-love" never seeks anything external for the sake of the thing, but only as a means of happiness or good; particular affections rest in the external things themselves. One belongs to man as a reasonable creature reflecting upon his own interest or happiness. The other, though quite distinct from reason, are as much a part of human nature.

That all particular appetites and passions are *toward external things themselves*, distinct from the *pleasure arising from them*, is manifested from hence—that there could not be this pleasure were it not for that prior suitableness between the object and the passion; there could be no enjoyment or delight from one thing more than another, from eating food more than from swallowing a stone, if there were not an affection or appetite to one thing more than another.

Every particular affection, even the love of our neighbor, is as really our own affection as self-love; and the pleasure arising from its gratification is as much my own pleasure as the pleasure self-love would have from knowing I myself should be happy some time hence, would be my own pleasure. And if, because every particular affection is a man's own, and the pleasure arising from its gratification his own pleasure, or pleasure to himself, such particular affection must be called self-love, according to this way of speaking no creature whatever can possibly act but merely from self-love; and every action and every affection whatever is to be resolved up into this one principle. But then this is not the language of mankind; or if it were, we should want words to express the difference between the principle of an action proceeding from cool consideration that it will be to my own advantage, and an action, suppose of revenge or of friendship, by which a man runs upon certain ruin to do evil or good to another. It is manifest the principles of these actions are totally different, and so want different words to be distinguished by; all that they agree in is that they both proceed from and are done to gratify an inclination in a man's self. But the principle or inclination in one case is self-love, in the other, hatred or love of another. There is then a distinction between the cool principle of self-love or general desire of our happiness, as one part of our nature and one principle of action, and the particular affections toward particular external objects, as another part of our nature and another principle of action. How much soever therefore is to be allowed to self-love, yet it cannot be allowed to be the whole of our inward constitution, because, you see, there are other parts or principles which come into it.

Further, private happiness or good is all which self-love can make us desire or be concerned about; in having this consists its gratification: it is an affection to ourselves, a regard to our own interest, happiness, and private good; and in the proportion a man hath this, he is interested, or a lover of himself. Let this be kept in mind; because there is commonly, as I shall presently have occasion to observe, another sense put upon these words. On the other hand, particular affections tend toward particular external things; these are their objects; having these is their end—in this consists their gratification, no matter whether it be, or be not, upon the whole, our interest or happiness. An action done from the former of these principles is called an interested action. An action proceeding from any of the latter has its denomination of passionate, ambitious, friendly, revengeful, or any other, from the particular appetite or affection from which it proceeds. Thus self-love as one part of human nature and the several particular principles as the other part are, themselves, their objects and ends, stated and shown.

From hence it will be easy to see how far, and in what ways, each of these can contribute and be subservient to the private good of the individual. Happiness does not consist in self-love. The desire of happiness is no more the thing itself than the desire of riches is the possession or enjoyment of them. People may love themselves with the most entire and unbounded affection, and yet be extremely miserable. Neither can self-love anyway help them out, but by setting them on work to get rid of the causes of their misery, to gain or make use of those objects which are by nature adapted to afford satisfaction. Happiness or satisfaction consists only in the enjoyment of those objects which are by nature suited to our several particular appetites, passions, and affections. So that if self-love wholly engrosses us, and leaves no room for any other principle, there can be absolutely no such thing at all as happiness, or enjoyment of any kind whatever, since happiness consists in the gratification of particular passions, which supposes the having of them. Self-love then does not constitute this or that to be our interest or good; but, our interest or good being constituted by nature and supposed, self-love only puts us upon obtaining and securing it. Therefore, if it be possible that self-love may prevail and exert itself in a degree or manner which is not subservient to this end, then it will not follow that our interest will be promoted in proportion to the degree in which that principle engrosses us, and prevails over others. Nay further, the private and contracted affection, when it is not subservient to this end, private good, may, for anything that appears, have a direct contrary tendency and effect. And if we will consider the matter, we shall see that it often really has. *Disengagement* is absolutely necessary to enjoyment; and a person may have so steady and fixed an eye upon his own interest, whatever he places it in, as may hinder him from *attending* to many gratifications within his reach, which others have their minds free and open to. Overfondness for a child is not generally thought to be for its advantage; and if there be any guess to be made from appearances, surely that character we call selfish is not the most promising for happiness. Such a temper may plainly be, and exert itself in a degree and manner which may give unnecessary and useless solicitude and anxiety, in a degree and manner which may prevent obtaining the means and materials of enjoyment, as well as the making use of them. Immoderate self-love does very ill consult its own interest; and how much soever a paradox it may appear, it is certainly true that even from self-love we should endeavor to get over all inordinate regard to and consideration of ourselves. Every one of our passions and affections hath its natural stint and bound, which may easily be exceeded;

whereas our enjoyments can possibly be but in a determinate measure and degree. Therefore such excess of the affection, since it cannot procure any enjoyment, must in all cases be useless, but is generally attended with inconveniences, and often is downright pain and misery. This holds as much with regard to self-love as to all other affections. The natural degree of it, so far as it sets us on work to gain and make use of the materials of satisfaction, may be to our real advantage; but beyond or besides this, it is in several respects an inconvenience and disadvantage. Thus it appears that private interest is so far from being likely to be promoted in proportion to the degree in which self-love engrosses us, and prevails over all other principles, that the contracted affection may be so prevalent as to disappoint itself, and even contradict its own end, private good.

"But who, except the most sordidly covetous, ever thought there was any rivalship between the love of greatness, honor, power, or between sensual appetites and self-love? No, there is a perfect harmony between them. It is by means of these particular appetites and affections that self-love is gratified in enjoyment, happiness, and satisfaction. The competition and rivalship is between self-love and the love of our neighbor, that affection which leads us out of ourselves, makes us regardless of our own interest, and substitute that of another in its stead." Whether then there be any peculiar competition and contrariety in this case, shall now be considered.

Self-love and interestedness was stated to consist in or be an affection to ourselves, a regard to our own private good; it is therefore distinct from benevolence, which is an affection to the good of our fellow creatures. But that benevolence is distinct from, that is, not the same thing with self-love, is no reason for its being looked upon with any peculiar suspicion; because every principle whatever, by means of which self-love is gratified, is distinct from it; and all things which are distinct from each other are equally so. A man has an affection or aversion to another; that one of these tends to and is gratified by doing good, that the other tends to and is gratified by doing harm, does not in the least alter the respect which either one or the other of these inward feelings has to self-love. We use the word "property" so as to exclude any other persons having an interest in that of which we say a particular man has the property. And we often use the word "selfish" so as to exclude in the same manner all regards to the good of others. But the cases are not parallel; for though that exclusion is really part of the idea of property, yet such positive exclusion, or bringing this peculiar disregard to the good of others into the idea of self-love, is in reality adding to the idea, or changing it from what it was before stated to consist in, namely, in an affection to ourselves. This being the whole idea of self-love, it can no otherwise exclude goodwill or love of others than merely by not including it, no otherwise than it excludes love of arts or reputation, or of anything else. Neither, on the other hand, does benevolence, any more than love of arts or of reputation, exclude self-love. Love of our neighbor then has just the same respect to, is no more distant from, self-love than hatred of our neighbor, or than love or hatred of anything else. Thus the principles from which men rush upon certain ruin for the destruction of an enemy, and for the preservation of a friend, have the same respect to the private affection, and are equally interested or equally disinterested; and it is of no avail whether they are said to be one or the other. Therefore, to those that are shocked to hear virtue spoken of as disinterested, it may be allowed that it is indeed absurd to speak thus of it, unless hatred, several particular instances of vice, and all the common affections and aversions in mankind are acknowledged to be disinterested too. Is there any less inconsistency between the love of inanimate things, or of creatures merely sensitive, and self-love than between self-love and the love of our neighbor? Is desire of the love of inanimate things, or of creatures merely sensitive, and self-love than desire of and delight in the esteem of another? They are both equally desire of and delight in somewhat external to ourselves: either both or neither are so. The object of self-love is expressed in the term "self"; and every appetite of sense and every particular affection of the heart are equally interested or disinterested, because the objects of them are all equally self or somewhat else. Whatever ridicule therefore the mention of a disinterested principle or action may be supposed to lie open to, must, upon the matter being thus stated, relate to ambition and every appetite and particular affection, as much as to benevolence. And indeed all the ridicule and all the grave perplexity, of which this subject hath had its full share, is merely from words. The most intelligible way of speaking of it seems to be this: that self-love and the actions done in consequence of it (for these will presently appear to be the same as to this question) are interested; that particular affections toward external objects, and the actions done in consequence of those affections, are not so. But everyone is at liberty to use words as he pleases. All that is here insisted upon is that ambition, revenge, benevolence, all particular passions whatever, and the actions they produce, are equally interested or disinterested.

Thus it appears that there is no peculiar contrariety between self-love and benevolence, no greater competition between these than between any other particular affections and self-love. . . .

David Hume, *An Enquiry Concerning the Principles of Morals*, 1751

Morality and the Emotions
David Hume

OF THE GENERAL PRINCIPLES OF MORALS

There has been a controversy started of late, much better worth examination, concerning the general foundation of Morals; whether they be derived from Reason, or from Sentiment; whether we attain the knowledge of them by a chain of argument and induction, or by an immediate feeling and finer internal sense; whether, like all sound judgment of truth and falsehood, they should be the same to every rational intelligent being; or whether, like the perception of beauty and deformity, they be founded entirely on the particular fabric and constitution of the human species.

The ancient philosophers, though they often affirm, that virtue is nothing but conformity to reason, yet, in general, seem to consider morals as deriving their existence from taste and sentiment. On the other hand, our modern enquirers, though they also talk much of the beauty of virtue, and deformity of vice, yet have commonly endeavoured to account for these distinctions by metaphysical reasonings, and by deductions from the most abstract principles of the understanding. . . .

It must be acknowledged, that both sides of the question are susceptible of specious arguments. Moral distinctions, it may be said, are discernible by pure *reason*: else, whence the many disputes that reign in common life, as well as in philosophy, with regard to this subject: the long chain of proofs often produced on both sides; the examples cited, the authorities appealed to, the analogies employed, the fallacies detected, the inferences drawn, and the several conclusions adjusted to their proper principles. Truth is disputable: not taste: what exists in the nature of things is the standard of our judgment; what each man feels within himself is the standard of sentiment. . . .

On the other hand, those who would resolve all moral determinations into sentiment, may endeavor to show, that it is impossible for reason ever to draw conclusions of this nature. To virtue, say they, it belongs to be *amiable* and vice *odious*. This forms their very nature or essence. But can reason or argumentation distribute these different epithets to any subjects, and pronounce beforehand, that this must produce love, and that hatred? Or what other reason can we ever assign for these affections, but the original fabric and formation of the human mind, which is naturally adapted to receive them?

The end of all moral speculations is to teach us our duty; and, by proper representations of the deformity of vice and beauty of virtue, beget correspondent habits, and engage us to avoid the one, and embrace the other. But is this ever to be expected from inferences and conclusions of the understanding, which of themselves have no hold of the affections or set in motion the active powers of men? . . .

What is honourable, what is fair, what is becoming, what is noble, what is generous, takes possession of the heart, and animates us to embrace and maintain it. What is intelligible, what is evident, what is probable, what is true, procures only the cool asset of the understanding: and gratifying a speculative curiosity, puts an end to our researches.

Extinguish all the warm feelings and prepossessions in favour of virtue, and all disgust or aversion to vice: render men totally indifferent towards these distinctions; and morality is no longer a practical study, nor has any tendency to regulate our lives and actions.

These arguments on each side (and many more might be produced) are so plausible, that I am apt to suspect, they may, the one as well as the other, be solid and satisfactory, and that *reason* and *sentiment* concur in almost all moral determinations and conclusions. The final sentence, it is probable, which pronounces characters and actions amiable or odious, praiseworthy or blameable; that which stamps on them the mark of honour or infamy. approbation or censure; that which renders morality an active principle and constitutes virtue our happiness and vice our misery; it is probable, I say, that this final sentence depends on some internal sense or feeling, which nature has made universal in the whole species. For what else can have an influence of this nature? But in order to pave the way for such a sentiment, and give a proper discernment of its object, it is often necessary, we find, that much reasoning should precede, that nice distinctions be made, just conclusions drawn, distant comparisons formed, complicated relations examined, and general facts fixed and ascertained. . . .

But though this question, concerning the general principles of morals, be curious and important, it is needless for us, at present, to employ farther care in our researches concerning it. For if we can be so happy, in the course of this enquiry, as to discover the true origin of morals, it will then easily appear how far either sentiment or reason enters into all determinations of this nature. In order to attain this purpose, we shall endeavor to follow a very simple method: we shall analyse that complication of mental qualities, which form what, in common life, we call Personal Merit: we shall consider every attribute of the mind, which renders a man an object either of esteem and affection, or of hatred and contempt; every habit or sentiment or faculty, which, if ascribed to any person, implies either praise or blame, and may enter into any panegyric or satire of his character and manners. . . .

We shall begin our enquiry on this head by the consideration of the social virtues, Benevolence and Justice. The explication of them will probably give us an opening by which the others may be accounted for.

OF BENEVOLENCE

Part I

It may be esteemed, perhaps, a superfluous task to prove, that the benevolent or softer affections are estimable; and wherever they appear, engage the approbation and good-will of mankind. The epithets *sociable*, *good-natured*, *humane*, *merciful*, *grateful*, *friendly*, *generous*, *beneficent*, or their equivalents, are known in all languages, and universally express the highest merit, which *human nature* is capable of attaining. Where these amiable qualities are attended with birth and power and eminent abilities, and display themselves in the good government or useful instruction of mankind, they seem even to raise the possessors of them above the rank of *human nature*, and make them approach in some measure to the divine. Exalted capacity, undaunted courage, prosperous success; these may only expose a hero or politician to the envy and ill-will of the public: but as soon as the praises are added of humane and beneficent; when instances are displayed of lenity, tenderness or friendship; envy itself is silent, or joins the general voice of approbation and applause. . . .

[N]o qualities are more intitled to the general good-will and approbation of mankind than beneficence and humanity, friendship and gratitude, natural affection and public spirit, or whatever proceeds from a tender sympathy with others, and a generous concern for our kind and species. These wherever they appear seem to transfuse themselves, in a manner, into each beholder, and to call forth, in their own behalf, the same favourable and affectionate sentiments, which they exert on all around.

Part II

We may observe that, in displaying the praises of any humane, beneficent man, there is one circumstance which never fails to be amply insisted on, namely, the happiness and satisfaction, derived to society from his intercourse and good offices. To his parents, we are apt to say, he endears himself by his pious attachment and duteous care still more than by the connexions of nature. His children never feel his authority, but when employed for their advantage. With him, the ties of love are consolidated by beneficence and friendship. The ties of friendship approach, in a fond observance of each obliging office, to those of love and inclination. His domestics and dependants have in him a sure resource; and no longer dread the power of fortune, but so far as she exercises it over him. From him the hungry receive food, the naked clothing, the ignorant and slothful skill and industry. Like the sun, an inferior minister of providence he cheers, invigorates, and sustains the surrounding world.

If confined to private life, the sphere of his activity is narrower; but his influence is all benign and gentle. If exalted into a higher station, mankind and posterity reap the fruit of his labours.

As these topics of praise never fail to be employed, and with success, where we would inspire esteem for any one; may it not thence be concluded, that the utility, resulting from the social virtues, forms, at least, a *part* of their merit, and is one source of that approbation and regard so universally paid to them?

Upon the whole, then, it seems undeniable, *that* nothing can bestow more merit on any human creature than the sentiment of benevolence in an eminent degree; and *that* a *part*, at least, of its merit arises from its tendency to promote the interests of our species, and bestow happiness on human society. We carry our view into the salutary consequences of such a character and disposition; and what ever has so benign an influence, and forwards so desirable an end, is beheld with complacency and pleasure. The social virtues are never regarded without their beneficial tendencies, nor viewed as barren and unfruitful. The happiness of mankind, the order of society, the harmony of families, the mutual support of friends, are always considered as the result of their gentle dominion over the breasts of men. . . .

OF JUSTICE

Part I

That Justice is so useful to society, and consequently that *part* of its merit, at least, must arise from that consideration, it would be a superfluous undertaking to prove. That public utility is the *sole* origin of justice, and that reflections on the beneficial consequences of this virtue are the *sole* foundation of its merit; this proposition, being more curious and important, will better deserve our examination and enquiry.

Let us suppose that nature has bestowed on the human race such profuse *abundance* of all *external* conveniences, that, without any uncertainty in the event, without any care or industry on our part, every individual finds himself fully provided with whatever his most voracious appetites can want, or luxurious imagination wish or desire. His natural beauty, we shall suppose, surpasses all acquired ornaments: the perpetual elemency of the seasons renders useless all clothes or covering; the raw herbage affords him the most delicious fare; the clear fountain, the richest beverage. No laborious occupation required: no tillage: no navigation. Music, poetry, and contemplation form his sole business: conversation, mirth, and friendship his sole amusement.

It seems evident that, in such a happy state, every other social virtue would flourish, and receive tenfold increase; but the cautious, jealous virtue of justice would never once have been dreamed of. For what purpose make a partition of goods, where every one has already more than enough? Why give rise to property, where there cannot possibly be any injury? Why call this object mine, when upon the seizing of it by another, I need but stretch out my hand to possess myself to what is equally valuable? Justice, in that case, being totally useless, would be an idle ceremonial, and could never possibly have place in the catalogue of virtues.

We see, even in the present necessitous condition of mankind, that, wherever any benefit is bestowed by nature in an unlimited abundance, we leave it always in common among the whole human race, and make no subdivisions of right and property. Water and air, though the most necessary of all objects, are not challenged as the property of individuals; nor can any man commit injustice by the most lavish use and enjoyment of these blessings. In fertile extensive countries, with few inhabitants, land is regarded on the same footing. . . .

Again; suppose, that, though the necessities of human race continue the same as at present, yet the mind is so enlarged, and so replete with friendship and generosity, that every man has the utmost tenderness for every man, and feels no more concern for his own interest than for that of his fellows; it seems evident, that the use of justice would, in this case, be suspended by such an extensive benevolence, nor would the divisions and barriers of property and obligation have ever been thought of. Why should I bind another, by a deed or promise, to do me any good office, when I know that he is already prompted, by the strongest inclination, to seek my happiness, and would, of himself, perform the desired service; except the hurt, he thereby receives, be greater than the benefit accruing to me? In which case, he knows, that, from my innate humanity and friendship, I should be first to oppose myself to his impudent generosity. Why raise land marks between my neighbour's field and mine, when my heart has made no division between our interests; but shares all his joys and sorrows with the same force and vivacity as if originally my own? Every man, upon this supposition, being a second self to another, would trust all his interests to the discretion of every man; without jealousy, without partition, without distinction. And the whole human race would form only one family; where all would lie in common, and be used freely, without regard to property; but cautiously too, with as entire regard to the necessities of each individual as if our own interests were most intimately concerned.

In the present disposition of the human heart, it would, perhaps, be difficult to find complete instances of such enlarged affections; but still we may observe, that the case of families approaches towards it; and the stronger the mutual benevolence is among the individuals, the nearer it approaches; till all distinction of property be, in a great measure, lost and confounded among them. Between married persons, the cement of friendship is by the laws supposed so strong as to abolish all division of possessions; and has often, in reality, the force ascribed to it. . . .

To make this truth more evident, let us reverse the foregoing suppositions; and carrying everything to the opposite extreme, consider what would be the effect of these new situations. Suppose a society to fall into such want of all common necessaries, that the utmost frugality and industry cannot preserve the greater number from perishing, and the whole from extreme misery; it will readily, I believe, be admitted, that the strict laws of justice are suspended, in such a pressing emergence, and give place to the stronger motives of necessity and self-preservation. Is it any crime, after a shipwreck, to seize whatever means or instrument of safety one can lay hold of, without regard to former limitations of property? Or if a city besieged were perishing with hunger; can we imagine, that men will see any means of preservation before them, and lose their lives, from a scrupulous regard to what, in other situations, would be the rules of equity and justice? The use and tendency of that virtue is to procure happiness and security, by preserving order in society: but where the society is ready to perish from extreme necessity, no greater evil can be dreaded from violence and injustice; and every man may now provide for himself by all the means, which prudence can dictate, or humanity permit. . . .

Suppose likewise, that it should be a virtuous man's fate to fall into the society of ruffians, remote from the protection of laws and government; what conduct must he embrace in that melancholy situation? He sees such a desperate rapaciousness prevail; such a disregard to equity, such contempt of order, such stupid blindness to future consequences, as must immediately have the most tragical conclusion, and must terminate in destruction to the greater number, and in a total dissolution of society to the rest. He, meanwhile, can have no other expedient than to arm himself, to whomever the sword he seizes, or the buckler may belong: To make provision of all means of defence and security: And his particular regard to justice being no longer of use to his own safety or that of others, he must consult the dictates of self-preservation alone, without concern for those who no longer merit his care and attention. . . .

Thus, the rules of equity or justice depend entirely on the particular state and condition in which men are placed, and owe their origin and existence to that utility, which results to the public from their strict and regular observance. Reverse, in any considerable circumstance, the condition of men: Produce extreme abundance or extreme necessity: Implant in the human breast perfect moderation and humanity, or perfect rapaciousness and malice: By rendering justice totally *useless*, you thereby totally destroy its essence, and suspend its obligation upon mankind.

The common situation of society is a medium amidst all these extremes. We are naturally partial to ourselves, and to our friends; but are capable of learning the advantage resulting from a more equitable conduct. Few enjoyments are given us from the open and liberal hand of nature; but by art, labour, and industry, we can extract them in great abundance. Hence the ideas of property become necessary in all civil society: Hence justice derives its usefulness to the public: And hence alone arises its merit and moral obligation. . . .

Were the human species so framed by nature as that each individual possessed within himself every faculty, requisite both for his own preservation and for the propagation of his kind: Were all society and intercourse cut off between man and man, by the primary intention of the supreme Creator: It seems evident, that so solitary a being would be as much incapable of justice, as of social justice and conversation. . . .

But suppose the conjunction of the sexes to be established in nature, a family immediately arises; and particular rules being found requisite for its subsistence, these are immediately embraced; though without comprehending the rest of mankind within their prescriptions. Suppose that several families unite together into one society, which is totally disjoined from all others, the rules, which preserve peace and order, enlarge themselves to the utmost extent of that society; but becoming then entirely useless, lose their force when carried one step farther. But again suppose, that several distinct societies maintain a kind of intercourse for mutual convenience and advantage, the boundaries of justice still grow larger, in proportion to the largeness of men's views, and the force of their mutual connexions. History, experience, reason sufficiently instruct us in this natural progress of human sentiments, and in the gradual enlargement of our regards to justice, in proportion as we become acquainted with the extensive utility of that virtue.

Part II

If we examine the *particular* laws, by which justice is directed, and property determined; we shall still be presented with the same conclusion. The good of mankind is the only object of all these laws and regulations. Not only is it requisite, for the peace and interest of society, that men's possessions should be separated; but the rules, which we follow, in making the separation, are such as can best be contrived to serve farther the interests of society. . . . Render possessions ever so equal, men's different degrees of art, care, and industry will immediately break that equality. Or if you check these virtues, you reduce society to the most extreme indigence; and instead of preventing want and beggary in a few, render it unavoidable to the whole community. The most rigorous inquisition too is requisite to watch every inequality on its first appearance; and the most severe jurisdiction, to punish and redress it. But besides, that so much authority must soon degenerate into tyranny, and be exerted with great partialities; who can possibly be possessed of it, in such a situation as is here supposed? Perfect equality of possessions, destroying all subordination, weakens extremely the authority of magistracy, and must reduce all power nearly to a level, as well as property.

We may conclude, therefore, that, in order to establish laws for the regulation of property, we must be acquainted with the nature and situation of man; must reject appearances, which may be false, though specious; and must search for those rules, which are, on the whole, most *useful* and *beneficial*. Vulgar sense and slight experience are sufficient for this purpose; where men give not way to too selfish avidity, or too extensive enthusiasm.

Who sees not, for instance. that whatever is produced or improved by man's art or industry ought, for ever, to be secured to him, in order to give encouragement to such *useful* habits and accomplishments? That the property ought to also descend to children and relations, for the same *useful* purpose? That it may be alienated by consent, in order to beget that commerce and intercourse, which is so *beneficial* to human society? And that all contracts and promises ought carefully to be fulfilled, in order to secure mutual trust and confidence, by which the general *interest* of mankind is so much promoted?

Examine the writers on the laws of nature: and you will always find. that. whatever principles they set out with, they are sure to terminate here at last, and to assign, as the ultimate reason for every rule which they establish, the convenience and necessities of mankind. . . .

What is man's property? Anything which it is lawful for him, and for him alone, to use. *But what rule have we by which we can distinguish these objects?* Here we must have recourse to statutes, customs, precedents, analogies, and a hundred other circumstances; some of which are constant and inflexible, some variable and arbitrary. But the ultimate point, in which they all professedly terminate, is the interest and happiness of human society. Where this enters not into consideration, nothing can appear more whimsical, unnatural, and even superstitious, than all or more of the laws of justice and of property.

Those who ridicule vulgar superstitions, and expose the folly of particular regards to meats, days, places, postures, apparel, have an easy task; while they consider all the qualities and relations of the objects, and discover no adequate cause for that affection or antipathy, veneration of horror, which have so mighty an influence over a considerable part of mankind. A Syrian would have starved rather than taste pigeon: an Egyptian would not have approached bacon: But if these species of food be examined by the senses of sight, smell, or taste, or scrutinized by the sciences of chemistry, medicine, or physics, no difference is ever found between them and any other species, nor can that precise circumstance be pitched on, which may afford a just foundation for the religious passion. A fowl on Thursday is lawful food; on Friday abominable: Eggs in this house and in this diocese, are permitted during Lent; a hundred paces farther, to eat them is a damnable sin. This earth or building, yesterday was profane; today, by the muttering of certain words, it has become holy and sacred. . . .

But there is this material difference between *superstition* and *justice*, that the former is frivolous, useless, and burdensome; the latter is absolutely requisite to the well-being of mankind and existence of society. When we abstract from this circumstance (for it is too apparent ever to be overlooked) it must be confessed, that all regards to right and property, seem entirely without foundation, as much as the grossest and most vulgar superstition. Were the interests of society nowise concerned, it is as unintelligible why another's articulating certain sounds implying consent, should change the nature of my actions with regard to a particular object, as why the reciting of a liturgy by a priest, in a certain habit and posture, should dedicate a heap of brick and timber, and render it, thenceforth and for ever, sacred.

These reflections are far from weakening the obligations of justice, or diminishing anything from the most sacred attention to property. On the contrary, such sentiments must acquire new force from the present reasoning. For what stronger foundation can be desired or conceived for any duty, than to observe, that human society, or even human nature, could not subsist without the establishment of it; and will still arrive at greater degrees of happiness and perfection, the more inviolable the regard is, which is paid to that duty? . . .

All birds of the same species in every age and country, built their nests alike: In this we see the force of instinct. Men, in different times and places, frame their houses differently: Here we perceive the influence of reason and custom. A like inference may be drawn from comparing the instinct of generation and the institution of property.

How great soever the variety of municipal laws, it must be confessed, that their chief outlines pretty regularly concur; because the purposes, to which they tend, are everywhere exactly similar. In like manner, all houses have a roof and walls, windows and chimneys;

though diversified in their shape, figure, and materials. The purposes of the latter, directed to the conveniences of human life, discover not more plainly their origin from reason and reflection, than do those of the former, which points all to a like end. . . .

The convenience, or rather necessity, which leads to justice is so universal, and everywhere points so much to the same rules, that the habit takes place in all societies; and it is not without some scrutiny, that we are able to ascertain its true origin. The matter, however, is not so obscure, but that even in common life we have every moment recourse to the principle of public utility, and ask, *What must become of the world, if such practices prevail? How could society subsist under such disorders?* Were the distinction or separation of possessions entirely useless, can any one conceive, that it ever should have obtained in society?

Thus we seem, upon the whole, to have attained a knowledge of the force of that principle here insisted on, and can determine what degree of esteem or moral approbation may result from reflections on public interest and utility. The necessity of justice to the support of society is the sole foundation of that virtue; and since no moral excellence is more highly esteemed, we may conclude that this circumstance of usefulness has, in general, the strongest energy, and most entire command over our sentiments. . . .

WHY UTILITY PLEASES

Part I

It seems so natural a thought to ascribe to their utility the praise, which we bestow on the social virtues, that one would expect to meet with this principle everywhere in moral writers, as the chief foundation of their reasoning and enquiry. In common life, we may observe, that he circumstance of utility is always appealed to; nor is it supposed, that a greater eulogy can be given to any man, than to display his usefulness to the public, and enumerate the services, which he has performed to mankind and society. . . . A building, whose doors and windows were exact squares, would hurt the eye by that very proportion; as ill adapted to the figure of a human creature, for whose service the fabric was intended. What wonder then, that a man, whose habits and conduct are hurtful to society, and dangerous or pernicious to every one who has an intercourse with him, should, on that account, be an object of disapprobation, and communicate to every spectator the strongest sentiment of disgust and hatred. . . .

The social virtues must, therefore, be allowed to have a natural beauty and amiableness, which, at first, antecedent to all precept or education, recommends them to the esteem of uninstructed mankind, and engages their affections. And as the public utility of these virtues is the chief circumstance whence they derive their merit, it follows, that the end, which they have a tendency to promote, must be some way agreeable to us, and take hold of some natural affection. It must please, either from considerations of self-interest or from more generous motives and regards.

It has often been asserted, that, as every man has a strong connexion with society, and perceives the impossibility of his solitary subsistence, he becomes, on that account, favourable to all those habits or principles, which promote order in society, and insure to him the quiet possession of so inestimable a blessing. As much as we value our own happiness and welfare, as much must we applaud the practice of justice and humanity, by which alone the social confederacy can be maintained, and every man reap the fruits of mutual protection and assistance.

This deduction of morals from self-love, or a regard to private interest, is an obvious thought. . . . [Y]et is not this an affair to be decided by authority, and the voice of nature and experience seems plainly to oppose the selfish theory.

We frequently bestow praise on virtuous actions, performed in very distant ages and remote countries; where the utmost subtilty of imagination would not discover any appearance of self-interest, or find any connexion of our present happiness and security with events so widely separated from us.

A generous, a brave, a noble deed, performed by an adversary, commands our approbation; while in its consequences it may be acknowledged prejudicial to our particular interest. . . .

Usefulness is agreeable, and engages our approbation. This is a matter of fact, confirmed by daily observation. But, useful? For what? For somebody's interest, surely. Whose interest then? Not our own only: For our approbation frequently extends farther. It must, therefore, be the interest of those, who are served by the character of action approved of; and these we may conclude, however remote, are not totally indifferent to us. By opening up this principle, we shall discover one great source of moral distinctions.

Part II

. . . We have found instances, in which private interest was separate from public; in which it was even contrary: And yet we observed the moral sentiment to continue, notwithstanding this disjunction of interests. . . .

Have we any difficulty to comprehend the force of humanity and benevolence? Or to conceive, that the very aspect of happiness, joy, prosperity, gives pleasure; that of pain, suffering, sorrow, communicates uneasiness? The human countenance, says Horace, borrows smiles or tears from the human countenance. Reduce a person to solitude, and he loses all enjoyment, except either of the sensual or speculative kind; and that because the movements of his heart are not forwarded by correspondent movements in his fellow-creatures. The signs of sorrow and mourning, though arbitrary, affect us with melancholy; but the natural symptoms, tears and cries and groans, never fail to infuse compassion and uneasiness. And if the effects of misery touch us in so lively a manner: can we be supposed altogether insensible or indifferent towards its causes; when a malicious or treacherous character and behaviour are presented to us?

We enter, I shall suppose, into a convenient, warm, well-contrived apartment: We necessarily receive a pleasure from its very survey; because it presents us with the pleasing ideas of ease, satisfaction, and enjoyment. The hospitable, good-humoured, humane landlord appears. This circumstance surely must embellish the whole; nor can we easily forbear reflecting, with pleasure, on the satisfaction which results to every one from his intercourse and good-offices.

His whole family, by the freedom, ease, confidence, and calm enjoyment, diffused over their countenances, sufficiently express their happiness. I have a pleasing sympathy in the prospect of so much joy, and can never consider the source of it, without the most agreeable emotions.

He tells me, that an oppressive and powerful neighbour had attempted to dispossess him of his inheritance, and had long disturbed all his innocent and social pleasures. I feel an immediate indignation arise in me against such violence and injury.

But it is no wonder, he adds, that a private wrong should proceed from a man, who had enslaved provinces, depopulated cities, and made the field and scaffold stream with human blood. I am struck with horror at the prospect of so much misery, and am actuated by the strongest antipathy against its author.

In general, it is certain, that, wherever we go, whatever we reflect on or converse about, everything still presents us with the view of human happiness or misery, and excites in our breast a sympathetic movement of pleasure or uneasiness. In our serious occupations, in our careless amusements, this principle still exerts its active energy. . . . We surely take into consideration the happiness and misery of others, in weighing the several motives of action, and incline to the former, where no private regards draw us to seek our own promotion or advantage by the injury of our fellow-creatures. And if the principles of humanity are capable, in many instances, of influencing our actions, they must, at all times, have *some* authority over our sentiments, and give us a general approbation of what is useful to society, and blame of what is dangerous or pernicious. The degrees of these sentiments may be the subject of controversy; but the reality of their existence, one should think, must be admitted in every theory or system. . . . Sympathy, we shall allow, is much fainter than our concern for ourselves, and sympathy with persons remote from us much fainter than that with persons near and contiguous; but for this very reason it is necessary for us, in our calm judgments and discourse concerning the characters of men, to neglect all these differences, and render our sentiments more public and social. Besides, that we ourselves often change our situation in this particular, we every day meet with persons who are in a situation different from us, and who could never converse with us were we to remain constantly in that position and point of view, which is peculiar to ourselves. The intercourse of sentiments, therefore, in society and conversation, makes us form some general unalterable standard, by which we may approve or disapprove of characters and manners. And though the heart takes not part entirely with these general notions, nor regulates all its love and hatred by the universal abstract differences of vice and virtue, without regard to self, or the persons with whom we are more intimately connected; yet have these moral differences a considerable influence, and being sufficient, at least for discourse, serve all our purposes in company, in the pulpit, on the theatre, and in the schools.

Thus, in whatever light we take this subject, the merit, ascribed to the social virtues, appears still uniform, and arises chiefly from that regard, which the natural sentiment of benevolence engages us to pay to the interests of mankind and society. . . .

Were it doubtful, whether there were any such principle in our nature as humanity or a concern for others, yet when we see, in numberless instances, that whatever has a tendency to promote the interests of society, is so highly approved of, we ought thence to learn the force of the benevolent principle; since it is impossible for anything to please as means to an end, where the end is totally indifferent. On the other hand, were it doubtful, whether there were, implanted in our nature, any general principle of moral blame and approbation, yet when we see, in numberless instances, the influence of humanity, we ought hence to conclude, that it is impossible, but that everything which promotes the interest of society must communicate pleasure, and what is pernicious gives uneasiness. But when these different reflections and observations concur in establishing the same conclusion, must they not bestow an undisputed evidence upon it? . . .

CONCLUSION

. . . It is sufficient for our present purpose, if it be allowed, what surely, without the greatest absurdity cannot be disputed, that there is some benevolence, however small, infused into our bosom; some spark of friendship for human kind; some particle of the dove kneaded into our frame, along with the elements of the wolf and serpent. Let these generous sentiments be supposed ever so weak; let them be insufficient to move even a hand or finger of our body, they must still direct the determinations of our mind, and where everything else is equal, produce a cool preference of what is useful and serviceable to mankind, above what is pernicious and dangerous. A *moral distinction*, therefore, immediately arises; a general sentiment of blame and approbation; a tendency, however faint, to the objects of the one, and a proportionable aversion to those of the other. . . .

Avarice, ambition, vanity, and all passions vulgarly though improperly, comprised under the denomination of *self-love*, are here excluded from our theory concerning the origin of morals, not because they are too weak, but because they have not a proper direction for that purpose. The notion of morals implies some sentiment common to all mankind, which recommends the same object to general approbation, and makes every man, or most men, agree in the same opinion or decision concerning it. It also implies some sentiment, so universal and comprehensive as to extend to all mankind, and render the actions and conduct, even of the persons the most remote, an object of applause or censure, according as they agree or disagree with that rule of right which is established. . . .

When a man denominates another his *enemy*, his *rival*, his *antagonist*, his *adversary*, he is understood to speak the language of self-love, and to express sentiments, peculiar to himself, and arising from his particular circumstances and situation. But when he bestows on any man the epithets of *vicious* or *odious* or *depraved*, he then speaks another language and expresses sentiments, in which he expects all his audience to concur with him. He must here, therefore, depart from his private and particular situation, and must choose a point of view, common to him with others; he must move some universal principle of the human frame, and touch a string to which all mankind have an accord and symphony. If he mean, therefore, to express that this man possesses qualities, whose tendency is pernicious to society, he has chosen this common point of view, and has touched the principle of humanity, in which every man, in some degree, concurs. While the human heart is compounded of the same elements as at present, it will never be wholly indifferent to public good, nor entirely unaffected with the tendency of characters and manners. And though this affection of humanity may not generally be esteemed so strong as vanity or ambition, yet, being common to all men, it can alone be the foundation of morals, or of any general system of blame or praise. . . .

What more, therefore, can we ask to distinguish the sentiments, dependent on humanity, from those connected with any other passion, or to satisfy us, why the former are the origin of morals, not the latter? Whatever conduct gains my approbation, by touching my humanity, procures also the applause of all mankind, by affecting the same principle in them; by what serves my avarice or ambition pleases these passions in me alone, and affects not the avarice and ambition of the rest of mankind. There is no circumstance of conduct in any man, provided it have a beneficial tendency, that is not agreeable to my humanity, however remote the person; but every man. so far removed as neither to cross nor serve my avarice and ambition, is regarded as wholly indifferent by those passions. The distinction, therefore, between these species of sentiment being so great and evident, language must soon be moulded upon it, and must invent a peculiar set of terms, in order to express those universal sentiments of censure or approbation, which arise from humanity, or from views of general usefulness and its contrary. Virtue and Vice become then known; morals are recognized; certain general ideas are framed of human conduct and behaviour; such measures are expected from men in such situations. This action is determined to be conformable to our abstract rule; that other, contrary. And by such universal principles are the particular sentiments of self love frequently controlled and limited. . . .

One principal foundation of moral praise being supposed to lie in the usefulness of any quality or action, it is evident that reason must enter for a considerable share in all decisions of this kind; (since nothing but that faculty can instruct us in the tendency of qualities and actions] and point out their beneficial consequences to society and to their possessor. In many cases this is an affair liable to great controversy: doubts may arise; opposite interests may occur; and a preference must be given to one side, from very nice views, and a small overbalance of utility. This is particularly remarkable in questions with regard to justice; as is, indeed, natural to suppose, from that species of utility which attends this virtue. Were every single instance of justice, like that of benevolence, useful to society; this would be a more simple state of the case, and seldom liable to great controversy. But as single instances of justice are often pernicious in their first and immediate tendency, and as the advantage to society results only from the observance of the general rule, and from the concurrence and combination of several persons in the same equitable conduct; the case here becomes more intricate and involved. The various circumstances of society; the various consequences of any practice; the various interests which may be proposed; these, on many occasions are doubtful, and subject to great discussion and inquiry. The object of municipal laws is to fix all the questions with regard to justice: the debates of civilians; the reflections of politicians; the precedents of history and public records, are all directed to the same purpose. And a very accurate *reason* or *judgement* is often requisite, to give the true determination, amidst such intricate doubts arising from obscure or opposite utilities.

But though reason, when fully assisted and improved, be sufficient to instruct us in the pernicious or useful tendency of qualities and actions; it is not alone sufficient to produce any moral blame or approbation. Utility is only a tendency to a certain end; and were the end totally indifferent to us, we should feel the same indifference towards the means. It is requisite a *sentiment* should here display itself, in order to give a preference to the useful above the pernicious tendencies. This sentiment can be no other than a feeling for the happiness of mankind, and a resentment of their misery; since these are the different ends which virtue and vice have a tendency to promote. Here therefore reason instructs us in the several tendencies of actions, and *humanity* makes a distinction in favour of those which are useful and beneficial. . . .

Immanuel Kant, *The Fundamental Principles of the Metaphysic of Morals,* Thomas K. Abbott (trans.), 1785

Deontology: The Ethics of Duty
Immanuel Kant

THE GOOD WILL

Nothing can possibly be conceived in the world, or even out of it, which can be called good without qualification, except a good will. Intelligence, wit, judgment, and the other talents of the mind, however they may be named, or courage, resolution, perseverance, as qualities of temperament, are undoubtedly good and desirable in many respects; but these gifts of nature may also become extremely bad and mischievous if the will which is to make use of them, and which, therefore, constitutes what is called character, is not good. It is the same with the gifts of fortune. Power, riches, honor, even health, and the general well-being and contentment with one's condition which is called happiness, inspire pride, and often presumption, if there is not a good will to correct the influence of these on the mind, and with this also to rectify the whole principle of acting, and adapt it to its end. The sight of a being who is not adorned with a single feature of a pure and good will, enjoying unbroken prosperity, can never give pleasure to an impartial rational spectator. Thus a good will appears to constitute the indispensable condition even of being worthy of happiness.

There are even some qualities which are of service to this good will itself, and may facilitate its action, yet which have no intrinsic unconditional value, but always presuppose a good will, and this qualifies the esteem that we justly have for them, and does not permit us to regard them as absolutely good. Moderation in the affections and passions, self-control, and calm deliberation are not only good in many respects, but even seem to constitute part of the intrinsic worth of the person; but they are far from deserving to be called good without qualification, although they have been so unconditionally praised by the ancients. For without the principles of a good will, they may become extremely bad; and the coolness of a villain not only makes him far more dangerous, but also directly makes him more abominable in our eyes than he would have been without it.

A good will is good not because of what it performs or effects, not by its aptness for the attainment of some proposed end, but simply by virtue of the volition—that is, it is good in itself, and considered by itself is to be esteemed much higher than all that can be brought about by it in favor of any inclination, nay, even of the sum-total of all inclinations. Even if it should happen that, owing to special disfavor of fortune, or the niggardly provision of a stepmotherly nature, this will should wholly lack power to accomplish its purpose, if with its greatest efforts it should yet achieve nothing, and there should remain only the good will (not, to be sure, a mere wish, but the summoning of all means in our power), then, like a jewel, it would still shine by its own light, as a thing which has its whole value in itself. Its usefulness or fruitlessness can neither add to nor take away anything from this value. It would be, as it were, only the setting to enable us to handle it the more conveniently in common commerce, or to attract to it the attention of those who are not yet connoisseurs, but not to recommend it to true connoisseurs, or to determine its value. . . .

THE FIRST PROPOSITION OF MORALITY

We have then to develop the notion of a will which deserves to be highly esteemed for itself, and is good without a view to anything further. . . . [Consider] that it is always a matter of duty that a tradesman should not overcharge an inexperienced purchaser; and wherever there is much commerce the prudent tradesman does not overcharge, but keeps a fixed price of everyone, so that a child buys of him as well as any other. Men are thus honestly served, but this is not enough to make us believe that the tradesman acted from duty and from principles of honesty: his own advantage required it. Accordingly the action was done neither from duty nor from direct inclination, but merely with a selfish view. . . .

On the other hand, it is a duty to maintain one's life; and, in addition, everyone also has a direct inclination to do so. But on this account the often anxious care which most men take for it has no intrinsic worth, and their maxim has no moral import. They preserve their life *as duty requires*, no doubt, but not *because duty requires*. On the other hand, if adversity and hopeless sorrow have completely taken away the relish for life; if the unfortunate one, strong in mind, indignant at his fate rather than desponding or dejected, wishes for death, and yet preserves his life without loving it—not from inclination of fear, but from duty—then his maxim has a moral worth.

To be beneficent when we can is a duty; and besides this, there are many minds so sympathetically constituted that, without any other motive of vanity or self-interest, they find a pleasure in spreading joy around them, and can take delight in the satisfaction of others so far as it is their own work. But I maintain that in such a case an action of this kind, however proper, however amiable it may be, has nevertheless no true moral worth, but is on a level with other inclinations. For the maxim lacks the moral import, namely, that such actions be done *from duty*, not from inclination. Put the case that the mind of a philanthropist was clouded by sorrow of his own, extinguishing all sympathy with the lot of others, and that while he still has the power to benefit others in distress, he is not touched by their trouble because he is absorbed with his own; and now suppose that he tears himself out of this dead sensibility, and performs the action without any inclination to it, but simply from duty—then does his action have a genuine moral worth. Further still; if nature has put little sympathy in the heart of this or that man; if he, supposed to be an upright man, is by temperament cold and indifferent to the sufferings of others, perhaps because in respect of his own he is provided with a special gift of patience and fortitude, and supposes, or even requires, that others should have the same—and such a man would certainly not be the meanest product of nature—but would he not still find in himself a source from whence to give himself a far higher worth than that of a good natured temperament would be? Unquestionably. It is just in this that the moral worth of character is brought out which is incomparably the highest of all, namely, that he is beneficent, not from inclination, but from duty. . . .

It is in this manner, undoubtedly, that we are to understand those passages of Scripture in which we are commanded to love our neighbour, even our enemy. For love, as an affection, cannot be commanded, but beneficence for duty's sake may. This is *practical* love, and not *pathological*—a love that is seated in the will, and not in the propensies of feeling— in principles of action and not of tender sympathy; and it is this love alone which can be commanded.

THE SECOND AND THIRD PROPOSITIONS OF MORALITY

The second proposition is: That an action done from duty derives its moral worth, not from the purpose which is to be attained by it, but from the maxim by which it is determined, and therefore does not depend on the realization of the object of the action, but merely on the principle of volition by which the action has taken place, without regard to any object of desire. It is clear from what precedes that the purposes which we may have in view in our actions, or their effects regarded as ends and springs of the will, cannot give to actions any unconditional or moral worth. In what, then, can their worth lie if it is not to consist in the will and in reference to its expected effect? It cannot lie anywhere but in the principle of the will without regard to the ends which can be attained by the action. . . .

The third proposition, which is a consequence of the two preceding, I would express thus: *Duty is the necessity of acting from respect for the law.* I may have *inclination* for an object as the effect of my proposed action, but I cannot have *respect* for it just for this reason that it is an effect and not an energy of will. Similarly, I cannot have respect for inclination, whether my own or another's; I can at most, if my own, approve it; if another's, sometimes even love it, that is, look on it as favorable to my own interest. It is only what is connected with my will as a principle, by no means as an effect—what does not subserve my inclination, but overpowers it, or at least in case of choice excludes it from its calculation—in other words, simply the law of itself, which can be an object of command. Now an action done from duty must wholly exclude the influence of inclination, and with it every object of the will, so that nothing remains which can determine the will except objectively the *law*, and subjectively *pure respect* for this practical law, and consequently the maxim[1] that I should follow this law even to the thwarting of all my inclinations.

Thus the moral worth of an action does not lie in the effect expected from it, nor in any principle of action which requires to borrow its motive from this expected effect. For all these effects—agreeableness of one's condition, and even the promotion of the happiness of others— could have been also brought about by other causes, so that for this there would have been no need of the will of a rational being; whereas it is in this alone that the supreme and unconditional good can be found. The pre-eminent good which we call moral can therefore consist in nothing else than *the conception of law* in itself, *which certainly is only possible in a rational being,* in so far as this conception, and not the expected effect, determines the will. This is a good which is already present in the person who acts accordingly, and we have not to wait for it to appear first in the result.

THE SUPREME PRINCIPLE OF MORALITY:
THE CATEGORICAL IMPERATIVE

But what sort of law can that be the conception of which must determine the will, even without paying any regard to the effect expected from it, in order that this will may be called good absolutely and without qualification? As I have deprived the will of every impulse which could arise to it from obedience to any law, there remains nothing but the universal conformity of its actions to law in general, which alone is to serve the will as a principle, that is, I am never to act otherwise than so *that I could also will my maxim should become a universal law.* Here, now, it is the simple conformity to law in general, without assuming any particular law applicable to certain actions, that serves the will as its principle, and must so serve it if duty is not to be a vain delusion and a chimerical notion. The common reason of men in its practical judgments perfectly coincides with this, and always has in view the principle here suggested. Let the question be, for example: May I when in distress make a promise with the intention not to keep it? I readily distinguish here between the two significations which the question may have: whether it is prudent or whether it is right to make a false promise? The former may undoubtedly often be the case. I see clearly indeed that it is not enough to extricate myself from a present difficulty by means of this subterfuge, but it must be well considered whether there may not hereafter spring from this lie much greater inconvenience than that from which I now free myself, and as, with all my supposed *cunning*, the consequences cannot be so easily foreseen but that credit once lost may be much more injurious to me than any mischief which I seek to avoid at present, it should be considered whether it would not be more *prudent* to act herein according to a universal maxim, and to make it a habit to promise nothing except with the intention of keeping it. But it is soon clear to me that such a maxim will still only be based on the fear of consequences. Now it is a wholly different thing to be truthful from duty, and to be so from apprehension of injurious consequences. In the first case, the very notion of the action already implies a law for me; in the second case, I must first look about elsewhere to see what results may be combined with it which would affect myself. For to deviate from the principle of duty is beyond all doubt wicked; but to be unfaithful to my maxim of prudence may often be very advantageous to me, although to abide by it is certainly safer. The shortest way, however, and an unerring one, to discover the answer to this question whether a lying promise is consistent with duty, is to ask myself, Should I be content that my maxim (to extricate myself from difficulty by a false promise) should hold good as a universal law, for myself as well as for others; and should I be able to say to myself, "Every one may make a deceitful promise when he finds himself in a difficulty from which he cannot otherwise extricate himself"? Then I presently become aware that, while I can will the lie, I can by no means will that lying should be a universal law. For with such a law there would be no promises at all, since it would be in vain to allege my intention in regard to my future actions to those who would not believe this allegation, or if they over-hastily did so, would pay me back in my own coin. Hence my maxim, so soon as it should be made a universal law, would necessarily destroy itself.

I do not, therefore, need any far-reaching penetration to discern what I have to do in order that my will may be morally good. Inexperienced in the course of the world, incapable of being prepared for all its contingencies, I only ask myself: Canst thou also will that thy maxim should be a universal law? If not, then it must be rejected, and that not because of a disadvantage accruing from it to myself or even to others, but because it cannot enter as a principle into a possible universal legislation, and reason extorts from me immediate respect for such legislation. I do not indeed as yet *discern* on what this respect is based (this the philosopher may inquire), but at least I understand this—that it is an estimation of the worth which far outweighs all worth of what is recommended by inclination, and that the necessity of acting from pure respect for the practical law is what constitutes duty, to which every other motive must give place because it is the condition of a will being good *in itself*, and the worth of such a will is above everything.

Thus, then, without quitting the moral knowledge of common human reason, we have arrived at its principle. And although, no doubt, common men do not conceive it in such an abstract and universal form, yet they always have it really before their eyes and use it as the standard of their decision. Here it would be easy to show how, with this compass in hand, men are well able to distinguish, in every case that occurs, what is good, what bad, conformably to duty or inconsistent with it. . . .

IMPERATIVES: HYPOTHETICAL AND CATEGORICAL

Everything in nature works according to laws. Rational beings alone have the faculty of acting according *to the conception* of laws, that is according to principles, *i.e.*, have a *will*. Since the deduction of actions from principles requires *reason*, the will is nothing but practical reason. . . .

The conception of an objective principle, in so far as it is obligatory for a will, is called a command (of reason), and the formula of the command is called an Imperative.

All imperatives are expressed by the word *ought* [or *shall*], and thereby indicate the relation of an objective law of reason to a will, which from its subjective constitution is not necessarily determined by it (an obligation). . . .

Now all *imperatives* command either *hypothetically* or *categorically*. The former represent the practical necessity of a possible action as means to something else that is willed (or at least which one might possibly will). The categorical imperative would be that which represented an action as necessary of itself without reference to another end, that is, as objectively necessary. . . .

If now the action is good only as a means to *something else*, then the imperative is *hypothetical*; if it is conceived as good *in itself* and consequently as being necessarily the principle of a will which of itself conforms to reason, then it is *categorical*. . . .

Accordingly the hypothetical imperative only says that the action is good for some purpose, *possible or actual*. In the first case it is a *problematical*, in the second an *assertorial* practical principle. The categorical imperative which declares an action to be objectively necessary in itself without reference to any purpose, that is, without any other end, is valid as an *apodictic* (practical) principle. . . .

FIRST FORMULATION OF THE CATEGORICAL IMPERATIVE: UNIVERSAL LAW

When I conceive a hypothetical imperative, in general I do not know beforehand what it will contain until I am given the condition. But when I conceive a categorical imperative, I know at once what it contains. For as the imperative contains besides the law only the necessity that the maxims[2] shall conform to this law, while the law contains no conditions restricting it, there remains nothing but the general statement that the maxim of the action should conform to a universal law, and it is this conformity alone that the imperative properly represents as necessary.

There is therefore but one categorical imperative, namely, this: *Act only on that maxim whereby thou canst at the same time will that it should become a universal law.*

Now if all imperatives of duty can be deduced from this one imperative as from their principle, then, although it should remain undecided whether what is called duty is not merely a vain notion, yet at least we shall be able to show what we understand by it and what this notion means. . . .

Four Illustrations

We will now enumerate a few duties, adopting the usual division of them into duties to ourselves and to others, and into perfect and imperfect duties.

1. A man reduced to despair by a series of misfortunes feels wearied of life, but is still so far in possession of his reason that he can ask himself whether it would not be contrary to his duty to himself to take his own life. Now he inquires whether the maxim of his action could become a universal law of nature. His maxim is: From self-love I adopt it as a principle to shorten my life when its longer duration is likely to bring more evil than satisfaction. It is asked then simply whether this principle founded on self-love can become a universal law of nature. Now we see at once that a system of nature of which it should be a law to destroy life by means of the very feeling whose special nature it is to impel to the improvement of life would contradict itself, and therefore could not exist as a system of nature; hence that maxim cannot possibly exist as a universal law of nature, and consequently would be wholly inconsistent with the supreme principle of all duty.

2. Another finds himself forced by necessity to borrow money. He knows that he will not be able to repay it, but sees also that nothing will be lent to him unless he promises stoutly to repay it in a definite time. He desires to make this promise, but he has still so much conscience as to ask himself: Is it not unlawful and inconsistent with duty to get out of a difficulty in this way? Suppose, however, that he resolves to do so, then the maxim of his action would be expressed thus: When I think myself in want of money, I will borrow money and promise to repay it, although I know that I never can do so. Now this principle of self-love or of one's own advantage may perhaps be consistent with my whole future welfare; but the question now is, Is it right? I change then the suggestion of self-love into a universal law, and state the question thus: How would it be if my maxim were a universal law? Then I see at once that it could never hold as a universal law of nature, but would necessarily contradict itself. For supposing it to be a universal law that everyone when he thinks himself in a difficulty should be able to promise whatever he pleases, with the purpose of not keeping his promise, the promise itself would become impossible, as well as the end that one might have in view in it, since no one would consider that anything was promised to him, but would ridicule all such statements as vain pretenses.

3. A third finds in himself a talent which with the help of some culture might make him a useful man in many respects. But he finds himself in comfortable circumstances and prefers to indulge in pleasure rather than to take pains in enlarging and improving his happy natural capacities. He asks, however, whether his maxim of neglect of his natural gifts, besides agreeing with his inclination to indulgence, agrees also with

what is called duty. He sees then that a system of nature could indeed subsist with such a universal law, although men (like the South Sea islanders) should let their talents rest and resolve to devote their lives merely to idleness, amusement, and propagation of their species—in a word, to enjoyment; but he cannot possibly will that this should be a universal law of nature, or be implanted in us as such by a natural instinct. For, as a rational being, he necessarily wills that his faculties be developed, since they serve him, and have been given him, for all sorts of possible purposes.

4. A fourth, who is in prosperity, while he sees that others have to contend with great wretchedness and that he could help them, thinks: "What concern is it of mine? Let everyone be as happy as Heaven pleases, or as he can make himself; I will take nothing from him nor even envy him, only I do not wish to contribute anything to his welfare or to his assistance in distress!" Now no doubt, if such a mode of thinking were a universal law, the human race might very well subsist, and doubtless even better than in a state in which everyone talks of sympathy and good-will, or even takes care occasionally to put it into practice, but, on the other side, also cheats when he can, betrays the rights of men, or otherwise violates them. But although it is possible that a universal law of nature might exist in accordance with that maxim, it is impossible to *will* that such a principle should have the universal validity of a law of nature. For a will which resolved this would contradict itself, inasmuch as many cases might occur in which one would have need of the love and sympathy of others, and in which, by such a law of nature, sprung from his own will, he would deprive himself of all hope of the aid he desires.

These are a few of the many actual duties, or at least what we regard as such, which obviously fall into two classes on the one principle that we have laid down. We must be *able to will* that a maxim of our action should be a universal law. This is the canon of the moral appreciation of the action generally. Some actions are of such a character that their maxim cannot without contradiction be even *conceived* as a universal law of nature, far from it being possible that we should *will* that it *should* be so. In others, this intrinsic impossibility is not found, but still it is impossible to will that their maxim should be raised to the universality of a law of nature, since such a will would contradict itself. . . .

SECOND FORMULATION OF THE CATEGORICAL IMPERATIVE: HUMANITY AS END IN ITSELF

The will is conceived as a faculty of determining oneself to action *in accordance with the conception of certain laws*. And such a faculty can be found only in rational beings. The ends which a rational being proposes to himself at pleasure as *effects* of his actions are all only relative, for it is only their relation to the particular desires of the subject that gives them their worth, which therefore cannot furnish principles universal and necessary for all rational beings and every volition, that is to say practical laws. Hence all these relative ends can give only hypothetical imperatives. Supposing, however, that there were something *whose existence* has *in itself* an absolute worth, something which, being *an end in itself*, could be a source of definite laws, then in this and this alone would lie the source of a possible categorical imperative, i.e. a practical law. . . .

Now I say: man and generally any rational being exists as an end in himself, *not merely as a means* to be arbitrarily used by this or that will, but in all his actions, whether they concern himself or other rational beings, must be always regarded at the same time as an end. All objects of the inclinations have only a conditional worth, for if the inclinations and the wants founded on them did not exist, then their object would be without value. Thus the worth of any object which *is to be acquired* by our action is always conditional. Beings whose existence depends not on our will but on nature's, have nevertheless, if they are nonrational beings, only a relative value as means, and are therefore called *things;* rational beings, on the contrary, are called *persons,* because their very nature points them out as ends in themselves, that is, as something which must not be used merely as means, and so far therefore restricts freedom of action (and is an object of respect). These, therefore, are not merely subjective ends whose existence has a worth *for us* as an effect of our action, but *objective ends,* that is, things whose existence is an end in itself—an end, moreover, for which no other can be substituted, which they should subserve *merely* as means, for otherwise nothing whatever would possess *absolute* worth; . . . .

If then there is a supreme practical principle or, in respect of the human will, a categorical imperative, it must be one which, being drawn from the conception of that which is necessarily an end for everyone because it is *an end in itself,* constitutes an objective principle of will, and can therefore serve as a universal practical law. The foundation of this principle is: *rational nature exists as an end in itself.* Man necessarily conceives his own existence as being so: so far then this is a *subjective* principle of human actions. But every other rational being regards its existence similarly, just on the same rational principle that holds for me: so that it is at the same time an objective principle, from which as a supreme practical law all laws of the will must be capable of being deduced. Accordingly the practical imperative will be as follows: *So act as to treat humanity, whether in thine own person or in that of any other, in every case as an end withal, never as means only.* We will now inquire whether this can be practically carried out. . . .

THE KINGDOM OF ENDS

The conception of the will of every rational being as one which must consider itself as giving in all the maxims of its will universal laws, so as to judge itself and its actions from this point of view—this conception leads to another which depends on it and is very fruitful, namely that of a kingdom of ends.

By a *kingdom* I understand the union of different rational beings in a system by common laws. Now since it is by laws that ends are determined as regards their universal validity, hence, if we abstract from the personal differences of rational beings and likewise from all the content of their private ends, we shall be able to conceive all ends combined in a systematic whole (including both rational beings as ends in themselves, and also the special ends which each may propose to himself), that is to say, we can conceive a kingdom of ends, which on the preceding principles is possible.

For all rational beings come under the *law* that each of them must treat itself and all others *never merely as means,* but in every case *at the same time as ends in themselves.* Hence results a systematic union of rational beings by common objective laws, *i.e.,* a kingdom which may be called a kingdom of ends, since what these laws have in view is just the relation of these beings to one another as ends and means. It is certainly only an ideal.

A rational being belongs as a *member* to the kingdom of ends when although giving universal laws in it he is also himself subject to these laws. He belongs to it *as sovereign,* when while giving laws he is not subject to the will of any other.

A rational being must always regard himself as giving laws in a kingdom of ends which freedom of the will makes possible, whether it be as member or as sovereign. He cannot, however, maintain the latter position merely by the maxims of his will, but only in case he is a completely independent being without wants and with unrestricted power adequate to his will.

Morality consists then in the reference of all action to the legislation which alone can render a kingdom of ends possible. This legislation must be capable of existing in every rational being, and of emanating from his will, so that the principle of this will, is never to act on any maxim which could not without contradiction be also a universal law, and accordingly always so to act *that the will could at the same time regard itself as giving in its maxims universal laws.* If now the maxims of rational beings are not by their own nature coincident with this objective principle, then the necessity of acting on it is called practical obligation, *i.e., duty.* Duty does not apply to the sovereign in the kingdom of ends, but it does to every member of it and to all in the same degree.

The practical necessity of acting on this principle, i.e. duty, does not rest at all on feelings, impulses, or inclinations, but solely on the relation of rational beings to one another, a relation in which the will of a rational being must always be regarded as *legislative* . . . .

In the kingdom of ends everything has either Value or Dignity. Whatever has a value can be replaced by something else which is *equivalent;* whatever on the other hand is above all value, and therefore admits of no equivalent, has a dignity.

Whatever has reference to the general inclinations and wants of mankind has a *market value;* whatever without presupposing a want, corresponds to a certain taste, that is to a satisfaction in the mere purposeless play of our faculties, has a *fancy value;* but that which constitutes the condition under which alone anything can be an end in itself, this has not merely a relative worth, *i.e.,* value, but an intrinsic worth, that is, *dignity.*

Now morality is the condition under which alone a rational being can be an end in himself, since by this alone is it possible that he should be a legislating member in the kingdom of ends. Thus morality, and humanity as capable of it, is that which alone has dignity. Skill and diligence in labour have a market value; wit, lively imagination, and humour have a fancy value; on the other hand, fidelity to promises, benevolence from principle (not from instinct) have an intrinsic worth. Neither nature nor art contains anything which in default of these it could put in their place, for their worth consists not in the effects which spring from them, not in the use and advantage which they secure, but in the disposition of mind, that is the maxims of the will which are ready to manifest themselves in such actions, even though they should not have the desired effect. These actions also need no recommendation from any subjective taste or sentiment, that they may be looked on with immediate favour and satisfaction: they need no immediate propensities or feeling for them; they exhibit the will that performs them as an object of an immediate respect, and nothing but reason is required to *impose* them on the will; not to *flatter* it into them, which in the case of duties would be a contradiction. This estimation therefore shows that the worth of such a disposition is dignity, and places it infinitely above all value, with which it cannot for a moment be brought into comparison or competition without as it were violating its sanctity.

What then is it which justifies virtue or the morally good disposition, in making such lofty claims? It is nothing less than the privilege it secures to the rational being of participating in the giving of universal laws, by which it qualifies him to be a member of a possible kingdom of ends, a privilege to which he was already destined by his own nature as being an end in himself, and on that account legislating in the kingdom of ends; free as regards all laws of physical nature, and obeying those only which he himself gives, and by which his maxims can belong to a system of universal law, to which at the same time he submits himself. For nothing has any worth except what the law assigns it. Now the legislation itself which assigns the worth of everything, must for that very reason possess dignity, that is an unconditional incomparable worth, and the word *respect* alone supplies a becoming expression for the esteem which a rational being must have for it. *Autonomy* then is the basis of the dignity of human and of every rational nature. . . .

The Autonomy of the Will

Autonomy of the will is the property that the will has of being a law to itself (independently of any property of the objects of volition). The principle of autonomy is this: Always choose in such a way that in the same volition the maxims of the choice are at the same time present as universal law.

If the will seeks the law that is to determine it anywhere but in the fitness of its maxims for its own legislation of universal laws, and if it thus goes outside of itself and seeks this law in the character of any of its objects, then heteronomy always results. The will in that case does not give itself the law, but the object does so because of its relation to the will. This relation, whether it rests on inclination or on representations of reason, admits only of hypothetical imperatives: I ought to do something because I will something else. On the other hand, the moral, and hence categorical, imperative says that I ought to act in this way or that way, even though I did not will something else. . . .

The Concept of Freedom Is the Key
That Explains the Autonomy of the Will

The will is a kind of causality belonging to living beings in so far as they are rational, and freedom would be this property of such causality that it can be efficient, independently of foreign causes determining it; just as physical necessity is the property that the causality of all rational beings has of being determined to activity by the influence of foreign causes . . . .

What else then can freedom of the will be but autonomy, that is, the property of the will to be a law to itself? But the proposition: The will is in every action a law to itself, only expresses the principle to act on no other maxim than that which can also have as an object itself as a universal law. Now this is precisely the formula of the categorical imperative and is the principle of morality, so that a free will and a will subject to moral laws are one and the same.

Freedom Must Be Presupposed as a
Property of the Will of All Rational Beings

It is not enough to predicate freedom of our own will, from whatever reason, if we have not sufficient grounds for predicating the same of all rational beings. For as morality serves as a law for us only because we are rational beings, it must also hold for all rational beings. Now I say every being that cannot act except under the idea of freedom is just for that reason in a practical point of view really free, that is to say, all laws which are inseparably connected with freedom have the same force for him as if his will had been shown to be free in itself by a proof theoretically conclusive. (I adopt this method of assuming freedom merely as an idea which rational being suppose in their actions, in order to avoid the necessity of proving it in theory. The form is sufficient for my purpose; for even though the speculative proof should not be made out yet a being that cannot act except with the idea of freedom is bound by the same laws that would oblige a being who is actually free.) Now I affirm that we must attribute to every rational being which has a will that it has also the idea of freedom and acts entirely under this idea. For in such a being we conceive a reason that is practical, that is, has causality in reference to its objects. It must regard itself as the author of its principles independent on foreign influences. Consequently, as practical reason or as the will of a rational being it must regard itself as free, that is to say, the will of such a being cannot be a will of its own except under the idea of freedom. This idea must therefore in a practical point of view be ascribed to every rational being.

Notes

1. A *maxim* is the subjective principle of volition. The objective principle (i.e., that which would also serve subjectively as a practical principle to all rational beings if reason had full power over the faculty of desire) is the practical law.

2. A *maxim* is a subjective principle of action, and must be distinguished from the objective principle, namely, practical law. The former contains the practical rule set by reason according to the conditions of the subject (often its ignorance or its inclinations), so that it is the principle on which the subject acts; but the law is the objective principle valid for every rational being, and is the principle which it *ought to act*—that is, an imperative.

Adam Smith, *Wealth of Nations*, 1776

The Ethics of the Profit Motive
Adam Smith

The greatest improvement in the productive powers of labor, and the greater part of the skill, dexterity, and judgment with which it is anywhere directed, or applied, seem to have been the effects of the division of labor. . . .

To take an example, therefore, from a very trifling manufacture, but one in which the division of labor has been very often taken notice of, the trade of the pin-maker; a workman not educated to this business (which the division of labor has rendered a distinct trade), nor acquainted with the use of the machinery employed in it (to the invention of which the same division of labor has probably given occasion), could scarce, perhaps, with his utmost industry, make one pin a day, and certainly could not make twenty. But in the way in which this business is now carried on, not only the whole work is a peculiar trade, but it is divided into a number of branches, of which the greater part are likewise peculiar trades. One man draws out the wire, another sleights it, a third cuts it, a fourth points it, a fifth grinds it at the top for receiving the head; to make the head requires two or three distinct operations; to put it on is a peculiar business, to whiten the pins is another; it is even a trade by itself to put them into the paper; and the important business of making a pin is, in this manner, divided into about eighteen distinct operations, which, in some manufactories, are all performed by distinct hands, though in others the same man will sometimes perform two or three of them. I have seen a small manufactory of this kind where ten men only were employed, and where some of them consequently performed two or three distinct operations. But though they were very poor, and therefore but indifferently accommodated with the necessary machinery, they could, when they exerted themselves, make among them about twelve pounds of pins in a day. There are in a pound upwards of four thousand pins of a middling size. Those ten persons, therefore, could make among them upwards of forty-eight thousand pins in a day. Each person, therefore, making a tenth part of forty-eight thousand pins, might be considered as making four thousand eight hundred pins in a day. But if they had all wrought separately and independently, and without any of them having been educated to this peculiar business, they certainly could not each of them have made twenty, perhaps not one pin in a day; that is, certainly, not the two hundred and fortieth, perhaps not the four thousand eight hundredth part, of what they are at present capable of performing in consequence of a proper division and combination of their different operations.

In every other art and manufacture, the effects of the division of labor are similar to what they are in this very trifling one; though in many of them, the labor can neither be so much subdivided, nor reduced to so great a simplicity of operation. The division of labor, however, so far as it can be introduced, occasions, in every art, a proportionable increase of the productive powers of labor. . . .

This great increase of the quantity of work, which, in consequence of the division of labor, the same number of people are capable of performing, is owing to three different circumstances: first, to the increase of dexterity in every particular workman; secondly, to the saving of the time which is commonly lost in passing from one species of work to another; and lastly, to the invention of a great number of machines which facilitate and abridge labor, and enable one man to do the work of many.

First, the improvement of the dexterity of the workman necessarily increases the quantity of the work he can perform; and the division of labor, by reducing every man's business to some one simple operation and by making this operation the sole employment of his life, necessarily increases very much the dexterity of the workman. A common smith, who, though accustomed to handle the hammer, has never been used to make nails, if upon some particular occasion he is obliged to attempt it, will scarce, I am assured, be able to make about two or three hundred nails in a day, and those too very bad ones. A smith who has been accustomed to make nails, but whose sole or principal business has not been that of a nailer, can seldom with his utmost diligence make more than eight hundred or a thousand nails in a day. I have seen several boys under twenty years of age who had never exercised any other trade but that of making nails, and who, when they exerted themselves, could make, each of them, upwards of two thousand three hundred nails in a day. The making of a nail, however, is by no means one of the simplex operations. The same person blows the bellows, stirs or mends the fire as there is occasion, heats the iron, and forges every part of the nail: In forging the head too he is obliged to change his tools. The different operations into which the making of a pin or of a metal button is subdivided, are all of them much more simple; and the dexterity of the person, of whose life it has been the sole business to perform them, is usually much greater. The rapidity with which some of the operations of those manufactures are performed exceeds what the human hand could, by those who had never seen them, be supposed capable of acquiring.

Secondly, the advantage which is gained by saving the time commonly lost in passing from one sort of work to another is much greater than we should at first view be apt to imagine it. It is impossible to pass very quickly from one kind of work to another, that is carried on in a different place, and with quite different tools. A country weaver who cultivates a small farm must lose a good deal of time in passing from his loom to the field, and from the field to his loom. When the two trades can be carried on in the same workhouse, the loss of time is no doubt much less. It is even in this case, however, very considerable. . . .

Thirdly, and lastly, every body must be sensible how much labor is facilitated and abridged by the application of proper machinery. . . .

. . . A great part of the machines made use of in those manufactures in which labor is most subdivided were originally the inventions of common workmen, who, being each of them employed in some very simple operation, naturally turned their thoughts toward finding out easier and readier methods of performing it. Whoever has been much accustomed to visit such manufacturers must frequently have been shown very pretty machines which were the inventions of such workmen in order to facilitate and quicken their own particular part of the work. In the first fire-engines, a boy was constantly employed to open and shut alternately the communication between the boiler and the cylinder, according as the piston either ascended or descended. One of those boys, who loved to play with his companions, observed that, by tying a string from the handle of the valve which opened this communication to another part of the machine, the valve would open and shut without his assistance, and leave him at liberty to divert himself with his play-fellows. One of the greatest improvements that has been made upon this machine, since it was first invented, was in this manner the discovery of a boy who wanted to save his own labor. . . .

It is the great multiplication of the productions of all the different arts, in consequence of the division of labor, which occasions, in a well-governed society, that universal opulence which extends itself to the lowest ranks of the people. Every workman has a great quantity of his own work to dispose of beyond what he himself has occasion for; and every other workman being exactly in the same situation, he is enabled to exchange a great quantity of his own goods for a great quantity, or, what comes to the same thing, for the price of a great quantity of theirs. He supplies them abundantly with what they have occasion for, and they accommodate him as amply with what he has occasion for, and a general plenty diffuses itself through all the different ranks of the society. . . .

This division of labor, from which so many advantages are derived, is not originally the effect of any human wisdom which foresees and intends that general opulence to which it gives occasion. It is the necessary, though very slow and gradual, consequence of a certain propensity in human nature which has in view no such extensive utility: the propensity to truck, barter, and exchange one thing for another.

. . . In almost every other race of animals each individual, when it is grown up to maturity, is entirely independent, and in its natural state has occasion for the assistance of no other living creature. But man has almost constant occasion for the help of his brethren, and it is in vain for him to expect it from their benevolence only. He will be more likely to prevail if he can increase their self-love in his favor, and show them that it is for their own advantage to do for him what he requires of them. Whoever offers to another a bargain of any kind, proposes to do this. Give me that which I want, and you shall have this which you want, is the meaning of every such offer; and it is in the manner that we obtain from one another the far greater part of those good offices which we stand in need of. It is not from the benevolence of the butcher, the brewer, or the baker, that we expect our dinner, but from their regard to their own interest. We address ourselves, not to their humanity but to their self-love, and never talk to them of our own necessities but of their advantages. Nobody but a beggar chooses to depend chiefly upon the benevolence of his fellow-citizens. Even a beggar does not depend on it entirely. The charity of well-disposed people, indeed, supplies him with the whole fund of his subsistence. But though this principle ultimately provides him with all the necessaries of life which he has occasion for, it neither does nor can provide him with them as he has occasion for them. The greater part of his occasional wants are supplied in the same manner as those of other people, by treaty, by barter, and by purchase. With the money which one man gives him he purchases food. The old clothes which another bestows upon him he exchanges for other old clothes which suit him better, or for lodging, or for food, or for money, with which he can buy either food, clothes, or lodging, as he has occasion.

As it is by treaty, by barter, and by purchase that we obtain from one another the greater part of those mutual good offices which we stand in need of, so it is this same trucking disposition which originally gives occasion to the division of labor. In a tribe of hunters or shepherds a particular person makes bows and arrows, for example, with more readiness and dexterity than any other. He frequently exchanges them for cattle or for venison with his companions; and he finds at last that he can in this manner get more cattle and venison than if he himself went to the field to catch them. From a regard to his own interest, therefore, the making of bows and arrows grows to be his chief business, and he becomes a sort of armorer. Another excels in making the frames and covers of their little huts or movable houses. He is accustomed to be of use in this way to his neighbors, who reward him in the same manner with cattle and with venison till at last he finds it his interest to dedicate himself entirely to this employment, and to become a sort of house carpenter. In the same manner a third becomes a smith or a brazier; a fourth a tanner or dresser of hides or skins, the principal part of the clothing of savages. And thus the certainty of being able to exchange all that surplus part of the produce of his own labor, which is over and above his own consumption, for such parts of the produce of other men's labor as he may have occasion for, encourages every man to apply himself to a particular occupation, and to cultivate and bring to perfection whatever talent or genius he may possess for that particular species of business.

The difference of natural talents in different men is, in reality, much less than we are aware of; and the very different genius which appears to distinguish men of different professions, when grown up to maturity, is not upon many occasions so much the cause as the effect of the division of labor. The difference between the most dissimilar characters, between a philosopher and a common street porter, for example, seems to arise not so much from nature as from habit, custom, and education. When they came into the world, and for the first six or eight years of their existence, they were, perhaps, very much alike, and neither their parents nor play-fellows could perceive any remarkable difference. About that age, or soon after, they come to be employed in very different occupations. The difference of talents comes then to be taken notice of, and widens by degrees, till at last the vanity of the philosopher is willing to acknowledge scarce any resemblance. But without the disposition to truck, barter and exchange, every man must have procured to himself every necessary and conveniency of life which he wanted. All must have had the same duties to perform, and the same work to do, and there could have been no such difference of employment as could alone give occasion to any great difference of talents. . . .

Every individual is continually exerting himself to find out the most advantageous employment for whatever capital he can command. It is his own advantage, indeed, and not that of the society, which he has in view. But the study of his own advantage, naturally, or rather necessarily, leads him to prefer that employment which is most advantageous to the society. . . .

As every individual, therefore, endeavors as much as he can both to employ his capital in the support of domestic industry, and so to direct that industry that its produce may be of the greatest value, every individual necessarily labors to render the annual revenue of the society as great as he can. He generally, indeed, neither intends to promote the public interest, nor knows how much he is promoting it. By preferring the support of domestic to that of foreign industry, he intends only his own security: and by directing that industry in such a manner as its produce may be of the greatest value, he intends only his own gain, and he is in this, as in many other cases, led by an invisible hand to promote an end which was no part of his intention. Nor is it always the worse for the society that it was no part of it. By pursuing his own interest he frequently promotes that of the society more effectually than when he really intends to promote it. I have never known much good done by those who affected to trade for the public good. It is an affectation, indeed, not very common among merchants, and very few words need be employed in dissuading them from it. . . .

   If we examine, I say, all those things . . . we shall be sensible that without the assistance and cooperation of many thousands, the very meanest person in a civilized country could not be provided, even according to what we very falsely imagine, the easy and simple manner in which he is commonly accommodated. Compared indeed with the more extravagant luxury of the great, his accommodation must no doubt appear extremely simple and easy; and yet it may be true, perhaps, that the accommodation of a European prince does not always so much exceed that of an industrious and frugal peasant, as the accommodation of the latter exceeds that of many an African king, the absolute master of the lives and liberties of ten thousand naked savages.

John Stuart Mill, *Utilitarianism*, 1861

Utilitarianism
John Stuart Mill

General Remarks

On the present occasion, I shall attempt to contribute something towards the understanding and appreciation of the Utilitarian or Happiness theory, and towards such proof as it is susceptible of. It is evident that this cannot be proof in the ordinary and popular meaning of the term. Questions of ultimate ends are not amenable to direct proof. We are not, however, to infer that its acceptance or rejection must depend on blind impulse, or arbitrary choice. Considerations may be presented capable of determining the intellect either to give or withhold its assent to the doctrine; and this is equivalent of proof.

WHAT UTILITARIANISM IS

The creed which accepts as the foundation of morals utility or the greatest happiness principle holds that actions are right in proportion as they tend to promote happiness, wrong as they tend to produce the reverse of happiness. By "happiness" is intended pleasure, and the absence of pain; by "unhappiness," pain, and the privation of pleasure. To give a clear view of the moral standard set up by the theory, much more requires to be said; in particular, what things it includes in the ideas of pain and pleasure, and to what extent this is left an open question. But these supplementary explanations do not affect the theory of life on which this theory of mortality is grounded—namely, that pleasure, and freedom from pain, are the only things desirable as ends; and that all desirable things (which are as numerous in the utilitarian as in any other scheme) are desirable either for the pleasure inherent in themselves, or as means to the promotion of pleasure and the prevention of pain.

Now such a theory of life excites in many minds, and among them in some of the most estimable in feeling and purpose, inveterate dislike. To suppose that life has (as they express it) no higher end than pleasure—no better and nobler object of desire and pursuit—they designate as utterly mean and groveling; as a doctrine worthy only of swine. . . .

[But it] is quite compatible with the principle of utility to recognize the fact, that some *kinds* of pleasure are more desirable and more valuable than others. It would be absurd that while, in estimating all other things, quality is considered as well as quantity, the estimation of pleasures should be supposed to depend on quantity alone.

If I am asked what I mean by difference of quality in pleasures, or what makes one pleasure more valuable than another merely as a pleasure, except its being greater in amount, there is but one possible answer. Of two pleasures, if there be one to which all or almost all who have experience of both give a decided preference, irrespective of any feeling of moral obligation to prefer it, that is the more desirable pleasure. If one of the two is, by those who are competently acquainted with both, placed so far above the other that they prefer it, even though knowing it to be attended with a greater amount of discontent, and would not resign it for any quantity of the other pleasure which their nature is capable of, we are justified in ascribing to the preferred enjoyment a superiority in quality, so far outweighing quantity as to render it, in comparison, of small account.

Now it is an unquestionable fact that those who are equally acquainted with, and equally capable of appreciating and enjoying, both, do give a most marked preference to the manner of existence which employs their higher faculties. Few human creatures would consent to be changed into any of the lower animals, for a promise of the fullest allowance of a beast's pleasures; no intelligent human being would consent to be a fool, no instructed person would be an ignoramus, no person of feeling and conscience would be selfish and base, even though they should be persuaded that the fool, the dunce, or the rascal is better satisfied with his lot than they are with theirs. They would not resign what they possess more than he for the most complete satisfaction of all the desires which they have in common with him. If they ever fancy they would, it is only in cases of unhappiness so extreme, that to escape from it they would exchange their lot for almost any other, however undesirable in their own eyes. A being of higher faculties requires more to make him happy, is capable probably of more acute suffering, and certainly accessible to it at more points, than one of an inferior type; but in spite of these liabilities, he can never really wish to sink into what he feels to be a lower grade of existence. We may give what explanation we please of this unwillingness: we may attribute it to pride, a name which is given indiscriminately to some of the most and to some of the least estimable feelings of which mankind are capable, we may refer it to the love of liberty and personal independence, an appeal to which was with the Stoics one of the most effective means for the inculcation of it; to the love of power, or to the love of excitement, both of which do really enter into and contribute to it: but its most appropriate appellation is a sense of dignity, which all human beings possess in one form or other, and in some, though by no means in exact, proportion to their higher faculties, and which is so essential a part of the happiness of those in whom it is strong, that nothing which conflicts with it could be, otherwise than momentarily, an object of desire to them[.] It is better to be a human being dissatisfied than a pig satisfied; better to be Socrates dissatisfied than a fool satisfied. And if the fool, or the pig, is of a different opinion, it is because they only know their own side of the question. The other party to the comparison knows both sides. . .

From this verdict of the only competent judges I apprehend there can be no appeal. On a question which is the best worth having of two pleasures, or which of two modes of existence is the most grateful to the feelings, apart from its moral attributes and from its consequences, the judgment of those who are qualified by knowledge of both, or, if they differ, that of the majority among them, must be admitted as final. And there need be the less hesitation to accept this judgment respecting the quality of pleasures, since there is no other tribunal to be referred to even on the question of quantity. What means are there of determining which is the acutest of two pains, or the intensest of two pleasurable sensations, except the general suffrage of those who are familiar with both? Neither pains nor pleasures are homogeneous, and pain is always heterogeneous with pleasure. What is there to decide whether a particular pleasure is worth purchasing at the cost of a particular pain, except the feelings and judgment of the experienced? When, therefore, those feelings and judgment declare the pleasures derived from the higher faculties to be preferable in kind, apart from the question of intensity, to those of which the animal nature, disjoined from the higher faculties, is susceptible, they are entitled on this subject to the same regard. . . .

Utilitarianism, therefore, could only attain its end by the general cultivation of nobleness of character, even if each individual were only benefited by the nobleness of others, and his own, so far as happiness is concerned, were a sheer deduction from the benefit. But the bare enunciation of such an absurdity as this last renders refutation superfluous. . . .

Though it is only in a very imperfect state of the world's arrangements that anyone can best serve the happiness of others by the absolute sacrifice of his own, yet so long as the world is in that imperfect state, I fully acknowledge that the readiness to make such a sacrifice is the highest virtue which can be found in man. I will add that in this condition of the world, paradoxical as the assertion may be, the conscious ability to do without happiness gives the best prospect of realizing such happiness as is attainable. For nothing except that consciousness can raise a person above the chances of life, by making him feel that, let fate and fortune do their worst, they have not power to subdue him. . . .

The utilitarian morality does recognize in human beings the power of sacrificing their own greatest good for the good of others. It only refuses to admit that the sacrifice is itself a good. A sacrifice which does not increase, or tend to increase, the sum total of happiness, it considers as wasted. . . .

The assailants of utilitarianism seldom have the justice to acknowledge, that the happiness which forms the utilitarian standard of what is right in conduct is not the agent's own happiness but that of all concerned. As between his own happiness and that of others, utilitarianism requires him to be as strictly impartial as a disinterested and benevolent spectator. In the golden rule of Jesus of Nazareth, we read the complete spirit of the ethics of utility. "To do as you would be done by," and "to love your neighbor as yourself," constitute the ideal perfection of utilitarian morality. As the means of making the nearest approach to this ideal, utility would enjoin, first, that laws and social arrangements should place the happiness or (as speaking practically, it may be called) the interest of every individual as nearly as possible in harmony with the interest of the whole; and, secondly, that education and opinion, which have so vast a power over human character, should so use that power as to establish in the mind of every individual an indissoluble association between his own happiness and the good of the whole, especially between his own happiness and the practice of such modes of conduct, negative and positive, as regard for the universal happiness prescribes; so that not only he may be unable to conceive the possibility of happiness to himself, consistent with the conduct opposed to the general good, but also that a direct impulse to promote the general good may be every individual one of the habitual motives of action, and the sentiments connected therewith may fill a large and prominent place in every human being's sentient existence. . . .

We not uncommonly hear the doctrine of utility inveighed against as a *godless* doctrine. If it be necessary to say anything at all against so mere an assumption, we may say that the question depends upon what idea we have formed of the moral character of the Deity. If it be a true belief that God desires, above all things, the happiness of his creatures, and that this was his purpose in their creation, utility is not only not a godless doctrine, but more profoundly religious than any other. If it be meant that utilitarianism does not recognize the revealed will of God as the supreme law of morals, I answer that a utilitarian who believes in the perfect goodness and wisdom of God necessarily believes that whatever God has thought fit to reveal on the subject of morals must fulfill the requirements of utility in a supreme degree. . . .

Again, defenders of utility often find themselves called upon to reply to such objections as this—that there is not time, previous to action, for calculating and weighing the effects of any line of conduct on the general happiness. This is exactly as if anyone were to say that it is impossible to guide our conduct by Christianity because there is not time, on every occasion on which anything has to be done, to read through the Old and New Testaments. The answer to the objection is that there has been ample time, namely, the whole past duration of the human species. During all that time mankind have been learning by experience the tendencies of actions; on which experience all the prudence as well as all the morality of life are dependent. The corollaries from the principle of utility, like the precepts of every practical art, admit of indefinite improvement, and, in a progressive state of the human mind, their improvement is perpetually going on. But to consider the rules of morality as improvable is one thing; to pass over the intermediate generalization entirely and endeavor to test each individual action directly by the first principle is another. It is a strange notion that the acknowledgment of a first principle is inconsistent with the admission of secondary ones. To inform a traveler respecting the place of his ultimate destination is not to forbid the use of landmarks and direction-posts on the way. . . .

There exists no moral system under which there do not arise unequivocal cases of conflicting obligation. These are real difficulties, the knotty points both in the theory of ethics and in the conscientious guidance of personal conduct. They are overcome practically, with greater or with less success, according to the intellect and virtue of the individual; but it can hardly be pretended that anyone will be the less qualified for dealing with them, from possessing an ultimate standard to which conflicting rights and duties can be referred. If utility is the ultimate source of moral obligations, utility may be invoked to decide between them when their demands are incompatible. Though the application of the [utilitarian] standard may be difficult, it is better than none at all; while in other systems, the moral laws all claiming independent authority, there is no common umpire entitled to interfere between them; their claims to precedence one over another rest on little better than sophistry, and, unless determined, as they generally are, by the unacknowledged influence of consideration of utility, afford a free scope for the action of personal desires and partialities. We must remember that only in these cases of conflict between secondary principles is it requisite that first principles should be appealed to. There is no case of moral obligation in which some secondary principle is not involved; and if only one, there can seldom be any real doubt which one it is, in the mind of any person by whom the principle itself is recognized.

OF WHAT SORT OF PROOF THE PRINCIPLE OF UTILITY IS SUSCEPTIBLE

It has already been remarked that questions of ultimate ends do not admit of proof, in the ordinary acceptation of the term. To be incapable of proof by reasoning is common to all first principles; to the first premises of our knowledge, as well as to those of our conduct. But the former, being matters of fact, may be the subject of a direct appeal to the faculties which judge of fact—namely, our senses, and our internal consciousness. Can an appeal be made to the same faculties on questions of practical ends? Or by what other faculty is cognizance taken of them?

Questions about ends are, in other words, questions about what things are desirable. The utilitarian doctrine is, that happiness is desirable, and the only thing desirable, as an end; all other things being only desirable as means to that end. What ought to be required of this doctrine—what conditions is it requisite that the doctrine should fulfill—to make good its claim to be believed?

The only proof capable of being given that an object is visible, is that people actually see it. The only proof that a sound is audible, is that people hear it: and so of the other sources of our experience. In like manner, I apprehend, the sole evidence it is possible to produce that anything is desirable, is that people do actually desire it. If the end which the utilitarian doctrine proposes to itself were not, in theory and in practice, acknowledged to be an end, nothing could ever convince any person that it was so. No reason can be given why the general happiness is desirable, except that each person, so far as he believes it to be attainable, desires his own happiness. This, however, being a fact, we have not only all the proof which the case admits of, but all which it is possible to require, that happiness is a good: that each person's happiness is a good to that person, and the general happiness, therefore, a good to the aggregate of all persons. Happiness has made out its title as *one* of the ends of conduct, and consequently one of the criteria of morality.

But it has not, by this alone, proved itself to be the sole criterion. To do that, it would seem, by the same rule, necessary to show, not only that people desire happiness, but that they never desire anything else. Now it is palpable that they do desire things which, in common language, are decidedly distinguished from happiness. They desire, for example, virtue, and the absence of vice, no less really than pleasure and the absence of pain. The desire of virtue is not as universal, but it is as authentic a fact, as the desire of happiness. And hence the opponents of the utilitarian standard deem that they have a right to infer that there are other ends of human action besides happiness, and that happiness is not the standard of approbation and disapprobation.

The ingredients of happiness are very various, and each of them is desirable in itself, and not merely when considered as swelling an aggregate. The principle of utility does not mean that any given pleasure, as music, for instance, or any given exemption from pain, as for example health, is to be looked upon as means to a collective something termed happiness, and to be desired on that account. They are desired and desirable in and for themselves, besides being a means, they are part of the end. Virtue, according to the utilitarian doctrine, is not naturally and originally part of the end, but is capable of becoming so; and in those who live disinterestedly it has become so, and is desired and cherished, not as a means to happiness, but as part of their happiness.

To illustrate this further, we may remember that virtue is not the only thing originally a means, and which if it were not a means to anything else would be and remain indifferent, but which by association with what it is a means to comes to be desired for itself, and that too with the utmost intensity. What, for example, shall we say of the love of money? There is nothing originally more desirable about money than about any heap of glittering pebbles. Its worth is solely that of the things which it will buy; the desires for other things than itself, which it is a means of gratifying. Yet the love of money is not only one of the strongest moving forces of human life, but money is, in many cases, desired in and for itself; the desire to possess it is often stronger than the desire to use it, and goes on increasing when all the desires which point to ends beyond it, to be compassed by it, are falling off. It may, then, be said truly that money is desired not for the sake of an end, but as part of the end, From being a means to happiness, it has come to be itself a principal ingredient of the individual's conception of happiness. The same may be said of the majority of the great objects of human life: power, for example, or fame, except that to each of these there is a certain amount of immediate pleasure annexed, which has at least the semblance of being naturally inherent in them—a thing which cannot be said of money. . . .

It results from the preceding considerations that there is in reality nothing desired except happiness. Whatever is desired otherwise than as a means to some end beyond itself, and ultimately to happiness, is desired as itself a part of happiness, and is not desired for itself until it has become so. . . .

We have now. then, an answer to the question, of what sort of proof the principle of utility is susceptible. If the opinion which I have now stated is psychologically true—if human nature is so constituted as to desire nothing which is not either a part of happiness or a means of happiness—we can have no other proof, and we require no other, that these are the only things desirable. If so, happiness is the sole end of human action, and the promotion of it the test by which to judge of all human conduct; from whence it necessarily follows that it must be the criterion of morality, since a part is included in the whole. . . .

On the Connection Between Justice and Utility

In all ages of speculation, one of the strongest obstacles to the reception of the doctrine that Utility or Happiness is the criterion of right and wrong, has been drawn from the idea of Justice. . . .

To throw light upon this question, it is necessary to attempt to ascertain what is the distinguishing or character of justice, or of injustice: . . . .

In the first place is mostly considered unjust to deprive anyone of his personal liberty, his property, or any other thing which belongs to him by law. Here, therefore, is one instance of the application of the terms just and unjust in a perfectly definite sense, namely, that it is just to respect, unjust to violate, the *legal rights* of any one. . . .

Secondly; the legal rights of which he is deprived, may be rights which *ought* not to have belonged to him; in other words, the law which confers on him these rights, may be a bad law. . . . When, however, a law is thought to be unjust, it seems to be regarded as being so in the same way in which a breach of law is unjust, namely, by infringing somebody's right; which, as it cannot in this case be a legal right . . . is called a moral right. We may say, therefore, that a second case of injustice consists in taking or withholding from any person that to which he has a *moral right.*

Thirdly, it is universally considered just that each person should obtain that (whether good or evil) which he *deserves;* and unjust that he should obtain a good, or be made to undergo an evil, which he does not deserve. . . . Speaking in a general way, a person is understood to deserve good if he does right, evil if he does wrong; and in a more particular sense, to deserve good from those to whom he does or has done good, and evil from those to whom he does or has done evil. . . .

Fourthly, it is confessedly unjust to *break faith* with any one: to violate an engagement, either express or implied, or disappoint expectations raised by our own conduct, at least if we have raised those expectations knowingly and voluntarily. . . .

Fifthly, it is, by universal admission, inconsistent with justice to be *partial*—to show favor or preference to one person over another in matters in which favor and preference do not apply. . . .

Among the many diverse applications of the term "justice" it is a matter of some difficulty to seize the mental link which holds them together. We must observe that it contains as yet nothing to distinguish that obligation [justice] from moral obligation in general. We do not call anything wrong unless we mean to imply that a person ought to be punished in some way or other for not doing it—if not by law, by the opinion of his fellow creatures; if not by opinion, by the reproaches of his own conscience. This seems the real turning point between morality and simple expediency. It is part of the notion of duty in every one of its forms that a person may rightfully be compelled to fulfill it. Duty is a thing which may be *exacted* from a person, as one exacts a debt. . . .

This, therefore, being the characteristic difference which marks off, not justice, but morality in general from the remaining provinces of expedience and worthiness, the character is still to be sought which distinguishes justice from other branches of morality . . . In our survey of the various popular acceptations of justice, the term appeared generally to involve the idea of a personal right—a claim on the part of one or more individuals, light that which the law gives when it confers a proprietary or other legal rights. Whether the injustice consists in depriving a person of a possession, or in breaking faith with him, or in treating worse than he deserves, or worse than other people who have no greater claims—in each case the supposition implies two things: a wrong done, and some assignable person who is wronged. Injustice may also be done by treating a person better than others; but the wrong in this case is to the competitor, or are also assignable persons. It seems to me that this feature in the case— a right in some person, correlative to the moral obligation—constitutes the specific difference between justice and generosity or beneficence. Justice implies something which is not only right to do, and wrong not to do, but which some individual person can claim from us as his moral right. No one has a moral right to our generosity or beneficence because we are not morally bound to practice those virtues toward any given individual. . . .

We have seen that the two essential ingredients in the sentiment of justice are, the desire to punish a person who has done harm, and the knowledge or belief that there is some definite individual or individuals to whom harm has been done.

Now it appears to me, that the desire to punish a person who has done harm to some individual is a spontaneous outgrowth from two sentiments, both in the highest degree natural, and which either are or resemble instincts; the impulse of self-defense, and the feeling of sympathy.

It is natural to resent, and to repel or retaliate, any harm done or attempted against ourselves, or against those with whom we sympathize. The origin of this sentiment it is not necessary here to discuss. Whether it be an instinct or a result of intelligence, it is, we know, common to all animal nature; for every animal tries to hurt those who have hurt, or who it thinks are about to hurt, itself or its young. Human beings, on this point, only differ from other animals in two particulars. First, in being capable of sympathizing, not solely with their offspring, or, like some of the more noble animals, with some superior animal who is kind to them, but with all human, and even with all sentient beings. Secondly, in having a more developed intelligence, which gives a wider range to the whole of their sentiments, whether self-regarding or sympathetic. By virtue of his superior intelligence, even apart from his superior range of sympathy, a human being is capable of apprehending a community of interest between himself and the human society of which he forms a part, such that any conduct which threatens the security of the society generally, is threatening to his own, and calls forth his instinct (if instinct it be) of self-defense. The same superiority of intelligence, joined to the power of sympathizing with human beings generally, enables him to attach himself to the collective idea of his tribe, his country, or mankind, in such a manner that any act hurtful to them, raises his instinct of sympathy, and urges him to resistance.

The sentiment of justice, in that one of its elements which consists of the desire to punish, is thus, I conceive, the natural feeling of retaliation or vengeance, rendered by intellect and sympathy applicable to those injuries, that is, to those hurts, which wound us through, or in common with, society at large. This sentiment, in itself, has nothing moral in it; what is moral is, the exclusive subordination of it to the social sympathies, so as to wait on and obey their call. For the natural feeling would make us resent indiscriminately whatever any one does that is disagreeable to us; but when moralized by the social feeling, it only acts in the directions conformable to the general good: just persons resenting a hurt to society, though not otherwise a hurt to themselves, and not resenting a hurt to themselves, however painful, unless it be of the kind which society has a common interest with them in the repression of.

It is no objection against this doctrine to say that, when we feel our sentiment of justice outraged, we are not thinking of society at large or of any collective interest, but only of the individual case. It is common enough, certainly, though the reverse is commendable, to feel resentment merely because we have suffered pain; but a person whose resentment is really a moral feeling, that is, who considers whether an act is blamable before he allows himself to resent it—such a person, though he may not say expressly to himself that he is standing up for the interests of society, certainly does feel that he is asserting a rule which is for the benefit of others as well as for his own. If he is not feeling this, if he is regarding the act solely as it affects him individually, he is not consciously just; he is not concerning himself about the justice of his actions. This is admitted even by anti-utilitarian moralists. When Kant propounds as the fundamental principle of morals, "So act that thy rule of conduct might be adopted as a law by all rational beings," he virtually acknowledged that the interest of mankind collectively, or at least mankind indiscriminately, must be in the mind of the agent when conscientiously deciding on the morality of an act. To give any meaning to Kant's principle, the sense put upon it must be that we ought to shape our conduct by a rule which all rational beings might adopt *with the benefit of their collective interest.*

To recapitulate: the idea of justice supposes two things; a rule of conduct, and a sentiment which sanctions the rule. The first must be supposed common to all mankind, and intended for their good. The other (the sentiment) is a desire that punishment may be suffered by those who infringe the rule. There is involved, in addition, the conception of some definite person who suffers by the infringement; whose rights (to use the expression appropriated to the case) are violated by it. And the sentiment of justice appears to me to be, the animal desire to repel or retaliate a hurt or damage to oneself, or to those with whom one sympathizes, widened so as to include all persons, by the human capacity of enlarged sympathy, and the human conception of intelligent self-interest.

From the latter elements, the feeling derives its morality; from the former, its peculiar impressiveness, and energy of self-assertion.

I have, throughout, treated the idea of a *right* residing in the injured person, and violated by the injury, not as a separate element in the composition of the idea and sentiment, but as one of the forms in which the other two elements clothe themselves. These elements are, a hurt to some assignable person or persons on the one hand, and a demand for punishment on the other. An examination of our own minds, I think, will show, that these two things include all that we mean when we speak of violation of a right. When we call anything a person's right, we mean that he has a valid claim on society to protect him in the possession of it, either by the force of law, or by that of education and opinion. If he has what we consider a sufficient claim, on whatever account, to have something guaranteed to him by society, we say that he has a right to it. If we desire to prove that anything does not belong to him by right, we think this done as soon as it is admitted that society ought not to take measures for securing it to him, but should leave him to chance, or to his own exertions. Thus, a person is said to have a right to what he can earn in fair professional competition; because society ought not to allow any other person to hinder him from endeavoring to earn in that manner as much as he can. But he has not a right to three hundred a year, though he may happen to be earning it; because society is not called on to provide that he shall earn that sum. On the contrary, if he owns ten thousand pounds three per cent, stock, he *has* a right to three hundred a year; because society has come under an obligation to provide him with an income of that amount.

To have a right, then, is, I conceive, to have something which society ought to defend me in the possession of. If the objector goes on to ask, why it ought? I can give him no other reason than general utility. If that expression does not seem to convey a sufficient feeling of the strength of the obligation, nor to account for the peculiar energy of the feeling, it is because there goes to the composition of the sentiment, not a rational only but also an animal element—the thirst for retaliation; and this thirst derives its intensity, as well as its moral justification, from the extraordinarily important and impressive kind of utility which is concerned. The interest involved is that of security, to everyone's feelings the most vital of all interests. . . .

We are continually informed that utility is an uncertain standard, which every different person interprets differently, and that there is no safety but in the immutable, ineffaceable, and unmistakable dictates of justice, which carry their evidence in themselves. [But] not only have different nations and individuals different notions of justice, but in the mind of one and the same individual, justice is not some one rule, principle, or maxim but many which do not always coincide in their dictates, and, in choosing between which, he is guided either by some extraneous standard or by his own personal predilections.

For instance, there are some who say that it is unjust to punish anyone for the sake of example to others. Others maintain the extreme reverse, contending that to punish persons who have attained years of discretion for their own benefit, is despotism and injustice since, if the matter is solely their own good, no one has a right to control their own judgment of it; but that they may justly be punished to prevent evil to others. . . .

To escape these and other difficulties, a favorite contrivance has been the fiction of a contract whereby at some unknown period all members of society engaged to obey the laws and consented to be punished for any disobedience to them, thereby giving to their legislators the right, which it is assumed they would not otherwise have had, of punishing them, either for their own good or for that of the society. This happy thought was considered to get rid of the whole difficulty and to legitimate the infliction of punishment, in virtue of another received maxim of justice—that is not unjust which is done with the consent of the person who is supposed to be hurt by it. I need hardly remark that, even if consent were not a mere fiction, this maxim is not superior in authority to others which it is brought in to supersede. It is, on the contrary, an instructive specimen of the loose and irregular matter in which supposed principles of justice grow up. . . .

Again, . . . how many conflicting conceptions of justice come to light in discussing the proper apportionment of punishment to offenses. [One is] an eye for an eye, a tooth for a tooth. [Others think] it should be measured by the moral guilt of the culprit, [or] what amount of punishment is necessary to deter the offense. To take another example, . . . in a cooperative industrial association is it just or not that talent or skill should give the title to superior remuneration? On the negative side of the question it is argued that whoever does the best he can deserves equally well, and ought not injustice to be put in a position of inferiority for no fault of his own; that superior abilities have already advantages more than enough, in the admiration they excite, the personal influence they command, and the internal sources of satisfaction attending them, without adding to these a superior share of the world's goods; and that society is bound in justice rather to make compensation to the less favored for this unmerited inequality of advantages than to aggravate it. On the contrary side it is contended that society receives more from the efficient laborer; that, his services being more useful, society owes him the larger return for them; that a greater share of the joint result is actually his work, and not to allow his claim to it is a kind of robbery; that, if he is only to receive as much as others, he can only be justly required to produce as much, and to give a smaller amount of time and exertion, proportioned to his superior efficiency. Who shall decide between these appeals to conflicting principles of justice? Each, from his own point of view, is unanswerable; and any choice between them, on grounds of justice, must be perfectly arbitrary. Social utility alone can decide the preference. . . .

Has society been under a delusion in thinking that justice is a more sacred thing than policy, and that the latter ought only to be listened to after the former has been satisfied? By no means. . . . Justice is a name for certain classes of moral rules which concern the essential of human well-being more nearly, and are therefore of more absolute obligation, than any other rules for the guidance of life. The moral rules which forbid mankind to hurt one another (in which we must never forget to include a wrongful interference with each other's freedom) are more vital to human well-being than any maxims, however important, which only point out the best mode of managing some department of human affairs. The moralities which protect every individual from being harmed by others, either directly or by being hindered in his freedom of pursuing his own good, are at once those which he himself has most at heart and those which he has the strongest interest in publishing and enforcing by word and deed. Now it is these moralities primarily which compose obligations of justice.

Søren Kiekegaard, *Concluding Unscientific Postscript*, David F. Swenson (trans.), 1941

Radical Subjectivity
Søren Kierkegaard

PART TWO

How the Subjectivity of the Individual Must Be Qualified in Order that the Problem May Exist for Him

The Task of Becoming Subjective

The conclusion that would be forced upon ethics if the attainment of subjectivity were not the highest task confronting a human being—Considerations left out of account in connection with the closer understanding of this—Examples of thinking directed towards becoming subjective

Objectively we consider only the matter at issue, subjectively we have regard to the subject and his subjectivity; and behold, precisely this subjectivity is the matter at issue. This must constantly be borne in mind, namely, that the subjective problem is not something about an objective issue, but is the subjectivity itself. For since the problem in question poses a decision, and since all decisiveness as shown above, inheres in subjectivity, it is essential that every trace of an objective issue should be eliminated. If any such trace remains, it is at once a sign that the subject seeks to shirk something of the pain and crisis of the decision; that is, he seeks to make the problem to some degree objective. If the Introduction still awaits the appearance of another work before bringing the matter up for judgment, if the System still lacks a paragraph, if the speaker has still another argument up his sleeve, it follows that the decision is postponed. Hence we do not here raise the question of the truth of Christianity in the sense that when this has been determined, the subject is assumed ready and willing to accept it. No, the question is as to the mode of the subject's acceptance; and it must be regarded as an illusion rooted in the demoralization which remains ignorant of the subjective nature of the decision, or as an evasion springing from the disingenuousness which seeks to shirk the decision by an objective mode of approach, wherein there can in all eternity be no decision, to assume that the transition from something objective to the subjective acceptance is a direct transition, following upon the objective deliberation as a matter of course. On the contrary, the subjective acceptance is precisely the decisive factor; and an objective acceptance of Christianity (*sit venia verbo*) is paganism or thoughtlessness. . . .

The subjective reflection turns its attention inwardly to the subject, and desires in this intensification of inwardness to realize the truth. And it proceeds in such fashion that, just as in the preceding objective reflection, when the objectivity had come into being, the subjectivity had vanished, so here the subjectivity of the subject becomes the final stage, and objectivity a vanishing factor. Not for a single moment is it forgotten that the subject is an existing individual, and that existence is a process of becoming, and that therefore the notion of the truth as identity of thought and being is a chimera of abstraction, in its truth only an expectation of the creature; not because the truth is not such an identity, but because the knower is an existing individual for whom the truth cannot be such an identity as long as he lives in time. Unless we hold fast to this, speculative philosophy will immediately transport us into the fantastic realism of the I-am-I, which modern speculative thought has not hesitated to use without explaining how a particular individual is related to it; and God knows, no human being is more than such a particular individual.

If an existing individual were really able to transcend himself, the truth would be for him something final and complete; but where is the point at which he is outside himself? The I-am-I is a mathematical point which does not exist, and in so far there is nothing to prevent everyone from occupying this standpoint; the one will not be in the way of the other. It is only momentarily that the particular individual is able to realize existentially a unity of the infinite and the finite which transcends existence. This unity is realized in the moment of passion. Modern philosophy has tried anything and everything in the effort to help the individual to transcend himself objectively, which is a wholly impossible feat; existence exercises its restraining influence, and if philosophers nowadays had not become mere scribblers in the service of a fantastic thinking and its preoccupation, they would long ago have perceived that suicide was the only tolerable practical interpretation of its striving. But the scribbling modern philosophy holds passion in contempt; and yet passion is the culmination of existence for an existing individual—and we are all of us existing individuals. In passion the existing subject is rendered infinite in the eternity of the imaginative representation, and yet he is at the same time most definitely himself. The fantastic I-am-I is not an identity of the infinite and the finite, since neither the one nor the other is real; it is a fantastic rendezvous in the clouds,[5] an unfruitful embrace, and the relationship of the individual self to this mirage is never indicated.

All essential knowledge relates to existence, or only such knowledge as has an essential relationship to existence is essential knowledge, All knowledge which does not inwardly relate itself to existence, in the reflection of inwardness, is, essentially viewed, accidental knowledge; its degree and scope is essentially indifferent. That essential knowledge is essentially related to existence does not mean the above-mentioned identity which abstract thought postulates between thought and being; nor does it signify, objectively, that knowledge corresponds to something existent as its object. But it means that knowledge has a relationship to the knower, who is essentially an existing individual, and that for this reason all essential knowledge is essentially related to existence. Only ethical and ethico-religious knowledge has an essential relationship to the existence of the knower.

Mediation is a mirage, like the I-am-I. From the abstract point of view everything is and nothing comes into being. Mediation can therefore have no place in abstract thought because it presupposes *movement*. Objective knowledge may indeed have the existent for its object; but since the knowing subject is an existing individual, and through the fact of his existence in process of becoming, philosophy must first explain how a particular existing subject is related to a knowledge of mediation. It must explain what he is in such a moment, if not pretty nearly *distrait;* where he is, if not in the moon? There is constant talk of mediation and mediation; is mediation then a man, as Peter Deacon[6] believes that *Imprimatur* is a man? How does a human being manage to become something of this kind? Is this dignity, this great *philosophicum,* the fruit of study, or does the magistrate give it away, like the office of deacon or grave-digger? Try merely to enter into these and other such plain questions of a plain man, who would gladly become mediation if it could be done in some lawful and honest manner, and not either by saying *ein zwei drei kokolorum,* or by forgetting that he is himself an existing human being, for whom existence is therefore something essential, and an ethico-religious existence a suitable *quantum satis.* A speculative philosopher may perhaps find it in bad taste to ask such questions. But it is important not to direct the polemic to the wrong point, and hence not to begin in a fantastic objective manner to discuss *pro* and *contra* whether there is a mediation or not, but to hold fast what it means to be a human being.

In an attempt to make clear the difference of way that exists between an objective and a subjective reflection, I shall now proceed to show how a subjective reflection makes its way inwardly in inwardness. Inwardness in an existing subject culminates in passion; corresponding to passion in the subject the truth becomes a paradox; and the fact that the truth becomes a paradox is rooted precisely in its having a relationship to an existing subject. Thus the one corresponds to the other. By forgetting that one is an existing subject, passion goes by the board and the truth is no longer a paradox; the knowing subject becomes a fantastic entity rather than a human being, and the truth becomes a fantastic object for the knowledge of this fantastic entity.

When the question of truth is raised in an objective manner, reflection is directed objectively to the truth, as an object to which the knower is related. Reflection is not focussed upon the relationship, however, but upon the question of whether it is the truth to which the knower is related. If only the object to which he is related is the truth, the subject is accounted to be in the truth. When the question of the truth is raised subjectively, reflection is directed subjectively to the nature of the individual's relationship; if only the mode of this relationship is in the truth, the individual is in the truth even if he should happen to be thus related to what is not true. Let us take as an example the knowledge of God. Objectively, reflection is directed to the problem of whether this object is the true God; subjectively, reflection is directed to the question whether the individual is related to a something *in such a manner* that his relationship is in truth a God-relationship. On which side is the truth now to be found? Ah, may we not here resort to a mediation, and say: It is on neither side, but in the mediation of both? Excellently well said, provided we might have it explained how an existing individual manages to be in a state of mediation. For to be in a state of mediation is to be finished, while to exist is to become. Nor can an existing individual be in two places at the same time—he cannot be an identity of subject and object. When he is nearest to being in two places at the same time he is in passion; but passion is momentary, and passion is also the highest expression of subjectivity.

The existing individual who chooses to pursue the objective way enters upon the entire approximation-process by which it is proposed to bring God to light objectively. But this is in all eternity impossible, because God is a subject, and therefore exists only for subjectivity in

*The reader will observe that the question here is about essential truth, or about the truth which is essentially related to existence, and that it is precisely for the sake of clarifying it as inwardness or as subjectivity that this contrast is drawn.

inwardness. The existing individual who chooses the subjective way apprehends instantly the entire dialectical difficulty involved in having to use some time, perhaps a long time, in finding God objectively; and he feels this dialectical difficulty in all its painfulness, because every moment is wasted in which he does not have God. That very instant he has God, not by virtue of any objective deliberation, but by virtue of the infinite passion of inwardness. The objective inquirer, on the other hand, is not embarrassed by such dialectical difficulties as are involved in devoting an entire period of investigation to finding God—since it is possible that the inquirer may die tomorrow; and if he lives he can scarcely regard God as something to be taken along if convenient, since God is precisely that which one takes *a tout prix*, which in the understanding of passion constitutes the true inward relationship to God.

It is at this point, so difficult dialectically, that the way swings off for everyone who knows what it means to think, and to think existentially; which is something very different from sitting at a desk and writing about what one has never done, something very different from writing *de omnibus dubitandum* and at the same time being as credulous existentially as the most sensuous of men. Here is where the way swings off, and the change is marked by the fact that while objective knowledge rambles comfortably on by way of the long road of approximation without being impelled by the urge of passion, subjective knowledge counts every delay a deadly peril, and the decision so infinitely important and so instantly pressing that it is as if the opportunity had already passed. . . .

In our own day the ethical tends more and more to be ignored. This has had among other things the harmful consequence that poetry and speculative thought have become unsettled, and have deserted the lofty disinterestedness of the possible in order to reach out for reality. Instead of assigning to each sphere its own proper scale of values, a double confusion has been introduced. Poetry makes one attempt after the other to play the role of reality, which is entirely unpoetical. Speculative thought repeatedly attempts to reach reality within its own domain, assuring us that whatever is thought is real, that thought is not only capable of thinking reality but of bestowing it, while the truth is the direct opposite; and simultaneously a forgetfulness of what it means to exist, extends itself more and more. The age becomes increasingly unreal, and the people in it; hence these substitutes to make up for what is lacking. The ethical tends more and more to be abandoned; the life of the individual not only becomes poetic, but is unsettled by an abnormal historical consciousness that prevents him from existing ethically. It follows that reality must be provided in other ways. But this spurious reality resembles what would happen if a generation and its members had become prematurely old, and sought to obtain an artificial youth. Instead of recognizing that ethical existence is reality, the age has grown overwhelmingly contemplative, so that not only is everyone engrossed in contemplation, but this has finally become falsified as if it were reality. We smile at the life of the cloister, and yet no hermit ever lived so unreal a life as is common nowadays. For the hermit abstracted from the entire world, but he did not abstract from himself. We know how to describe the fantastic situation of the cloister, far from the haunts of men, in the solitude of the forest, in the distant blue of the horizon; but we take no notice of the fantastic situation of pure thought. And yet, the pathetic unreality of the hermit is far preferable to the comic unreality of the pure thinker; and the passionate forgetfulness of the hermit, which takes from him the entire world, is much to be preferred to the comical distraction of the philosopher engrossed in the contemplation of universal history, which leads him to forget himself.

Ethically regarded, reality is higher than possibility. The ethical proposes to do away with the disinterestedness of the possible, by making existence the infinite interest. It therefore opposes every confusing attempt, like that of proposing ethically to *contemplate* humanity and the world. Such ethical contemplation is impossible, since there is only one kind of ethical contemplation, namely, self-contemplation. Ethics closes immediately about the individual, and demands that he exist ethically; it does not make a parade of millions, or of generations of men; it does not take humanity in the lump, any more than the police arrest humanity at large. The ethical is concerned with particular human beings, and with each and every one of them by himself. If God knows how many hairs there are on a man's head, the ethical knows how many human beings there are; and its enumeration is not in the interest of a total sum, but for the sake of each individual. The ethical requirement is imposed upon each individual, and when it judges, it judges each individual by himself; only a tyrant or an impotent man is content to decimate. The ethical lays hold of each individual and demands that he refrain from all contemplation, especially of humanity and the world; for the ethical, as being the internal, cannot be observed by an outsider. It can be realized only by the individual subject, who alone can know what it is that moves within him. This ethical reality is the only reality which does not become a mere possibility through being known, and which can be known only through being thought; for it is the individual's own reality. Before it became a reality it was known by him in the form of a conceived reality, and hence as a possibility. But in the case of another person's reality he could have no knowledge about it until he conceived it in coming to know it, which means that he transformed it from a reality into a possibility.

With respect to every reality external to myself, I can get hold of it only through thinking it. In order to get hold of it really, I should have to be able to make myself into the other, the acting individual, and make the foreign reality my own reality, which is impossible. For if I make the foreign reality my own, this does not mean that I become the other through knowing his reality, but it means that I acquire a new reality, which belongs to me as opposed to him.

Karl Marx, *The Marx-Engels Reader,* Second edition, Robert C. Tucker (ed.), 1978

The Economic Basis of Morality
Karl Marx

[FROM *ECONOMIC AND PHILOSOPHIC MANUSCRIPTS* OF 1844]

We proceed from an *actual* economic fact.

The worker becomes all the poorer the more wealth he produces, the more his production increases in power and range. The worker becomes an ever cheaper commodity the more commodities he creates. With the *increasing value* of the world of things proceeds in direct proportion the *devaluation* of the world of men. Labour produces not only commodities; it produces itself and the worker as a *commodity*—and does so in the proportion in which it produces commodities, generally.

This fact expresses merely that the object which labour produces—labour's product—confronts it as *something alien,* as a *power independent* of the producer. The product of labour is labour which has been congealed in an object, which has become material: it is the *objectification* of labour. Labour's realization is its objectification. In the conditions dealt with by political economy this realization of labour appears as *loss of reality* for the workers; objectification as *loss of the object* and *object-bondage;* appropriation as *estrangement,* as *alienation.*

So much does labour's realization appear as loss of reality that the worker loses reality to the point of starving to death. So much does objectification appear as loss of the object that the worker is robbed of the objects most necessary not only for his life but for his work. Indeed, labour itself becomes an object which he can get hold of only with the greatest effort and with the most irregular interruptions. So much does the appropriation of the object appear as estrangement that the more objects the worker produces the fewer can he possess and the more he falls under the dominion of his product, capital.

All these consequences are contained in the definition that the worker is related to the *product of his labour* as to an *alien* object. For on this premise it is clear that the more the worker spends himself, the more powerful the alien objective world becomes which he creates over-against himself the poorer he himself—his inner world—becomes: the less belongs to him as his own. It is the same in religion. The more man puts into God, the less he retains in himself. The worker puts his life into the object; but now his life no longer belongs to him but to the object. Hence, the greater this activity, the greater is the worker's lack of objects. Whatever the product of his labour is, he is not. Therefore the greater this product, the less is he himself. The *alienation* of the worker in his product means not only that his labour becomes an object, an *external* existence, but that it exists *outside him*, independently, as something alien to him, and that it becomes a power of its own confronting him; it means that the life which he has conferred on the object confronts him as something hostile and alien.

Let us now look more closely at the *objectification*, at the production of the worker; and therein at the *estrangement*, the *loss* of the object, his product.

The worker can create nothing without *nature*, without the *sensuous external world*. It is the material on which his labor is manifested, in which it is active, from which and by means of which it produces. . . .

What, then, constitutes the alienation of labour?

First, the fact that labour is *external* to the worker, i.e., it does not belong to his essential being; that in his work, therefore, he does not affirm himself but denies himself, does not feel content but unhappy, does not develop freely his physical and mental energy but mortifies his body and ruins his mind. The worker therefore only feels himself outside his work, and in his work feels outside himself. He is at home when he is not working, and when he is working he is not at home. His labour is therefore not voluntary, but coerced; it is *forced labour*. It is therefore not the satisfaction of a need; it is merely a *means* to satisfy needs external to it. Its alien character emerges clearly in the fact that as soon as no physical or other compulsion exists, labour is shunned like the plague. External labour, labour in which man alienates himself, is a labour of self-sacrifice, of mortification. Lastly, the external character of labour for the worker appears in the fact that it is not his own, but someone else's, that it does not belong to him, that in it he belongs, not to himself, but to another. Just as in religion the spontaneous activity of the human imagination, of the human brain and the human heart, operates independently of the individual—that is, operates on him as an alien, divine or diabolical activity—in the same way the worker's activity is not his spontaneous activity. It belongs to another; it is the loss of his self.

As a result, therefore, man (the worker) no longer feels himself to be freely active in any but his animal functions—eating, drinking, procreating, or at most in his dwelling and in dressing-up, etc.; and in his human functions he no longer feels himself to be anything but an animal. What is animal becomes human and what is human becomes animal.

Certainly eating, drinking, procreating, etc., are also genuinely human functions. But in the abstraction which separates them from the sphere of all other human activity and turns them into sole and ultimate ends, they are animal.

We have considered the act of estranging practical human activity, labour, in two of its aspects. (1) The relation of the worker to the *product of labour* as an alien object exercising power over him. This relation is at the same time the relation to the sensuous external world, to the objects of nature as an alien world antagonistically opposed to him. (2) The relation of labour to the *act of production* within the *labour* process. This relation is the relation of the worker to his own activity as an alien activity not belonging to him; it is activity as suffering, strength as weakness, begetting as emasculating, the worker's own physical and mental energy, his personal life or what is life other than activity—as an activity, which is turned against him, neither depends on nor belongs to him. Here we have *self-estrangement*, as we had previously the estrangement of the *thing*. . . .

[FROM *THE GERMAN IDEOLOGY*]

The premises from which we begin are not arbitrary ones, not dogmas, but real premises from which abstraction can only be made in the imagination. They are the real individuals, their activity and the material conditions under which they live, both those which they find already existing and those produced by their activity. These premises can thus be verified in a purely empirical way.

The first premise of all human history is, of course, the existence of living human individuals. Thus the first fact to be established is the physical organisation of these individuals and their consequent relation to the rest of nature. Of course, we cannot here go either into the actual physical nature of man, or into the natural conditions in which man finds himself—geological, orohydrographical, climatic and so on. The writing of history must always set out from these natural bases and their modification in the course of history through the action of men.

Men can be distinguished from animals by consciousness, by religion or anything else you like. They themselves begin to distinguish themselves from animals as soon as they begin to *produce* their means of subsistence, a step which is conditioned by their physical organisation. By producing their means of subsistence men are indirectly producing their actual material life.

The way in which men produce their means of subsistence depends first of all on the nature of the actual means of subsistence they find in existence and have to reproduce. This mode of production must not be considered simply as being the reproduction of the physical existence of the individuals. Rather it is a definite form of activity of these individuals, a definite form of expressing their life, a definite *mode of life* on their part. As individuals express their life, so they are. What they are, therefore, coincides with their production, both with *what* they produce and with *how* they produce. The nature of individuals thus depends on the material conditions determining their production. . . .

The production of ideas, of conceptions, of consciousness, is at first directly interwoven with the material activity and the material intercourse of men, the language of real life. Conceiving, thinking, the mental intercourse of men, appear at this stage as the direct efflux of their material behaviour. The same applies to mental production as expressed in the language of politics, laws, morality, religion, metaphysics, etc., of a people. Men are the producers of their conceptions, ideas, etc.—real, active men, as they are conditioned by a definite development of their productive forces and of the intercourse corresponding to these, up to its furthest forms. Consciousness can never be anything else than conscious existence, and the existence of men is their actual life-process. If in all ideology men and their circumstances appear upside-down as in a *camera obscura*, this phenomenon arises just as much from their historical life-process as the inversion of objects on the retina does from their physical life-process.

In direct contrast to German philosophy which descends from heaven to earth, here we ascend from earth to heaven. That is to say, we do not set out from what men say, imagine, conceive, nor from men as narrated, thought of, imagined, conceived, in order to arrive at men in the flesh. We set out from real, active men, and on the basis of their real life-process we demonstrate the development of the ideological reflexes and echoes of this life-process. The phantoms formed in the human brain are also, necessarily, sublimates of their material life-process, which is empirically verifiable and bound to material premises. Morality, religion, metaphysics, all the rest of ideology and their corresponding forms of consciousness, thus no longer retain the semblance of independence. They have no history, no development; but men, developing their material production and their material intercourse, alter, along with this their real existence, their thinking and the products of their thinking. Life is not determined by consciousness, but consciousness by life. In the first method of approach the starting-point, is consciousness taken as the living individual; in the second method, which conforms to real life, it is the real living individuals themselves, and consciousness is considered solely as *their* consciousness.

This method of approach is not devoid of premises. It starts out from the real premises and does not abandon them for a moment. Its premises are men, not in any fantastic isolation and rigidity, but in their actual, empirically perceptible process of development under definite conditions. As soon as this active life-process is described, history ceases to be a collection of dead facts as it is with the empiricists (themselves still abstract); or an imagined activity of imagined subjects, as with the idealists.

Where speculation ends—in real life—there real, positive science begins: the representation of the practical activity, of the practical process of development of men. Empty talk about consciousness ceases, and real knowledge has to take its place. When reality is depicted, philosophy as an independent branch of knowledge loses its medium of existence. At the best its place can only the taken by a summing-up of the most general results, abstractions which arise from the observation of the historical development of men. Viewed apart from real history, these abstractions have in themselves no value whatsoever. They can only serve to facilitate the arrangement of historical material, to indicate the sequence of its separate strata. . . .

Our investigation hitherto started from the instruments of production, and it has already shown that private property was a necessity for certain industrial stages. In *industrie extractive* private property still coincides with labour; in small industry and all agriculture up till now property is the necessary consequence of the existing instruments of production; in big industry the contradiction between the instrument of production and private property appears for the first time and is the product of big industry; moreover, big industry must be highly developed to produce this contradiction.

And thus only with big industry does the abolition of private property, become possible.

In big industry and competition the whole mass of conditions of existence, limitations, biases of individuals, are fused together into the two simplest forms: private property and labour. With money every form of intercourse, and intercourse itself, is considered fortuitous for the individuals. Thus money implies that all previous intercourse was only intercourse of individuals under particular conditions, not of individuals as individuals. These conditions are reduced to two: accumulated labour or private property, and actual labour. If both or one of these ceases, then intercourse comes to a standstill. The modern economists themselves, e.g., Sismondi, Cherbuliez, etc., oppose "association of individuals" to "association of capital." On the other hand, the individuals themselves are entirely subordinated to the division of labour and hence are brought into the most complete dependence on one another. Private property, insofar as within labour itself it is opposed to labour, evolves out of the necessity of accumulation, and has still, to begin with, rather the form of the communality; but in its further development it approaches more and more the modern form of private property. The division of labour implies from the outset the division of the *conditions* of labour, of tools and materials, and thus the splitting-up of accumulated capital among different owners, and thus, also, the division between capital and labour, and, the different forms of property itself. The more the division of labour develops and accumulation grows, the sharper are the forms that this process of differentiation assumes. Labour itself can only exist on the premise of this fragmentation.

Thus two facts are here revealed. First the productive forces appear as a world for themselves, quite independent of and divorced from the individuals, alongside the individuals: the reason for this is that the individuals, whose forces they are, exist split up and in opposition to one another, whilst, on the other hand, these forces are only real forces in the intercourse and association of these individuals. Thus, on the one hand, we have a totality of productive forces, which have, as it were, taken on a material form and are for the individuals no longer the forces of the individuals but of private property, and hence of the individuals only insofar as they are owners of private property themselves. Never, in any earlier period, have the productive forces taken on a form so indifferent to the intercourse of individuals *as individuals*, because their intercourse itself was formerly a restricted one. On the other hand, standing over against these productive forces, we have the majority of the individuals from whom these forces have been wrested away, and who, robbed thus of all real life-content, have become abstract individuals, but who are, however, only by this fact put into a position to enter into relation with one another *as individuals*.

The only connection which still links them with the productive forces: and with their own existence—labour—has lost all semblance of self-activity and only sustains their life by stunting it. While in the earlier periods self-activity and the production of material life were separated, in that they devolved on different persons, and while on account of the narrowness of the individuals themselves, the production of material life was considered as a subordinate mode of self-activity, they now diverge to such an extent that altogether material life appears as the end, and what produces this material life, labour (which is now the only possible but, as we see, negative form of self-activity), as the means.

Thus things have now come to such a pass, that the individuals must appropriate the existing totality of productive forces, not only to achieve self-activity, but also merely to safeguard their very existence. This appropriation is first determined by the object to be appropriated, the productive forces, which have been developed to a totality and which only exist within a universal intercourse. From this aspect alone, therefore, this appropriation must have a universal character corresponding to the productive forces and the intercourse. The appropriation of these forces is itself nothing more than the development of the individual capacities corresponding to the material instruments of production. The appropriation of a totality of instruments of production is, for this very reason, the development of a totality of capacities in the individuals themselves. This appropriation is further determined by the persons appropriating. Only the proletarians of the present day, who are completely shut off from all self-activity, are in a position to achieve a complete and no longer restricted self-activity, which consists in the appropriation of a totality of productive forces and in the thus postulated development of a totality of capacities. All earlier revolutionary appropriations were restricted; individuals, whose self-activity was restricted by a crude instrument of production and a limited intercourse, appropriated this crude instrument of production, and hence merely achieved a new state of limitation. Their instrument of production became their property, but they themselves remained subordinate to the division of labour and their own instrument of production. In all expropriations up to now, a mass of individuals remained subservient to a single instrument of production; in the appropriation by the proletarians, a mass of instruments of production must be made subject to each individual, and property to all. Modern universal intercourse can be controlled by individuals, therefore, only when controlled by all.

This appropriation is further determined by the manner in which it must be effected. It can only be effected through a union, which by the character of the proletariat itself can again only be a universal one, and through a revolution, in which, on the one hand, the power of the earlier mode of production and intercourse and social organisation is overthrown, and, on the other hand, there develops the universal character and the energy of the proletariat without which the revolution cannot be accomplished; and in which, further, the proletariat rids itself of everything that still clings to it from its previous position in society. Only at this stage does self-activity coincide with material life, which corresponds to the development of individuals into complete individuals and the casting-off of all natural limitations. The transformation of labour into self-activity corresponds to the transformation of the earlier limited intercourse into the intercourse of individuals as such. With the appropriation of the total productive forces through united individuals, private property comes to an end. Whilst previously in history a particular condition always appeared as accidental, now the isolation of individuals and the particular private gain of each man have themselves become accidental. . . .

[FROM *CAPITAL, VOLUME I*]

[W]ithin the capitalist system all methods for raising the social productiveness of labour are brought about at the cost of the individual labourer; all means for the development of production transform themselves into means of domination over, and exploitation of, the producers; they mutilate the labourer into a fragment of a man, degrade him to the level of an appendage of a machine, destroy every remnant of charm in his work and turn it into a hated toil; they estrange from him the intellectual potentialities of the labour-process in the same proportion as science is incorporated in it as an independent power; they distort the conditions under which he works, subject him during the labour-process to a despotism the more hateful for its meanness; they transform his life-time into working-time, and drag his wife and child beneath the wheels of the Juggernaut of capital. But all methods for the production of surplus-value are at the same time methods of accumulation; and every extension of accumulation becomes again a means for the development of those methods. It follows therefore that in proportion as capital accumulates, the lot of the labourer, be his payment high or low, must grow worse. The law, finally, that always equilibrates the relative surplus-population, or industrial reserve army, to the extent and energy of accumulation, this law rivets the labourer to capital more firmly than the wedges of Vulcan did Prometheus to the rock. It establishes an accumulation of misery, corresponding with accumulation of capital. Accumulation of wealth at one pole is, therefore, at the same time accumulation of misery, agony of toil, slavery, ignorance, brutality, mental degradation, at the opposite pole, *i.e.*, on the side of the class that produces its own product in the form of capital. . . .

Karl Marx and Friedrich Engels, *The Communist Manifesto,* 1848

The Immorality of Capitalism
Karl Marx and Friedrich Engels

The history of all hitherto existing society is the history of class struggles.

Freeman and slave, patrician and plebeian, lord and serf, guildmaster and journeyman, in a word, oppressor and oppressed, stood in constant opposition to one another, carried on an uninterrupted, now hidden, now open fight, a fight that each time ended, either in a revolutionary reconstitution of society at large, or in the common ruin of the struggling classes.

In the earlier epochs of history, we find almost everywhere a complicated arrangement of society into various orders, a manifold gradation of social rank. In ancient Rome we have patricians, knights, plebeians, slaves; in the Middle Ages, feudal lords, vassals, guildmasters, journeymen, apprentices, serfs; and in almost all of these particular classes, again, other subordinate gradations.

The modern bourgeois society that has sprouted from the ruins of feudal society has not done away with class antagonisms. It has only established new classes, new conditions of oppression, new forms of struggle in place of the old ones.

Our epoch, the epoch of the bourgeoisie, shows, however, this distinctive feature: it has simplified the class antagonisms. Society as a whole is more and more splitting up into two great hostile camps, into two great classes directly facing each other: *bourgeoisie* and *proletariat*.

From the serfs of the Middle Ages sprang the chartered burghers of the earliest towns. From these burghers the first elements of the bourgeoisie were developed.

The discovery of America, the rounding of the Cape, opened up fresh ground for the rising bourgeoisie. The East-Indian and Chinese markets, the colonization of America, trade with the colonies, the increase in the means of exchange and in commodities generally, gave to commerce, to navigation, to industry, an impulse never before known, and thereby, to the revolutionary element in the tottering feudal society, a rapid development.

The feudal system of industry, under which industrial production was monopolized by closed guilds, now no longer sufficed for the growing wants of the new markets. The manufacturing system took its place. The guildmasters were pushed on one side by the manufacturing middle class; division of labor between the different corporate guilds vanished in the face of division of labor in each single workshop.

Meanwhile the markets kept on growing; demand went on rising. Manufacturing no longer was able to keep up with this growth. Then, steam and machinery revolutionized industrial production. The place of manufacture was taken by the giant, *modern industry*; the place of the industrial middle class, by industrial millionaires, the leaders of whole industrial armies, the modern bourgeois.

Modern industry has established the world market, for which the discovery of America paved the way. This market has given an immense development to commerce, to navigation, to communication by land. This development has, in its turn, reacted on the extension of industry; and in proportion as industry, commerce, navigation, railways extended, in the same proportion the bourgeoisie developed, increased its capital, and pushed into the background every class handed down from the Middle Ages.

We see, therefore, how the modern bourgeoisie is itself the product of a long course of development, of a series of revolutions in the modes of production and of exchange. . . .

The need of a constantly expanding market for its products chases the bourgeoisie over the whole surface of the globe. It must nestle everywhere, settle everywhere, establish connections everywhere.

The bourgeoisie has through its exploitation of the world market given a cosmopolitan character to production and consumption in every country. To the great chagrin of reactionaries, it has drawn from under the feet of industry the national ground on which it stood. All old-established national industries have been destroyed or are daily being destroyed. They are dislodged by new industries, whose introduction becomes a life and death question for all civilized nations, by industries that no longer work up indigenous raw material, but raw material drawn from the remotest zones; industries whose products are consumed, not only at home, but in every quarter of the globe. In place of the old wants, satisfied by the productions of the country, we find new wants requiring for their satisfaction the products of distant lands and climates. In place of the old local and national seclusion and self-sufficiency, we have intercourse in every direction, universal inter-dependence of nations. And as in material, so also in intellectual production. The intellectual creations of individual nations become common property. National one-sidedness and narrow-mindedness become more and more impossible, and from the numerous national and local literatures, there emerges a world literature.

The bourgeoisie, by the rapid improvement of all instruments of production, by the immensely facilitated means of communications, draws all, even the most backward, nations into civilization. The cheap prices of its commodities are the heavy artillery with which it batters down all Chinese walls, with which it forces the underdeveloped nations' intensely obstinate hatred of foreigners to capitulate. It compels all nations', on pain of extinction, to adopt the bourgeois mode of production; it compels them to introduce what it calls civilization into their midst, *i.e.,* to become bourgeois themselves. In one word, it creates a world in its own image.

The bourgeoisie has subjected rural areas to the rule of cities. It has created enormous cities, has greatly increased the urban population as compared with the rural, and has thus rescued a considerable part of the population from the idiocy of rural life. Just as it has made the country dependent on the cities. so has it made barbarian and semi-underdeveloped countries dependent on the civilized ones, nations of peasants on nations of bourgeois, the East on the West.

The bourgeoisie keeps more and more doing away with the scattered state of the population, of the means of production, and of property. It has agglomerated population, centralized means of production, and has concentrated property in a few hands. The necessary consequence of this was political centralization. Independent, or but loosely connected, provinces with separate interests, laws, governments, and systems of taxation became lumped together into one nation, with one government, one code of laws, one national class-interest, one frontier, and one customs-tariff.

The bourgeoisie, during its rule of scarcely one hundred years, has created more massive and more colossal productive forces than have all preceding generations together. Subjection of Nature's forces to man, machinery, application of chemistry to industry and agriculture, steam-navigation, railways, electric telegraphs, clearing of whole continents for cultivation, canalization of rivers, whole populations conjured out of the ground—what earlier century had even a presentiment that such productive forces slumbered in the lap of social labor?

We see then: the means of production and of exchange, on whose foundation the bourgeoisie built itself up, were generated in feudal society. At a certain stage in the development of these means of production and of exchange, the conditions under which feudal society produced and exchanged, the feudal organization of agriculture and manufacturing industry, in one word, the feudal relations of property became no longer compatible with the already developed productive forces; they became so many fetters. They had to be burst asunder; they were burst asunder.

Into their place stepped free competition, accompanied by a social and political constitution adapted to it, and by the economical and political sway of the bourgeois class.

A similar movement is going on before our own eyes. Modern bourgeois society with its relations of production, of exchange and of property, a society that has conjured up such gigantic means of production and of exchange, is like the sorcerer, who is no longer able to control the powers of the subterranean world which he has called up by his spells. For many decades now the history of industry and commerce has been but the history of the revolt of modern productive forces against modern conditions of production, against the property relations that are the conditions for the existence of the bourgeoisie and of its rule. It is enough to mention the commercial crises that by their periodical return put on trial, each time more threateningly, the existence of the entire bourgeois society. In these crises a great part not only of the existing products, but also of the previously created productive forces, are periodically destroyed. In these crises there breaks out an epidemic that, in all earlier epochs, would have seemed an absurdity—the epidemic of overproduction. Society suddenly finds itself put back into a state of momentary barbarism; it appears as if a famine, a universal war of devastation had cut off the supply of every means of subsistence; industry and commerce seem to be destroyed; and why? Because there is too much civilization, too much means of subsistence, too much industry, too much commerce. The productive forces at the disposal of society no longer tend to further the development of the conditions of bourgeois property; on the contrary, they have become too powerful for these conditions, by which they are fettered, and so soon as they overcome these fetters, they bring disorder into the whole of bourgeois society, endanger the existence of bourgeois property. The conditions of bourgeois society are too narrow to comprise the wealth created by them. And how does the bourgeoisie get over these crises? On the one hand by enforced destruction of a mass of productive forces; on the other, by the conquest of new markets, and by the more thorough exploitation of the old ones. That is to say, by paving the way for more extensive and more destructive crises, and by diminishing the means whereby crises are prevented.

The weapons with which the bourgeoisie felled feudalism to the ground are now turned against the bourgeoisie itself.

But not only has the bourgeoisie forged the weapons that bring death to itself; it has also called into existence the men who are to wield those weapons—the modern working class—the proletarians.

In proportion as the bourgeoisie, *i.e.*, capital, is developed, in the same proportion is the proletariat, the modern working class, developed—a class of laborers, who live only so long as they find work, and who find work only so long as their labor increases capital. These laborers, who must sell themselves piecemeal, are a commodity, like every other article of commerce, and are consequently exposed to all the vicissitudes of competition, to all the fluctuations of the market.

Owing to the extensive use of machinery and division of labor, the work of the proletarians has lost all individual character, and, consequently, all charm for the workman. He becomes an appendage of the machine, and it is only the most simple, most monotonous, and most easily acquired knack that is required of him. Hence, the cost of production of a workman is restricted, almost entirely, to the means of subsistence that he requires for his maintenance, and for the propagation of his race. But the price of a commodity, and therefore also of labor, is equal to its cost of production. In proportion, therefore, as the repulsiveness of the work increases, the wage decreases. What is more, in proportion as the use of machinery and division of labor increases, in the same proportion the burden of toil also increases, whether by prolongation of the working hours, by increase of the work exacted in a given time or by increased speed of the machinery, etc.

Modern industry has converted the little workshop of the patriarchal master into the great factory of the industrial capitalist. Masses of laborers, crowded into the factory, are organized like soldiers. As privates of the industrial army they are placed under the command of a perfect hierarchy of officers and sergeants. Not only are they slaves of the bourgeois class, and of the bourgeois state; they are daily and hourly enslaved by the machine, by the foreman, and, above all, by the individual bourgeois manufacturer himself. The more openly this despotism proclaims gain to be its end and aim, the more petty, the more hateful, and the more embittering it is. . . .

But with the development of industry the proletariat not only increases in number; it becomes concentrated in greater masses, its strength grows, and it feels that strength more. The various interests and conditions of life within the ranks of the proletariat are more and more equalized, in proportion as machinery obliterates all distinctions of labor, and nearly everywhere reduces wages to the same low level. The growing competition among the bourgeoisie, and the resulting commercial crises, make the wages of the workers ever more fluctuating. The unceasing improvement of machinery, ever more rapidly developing, makes their livelihood more and more precarious; the collisions between individual workmen and individual bourgeoisie take more and more the character of collisions between two classes. Thereupon the workers begin to form combinations (trade unions) against the bourgeoisie; they club together in order to keep up the rate of wages; they found permanent associations in order to make provision beforehand for these occasional revolts. Here and there the contest breaks out into riots.

From time to time the workers are victorious, but only for a time. The real fruit of their battles lies not in the immediate results, but in the ever-expanding union of the workers. This union is helped by the improved means of communication that are created by modern industry and that place the workers of different localities in contact with one another. It was just this contact that was needed to centralize the numerous local struggles, all of the same characters, into one national struggle between classes. But every class struggle is a political struggle. And that union, to attain which the burghers of the Middle Ages, with their miserable highways, required centuries, the modern proletarians, thanks to railways, achieve in a few years. . . .

Hitherto, every form of society has been based, as we have already seen, on the antagonism of oppressing and oppressed classes. But in order to oppress a class, certain conditions must be assured to it under which it can, at least, continue its slavish existence. The serf, in the period of serfdom, raised himself to membership in the commune, just as the petty bourgeois, under the yoke of feudal absolutism, managed to develop into a bourgeois. The modern laborer, on the contrary, instead of rising with the progress of industry, sinks deeper and deeper below the conditions of existence of his own class. He becomes a pauper, and pauperism develops more rapidly than population and wealth. And here it becomes evident that the bourgeoisie is unfit any longer to be the ruling class in society, and to impose its conditions of existence upon society as an overriding law. It is unfit to rule because it is incompetent to assure an existence to its slave within his slavery, because it cannot help letting him sink into such a state, that it has to feed him, instead of being fed by him. Society can no longer live under this bourgeoisie, in other words, its existence is no longer compatible with society.

The essential condition for the existence, and for the sway of the bourgeois class, is the formation and augmentation of capital; the condition for capital is wage labor. Wage labor rests exclusively on competition between laborers. The advance of industry, whose involuntary promoter is the bourgeoisie, replaces the isolation of the laborers, due to competition, by their revolutionary combination, due to association. The development of modern industry, therefore, cuts from under its feet the very foundation on which the bourgeoisie produces and appropriates products. What the bourgeoisie, therefore, produces, above all, is its own grave-diggers. Its fall and the victory of the proletariat are equally inevitable.

Friedrich Nietzsche, *Beyond Good and Evil: Prelude to a Philosophy of the Future* and *The Gay Science*, H. Zimmern (trans.), 1923

The Transvaluation of All Values
Friedrich Nietzsche

[FROM *BEYOND GOOD AND EVIL*]

Whether it be hedonism, pessimism, utilitarianism or eudaemonism, all those modes of thinking which measure the worth of things according to *pleasure* and *pain,* that is, according to accompanying circumstances and secondary considerations, are plausible modes of thought and naïvetés, which every one conscious of *creative* powers and an artist's conscience will look down upon with scorn, though not without sympathy. Sympathy for *you!*—to be sure, that is not sympathy as you understand it: it is not sympathy for social "distress," for "society" with its sick and misfortuned, for the hereditarily vicious and defective who lie on the ground around us; still less is it sympathy for the grumbling, vexed, revolutionary slave-classes who strive after power—they call it "freedom." *Our* sympathy is a loftier and further-sighted sympathy:—we see how *man* dwarfs himself, how *you* dwarf him! and there are moments when we view *your* sympathy with an indescribable anguish, when we resist it,—when we regard your seriousness as more dangerous than any kind of levity. You want, if possible—and there is not a more foolish "if possible"—*to do away with suffering;* and we?—it really seems that *we* would rather have it increased and made worse than it has ever been! Well-being, as you understand it—is certainly not a goal; it seems to us an *end;* a condition which at once renders man ludicrous and contemptible—and makes his destruction *desirable!* The discipline of suffering, of *great* suffering—know ye not that it is only *this* discipline that has produced all the elevations of humanity hitherto? The tension of soul in misfortune which communicates to it its energy, its shuddering in view of rack and ruin, its inventiveness and bravery in undergoing, enduring, interpreting, and exploiting misfortune, and whatever depth, mystery, disguise, spirit, artifice or greatness has been bestowed upon the soul—has it not been bestowed through suffering, through the discipline of great suffering? In man *creature* and *creator* are united: in man there is not only matter, shred, excess, clay, mire, folly, chaos; but there is also the creator, the sculptor, the hardness of the hammer, the divinity of the spectator, and the seventh day—do ye understand this contrast? And that *your* sympathy for the "creature in man" applies to that which has to be fashioned, bruised, forged, stretched, roasted, annealed, refined—to that which must necessarily *suffer,* and *is meant* to suffer? And *our* sympathy—do ye not understand what our *reverse* sympathy applies to, when it resists your sympathy as the worst of all pampering and enervation?—So it is sympathy *against* sympathy!—But to repeat it once more, there are higher problems than the problems of pleasure and pain and sympathy; and all systems of philosophy which deal only with these are naïvetés. . . .

I hope to be forgiven for discovering that all moral philosophy hitherto has been tedious and has belonged to the soporific appliances—and that "virtue," in my opinion, has been *more* injured by the *tediousness* of its advocates than by anything else; at the same time, however, I would not wish to overlook their general usefulness. It is desirable that as few people as possible should reflect upon morals, and consequently it is *very* desirable that morals should not some day become interesting! But let us not be afraid! Things still remain today as they have always been. I see no one in Europe who has (or *discloses*) an idea of the fact that philosophising concerning morals might be conducted in a dangerous, captious, and ensnarling manner—that *calamity* might be involved therein. Observe, for example, the indefatigable, inevitable English utilitarians: how ponderously and respectably they stalk on, (a Homeric metaphor expresses it better) in the footsteps of Bentham, just as he had already stalked in the footsteps of the respectable Helvétius! (no, he was not a dangerous man, Helvétius, *ce sénateur Pococurante,* to use an expression of Galiani). No new thought, nothing of the nature of a finer turning or better expression of an old thought, not even a proper history of what has been previously thought on the subject: an *impossible* literature, taking it all in all, unless one knows how to leaven it with some mischief. In effect, the old English vice called *cant,* which is *moral Tartuffism,* has insinuated itself also into these moralists (whom one must certainly read with an eye to their motives if one *must* read them), concealed this time under the new form of the scientific spirit; moreover, there is not absent from them a secret struggle with the pangs of conscience, from which a race of former Puritans must naturally suffer, in all their scientific tinkering with morals. (Is not a moralist the opposite of a Puritan? That is to say, as a thinker who regards morality as questionable, as worthy of interrogation, in short, as a problem? Is moralising not—immoral?) In the end, they all want *English* morality to be recognised as authoritative, inasmuch as mankind, or the "general utility," or "the happiness of the greatest number,"—no! the happiness of *England,* will be best served thereby. They would like, by all means, to convince themselves that the striving after *English* happiness, I mean after *comfort* and *fashion* (and in the highest instance, a seat in Parliament), is at the same time the true path of virtue; in fact, that in so far as there has been virtue in the world hitherto, it has just consisted in such striving. Not one of those ponderous, conscience-stricken herding-animals (who undertake to advocate the cause of egoism as conducive to the general welfare) wants to have any knowledge or inkling of the facts that the "general welfare" is no ideal, no goal, no notion that can be at all grasped, but is only a nostrum,—that what is fair to one *may not* be fair to another, the requirement of one morality for all is really a detriment to higher men, in short, that there is a *distinction of rank* between man and man, and consequently between morality and morality. They are an unassuming and fundamentally mediocre species of men, these utilitarian Englishmen, and, as already remarked, in so far as they arc tedious, one cannot think highly enough of their utility. . . .

To refrain mutually from injury, from violence, from exploitation, and put one's will on a par with that of others: this may result in a certain rough sense in good conduct among individuals when the necessary conditions are given (namely, the actual similarity of the individuals in amount of force and degree of worth, and their co-relation within one organisation). As soon, however, as one wished to take this principle more generally, and if possible even as *the fundamental principle of society*, it would immediately disclose what it really is—namely, a Will to the *denial* of life, a principle of dissolution and decay. Here one must think profoundly to the very basis and resist all sentimental weakness: life itself is *essentially* appropriation, injury, conquest of the strange and weak, suppression, severity, obtrusion of peculiar forms, incorporation, and at the least, putting it mildest, exploitation;—but why should one for ever use precisely these words on which for ages a disparaging purpose has been stamped? Even the organisation within which, as was previously supposed, the individuals treat each other as equal—it takes place in every healthy aristocracy—must itself, if it be a living and not a dying organisation, do all that towards other bodies, which the individuals within it refrain from doing to each other: it will have to be the incarnated Will to Power, it will endeavour to grow, to gain ground, attract to itself and acquire ascendency— not owing to any morality or immorality, but because it *lives,* and because life *is* precisely Will to Power. On no point, however, is the ordinary consciousness of Europeans more unwilling to be corrected than on this matter; people now rave everywhere, even under the guise of science, about coming conditions of society in which "the exploiting character" is to be absent:—that sounds to my ears as if they promised to invent a mode of life which should refrain from all organic functions. "Exploitation" does not belong to a depraved, or imperfect and primitive society: it belongs to the *nature* of the living being as a primary organic function; it is a consequence of the intrinsic Will to Power, which is precisely the Will to Life.—Granting that as a theory this is a novelty—as a reality it is the *fundamental fact* of all history: let us be so far honest towards ourselves!

In a tour through the many finer and coarser moralities which have hitherto prevailed or still prevail on the earth, I found certain traits recurring regularly together, and connected with one another, until finally two primary types revealed themselves to me, and a radical distinction was brought to light. There is *master-morality* and *slave-morality;*—I would at once add, however, that in all higher and mixed civilisations, there are also attempts at the reconciliation of the two moralities; but one finds still oftener the confusion and mutual misunderstanding of them, indeed, sometimes their close juxtaposition—even in the same man, within one soul. The distinctions of moral values have either originated in a ruling caste, pleasantly conscious of being different from the ruled—or among the ruled class, the slaves and dependents of all sorts. In the first case, when it is the rulers who determine the conception "good," it is the exalted, proud disposition which is regarded as the distinguishing feature, and that which determines the order of rank. The noble type of man separates from himself the beings in whom the opposite of this exalted, proud disposition displays itself: he despises them. Let it at once be noted that in this first kind of morality the antithesis "good" and "bad" means practically the same as "noble" and "despicable";—the antithesis "good" and *"evil"* is of a different origin. The cowardly, the timid, the insignificant, and those thinking merely of narrow utility are despised; moreover, also, the distrustful, with their constrained glances, the self-abasing, the dog-like kind of men who let themselves be abused, the mendicant flatterers, and above all the liars:—it is a fundamental belief of all aristocrats that the common people are untruthful. "We truthful ones"—the nobility in ancient Greece that everywhere the designations of moral value were at first applied to *men,* and were only derivatively and at a later period applied to *actions;* it is a gross mistake, therefore, when historians of morals start questions like, "Why have sympathetic actions been praised?" The noble type of man regards *himself* as a determiner of values; he does not require to be approved of; he passes the judgment: "What is injurious to me is injurious in itself"; he knows that it is he himself only who confers honour on things; he is a *creator of values.* He honours whatever he recognises in himself: such morality is self-glorification. In the foreground there is the feeling of plenitude, of power, which seeks to overflow, the happiness of high tension, the consciousness of a wealth which would fain give and bestow:—the noble man also helps the unfortunate, but not—or scarcely—out of pity, but rather from an impulse generated by the super-abundance of power. The noble man honours in himself the powerful one, him also who has power over himself, who knows how to speak and how to keep silence, who takes pleasure in subjecting himself to severity and hardness, and has reverence for all that is severe and hard. "Wotan placed a hard heart in my breast," says an old Scandinavian Saga: it is thus rightly expressed from the soul of a proud Viking. Such a type of man is even proud of *not* being made for sympathy; the hero of the Saga therefore adds warningly: "He who has not a hard heart when young, will never have one." The noble and brave who think thus are the furthest removed from the morality which sees precisely in sympathy, or in acting for the good of others, or in *désintéressement*, the characteristic of the moral; faith in oneself, pride in oneself, a radical enmity and irony towards "selflessness," belong as definitely to noble morality, as do a careless scorn and precaution in presence of sympathy and the "warm heart."—It is the powerful who *know* how to honor, it is their art, their domain for invention. The profound reverence for age and for tradition—all law rests on this double reverence,—the belief and prejudice in favour of ancestors and unfavourable to newcomers, is typical in the morality of the powerful; and if, reversely, men of "modern ideas" believe almost instinctively in "progress" and the "future," and are more and more lacking in respect for old age, the ignoble origin of these "ideas" has complacently betrayed itself thereby. A morality of the ruling class, however, is more especially foreign and irritating to present-day taste in the sternness of its principle that one has duties only to one's equals; that one may act towards beings of a lower rank, towards all that is foreign, just as seems good to one, or "as the heart desires," and in any case "beyond good and evil": it is here that sympathy and similar sentiments can have a place. The ability and obligation to exercise prolonged gratitude and prolonged revenge—both only within the circle of equals,—artfulness in retaliation, *raffinement* of the idea in friendship, a certain necessity to have enemies (as outlets for the emotions of envy, quarrelsomeness, arrogance—in fact, in order to be a good *friend*): all these are typical characteristics of the noble morality, which, as has been pointed out, is not the morality of "modern ideas," and is therefore at present difficult to realise, and also to unearth and disclose.—It is otherwise with the second type of morality, *slave-morality*. Supposing that the abused, the oppressed, the suffering, the unemancipated, the weary, and those uncertain of themselves, should moralise, what will be the common element of their moral estimates? Probably a pessimistic suspicion with regard to the entire situation of man will find expression, perhaps a condemnation of man, together with his situation. The slave has an unfavourable eye for the virtues of the powerful; he has a scepticism and distrust, a *refinement* of distrust of everything "good" that is there honoured—he would fain persuade himself that the very happiness there is not genuine. On the other hand, *those* qualities which serve to alleviate the existence of sufferers are brought into prominence and flooded with light; it is here that sympathy, the kind, helping hand, the warm heart, patience, diligence, humility, and friendliness attain to honour; for here these are the most useful qualities, and almost the only means of supporting the burden of existence. Slave-morality is essentially the morality of utility. Here is the seat of the origin of the famous antithesis "good" and "*evil*":—power and dangerousness are assumed to reside in the evil, a certain dreadfulness, subtlety, and strength, which do not admit of being despised. According to slave-morality, therefore, the "evil" man arouses fear; according to master-morality, it is precisely the "good" man who arouses fear and seeks to arouse it, while the bad man is regarded as the despicable being. The contrast attains its maximum when, in accordance with the logical consequences of slave-morality, a shade of depreciation—it may be slight and well-intentioned—at last attaches itself to the "good" man of this morality;

because, according to the servile mode of thought, the good man must in any case be the *safe* man: he is good-natured, easily deceived, perhaps a little stupid, *un bonhomme.* Everywhere that slave-morality gains the ascendency, language shows a tendency to approximate the significations of the words "good" and "stupid."—A last fundamental difference: the desire for *freedom,* the instinct for happiness and the refinements of the feeling of liberty belong as necessarily to slave-morals and morality, as artifice and enthusiasm in reverence and devotion are the regular symptoms of an aristocratic mode of thinking and estimating.—Hence we can understand without further detail why love *as a passion*—it is our European specialty—must absolutely be of noble origin; as is well known, its invention is due to the Provençal poet-cavaliers, those brilliant, ingenious men of the *"gai saber,"* to whom Europe owes so much, and almost owes itself.

[FROM *THE GAY SCIENCE*]

Preparatory men. I welcome all signs that a more manly, a warlike, age is about to begin, an age which, above all, will give honor to valor once again. For this age shall prepare the way for one yet higher, and it shall gather the strength which this higher age will need one day— this age which is to carry heroism into the pursuit of knowledge and *wage wars* for the sake of thoughts and their consequences. To this end we now need many preparatory valorous men who cannot leap into being out of nothing—any more than out of the sand and slime of our present civilization and metropolitanism: men who are bent on seeking for that aspect in all things which must be *overcome;* men characterized by cheerfulness, patience, unpretentious-ness, and contempt for all great vanities, as well as by magnanimity in victory and forbearance regarding the small vanities of the vanquished; men possessed of keen and free judgment concerning all victors and the share of chance in every victory and every fame; men who have their own festivals, their own weekdays, their own periods of mourning, who are accustomed to command with assurance and are no less ready to obey when necessary, in both cases equally proud and serving their own cause; men who are in greater danger, more fruitful, and happier! For, believe me, the secret of the greatest fruitfulness and the greatest enjoyment of existence is: to *live dangerously!* Build your cities under Vesuvius! Send your ships into uncharted seas! Live at war with your peers and yourselves! Be robbers and conquerors, as long as you cannot be rulers and owners, you lovers of knowledge! Soon the age will be past when you could be satisfied to live like shy deer, hidden in the woods! At long last the pursuit of knowledge will reach out for its due: it will want to *rule* and *own,* and you with it! . . .

One thing is needful. "Giving style" to one's character—a great and rare art! It is exercised by those who see all the strengths and weaknesses of their own natures and then comprehend them in an artistic plan until everything appears as art and reason and even weakness delights the eye. Here a large mass of second nature has been added; there a piece of original nature has been removed: both by long practice and daily labor. Here the ugly which could not be removed is bidden; there it has been reinterpreted and made sublime . . . It will be the strong and domineering natures who enjoy their finest gaiety in such compulsion, in such constraint and perfection under a law of their own; the passion of their tremendous will relents when confronted with stylized, conquered, and serving nature; even when they have to build palaces and lay out gardens, they demur at giving nature a free hand. Conversely, it is the weak characters without power over themselves who *hate* the constraint of style . . . They become slaves as soon as they serve; they hate to serve. Such spirits—and they may be of the first rank—are always out to interpret themselves and their environment as *free* nature—wild, arbitrary, fantastic, disorderly, astonishing; and they do well because only in this way do they please themselves. For one thing is needful: that a human being attain his satisfaction with himself—whether it be by this or by that poetry and art; only then is a human being at all tolerable to behold. Whoever is dissatisfied with himself is always ready to revenge himself therefor; we others will be his victims, if only by always having to stand his ugly sight. For the sight of the ugly makes men bad and gloomy.

Perhaps premature . . . There is no morality that alone makes moral, and every ethic that affirms itself exclusively kills too much good strength and costs humanity too dearly. The deviants, who are so frequently the inventive and fruitful ones, shall no longer be sacrificed; it shall not even be considered infamous to deviate from morality, in thought and deed; numerous new experiments of life and society shall be made; a tremendous burden of bad conscience shall be removed from the world—these most general aims should be recognized and promoted by all who are honest and seek truth.

If we have our own *why* of life, we shall get along with almost any *how*. Man does *not* strive for pleasure; only the Englishman does.

What is good? Everything that heightens the feeling of power in man, the will to power, power itself.

What is bad? Everything that is born of weakness.

What is happiness? The feeling that power is *growing*, that resistance is overcome.

Not contentedness but more power; not peace but war; not virtue but fitness. . . .

My demand upon the philosopher is known, that he take his stand *beyond* good and evil and leave the illusion of moral judgment *beneath* himself. This demand follows from an insight which I was the first to formulate: that *there are altogether no moral facts*. Moral judgments agree with religious ones in believing in realities which are no realities. Morality is merely an interpretation of certain phenomena—more precisely, a misinterpretation. Moral judgments, like religious ones, belong to a stage of ignorance at which the very concept of the real and the distinction between what is real and imaginary, are still lacking; thus "truth," at this stage, designates all sorts of things which we today call "imaginings." Moral judgments are therefore never to be taken literally: so understood, they always contain mere absurdity. Semeiotically, however, they remain invaluable: they reveal, at least for those who know, the most valuable realities of cultures and inwardnesses which did not know enough to "understand" themselves. Morality is mere sign language, mere symptomatology: one must know what it is all about to be able to profit from it.

G. E. Moore, *Principia Ethica*, 1903

Intuitionism:
The Indefinability of Moral Goodness
G. E. Moore

6.   What, then, is good? How is good to be defined? Now, it may be thought that this is a verbal question. A definition does indeed often mean the expressing of one word's meaning in other words. But this is not the sort of definition I am asking for. Such a definition can never be of ultimate importance in any study except lexicography. If I wanted that kind of definition I should have to consider in the first place how people generally used the word "good"; but my business is not with its proper usage, as established by custom. I should, indeed, be foolish, if I tried to use it for something Which it did not usually denote: if, for instance, I were to announce that, whenever I used the word "good," I must be understood to be thinking of that object which is usually denoted by the word "table." I shall, therefore, use the word in the sense in which I think it is ordinarily used; but at the same time I am not anxious to discuss whether I am right in thinking that it is so used. My business is solely with that object or idea, which I hold, rightly or wrongly, that the word is generally used to stand for. What I want to discover is the nature of that object or idea, and about this I am extremely anxious to arrive at an agreement.

But, if we understand the question in this sense, my answer to it may seem a very disappointing one. If I am asked "What is good?" my answer is that good is good, and that is the end of the matter. Or if I am asked "How is good to be defined?" my answer is that it cannot be defined, and that is all I have to say about it. But disappointing as these answers may appear, they are of the very last importance. To readers who are familiar with philosophic terminology, I can express their importance by saying that they amount to this: That propositions about the good are all of them synthetic and never analytic; and that is plainly no trivial matter. And the same thing may be expressed more popularly, by saying that, if I am right, then nobody can foist upon us such an axiom as that "Pleasure is the only good" or that "The good is the desired" on the pretence that this is "the very meaning of the word."

7.   Let us, then, consider this position. My point is that "good" is a simple notion, just as "yellow" is a simple notion; that, just as you cannot, by any manner of means, explain to any

one who does not already know it, what yellow is, so you cannot explain what good is. Definitions of the kind that I was asking for, definitions which describe the real nature of the object or notion denoted by a word, and which do not merely tell us what the word is used to mean, are only possible when the object or notion in question is something complex. You can give a definition of a horse, because a horse has many different properties and qualities, all of which you can enumerate. But when you have enumerated them all, when you have reduced a horse to his simplest terms, then you can no longer define those terms. They are simply something which you think of or perceive, and to any one who cannot think of or perceive them, you can never, by any definition, make their nature known. It may perhaps be objected to this that we are able to describe to others, objects which they have never seen or thought of. We can, for instance, make a man understand what a chimaera is, although he has never heard of one or seen one. You can tell him that it is an animal with a lioness's head and body, with a goat's head growing from the middle of its back, and with a snake in place of a tail. But here the object which you are describing is a complex object; it is entirely composed of parts, with which we are all perfectly familiar—a snake, a goat, a lioness; and we know, too, the manner in which those parts are to be put together, because we know what is meant by the middle of a lioness's back, and where her tail is wont to grow. And so it is with all objects, not previously known, which we are able to define: they are all complex; all composed of parts, which may themselves, in the first instance, be capable of similar definition, but which must in the end be reducible to simplest parts, which can no longer be defined. But yellow and good, we say, are not complex: they are notions of that simple kind, out of which definitions are composed and with which the power of further defining ceases.

8.   When we say, as Webster says, "The definition of horse is 'A hoofed quadruped of the genus Equus,'" we may, in fact, mean three different things. (1) We may mean merely: "When I say 'horse,' you are to understand that I am talking about a hoofed quadruped of the genus Equus." This might be called the arbitrary verbal definition: and I do not mean that good is indefinable in that sense. (2) We may mean, as Webster ought to mean: "When most English people say 'horse,' they mean a hoofed quadruped of the genus Equus." This may be called the verbal definition proper, and I do not say that good is indefinable in this sense either; for it is certainly possible to discover how people use a word: otherwise, we could never have known that "good" may be translated by "gut" in German and by "bon" in French. But (3) we may, when we define horse, mean something much more important. We may mean that a certain object, which we all of us know, is composed in a certain manner: that it has four legs, a head, a heart, a liver, etc., etc., all of them arranged in definite relations to one another. It is in this sense that I deny good to be definable. I say that it is not composed of any parts which we can substitute for it in our minds when we are thinking of it. We might think just as clearly and correctly about a horse, if we thought of all its parts and their arrangements instead of thinking of the whole: we could, I say, think how a horse differed from a donkey just as well, just as truly, in this way, as now we do, only not so easily; but there is nothing whatsover which we could so substitute for good; and that is what I mean when I say that good is indefinable.

9.   But I am afraid I have still not removed the chief difficulty which may prevent acceptance of the proposition that good is indefinable. I do not mean to say that *the* good, that which is good, is thus indefinable; if I did think so, I should not be writing on Ethics, for my main object is to help towards discovering that definition. It is just because I think there will be less risk of error in our search for a definition of "the good," that I am now insisting that *good* is indefinable. I must try to explain the difference between these two. I suppose it may be

granted that "good" is an adjective. Well "the good," "that which is good," must therefore be the substantive to which the adjective "good" will apply: it must be the whole of that to which the adjective will apply, and the adjective must *always* truly apply to it. But if it is that to which the adjective will apply, it must be something different from that adjective itself; and the whole of that something different, whatever it is, will be our definition of *the* good. Now it may be that this something will have other adjectives, beside "good," that will apply to it. It may be full of pleasure, for example; it may be intelligent; and if these two adjectives are really part of its definition, then it will certainly be true, that pleasure and intelligence are good. And many people appear to think that, if we say "Pleasure and intelligence are good," or if we say "Only pleasure and intelligence are good," we are defining "good." Well, I cannot deny that propositions of this nature may sometimes be called definitions; I do not know well enough how the word is generally used to decide upon this point. I only wish it to be understood that that is not what I mean when I say there is no possible definition of good and that I shall not mean this if I use the word again. I do most fully believe that some true proposition of the form "Intelligence is good and intelligence alone is good" can be found; if none could be found, our definition of *the* good would be impossible. As it is, I believe *the* good to be definable; and yet I still say that good itself is indefinable.

10. "Good," then, if we mean by it that quality which we assert to belong to a thing, when we say that the thing is good, is incapable of any definition, in the most important sense of that word. The most important sense of "definition" is that in which a definition states what are the parts which invariably compose a certain whole; and in this sense has no definition because it is simple and has no parts. It is one of those innumerable objects of thought which are themselves incapable of definition, because they are the ultimate terms by reference to which whatever *is* capable of definition must be defined. That there must be an indefinite number of such terms is obvious, on reflection; since we cannot define anything except by an analysis, which, when carried as far as it will go, refers us to something, which is simply different from anything else, and which by that ultimate difference explains the peculiarity of the whole which we are defining: for every whole contains some parts which are common to other wholes also. There is, therefore, no intrinsic difficulty in the contention that "good" denotes a simple and indefinable quality. There are many other instances of such qualities.

Consider yellow, for example. We may try to define it, by describing its physical equivalent; we may state what kind of light-vibrations must stimulate the normal eye, in order that we may perceive it. But a moment's reflection is sufficient to shew that those light-vibrations are not themselves what we mean by yellow. *They* are not what we perceive. Indeed we should never have been able to discover their existence, unless we had first been struck by the patent difference of quality between the different colours. The most we can be entitled to say of those vibrations is that they are what corresponds in space to the yellow which we actually perceive.

Yet a mistake of this simple kind has commonly been made about "good." It may be true that all things which are good are *also* something else, just as it is true that all things which are yellow produce a certain kind of vibration in the light. And it is a fact, that Ethics aims at discovering what are those other properties belonging to all things which are good. But far too many philosophers have thought that when they named those other properties they were actually defining good; that these properties, in fact, were simply not "other," but absolutely and entirely the same with goodness. This view I propose to call the "naturalistic fallacy" and of it I shall now endeavour to dispose.

11. Let us consider what it is such philosophers say. And first it is to be noticed that they do not agree among themselves. They not only say that they are right as to what good is, but they endeavour to prove that other people who say that it is something else, are wrong. One, for instance, will affirm that good is another, perhaps, that pleasure, is that which is desired; and each of these will argue eagerly to prove that the other is wrong. But how is that possible? One of them says that good is nothing but the object of desire, and at the same time tries to prove that it is not pleasure. But from his first assertion, that good means the object of desire, one of two things must follow as regards his proof:

(1) He may be trying to prove that the object of desire is not pleasure. But, if this be all, where is his Ethics? The position he is maintaining is merely a psychological one. Desire is something which occurs in our minds, and pleasure is something else which so occurs; and our would-be ethical philosopher is merely holding that the latter is not the object of the former. But what has that to do with the question in dispute? His opponent held the ethical proposition that pleasure was the good, and although he should prove a million times over the psychological proposition that pleasure is not the object of desire, he is no nearer proving his opponent to be wrong. The position is like this. One man says a triangle is a circle: another replies "A triangle is a straight line, and I will prove to you that I am right: *for*" (this is the only argument) "a straight line is not a circle." "That is quite true," the other may reply; "but nevertheless a triangle is a circle, and you have said nothing whatever to prove the contrary. What is proved is that one of us is wrong, for we agree that a triangle cannot be both a straight line and a circle: but which is wrong, there can be no earthly means of proving, since you define triangle as straight line and I define it as circle"—Well, that is one alternative which any naturalistic Ethics has to face; if good is *defined* as something else, it is then impossible either to prove that any other definition is wrong or even to deny such definition.

(2) The other alternative will scarcely be more welcome. It is that the discussion is afterall a verbal one. When A says "Good means pleasant" and B says "Good means desired," they may merely wish to assert that most people have used the word for what is pleasant and for what is desired respectively. And this is quite an interesting subject for discussion: only it is not a whit more an ethical discussion than the last was. Nor do I think that any exponent of naturalistic Ethics would be willing to allow that this was all he meant. They are all so anxious to persuade us that what they call the good is what we really ought to do. "Do, pray, act so, because the word 'good' is generally used to denote actions of this nature": such, on this view, would be the substance of their teaching. And in so far as they tell us how we ought to act, their teaching is truly ethical, as they mean it to be. But how perfectly absurd is the reason they would give for it! "You are to do this, because most people use a certain word to denote conduct such as this." "You are to say the thing which is not, because most people call it lying." That is an argument just as good!—My dear sirs, what we want to know from you as ethical teachers, is not how people use a word; it is not even, what kind of actions they approve, which the use of this word "good" may certainly imply: what we want to know is simply what *is* good. We may indeed agree that what most people do think good, is actually so; we shall at all events be glad to know their opinions: but when we say their opinions about what is good, we do mean what we say; we do not care whether they call that thing which they mean "horse" or "table" or "chair," "gut," or "bon" or "αγαθός," we want to know what it is that they so call. When they say "Pleasure is good," we cannot believe that they merely mean "Pleasure is pleasure" and nothing more than that.

12. Suppose a man says "I am pleased"; and suppose that is not a lie or a mistake but the truth. Well, if it is true, what does that mean? It means that his mind, a certain definite mind, distinguished by certain definite marks from all others, has at this moment a certain definite feeling called pleasure. "Pleased" *means* nothing but having pleasure, and though we may be more pleased or less pleased, and even, we may admit for the present, have one or another kind of pleasure; yet in so far as it is pleasure we have, whether there be more or less of it, and whether it be of one kind or another, what we have is one definite thing, absolutely indefinable, some one thing that is the same in all the various degrees and in all the various kinds of it that there may be. We may be able to say how it is related to other things: that, for example, it is in the mind, that it causes desire, that we are conscious of it, etc., etc. We can, I say, describe its relations to other things, but define it we can *not*. And if anybody tried to define pleasure for us as being any other natural object; if anybody were to say, for instance, that pleasure *means* the sensation of red, and were to proceed to deduce from that that pleasure is a colour, we should be entitled to laugh at him and to distrust his future statements about pleasure. Well, that would be the same fallacy which I have called the naturalistic fallacy. That "pleased" does not mean "having the sensation of red," or anything else whatever, does not prevent us from understanding what it does mean. It is enough for us to know that "pleased" does mean "having the sensation of pleasure," and though pleasure is absolutely indefinable, though pleasure is pleasure and nothing else whatever, yet we feel no difficulty in saying that we are pleased. The reason is, of course, that when I say "I am pleased," I do *not* mean that "I" am the same thing as "having pleasure." And similarly no difficulty need be found in my saying that "pleasure is good" and yet not meaning that "pleasure" is the same thing as "good," that pleasure *means* good, and that good *means* pleasure. If I were to imagine that when I said "I am pleased," I meant that I was exactly the same thing as "pleased," I should not indeed call that a naturalistic fallacy, although it would be the same fallacy as I have called naturalistic with reference to Ethics. The reason of this is obvious enough. When a man confuses two natural objects with one another, defining the one by the other, if for instance, he confuses himself, who is one natural object, with "pleased" or with "pleasure" which are others, then there is no reason to call the fallacy naturalistic. But if be confuses "good," which is not in the same sense a natural object, with any natural object whatever, then there is a reason for calling that a naturalistic fallacy; its being made with regard to "good" marks it as something quite specific, and this specific mistake deserves a name because it is so common. As for the reasons why good is not to be considered a natural object, they may be reserved for discussion in another place. But, for the present, it is sufficient to notice this: Even if it were a natural object, that would not alter the nature of the fallacy nor diminish its importance one whit. All that I have said about it would remain quite equally true: only the name which I have called it would not be so appropriate as I think it is. And I do not care about the name: what I do care about is the fallacy. It does not matter what we call it, provided we recognise it when we meet with it. It is to be met with in almost every book on Ethics; and yet it is not recognised: and that is why it is necessary to multiply illustrations of it, and convenient to give it a name. It is a very simple fallacy indeed. When we say that an orange is yellow, we do not think our statement binds us to hold that "orange" means nothing else than "yellow," or that nothing can be yellow but an orange. Supposing the orange is also sweet! Does that bind us to say that "sweet" is exactly the same thing as "yellow," that "sweet" must be defined as "yellow"? And supposing it be recognised that "yellow" just means "yellow" and nothing else whatever, does that make it any more difficult to hold that oranges are yellow? Most certainly it does not: on the contrary, it would be absolutely meaningless to say that oranges were yellow, unless yellow did in the end mean just "yellow" and nothing else whatever—unless it was absolutely

indefinable. We should not get any very clear notion about things, which are yellow—we should not get very far with our science, if we were bound to hold that everything which was yellow, *meant* exactly the same thing as yellow. We should find we had to hold that an orange was exactly the same thing as a stool, a piece of paper, a lemon, anything you like. We could prove any number of absurdities; but should we be the nearer to the truth? Why, then, should it be different with "good"? Why, if good is good and indefinable, should I be held to deny that pleasure is good? Is there any difficulty in holding both to be true at once? On the contrary, there is no meaning in saying that pleasure is good, unless good is something different from pleasure. It is absolutely useless, so far as Ethics is concerned, to prove, as Mr. Spencer tries to do, that increase of pleasure coincides with increase of life, unless good *means* something different from either life or pleasure. He might just as well try to prove that an orange is yellow by shewing that it always is wrapped up in paper.

13. In fact, if it is not the case that "good" denotes something simple and indefinable, only two alternatives are possible: either it is a complex, a given whole, about the correct analysis of which there may be disagreement; or else it means nothing at all, and there is no such subject as Ethics. In general, however, ethical philosophers have attempted to define good, without recognising what such an attempt must mean. We are, therefore, justified in concluding that the attempt to define good is chiefly due to want of clearness as to the possible nature of definition. There are, in fact, only two serious alternatives to be considered, in order to establish the conclusion that "good" does denote a simple and indefinable notion. It might possibly denote a complex, as "horse" does; or it might have no meaning at all. Neither of these possibilities has, however, been clearly conceived and seriously maintained, as such, by those who presume to define good; and both may be dismissed by a simple appeal to facts.

(1) The hypothesis that disagreement about the meaning of good is disagreement with regard to the correct analysis of a given whole, may be most plainly seen to be incorrect by consideration of the fact that, whatever definition be offered, it may be always asked, with significance, of the complex so defined, whether it is itself good. To take, for instance, one of the more plausible, because one of the more complicated, of such proposed definitions, it may easily be thought, at first sight, that to be good may mean to be that which we desire to desire. Thus if we apply this definition to a particular instance and say "When we think that A is good, we are thinking that A is one of the things which we desire to desire," our proposition may seem quite plausible. But, if we carry the investigation further, and ask ourselves "Is it good to desire to desire A?" it is apparent, on a little reflection, that this question is itself as intelligible, as the original question "Is A good?"—that we are, in fact, now asking for exactly the same information about the desire to desire A, for which we formerly asked with regard to A itself. But it is also apparent that the meaning of this second question cannot be correctly analysed into "Is the desire to desire A one of the things which we desire to desire?": we have not before our minds anything so complicated as the question "Do we desire to desire to desire to desire A?" Moreover any one can easily convince himself by inspection that the predicate of this proposition—"good"—is positively different from the notion of "desiring to desire" which enters into its subject: "That we should desire to desire A is good" is *not* merely equivalent to "That A should be good is good." It may indeed be true that what we desire to desire is always also good; perhaps, even the converse may be true: but it is very doubtful whether this is the case, and the mere fact that we understand very well what is meant by doubting it, shews clearly that we have two different notions before our minds.

(2) And the same consideration is sufficient to dismiss the hypothesis that "good" has no meaning whatsoever. It is very natural to make the mistake of supposing that what is universally true is of such a nature that its negation would be self-contradictory: the importance which has been assigned to analytic propositions in the history of philosophy shews how easy such a mistake is. And thus it is very easy to conclude that what seems to be a universal ethical principle is in fact an identical proposition; that, if, for example, whatever is called "good" seems to be pleasant, the proposition "Pleasure is the good" does not assert a connection between two different notions, but involves only one, that of pleasure, which is easily recognised as a distinct entity. But whoever will attentively consider with himself what is actually before his mind when he asks the question "Is pleasure (or whatever it may be) after all good?" can easily satisfy himself that be is not merely wondering whether pleasure is pleasant. And if he will try this experiment with each suggested definition in succession, he may become expert enough to recognise that in every case he has before his mind a unique object, with regard to the connection of which with any other object, a distinct question may be asked. Every one does in fact understand the question "Is this good?" When he thinks of it, his state of mind is different from what it would be, were he asked "Is this pleasant, or desired, or approved?" It has a distinct meaning for him, even though he may not recognise in what respect it is distinct. Whenever he thinks of "intrinsic value," or "intrinsic worth," or says that a thing "ought to exist," he has before his mind the unique object—the unique property of things—which I mean by "good." Everybody is constantly aware of this notion, although he may never become aware at all that it is different from other notions of which he is also aware. But, for correct ethical reasoning, it is extremely important that he should become aware of this fact; and, as soon as the nature of the problem is clearly understood, there should be little difficulty in advancing so far in analysis. . . .

14. My objections to Naturalism are then, in the first place, that it offers no reason at all, far less any valid reason, for any ethical principle whatever; and in this it already fails to satisfy the requirements of Ethics, as a scientific study. But in the second place I contend that, though it gives a reason for no ethical principle, it is a *cause* of the acceptance of false principles—it deludes the mind into accepting ethical principles, which are false; and in this it is contrary to every aim of Ethics. It is easy to see that if we start with a definition of right conduct as conduct conducive to general happiness; then, knowing that right conduct is universally conduct conducive to the good, we very easily arrive at the result that the good is general happiness. If, on the other hand, we once recognise that we must start our Ethics without a definition, we shall be much more apt to look about us, before we adopt any ethical principle whatever; and the more we look about us, the less likely are we to adopt a false one. It may be replied to this: Yes, but we shall look about us just as much, before we settle on our definition, and are therefore just as likely to be right. But I will try to shew that this is not the case. If we start with the conviction that a definition of good can be found, we start with the conviction that good *can mean* nothing else than some one property of things; and our only business will then be to discover what that property is. But if we recognise that, so far as the meaning of good goes, anything whatever may be good, we start with a much more open mind. Moreover, apart from the fact that, when we think we have a definition, we cannot logically defend our ethical principles in any way whatever, we shall also be much less apt to defend them well, even if illogically. For we shall start with the conviction that good must mean so and so, and shall therefore be inclined either to misunderstand our opponent's arguments or to cut them short

with the reply, "This is not an open question: the very meaning of the word decides it; no one can think otherwise except through confusion." . . .

86. . . . I [have] tried to shew what "good"—the adjective "good"—*means*. This appeared to be the first point to be settled in any treatment of Ethics, that should aim at being systematic. It is necessary we should know this, should know what good means, before we can go on to consider what is good—what things or qualities are good. It is necessary we should know it for two reasons. The first reason is that "good" is the notion upon which all Ethics depends. We cannot hope to understand what we mean, when we say that this is good or that is good, until we understand quite clearly, not only what "this" is or "that" is (which the natural sciences and philosophy can tell us) but also what is meant by calling them good, a matter which is reserved for Ethics only. Unless we are quite clear on this point, our ethical reasoning will be always apt to be fallacious. We shall think that we are proving that a thing is "good," when we are really only proving that it is something else; since unless we know what "good" means, unless we know what is meant by that notion in itself, as distinct from what is meant by any other notion, we shall not be able to tell when we are dealing with it and when we are dealing with something else, which is perhaps like it, but yet not the same. And the second reason why we should settle first of all this question "What good means?" is a reason of method. It is this, that we can never know on what *evidence* an ethical proposition rests, until we know the nature of the notion which makes the proposition ethical. We cannot tell what is possible, by way of proof, in favour of one judgment that "This or that is good," or against another judgment "That this or that is bad," until we have recognised what the nature of such propositions must always be. In fact, it follows from the meaning of good and bad, that such propositions are all of them, in Kant's phrase, "synthetic": they all must rest in the end upon some proposition which must be simply accepted or rejected, which cannot be logically deduced from any other proposition. This result, which follows from our first investigation, may be otherwise expressed by saying that the fundamental principles of Ethics must be self-evident. But I am anxious that this expression should not be misunderstood. The expression "self- evident" means properly that the proposition so called is evident or true, *by itself* alone; that it is not an inference from some proposition other than *itself*. The expression does *not* mean that the proposition is true, because it is evident to you or me or all mankind, because in other words it appears to us to be true. That a proposition appears to be true can never be a valid argument that true it really is. By saying that a proposition is self-evident, we mean emphatically that its appearing so to us, is *not* the reason why it is true: for we mean that it has absolutely no reason. It would not be a self-evident proposition, if we could say of it: I cannot think otherwise and therefore it is true. For then its evidence or proof would not lie in itself, but in something else, namely our conviction of it. That it appears true to us may indeed be the *cause* of our asserting it, or the reason why we think and say that it is true: but a reason in this sense is something utterly different from a logical reason, or reason why something is true. Moreover, it is obviously not a reason of the same thing. The *evidence* of a proposition to us is only a reason for *our holding it* to be true: whereas a logical reason, or reason in the sense in which self-evident propositions have no reason, is a reason why the *proposition itself* must be true, not why we hold it so to be. Again that a proposition is evident to us may not only be the reason why we do think or affirm it, it may even be a *reason* why we ought to think it or affirm it. But a reason, in this sense too, is not a logical reason for the truth of the proposition, though it is a logical reason for the rightness of holding the proposition. In our common language, however, these three meanings of "reason" are constantly confused, whenever we say "I have a reason for thinking that true." But it is absolutely essential, if we are to get clear notions about Ethics or, indeed, about any other, especially any philosophical, study, that we should

distinguish them. When, therefore, I talk of Intuitionistic Hedonism, I must not be understood to imply that my denial that "Pleasure is the only good" is *based* on my Intuition of its falsehood. My Intuition of its falsehood is indeed *my* reason for *holding* and declaring it untrue; it is indeed the only valid reason for so doing. But that is just because there is *no* logical reason for it; because there is no proper evidence or reason of its falsehood except itself alone. It is untrue, because it is untrue, and there is no other reason: but I *declare* it untrue, because its untruth is evident to me, and I hold that that is a sufficient reason for my assertion. We must not therefore look on Intuition, as if it were an alternative to reasoning. Nothing whatever can take the place of *reasons* for the truth of any proposition: intuition can only furnish a reason for *holding* any proposition to be true: this however it must do when any proposition is self-evident, when, in fact, there are no reasons which prove its truth.

William David Ross, *The Right and the Good*, 1930

Prima Facie Duties
W. D. Ross

. . . When a plain man fulfills a promise because he thinks he ought to do so, it seems clear that he does so with no thought of its total consequences, still less with any opinion that these are likely to be the best possible. He thinks in fact much more of the past than of the future. What makes him think it right to act in a certain way is the fact that he has promised to do so—that and, usually, nothing more. That his act will produce the best possible consequences is not his reason for calling it right. What lends colour to the theory we are examining [i.e., utilitarianism], then, is not the actions (which form probably a great majority of our actions) in which some such reflection as "I have promised" is the only reason we give ourselves for thinking a certain action right, but the exceptional cases in which the consequences of fulfilling a promise (for instance) would be so disastrous to others that we judge it right not to do so. It must of course be admitted that such cases exist. If I have promised to meet a friend at a particular time for some trivial purpose, I should certainly think myself justified in breaking my engagement if by doing so I could prevent a serious accident or bring relief to the victims of one. And the supporters of the view we are examining hold that my thinking so is due to my thinking that I shall bring more good into existence by the one action than by the other. A different account may, however, be given of the matter, an account which will, I believe, show itself to be the true one. It may be said that besides the duty of fulfilling promises I have and recognize a duty of relieving distress, and that when I think it right to do the latter at the cost of not doing the former, it is not because I think I shall produce more good thereby but because I think it the duty which is in the circumstances more of a duty. This account surely corresponds much more closely with what we really think in such a situation. If, so far as I can see, I could bring equal amounts of good into being by fulfilling my promise and by helping some one to whom I had made no promise, I should not hesitate to regard the former as my duty. Yet on the view that what is right is right because it is productive of the most good I should not so regard it. . . .

In fact the theory of "ideal utilitarianism," if I may for brevity refer so to the theory of Professor Moore, seems to simplify unduly our relations to our fellows. It says, in effect, that the only morally significant relation in which my neighbours stand to me is that of being possible beneficiaries by my action. They do stand in this relation to me, and this relation is morally significant. But they may also stand to me in the relation of promisee to promiser, of creditor to debtor, of wife to husband, of child to parent, of friend to friend, of fellow countryman to fellow countryman, and the like; and each of these relations is the foundation of a *prima facie* duty, which is more or less incumbent on me according to the circumstances of the case. When I am in a situation, as perhaps I always am, in which more than one of these *prima facie* duties is incumbent on me, what I have to do is to study the situation as fully as I can until I form the considered opinion (it is never more) that in the circumstances one of them is more incumbent than any other; then I am bound to think that to do this *prima facie* duty is my duty *sans phrase* in the situation.

I suggest *"prima facie* duty" or "conditional duty" as a brief way of referring to the characteristic (quite distinct from that of being a duty proper) which an act has, in virtue of being of a certain kind (e.g. the keeping of a promise), of being an act which would be a duty proper if it were not at the same time of another kind which is morally significant. Whether an act is a duty proper or actual duty depends on *all* the morally significant kinds it is an instance of. . . .

There is nothing arbitrary about these *prima facie* duties. Each rests on a definite circumstance which cannot seriously be held to be without moral significance. Of *prima facie* duties I suggest, without claiming completeness or finality for it, the following division.

(1) Some duties rest on previous acts of my own. These duties seem to include two kinds, (a) those resting on a promise or what may fairly be called an implicit promise, such as the implicit undertaking not to tell lies which seems to be implied in the act of entering into conversation (at any rate by civilized men), or of writing books that purport to be history and not fiction. These may be called the duties of fidelity. (b) Those resting on a previous wrongful act. These may be called the duties of reparation. (2) Some rest on previous acts of other men, i.e., services done by them to me. These may be loosely described as the duties of gratitude. (3) Some rest on the fact or possibility of a distribution of pleasure or happiness (or of the means thereto) which is not in accordance with the merit of the persons concerned; in such cases there arises a duty to upset or prevent such a distribution. These are the duties of justice. (4) Some rest on the mere fact that there are other beings in the world whose condition we can make better in respect of virtue, or of intelligence, or of pleasure. These are the duties of beneficence. (5) Some rest on the fact that we can improve our own condition in respect of virtue or of intelligence. These are the duties of self-improvement. (6) I think that we should distinguish from (4) the duties that may be summed up under the title of "not injuring others." No doubt to injure others is incidentally to fail to do them good; but it seems to me clear that non-maleficence is apprehended as a duty distinct from that of beneficence, and as a duty of a more stringent character. It will be noticed that this alone among the types of duty has been stated in a negative way. An attempt might no doubt be made to state this duty, like the others, in a positive way. It might be said that it is really the duty to prevent ourselves from acting either from an inclination to harm others or from an inclination to seek our own pleasure, in doing which we should incidentally harm them. But on reflection it seems clear that the primary duty here is the duty not to harm others, this being a duty whether or not we have an inclination that if followed would lead to our harming them; and that when we have such an inclination the primary duty not to harm others gives rise to a consequential duty to resist the inclination. The recognition of this duty of non-maleficence is the first step on the way to the recognition of the duty of beneficence; and that accounts for the prominence of the commands "thou shalt not kill," "thou shalt not commit adultery," "thou shalt not steal," "thou shalt not bear false witness," in so early a code as the Decalogue. But even when we

have come to recognize the duty of beneficence, it appears to me that the duty of non-maleficence is recognized as a distinct one, and as *prima facie* more binding. We should not in general consider it justifiable to kill one person in order to keep another alive, or to steal from one in order to give alms to another.

The essential defect of the "ideal utilitarian" theory is that it ignores, or at least does not do full justice to, the highly personal character of duty. If the only duty is to produce the maximum of good, the question who is to have the good—whether it is myself, or my benefactor, or a person to whom I have made a promise to confer that good on him, or a mere fellow man to whom I stand in no such special relation—should make no difference to my having a duty to produce that good. But we are all in fact sure that it makes a vast difference.

One or two other comments must be made on this provisional list of the divisions of duty. (1) The nomenclature is not strictly correct. For by "fidelity" or "gratitude" we mean, strictly, certain states of motivation; and, as I have urged, it is not our duty to have certain motives, but to do certain acts. By "fidelity," for instance, is meant, strictly, the disposition to fulfill promises and implicit promises *because we have made them*. We have no general word to cover the actual fulfilment of promises and implicit promises *irrespective of motive;* and I use "fidelity," loosely but perhaps conveniently, to fill this gap. So too I use "gratitude" for the returning of services, irrespective of motive. The term "justice" is not so much confined, in ordinary usage, to a certain state of motivation, for we should often talk of a man as acting justly even when we did not think his motive was the wish to do what was just simply for the sake of doing so. Less apology is therefore needed for our use of "justice" in this sense. And I have used the word "beneficence" rather than "benevolence," in order to emphasize the fact that it is our duty to do certain things, and not to do them from certain motives.

(2) If the objection be made, that this catalogue of the main types of duty is an unsystematic one resting on no logical principle, it may be replied, first, that it makes no claim to being ultimate. It is a *prima facie* classification of the duties which reflection on our moral convictions seems actually to reveal. And if these convictions are, as I would claim that they are, of the nature of knowledge, and if I have not misstated them, the list will be a list of authentic conditional duties, correct as far as it goes though not necessarily complete. The list of *goods* put forward by the rival theory is reached by exactly the same method—the only sound one in the circumstances—viz. that of direct reflection on what we really think. Loyalty to the facts is worth more than a symmetrical architectonic or a hastily reached simplicity. If further reflection discovers a perfect logical basis for this or for a better classification, so much the better.

(3) It may, again, be objected that our theory that there are these various and often conflicting types of *prima facie* duty leaves us with no principle upon which to discern what is our actual duty in particular circumstances. But this objection is not one which the rival theory is in a position to bring forward. For when we have to choose between the production of two heterogeneous goods, say knowledge and pleasure, the "ideal utilitarian" theory can only fall back on an opinion, for which no logical basis can be offered, that one of the goods is the greater; and this is no better than a similar opinion that one of two duties is the more urgent. And again, when we consider the infinite variety of the effects of our actions in the way of pleasure, it must surely be admitted that the claim which *hedonism* sometimes makes, that it offers a readily applicable criterion of right conduct, is quite illusory.

I am unwilling, however, to content myself with an *argumentum ad hominem*, and I would contend that in principle there is no reason to anticipate that every act that is our duty is so for one and the same reason. Why should two sets of circumstances, or one set of circumstances, *not* possess different characteristics, any one of which makes a certain act our *prima facie* duty? When I ask what it is that makes me in certain cases sure that I have a *prima facie* duty to do so and so, I find that it lies in the fact that I have made a promise; when I ask the same question in another case, I find the answer lies in the fact that I have done a wrong. And if on reflection I find (as I think I do) that neither of these reasons is reducible to the other, I must not on any *a priori* ground assume that such a reduction is possible. . . .

It is necessary to say something by way of clearing up the relation between *prima facie* duties and the actual or absolute duty to do one particular act in particular circumstances. If, as almost all moralists except Kant are agreed, and as most plain men think, it is sometimes right to tell a lie or to break a promise, it must be maintained that there is a difference between *prima facie* duty and actual or absolute duty. When we think ourselves justified in breaking, and indeed morally obliged to break, a promise in order to relieve some one's distress, we do not for a moment cease to recognize a *prima facie* duty to keep our promise, and this leads us to feel, not indeed shame or repentance, but certainly compunction, for behaving as we do; we recognize further, that it is our duty to make up somehow to the promisee for the breaking of the promise. We have to distinguish from the characteristic of being our duty that of tending to be our duty. Any act that we do contains various elements in virtue of which it falls under various categories. In virtue of being the breaking of a promise, for instance, it tends to be wrong; in virtue of being an instance of relieving distress it tends to be right. Tendency to be one's duty may be called a parti-resultant attribute, i.e. one which belongs to an act in virtue of some one component in its nature. *Being* one's duty is a toti-resultant attribute, one which belongs to an act in virtue of its whole nature and of nothing less than this. . . .

Some of these general principles of *prima facie* duty may appear to be open to criticism. It may be thought, for example, that the principle of returning good for good is a falling off from the Christian principle, generally and rightly recognized as expressing the highest morality, of returning good for evil. To this it may be replied that I do not suggest that there is a principle commanding us to return good for good and forbidding us to return good for evil, and that I do suggest that there is a positive duty to seek the good of all men. What I maintain is that an act in which good is returned for good is recognized as *specially* binding on us just because it is of that character, and that *ceteris paribus* any one would think it his duty to help his benefactors rather than his enemies, if he could not do both; just as it is generally recognized that *ceteris paribus* we should pay our debts rather than give our money in charity, when we cannot do both. A benefactor is not only a man, calling for our effort on his behalf on that ground, but also our benefactor, calling for our *special* effort on *that* ground.

Our judgements about our actual duty in concrete situations have none of the certainty that attaches to our recognition of the general principles of duty. A statement is certain, i.e. is an expression of knowledge, only in one or other of two cases: when it is either self-evident, or a valid conclusion from self-evident premises. And our judgements about our particular duties have neither of these characters. (1) They are not self-evident. Where a possibile act is seen to have two characteristics, in virtue of one of which it is *prima facie* right, and in virtue of the other *prima facie* wrong, we are (I think) well aware that we are not certain whether we ought or ought not to do it; that whether we do it or not, we are taking a moral risk. We come in the long run, after consideration, to think one duty more pressing than the other, but we do not feel certain that it is so. And though we do not always recognize that a possible act has two such characteristics, and though there *may* be cases in which it has not, we are never certain that any particular possible act has not, and therefore never certain that it is right, nor certain that it is wrong. For, to go no further in the analysis, it is enough to point out that any particular act will in all probability in the course of time con-tribute to the bringing about of good or of evil for many human beings, and thus have a *prima facie* rightness or wrongness of which we know nothing. (2) Again, our judgements about our particular duties are not logical conclusions from self-evident premises. The only possible premises would be the general principles stating their *prima facie* rightness or wrongness *qua* having the different characteristics they do have; and even if we could (as we cannot) apprehend the extent to which an act will tend on the one hand, for example, to bring about advantages for our benefactors and on the other hand to bring about disadvantages for fellow men who are not our benefactors, there is no principle by which we can draw the conclusion that it is on the whole right or on the whole wrong. In this respect the judgement as to the rightness of a particular act is just like the judgement as to the beauty of a particular natural object or work of art. A poem is, for instance, in respect of certain qualities beautiful and in respect of certain others not beautiful; and our judgement as to the degree of beauty it possesses on the whole is never reached by logical reasoning from the apprehension of its particular beauties or particular defects. Both in this and in the moral case we have more or less probable opinions which are not logically justified conclusions from the general principles that are recognized as self-evident.

There is therefore much truth in the description of the right act as a fortunate act. If we cannot be certain that it is right, it is our good fortune if the act we do is the right act. This consideration does not, however, make the doing of our duty a mere matter of chance. There is a parallel here between the doing of duty and the doing of what will be to our personal advantage. We never *know* what act will in the long run be to our advantage. Yet it is certain that we are more likely in general to secure our advantage if we estimate to the best of our ability the probable tendencies of our actions in this respect, than if we act on caprice. And similarly we are more likely to do our duty if we reflect to the best of our ability on the *prima facie* rightness or wrongness of various possible acts in virtue of the characteristics we perceive them to have, than if we act without reflection. With this greater likelihood we must be content.

Many people would be inclined to say that the right act for me is not that whose general nature I have been describing, viz. that which if I were omniscient I should see to be my duty, but that which on all the evidence available to me I should think to be my duty. But suppose that from the state of partial knowledge in which I think act *A* to be my duty, I could pass to a state of perfect knowledge in which I saw act *B* to be my duty, should I not say "act *B* was the right act for me to do"? I should no doubt add "though I am not to be blamed for doing act *A*." But in adding this, am I not passing from the question "what is right" to the question "what is morally good"? At the same time I am not making the *full* passage from the one notion to the other; for in order that the act should be morally good, or an act I am not to be blamed for doing, it must not merely be the act which it is reasonable for me to think my duty; it must also be done for that reason, or from some other morally good motive. Thus the conception of the right act as the act which it is reasonable for me to think my duty is an unsatisfactory compromise between the true notion of the right act and the notion of the morally good action.

The general principles of duty are obviously not self-evident from the beginning of our lives. How do they come to be so? The answer is, that they come to be self-evident to us just as mathematical axioms do. We find by experience that this couple of matches and that couple make four matches, that this couple of balls on a wire and that couple make four balls; and by reflection on these and similar discoveries we come to see that it is of the nature of two and two to make four. In a precisely similar way, we see the *prima facie* rightness of an act which would be the fulfilment of a particular promise, and of another which would be the fulfilment of another promise, and when we have reached sufficient maturity to think in general terms, we apprehend *prima facie* rightness to belong to the nature of any fulfilment of promise. What comes first in time is the apprehension of the self-evident *prima facie* rightness of an individual act of a particular type. From this we come by reflection to apprehend the self-evident general principle of *prima facie* duty. From this, too, perhaps along with the apprehension of the self-evident *prima facie* rightness of the same act in virtue of its having another characteristic as well, and perhaps in spite of the apprehension of its *prima facie* wrongness in virtue of its having some third characteristic, we come to believe something not self-evident at all, but an object of probable opinion, viz. that this particular act is (not *prima facie* but) actually right. . . .

Supposing it to be agreed, as I think on reflection it must, that no one *means* by "right" just "productive of the best possible consequences," or "optimific," the attributes "right" and "optimific" might stand in either of two kinds of relation to each other. (1) They might be so related that we could apprehend *a priori*, either immediately or deductively, that any act that is optimific is right and any act that is right is optimific, as we can apprehend that any triangle that is equilateral is equiangular and *vice versa*. Professor Moore's view is, I think, that the coextensiveness of "right" and "optimific" is apprehended immediately. He rejects the possibility of any proof of it. Or (2) the two attributes might be such that the question whether they are invariably connected had to be answered by means of an inductive inquiry. Now at first sight it might seem as if the constant connexion of the two attributes could be immediately apprehended. It might seem absurd to suggest that it could be right for any one to do an act which would produce consequences less good than those which would be produced by some other act in his power. Yet a little thought will convince us that this is not absurd. The type of case in which it is easiest to see that this is so is, perhaps, that in which one has made a promise. In such a case we all think that *prima facie* it is our duty to fulfil the promise irrespective of the precise goodness of the total consequences. And though we do not think it is necessarily our actual or absolute duty to do so, we are far from thinking that any, even the slightest, gain in the value of the total consequences will necessarily justify us in doing something else instead. Suppose, to simplify the case by abstraction, that the fulfilment of a promise to *A* would produce 1,000 units of good for him, but that by doing some other act I could produce 1,001 units of good for *B*, to whom I have made no promise, the other consequences of the two acts being of equal value; should we really think it self-evident that it was our duty to do the second act and not the first? I think not. We should, I fancy, hold that only a much greater disparity of value between the total consequences would justify us in failing to discharge our *prima facie* duty to *A*. After all, a promise is a promise, and is not to be treated so lightly as the theory we are examining would imply. What, exactly, a promise is, is not so easy to determine, but we are surely agreed that it constitutes a serious moral limitation to our freedom of action. To produce the 1,001 units of good for *B* rather than fulfil our promise to *A* would be to take, not perhaps our duty as philanthropists too seriously, but certainly our duty as makers of promises too lightly. . . .

Such instances—and they might easily be added to—make it clear that there is no self-evident connexion between the attributes "right" and "optimific." The theory we are examining has a certain attractiveness when applied to our decision that a particular act is our duty (though I have tried to show that it does not agree with our actual moral judgements even here). But it is not even plausible when applied to our recognition of *prima facie* duty. For if it were self-evident that the right coincides with the optimific, it should be self-evident that what is *prima facie* right is *prima facie* optimific. But whereas we are certain that keeping a promise is *prima facie* right, we are not certain that it is *prima facie* optimific (though we are perhaps certain that it is *prima facie* bonific). Our certainty that it is *prima facie* right depends not on its consequences but on its being the fulfilment of a promise. The theory we are examining involves too much difference between the evident ground of our conviction about *prima facie* duty and the alleged ground of our conviction about actual duty.

The coextensiveness of the right and the optimific is, then, not self-evident.

I conclude that the attributes "right" and "optimific" are not identical, and that we do not know either by intuition, by deduction, or by induction that they coincide in their application, still less that the latter is the foundation of the former. It must be added, however, that if we are ever under no special obligation such as that of fidelity to a promisee or of gratitude to a benefactor, we ought to do what will produce most good; and that even when we are under a special obligation the tendency of acts to promote general good is one of the main factors in determining whether they are right.

Alfred Jules Ayer, *Language, Truth, and Logic*, 1950

The Emotive Theory of Ethics
A. J. Ayer

. . . it is our business to give an account of "judgements of value" which is both satisfactory in itself and consistent with our general empiricist principles. We shall set ourselves to show that in so far as statements of value are significant, they are ordinary "scientific" statements; and that in so far as they are not scientific, they are not in the literal sense significant, but are simply expressions of emotion which can be neither true nor false. In maintaining this view, we may confine ourselves for the present to the case of ethical statements. . . . What we are interested in is the possibility of reducing the whole sphere of ethical terms to non-ethical terms. We are enquiring whether statements of ethical value can be translated into statements of empirical fact.

That they can be so translated is the contention of those ethical philosophers who are commonly called subjectivists and of those who are known as utilitarians. For the utilitarian defines the rightness of actions, and the goodness of ends, in terms of the pleasure, or happiness, or satisfaction, to which they give rise; the subjectivist, in terms of the feelings of approval which a certain person, or group of people, has towards them. Each of these types of definition makes moral judgements into a sub-class of psychological or sociological judgements; and for this reason they are very attractive to us. For, if either was correct, it would follow that ethical assertions were not generically different from the factual assertions which are ordinarily contrasted with them; and the account which we have already given of empirical hypotheses would apply to them also.

Nevertheless we shall not adopt either a subjectivist or a utilitarian analysis of ethical terms. We reject the subjectivist view that to call an action right, or a thing good, is to say that it is generally approved of, because it is not self-contradictory to assert that some actions which are generally approved of are not right, or that some things which are generally approved of are not good. And we reject the alternative subjectivist view that a man who asserts that a certain action is right, or that a certain thing is good, is saying that he himself approves of it, on the ground that a man who confessed that he sometimes approved of what was bad or wrong would not be contradicting himself. And a similar argument is fatal to utilitarianism. We cannot agree that to call an action right is to say that of all the actions possible in the circumstances it would cause, or be likely to cause, the greatest happiness, or the greatest balance of pleasure over pain, or the greatest balance of satisfied over unsatisfied desire, because we find that it is not self-contradictory to say that it is sometimes wrong to perform the actually or probably I cause the greatest, happiness, or the greatest balance of pleasure over pain, or of satisfied over unsatisfied desire. And since it is not self-contradictory to say that some pleasant things are not good, or that some bad things are desired, it cannot be the case that the sentence "x is good" is equivalent to "x is pleasant," or to "x is desired." And to every other variant of utilitarianism with which I am acquainted the same objection can be made. And therefore we should, I think, conclude that the validity of ethical judgements is not determined by the felicific tendencies of actions, any more than by the nature of people's feelings; but that it must be regarded as "absolute" or "intrinsic," and not empirically calculable.

If we say this, we are not, of course, denying that it is possible to invent a language in which all ethical symbols are definable in non-ethical terms, or even that it is desirable to invent such a language and adopt it in place of our own; what we are denying is that the suggested reduction of ethical to non-ethical statements is consistent with the conventions of our actual language. That is, we reject utilitarianism and subjectivism, not as proposals to replace our existing ethical notions by new ones, but as analyses of our existing ethical notions. Our contention is simply that, in our language, sentences which contain normative ethical symbols are not equivalent to sentences which express psychological propositions, or indeed empirical propositions of any kind. . . .

In admitting that normative ethical concepts are irreducible to empirical concepts, we seem to be leaving the way clear for the "absolutist" view of ethics—that is, the view that statements of value are not controlled by observation, as ordinary empirical propositions are, but only by a mysterious "intellectual intuition." A feature of this theory, which is seldom recognized by its advocates, is that it makes statements of value unverifiable. For it is notorious that what seems intuitively certain to one person may seem doubtful, or even false, to another. So that unless it is possible to provide some criterion by which one may decide between conflicting intuitions, a mere appeal to intuition is worthless as a test of a proposition's validity. But in the case of moral judgements, no such criterion can be given. Some moralists claim to settle the matter by saying that they "know" that their own moral judgements are correct. But such an assertion is of purely psychological interest, and has not the slightest tendency to prove the validity of any moral judgement. For dissentient moralists may equally well "know" that their ethical views are correct. And, as far as subjective certainty goes, there will be nothing to choose between them. When such differences of opinion arise in connection with an ordinary empirical proposition, one may attempt to resolve them by referring to, or actually carrying out, some relevant empirical test. But with regard to ethical statements, there is, on the "absolutist" or "intuitionist" theory, no relevant empirical test. We are therefore justified in saying that on this theory ethical statements are held to be unverifiable. They are, of course, also held to be genuine synthetic propositions.

Considering the use which we have made of the principle that a synthetic proposition is significant only if it is empirically verifiable, it is clear that the acceptance of an "absolutist" theory of ethics would undermine the whole of our main argument. And as we have already rejected the "naturalistic" theories which are commonly supposed to provide the only alternative to "absolutism" in ethics, we seem to have reached a difficult position. We shall meet the difficulty by showing that the correct treatment of ethical statements is afforded by a third theory, which is wholly compatible with our radical empiricism.

We begin by admitting that the fundamental ethical concepts are unanalysable, inasmuch as there is no criterion by which one can test the validity of the judgements in which they occur. So far we are in agreement with the absolutists. But, unlike the absolutists, we are able to give an explanation of this fact about ethical concepts. We say that the reason why they are unanalysable is that they are mere pseudo-concepts. The presence of an ethical symbol in a proposition adds nothing to its factual content. Thus if I say to someone, "You acted wrongly in stealing that money," I am not stating anything more than if I had simply said, "You stole that money." In adding that this action is wrong I am not making any further statement about it. I am simply evincing my moral disapproval of it. It is as if I had said, "You stole that money," in a peculiar tone of horror, or written it with the addition of some special exclamation marks. The tone, or the exclamation marks, adds nothing to the literal meaning of the sentence. It merely serves to show that the expression of it is attended by certain feelings in the speaker.

If now I generalise my previous statement and say, "Stealing money is wrong," I produce a sentence which has no factual meaning—that is expresses no proposition which can be either true or false. It is as if I had written "Stealing money!!"—where the shape and thickness of the exclamation marks show, by a suitable convention, that a special sort of moral disapproval is the feeling which is being expressed. It is clear that there is nothing said here which can be true or false. Another man may disagree with me about the wrongness of stealing, in the sense that he may not have the same feelings about stealing as I have, and he may quarrel with me on account of my moral sentiments. But he cannot, strictly speaking, contradict me. For in saying that a certain type of action is right or wrong, I am not making any factual statement, not even a statement about my own state of mind. I am merely expressing certain moral sentiments. And the man who is ostensibly contradicting me is merely expressing his moral sentiments. So that there is plainly no sense in asking which of us is in the right. For neither of us is asserting a genuine proposition.

What we have just been saying about the symbol "wrong" applies to all normative ethical symbols. Sometimes they occur in sentences which record ordinary empirical facts besides expressing ethical feeling about those facts: sometimes they occur in sentences which simply express ethical feeling about a certain type of action, or situation, without making any statement of fact. But in every case in which one would commonly be said to be making an ethical judgement, the function of the relevant ethical word is purely "emotive." It is used to express feeling about certain objects, but not to make any assertion about them.

It is worth mentioning that ethical terms do not serve only to express feeling. They are calculated also to arouse feeling, and so to stimulate action. Indeed some of them are used in such a way as to give the sentences in which they occur the effect of commands. Thus the sentence "It is your duty to tell the truth" may be regarded both as the expression of a certain sort of ethical feeling about truthfulness and as the expression of the command "Tell the truth." The sentence "You ought to tell the truth" also involves the command "Tell the truth," but here the tone of the command is less emphatic. In the sentence "It is good to tell the truth" the command has become little more than a suggestion. And thus the "meaning" of the word "good," in its ethical usage, is differentiated from that of the word "duty" or the word "ought." In fact we may define the meaning of the various ethical words in terms both of the different feelings they are ordinarily taken to express, and also the different responses which they are calculated to provoke.

We can now see why it is impossible to find a criterion for determining the validity of ethical judgements. It is not because they have an "absolute" validity which is mysteriously independent of ordinary sense-experience, but because they have no objective validity whatsoever. If a sentence makes no statement at all, there is obviously no sense in asking whether what it says is true or false. And we have seen that sentences which simply express moral judgements do not say anything. They are pure expressions of feeling and as such do not come under the category of truth and falsehood. They are unverifiable for the same reason as a cry of pain or a word of command is unverifiable—because they do not express genuine propositions.

Thus, although our theory of ethics might fairly be said to be radically subjectivist, it differs in a very important respect from the orthodox subjectivist theory. For the orthodox subjectivist does not deny, as we do, that the sentences of a moralizer express genuine propositions. All he denies is that they express propositions of a unique non-empirical character. His own view is that they express propositions about the speaker's feelings. If this were so, ethical judgements clearly would be capable of being true or false. They would be true if the speaker had the relevant feelings, and false if he had not. And this is a matter which is, in principle, empirically verifiable. Furthermore they could be significantly contradicted. For if I say, "Tolerance is a virtue," and someone answers, "You don't approve of it," he would, on the ordinary subjectivist theory, be contradicting me. On our theory, he would not be contradicting me, because, in saying that tolerance was a virtue, I should not be making any statement about my own feelings or about anything else. I should simply be evincing my feelings, which is not at all the same thing as saying that I have them.

The distinction between the expression of feeling and the assertion of feeling is complicated by the fact that the assertion that one has a certain feeling often accompanies the expression of that feeling, and is then, indeed, a factor in the expression of that feeling. Thus I may simultaneously express boredom and say that I am bored, and in that case my utterance of the word, "I am bored," is one of the circumstances which make it true to say that I am expressing or evincing boredom. But I can express boredom without actually saying that I am bored. I can express it by my tone and gestures, while making a statement about something wholly unconnected with it, or by an ejaculation, or without uttering any words at all. So that even if the assertion that one has a certain feeling always involves the expression of that feeling, the expression of a feeling assuredly does not always involve the assertion that one has it. And this is the important point to grasp in considering the distinction between our theory and the ordinary subjectivist theory. For whereas the subjectivist holds that ethical statements actually assert the existence of certain feelings, we hold that ethical statements are expressions and excitants, of feeling which do not necessarily involve any assertions.

We have already remarked that the main objection to the ordinary subjectivist theory is that the validity of ethical judgements is not determined by the nature of their author's feelings. And this is an objection which our theory escapes. For it does not imply that the existence of any feelings is a necessary and sufficient condition of the validity of an ethical judgement. It implies, on the contrary, that ethical judgements have no validity.

There is, however, a celebrated argument against subjectivist theories which our theory does not escape. It has been pointed out by Moore that if ethical statements were simply statements about the speaker's feelings, it would be impossible to argue about questions of value.[1] To take a typical example: if a man said that thrift was a virtue, and another replied that it was a vice, they would not, on this theory, be disputing with one another. One would be saying that he approved of thrift, and the other that *he* didn't; and there is no reason why both these statements should not be true. Now Moore held it to be obvious that we do dispute about questions of value, and accordingly concluded that the particular form of subjectivism which he was discussing was false.

It is plain that the conclusion that it is impossible to dispute about questions of value follows from our theory also. For as we hold that such sentences as "Thrift is a virtue" and "Thrift is a vice" do not express propositions at all, we clearly cannot hold that they express incompatible propositions. We must therefore admit that if Moore's argument really refutes the ordinary subjectivist theory, it also refutes ours. But, in fact, we deny that it does refute even the ordinary subjectivist theory. For we hold that one really never does dispute about questions of value.

This may seem, at first sight, to be a very paradoxical assertion. For we certainly do engage in disputes which are ordinarily regarded as disputes about questions of value. But, in all such cases, we find, if we consider the matter closely, that the dispute is not really about a question of value, but about a question of fact. When someone disagrees with us about the moral value of a certain action or type of action, we do admittedly resort to argument in order to win him over to our way of thinking. But we do not attempt to show by our arguments that he has the "wrong" ethical feeling towards a situation whose nature he has correctly apprehended. What we attempt to show is that he is mistaken about the facts of the case. We argue that he has misconceived the agent's motive: or that he has misjudged the effects of the action, or its probable effects in view of the agent's knowledge; or that he has failed to take into account the special circumstances in which the agent was placed. Or else we employ more general arguments about the effects which actions of a certain type tend to produce, or the qualities which are usually manifested in their performance. We do this in the hope that we have only to get our opponent to agree with us about the nature of the empirical facts for him to adopt the same moral attitude towards them as we do. And as the people with whom we argue have generally received the same moral education as ourselves, and live in the same social order, our expectation is usually justified. But if our opponent happens to have undergone a different process of moral "conditioning" from ourselves, so that, even when he acknowledges all the facts, he still disagrees with us about the moral value of the actions under discussion, then we abandon the attempt to convince him by argument. We say that it is impossible to argue with him because he has a distorted or undeveloped moral sense; which signifies merely that he employs a different set of values from our own. We feel that our own system of values is superior, and therefore speak in such derogatory terms of his. But we cannot bring forward any arguments to show that our system is superior. For our judgement that it is so is itself a judgement of value, and accordingly outside the scope of argument. It is because argument fails us when we come to deal with pure questions of value, as distinct from questions of fact, that we finally resort to mere abuse.

In short, we find that argument is possible on moral questions only if some system of values is presupposed. If our opponent concurs with us in expressing moral disapproval of all actions of a given type *t*, then we may get him to condemn a particular action A, by bringing forward arguments to show that A is of type *t*. For the question whether A does or does not belong to that type is a plain question of fact. Given that a man has certain moral principles, we argue that he must, in order to be consistent, react morally to certain things in a certain way. What we do not and cannot argue about is the validity of these moral principles. We merely praise or condemn them in the light of our own feelings.

If anyone doubts the accuracy of this account of moral disputes, let him try to construct even an imaginary argument on a question of value which does not reduce itself to an argument about a question of logic or about an empirical matter of fact. I am confident that he will not succeed in producing a single example, And if that is the case, be must allow that its involving the impossibility of purely ethical arguments is not, as Moore not, as Moore thought, a ground of objection to our theory, but rather a point in favour of it.

Carl F. Henry, *Christian Personal Ethics*, 1957

Divine Command Ethics
C. F. Henry

... The good in Hebrew-Christian theistic ethics is not that which is adapted to human nature, but it is that to which the Creator obliges human nature.

The doctrine that the good is to be identified with the will of God cuts across secular ethics at almost every point. It protests against Utilitarianism, and its validation of the good by an appeal to consequences alone. It indicts Kant's supposition that duty and obligation rest upon a wholly immanental basis. According to Kant, the human will alone imposes man's duties upon him and affirms for him the categorical imperative. This theory of morality mediated to the modern man the artificial hope that the objectivity of the moral order could be maintained by a deliberate *severance* of duty and the good *from* the will of God. The Hebrew-Christian ethical perspective also challenges the many species of humanistic ethics so influential in the Western world today. Biblical ethics discredits an autonomous morality. It gives theonomous ethics its classic form—the identification of the moral law with the Divine will. In Hebrew-Christian revelation, distinctions in ethics reduce to what is good or what is pleasing, and to what is wicked or displeasing to the Creator-God alone. ...

That the essence of true morality is to be found primarily in complete obedience to the sovereign Lord provided the climate of thought which Hobbes secularized and perverted. in the *Leviathan.* His contemporary, Ralph Cudworth (1617–1688), who wrote *Eternal and Immutable Morality,* sought to place all men, including Hobbes and his sovereign, under an obligation to act for the common good. Cudworth argued that the distinction between right and wrong does not depend upon sovereign will, but on the moral order which confronts the whole of reality. Cudworth did not hesitate to insist that the principles of morality are addressed even to the Divine will and hence are determinative of it. By moralists under Cudworth's influence, man's obligation to obey the injunctions of Scripture was no longer suspended exclusively on the fact that God commands obedience, but correlative reasons for man's conformity were introduced, e.g., that obedience involves the common good. British moralists especially contributed to this Platonic rather than Hebraic orientation of values. The erroneous notion gained ground swiftly that the best device for thwarting political Naturalism, and for protecting the idea of duty from arbitrary perversion, is to assert the

146

independent existence of moral values, rather than to defend the good as the will of God. God is himself thereby assertedly obliged to uphold these values, and hence precluded from acting in an arbitrary detachment of the content of morality from the will of God became the optimistic basis of a reply to political Naturalism and all forms of moral autonomy.

Thereafter, the phrase "I ought" no longer means "the sovereign Lord commands." Rather, it is informed by self-evident truths or by intuitions of the moral order, as by the Cambridge Platonists, and finally it loses its connection with a transcendent moral order no less than with the sovereign Divine will. Thus the Christian West enters into a non-Christian orientation of the account of duty, and the outcome of this transition is that the doctrine of obligation is sketched independently of both the will of God and of theism. At first it was thought that, while separated from the will of God, moral obligations were as secure as mathematical axioms. They were safeguarded by universal and necessary implications of conscience or by some other immanentistic device. In place of the God-spoken moral imperative there arose a categorical imperative. This endured as an effective rallying point for ethical Idealism for less than a century. When the empirical and evolutionary movements in modern thought were felt, the attempt to secure the absolute obligation to perform every duty within an autonomous ethics dissolved, and with it the absoluteness of duty. Instead of exhibiting the inner unity of duty and goodness in their ultimate basis in the will of God, it lost the sanctity of moral obligation.

Yet the failure to identify duty and the good with the will of God is characteristic of idealistic ethics both in ancient and in modern times. Even those moral philosophies that professed hostility to an autonomous ethic and championed the transcendent objectivity of the moral order regarded the good as something given to God. They viewed the good as something to which God was bound rather than as something legislated by him. This prepared the way for an objectionable doctrine of the "good in itself." The good then is superior to God. It is a content which is externally addressed to him as it is to us. This thesis runs through Oriental religion as well as early Western philosophy. It underlies the Zoroastrian notion that Ormazd becomes supreme through his furtherance of the good. This view assumes the existence of an ethical law superior to God himself. It is found also in the Hindu conception of the law of Karma. God is the author of sovereign causality in an impersonal moral universe. Yet not even he can interfere with its autonomous operation now that it is in movement. The same idea becomes influential in Western thought through the moral philosophy of Plato, as expressed in the *Euthyphro*. Plato did not clearly identify the Idea of the Good with God, but it stood at the apex of the Divine Ideas. Hence the good can only be regarded as confronting the eternal spiritual world.

This notion of an "intrinsic good" is alien to biblical theology. The God of Hebrew-Christian revelation is the ground of ethics. He is the supreme rule of right. He defines the whole content of morality by his own revealed will. It is not merely because "in God is the perfect realization of the Ideal Righteousness," but because God legislates the nature of the good that biblical ethics is a radical departure from the pagan view of the moral order. . . . It is the will of God that defines the nature of intrinsic goodness. There exists no intrinsic good that is distinguishable from the will of God and to which God must conform.

Therefore the good must be conceived in wholly personal dimensions. The good-in-itself is none other than God-in-himself. . . . Kant's insistence that there is nothing good in the last analysis but a good will is formally right. His error was his displacement of the Divine by the human and his staggering moral optimism about human nature. The will of God is the source of the ethical law and supplies the content of morality. It alone is intrinsically good. Man's life is not to be oriented to impersonal eternal values, to objective norms, to ethical laws, to principles of conduct, to abiding virtues, viewed abstractly or independently of the Divine will. These place obligation upon men only insofar as they may be traced to the will of God. . . .

The question whether the good is to be conceived as identical with the nature of God has supplied fuel for theological debate in numerous Christian controversies. . . . It is possible to hold a view that transcends the conflict, yet it is important to rule out dangerous and misleading views. It is obvious enough that unless there is an ultimate ethical tension in the being of God, the Divine nature and will cannot be thought of as in competition with each other, but as morally identical. From this standpoint the good is conformity to God's being and to his will. But the nature of God must not be regarded as necessarily good in the sense that it gains its goodness independently of his will, nor that his good nature determines his will so that the will bows to the good by a sort of pantheistic inevitability. The good is what God wills, and what he freely wills. The good is what the Creator-Lord does and commands. He is the creator of the moral law, and defines its very nature.

At the same time no suggestion is conveyed that the good is arbitrary or a matter of Divine "caprice." That term frequently suits the propaganda purposes of those who caricature Divine sovereignty. Biblical morality itself has supplied a perspective from which the capriciousness of the polytheistic gods of Greek mythology may be judged. The moral activity of God is a closer definition of his nature. It is the constancy of God's will in its ethical affirmations and claims that supplies the durable basis for moral distinctions. Hovey declares, "The moral law is a free expression of his will to others, and therefore in the fullest and strictest sense it is from him, under him, dependent on him, and immutable only as he is immutable; while the same law comes down upon us from his mind and will, imposing itself on our consciences, and therefore is over us, and independent of us."[1] In stipulating the moral law, the Creator-God lay under no necessity other than to form it according to his own pleasure, and hence in conformity with his real character and purpose. The will of God so reveals his character that the man who conforms to his commandments will exhibit the image of God in his life. The Hebrew-Christian knowledge of God is a knowledge of the Righteous One. The commandments are manifestations of his character, and righteousness is what he prizes as his special glory (Ex. 33:18f., 34:6f.). . . .

The question what makes an act a duty has been answered ambiguously throughout the whole history of ethics. The view that finds in consequences or good results the obligatory basis of our actions, and conceives the ethical act merely as instrumentally good is inadequate. The view that regards an action itself as intrinsically good with total indifference to its consequences, and derives goodness from obligation, is equally inadequate. Both views fail to grasp the fact that obligation and virtue, goodness and happiness, find their common ground in the Divine will. They also fail to recognize that the notions of duty and goodness cannot be analyzed so as to enforce their interlocking nature when this fundamental reference is ignored. Why should man be obliged to do what is regarded as intrinsically good without regard to the consequences? Why is he obliged to do what leads to good consequences if he is in doubt regarding the basic rightness of his action? Speculative ethics furnishes a running commentary on this tension and fails to resolve it.

Hebrew-Christian ethics centers in the Divine revelation of the statutes, commandments, and precepts of the Living God. Its whole orientation of the moral life may be summarized by what the Holy Lord commands and what he forbids: what accords with his edicts is right, what opposes his holy will is wicked. . . .[2]

The moral law that lays an imperative on the human conscience is nothing more or less than the manifested will of God. For man nothing is good but union with the sovereign holy will of God. Sin therefore must not be defined primarily as social irresponsibility. Rather, it is repudiation of a Divine claim. David's words "against thee only have I sinned" (Psa. 51:4) echo the penitent's confession at its deepest level. Since God fashioned man to bear his moral likeness, nothing other than the fulfillment of this Divine purpose is man's supreme good. This purpose of God is the moral standard by which man throughout all history will be judged. Society in all its breadth and depth is responsible to the will of God. According to Christianity, to be morally good is to obey God's commands. The performance of God's will alone constitutes man's highest good. The rule of life is to "seek first the kingdom of God and his righteousness" (Mt. 6:33).

---

1. Alvah Hovey, *Manual of Systematic Theology and Christian Ethics* (Philadelphia: American Baptist Publication Society, 1877), p. 369.

2. "The good is what God rewards and the bad is what He punishes." Edward John Carnell, *An Introduction to Christian Apologetics.* (Grand Rapids: Eerdmans, 1948), p. 154.

Carol Gilligan, "Moral Orientation and Moral Development" in *Women and Moral Theory,* Eva Kittay and Diana Meyers (eds.), 1987

Gender and Ethical Perspective
Carol Gilligan

When one looks at an ambiguous figure like the drawing that can be seen as a young or old woman, or the image of the vase and the faces, one initially sees it in only one way. Yet even after seeing it in both ways, one way often seems more compelling. This phenomenon reflects the laws of perceptual organization that favor certain modes of visual grouping. But it also suggests a tendency to view reality as unequivocal and thus to argue that there is one right or better way of seeing.

The experiments of the Gestalt psychologists on perceptual organization provide a series of demonstrations that the same proximal pattern can be organized in different ways so that, for example, the same figure can be seen as a square or a diamond, depending on its orientation in relation to a surrounding frame. Subsequent studies show that the context influencing which of two possible organizations will be chosen may depend not only on the features of the array presented but also on the perceiver's past experience or expectation. Thus, a birdwatcher and a rabbit-keeper are likely to see the duck-rabbit figure in different ways; yet this difference does not imply that one way is better or a higher form of perceptual organization. It does, however, call attention to the fact that the rabbit-keeper, perceiving the rabbit, may not see the ambiguity of the figure until someone points out that it can also be seen as a duck.

This paper presents a similar phenomenon with respect to moral judgment, describing two moral perspectives that organize thinking in different ways. The analogy to ambiguous figure perception arises from the observation that although people are aware of both perspectives, they tend to adopt one or the other in defining and resolving moral conflict. Since moral judgments organize thinking about choice in difficult situations, the adoption of a single perspective may facilitate clarity of decision. But the wish for clarity may also imply a compelling human need for resolution or closure, especially in the face of decisions that give rise to discomfort or unease. Thus, the search for clarity in seeing may blend with a search for justification, encouraging the position that there is one right or better way to think about moral problems. This question, which has been the subject of intense theological and philosophical debate, becomes of interest to the psychologist not only because of its psychological dimensions—the tendency to focus on one perspective and the wish for justification—but also because one moral perspective currently dominates psychological thinking and is embedded in the most widely used measure for assessing the maturity of moral reasoning.

In describing an alternative standpoint, I will reconstruct the account of moral development around two moral perspectives, grounded in different dimensions of relationship that give rise to moral concern. The justice perspective, often equated with moral reasoning, is recast as one way of seeing moral problems and a care perspective is brought forward as an alternate vision or frame. The distinction between justice and care as alternative perspectives or moral orientations is based empirically on the observation that a shift in the focus of attention from concerns about justice to concerns about care changes the definition of what constitutes a moral problem, and leads the same situation to be seen in different ways. Theoretically, the distinction between justice and care cuts across the familiar divisions between thinking and feeling, egoism and altruism, theoretical and practical reasoning. It calls attention to the fact that all human relationships, public and private, can be characterized *both* in terms of equality and in terms of attachment, and that both inequality and detachment constitute grounds for moral concern. Since everyone is vulnerable both to oppression and to abandonment, two moral visions—one of justice and one of care—recur in human experience. The moral injunctions, not to act unfairly toward others, and not to turn away from someone in need, capture these different concerns.

The conception of the moral domain as comprised of at least two moral orientations raises new questions about observed differences in moral judgment and the disagreements to which they give rise. Key to this revision is the distinction between differences in developmental stage (more or less adequate positions within a single orientation) and differences in orientation (alternative perspectives or frameworks). The findings reported in this paper of an association between moral orientation and gender speak directly to the continuing controversy over sex differences in moral reasoning. In doing so, however, they also offer an empirical explanation for why previous thinking about moral development has been organized largely within the justice framework.

My research on moral orientation derives from an observation made in the course of studying the relationship between moral judgment and action. Two studies, one of college students describing their experiences of moral conflict and choice, and one of pregnant women who were considering abortion, shifted the focus of attention from the ways people reason about hypothetical dilemmas to the ways people construct moral conflicts and choices in their lives. This change in approach made it possible to see what experiences people define in moral terms, and to explore, the relationship between the understanding of moral problems and the reasoning strategies used and the actions taken in attempting to resolve them. In this context, I observed that women, especially when speaking about their own experiences of moral conflict and choice, often define moral problems in a way that eludes the categories of moral theory and is at odds with the assumptions that shape psychological thinking about morality and about the self.[1] This discovery, that a different voice often guides the moral judgments and the actions of women, called attention to a major design problem in previous moral judgment research: namely, the use of all-male samples as the empirical basis for theory construction.

The selection of an all-male sample as the basis for generalizations that are applied to both males and females is logically inconsistent. As a research strategy, the decision to begin with a single-sex sample is inherently problematic, since the categories of analysis will tend to be defined on the basis of the initial data gathered and subsequent studies will tend to be restricted to these categories. Piaget's work on the moral judgment of the child illustrates these problems since he defined the evolution of children's consciousness and practice of rules on the basis of his study of boys playing marbles, and then undertook a study of girls to assess the generality of his findings. Observing a series of differences both in the structure of girls' games and "in the actual mentality of little girls," he deemed these differences not of interest because "it was not this contrast which we proposed to study." Girls, Piaget found, "rather complicated our interrogatory in relation to what we know about boys," since the changes in their conception of rules, although following the same sequence observed in boys, did not stand in the same relation to social experience. Nevertheless, he concluded that "in spite of these differences in the structure of the game and apparently in the players" mentality, we find the same process at work as in the evolution of the game of marbles."[2]

Thus, girls were of interest insofar as they were similar to boys and confirmed the generality of Piaget's findings. The differences noted, which included a greater tolerance, a greater tendency toward innovation in solving conflicts, a greater willingness to make exceptions to rules, and a lesser concern with legal elaboration, were not seen as germane to "the psychology of rules," and therefore were regarded as insignificant for the study of children's moral judgment. Given the confusion that currently surrounds the discussion of sex differences in moral judgment, it is important to emphasize that the differences observed by Piaget did not pertain to girls' understanding of rules *per se* or to the development of the idea of justice in their thinking, but rather to the way girls structured their games and their approach to conflict resolution—that is, to their use rather than their understanding of the logic of rules and justice.

Kohlberg, in his research on moral development, did not encounter these problems since he equated moral development with the development of justice reasoning and initially used an all-male sample as the basis for theory and test construction. In response to his critics, Kohlberg has recently modified his claims, renaming his test a measure of "justice reasoning" rather than of "moral maturity" and acknowledging the presence of a care perspective in people's moral thinking.[3] But the widespread use of Kohlberg's measure as a measure of moral development together with his own continuing tendency to equate justice reasoning with moral judgment leaves the problem of orientation differences unsolved. More specifically, Kohlberg's efforts to assimilate thinking about care to the six-stage developmental sequence he derived and refined by analyzing changes in justice reasoning (relying centrally on his all-male longitudinal sample), underscores the continuing importance of the points raised in this paper concerning (1) the distinction between differences in developmental stage within a single orientation and differences in orientation, and (2) the fact that the moral thinking of girls and women was not examined in establishing either the meaning or the measurement of moral judgment within contemporary psychology.

An analysis of the language and logic of men's and women's moral reasoning about a range of hypothetical and real dilemmas underlies the distinction elaborated in this paper between a justice and a care perspective. The empirical association of care reasoning with women suggests that discrepancies observed between moral theory and the moral judgments of girls and women may reflect a shift in perspective, a change in moral orientation. Like the figure-ground shift in ambiguous figure perception, justice and care as moral perspectives are not opposites or mirror-images of one another, with justice uncaring and care unjust. Instead, these perspectives denote different ways of organizing the basic elements of moral judgment: self, others, and the relationship between them. With the shift in perspective from justice to care, the organizing dimension of relationship changes from inequality/equality to attachment/detachment, reorganizing thoughts, feelings and language so that words connoting relationship like "dependence" or "responsibility" or even moral terms such as "fairness" and "care" take on different meanings. To organize relationships in terms of attachment rather than in terms of equality changes the way human connection is imagined, so that the images or metaphors of relationship shift from hierarchy or balance to network or web. In addition, each organizing framework leads to a different way of imagining the self as a moral agent.

From a justice perspective, the self as moral agent stands as the figure against a ground of social relationships, judging the conflicting claims of self and others against a standard of equality or equal respect (the Categorical Imperative, the Golden Rule). From a care perspective, the relationship becomes the figure, defining self and others. Within the context of relationship, the self as a moral agent perceives and responds to the perception of need. The shift in moral perspective is manifest by a change in the moral question from "What is just?" to "How to respond?"

For example, adolescents asked to describe a moral dilemma often speak about peer or family pressure in which case the moral question becomes how to maintain moral principles or standards and resist the influence of one's parents or friends. "I have a right to my religious opinions," one teenager explains, referring to a religious difference with his parents. Yet, he adds, "I respect their views." The same dilemma, however, is also construed by adolescents as a problem of attachment, in which case the moral question becomes: how to respond both to oneself and to one's friends or one's parents, how to maintain or strengthen connection in the face of differences in belief. "I understand their fear of my new religious ideas," one teenager explains, referring to her religious disagreement with her parents, "but they really ought to listen to me and try to understand my beliefs."

One can see these two statements as two versions of essentially the same thing. Both teenagers present self-justifying arguments about religious disagreement; both address the claims of self and of others in a way that honors both. Yet each frames the problem in different terms, and the use of moral language points to different concerns. The first speaker casts the problem in terms of individual rights that must be respected within the relationship. In other words, the figure of the considering is the self looking on the disagreeing selves in relationship, and the aim is to get the other selves to acknowledge the right to disagree. In the case of the second speaker, figure and ground shift. The relationship becomes the figure of the considering, and relationships are seen to require listening and efforts at understanding differences in belief. Rather than the right to disagree, the speaker focuses on caring to hear and to be heard. Attention shifts from the grounds for agreement (rights and respect) to the grounds for understanding (listening and speaking, hearing and being heard). This shift is marked by a change in moral language from the stating of separate claims to rights and respect ("I have a right . . . I respect their views.") to the activities of relationship—the injunction to listen and try to understand ("I understand . . . they ought to listen . . . and try to understand."). The metaphor of moral voice itself carries the terms of the care perspective and reveals how the language chosen for moral theory is not orientation neutral.

The language of the public abortion debate, for example, reveals a justice perspective. Whether the abortion dilemma is cast as a conflict of rights or in terms of respect for human life, the claims of the fetus and of the pregnant woman are balanced or placed in opposition. The morality of abortion decisions thus construed hinges on the scholastic or metaphysical question as to whether the fetus is a life or a person, and whether its claims take precedence over those of the pregnant woman. Framed as a problem of care, the dilemma posed by abortion shifts. The connection between the fetus and the pregnant woman becomes the focus of attention and the question becomes whether it is responsible or irresponsible, caring or careless, to extend or to end this connection. In this construction, the abortion dilemma arises because there is no way not to act, and no way of acting that does not alter the connection between self and others. To ask what actions constitute care or are more caring directs attention to the parameters of connection and the costs of detachment, which become subjects of moral concern.

Finally, two medical students, each reporting a decision not to turn in someone who has violated the school rules against drinking, cast their decision in different terms. One student constructs the decision as an act of mercy, a decision to override justice in light of the fact that the violator has shown "the proper degrees of contrition." In addition, this student raises the question as to whether or not the alcohol policy is just. i.e., whether the school has the right to prohibit drinking. The other student explains the decision not to turn in a proctor who was drinking on the basis that turning him in is not a good way to respond to this problem, since it would dissolve the relationship between them and thus cut off an avenue for help. In addition, this student raises the question as to whether the proctor sees his drinking as a problem.

This example points to in important distinction, between care as understood or construed within a justice framework and care as a framework or a perspective on moral decision. Within a justice construction, care becomes the mercy that tempers justice; or connotes the special obligations or supererogatory duties that arise in personal relationships: or signifies altruism freely chosen—a decision to modulate the strict demands of justice by considering equity or showing forgiveness; or characterizes a choice to sacrifice the claims of the self. All of these interpretations of care leave the basic assumptions of a justice framework intact: the division between the self and others. the logic of reciprocity or equal respect.

As a moral perspective, care is less well elaborated, and there is no ready vocabulary in moral theory to describe its terms. As a framework for moral decision, care is grounded in the assumption that self and other are interdependent, an assumption reflected in a view of action as responsive and, therefore, as arising in relationship rather than the view of action as emanating from within the self and, therefore, "self governed." Seen as responsive, the self is by definition connected to others, responding to perceptions, interpreting events, and governed by the organizing tendencies of human interaction and human language. Within this framework, detachment, whether from self or from others, is morally problematic, since it breeds moral blindness or indifference—a failure to discern or respond to need. The question of what responses constitute care and what responses lead to hurt draws attention to the fact that one's own terms may differ from those of others. Justice in this context becomes understood as respect for people in their own terms.

The medical student's decision not to turn in the proctor for drinking reflects a judgment that turning him in is not the best way to respond to the drinking problem, itself seen as a sign of detachment or lack of concern. Caring for the proctor thus raises the question of what actions are most likely to ameliorate this problem, a decision that leads to the question of what are the proctor's terms.

The shift in organizing perspective here is marked by the fact that the first student does not consider the terms of the other as potentially different but instead assumes one set of terms. Thus the student alone becomes the arbiter of what is *the* proper degree of contrition. The second student, in turn, does not attend to the question of whether the alcohol policy itself is just or fair. Thus each student discusses an aspect of the problem that the other does not mention.

These examples are intended to illustrate two cross-cutting perspectives that do not negate one another but focus attention on different dimensions of the situation, creating a sense of ambiguity around the question of what is the problem to be solved. Systematic research on moral orientation as a dimension of moral judgment and action initially addressed three questions: (1) Do people articulate concerns about justice and concerns about care in discussing a moral dilemma? (2) Do people tend to focus their attention on one set of concerns and minimally represent the other? and (3) is there an association between moral orientation and gender? Evidence from studies that included a common set of questions about actual experiences of moral conflict and matched samples of males and females provides affirmative answers to all three questions.

When asked to describe a moral conflict they had faced, 55 out of 80 (69 percent) educationally advantaged North American adolescents and adults raised considerations of both justice and care. Two-thirds (54 out of 80) however, focused their attention on one set of concerns, with focus defined as 75 percent or more of the considerations raised pertaining either to justice or to care. Thus the person who presented, say, two care considerations in discussing a moral conflict was more likely to give a third, fourth, and fifth than to balance care and justice concerns—a finding consonant with the assumption that justice and care constitute organizing frameworks for moral decision. The men and the women involved in this study (high school students, college students, medical students, and adult professionals) were equally likely to demonstrate the focus phenomenon (two-thirds of both sexes fell into the outlying focus categories). There were, however, sex differences in the direction of focus. With one exception, all of the men who focused, focused on justice. The women divided, with roughly one third focusing on justice and one third on care.[4]

These findings clarify the different voice phenomenon and its implications for moral theory and for women. First, it is notable that if women were eliminated from the research sample, care focus in moral reasoning would virtually disappear. Although care focus was by no means characteristic of all women, it was almost exclusively a female phenomenon in this sample of educationally advantaged North Americans. Second, the fact that the women were advantaged means that the focus on care cannot readily be attributed to educational deficit or occupational disadvantage—the explanation Kohlberg and others have given for findings of lower levels of justice reasoning in women.[5] Instead, the focus on care in women's moral reasoning draws attention to the limitations of a justice-focused moral theory and highlights the presence of care concerns in the moral thinking of both women and men. In this light, the Care/Justice group composed of one third of the women and one third of the men becomes of particular interest, pointing to the need for further research that attends to the way people organize justice and care in relation to one another—whether, for example, people alternate perspectives, like seeing the rabbit and the duck in the rabbit-duck figure, or integrate the two perspectives in a way that resolves or sustains ambiguity.

Third, if the moral domain is comprised of at least two moral orientations, the focus phenomenon suggests that people have it tendency to lose sight of one moral perspective in arriving at moral decision—a liability equally shared by both sexes. The present findings further suggest that men and women tend to lose sight of different perspectives. The most striking result is the virtual absence of care-focus reasoning among the men. Since the men raised concerns about care in discussing moral conflicts and thus presented care concerns as morally relevant, a question is why they did not elaborate these concerns to a greater extent.

In summary, it becomes clear why attention to women's moral thinking led to the identification of a different voice and raised questions about the place of justice and care within a comprehensive moral theory. It also is clear how the selection of an all-male sample for research on moral judgment fosters an equation of morality with justice, providing little data discrepant with this view. In the present study, data discrepant with a justice-focused moral theory comes from a third of the women. Previously, such women were seen as having a problem understanding "morality." Yet these women may also be seen as exposing the problem in a justice-focused moral theory. This may explain the decision of researchers to exclude girls and women at the initial stage of moral judgment research. If one begins with the premise that "all morality consists in respect for rules,"[6] or "virtue is one and its name is justice,"[7] then women are likely to appear problematic within moral theory. If one begins with women's moral judgments, the problem becomes how to construct a theory that encompasses care as a focus of moral attention rather than as a subsidiary moral concern.

The implications of moral orientation for moral theory and for research on moral development are extended by a study designed and conducted by Kay Johnston.[8] Johnston set out to explore the relationship between moral orientation and problem-solving strategies, creating a standard method using fables for assessing spontaneous moral orientation and orientation preference. She asked 60 eleven- and fifteen-year-olds to state and to solve the moral problem posed by the fable. Then she asked: "Is there another way to solve this problem?" most of the children initially constructed the fable problems either in terms of justice or in terms of care; either they stood back from the situation and appealed to a rule or principle for adjudicating the conflicting claims or they entered the situation in an effort to discover or create a way of responding to all of the needs. About half of the children, slightly more fifteen- than eleven-year-olds, spontaneously switched moral orientation when asked whether there was another way to solve the problem. Others did so following an interviewer's cue as to the form such a switch might take. Finally, the children were asked which of the solutions they described was the best solution. Most of the children answered the question and explained why one way was preferable.

Johnston found gender differences parallel to those previously reported, with boys more often spontaneously using and preferring justice solutions and girls more often spontaneously using and preferring care solutions. In addition, she found differences between the two fables she used, confirming Langdale's finding that moral orientation is associated both with the gender of the reasoner and with the dilemma considered.[9] Finally, the fact that children, at least by the age of eleven, are able to shift moral orientation and can explain the logic of two moral perspectives, each associated with a different problem-solving strategy, heightens the analogy to ambiguous figure perception and further supports the conception of justice and care as organizing frameworks for moral decision.

The demonstration that children know both orientations and can frame and solve moral problems in at least two different ways means that the choice of moral standpoint is an element of moral decision. The role of the self in moral judgment thus includes the choice of moral standpoint, and this decision, whether implicit or explicit, may become linked with self-respect and self-definition. Especially in adolescence when choice becomes more self-conscious and self-reflective, moral standpoint may become entwined with identity and self-esteem. Johnston's finding that spontaneous moral orientation and preferred orientation are not always the same raises a number of questions as to why and under what conditions a person may adopt a problem-solving strategy that he or she sees as not the best way to solve the problem.

The way people chose to frame or solve a moral problem is clearly not the only way in which they can think about the problem, and is not necessarily the way they deem preferable. Moral judgments thus do not reveal *the* structure of moral thinking, since there are at least two ways in which people can structure moral problems. Johnston's demonstration of orientation-switch poses a serious challenge to the methods that have been used in moral judgment and moral development research, introducing a major interpretive caution. The fact that boys and girls at eleven and fifteen understand and distinguish the logics of justice and care reasoning directs attention to the origins and the development of both ways of thinking. In addition, the tendency for boys and girls to use and prefer different orientations when solving the same problem raises a number of questions about the relationship between these orientations and the factors influencing their representation. The different patterns of orientation use and preference, as well as the different conceptions of justice and of care implied or elaborated in the fable judgments, suggest that moral development cannot be mapped along a single linear stage sequence.

One way of explaining these findings, suggested by Johnston, joins Vygotsky's theory of cognitive development with Chodorow's analysis of sex differences in early childhood experiences of relationship.[10] Vygotsky posits that all of the higher cognitive functions originate as actual relations between individuals. Justice and care as moral ideas and as reasoning strategies thus would originate as relationships with others—an idea consonant with the derivation of justice and care reasoning from experiences of inequality and attachment in early childhood. All children are born into a situation of inequality in that they are less capable than the adults and older children around them and, in this sense, more helpless and less powerful. In addition, no child survives in the absence of some kind of adult attachment—or care, and through this experience of relationship children discover the responsiveness of human connection including their ability to move and affect one another.

Through the experience of inequality, of being in the less powerful position, children learn what it means to depend on the authority and the good will of others. As a result, they tend to strive for equality of greater power, and for freedom. Through the experience of attachment, children discover the ways in which people are able to care for and to hurt one another. The child's vulnerability to oppression and to abandonment thus can be seen to lay the groundwork for the moral visions of justice and care, conceived as ideals of human relationship and defining the ways in which people "should" act toward one another.

Chodorow's work then provides a way of explaining why care concerns tend to be minimally represented by men and why such concerns are less frequently elaborated in moral theory. Chodorow joins the dynamics of gender identity formation (the identification of oneself as male or female) to an analysis of early childhood relationships and examines the effects of maternal child care on the inner structuring of self in relation to others. Further, she differentiates a positional sense of self from a personal sense of self, contrasting a self defined in terms of role or position from a self known through the experience of connection. Her point is that maternal child care fosters the continuation of a relational sense of self in girls, since female gender identity is consonant with feeling connected with one's mother. For boys, gender identity is in tension with mother-child connection, unless that connection is structured in terms of sexual opposition (e.g., as an Oedipal drama). Thus, although boys experience responsiveness or care in relationships, knowledge of care or the need for care, when associated with mothers, poses a threat to masculine identity.[11]

Chodorow's work is limited by her reliance on object relations theory and problematic on that count. Object relations theory ties the formation of the self to the experience of separation, joining separation with individuation and thus counterposing the experience of self to the experience of connection with others. This is the line that Chodorow traces in explicating male development. Within this framework, girls' connections with their mothers can only be seen as problematic. Connection with others or the capacity to feel and think *with* others is, by definition, in tension with self-development when self-development or individuation is linked to separation. Thus, object-relations theory sustains a series of oppositions that have been central in Western thought and moral theory, including the opposition between thought and feelings, self and relationship, reason and compassion, justice and love. Object relations theory also continues the conventional division of psychological labor between women and men. Since the idea of a self, experienced in the context of attachment with others, is theoretically impossible, mothers. described as objects, are viewed as selfless, without a self. This view is essentially problematic for women, divorcing the activity of mothering from desire, knowledge, and agency, and implying that insofar as a mother experiences herself as a subject rather than as an object (a mirror reflecting her child), she is "selfish" and not a good mother. Winnicott's phrase "good-enough mother" represents an effort to temper this judgment.

Thus, psychologists and philosophers, aligning the self and morality with separation and autonomy—the ability to be self-governing—have associated care with self-sacrifice, or with feelings—a view at odds with the current position that care represents a way of knowing and a coherent moral perspective. This position, however, is well represented in literature written by women. For example the short story "A Jury of Her Peers," written by Susan Glaspell in 1917, a time when women ordinarily did not serve on juries, contrasts two ways of knowing that underlie two ways of interpreting and solving a crime.[12] The story centers on a murder; Minnie Foster is suspected of killing her husband.

A neighbor woman and the sheriff's wife accompany the sheriff and the prosecutor to the house of the accused woman. The men, representing the law, seek evidence that will convince a jury to convict the suspect. The women, collecting things to bring Minnie Foster in jail, enter in this way into the lives lived in the house. Taking in rather than taking apart, they begin to assemble observations and impressions, connecting them to past experience and observations until suddenly they compose a familiar pattern, like the log-cabin pattern they recognize in the quilt Minnie Foster was making. "Why do we *know*—what we know this minute?" one woman asks the other, but she also offers the following explanation:

> We live close together, and we live far apart. We all go through the same things— it's all just a different kind of the same thing! If it weren't—why do you and I *understand*.[13]

The activity of quilt-making—collecting odd scraps and piecing them together until they form a pattern—becomes the metaphor for this way of knowing. Discovering a strangled canary buried under pieces of quilting, the women make a series of connections that lead them to understand what happened.

The logic that says you don't kill a man because he has killed a bird, the judgment that finds these acts wildly incommensurate, is counterposed to the logic that sees both events as part of a larger pattern—a pattern of detachment and abandonment that led finally to the strangling. "I *wish* I'd come over here once in a while," Mrs. Hale, the neighbor, exclaims. "That was a crime! Who's going to punish that?" Mrs. Peters, the sheriff's wife, recalls that when she was a girl and a boy killed her cat, "If they hadn't held me back I would have—"and realizes that there had been no one to restrain Minnie Foster. John Foster was known as "a good man . . . He didn't drink, and he kept his word as well as most, I guess, and paid his debts." But he also was "a hard man," Mrs. Hale explains, "like a raw wind that gets to the bone."

Seeing detachment as the crime with murder as its ultimate extension, implicating themselves and also seeing the connection between their own and Minnie Foster's actions, the women solve the crime by attachment—by joining together, like the "knotting" that joins pieces of a quilt. In the decision to remove rather than to reveal the evidence, they separate themselves from a legal system in which they have no voice but also no way of voicing what they have come to understand. In choosing to connect themselves with one another and with Minnie, they separate themselves from the law that would use their understanding and their knowledge as grounds for further separation and killing.

In a law school class where a film-version of this story was shown, the students were divided in their assessment of the moral problem and in their evaluation of the various characters and actions. Some focused on the murder, the strangling of the husband. Some focused on the evidence of abandonment or indifference to others. Responses to a questionnaire showed a bi-modal distribution, indicating two ways of viewing the film. These different perspectives led to different ways of evaluating both the act of murder and the women's decision to remove the evidence. Responses to the film were not aligned with the sex of the viewer in an absolute way, thus dispelling any implication of biological determinism or of a stark division between the way women and men know or judge events. The knowledge gained inductively by the women in the film, however, was also gained more readily by women watching the film, who came in this way to see a logic in the women's actions and to articulate a rationale for their silence.

The analogy to ambiguous figure perception is useful here in several ways. First, it suggests that people can see a situation in more than one way, and even alternate ways of seeing, combining them without reducing them—like designating the rabbit-duck figure both duck and rabbit. Second, the analogy argues against the tendency to construe justice and care as opposites or mirror-images and also against the implication that these two perspectives are readily integrated or fused. The ambiguous figure directs attention to the way in which a change in perspective can reorganize perception and change understanding, without implying an underlying reality or pure form. What makes seeing both moral perspectives so difficult is precisely that the orientations are not opposites nor mirror images or better and worse representations of a single moral truth. The terms of one perspective do not contain the terms of the other. Instead, a shift in orientation denotes a restructuring of moral perception, changing the meaning of moral language and thus the definition of moral conflict and moral action. For example, detachment is considered the hallmark of mature moral thinking within a justice perspective, signifying the ability to judge dispassionately, to weigh evidence in an even-handed manner, balancing the claims of others and self. From a care perspective, detachment is *the* moral problem.

> "I could've come," retorted Mrs. Hale . . . "I wish I had come over to see Minnie Foster sometimes. I can see now . . . If there had been years and years of—nothing, then a bird to sing to you, it would be awful—still—after the bird was still. . . . I know what stillness is."

The difference between agreement and understanding captures the different logics of justice and care reasoning, one seeking grounds for agreement, one seeking grounds for understanding, one assuming separation and thus the need for some external structure of connection, one assuming connection and thus the potential for understanding. These assumptions run deep, generating and reflecting different views of human nature and the human condition. They also point to different vulnerabilities and different sources of error. The potential error in justice reasoning lies in its latent egocentrism, the tendency to confuse one's perspective with an objective standpoint or truth, the temptation to define others in one's own terms by putting oneself in their place. The potential error in care reasoning lies in the tendency to forget that one has terms, creating a tendency to enter into another's perspective and to see oneself as "selfless" by defining oneself in other's terms. These two types of error underlie two common equations that signify distortions or deformations of justice and care: the equation of human with male, unjust in its omission of women; and the equation of care with self sacrifice, uncaring in its failure to represent the activity and the agency of care.

The equation of human with male was assumed in the Platonic and in the Enlightenment tradition as well as by psychologists who saw all-male samples as "representative" of human experience. The equation of care with self-sacrifice is in some ways more complex. The premise of self-interest assumes a conflict of interest between self and other manifest in the opposition of egoism and altruism. Together, the equations of male with human and of care with self-sacrifice form a circle that has had a powerful hold on moral philosophy and psychology. The conjunction of women and moral theory thus challenges the traditional definition of human and calls for a reconsideration of what is meant by both justice and care.

To trace moral development along two distinct although intersecting dimensions of relationship suggests the possibility of different permutations of justice and care reasoning, different ways these two moral perspectives can be understood and represented in relation to one another. For example, one perspective may overshadow or eclipse the other, so that one is brightly illuminated while the other is dimly remembered, familiar but for the most part forgotten. The way in which one story about relationship obscures another was evident in high-school girls' definitions of dependence. These definitions highlighted two meanings— one arising from the opposition between dependence and independence, and one from the opposition of dependence to isolation ("No woman," one student observed, "is an island.") As the word "dependence" connotes the experience of relationship, this shift in the implied opposite of dependence indicates how the valence of relationship changes, when connection with others is experienced as an impediment to autonomy or independence, and when it is experienced as a source of comfort and pleasure, and a protection against isolation. This essential ambivalence of human connection provides a powerful emotional grounding for two moral perspectives, and also may indicate what is at stake in the effort to reduce morality to a single perspective.

It is easy to understand the ascendance of justice reasoning and of justice-focused moral theories in a society where care is associated with personal vulnerability in the form of economic disadvantage. But another way of thinking about the ascendance of justice reasoning and also about sex differences in moral development is suggested in the novel *Masks*, written by Fumiko Enchi, a Japanese woman.[14] The subject is spirit possession, and the novel dramatizes what it means to be possessed by the spirits of others. Writing about the Rokujo lady in the *Tales of Genji,* Enchi's central character notes that:

> Her soul alternates uncertainly between lyricism and spirit possession, making no philosophical distinction between the self alone and in relation to others, and is unable to achieve the solace of a religious indifference.[15]

The option of transcendence, of a religious indifference or a philosophical detachment, may be less available to women because women are more likely to be possessed by the spirits and the stories of others. The strength of women's moral perceptions lies in the refusal of detachment and depersonalization, and insistence on making connections that can lead to seeing the person killed in war or living in poverty as someone's son or father or brother or sister, or mother, or daughter, or friend. But the liability of women's development is also underscored by Enchi's novel in that women, possessed by the spirits of others, also are more likely to be caught in a chain of false attachments. If women are at the present time the custodians of a story about human attachment and interdependence, not only within the family but also in the world at large, then questions arise as to how this story can be kept alive and how moral theory can sustain this story. In this sense, the relationship between women and moral theory itself becomes one of interdependence.

By rendering a care perspective more coherent and making its terms explicit, moral theory may facilitate women's ability to speak about their experiences and perceptions and may foster the ability of others to listen and to understand. At the same time, the evidence of care focus in women's moral thinking suggests that the study of women's development may provide a natural history of moral development in which care is ascendant, revealing the ways in which creating and sustaining responsive connection with others becomes or remains a central moral concern. The promise in joining women and moral theory lies in the fact that human survival, in the late twentieth century, may depend less on formal agreement than on human connection.

Notes

1. Gilligan, C. (1977). "In a Different Voice: Women's Conceptions of Self and of Morality." *Harvard Educational Review* 47 (1982):481–517; *In a Different Voice: Psychological Theory and Women's Development.* Cambridge, Mass.: Harvard University Press.

2. Piaget, J. (1965). *The Moral Judgment of the Child.* New York, N.Y.: The Free Press Paperback Edition, pp. 76–84.

3. Kohlberg, L. (1984). *The Psychology of Moral Development.* San Francisco, Calif.: Harper & Row, Publishers, Inc.

4. Gilligan, C. and J. Attanucci. (1986). *Two Moral Orientations.* Harvard University, unpublished manuscript.

5. See Kohlberg, L. *op. cit.,* also Walker, L. (1984). "Sex Differences in the Development of Moral Reasoning: A Critical Review of the Literature." *Child Development* 55 (3):677–91.

6. Piaget. J., *op. cit.*

7. Kohlberg, L., *op. cit.*

8. Johnston, K. (1985). *Two Moral Orientations—Two Problem-solving Strategies: Adolescents' Solutions to Dilemmas in Fables.* Harvard University, unpublished doctoral dissertation.

9. Langdale, C. (1983). *Moral Orientation and Moral Development: The Analysis of Care and Justice Reasoning Across Different Dilemmas in Females and Males from Childhood through Adulthood.* Harvard University, unpublished doctoral dissertation.

10. Johnston, K., *op. cit.*; Vygotsky, L. (1978). *Mind in Society,* Cambridge, Mass.: Harvard University Press; Chodorow, N. (1974). "Family Structure and Feminine Personality" in *Women, Culture and Society,* L. M. Rosaldo and L. Lamphere, eds., Stanford, Calif.: Stanford University Press; see also Chodorow, N. (1978). *The Reproduction of Mothering: Psychoanalysis and the Sociology of Gender.* Berkeley, Calif.: University of California Press.

11. Chodorow, N., *op. cit.*

12. Glaspell, S. (1927). *A Jury of Her Peers.* London: E. Benn.

13. *Ibid.*

14. Fumiko, E. (1983). *Masks.* New York: Random House.

15. *Ibid.* p. 54.

John Ladd, "On Relativisim" in *Ethics and the Environment*, Vol. 2, No. 2, Victoria Davion (ed.), 1997

Ethical Relativism
John Ladd

Any discussion of the relations between anthropology and ethics leads inevitably to the ticklish issue of relativism. Even when not explicitly recognized as such, this issue has been the skeleton in the closet for every philosophical moralist since the time of Plato and the Sophists: for the critical implications of the fact of the diversity and discordance between moral precepts and moral codes in different societies are inescapable. Yet it is difficult to pin down the precise relevance of these differences for morals. To the layman it seems obvious that the lack of universal agreement concerning morals derogates somehow from their validity; in particular he is ready to think twice about a moral precept if it appears to him as a purely local or provincial custom. And yet, on the other hand, he is willing to acknowledge some truth in the ancient maxim: "When in Rome do as the Romans do"! Thus already for the layman there is a kind of ambiguous message conveyed by the facts of cultural relativism. Quite significantly, however, this same kind of ambiguity is incorporated into the leading ideology of our times, namely Marxism, which, as 'scientific socialist,' is based on the relativity of ideologies and social relations.

Despite the natural perplexities and practical challenges that appear to arise from the facts of cultural diversity and relativity, discussions by moral philosophers of their relevance to ethics are curiously vapid and, it seems to me, beside the point. If, as is maintained by some, cultural relativism somehow undermines ethics, it is necessary to show how and why it does so, and this has not been done. On the other hand, if, as others maintain, cultural relativism is totally irrelevant to ethics, as irrelevant, perhaps, as is the fact of diversity of human beliefs concerning the causes of tuberculosis to the latest expert opinion or medical science, then why does this fact create so much uneasiness among philosophers and laymen alike? Finally, there are some who try to cope with cultural relativity by denying it, that is, by maintaining that basically there is no real disagreement between people of different cultures concerning morals. Why, we may ask, are they so anxious to refute cultural relativism? These three attitudes appear to comprehend all of the prevalent conceptions of the relevance of cultural relativity to ethics, yet none of them is very satisfactory. The reason for this is that the issue of relativism has never been stated clearly. . . .

Let us begin by defining 'cultural relativism.' I shall assume that this is an anthropological doctrine which is scientific and empirical in nature and which rests on actual observations of other cultures and on related psychological and sociological theories. Consequently, I regard cultural relativism as itself a descriptive theory and in this sense neutral as far as evaluations are concerned. (This is, of course, not to deny that it may be relevant to ethics and evaluations in general. If 'cultural relativism' is defined as an ethical doctrine, as it is by some anthropologists, then the issues I want to discuss are lost in verbal quibbles.)

Cultural relativism, I shall assume, consists of two different theses, which may respectively be called the *diversity thesis* and the *relativity thesis.* The first of these, the diversity thesis, asserts that there is a diversity of moral opinions from one society to another and hence there is no *consensus gentium* concerning morals: what is regarded as right in one society is regarded as wrong in another. Furthermore, it asserts that these ethical differences relate not only to the evaluations of particular acts, but also to rules, principles, ideals, goals and character evaluations.

The second thesis, the relativity thesis, maintains that the character of people's moral opinions is to be explained by cultural and social factors of some sort, such as linguistic structure, economic determinants, psychological conditioning, psychoanalytic mechanisms, historical factors, or the unique pattern of culture of the society in question. In other words, moral opinions are relative to cultural determinants of some kind in the sense that they are casually dependent upon them. Although most contemporary cultural relativists combine these two theses, it is possible to accept one without the other. Hume, for example, would subscribe to the relativity thesis inasmuch as he presents a psychology theory of the origin of moral sentiments (opinions), although more than likely he would have denied the diversity thesis.

The question with which we shall be concerned as simply this: supposing that cultural relativism in some form or other is true, what follows with regard to ethics? A survey of the conclusions of those who stress the significance of cultural relativism for ethics reveals nothing but confusion. If I am right, then it is easy to see why this should be so, for cultural relativism is not really used to establish any simple ethical conclusion at all. Instead, it is used as a form of argument, or rather, as several forms of argument that are quite peculiar to ethics. In order to show the absurdity of supposing that cultural relativism directly establishes a conclusion of some sort, let us briefly survey some of the conclusions that it is supposed to entail.

First, cultural relativism is supposed to show that what is right for one person in one social and cultural situation is wrong for another person in another social cultural situation. There is, however, nothing especially novel about the contention that the rightness or wrongness of acts is dependent upon the agent's situation, including his social and cultural situation. It is generally agreed by moral philosophers of every school that circumstances require us to apply moral principles differently to different cases. Elsewhere I have called this phenomenon *applicational relativity.* (The accusation by social scientists that the Western ethical tradition has paid no attention to the applicational relativity of morals merely reflects their ignorance of the history of ethics.)

Now it is quite clear that the facts of cultural relativism, and cultural anthropology in general, do not prove the principle of applicational relativity, nor do they need to do so, although they may help us to use this principle more intelligently by calling our attention to the differentials that require our principles to be applied differently. The question of which situational factors are ultimately to be taken as morally relevant is, of course, a question for ethics rather than anthropology. One cannot, for example, persuasively justify the institution of polygamy in a certain society on the grounds of its effectiveness in promoting social stability if such considerations are rejected as morally irrelevant to the proper or just conception of marriage. At any rate, what is and what is not a morally relevant factor in the evaluation of institutions like marriage is an open question and one I believe it is the role of moral philosophers to discuss.

Let us assume, therefore, that the issue of relativism is not related to questions involving the principle of applicational relativity as such. Indeed, the principle of applicational relativity itself presupposes the validity of some sort of moral principle to be applied, which cannot be established by anthropology. We must therefore search elsewhere in our effort to pin down the conclusions that are supposed to follow from cultural relativism.

Sometimes it is insinuated or implied that the facts of cultural relativity lead us in a new way to recognize the importance of tolerance and mutual understanding. Through the recognition of cultural relativity, we shall arrive then at a more realistic social faith, accepting as grounds of hope and as new bases for tolerance the coexisting and equally valid patterns of life which mankind has created for itself from the raw materials of existence. "The very core of cultural relativism is the social discipline that comes of respect for differences—of mutual respect." The principle of tolerance and of mutual respect is itself, however, an ethical principle, not an anthropological truth, and if I am not mistaken, no one supposes that it is a principle which is established by cultural relativism. Rather, cultural relativism merely provides ammunition for the 'attack' on certain accepted ethical dogmas, namely, those that are incompatible with tolerance. . . .

It is obvious by now that the decisive and distinctive import for ethics of the facts of cultural relativity hinges on the assumption of an intimate, perhaps even logical connection between people's moral opinions and the rightness and wrongness of their actions; for it is clear that cultural relativism, insofar as it relates to what is thought to be right or wrong in different societies, will be relevant to ethics only if it is assumed that moral opinion reflects, constitutes, validates or in some other way determines moral principle. Science and other standard types of knowledge do not admit this kind of assumption; it would be highly irregular indeed to try to prove or disprove a scientific hypothesis by reference to popular opinion! (This statement will require slight modification later.) The kind of assumed relationship between moral opinion and moral principle that we are concerned with here is much more like the relationship holding between opinion and rule, say, in etiquette. In matters of etiquette the opinion of the upper social classes is authoritative and determines what is socially proper or improper: what is considered to be proper or improper is no different from what actually is proper or improper. (To quote Hamlet: "There is nothing either good or bad but thinking makes it so.")

Marilyn Friedman, "Beyond Caring: The Demoralization of Gender" in *Canadian Journal of Philosophy,*
Supp. Vol. 13, M. Haner and K. Nielsen (eds.), 1987

Overcoming Gender in Ethics
Marilyn Friedman

Carol Gilligan heard a "distinct moral language" in the voices of women who were subjects in her studies of moral reasoning.[1] Though herself a developmental psychologist, Gilligan has put her mark on contemporary feminist moral philosophy by daring to claim the competence of this voice and the worth of its message. Her book, *In a Different Voice,* which one theorist has aptly described as a bestseller[2] explored the concern with care and relationships which Gilligan discerned in the moral reasoning of women and contrasted it with the orientation toward justice and rights which she found to typify the moral reasoning of men.

According to Gilligan, the standard (or "male") moral voice articulated in moral psychology derives moral judgments about particular cases from abstract, universalized moral rules and principles which are substantively concerned with justice and rights. For justice reasoners: the major moral imperative enjoins respect for the rights of others (100); the concept of duty is limited to reciprocal noninterference (147); the motivating vision is one of the equal worth of self and other (63); and one important underlying presupposition is a highly individuated conception of persons.

By contrast, the other (or "female") moral voice which Gilligan heard in her studies eschews abstract rules and principles. This moral voice derives moral judgments from the contextual detail of situations grasped as specific and unique (100). The substantive concern for this moral voice is care and responsibility, particularly as these arise in the context of interpersonal relationships (19). Moral judgments, for care reasoners, are tied to feelings of empathy and compassion (69); the major moral imperatives center around caring, not hurting others, and avoiding selfishness (90); and the motivating vision of this ethic is "that everyone will be responded to and included, that no one will be left alone or hurt" (63).

While these two voices are not necessarily contradictory in all respects, they seem, at the very least, to be different in their orientation. Gilligan's writings about the differences have stimulated extensive feminist reconsideration of various ethical themes.[3] In this paper, I use Gilligan's work as a springboard for extending certain of those themes in new directions . . . I will explore a different reason why actual women and men may not show a divergence of reasoning along the care-justice dichotomy, namely, that the notions of care and justice overlap more than Gilligan, among others, has realized. I will suggest, in particular, that morally adequate care involves considerations of justice. Thus, the concerns captured by these two moral categories do not define necessarily distinct moral perspectives, in practice . . . People who treat each other justly can also care about each other. Conversely, personal relationships are arenas in which people have rights to certain forms of treatment, and in which fairness can be reflected in ongoing interpersonal mutuality. It is this latter insight—the relevance of justice to close personal relationships—which I will emphasize here.

Justice, at the most general level, is a matter of giving people their due, of treating them appropriately. Justice is relevant to personal relationships and to care precisely to the extent that considerations of justice itself determine appropriate ways to treat friends or intimates. Justice as it bears on relationships among friends or family, or on other close personal ties, might not involve duties which are universalizable, in the sense of being owed to all persons simply in virtue of shared moral personhood. But this does not entail the irrelevance of justice among friends or intimates.

Moral thinking has not always dissociated the domain of justice from that of close personal relationships. The earliest Greek code of justice placed friendship at the forefront of conditions for the realization of justice, and construed the rules of justice as being coextensive with the limits of friendship. The reader will recall that one of the first definitions of justice which Plato sought to contest, in the *Republic*, is that of "helping one's friends and harming one's enemies."[4] Although the ancient Greek model of justice among friends reserved that moral privilege for free-born Greek males, the conception is, nevertheless, instructive for its readiness to link the notion of justice to relationships based on affection and loyalty. This provides an important contrast to modern notions of justice which are often deliberately constructed so as to avoid presumptions of mutual concern on the parts of those to whom the conception is to apply.

As is well known, John Rawls, for one, requires that the parties to the original position in which justice is to be negotiated be mutually disinterested.[5] Each party is assumed, first and foremost, to be concerned for the advancement of her own interests and to care about the interests of others only to the extent that her own interests require it. This postulate of mutual disinterestedness is intended by Rawls to ensure that the principles of justice do not depend on what he calls "strong assumptions," such as "extensive ties of natural sentiment."[6] Rawls is seeking principles of justice which apply to everyone in all their social interrelationships, *whether or not* characterized by affection and a concern for each other's well-being. While such an account promises to disclose duties of justice owed to all other parties to the social contract, it may fail to uncover special duties of justice which arise in close personal relationships the foundation of which is affection or kinship, rather than contract. The methodological device of assuming mutual disinterest might blind us to the role of justice among mutually interested and/or intimate parties.

Gilligan herself has suggested that mature reasoning about care incorporates considerations of justice and rights. But Gilligan's conception of what this means is highly limited. It appears to involve simply the recognition "that self and other are equal," a notion which serves to override the problematic tendency of the ethic of care to become *self-sacrificing* care in women's practices. However, important as it may be, this notion hardly does justice to justice.

There are several ways in which justice pertains to close personal relationships. The first two ways which I will mention are largely appropriate only among friends, relatives, or intimates who are of comparable development in their realization of moral personhood, for example, who are both mature responsible adults. The third sort of relevance of justice to close relationships, which I will discuss shortly, pertains to families, in which adults often interrelate with children—a more challenging domain for the application of justice. But first the easier task.

One sort of role for justice in close relationships among people of comparable moral personhood may be discerned by considering that a personal relationship is a miniature social system, which provides valued mutual intimacy, support, and concern for those who are involved. The maintenance of a relationship requires effort by the participants. One intimate may bear a much greater burden for sustaining a relationship than the other participant(s) and may derive less support, concern, and so forth than she deserves for her efforts. Justice sets a constraint on such relationships by calling for an appropriate sharing, among the participants, of the benefits and burdens which constitute their relationship.

Marilyn Frye, for example, has discussed what amounts to a pattern of *violation* of this requirement of justice in heterosexual relationships. She has argued that women of all races, social classes, and societies can be defined as a coherent group in terms of a distinctive function which is culturally assigned to them. This function is, in Frye's words, "the service of men and men's interests as men define them."[7] This service work includes personal service (satisfaction of routine bodily needs, such as hunger, and other mundane tasks), sexual and reproductive service, and ego service. Says Frye,". . . at every race/class level and even across race/class lines men do not serve women as women serve men."[8] Frye is, of course, generalizing over society and culture, and the sweep of her generalization encompasses both ongoing close personal relationships as well as other relationships which are not close or are not carried on beyond specific transactions, for example, that of prostitute to client. By excluding those latter cases for the time being, and applying Frye's analysis to familial and other close ties between women and men, we may discern the sort of one-sided relational exploitation, often masquerading in the guise of love or care, which constitutes this first sort of injustice.

Justice is relevant to close personal relationships among comparable moral persons in a second way as well. The trust and intimacy which characterize special relationships create special vulnerabilities to harm. Commonly recognized harms, such as physical injury and sexual assault, become more feasible; and special relationships, in corrupt, abusive, or degenerate forms, make possible certain uncommon emotional harms not even possible in impersonal relationships. When someone is harmed in a personal relationship, she is owed a rectification of some sort, a righting of the wrong which has been done her. The notion of justice emerges, once again, as a relevant moral notion.

Thus, in a close relationship among persons of comparable moral personhood, care may degenerate into the injustices of exploitation, or oppression. Many such problems have been given wide public scrutiny recently as a result of feminist analysis of various aspects of family life and sexual relationships. Woman-battering, acquaintance rape, and sexual harassment are but a few of the many recently publicized injustices of "personal" life. The notion of distributive or corrective injustice seems almost too mild to capture these indignities, involving, as they do, violation of bodily integrity and an assumption of the right to assault and injure. But to call these harms injustices is certainly not to rule out impassioned moral criticism in other terms as well.

The two requirements of justice which I have just discussed exemplify the standard distinction between distributive and corrective justice. They illustrate the role of justice in personal relationships regarded in abstraction from a social context. Personal relationships may also be regarded in the context of their various institutional settings, such as marriage and family. Here justice emerges again as a relevant ideal, its role being to define appropriate institutions to structure interactions among family members, other household cohabitants, and intimates in general. The family, for example,[9] is a miniature society, exhibiting all the major facets of large-scale social life: decision-making affecting the whole unit; executive action; judgments of guilt and innocence; reward and punishment; allocation of responsibilities and privileges, of burdens and benefits; and monumental influences on the life-chances of both its maturing and its matured members. Any of these features *alone* would invoke the relevance of justice; together, they make the case overwhelming.

Women's historically paradigmatic role of mothering has provided a multitude of insights which can be reconstructed as insights about the importance of justice in family relationships, especially those relationships involving remarkable disparities in maturity, capability, and power.[10] In these familial relationships, one party grows into moral personhood over time, gradually acquiring the capacity to be a responsible moral agent. Considerations of justice pertain to the mothering of children in numerous ways. For one thing, there may be siblings to deal with, whose demands and conflicts create the context for parental arbitration and the need for a fair allotment of responsibilities and privileges. Then there are decisions to be made, involving the well-being of all persons in the family unit, whose immature members become increasingly capable over time of participating in such administrative affairs. Of special importance in the practice of raising children are the duties to nurture and to promote growth and maturation. These duties may be seen as counterparts to the welfare rights viewed by many as a matter of social justice.[11] Motherhood continually presents its practitioners with moral problems best seen in terms of a complex framework which integrates justice with care, even though the politico-legal discourse of justice has not shaped its domestic expression.[12]

I have been discussing the relevance of justice to close personal relationships. A few words about my companion thesis—the relevance of care to the public domain—is also in order.[13] In its more noble manifestation, care in the public realm would show itself, perhaps, in foreign aid, welfare programs, famine or disaster relief, or other social programs designed to relieve suffering and attend to human needs. If untempered by justice in the public domain, care degenerates precipitously. The infamous "boss" of Chicago's old-time Democratic machine, Mayor Richard J. Daley, was legendary for his nepotism and political partisanship; he cared extravagantly for his relatives, friends, and political cronies.[14]

In recounting the moral reasoning of one of her research subjects, Gilligan once wrote that the "justice" perspective fails "to take into account the reality of relationships" (147). What she meant is that the "justice" perspective emphasizes a self's various rights to noninterference by others. Gilligan worried that if this is all that a concern for justice involved, then such a perspective would disregard the moral value of positive interaction, connection, and commitment among persons.

However, Gilligan's interpretation of justice is far too limited. For one thing, it fails to recognize positive rights, such as welfare rights, which may be endorsed from a "justice" perspective. But beyond this minor point, a more important problem is Gilligan's failure to acknowledge the potential for *violence and harm* in human interrelationships and human community.[15] The concept of justice, in general, arises out of relational conditions in which most human beings have the capacity, and many have the inclination, to treat each other badly.

Thus, notions of distributive justice are impelled by the realization that people who together comprise a social system may not share fairly in the benefits and burdens of their social cooperation. Conceptions of rectificatory, or corrective, justice are founded on the concern that when harms are done, action should be taken either to restore those harmed as fully as possible to their previous state, or to prevent further similar harm, or both. And the specific rights which people are variously thought to have are just so many manifestations of our interest in identifying ways in which people deserve protection against harm by others. The complex reality of social life encompasses the human potential for helping, caring for, and nurturing others *as well as* the potential for harming, exploiting, and oppressing others. Thus, Gilligan is wrong to think that the justice perspective completely neglects "the reality of relationships." Rather, it arises from a more complex, and more realistic, estimate of the nature of human interrelationship.

In light of these reflections, it seems wise both to reconsider the seeming dichotomy of care and justice, and to question the moral adequacy of either orientation dissociated from the other. Our aim would be to advance "beyond caring," that is, beyond *mere* caring dissociated from a concern for justice. In addition, we would do well to progress beyond gender stereotypes which assign distinct and different moral roles to women and men. Our ultimate goal should be a non-gendered, non-dichotomized, moral framework in which all moral concerns could be expressed. We might, with intentional irony, call this project, "de-moralizing the genders."

Notes

1. *In a Different Voice* (Cambridge, MA: Harvard University Press 1982), 73. More recently, the following works by Gilligan on related issues have also appeared: "Do the Social Sciences Have an Adequate Theory of Moral Development?" in Norma Haan, Robert N. Bellah, Paul Rabinow and William M. Sullivan, eds., *Social Science as Moral Inquiry* (New York: Columbia University Press 1983), 33–51; "Reply," *Signs* 11 (1986), 324–33; and "Remapping the Moral Domain: New Images of the Self in Relationship," in Thomas C. Heller, Morton Sosna and David E. Wellbery, eds., *Reconstructing Individualism* (Stanford, CA: Stanford University Press 1986) 237–52. Throughout this paper, all page references inserted in the text are to *In a Different Voice*.

2. Frigga Haug, "Morals Also Have Two Genders," trans. Rodney Livingstone, *New Left Review* 143 (1984), 55.

3. These sources include: Owen J. Flanagan, Jr. and Jonathan E. Adler, "Impartiality and Particularity," *Social Research* 50 (1983), 576–96; Nel Noddings, *Caring* (Berkeley: University of California Press 1984); Claudia Card, "Virtues and Moral Luck" (unpublished paper presented at American Philosophical Association, Western Division Meetings, Chicago, IL, April 1985, and at the Conference on Virtue Theory, University of San Diego, San Diego, CA, February 1986); Marilyn Friedman, *Care and Context in Moral Reasoning*, MOSAIC Monograph #1 (Bath, England: University of Bath 1985), reprinted in Carol Harding, ed., *Moral Dilemmas* (Chicago: Precedent 1986), 25–42, and in Diana T. Meyers and Eva Feder Kittay, eds., *Women and Moral Theory* (Totowa, NJ: Rowman and Littlefield 1987), 190–204; all the papers in Meyers and Kittay; Linda K. Kerber, "Some Cautionary Words for Historians," *Signs* 11 (1986), 304-10; Catherine G. Greeno and Eleanor E. Maccoby, "How Different IS the "Different Voice," *Signs* 11 (1986), 310–16; Zella Luria, "A Methodological Critique," *Signs* 11 (1986), 316–21; Carol B. Stack, "The Culture of Gender: Women and Men of Color," *Signs* 11 (1986), 321–4; Owen Flanagan and Kathryn Jackson, "Justice, Care, and Gender: The Kohlberg-Gilligan Debate Revisited," *Ethics* 97 (1987). 622–37. An analysis of this issue from an ambiguously feminist standpoint is to be found in: John M. Broughton, "Women's Rationality and Men's Virtues," *Social Research* 50 (1983), 597–642. For a helpful review of some of these issues, cf. Jean Grimshaw, *Philosophy and Feminist Thinking* (Minneapolis: University of Minnesota Press 1986). esp. chs. 7 and 8.

4. Book 1, 322–35. A thorough discussion of the Greek conception of justice in the context of friendship can be found in Horst Hutter, *Politics as Friendship* (Waterloo, ON: Wilfrid Laurier University Press 1978).

5. Rawls, *A Theory of Justice*, 13 and elsewhere.

6. Ibid., 129.

7. *The Politics of Reality* (Trumansburg, NY: The Crossing Press 1983) 9.

8. *Ibid.*, 10.

9. For an important discussion of the relevance of justice to the family, cf. Susan Moller Okin, "Justice and Gender," *Philosophy and Public Affairs* 16 (1987), 42–72.

10. For insightful discussions of the distinctive modes of thought to which mothering gives rise, cf. Sara Ruddick, "Maternal Thinking," *Feminist Studies* 6 (1980) 342-67; and her "Preservative Love and Military Destruction: Some Reflections on Mothering and Peace," in Joyce Trebilcot, ed., *Mothering: Essays in Feminist Theory* (Totowa, NJ: Rowman & Allanheld 1983) 231–62; also Virginia Held, "The Obligations of Mothers and Fathers," in Trebilcot, ed. 7–20.

11. This point was suggested to me by L. W. Sumner.

12. John Broughton also discusses the concern for justice and rights which appears in women's moral reasoning as well as the concern for care and relationships featured in men's moral reasoning; "Women's Rationality and Men's Virtues," esp. 603–22. For a historical discussion of male theorists who have failed to hear the concern for justice in women's voices, cf. Carole Pateman, "'The Disorder of Women': Women, Love, and the Sense of Justice," *Ethics* 91 (1980), 20–34.

13. This discussion owes a debt to Francesca M. Cancian's warning that we should not narrow our conception of love to the recognized ways in which women love, which researchers find to center around the expression of feelings and verbal disclosure. Such a conception ignores forms of love which are stereotyped as characteristically male, including instrumental help and the sharing of activities. Cf. "The Feminization of Love," *Signs* 11 (1986), 692–709.

14. Cf. Mike Royko. *Boss: Richard J. Daley of Chicago* (New York: New American Library 1971).

15. Claudia Card has critiqued Gilligan's work for ignoring, in particular, the dismaying harms to which women have historically been subjected in heterosexual relationships, including, but by no means limited to, marriage ("Virtues and Moral Luck," 15–17).

Part Two

ETHICS IN PRACTICE

WEALTH, POVERTY, AND SOCIAL INJUSTICE

Peter Singer, "Famine, Affluence, and Morality" in *Philosophy and Public Affairs*, Spring 1972

Famine, Affluence, and Morality
Peter Singer

As I write this, in November 1971, people are dying in East Bengal from lack of food, shelter, and medical care. The suffering and death that are occurring there now are not inevitable, not unavoidable in any fatalistic sense of the term. Constant poverty, a cyclone, and a civil war have turned at least nine million people into destitute refugees; nevertheless, it is not beyond the capacity of the richer nations to give enough assistance to reduce any further suffering to very small proportions. The decisions and actions of human beings can prevent this kind of suffering. Unfortunately, human beings have not made the necessary decisions. At the individual level, people have, with very few exceptions, not responded to the situation in any significant way. Generally speaking, people have not given large sums to relief funds; they have not written to their parliamentary representatives demanding increased government assistance; they have not demonstrated in the streets, held symbolic fasts, or done anything else directed toward providing the refugees with the means to satisfy their essential needs. At the government level, no government has given the sort of massive aid that would enable the refugees to survive for more than a few days. Britain, for instance, has given rather more than most countries. It has, to date, given £14,750,000. For comparative purposes, Britain's share of the nonrecoverable development costs of the Anglo-French Concorde project is already in excess of £275,000,000, and on present estimates will reach £440,000,000. The implication is that the British government values a supersonic transport more than thirty times as highly as it values the lives of the nine million refugees. Australia is another country which, on a per capita basis, is well up in the "aid to Bengal" table. Australia's aid, however, amounts to less than one-twelfth of the cost of Sydney's new opera house. The total amount given, from all sources, now stands at about £65,000,000. The estimated cost of keeping the refugees alive for one year is £464,000,000. Most of the refugees have now been in the camps for more than six months. The World Bank has said that India needs a minimum of £300,000,000 in assistance from other countries before the end of the year. It seems obvious that assistance on this scale will not be forthcoming. India will be forced to choose between letting the refugees starve or diverting funds from her own development program, which will mean that more of her own people will starve in the future.[1]

These are the essential facts about the present situation in Bengal. So far as it concerns us here, there is nothing unique about this situation except its magnitude. The Bengal emergency is just the latest and most acute of a series of major emergencies in various parts of the world, arising both from natural and from man-made causes. There are also many parts of the world in which people die from malnutrition and lack of food independent of any special emergency. I take Bengal as my example only because it is the present concern, and because the size of the problem has ensured that it has been given adequate publicity. Neither individuals nor governments can claim to be unaware of what is happening there.

What are the moral implications of a situation like this? In what follows, I shall argue that the way people in relatively affluent countries react to a situation like that in Bengal cannot be justified; indeed, the whole way we look at moral issues—our moral conceptual scheme— needs to be altered, and with it, the way of life that has come to be taken for granted in our society.

In arguing for this conclusion I will not, of course, claim to be morally neutral. I shall, however, try to argue for the moral position that I take, so that anyone who accepts certain assumptions, to be made explicit, will, I hope, accept my conclusion.

I begin with the assumption that suffering and death from lack of food, shelter, and medical care are bad. I think most people will agree about this, although one may reach the same view by different routes. I shall not argue for this view. People can hold all sorts of eccentric positions, and perhaps from some of them it would not follow that death by starvation is in itself bad. It is difficult, perhaps impossible, to refute such positions, and so for brevity I will henceforth take this assumption as accepted. Those who disagree need read no further.

My next point is this: if it is in our power to prevent something bad from happening, without thereby sacrificing anything of comparable moral importance, we ought, morally, to do it. By "without sacrificing anything of comparable moral importance" I mean without causing anything else comparably bad to happen, or doing something that is wrong in itself, or failing to promote some moral good, comparable in significance to the bad thing that we can prevent. This principle seems almost as uncontroversial as the last one. It requires us only to prevent what is bad, and not to promote what is good, and it requires this of us only when we can do it without sacrificing anything that is, from the moral point of view, comparably important. I could even, as far as the application of my argument to the Bengal emergency is concerned, qualify the point so as to make it: if it is in our power to prevent something very bad from happening, without thereby sacrificing anything morally significant, we ought, morally, to do it. An application of this principle would be as follows: if I am walking past a shallow pond and see a child drowning in it, I ought to wade in and pull the child out. This will mean getting my clothes muddy, but this is insignificant, while the death of the child would presumably be a very bad thing.

The uncontroversial appearance of the principle just stated is deceptive. If it were acted upon, even in its qualified form, our lives, our society, and our world would be fundamentally changed. For the principle takes, firstly, no account of proximity or distance. It makes no moral difference whether the person I can help is a neighbor's child ten yards from me or a Bengali whose name I shall never know, ten thousand miles away. Secondly, the principle makes no distinction between cases in which I am the only person who could possibly do anything and cases in which I am just one among millions in the same position.

I do not think I need to say much in defense of the refusal to take proximity and distance into account. The fact that a person is physically near to us, so that we have personal contact with him, may make it more likely that we *shall* assist him, but this does not show that we *ought* to help him rather than another who happens to be further away. If we accept any principle of impartiality, universalizability, equality, or whatever, we cannot discriminate against someone merely because he is far away from us (or we are far away from him). Admittedly, it is possible that we are in a better position to judge what needs to be done to help a person near to us than one far away, and perhaps also to provide the assistance we judge to be necessary. If this were the case, it would be a reason for helping those near to us first. This may once have been a justification for being more concerned with the poor in one's own town than with famine victims in India. Unfortunately for those who like to keep their moral responsibilities limited, instant communication and swift transportation have changed the situation. From the moral point of view, the development of the world into a "global village" has made an important, though still unrecognized, difference to our moral situation. Expert observers and supervisors, sent out by famine relief organizations or permanently stationed in famine-prone areas, can direct our aid to a refugee in Bengal almost as effectively as we could get it to someone in our own block. There would seem, therefore, to be no possible justification for discriminating on geographical grounds.

There may be a greater need to defend the second implication of my principle—that the fact that there are millions of other people in the same position, in respect to the Bengali refugees, as I am, does not make the situation significantly different from a situation in which I am the only person who can prevent something very bad from occurring. Again, of course, I admit that there is a psychological difference between the cases; one feels less guilty about doing nothing if one can point to others, similarly placed, who have also done nothing. Yet this can make no real difference to our moral obligations.[2] Should I consider that I am less obliged to pull the drowning child out of the pond if on looking around I see other people, no further away than I am, who have also noticed the child but are doing nothing? One has only to ask this question to see the absurdity of the view that numbers lessen obligation. It is a view that is an ideal excuse for inactivity; unfortunately most of the major evils—poverty, over-population, pollution—are problems in which everyone is almost equally involved.

The view that numbers do make a difference can be made plausible if stated in this way: if everyone in circumstances like mine gave £5 to the Bengal Relief Fund, there would be enough to provide food, shelter, and medical care for the refugees; there is no reason why I should give more than anyone else in the same circumstances as I am; therefore I have no obligation to give more than £5. Each premise in this argument is true, and the argument looks sound. It may convince us, unless we notice that it is based on a hypothetical premise, although the conclusion is not stated hypothetically. The argument would be sound if the conclusion were: if everyone in circumstances like mine were to give £5, I would have no obligation to give more than £5. If the conclusion were so stated, however, it would be obvious that the argument has no bearing on a situation in which it is not the case that everyone else gives £5. This, of course, is the actual situation. It is more or less certain that not everyone in circumstances like mine will give £5. So there will not be enough to provide the needed food, shelter, and medical care. Therefore by giving more than £5 I will prevent more suffering than I would if I gave just £5.

It might be thought that this argument has an absurd consequence. Since the situation appears to be that very few people are likely to give substantial amounts, it follows that I and everyone else in similar circumstances ought to give as much as possible, that is, at least up to the point at which by giving more one would begin to cause serious suffering for oneself and one's dependents—perhaps even beyond this point to the point of marginal utility, at which by giving more one would cause oneself and one's dependents as much suffering as one would prevent in Bengal. If everyone does this, however, there will be more than can be used for the benefit of the refugees, and some of the sacrifice will have been unnecessary. Thus, if everyone does what he ought to do, the result will not be as good as it would be if everyone did a little less than he ought to do, or if only some do all that they ought to do.

The paradox here arises only if we assume that the actions in question—sending money to the relief funds—are performed more or less simultaneously, and are also unexpected. For if it is to be expected that everyone is going to contribute something, then clearly each is not obliged to give as much as he would have been obliged to had others not been giving too. And if everyone is not acting more or less simultaneously, then those giving later will know how much more is needed, and will have no obligation to give more than is necessary to reach this amount. To say this is not to deny the principle that people in the same circumstances have the same obligations, but to point out that the fact that others have given, or may be expected to give, is a relevant circumstance: those giving after it has become known that many others are giving and those giving before are not in the same circumstances. So the seemingly absurd consequence of the principle I have put forward can occur only if people are in error about the actual circumstances—that is, if they think they are giving when others are not, but in fact they are giving when others are. The result of everyone doing what he really ought to do cannot be worse than the result of everyone doing less than he ought to do, although the result of everyone doing what he reasonably believes he ought to do could be.

If my argument so far has been sound, neither our distance from a preventable evil nor the number of other people who, in respect to that evil, are in the same situation as we are, lessens our obligation to mitigate or prevent that evil. I shall therefore take as established the principle I asserted earlier. As I have already said, I need to assert it only in its qualified form: if it is in our power to prevent something very bad from happening, without thereby sacrificing anything else morally significant, we ought, morally, to do it.

The outcome of this argument is that our traditional moral categories are upset. The traditional distinction between duty and charity cannot be drawn, or at least, not in the place we normally draw it. Giving money to the Bengal Relief Fund is regarded as an act of charity in our society. The bodies which collect money are known as "charities." These organizations see themselves in this way—if you send them a check, you will be thanked for your "generosity." Because giving money is regarded as an act of charity, it is not thought that there is anything wrong with not giving. The charitable man may be praised, but the man who is not charitable is not condemned. People do not feel in any way ashamed or guilty about spending money on new clothes or a new car instead of giving it to famine relief. (Indeed, the alternative does not occur to them.) This way of looking at the matter cannot be justified. When we buy new clothes not to keep ourselves warm but to look "well-dressed" we are not providing for any important need. We would not be sacrificing anything significant if we were to continue to wear our old clothes, and give the money to famine relief. By doing so, we would be preventing another person from starving. It follows from what I have said earlier that we ought to give money away, rather than spend it on clothes which we do not need to keep us warm. To do so is not charitable, or generous. Nor is it the kind of act which philosophers and theologians have called "supererogatory"—an act which it would be good to do, but not wrong not to do. On the contrary, we ought to give the money away, and it is wrong not to do so.

I am not maintaining that there are no acts which are charitable, or that there are no acts which it would be good to do but not wrong not to do. It may be possible to redraw the distinction between duty and charity in some other place. All I am arguing here is that the present way of drawing the distinction, which makes it an act of charity for a man living at the level of affluence which most people in the "developed nations" enjoy to give money to save someone else from starvation, cannot be supported. It is beyond the scope of my argument to consider whether the distinction should be redrawn or abolished altogether. There would be many other possible ways of drawing the distinction—for instance, one might decide that it is good to make other people as happy as possible, but not wrong not to do so.

Despite the limited nature of the revision in our moral conceptual scheme which I am proposing, the revision would, given the extent of both affluence and famine in the world today, have radical implications. These implications may lead to further objections, distinct from those I have already considered. I shall discuss two of these.

One objection to the position I have taken might be simply that it is too drastic a revision of our moral scheme. People do not ordinarily judge in the way I have suggested they should. Most people reserve their moral condemnation for those who violate some moral norm, such as the norm against taking another person's property. They do not condemn those who indulge in luxury instead of giving to famine relief. But given that I did not set out to present a morally neutral description of the way people make moral judgments, the way people do in fact judge has nothing to do with the validity of my conclusion. My conclusion follows from the principle which I advanced earlier, and unless that principle is rejected, or the arguments shown to be unsound, I think the conclusion must stand, however strange it appears.

It might, nevertheless, be interesting to consider why our society, and most other societies, do judge differently from the way I have suggested they should. In a well-known article, J. O. Urmson suggests that the imperatives of duty, which tell us what we must do, as distinct from what it would be good to do but not wrong not to do, function so as to prohibit behavior that is intolerable if men are to live together in society.[3] This may explain the origin and continued existence of the present division between acts of duty and acts of charity. Moral attitudes are shaped by the needs of society, and no doubt society needs people who will observe the rules that make social existence tolerable. From the point of view of a particular society, it is essential to prevent violations of norms against killing, stealing, and so on. It is quite inessential, however, to help people outside one's own society.

If this is an explanation of our common distinction between duty and supererogation, however, it is not a justification of it. The moral point of view requires us to look beyond the interests of our own society. Previously, as I have already mentioned, this may hardly have been feasible, but it is quite feasible now. From the moral point of view, the prevention of the starvation of millions of people outside our society must be considered at least as pressing as the upholding of property norms within our society.

It has been argued by some writers, among them Sidgwick and Urmson, that we need to have a basic moral code which is not too far beyond the capacities of the ordinary man, for otherwise there will be a general breakdown of compliance with the moral code. Crudely stated, this argument suggests that if we tell people that they ought to refrain from murder and give everything they do not really need to famine relief, they will do neither, whereas if we tell them that they ought to refrain from murder and that it is good to give to famine relief but not wrong not to do so, they will at least refrain from murder. The issue here is: Where should we drawn the line between conduct that is required and conduct that is good although not required, so as to get the best possible result? This would seem to be an empirical question, although a very difficult one. One objection to the Sidgwick-Urmson line of argument is that it takes insufficient account of the effect that moral standards can have on the decisions we make. Given a society in which a wealthy man who gives five percent of his income to famine relief is regarded as most generous, it is not surprising that a proposal that we all ought to give away half our incomes will be thought to be absurdly unrealistic. In a society which held that no man should have more than enough while others have less than they need, such a proposal might seem narrow-minded. What it is possible for a man to do and what he is likely to do are both, I think, very greatly influenced by what people around him are doing and expecting him to do. In any case, the possibility that by spreading the idea that we ought to be doing very much more than we are to relieve famine we shall bring about a general breakdown of moral behavior seems remote. If the stakes are an end to widespread starvation, it is worth the risk. Finally, it should be emphasized that these considerations are relevant only to the issue of what we should require from others, and not to what we ourselves ought to do.

The second objection to my attack on the present distinction between duty and charity is one which has from time to time been made against utilitarianism. It follows from some forms of utilitarian theory that we all ought, morally, to be working full time to increase the balance of happiness over misery. The position I have taken here would not lead to this conclusion in all circumstances, for if there were no bad occurrences that we could prevent without sacrificing something of comparable moral importance, my argument would have no application. Given the present conditions in many parts of the world, however, it does follow from my argument that we ought, morally, to be working full time to relieve great suffering of the sort that occurs as a result of famine or other disasters. Of course, mitigating circumstances can be adduced—for instance, that if we wear ourselves out through overwork, we shall be less effective than we would otherwise have been. Nevertheless, when all considerations of this sort have been taken into account, the conclusion remains: we ought to be preventing as much suffering as we can without sacrificing something else of comparable moral importance. This conclusion is one which we may be reluctant to face. I cannot see, though, why it should be regarded as a criticism of the position for which I have argued, rather than a criticism of our ordinary standards of behavior. Since most people are self-interested to some degree, very few of us are likely to do everything that we ought to do. It would, however, hardly be honest to take this as evidence that it is not the case that we ought to do it.

It may still be thought that my conclusions are so wildly out of line with what everyone else thinks and has always thought that there must be something wrong with the argument somewhere. In order to show that my conclusions, while certainly contrary to contemporary Western moral standards, would not have seemed so extraordinary at other times and in other places, I would like to quote a passage from a writer not normally thought of as a way-out radical, Thomas Aquinas.

> Now, according to the natural order instituted by divine providence, material goods are provided for the satisfaction of human needs. Therefore the division and appropriation of property, which proceeds from human law, must not hinder the satisfaction of man's necessity from such goods. Equally, whatever a man has in superabundance is owed, of natural fight, to the poor for their sustenance. So Ambrosius says, and it is also to be found in the *Decretum Gratiani:* "The bread which you withhold belongs to the hungry; the clothing you shut away, to the naked; and the money you bury in the earth is the redemption and freedom of the penniless."[4]

I now want to consider a number of points, more practical than philosophical, which are relevant to the application of the moral conclusion we have reached. These points challenge not the idea that we ought to be doing all we can to prevent starvation, but the idea that giving away a great deal of money is the best means to this end.

It is sometimes said that overseas aid should be a government responsibility, and that therefore one ought not to give to privately run charities. Giving privately, it is said, allows the government and the noncontributing members of society to escape their responsibilities.

This argument seems to assume that the more people there are who give to privately organized famine relief funds, the less likely it is that the government will take over full responsibility for such aid. This assumption is unsupported, and does not strike me as at all plausible. The opposite view—that if no one gives voluntarily, a government will assume that its citizens are uninterested in famine relief and would not wish to be forced into giving aid— seems more plausible. In any case, unless there were a definite probability that by refusing to give one would be helping to bring about massive government assistance, people who do refuse to make voluntary contributions are refusing to prevent a certain amount of suffering without being able to point to any tangible beneficial consequence of their refusal. So the onus of showing how their refusal will bring about government action is on those who refuse to give.

I do not, of course, want to dispute the contention that governments of affluent nations should be giving many times the amount of genuine, no-strings-attached aid that they are giving now. I agree, too, that giving privately is not enough, and that we ought to be campaigning actively for entirely new standards for both public and private contributions to famine relief. Indeed, I would sympathize with someone who thought that campaigning was more important than giving oneself, although I doubt whether preaching what one does not practice would be very effective. Unfortunately, for many people the idea that "it's the government's responsibility" is a reason for not giving which does not appear to entail any political action either.

Another, more serious reason for not giving to famine relief funds is that until there is effective population control, relieving famine merely postpones starvation. If we save the Bengal refugees now, others, perhaps the children of these refugees, will face starvation in a few years' time. In support of this, one may cite the now well-known facts about the population explosion and the relatively limited scope for expanded production.

This point, like the previous one, is an argument against relieving suffering that is happening now, because of a belief about what might happen in the future; it is unlike the previous point in that very good evidence can be adduced in support of this belief about the future. I will not go into the evidence here. I accept that the earth cannot support indefinitely a population rising at the present rate. This certainly poses a problem for anyone who thinks it important to prevent famine. Again, however, one could accept the argument without drawing the conclusion that it absolves one from any obligation to do anything to prevent famine. The conclusion that should be drawn is that the best means of preventing famine, in the long run, is population control. It would then follow from the position reached earlier that one ought to be doing all one can to promote population control (unless one held that all forms of population control were wrong in themselves, or would have significantly bad consequences). Since there are organizations working specifically for population control, one would then support them rather than more orthodox methods of preventing famine.

A third point raised by the conclusion reached earlier relates to the question of just how much we all ought to be giving away. One possibility, which has already been mentioned, is that we ought to give until we reach the level of marginal utility—that is, the level at which, by giving more, I would cause as much suffering to myself or my dependents as I would relieve by my gift. This would mean, of course, that one would reduce oneself to very near the material circumstances of a Bengali refugee. It will be recalled that earlier I put forward both a strong and a moderate version of the principle of preventing bad occurrences. The strong version, which required us to prevent bad things from happening unless in doing so we would be sacrificing something of comparable moral significance, does seem to require reducing ourselves to the level of marginal utility. I should also say that the strong version seems to me to be the correct one. I proposed the more moderate version—that we should prevent bad occurrences unless, to do so, we had to sacrifice something morally significant—only in order to show that even on this surely undeniable principle a great change in our way of life is required. On the more moderate principle, it may not follow that we ought to reduce ourselves to the level of marginal utility, for one might hold that to reduce oneself and one's family to this level is to cause something significantly bad to happen. Whether this is so I shall not discuss, since, as I have said, I can see no good reason for holding the moderate version of the principle rather than the strong version. Even if we accepted the principle only in its moderate form, however, it should be clear that we would have to give away enough to ensure that the consumer society, dependent as it is on people spending on trivia rather than giving to famine relief, would slow down and perhaps disappear entirely. There are several reasons why this would be desirable in itself. The value and necessity of economic growth are now being questioned not only by conservationists, but by economists as well.[5] There is no doubt, too, that the consumer society has had a distorting effect on the goals and purposes of its members. Yet looking at the matter purely from the point of view of overseas aid, there must be a limit to the extent to which we should deliberately slow down our economy; for it might be the case that if we gave away, say, forty percent of our Gross National Product, we would slow down the economy so much that in absolute terms we would be giving less than if we gave twenty-five percent of the much larger GNP than we would have if we limited our contribution to this smaller percentage.

I mention this only as an indication of the sort of factor that one would have to take into account in working out an ideal. Since Western societies generally consider one percent of the GNP an acceptable level for overseas aid, the matter is entirely academic. Nor does it affect the question of how much an individual should give in a society in which very few are giving substantial amounts.

It is sometimes said, though less often now than it used to be, that philosophers have no special role to play in public affairs, since most public issues depend primarily on an assessment of facts. On questions of fact, it is said, philosophers as such have no special expertise, and so it has been possible to engage in philosophy without committing oneself to any position on major public issues. No doubt there are some issues of social policy and foreign policy about which it can truly be said that a really expert assessment of the facts is required before taking sides or acting, but the issue of famine is surely not one of these. The facts about the existence of suffering are beyond dispute. Nor, I think, is it disputed that we can do something about it, either through orthodox methods of famine relief or through population control or both. This is therefore an issue on which philosophers are competent to take a position. The issue is one which faces everyone who has more money than he needs to support himself and his dependents, or who is in a position to take some sort of political action. These categories must include practically every teacher and student of philosophy in the universities of the Western world. If philosophy is to deal with matters that are relevant to both teachers and students, this is an issue that philosophers should discuss.

Discussion, though, is not enough. What is the point of relating philosophy to public (and personal) affairs if we do not take our conclusions seriously? In this instance, taking our conclusion seriously means acting upon it. The philosopher will not find it any easier than anyone else to alter his attitudes and way of life to the extent that, if I am right, is involved in doing everything that we ought to be doing. At the very least, though, one can make a start. The philosopher who does so will have to sacrifice some of the benefits of the consumer society, but he can find compensation in the satisfaction of a way of life in which theory and practice, if not yet in harmony, are at least coming together.

Notes

1.   There was also a third possibility: that India would go to war to enable the refugees to return to their lands. Since I wrote this paper, India has taken this way out. The situation is no longer that described above, but this does not affect my argument, as the next paragraph indicates.

2.   In view of the special sense philosophers often give to the term, I should say that I use "obligation" simply as the abstract noun derived from "ought," so that "I have an obligation to" means no more, and no less, than "I ought to." This usage is in accordance with the definition of ought" given by the *Shorter Oxford English Dictionary*: "the general verb to express duty or obligation." I do not think any issue of substance hangs on the way the term is used; sentences in which I use "obligation" could all be rewritten, although somewhat clumsily, as sentences in which a clause containing "ought" replaces the term "obligation."

3.   J. O. Urmson, "Saints and Heroes," in *Essays in Moral Philosophy,* ed. Abraham I. Melden (Seattle and London, 1958), p. 214. For a related but significantly different view see also Henry Sidgwick, *The Methods of Ethics,* 7th edn. (London, 1907), pp. 220–221, 492–493.

4.   *Summa Theologica,* II–II, Question 66, Article 7, in *Aquinas, Selected Political Writings,* ed. A. P. d'Entreves, trans. J. G. Dawson (Oxford, 1948), p. 171.

5.   See, for instance, John Kenneth Galbraith, *The New Industrial State* (Boston, 1967); and E. J. Mishan, *The Costs of Economic Growth* (London, 1967).

Garrett Hardin, "Lifeboat Ethics: The Case Against Helping the Poor" in *Psychology Today*, September 1974

Lifeboat Ethics: The Case Against Helping the Poor
Garrett Hardin

Environmentalists use the metaphor of the earth as a "spaceship" in trying to persuade countries, industries and people to stop wasting and polluting our natural resources. Since we all share life on this planet, they argue, no single person or institution has the right to destroy, waste, or use more than a fair share of its resources.

But does everyone on earth have an equal right to an equal share of its resources? The spaceship metaphor can be dangerous when used by misguided idealists to justify suicidal policies for sharing our resources through uncontrolled immigration and foreign aid. In their enthusiastic but unrealistic generosity, they confuse the ethics of a spaceship with those of a lifeboat.

A true spaceship would have to be under the control of a captain, since no ship could possibly survive if its course were determined by committee. Spaceship Earth certainly has no captain; the United Nations is merely a toothless tiger, with little power to enforce any policy upon its bickering members.

If we divide the world crudely into rich nations and poor nations, two thirds of them are desperately poor, and only one third comparatively rich, with the United States the wealthiest of all. Metaphorically each rich nation can be seen as a lifeboat full of comparatively rich people. In the ocean outside each lifeboat swim the poor of the world, who would like to get in, or at least to share some of the wealth. What should the lifeboat passengers do?

First, we must recognize the limited capacity of any lifeboat. For example, a nation's land has a limited capacity to support a population and as the current energy crisis has shown us, in some ways we have already exceeded the carrying capacity of our land.

ADRIFT IN A MORAL SEA

So here we sit, say fifty people in our lifeboat. To be generous, let us assume it has room for ten more, making a total capacity of sixty. Suppose the fifty of us in the lifeboat see 100 others swimming in the water outside, begging for admission to our boat or for handouts. We have several options: we may be tempted to live by the Christian ideal of being "our brother's

184

keeper," or by the Marxist ideal of "to each according to his needs." Since the needs of all in the water are the same, and since they can all be seen as "our brothers," we could take them all into our boat, making a total of 150 in a boat designed for sixty. The boat swamps, everyone drowns. Complete justice, complete catastrophe.

Since the boat has an unused excess capacity of ten more passengers, we could admit just ten more to it. But which ten do we let in? How do we choose? Do we pick the best ten, the neediest ten, "first come, first served"? And what do we say to the ninety we exclude? If we do let an extra ten into our lifeboat, we will have lost our "safety factor," an engineering principle of critical importance. For example, if we don't leave room for excess capacity as a safety factor in our country's agriculture, a new plant disease or a bad change in the weather could have disastrous consequences.

Suppose we decide to preserve our small safety factor and admit no more to the lifeboat. Our survival is then possible, although we shall have to be constantly on guard against boarding parties.

While this last solution clearly offers the only means of our survival, it is morally abhorrent to many people. Some say they feel guilty about their good luck. My reply is simple: "Get out and yield your place to others." This may solve the problem of the guilt-ridden person's conscience, but it does not change the ethics of the lifeboat. The needy person to whom the guilt-ridden person yields his place will not himself feel guilty about his good luck. If he did, he would not climb aboard. The net result of conscience-stricken people giving up their unjustly held seats is the elimination of that sort of conscience from the lifeboat.

This is the basic metaphor within which we must work out our solutions. Let us now enrich the image, step by step, with substantive additions from the real world, a world that must solve real and pressing problems of overpopulation and hunger.

The harsh ethics of the lifeboat become even harsher when we consider the reproductive differences between the rich nations and the poor nations. The people inside the lifeboats are doubling in numbers every eighty-seven years; those swimming around outside are doubling, on the average, every thirty-five years, more than twice as fast as the rich. And since the world's resources are dwindling, the difference in prosperity between the rich and the poor can only increase.

As of 1973, the U.S. had a population of 210 million people, who were increasing by 0.8 percent per year. Outside our lifeboat, let us imagine another 210 million people (say the combined populations of Colombia, Ecuador, Venezuela, Morocco, Pakistan, Thailand and the Philippines) who are increasing at a rate of 3.3 percent per year. Put differently, the doubling time for this aggregate population is twenty-one years, compared to eighty-seven years of the U.S.

MULTIPLYING THE RICH AND THE POOR

Now suppose the U.S. agreed to pool its resources with those seven countries, with everyone receiving an equal share. Initially the ratio of Americans to non-Americans in this model would be one-to-one. But consider what the ratio would be after eighty-seven years, by which time the Americans would have doubled to a population of 420 million. By then, doubling every twenty-one years, the other group would have swollen to 354 billion. Each American would have to share the available resources with more than eight people.

But, one could argue, this discussion assumes that current population trends will continue, and they may not. Quite so. Most likely the rate of population increase will decline much faster in the U.S. than it will in the other countries and there does not seem to be much we can do about it. In sharing with "each according to his needs," we must recognize that needs are determined by population size, which is determined by the rate of reproduction, which at present is regarded as a sovereign right of every nation, poor or not. This being so, the philanthropic load created by the sharing ethic of the spaceship can only increase.

The Tragedy of the Commons

The fundamental error of spaceship ethics, and the sharing it requires, is that it leads to what I call "the tragedy of the commons." Under a system of private property, the men who own property recognize their responsibility to care for it, for if they don't they will eventually suffer. A farmer, for instance, will allow no more cattle in a pasture than its carrying capacity justifies. If he overloads it, erosion sets in, weeds take over, and he loses the use of the pasture.

If a pasture becomes a commons open to all, the right of each to use it may not be matched by a corresponding responsibility to protect it. Asking everyone to use it with discretion will hardly do, for the considerate herdsman who refrains from overloading the commons suffers more than a selfish one who says his needs are greater. If everyone would restrain himself, all would be well; but it takes only one less than everyone to ruin a system of voluntary restraint. In a crowded world of less than perfect human beings, mutual ruin is inevitable if there are no controls. This is the tragedy of the commons.

One of the major tasks of education today should be the creation of such an acute awareness of the dangers of the commons that people will recognize its many varieties. For example, the air and water have become polluted because they are treated as commons. Further growth in the population or per capita conversion of natural resources into pollutants will only make the problem worse. The same holds true for the fish of the oceans. Fishing fleets have nearly disappeared in many parts of the world, technological improvements in the art of fishing are hastening the day of complete ruin. Only the replacement of the system of the commons with a responsible system of control will save the land, air, water and oceanic fisheries.

The World Food Bank

In recent years there has been a push to create a new commons called a World Food Bank, an international depository of food reserves to which nations would contribute according to their abilities and from which they would draw according to their needs. This humanitarian proposal has received support from many liberal international groups, and from such prominent citizens as Margaret Mead, U.N. Secretary General Kurt Waldheim, and senators Edward Kennedy and George McGovern.

A world food bank appeals powerfully to our humanitarian impulses. But before we rush ahead with such a plan, let us recognize where the greatest political push comes from, lest we be disillusioned later. Our experience with the "Food for Peace program," or Public Law 480, gives us the answer. This program moved billions of dollars worth of U.S. surplus grain to food-short, population-long countries during the past two decades. But when P.L. 480 first became law, a headline in the business magazine *Forbes* revealed the real power behind it: "Feeding the World's Hungry Millions: How It Will Mean Billions for U.S. Business."

And indeed it did. In the years 1960 to 1970, U.S. taxpayers spent a total of $7.9 billion on the Food for Peace program. Between 1948 and 1970, they also paid an additional $50 billion for other economic-aid programs, some of which went for food and food-producing machinery and technology. Though all U.S. taxpayers were forced to contribute to the cost of P.L. 480, certain special interest groups gained handsomely under the program. Farmers did not have to contribute the grain; the Government, or rather the taxpayers, bought it from them at full market prices. The increased demand raised prices of farm products generally. The manufacturers of farm machinery, fertilizers and pesticides benefited by the farmers' extra efforts to grow more food. Grain elevators profited from storing the surplus until it could be shipped. Railroads made money hauling it to ports, and shipping lines profited from carrying it overseas. The implementation of P.L. 480 required the creation of a vast Government bureaucracy, which then acquired its own vested interest in continuing the program regardless of its merits.

EXTRACTING DOLLARS

Those who proposed and defended the Food for Peace program in public rarely mentioned its importance to any of these special interests. The public emphasis was always on its humanitarian effects. The combination of silent selfish interests and highly humanitarian apologists made a powerful and successful lobby for extracting money from taxpayers. We can expect the same lobby to push now for the creation of a World Food Bank.

However great the potential benefit to selfish interests, it should not be a decisive argument against a truly humanitarian program. We must ask if such a program would actually do more good than harm, not only momentarily but also in the long run. Those who propose the food bank usually refer to a current "emergency" or "crisis" in terms of world food supply. But what is an emergency? Although they may be infrequent and sudden, everyone knows that emergencies will occur from time to time. A well-run family, company, organization or country prepares for the likelihood of accidents and emergencies. It expects them, it budgets for them, it saves for them.

LEARNING THE HARD WAY

What happens if some organizations or countries budget for accidents and others do not? If each country is solely responsible for its own wellbeing, poorly managed ones will suffer. But they can learn from experience. They may mend their ways, and learn to budget for infrequent but certain emergencies. For example, the weather varies from year to year, and periodic crop failures are certain. A wise and competent government saves out of the production of the good years in anticipation of bad years to come. Joseph taught this policy to Pharaoh in Egypt more than 2,000 years ago. Yet the great majority of the governments in the world today do not follow such a policy. They lack either the wisdom or the competence, or both. Should those nations that do manage to put something aside be forced to come to the rescue each time an emergency occurs among the poor nations?

"But it isn't their fault!" some kindhearted liberals argue. "How can we blame the poor people who are caught in an emergency? Why must they suffer for the sins of their governments?" The concept of blame is simply not relevant here. The real question is, what are the operational consequences of establishing a world food bank? If it is open to every country every time a need develops, slovenly rulers will not be motivated to take Joseph's advice. Someone will always come to their aid. Some countries will deposit food in the world food bank, and others will withdraw it. There will be almost no overlap. As a result of such solutions to food shortage emergencies, the poor countries will not learn to mend their ways, and will suffer progressively greater emergencies as their populations grow.

POPULATION CONTROL THE CRUDE WAY

On the average, poor countries undergo a 2.5 percent increase in population each year; rich countries, about 0.8 percent. Only rich countries have anything in the way of food reserves set aside, and even they do not have as much as they should. Poor countries have none. If poor countries received no food from the outside, the rate of their population growth would be periodically checked by crop failures and famines. But if they can always draw on a world food bank in time of need, their population can continue to grow unchecked, and so will their "need" for aid. In the short run, a world food bank may diminish that need, but in the long run it actually increases the need without limit.

Without some system of worldwide food sharing, the proportion of people in the rich and poor nations might eventually stabilize. The overpopulated poor countries would decrease in numbers, while the rich countries that had room for more people would increase. But with a well-meaning system of sharing, such as a world food bank, the growth differential between the rich and the poor countries will not only persist, it will increase. Because of the higher rate of population growth in the poor countries of the world, 88 percent of today's children are born poor, and only 12 percent rich. Year by year the ratio becomes worse, as the fast-reproducing poor outnumber the slow-reproducing rich.

A world food bank is thus a commons in disguise. People will have more motivation to draw from it than to add to any common store. The less provident and less able will multiply at the expense of the abler and more provident, bringing eventual ruin upon all who share in the commons. Besides, any system of "sharing" that amounts to foreign aid from the rich nations to the poor nations will carry the taint of charity, which will contribute little to the world peace so devoutly desired by those who support the idea of a world food bank.

As past U.S. foreign-aid programs have amply and depressingly demonstrated, international charity frequently inspires mistrust and antagonism rather than gratitude on the part of the recipient nation.

CHINESE FISH AND MIRACLE RICE

The modern approach to foreign aid stresses the export of technology and advice, rather than money and food. As an ancient Chinese proverb goes: "Give a man a fish and he will eat for a day; teach him how to fish and he will eat for the rest of his days." Acting on this advice, the Rockefeller and Ford Foundations have financed a number of programs for improving agriculture in the hungry nations. Known as the "Green Revolution," these programs have led to the development of "miracle rice" and "miracle wheat," new strains that offer bigger harvests and greater resistance to crop damage. Norman Borlaug, the Nobel Prize winning agronomist who, supported by the Rockefeller Foundation, developed "miracle wheat," is one of the most prominent advocates of a world food bank.

Whether or not the Green Revolution can increase food production as much as its champions claim is a debatable but possibly irrelevant point. Those who support this well-intended humanitarian effort should first consider some of the fundamentals of human ecology. Ironically, one man who did was the late Alan Gregg, a vice president of the Rockefeller Foundation. Two decades ago he expressed strong doubts about the wisdom of such attempts to increase food production. He likened the growth and spread of humanity over the surface of the earth to the spread of cancer in the human body, remarking that "cancerous growths demand food; but, as far as I know, they have never been cured by getting it."

OVERLOADING THE ENVIRONMENT

Every human born constitutes a draft on all aspects of the environment: food, air, water, forests, beaches, wildlife, scenery and solitude. Food can, perhaps, be significantly increased to meet a growing demand. But what about clean beaches, unspoiled forests, and solitude? If we satisfy a growing population's need for food, we necessarily decrease its per capita supply of the other resources needed by men.

India, for example, now has a population of 600 million, which increases by 15 million each year. This population already puts a huge load on a relatively impoverished environment. The country's forests are now only a small fraction of what they were three centuries ago, and floods and erosion continually destroy the insufficient farmland that remains. Every one of the 15 million new lives added to India's population puts an additional burden on the environment, and increases the economic and social costs of crowding. However humanitarian our intent, every Indian life saved through medical or nutritional assistance from abroad diminishes the quality of life for those who remain, and for subsequent generations. If rich countries make it possible, through foreign aid, for 600 million Indians to swell to 1.2 billion in a mere twenty-eight years, as their current growth rate threatens, will future generations of Indians thank us for hastening the destruction of their environment? Will our good intentions be sufficient excuse for the consequences of our actions?

My final example of a commons in action is one for which the public has the least desire for rational discussion—immigration. Anyone who publicly questions the wisdom of current U.S. immigration policy is promptly charged with bigotry, prejudice, ethnocentrism, chauvinism, isolationism or selfishness. Rather than encounter such accusations, one would rather talk about other matters, leaving immigration policy to wallow in the crosscurrents of special interests that take no account of the good of the whole, or the interests of posterity.

Perhaps we still feel guilty about things we said in the past. Two generations ago the popular press frequently referred to Dagos, Wops, Polacks, Chinks and Krauts, in articles about how America was being "overrun" by foreigners of supposedly inferior genetic stock. But because the implied inferiority of foreigners was used then as justification for keeping them out, people now assume that restrictive policies could only be based on such misguided notions. There are other grounds.

A NATION OF IMMIGRANTS

Just consider the numbers involved. Our Government acknowledges a net inflow of 400,000 immigrants a year. While we have no hard data on the extent of illegal entries, educated guesses put the figure at about 600,000 a year. Since the natural increase (excess of births over deaths) of the resident population now runs about 1.7 million per year, the yearly gain from immigration amounts to at least 19 percent of the total annual increase, and may be as much as 37 percent if we include the estimate for illegal immigrants. Considering the growing use of birth control devices, the potential effect of educational campaigns by such organizations as Planned Parenthood Federation of America and Zero Population Growth, and the influence of inflation and the housing shortage, the fertility rate of American women may decline so much that immigration could account for all the yearly increase in population. Should we not at least ask if that is what we want?

For the sake of those who worry about whether the "quality" of the average immigrant compares favorably with the quality of the average resident, let us assume that immigrants and nativeborn citizens are of exactly equal quality, however one defines that term. We will focus here only on quantity; and since our conclusions will depend on nothing else, all charges of bigotry and chauvinism become irrelevant.

IMMIGRATION VS. FOOD SUPPLY

World food banks *move food to the people,* hastening the exhaustion of the environment of the poor countries. Unrestricted immigration, on the other hand, *moves people to the food,* thus speeding up the destruction of the environment of the rich countries. We can easily understand why poor people should want to make this latter transfer, but why should rich hosts encourage it?

As in the case of foreign-aid programs, immigration receives support from selfish interests and humanitarian impulses. The primary selfish interest in unimpeded immigration is the desire of employers for cheap labor, particularly in industries and trades that offer degrading work. In the past, one wave of foreigners after another was brought into the U.S. to work at wretched jobs for wretched wages. In recent years the Cubans, Puerto Ricans and Mexicans have had this dubious honor. The interests of the employers of cheap labor mesh well with the guilty silence of the country's liberal intelligentsia. White Anglo-Saxon Protestants are particularly reluctant to call for a closing of the doors to immigration for fear of being called bigots.

But not all countries have such reluctant leadership. Most educated Hawaiians, for example, are keenly aware of the limits of their environment, particularly in terms of population growth. There is only so much room on the islands, and the islanders know it. To Hawaiians, immigrants from the other forty-nine states present as great a threat as those from other nations. At a recent meeting of Hawaiian government officials in Honolulu, I had the ironic delight of hearing a speaker, who like most of his audience was of Japanese ancestry, ask how the country might practically and constitutionally close its doors to further immigration. One member of the audience countered: "How can we shut the doors now? We have many friends and relatives in Japan we'd like to bring here some day so that they can enjoy Hawaii too." The Japanese-American speaker smiled sympathetically and answered; "Yes, but we have children now, and someday we'll have grandchildren too. We can bring people here from Japan only by giving away some of the land that we hope to pass on to our grandchildren some day. What right do we have to do that?"

At this point, I can hear U.S. liberals asking: "How can you justify slamming the door once you're inside? You say that immigrants should be kept out. But aren't we all immigrants, or the descendants of immigrants? If we insist on staying, must we not admit all others?" Our craving for intellectual order leads us to seek and prefer symmetrical rules and morals: a single rule for me and everybody else; the same rule yesterday, today, and tomorrow. Justice, we feel, should not change with time and place.

We Americans of non-Indian ancestry can look upon ourselves as the descendants of thieves who are guilty morally, if not legally, of stealing this land from its Indian owners. Should we then give back the land to the now living American descendants of those Indians? However morally or logically sound this proposal may be, I, for one, am unwilling to live by it and I know no one else who is. Besides, the logical consequence would be absurd. Suppose that, intoxicated with a sense of pure justice, we should decide to turn our land over to the Indians. Since all our wealth has also been derived from the land, wouldn't we be morally obliged to give that back to the Indians too?

PURE JUSTICE VS. REALITY

Clearly, the concept of pure justice produces an infinite regression to absurdity. Centuries ago, wise men invented statutes of limitations to justify the rejection of such pure justice, in the interest of preventing continual disorder. The law zealously defends property rights, but only relatively recent property rights. Drawing a line after an arbitrary time has elapsed may be unjust, but the alternatives are worse.

We are all the descendants of thieves, and the world's resources are inequitably distributed. But we must begin the journey to tomorrow from the point where we are today. We cannot remake the past. We cannot safely divide the wealth equitably among all peoples so long as people reproduce at different rates. To do so would guarantee that our grandchildren, and everyone else's grandchildren, would have only a ruined world to inhabit.

To be generous with one's own possessions is quite different from being generous with those of posterity. We should call this point to the attention of those who, from a commendable love of justice and equality, would institute a system of the commons, either in the form of a world food bank, or of unrestricted immigration. We must convince them if we wish to save at least some parts of the world from environmental ruin.

Without a true world government to control reproduction and the use of available resources, the sharing ethic of the spaceship is impossible. For the foreseeable future, our survival demands that we govern our actions by the ethics of a lifeboat, harsh though they may be. Posterity will be satisfied with nothing less.

The Social Responsibility of Business Is to Increase Its Profits
Milton Friedman

When I hear businessmen speak eloquently about the "social responsibilities of business in a free-enterprise system," I am reminded of the wonderful line about the French man who discovered at the age of 70 that he had been speaking prose all his life. The businessmen believe that they are defending free enterprise when they declaim that business is not concerned "merely" with profit but also with promoting desirable "social" ends; that business has a "social conscience" and takes seriously its responsibilities for providing employment, eliminating discrimination, avoiding pollution and whatever else may be the catchwords of the contemporary crop of reformers. In fact they are—or would be if they or anyone else took them seriously—preaching pure and unadulterated socialism. Businessmen who talk this way are unwitting puppets of the intellectual forces that have been undermining the basis of a free society these past decades.

The discussions of the "social responsibilities of business" are notable for their analytical looseness and lack of rigor. What does it mean to say that "business" has responsibilities? Only people can have responsibilities. A corporation is an artificial person and in this sense may have artificial responsibilities, but "business" as a whole cannot be said to have responsibilities, even in this vague sense. The first step toward clarity in examining the doctrine of the social responsibility of business is to ask precisely what it implies for whom.

Presumably, the individuals who are to be responsible are businessmen, which means individual proprietors or corporate executives. Most of the discussion of social responsibility is directed at corporations, so in what follows I shall mostly neglect the individual proprietor and speak of corporate executives.

In a free-enterprise, private-property system, a corporate executive is an employee of the owners of the business. He has direct responsibility to his employers. That responsibility is to conduct the business in accordance with their desires, which generally will be to make as much money as possible while conforming to the basic rules of the society, both those embodied in law and those embodied in ethical custom. Of course, in some cases his employers may have a different objective. A group of persons might establish a corporation for an eleemosynary purpose—for example, a hospital or a school. The manager of such a corporation will not have money profit as his objective but the rendering of certain services.

In either case, the key point is that, in his capacity as a corporate executive, the manager is the agent of the individuals who own the corporation or establish the eleemosynary institution, and his primary responsibility is to them.

Needless to say, this does not mean that. it is easy to judge how well he is performing his task. But at least the criterion of performance is straightforward, and the persons among whom a voluntary contractual arrangement exists are clearly defined.

Of course, the corporate executive is also a person in his own right. As a person, he may have many other responsibilities that he recognizes or assumes voluntarily—to his family, his conscience, his feelings of charity, his church, his clubs, his city, his country. He may feel impelled by these responsibilities to devote part of his income to causes he regards as worthy, to refuse to work for particular corporations, even to leave his job, for example, to join his country's armed forces. If we wish, we may refer to some of these responsibilities as "social responsibilities." But in these respects he is acting as a principal, not an agent; he is spending his own money or time or energy, not the money of his employers or the time or energy he has contracted to devote to their purposes. If these are "social responsibilities," they are the social responsibilities of individuals, not of business.

What does it mean to say that the corporate executive has a "social responsibility" in his capacity as businessman? If this statement is not pure rhetoric, it must mean that he is to act in some way that is not in the interest of his employers. For example, that he is to refrain from increasing the price of the product in order to contribute to the social objective of preventing inflation, even though a price increase would be in the best interests of the corporation. Or that he is to make expenditures on reducing pollution beyond the amount that is in the best interests of the corporation or that is required by law in order to contribute to the social objective of improving the environment. Or that, at the expense of corporate profits, he is to hire "hard-core" unemployed instead of better-qualified available workmen to contribute to the social objective of reducing poverty.

In each of these cases, the corporate executive would be spending someone else's money for a general social interest. Insofar as his actions in accord with his "social responsibility" reduce returns to stockholders, he is spending their money. Insofar as his actions raise the price to customers, he is spending the customers' money. Insofar as his actions lower the wages of some employees, he is spending their money.

The stockholders or the customers or the employees could separately spend their own money on the particular action if they wished to do so. The executive is exercising a distinct "social responsibility," rather than serving as an agent of the stockholders or the customers or the employees, only if he spends the money in a different way than they would have spent it.

But if he does this, he is in effect imposing taxes, on the one hand, and deciding how the tax proceeds shall be spent, on the other.

This process raises political questions on two levels: principle and consequences. On the level of political principle, the imposition of taxes and the expenditure of tax proceeds are governmental functions. We have established elaborate constitutional, parliamentary and judicial provisions to control these functions, to assure that taxes are imposed so far as possible in accordance with the preferences and desires of the public—after all, "taxation without representation" was one of the battle cries of the American Revolution. We have a system of checks and balances to separate the legislative function of imposing taxes and enacting expenditures from the executive function of collecting taxes and administering expenditure programs and from the judicial function of mediating disputes and interpreting the law.

Here the businessman—self-selected or appointed directly or indirectly by stockholders—is to be simultaneously legislator, executive and jurist. He is to decide whom to tax by how much and for what purpose, and he is to spend the proceeds—all this guided only by general exhortations from on high to restrain inflation , improve the environment, fight poverty and so on and on.

The whole justification for permitting the corporate executive to be selected by the stockholders is that the executive is an agent serving the interests of his principal. This justification disappears when the corporate executive imposes taxes and spends the proceeds for "social" purposes. He becomes in effect a public employee, a civil servant, even though he remains in name an employee of a private enterprise. On grounds of political principle, it is intolerable that such civil servants—insofar as their actions in the name of social responsibility are real and not just window-dressing—should be selected as they are now. If they are to be civil servants, then they must be selected through a political process. If they are to impose taxes and make expenditures to foster "social" objectives, then political machinery must be set up to guide the assessment of taxes and to determine through a political process the objectives to be served.

This is the basic reason why the doctrine of "social responsibility" involves the acceptance of the socialist view that political mechanisms, not market mechanisms, are the appropriate way to determine the allocation of scarce resources to alternative uses.

On the grounds of consequences, can the corporate executive in fact discharge his alleged "social responsibilities"? On the one hand, suppose he could get away with spending the stockholders' or customers' or employees' money. How is he to know how to spend it? He is told that he must contribute to fighting inflation. How is he to know what action of his will contribute to that end? He is presumably an expert in running his company—in producing a product or selling it or financing it. But nothing about his selection makes him an expert on inflation. Will his holding down the price of his product reduce inflationary pressure? Or, by leaving more spending power in the hands of his customers, simply divert it elsewhere? Or, by forcing him to produce less because of the lower price, will it simply contribute to shortages? Even *if* he could answer these questions, how much cost is he justified in imposing on his stockholders, customers and employees for this social purpose? What is his appropriate share and what is the appropriate share of others?

And, whether he wants to or not, can he get away with spending his stockholders', customers' or employees' money? Will not the stockholders fire him? (Either the present ones or those who take over when his actions in the name of social responsibility have reduced the corporation's profits and the price of its stock.) His customers and his employees can desert him for other producers and employers less scrupulous in exercising their social responsibilities.

This fact of "social responsibility" doctrine is brought into sharp relief when the doctrine is used to justify wage restraint by trade unions. The conflict of interest is naked and clear when union officials are asked to subordinate the interest of their members to some more general social purpose. If the union officials try to enforce wage restraint, the consequence is likely to be wildcat strikes, rank-and-file revolts and the emergence of strong competitors for their jobs. We thus have the ironic phenomenon that union leaders—at least in the U.S.—have objected to Government interference with the market far more consistently and courageously than have business leaders.

The difficulty of exercising "social responsibility" illustrates, of course, the great virtue of private competitive enterprise—it forces people to be responsible for their own actions and makes it difficult for them to "exploit" other people for either selfish or unselfish purposes. They can do good—but only at their own expense.

Many a reader who has followed the argument this far may be tempted to remonstrate that it is all well and good to speak of government's having the responsibility to impose taxes and determine expenditures for such "social" purposes as controlling pollution or training the hard-core unemployed, but that the problems are too urgent to wait on the slow course of political processes, that the exercise of social responsibility by businessmen is a quicker and surer way to solve pressing current problems.

Aside from the question of fact—I share Adam Smith's skepticism about the benefits that can be expected from "those who affected to trade for the public good"—this argument must be rejected on grounds of principle. What it amounts to is an assertion that those who favor the taxes and expenditures in question have failed to persuade a majority of their fellow citizens to be of like mind and that they are seeking to attain by undemocratic procedures what they cannot attain by democratic procedures. In a free society, it is hard for "good" people to do "good," but that is a small price to pay for making it hard for "evil" people to do "evil," especially since one man's good is another's evil.

I have, for simplicity, concentrated on the special case of the corporate executive, except only for the brief digression on trade unions. But precisely the same argument applies to the newer phenomenon of calling upon stockholders to require corporations to exercise social responsibility (the recent G.M. crusade for example). In most of these cases, what is in effect involved is some stockholders trying to get other stockholders (or customers or employees) to contribute against their will to "social" causes favored by the activists. Insofar as they succeed, they are again imposing taxes and spending the proceeds.

The situation of the individual proprietor is somewhat different. If he acts to reduce the returns of his enterprise in order to exercise his "social responsibility," he is spending his own money, not someone else's. If he wishes to spend his money on such purposes, that is his right, and I cannot see that there is any objection to his doing so. In the process, he, too, may impose costs on employees and customers. However, because he is far less likely than a large corporation or union to have monopolistic power, any such side effects will tend to be minor.

Of course, in practice the doctrine of social responsibility is frequently a cloak for actions that are justified on other grounds rather than a reason for those actions.

To illustrate, it may well be in the long-run interest of a corporation that is a major employer in a small community to devote resources to providing amenities to that community or to improving its government. That may make it easier to attract desirable employees, it may reduce the wage bill or lessen losses from pilferage and sabotage or have other worthwhile effects. Or it may be that given the laws about the deductibility of corporate charitable contributions, the stockholders can contribute more to charities they favor by having the corporation make the gift than by doing it themselves, since they can in that way contribute an amount that would otherwise have been paid as corporate taxes.

In each of these—and many similar—cases, there is a strong temptation to rationalize these actions as an exercise of "social responsibility." In the present climate of opinion, with its widespread aversion to "capitalism," "profits," the "soulless corporation" and so on, this is one way for a corporation to generate goodwill as a by-product of expenditures that are entirely justified in its own self-interest.

It would be inconsistent of me to call on corporate executives to refrain from this hypocritical window-dressing because it harms the foundations of a free society. That would be to call on them to exercise a "social responsibility"! If our institutions, and the attitudes of the public make it in their self-interest to cloak their actions in this way, I cannot summon much indignation to denounce them. At the same time, I can express admiration for those individual proprietors or owners of closely held corporations or stockholders of more broadly held corporations who disdain such tactics as approaching fraud.

Whether blameworthy or not, the use of the cloak of social responsibility, and the nonsense spoken in its name by influential and prestigious businessmen, does clearly harm the foundations of a free society. I have been impressed time and again by the schizophrenic character of many businessmen. They are capable of being extremely far-sighted and clear-headed in matters that are internal to their businesses. They are incredibly short-sighted and muddle-headed in matters that are outside their businesses but affect the possible survival of business in general. This short-sightedness is strikingly exemplified in the calls from many businessmen for wage and price guidelines or controls or incomes policies. There is nothing that could do more in a brief period to destroy a market system and replace it by a centrally controlled system than effective governmental control of prices and wages.

The short-sightedness is also exemplified in speeches by businessmen on social responsibility. This may gain them kudos in the short run. But it helps to strengthen the already too prevalent view that the pursuit of profits is wicked and immoral and must be curbed and controlled by external forces. Once this view is adopted, the external forces that curb the market will not be the social consciences, however highly developed, of the pontificating executives; it will be the iron fist of Government bureaucrats. Here, as with price and wage controls, businessmen seem to me to reveal a suicidal impulse.

The political principle that underlies the market mechanism is unanimity. In an ideal free market resting on private property, no individual can coerce any other, all cooperation is voluntary, all parties to such cooperation benefit or they need not participate. There are no "social" values, no "social" responsibilities in any sense other than the shared values and responsibilities of individuals. Society is a collection of individuals and of the various groups they voluntarily form.

The political principle that underlies the political mechanism is conformity. The individual must serve a more general social interest—whether that be determined by a church or a dictator or a majority. The individual may have a vote and a say in what is to be done, but if he is overruled, he must conform. It is appropriate for some to require others to contribute to a general social purpose whether they wish to or not.

Unfortunately, unanimity is not always feasible. There are some respects in which conformity appears unavoidable, so I do not see how one can avoid the use of the political mechanism altogether.

But the doctrine of "social responsibility" taken seriously would extend the scope of the political mechanism to every human activity. It does not differ in philosophy from the most explicitly collectivist doctrine. It differs only by professing to believe that collectivist ends can be attained without collectivist means. That is why, in my book "Capitalism and Freedom," I have called it a "fundamentally subversive doctrine" in a free society, and have said that in such a society, "there is one and only one social responsibility of business—to use its resources and engage in activities designed to increase its profits so long as it stays within the rules of the game, which is to say, engages in open and free competition without deception or fraud."

Introduction to Social Responsibility
Robert D. Hay and Edmund R. Gray

It was Jeremy Bentham, late eighteenth century English philosopher, who espoused the social, political, and economic goal of society to be "the greatest happiness for the greatest number." His cardinal principle was written into the Declaration of Independence as "the pursuit of happiness," which became a societal goal of the American colonists. Bentham's principle was also incorporated into the Constitution of the United States in the preamble where the goal was stated "to promote the general welfare."

The economic-political system through which we in America strive to achieve this societal goal emphasizes the economic and political freedom to pursue individual interests. Adam Smith, another English political economist of the late eighteenth century, stated that the best way to achieve social goals was as follows:

> Every individual is continually exerting himself to find out the most advantageous employment for whatever capital he can command. It is his own advantage, indeed, and not that of the society, which he has in view. But the study of his own advantage naturally, or rather necessarily, leads him to prefer that employment which is most advantageous to the society. . . .

> As every individual, therefore, endeavors as much as he can both to employ his capital in the support of domestic industry, and so to direct that industry that its produce may be of the greatest value, every individual necessarily labours to render the annual revenue of the society as great as he can. He generally, indeed, neither intends to promote the public interest, nor knows how much he is promoting it. By preferring the support of domestic to that of foreign industry, he intends only his own security; and by directing that industry in such a manner as its produce may be of the greatest value, he intends only his own gain, and he is in this, as in many other cases, led by an invisible hand to promote an end which was not part of his intention. Nor is it always the worse for the society that it was no part of it. By pursuing his own interest he frequently promotes that of the society more effectually than when he really intends to promote it. I have never known much good done by those who affected to trade for the public good. It is an affectation, indeed, not very common among merchants, and very few words need be employed in dissuading them from it.[1]

Adam Smith's economic values have had an important influence on American business thinking. As a result, most business people for the first hundred and fifty years of our history embraced the theory that social goals could be achieved by pursuing individual interests.

By 1930 American values were beginning to change from that of the individual owner ethic to that of the group or social ethic. As part of this changing mood, it was felt that Smith's emphasis on owner's interests was too predominant at the expense of other contributors to a business organization. Consequently, a new philosophy of management took shape which stated that the social goals could be achieved by balancing the interests of several groups of people who had an interest in a business. It was stated by Charles H. Percy, then president of Bell and Howell, in the 1950s as follows:

> There are over 64 million gainfully employed people in the United States. One half of these work directly for American corporations, and the other half are vitally affected by business directly or indirectly. Our entire economy, therefore, is dependent upon the type of business management we have. Business management is therefore in many respects a public trust charged with the responsibility of keeping America economically sound. We at Bell & Howell can best do this by keeping our own company's program on a firm foundation and by having a growing group of management leaders to direct the activities of the company.
>
> Management's role in a free society is, among other things, to prove that the real principles of a free society can work within a business organization.
>
> Our basic objective is the development of individuals. In our own present program we are doing everything conceivable to encourage, guide, and assist, and provide an opportunity to everyone to improve their abilities and skills, thus becoming more valuable to the company and enabling the company to improve the rewards paid to the individual for such additional efforts.
>
> Our company has based its entire program for the future on the development of the individual and also upon the building of an outstanding management group. This is why we have emphasized so strongly the supervisory training program recently completed by all Bell & Howell supervisors, and why we are now offering this program to others in the organization training for future management responsibilities.
>
> But a company must also have a creed to which its management is dedicated. I hope that we can all agree to the following:
>
> We believe that our company must develop and produce outstanding products that will perform a great service or fill a need for our customers.
>
> We believe that our business must be run at an adequate profit and that the services and products that we offer must be better than those offered by competitors.
>
> We believe that management must serve employees, stockholders, and customers, but that we cannot serve the interests of any one group at the undue expense of the other two. A proper and fair balance must be preserved.
>
> We believe that our business must provide stability of employment and job security for all those who depend on our company for their livelihood.
>
> We believe that we are failing in our responsibility if our wages are not sufficiently high to nor only meet the necessities of life but provide some of the luxuries as well. Wherever possible, we also believe that bonus earning should be paid for performance and output "beyond the call of duty."
>
> We believe that every individual in the company should have an opportunity for advancement and growth with the organization. There should be no dead-end streets any place in an organization.
>
> We believe in the necessity for constantly increasing productivity and output. Higher wages and greater benefits can never be "given" by management. Management can only see that they are paid out when "earned."

We believe in labor-saving machinery. We do not think human beings should perform operations that can be done by mechanical or electronic means. We believe in this because we believe in the human dignity and creative ability of the individual. We are more interested in the intellect, goodwill, initiative, enthusiasm, and cooperativeness of the individual than we are in his muscular energy.

We believe that every person in the company has a right to be treated with the respect and courtesy that is due a human being. It is for this reason that we have individual merit ratings, individual pay increases, job evaluation, and incentive pay; and it is why we keep every individual fully informed—through The Finder, through our annual report, through Family Night, and through individual letters—about the present program of the company and also about our future objectives.

We believe that our business must be conducted with the utmost integrity. We may fight the principle of confiscatory taxation, but we will pay our full share. We will observe every governmental law and regulation, local, state, and national. We will deal fairly with our customers, we will advertise our product truthfully, and we will make every attempt to maintain a friendly relationship with our competitors while at the same time waging the battle of free competition.

Some business leaders, on the one hand, preach the virtues of the free enterprise, democratic system and, on the other hand, run their own business in accordance with autocratic principles—all authority stemming from the top with little delegation of responsibility to individuals within the organization. We believe in democracy—in government and in our business.

We hope that every principle we believe in is right and is actually being practiced throughout the company as it affects every individual.[2]

Then in the late 1960s American business leaders began to take another look at the problems of society in light of the goal of "the greatest happiness for the greatest number." How could people be happy if they have to breathe foul air, drink polluted water, live in crowded cities, use very unsafe products, be misled by untruthful advertising, be deprived of a job because of race, and face many other problems? Thus, another philosophy of management emerged. It was voiced by several American business leaders:

Business must learn to look upon its social responsibilities as inseparable from its economic function. If it fails to do so, it leaves a void that will quickly be filled by others—usually by the government. (George Champion, Chase National Bank, 1966.)

I believe there is one basic principle that needs to be emphasized more than ever before. It is the recognition that business is successful in the long term only when it is directed toward the needs of the society. (Robert F. Hansberger, Boise Cascade, 1971.)

The actions of the great corporations have so profound an influence that the public has come to judge them not only by their profit-making record, but by the contribution of their work to society as a whole. Under a political democracy such as ours, if the corporation fails to perceive itself and govern its action in essentially the same manner as the public it large, it may find itself in serious trouble. (Louis B. Lundborg, Bank of America, 1971.)

With these remarks we can see that there has been a shift in managerial emphasis from owners' interests to group interests, and finally, to society's interests. Managers of some American businesses have come to recognize that they have a social responsibility.

HISTORICAL PERSPECTIVE OF SOCIAL RESPONSIBILITY

The concept of the social responsibility of business managers has in recent years become a popular subject of discussion and debate within both business and academic circles. Although the term itself is of relatively recent origin, the underlying concept has existed as long as there have been business organizations. It rests on the logical assumption that because the firm is a creation of society, it has a responsibility to aid in the accomplishment of society's goals. In the United States concepts of social responsibility have moved from three distinct phases which may be labeled Phases I, II, and III.[3]

Phase I—Profit Maximizing Management

The Phase I concept was based on the belief that business managers have but one single objective—maximize profits. The only constraint on this pursuit was the legal framework within which the firm operated. The origin of this view may be found in Adam Smith's *Wealth of Nations*. As previously noted, Smith believed that individual business people acting in their own selfish interest would be guided by an "invisible hand" to promote the public good. In other words, the individual's drive for maximum profits and the regulation of the competitive marketplace would interact to create the greatest aggregate wealth for a nation and therefore the maximum public good. In the United States this view was universally accepted throughout the nineteenth century and the early part of the twentieth century. Its acceptance rested not only on economic logic but also on the goals and values of society. America in the nineteenth and first half of the twentieth centuries was a society of economic scarcity; therefore, economic growth and the accumulation of aggregate wealth were primary goals. The business system with its emphasis on maximum profit was seen as a vehicle for eliminating economic scarcity. In the process employee abuses such as child labor, starvation wages, and unsafe working conditions could be tolerated. No questions were raised with regard to using up the natural resources and polluting streams and land. Nor was anyone really concerned about urban problems, unethical advertising, unsafe products, and poverty problems of minority groups.

The profit maximization view of social responsibility also complemented the Calvinistic philosophy which pervaded nineteenth and twentieth century American thinking. Calvinism stressed that the road to salvation was through hard work and the accumulation of wealth. It then logically followed that a business person could demonstrate diligence (and thus godliness) and accumulate a maximum amount of wealth by adhering to the discipline of profit maximization.

Phase II—Trusteeship Management

Phase II, which may be labeled the "trusteeship" concept, emerged in the 1920s and 30s. It resulted from structural changes in both business institutions and in society. According to this concept, corporate managers were responsible not simply for maximizing the stockholders' wealth but rather for maintaining an equitable balance among the competing claims of customers, employees, suppliers, creditors, and the community. In this view the manager was seen as "trustee" for the various contributor groups to the firm rather than simply an agent of the owners.[4]

The two structural trends largely responsible for the emergence of this newer view of social responsibility ,were: (1) the increasing diffusion of ownership of the shares of American corporations, and (2) the development of a pluralistic society. The extent of the diffusion of stock ownership may be highlighted by the fact that by the early 1930s the largest stockholders in corporations such as American Telephone and Telegraph, United States Steel, and the

Pennsylvania Railroad owned less than one percent of the total shares outstanding of these companies.[5] Similar dispersion of stock ownership existed in most other large corporations. In such situations management typically was firmly in control of the corporation. Except in rare circumstances, the top executives were able to perpetuate themselves in office through the proxy mechanism. If an individual shareholder was not satisfied with the performance of the firm, there was little recourse other than to sell the stock. Hence, although the stockholder's legal position was that of an owner—and thus a principal-agent relationship existed between the stockholder and the managers—the stockholder's actual position was more akin to bondholders and other creditors of the firm. Given such a situation it was only natural to ask, "To whom is management responsible?" The "trusteeship" concept provided an answer. Management was responsible to all the contributors to the firm—that is, stockholders, workers, customers, suppliers, creditors, and the community.

The emergence of a largely pluralistic society reinforced the logic of the "trusteeship" concept. A pluralistic society has been defined as "one which has many semi-autonomous and autonomous groups through which power is diffused. No one group has overwhelming power over all others, and each has direct or indirect impact on all others."[6] From the perspective of business firms this translated into the fact that exogenous groups had considerable impact upon and influence over them. In the 1930s the major groups exerting significant pressure on business were labor unions and the federal government. Today the list has grown to include numerous minority, environmental, and consumer groups among others. Clearly, one logical approach to such a situation is to consider that the firm has a responsibility to each interested group and that management's task is to reconcile and balance the claims of the various groups.

Phase III—"Quality of Life" Management

Phase III, which may be called the "quality of life" concept of social responsibility, has become popular in recent years.[7] The primary reason for the emergence of this concept is the very significant metamorphosis in societal goals which this nation is experiencing. Up to the middle part of this century, society's principal goal was to raise the standard of living of the American people, which could be achieved by producing more goods and services. The fact that the U.S. had become the wealthiest nation in the world was testimony to the success of business in meeting this expectation.

In this process, however, the U.S. has become what John Kenneth Galbraith calls an "affluent society" in which the aggregate scarcity of basic goods and services is no longer the fundamental problem.[8] Other social problems have developed as direct and indirect results of economic success. Thus, there are pockets of poverty in a nation of plenty, deteriorating cities, air and water pollution, defacement of the landscape, and a disregard for consumers to mention only a few of the prominent social problems. The mood of the country seems to be that things have gotten out of balance—the economic abundance in the midst of a declining social and physical environment does not make sense. As a result, a new set of national priorities which stress the "Quality of life" appear to be emerging.

Concomitant with the new priorities, societal consensus seems to be demanding that business, with its technological and managerial skills and its financial resources, assume broader responsibilities—responsibilities that extend beyond the traditional economic realm of the Phase I concept or the mere balancing of the competing demands of the sundry contributors and pressure groups of the Phase II concept. The socially responsible firm under Phase III reasoning is one that becomes deeply involved in the solution of society's major problems.

PERSONAL VALUES OF THE THREE STYLES OF MANAGERS

Values are the beliefs and attitudes which form one's frame of reference and help to determine the behavior which an individual displays. All managers have a set of values which affect their decisions, but the values are not the same for each manager; however, once values are ingrained in a manager, they do not change except over a period of time. It is possible to group these values into a general pattern of behavior which characterizes three styles of managers—the profit-maximizing style, the trusteeship style, and the "quality of life" style of management.

Phase I Managers

Phase I, profit-maximizing managers have a personal set of values which reflects their economic thinking. They believe that raw self-interest should prevail in society, and their values dictate that "What's good for me is good for my country." Therefore, Phase I managers rationalize that making as much profit as is possible would be good for society. They make every effort to become as efficient as possible and to make as much money as they can. To them money and wealth are the most important goals of their lives.

In the pursuit of maximum profit the actions of Phase I managers toward customers are reflected in a *caveat emptor* philosophy. "Let the buyer beware" characterizes decisions and actions in dealing with customers. They are not necessarily concerned with product quality or safety, or with sufficient and/or truthful information about products and services. A profit-maximizing manager's view toward employees can be stated as, "Labor is a commodity to be bought and sold in the marketplace." Thus, chief accountability lies with the owners of the business, and usually the Phase I manager is the owner or part owner of the organization.

To profit maximizers technology is very important. Machines and equipment rank high on their scale of values, Therefore, materialism characterizes their philosophy.

Social values do not predominate the thinking of Phase I managers. In fact, they believe that employee problems should be left at home. Economics should be separate from societal or family concerns. A Phase I manager's leadership style is one of the rugged individualist—"I'm my own boss, and I'll manage my business as I please." Values about minority groups dictate that such groups are inferior, so they must be treated accordingly.

Political values are based on the doctrine of laissez faire. "That government is best which governs the least" characterizes the thinking of Phase I managers. As a result, anything dealing with politicians and governments is foreign and distasteful to them.

Their beliefs about the environment can be stated, "The natural environment controls one's destiny; therefore, use it to protect your interests before it destroys you. Don't worry about the physical environment because there are plenty of natural resources which you can use."

Aesthetic values to the profit maximizer are minimal. In fact, Phase I managers would say, "Aesthetic values? What are they?" They have very little concern for the arts and cultural aspects of life. They hold musicians, artists, entertainers, and social scientists in low regard.

The values that a profit-maximizing manager holds were commonly accepted in the economic textbooks of the 1800s and early 1900s although they obviously did not apply to all managers of those times. It is easy to see how they conflict with the values of the other two styles of management.

Phase II Managers

Phase II, trusteeship managers have a somewhat different set of values. They recognize that self-interest plays a large role in their actions, but they also recognize the interests of those people who contribute to the organization—the customers, employees, suppliers, owners, creditors, government, and community. In other words, they operate with self-interest plus the interests of other groups. They believe that "What is good for my company is good for the country." They balance profits of the owners and the organization with wages for employees, taxes for the government, interest for the creditors, and so forth. Money is important to them but so are people, because their values tell them that satisfying people's needs is a better goal than just making money.

In balancing the needs of the various contributors to the organization, Phase II managers deal with customers as the chief providers of revenue to the firm. Their values tell them not to cheat the customers because cheating is not good for the firm.

They are concerned with providing sufficient quantities of goods as well as sufficient quality for customer satisfaction. They view employees as having certain rights which must be recognized and that employees are more than mere commodities to be traded in the marketplace. Their accountability as managers is to owners as well as to customers, employees, suppliers, creditors, government, and the community.

To the trusteeship-style manager, technology is important, but so are people. Innovation of technology is to be commended because new machines, equipment, and products are useful to people to create a high standard of living. Materialism is important, but so is humanism.

The social values held by trusteeship managers are more liberal than those held by profit maximizers. They recognize that employees have several needs beyond their economic needs. Employees have a desire for security and a sense of belonging as well as recognition. Phase II managers see themselves as individualists, but they also appreciate the value of group participation in managing the business. They view minority groups as having their place in society. But, a trusteeship manager would add: "Their place is usually inferior to mine; they are usually not qualified to hold their jobs but that's not my fault."

The political values of Phase II managers are reflected in recognizing that government and politics are important, but they view government and politics as necessary evils. They distrust both, recognizing that government serves as a threat to their existence if their firms do not live up to the laws passed since the 1930s.

The environmental beliefs of trusteeship managers are stated as follows: "People can control and manipulate their environment. Therefore, let them do it for their own benefit and incidentally for society's benefit."

Aesthetic values are all right to the trusteeship manager, but "they are not for our firm although someone has to support the arts and cultural values."

Phase III Managers

In contrast to profit maximizers and trustee managers, "quality of life" managers believe in enlightened self-interest. They agree that selfishness and group interests are important, but that society's interests are also important in making decisions. "What's good for society is good for our company" is their opinion. They agree that profit is essential for the firm, but that profit in and of itself is not the end objective of the firm. As far as money and wealth are concerned, their set of values tell them that money is important but people are more important than money.

In sharp contrast to *caveat emptor* in dealings with customers, the philosophy of Phase III managers is *caveat venditor*, that is, let the seller beware. The company should bear the responsibility for producing and distributing products and services in sufficient quantities at the right time and place with the necessary quality, information, and services necessary to satisfy customers' needs. Their views about employees are to recognize the dignity of each, not treating them as a commodity to be bought and sold. Their accountability as managers is to the owners, to the other contributors of the business, and to society in general.

Technological values are important but people are held in higher esteem than machines, equipment, computers, and esoteric products. A "quality of life" manager is a humanist rather than a materialist.

The social values of "quality of life" managers dictate that a person cannot be separated into an economic being or family being. Their philosophy is, "We hire the whole person including any problems that person might have." Phase III managers recognize that group participation rather than rugged individualism is a determining factor in an organization's success. Their values about minority groups are different from the other managers. Their view is that "A member of a minority group needs support and guidance like any other person."

The political values of "quality of life" managers dictate that government and politicians are necessary contributors to a quality of life. Rather than resisting government, they believe that business and government must cooperate to solve society's problems.

Their environmental beliefs are stated as, "A person must preserve the environment, not for the environment's sake alone, but for the benefit of people who want to lead a quality life."

As far as aesthetic values are concerned, Phase III managers recognize that the arts and cultural values reflect the lives of people whom they hold in high regard. Their actions support aesthetic values by committing resources to their preservation and presentation.

Figure 1 Comparison of Managerial Values

Phase I Profit Maximizing Management	Phase II Trusteeship Management	Phase III "Quality of Life" Management
Economic Values		
1) Raw self-interest	1) Self-interest 2) Contributor's interests	1) Enlightened self-interest 2) Contributor's interests 3) Society's interests
"What's good for me is good for my country."	"What's good for my company is good for our country."	"What's good for society is good for our company."
Profit maximizer.	Profit satisfier.	Profit is necessary, but . . .
Money and wealth are most important.	Money is important but so are people.	People are more important than money.
"Let the buyer beware." *(caveat emptor)*	"Let's not cheat the customer."	"Let the seller beware." *(caveat venditor)*
"Labor is a commodity to be bought and sold."	"Labor has certain rights which must be recognized."	"Employee dignity must be satisfied."
Accountability of management is to the owners.	Accountability of management is to the owners *and* customers, employees, suppliers, and other contributors.	Accountability of management is to the owners, contributors, and society.
Technological Values		
Technology is very important.	Technology is important but so are people.	People are more important than technology.
Social Values		
"Employee personal problems must be left at home."	"We recognize that employees have needs beyond their economic needs."	"We hire the whole person."
"I'm a rugged individualist, and I'll manage the business as I please."	"I am an individualist, but I recognize the value of group participation.	"Group participation is fundamental to our success."
"Minority groups are inferior. They must be treated accordingly."	"Minority groups have their place in society but their place is inferior to mine."	"Minority groups are people like you and I are."
Environmental Values		
"The natural environment controls one's destiny."	"One can control and manipulate one's environment."	"One must preserve the environment."
Political Values		
"The government is best which governs least."	"Government is a necessary evil."	"Business and government must cooperate to solve society's problems."
Aesthetic Values		
"Aesthetic values? What are they?"	"Aesthetic values are okay, but not for us."	"We must preserve our aesthetic values and we'll do our part."

Notes

1. Adam Smith. *Wealth of Nations*. Book IV, Chapter 2 (1776), as quoted in E. Bakke et al. *Unions, Management and the Public* (3d ed; New York: Harcourt, Brace & World, Inc. 1967), p. 22.

2. "Management Creeds and Philosophies," American Management Association Research Report No. 32.

3. A great portion of the discussion which follows is drawn from Robert D. Hay and Edmund R. Gray, "Social Responsibilities of Business Managers," *Academy of Management Journal* (March, 1974).

4. Howard R. Brown and William T. Greenwood. "Business Management: A Profession," *Issues in Business and Society* (2d ed., Boston: Houghton-Mifflin, 1971).

5. Adolph A. Berle and Gardiner C. Means. *The Modern Corporation and Private Property* (New York: Macmillan. 1932) , p. 47.

6. George A. Steiner. *Business and Society* (New York: Random House 1971). pp. 70–71.

7. Committee for Economic Development, Social Responsibilities of Business Corporations (New York: Research and Business Policy Committee. CED. June, 1971).

8. John K. Galbraith, *The Affluent Society* (Boston: Houghton Mifflin Company, 1958). Chapter 1. With emerging energy and raw material shortages we may be once again in the process of a fundamental economic change.

ABORTION

United States Supreme Court, 410 U.S. 113 (1973)

Majority Opinion in Roe v. Wade
Justice Harry A. Blackmun

In this case, a pregnant single woman, suing under the fictitious name of Jane Roe, challenged the constitutionality of the existing Texas criminal abortion law.

According to the Texas Penal Code, the performance of an abortion, except to save the life of the mother, constituted a crime that was punishable by a prison sentence of two to five years. At the time this case was finally resolved by the Supreme Court, abortion legislation varied widely from state to state. Some states, principally New York, had already legalized abortion on demand. Most other states, however, had legalized various forms of therapeutic abortion but had retained some measure of restrictive abortion legislation.

Justice Blackmun, writing an opinion concurred in by six other justices, argues that a woman's decision to terminate a pregnancy is encompassed by a *right to privacy*—but only up to a certain point in the development of the fetus. As the right to privacy is not an absolute right, it must yield at some point to the state's legitimate interests. Justice Blackmun contends that the state has a legitimate interest in protecting the health of the pregnant woman and that this interest becomes compelling at approximately the end of the first trimester in the development of the fetus. He also contends that the state has a legitimate interest in protecting potential life and that this interest becomes compelling at the point of viability.

It is . . . apparent that at common law, at the time of the adoption of our Constitution, and throughout the major portion of the 19th century, abortion was viewed with less disfavor than under most American statutes currently in effect. Phrasing it another way, a woman enjoyed a substantially brodader right to terminate a pregnancy than she does in most States today. At least with respect to the early stage of pregnancy, and very possibly without such a limitation, the opportunity to make this choice was present in this country well into the 19th century. Even later, the law continued for some time to treat less punitively an abortion procured in early pregnancy. . . .

Three reasons have been advanced to explain historically the enactment of criminal abortion laws in the 19th century and to justify their continued existence.

It has been argued occasionally that these laws were the product of a Victorian social concern to discourage illicit sexual conduct. Texas, however, does not advance this justification in the present case, and it appears that no court or commentator has taken the argument seriously. . . .

A second reason is concerned with abortion as a medical procedure. When most criminal abortion laws were first enacted, the procedure was a hazardous one for the woman. This was particularly true prior to the development of antisepsis. Antiseptic techniques, of course, were based on discoveries by Lister, Pasteur, and others first announced in 1867, but were not generally accepted and employed until about the turn of the century. Abortion mortality was high. Even after 1900, and perhaps until as late as the development of antibiotics in the 1940's, standard modern techniques such as dilatation and curettage were not nearly so safe as they are today. Thus it has been argued that a State's real concern in enacting a criminal abortion law was to protect the pregnant woman, that is, to restrain her from submitting to a procedure that placed her life in serious jeopardy.

Modern medical techniques have altered this situation. Appellants and various *amici* refer to medical data indicating that abortion in early pregnancy, that is, prior to the end of first trimester, although not without its risk, is now relatively safe. Mortality rates for women undergoing early abortion, where the procedure is legal, appear to be as low as or lower than the rates for normal childbirth. Consequently, any interest of the State in protecting the woman from an inherently hazardous procedure, except when it would be equally dangerous for her to forgo it, has largely disappeared. Of course, important state interests in the area of health and medical standards do remain. The State has a legitimate interest in seeing to it that abortion, like any other medical procedure, is performed under circumstances that insure maximum safety for the patient. This interest obviously extends at least to the performing physician and his staff, to the facilities involved, to the availability of after-care, and to adequate provision for any complication or emergency that might arise. The prevalence of high mortality rates at illegal "abortion mills" strengthens, rather than weakens, the State's interest in regulating the conditions under which abortions are performed. Moreover, the risk to the woman increases as her pregnancy continues. Thus the State retains a definite interest in protecting the woman's own health and safety when an abortion is performed at a late stage of pregnancy.

The third reason is the State's interest—some phrase it in terms of duty—in protecting prenatal life. Some of the argument for this justification rests on the theory that a new human life is present from the moment of conception. The State's interest and general obligation to protect life then extends, it is argued, to prenatal life. Only when the life of the pregnant mother herself is at stake, balanced against the life she carries within her, should the interest of the embryo or fetus not prevail. Logically, of course, a legitimate state interest in this area need not stand or fall on acceptance of the belief that life begins at conception or at some other point prior to live birth. In assessing the State's interest, recognition may be given to the less rigid claim that as long as at least *potential* life is involved, the State may assert interests beyond the protection of the pregnant woman alone.

Parties challenging state abortion laws have sharply disputed in some courts the contention that a purpose of these laws, when enacted, was to protect prenatal life. Pointing to the absence of legislative history to support the contention, they claim that most state laws were designed solely to protect the woman. Because medical advances have lessened this concern, at least with respect to abortion in early pregnancy, they argue that with respect to such abortions the laws can no longer be justified by any state interest. There is some scholarly support for this view of original purpose. The few state courts called upon to interpret their laws in the late 19th and early 20th centuries did focus on the State's interest in protecting the woman's health rather than in preserving the embryo and fetus. . . .

The Constitution does not explicitly mention any right of privacy. In a line of decisions, however, going back perhaps as far as *Union Pacific R. Co. v. Botsford* (1891), the Court has recognized that a right of personal privacy, or a guarantee of certain areas or zones of privacy, does exist under the Constitution. In varying contexts the Court or individual Justices have indeed found at least the roots of that right in the First Amendment, . . . in the Fourth and Fifth Amendments . . . in the penumbras of the Bill of Rights . . . in the Ninth Amendment . . . or in the concept of liberty guaranteed by the first section of the Fourteenth Amendment. . . . These decisions make it clear that only personal rights that can be deemed "fundamental" or "implicit in the concept of ordered liberty," . . . are included in this guarantee of personal privacy. They also make it clear that the right has some extension to activities relating to marriage, . . . procreation, . . . contraception, . . . family relationships, . . . and child rearing and education. . . .

This right of privacy, whether it be founded in the Fourteenth Amendment's concept of personal liberty and restrictions upon state action, as we feel it is, or, as the District Court determined, in the Ninth Amendment's reservation of rights to the people, is broad enough to encompass a woman's decision whether or not to terminate her pregnancy. . . .

. . . [A]ppellants and some *amici* argue that the woman's right is absolute and that she is entitled to terminate her pregnancy at whatever time, in whatever way, and for whatever reason she alone chooses. With this we do not agree. Appellants' arguments that Texas either has no valid interest at all in regulating the abortion decision, or no interest strong enough to support any limitation upon the woman's sole determination, is unpersuasive. The Court's decisions recognizing a right of privacy also acknowledge that some state regulation in areas protected by that right is appropriate. As noted above, a state may properly assert important interests in safe-guarding health, in maintaining medical standards, and in protecting potential life. At some point in pregnancy, these respective interests become sufficiently compelling to sustain regulation of the factors that govern the abortion decision. The privacy right involved, therefore, cannot be said to be absolute. . . .

We therefore conclude that the right of personal privacy includes the abortion decision, but that this right is not unqualified and must be considered against important state interests in regulation.

We note that those federal and state courts that have recently considered abortion law challenges have reached the same conclusion. . . .

Although the results are divided, most of these courts have agreed that the right of privacy, however based, is broad enough to cover the abortion decision; that the right, nonetheless, is not absolute and is subject to some limitations; and that at some point the state interests as to protection of health, medical standards, and prenatal life, become dominant. We agree with this approach. . . .

The appellee and certain *amici* argue that the fetus is a "person" within the language and meaning of the Fourteenth Amendment. In support of this they outline at length and in detail the well-known facts of fetal development. If this suggestion of personhood is established, the appellant's case, of course, collapses, for the fetus' right to life is then guaranteed specifically by the Amendment. The appellant conceded as much on reargument. On the other hand, the appellee conceded on reargument that no case could be cited that holds that a fetus is a person within the meaning of the Fourteenth Amendment. . . .

All this, together with our observation, *supra*, that throughout the major portion of the 19th century prevailing legal abortion practices were far freer than they are today, persuades us that the word "person," as used in the Fourteenth Amendment, does not include the unborn. . . . Indeed, our decision in *United States v. Vuitch* (1971) inferentially is to the same effect, for we there would not have indulged in statutory interpretation favorable to abortion in specified circumstances if the necessary consequence was the termination of life entitled to Fourteenth Amendment protection.

. . . As we have intimated above, it is reasonable and appropriate for a State to decide that at some point in time another interest, that of health of the mother or that of potential human life, becomes significantly involved. The woman's privacy is no longer sole and any right of privacy she possesses must be measured accordingly.

Texas urges that, apart from the Fourteenth Amendment, life begins at conception and is present throughout pregnancy, and that, therefore, the State has a compelling interest in protecting that life from and after conception. We need not resolve the difficult question of when life begins. When those trained in the respective disciplines of medicine, philosophy, and theology are unable to arrive at any consensus, the judiciary, at this point in the development of man's knowledge, is not in a position to speculate as to the answer.

It should be sufficient to note briefly the wide divergence of thinking on this most sensitive and difficult question. There has always been strong support for the view that life does not begin until live birth. This was the belief of the Stoics. It appears to be the predominant, though not the unanimous, attitude of the Jewish faith. It may be taken to represent also the position of a large segment of the Protestant community, insofar as that can be ascertained; organized groups that have taken a formal position on the abortion issue have generally regarded abortion as a matter for the conscience of the individual and her family. As we have noted, the common law found greater significance in quickening. Physicians and their scientific colleagues have regarded that event with less interest and have tended to focus either upon conception or upon live birth or upon the interim point at which the fetus becomes "viable," that is, potentially able to live outside the mother's womb, albeit with artificial aid. Viability is usually placed at about seven months (28 weeks) but may occur earlier, even at 24 weeks. . . .

In areas other than criminal abortion the law has been reluctant to endorse any theory that life, as we recognize it, begins before live birth or to accord legal rights to the unborn except in narrowly defined situations and except when the rights are contingent upon live birth. . . . In short, the unborn have never been recognized in the law as persons in the whole sense.

In view of all this, we do not agree that, by adopting one theory of life, Texas may override the rights of the pregnant woman that are at stake. We repeat, however, that the State does have an important and legitimate interest in preserving and protecting the health of the pregnant woman, whether she be a resident of the State or a nonresident who seeks medical consultation and treatment there, and that it has still *another* important and legitimate interest in protecting the potentiality of human life. These interests are separate and distinct. Each grows in substantiality as the woman approaches term and, at a point during pregnancy, each becomes "compelling."

With respect to the State's important and legitimate interest in the health of the mother, the "compelling" point, in the light of present medical knowledge, is at approximately the end of the first trimester. This is so because of the now established medical fact . . . that until the end of the first trimester mortality in abortion is less than mortality in normal childbirth. It follows that, from and after this point, a State may regulate the abortion procedure to the extent that the regulation reasonably relates to the preservation and protection of maternal health. Examples of permissible state regulation in this area are requirements as to the qualifications of the person who is to perform the abortion; as to the licensure of that person; as to the facility in which the procedure is to be performed, that is, whether it must be a hospital or may be a clinic or some other place of less-than-hospital status; as to the licensing of the facility; and the like.

This means, on the other hand, that, for the period of pregnancy prior to this "compelling" point, the attending physician, in consultation with his patient, is free to determine, without regulation by the State, that in his medical judgment the patient's pregnancy should be terminated. If that decision is reached, the judgment may be effectuated by an abortion free of interference by the State.

With respect to the State's important and legitimate interest in potential life, the "compelling" point is at viability. This is so because the fetus then presumably has the capability of meaningful life outside the mother's womb. State regulation protective of fetal life after viability thus has both logical and biological justifications. If the State is interested in protecting fetal life after viability, it may go so far as to proscribe abortion during that period except when it is necessary to preserve the life or health of the mother. . . .

To summarize and repeat:

1. A state criminal abortion statute of the current Texas type, that excepts from criminality only a *life saving* procedure on behalf of the mother, without regard to pregnancy stage and without recognition of the other interests involved, is violative of the Due Process Clause of the Fourteenth Amendment.

   (a) For the stage prior to approximately the end of the first trimester, the abortion decision and its effectuation must be left to the medical judgment of the pregnant woman's attending physician.

   (b) For the stage subsequent to approximately the end of the first trimester, the State, in promoting its interests in the health of the mother, may, if it chooses, regulate the abortion procedure in ways that are reasonably related to maternal health.

   (c) For the stage subsequent to viability the State, in promoting its interest in the potentiality of human life, may, if it chooses, regulate, and even proscribe, abortion except where it is necessary, in appropriate medical judgment, for the preservation of the life or health of the mother.

2. The State may define the term "physician," as it has been employed [here], to mean only a physician currently licensed by the State, and may proscribe any abortion by a person who is not a physician as so defined.

. . . The decision leaves the State free to place increasing restrictions on abortion as the period of pregnancy lengthens, so long as those restrictions are tailored to the recognized state interests. The decision vindicates the right of the physician to administer medical treatment according to his professional judgment up to the points where important state interests provide compelling justifications for intervention. Up to those points the abortion decision in all its aspects is inherently, and primarily, a medical decision, and basic responsibility for it must rest with the physician. If an individual practitioner abuses the privilege of exercising proper medical judgment, the usual remedies, judicial and intraprofessional, are available. . . .

Questions

1. Justice Blackmun contends that the state's legitimate interest in protecting the health of the mother becomes *compelling* at the end of the first trimester. Does the Court's choice of this particular point as "compelling" have any substantial justification, or is the choice fundamentally arbitrary?

2. Justice Blackmun contends that the state's legitimate interest in protecting potential life becomes *compelling* at the point of viability. Does the Court's choice of this particular point as "compelling" have any substantial justification, or is the choice fundamentally arbitrary?

3. Justice Blackmun *explicitly* disavows entering into philosophical speculation on the problem of the beginning of human life. To what extent could it be said that he *implicitly* takes a philosophical position on this problem?

Opinion in Webster v. Reproductive Health Services

Justice William H. Rehnquist

At issue in this case is the constitutionality of certain provisions of a Missouri statute designed to place restrictions on abortion. Of special importance are provisions banning the use of public facilities and public employees in the performance of abortions and a provision requiring physicians to perform tests to determine the viability of any fetus believed to be twenty weeks or older.

In announcing the judgment of a bitterly divided Court, Chief Justice Rehnquist argues that just as it is constitutionally acceptable for a state to refuse to fund abortions directly (e.g., through Medicaid), it is constitutionally acceptable for a state to prohibit the use of public facilities and employees in the performance of abortions. In upholding the constitutionality of the viability-testing provisions, he maintains that this provision "permissibly furthers" the state's interest in protecting potential human life. Chief Justice Rehnquist also argues that the present case does not call for a reexamination of Roe v. Wade, but he makes very clear his view that the Roe trimester framework is both "unsound in principle and unworkable in practice."

This appeal concerns the constitutionality of a Missouri statute regulating the performance of abortions. The United States Court of Appeals for the Eighth Circuit struck down several provisions of the statute on the ground that they violated this Court's decision in *Roe v. Wade* (1973) and cases following it. We noted probable jurisdiction and now reverse.

I

In June 1986, the Governor of Missouri signed into law Missouri Senate Committee Substitute for House Bill No. 1596 (hereinafter Act or statute), which amended existing state law concerning unborn children and abortions. The Act consisted of 20 provisions, 5 of which are now before the Court. The first provision, or preamble, contains "findings" by the state legislature that "[t]he life of each human being begins at conception," and that "unborn children have protectable interests in life, health, and well-being." The Act further requires that all Missouri laws be interpreted to provide unborn children with the same rights enjoyed by other persons, subject to the Federal Constitution and this Court's precedents. Among its other provisions, the Act requires that, prior to performing an abortion on any woman whom a physician has reason to believe is 20 or more weeks pregnant, the physician ascertain whether the fetus is viable by performing "such medical examinations and tests as are necessary to make a finding of the gestational age, weight, and lung maturity of the unborn child." The Act also prohibits the use of public employees and facilities to perform or assist abortions not necessary to save the mother's life, and it prohibits the use of public funds, employees, or facilities for the purpose of "encouraging or counseling" a woman to have an abortion not necessary to save her life.

In July 1986, five health professionals employed by the State and two nonprofit corporations brought this class action in the United States District Court for the Western District of Missouri to challenge the constitutionality of the Missouri statute, Plaintiffs, appellees in this Court, sought declaratory and injunctive relief on the ground that certain statutory provisions violated the First, Fourth, Ninth, and Fourteenth Amendments to the Federal Constitutions. . . .

Plaintiffs filed this suit "on their own behalf and on behalf of the entire class consisting of facilities and Missouri licensed physicians or other health care professionals offering abortion services or pregnancy counseling and on behalf of the entire class of pregnant females seeking abortion services or pregnancy counseling within the State of Missouri." The two nonprofit corporations are Reproductive Health Services, which offers family planning and gynecological services to the public, including abortion services up to 22 weeks "gestational age,"[1] and Planned Parenthood of Kansas City, which provides abortion services up to 14 weeks gestational age. . . .

Several weeks after the complaint was filed, the District Court temporarily restrained enforcement of several provisions of the Act. . . .

The court of Appeals for the Eight Circuit affirmed, with one exception not relevant to this appeal. The Court of Appeals determined that Missouri's declaration that life begins at conception was "simple an impermissible state adoption of theory of when life begins to justify its abortion regulations." Relying on *Colautti* v. *Franklin* (1979), it further held that the requirement that physicians perform viability tests was an unconstitutional legislative intrusion on a matter of medical skill and judgment. The Court of Appeals invalidated Missouri's prohibition on the use of public facilities and employees to perform or assist abortions not necessary to save the mother's life. It distinguished our decisions in *Harris* v. *McRae* (1980) and *Maher* v. *Roe* (1977), on the ground that "'[t]here is a fundamental difference between providing direct funding to effect the abortion decision and allowing staff physicians to perform abortions at an existing publicly owned hospital.'" The Court of Appeals struck down the provision prohibiting the use of public funds for "encouraging or counseling" women to have nontherapeutic abortions, for the reason that this provision was both overly vague and inconsistent with the right to an abortion enunciated in *Roe* v. *Wade*. . . .

II

Decision of this case requires us to address four sections of the Missouri Act: (a) the preamble; (b) the prohibition on the use of public facilities or employees to perform abortions; (c) the prohibitions on public funding of abortion counseling; and (d) the requirement that physicians conduct viability tests prior to performing abortions. We address these *seriatim*.

A

The Act's preamble, as noted, sets forth "findings" by the Missouri legislature that "[t]he life of each human being begins at conception," and that "[u]nborn children have protectable interests in life, health, and well-being." The Act then mandates that state laws be interpreted to provide unborn children with "all the rights, privileges, and immunities available to other persons, citizens, and residents of this state," subject to the Constitution and this Court's precedents. In invalidating the preamble, the Court of Appeals relied on this Court's dictum that "'a State may not adopt one theory of when life begins to justify its regulation of abortions.'" It rejected Missouri's claim that the preamble was "abortion-neutral," and "merely determine[d] when life begins in a nonabortion context, a traditional state prerogative." The court thought that "[t]he only plausible inference" from the fact that "every remaining section of the bill save one regulates the performance of abortions" was that "the state intended its abortion regulations to be understood against the backdrop of its theory of life."

The State contends that the preamble itself is precatory and imposes no substantive restrictions on abortions. . . .

. . . Certainly the preamble does not by its terms regulate abortion or any other aspects of appellees' medical practice. The Court has emphasized that *Roe* v. *Wade* "implies no limitation on the authority of a State to make a value judgment favoring childbirth over abortion." The preamble can be read simply to express that sort of value judgment.

We think the extent to which the preamble's language might be used to interpret other state statutes or regulations is something that only the courts of Missouri can definitively decide. . . .

It will be time enough for federal courts to address the meaning of the preamble should it be applied to restrict the activities of appellees in some concrete way. . . . We therefore need not pass on the constitutionality of the Act's preamble.

B

Section 188.210 provides that "[i]t shall be unlawful for any public employee within the scope of his employment to perform or assist an abortion, not necessary to save the life of the mother," while § 188.215 makes it "unlawful for any public facility to be used for the purpose of performing or assisting an abortion not necessary to save the life of the mother." The Court of Appeals held that these provisions contravened this Court's abortion decisions. We take the contrary view.

As we said earlier this Term . . . , "our cases have recognized that the Due Process Clauses generally confer no affirmative right to governmental aid, even where such aid may be necessary to secure life, liberty, or property interests of which the government itself may not deprive the individual." In *Maher* v. *Roe, supra,* the Court upheld a Connecticut welfare regulation under which Medicaid recipients received payments for medical services related to childbirth, but not for nontherapeutic abortions. The Court rejected the claim that this unequal subsidization of childbirth and abortion was impermissible under *Roe* v. *Wade.* As the court put it:

> "The Connecticut regulation before us is different in kind from the laws invalidated in our previous abortion decisions. The Connecticut regulation places no obstacles—absolute or otherwise—in the pregnant woman's path to an abortion. An

indigent woman who desires an abortion suffers no disadvantage as a consequence of Connecticut's decision to fund childbirth; she continues as before to be dependent on private sources for the service she desires. The State may have made childbirth a more attractive alternative, thereby influencing the woman's decision, but it has imposed no restriction on access to abortions that was not already there. The indigency that may make it difficult—and in some cases, perhaps, impossible—for some women to have abortions is neither created nor in any way affected by the Connecticut regulation."

Relying on *Maher*, the Court in *Poelker* v. *Doe* (1977) held that the city of St. Louis committed "no constitutional violation . . . in electing, as a policy choice, to provide publicly financed hospital services for childbirth without providing corresponding services for nontherapeutic abortions."

More recently, in *Harris* v. *McRae* (1980), the Court upheld "the most restrictive version of the Hyde Amendment," which withheld from States federal funds under the Medicaid program to reimburse the costs of abortions, "'except where the life of the mother would be endangered if the fetus were carried to term.'" As in *Maher* and *Poelker*, the Court required only a showing that Congress' authorization of "reimbursement for medically necessary services generally, but not for certain medically necessary abortions" was rationally related to the legitimate governmental goal of encouraging childbirth.

The Court of Appeals distinguished these cases on the ground that "[t]o prevent access to a public facility does more than demonstrate a political choice in favor of childbirth; it clearly narrows and in some cases forecloses the availability of abortion to women." The court reasoned that the ban on the use of public facilities "could prevent a woman's chosen doctor from performing an abortion because of his unprivileged status at other hospitals or because a private hospital adopted a similar anti-abortion stance." It also thought that "[s]uch a rule could increase the cost of obtaining an abortion and delay the timing of it as well."

We think that this analysis is much like that which we rejected in *Maher, Poelker*, and *McRae*. As in those cases, the State's decision here to use public facilities and staff to encourage childbirth over abortion "places no governmental obstacle in the path of a woman who chooses to terminate her pregnancy." Just as Congress' refusal to fund abortions in *McRae* left "an indigent woman with at least the same range of choice in deciding whether to obtain a medically necessary abortion as she would have had if Congress had chosen to subsidize no health care costs at all." Missouri's refusal to allow public employees to perform abortions in public hospitals leaves a pregnant woman with the same choices as if the State had chosen not to operate any public hospitals at all. The challenged provisions only restrict a woman's ability to obtain an abortion to the extent that she chooses to use a physician affiliated with a public hospital. This circumstance is more easily remedied, and thus considerably less burdensome, than indigency, which "may make it difficult—and in some cases, perhaps, impossible—for some women to have abortions" without public funding. Having held that the State's refusal to fund abortions does not violate *Roe* v. *Wade*, it strains logic to reach a contrary result for the use of public facilities and employees. If the State may "make a value judgment favoring childbirth over abortion and . . . implement that judgment by the allocation of public funds," surely it may do so through the allocation of other public resources, such as hospitals and medical staff. . . .

. . . Thus we uphold the Act's restrictions on the use of public employees and facilities for the performance or assistance of nontherapeutic abortions.

C

The Missouri Act contains three provisions relating to "encouraging or counseling a woman to have an abortion not necessary to save her life." Section 188.205 states that no public funds can be used for this purpose; § 188.210 states that public employees cannot, within the scope of their employment, engage in such speech; and § 188.215 forbids such speech in public facilities. The Court of Appeals did not consider § 188.205 separately from §§ 188.210 and 188.215. It held that all three of these provisions were unconstitutionally vague, and that "the ban on using public funds, employees, and facilities to encourage or counsel a woman to have an abortion is an unacceptable infringement of the woman's fourteenth amendment right to choose an abortion after receiving the medical information necessary to exercise the right knowingly and intelligently."

Missouri has chosen only to appeal the Court of Appeals' invalidation of the public funding provision, § 188.205. A threshold question is whether this provision reaches primary conduct, or whether it is simply an instruction to the State's fiscal officers not to allocate funds for abortion counseling. We accept, for purposes of decision, the State's claim that § 188.205 "is not directed at the conduct of any physician or health care provider, private or public," but "is directed solely at those persons responsible for expending public funds."

Appellees contend that they are not "adversely" affected under the State's interpretation of § 188.205, and therefore that there is no longer a case or controversy before us on this question. . . . A majority of the Court agrees with appellees that the controversy over § 188.205 is now moot. . . .

D

Section 188.029 of the Missouri Act provides:

> "Before a physician performs an abortion on a woman he has reason to believe is carrying an unborn child of twenty or more weeks gestational age, the physician shall first determine if the unborn child is viable by using and exercising that degree of care, skill, and proficiency commonly exercised by the ordinarily skillful, careful, and prudent physician engaged in similar practice under the same or similar conditions. In making this determination of viability, the physician shall perform or cause to be performed such medical examinations and tests as are necessary to make a finding of the gestational age, weight, and lung maturity of the unborn child and shall enter such findings and determination of viability in the medical record of the mother."

As with the preamble, the parties disagree over the meaning of this statutory provision. The State emphasizes the language of the first sentence, which speaks in terms of the physician's determination of viability being made by the standards of ordinary skill in the medical profession. Appellees stress the language of the second sentence, which prescribes such "tests as are necessary" to make a finding of gestational age, fetal weight, and lung maturity.

The Court of Appeals read § 188.029 as requiring that after 20 weeks "doctors *must* perform tests to find gestational age, fetal weight and lung maturity." The court indicated that the tests needed to determine fetal weight at 20 weeks are "unreliable and inaccurate" and would add $125 to $250 to the cost of an abortion. It also stated that "amniocentesis, the only method available to determine lung maturity, is contrary to accepted medical practice until 28–30 weeks of gestation, expensive, and imposes significant health risks for both the pregnant woman and the fetus."

We must first determine the meaning of § 188.029 under Missouri law. Our usual practice is to defer to the lower court's construction of a state statute, but we believe the Court of Appeals has "fallen into plain error" in this case. "'In expounding a statute, we must not be guided by a single sentence or member of a sentence, but look to the provisions of the whole law, and to its object and policy.'" The Court of Appeals' interpretation also runs "afoul of the well-established principle that statutes will be interpreted to avoid constitutional difficulties."

We think the viability-testing provision makes sense only if the second sentence is read to require only those tests that are useful to making subsidiary findings as to viability. If we construe this provision to require a physician to perform those tests needed to make the three specified findings *in all circumstances*, including when the physician's reasonable professional judgment indicates that the tests would be irrelevant to determining viability or even dangerous to the mother and the fetus, the second sentence of § 188.029 would conflict with the first sentence's *requirement* that a physician apply his reasonable professional skill and judgment. It would also be incongruous to read this provision, especially the word "necessary," to require the performance of tests irrelevant to the expressed statutory purpose of determining viability. It thus seems clear to us that the Court of Appeals' construction of § 188.029 violates well-accepted canons of statutory interpretation used in the Missouri courts. . . .

The viability-testing provision of the Missouri Act is concerned with promoting the State's interest in potential human life rather than in maternal health. Section 188.029 creates what is essentially a presumption of viability at 20 weeks, which the physician must rebut with tests indicating that the fetus is not viable prior to performing an abortion. It also directs the physician's determination as to viability by specifying consideration, if feasible, of gestational age, fetal weight, and lung capacity. The District Court found that "the medical evidence is uncontradicted that a 20-week fetus is *not* viable, and that "23 1/2 to 24 weeks gestation is the earliest point in pregnancy where a reasonable possibility of viability exists." But it also found that there may be a 4-week error in estimating gestational age, which supports testing at 20 weeks.

In *Roe* v. *Wade,* the Court recognized that the State has "important and legitimate" interests in protecting maternal health and in the potentiality of human life. During the second trimester, the State "may, if it chooses, regulate the abortion procedure in ways that are reasonably related to maternal health." After viability, when the State's interest in potential human life was held to become compelling, the State "may, if it chooses, regulate, and even proscribe, abortion except where it is necessary, in appropriate medical judgment, for the preservation of the life or health of the mother."

In *Colautti* v. *Franklin, supra,* upon which appellees rely, the Court held that a Pennsylvania statute regulating the standard of care to be used by a physician performing an abortion of a possibly viable fetus was void for vagueness. But in the course of reaching that conclusion, the Court reaffirmed its earlier statement in *Planned Parenthood of Central Missouri* v. *Danforth* (1976), that "'the determination of whether a particular fetus is viable is, and must be, a matter for the judgment of the responsible attending physician.'" The dissent ignores the statement in *Colautti* that "neither the legislature nor the courts may proclaim one of the elements entering into the ascertainment of viability—be it weeks of gestation or fetal weight or any other single factor—as the determinant of when the State has a compelling interest in the life or health of the fetus." To the extent that § 188.029 regulates the method for determining viability, it undoubtedly does superimpose state regulation on the medical determination of whether a particular fetus is viable. The Court of Appeals and the District Court thought it unconstitutional for this reason. To the extent that the viability tests increase the cost of what are in fact second-trimester abortions, their validity may also be questioned under *Akron v. Akron Center for Reproductive Health* (1983), where the Court held that a requirement that second trimester abortions must be performed in hospitals was invalid because it substantially increased the expense of those procedures.

We think that the doubt cast upon the Missouri statute by these cases is not so much a flaw in the statute as it is a reflection of the fact that the rigid trimester analysis of the course of a pregnancy enunciated in *Roe* has resulted in subsequent cases like *Colautti* and *Akron* making constitutional law in this area a virtual Procrustean bed. Statutes specifying elements of informed consent to be provided abortion patients, for example, were invalidated if they were thought to "structur[e] . . . the dialogue between the woman and her physician." *Thornburgh v. American College of Obstetricians and Gynecologists* (1986). As the dissenters in *Thornburgh* pointed out, such a statute would have been sustained under any traditional standard of judicial review, or for any other surgical procedure except abortion.

Stare decisis is a cornerstone of our legal system, but it has less power in constitutional cases, where, save for constitutional amendments, this Court is the only body able to make needed changes. We have not refrained from reconsideration of a prior construction of the Constitution that has proved "unsound in principle and unworkable in practice." We think the *Roe* trimester framework falls into that category.

In the first place, the rigid *Roe* framework is hardly consistent with the notion of a Constitution cast in general terms, as ours is, and usually speaking in general principles, as ours does. The key elements of the *Roe* framework—trimesters and viability—are not found in the text of the Constitution or in any place else one would expect to find a constitutional principle. Since the bounds of the inquiry are essentially indeterminate, the result has been a web of legal rules that have become increasingly intricate, resembling a code of regulations rather than a body of constitutional doctrine. As Justice White has put it, the trimester framework has left this Court to serve as the country's "*ex officio* medical board with powers to approve or disapprove medical and operative practices and standards throughout the United States."

In the second place, we do not see why the State's interest in protecting potential human life should come into existence only at the point of viability, and that there should therefore be a rigid line allowing state regulation after viability but prohibiting it before viability. The dissenters in *Thornburgh*, writing in the context of the *Roe* trimester analysis, would have recognized this fact by positing against the "fundamental right" recognized in *Roe* the State's "compelling interest" in protecting potential human life throughout pregnancy. . . .

The tests that § 188.029 requires the physician to perform are designed to determine viability. The State here has chosen viability as the point at which its interest in potential human life must be safeguarded. It is true that the tests in question increase the expense of abortion, and regulate the discretion of the physician in determining the viability of the fetus. Since the tests will undoubtedly show in many cases that the fetus is not viable, the tests will have been performed for what were in fact second-trimester abortions. But we are satisfied that the requirement of these tests permissibly furthers the State's interest in protecting potential human life, and we therefore believe § 188.029 to be constitutional.

The dissent takes us to task for our failure to join in a "great issues" debate as to whether the Constitution includes an "unenumerated" general right to privacy as recognized in cases such as *Griswold v. Connecticut* (1965) and *Roe*. But *Griswold v. Connecticut*, unlike *Roe*, did not purport to adopt a whole framework, complete with detailed rules and distinctions, to govern the cases in which the asserted liberty interest would apply. As such, it was far different from the opinion, if not the holding, of *Roe v. Wade,* which sought to establish a constitutional framework for judging state regulation of abortion during the entire term of pregnancy. That framework sought to deal with areas of medical practice traditionally subject to state regulation, and it sought to balance once and for all by reference only to the calendar the claims of the State to protect the fetus as a form of human life against the claims of a woman to decide for herself whether or not to abort a fetus she was carrying. The experience of the Court in applying *Roe v. Wade* in later cases suggests to us that there is wisdom in not unnecessarily attempting to elaborate the abstract differences between a "fundamental right" to abortion, as the Court described it in *Akron,* a "limited fundamental constitutional right," which Justice Blackmun's dissent today treats *Roe* as having established, or a liberty interest protected by the Due Process Clause, which we believe it to be. The Missouri testing requirement here is reasonably designed to ensure that abortions are not performed where the fetus is viable—an end which all concede is legitimate—and that is sufficient to sustain its constitutionality.

The dissent also accuses us, *inter alia,* of cowardice and illegitimacy in dealing with "the most politically divisive domestic legal issue of our time." There is no doubt that our holding today will allow some governmental regulation of abortion that would have been prohibited under the language of cases such as *Colautti v. Franklin* and *Akron v. Akron Center for Reproductive Health, Inc., supra.* But the goal of constitutional adjudication is surely not to remove inexorably "politically divisive" issues from the ambit of the legislative process, whereby the people through their elected representatives deal with matters of concern to them. The goal of constitutional adjudication is to hold true the balance between that which the Constitution puts beyond the reach of the democratic process and that which it does not. We think we have done that today. The dissent's suggestion that legislative bodies, in a Nation where more than half of our population is women, will treat our decision today as an invitation to enact abortion regulation reminiscent of the dark ages not only misreads our views but does scant justice to those who serve in such bodies and the people who elect them.

III

Both appellants and the United States as *Amicus Curiae* have argued that we overrule our decision in *Roe v. Wade.* The facts of the present case, however, differ from those at issue in *Roe.* Here, Missouri has determined that viability is the point at which its interest in potential human life must be safeguarded. In *Roe,* on the ot her hand, the Texas statute criminalized the performance of *all* abortions, except when the mother's life was at stake. This case therefore affords us no occasion to revisit the holding of *Roe,* which was that the Texas statute unconstitutionally infringed the right to an abortion derived from the Due Process Clause, and we leave it undisturbed. To the extent indicated in our opinion, we would modify and narrow *Roe* and succeeding cases.

Because none of the challenged provisions of the Missouri Act properly before us conflict with the Constitution, the judgment of the Court of Appeals is *Reversed.*

Notes

1.   The Act defines "gestational age" as the "length of pregnancy as measured from the first day of the woman's last menstrual period."

Questions

1. It is constitutionally permissible for a state to ban the use of *public* facilities and *public* employees in the performance of abortions, but is it advisable for a state to do so? Is it advisable for state to refuse to provide Medicaid funding for abortions?
2. What would be the basic elements of an ideal social policy on abortion? Why?

Abortion: Suggested Additional Readings

Bolton, Martha Brandt: "Responsible Women and Abortion Decisions." In Onora O'Neill and William Ruddick, eds., *Having Children: Philosophical and Legal Reflections on Parenthood*, New York: Oxford University Press, 1979, pp. 40–51. In defending a moderate view on the morality of abortion, Bolton emphasizes the importance of contextual features in the life of a pregnant woman. She argues that the decision to bear a child must "fit" into a woman's life and make sense in terms of her responsibilities to her family and to the larger society.

Brody, Baruch: "On the Humanity of the Foetus." In Robert L. Perkins, ed., *Abortion: Pro and Con.* Cambridge, Mass.: Schenkman, 1974, pp. 69–90. Brody critically examines the various proposals for "drawing the line" on the humanity of the fetus, ultimately suggesting that the most defensible view would draw the line at the pint where fetal brain activity begins.

Engelhardt, H. Tristram, Jr.: "The Ontology of Abortion." *Ethics*, vol. 84, April 1974, pp. 217–234. Engelhardt focuses attention on the issue of "whether or to what extent the fetus is a person." He argues that, strictly speaking, a human person is not present until the later stages of infancy. However, he finds the point of viability significant in that, with viability, an infant can play the social role of "child" and thus be treated "as if it were a person."

Feinberg, Joel: "Abortion." In Tom Regan, ed., *Matters of Life and Death.* New York: Random House, 1980, pp. 183–217. In this long essay, Feinberg analyzes the strengths and weaknesses of alternative views of the moral status of the fetus. He also considers the extent to which abortion is morally justifiable *if* it is granted that the fetus is a person.

Feinberg, Joel, ed.: *The Problem of Abortion*, 2d ed. Belmont, Calif.: Wadsworth, 1984. This excellent anthology features a wide range of articles on the moral justifiability of abortion.

Humber, James M.: "Abortion: The Avoidable Moral Dilemma." *Journal of Value Inquiry*, vol. 9, Winter 1975, pp. 282–302. Humber, defending the conservative view on the morality of abortion, examines and rejects what he identifies as the major defense of abortion. He also contends that proabortion arguments are typically so poor that they can only be viewed as "after-the-fact-rationalizations."

Langerak, Edward A.: "Abortion: Listening to the Middle." *Hastings Center Report*, vol. 9, October 1979, pp. 24–28. Langerak suggests a theoretical framework for a moderate view that incorporates two "widely shared beliefs": (1) that there is something about the fetus *itself* that makes abortion morally problematic and (2) that late abortions are significantly more problematic than early abortions.

Noonan, John T., Jr.: "An Almost Absolute Value in History." In John T. Noonan, Jr., ed., *The Morality of Abortion: Legal and Historical Perspectives.* Cambridge, Mass.: Harvard University Press, 1970, pp. 51–59. In this well-known statement of the conservative view on the morality of abortion, Noonan argues that conception is the only objectively based and nonarbitrary point at which to "draw the line" between the nonhuman and the human.

Ross, Steven L.: "Abortion and the Death of the Fetus." *Philosophy and Public Affairs,* vol. 11, Summer 1982, pp. 232–245. Ross draws a distinction between abortion as the termination of pregnancy and abortion as the termination of the life of the fetus. He proceeds to defend abortion in the latter sense, insisting that it is justifiable for a woman to desire not only the termination of pregnancy but also the death of the fetus.

Thomson, Judith Jarvis: "A Defense of Abortion." *Philosophy and Public Affairs,* vol. 1, Fall 1971, pp. 47–66. In this widely discussed article, Thomson attempts to "moderate the conservative view." For the sake of argument, she grants the premise that the fetus (from conception) is a person. Still, she argues, under certain conditions abortion remains morally permissible.

Tooley, Michael: *Abortion and Infanticide.* New York: Oxford University Press, 1983. In this long book, Tooley defends the liberal view on the morality of abortion. He insists that the question of the morality of abortion cannot be satisfactorily resolved "in isolation from the questions of the morality of infanticide and of the killing of nonhuman animals."

EUTHANASIA

Arthur J. Dyck, "An Alternative to the Ethic of Euthanasia" in *To Live and to Let Die*, 1973

An Alternative to the Ethic of Euthanasia
Arthur J. Dyck

The arguments for euthanasia focus upon two humane and significant concerns: compassion for those who are painfully and terminally ill; and concern for the human dignity associated with freedom of choice. Compassion and freedom are values that sustain and enhance the common good. The question here, however, is how these values affect our behavior toward the dying.

The argument for compassion usually occurs in the form of attacking the inhumanity of keeping dying people alive when they are in great pain or when they have lost almost all of their usual functions, particularly when they have lost the ability or will to communicate with other. . . . The argument for compassion is supplemented by an argument for greater freedom for a patient to choose how and when he or she will die. For one thing, the patient should not be subjected to medical treatment to which that patient does not consent. Those who argue for voluntary euthanasia extend this notion by arguing that the choice to withhold techniques that would prolong life is a choice to shorten life. Hence, if one can choose to shorten one's life, why cannot one ask a physician by a simple and direct act of intervention to put an end to one's life? Here it is often argued that physicians already curtail life by means of pain-killing drugs, which in the doses administered, will hasten death. Why should not the law recognize and sanction a simple and direct hastening of death, should the patient wish it?

How do the proponents of euthanasia view the general prohibition against killing? First of all, they maintain that we are dealing here with people who will surely die regardless of the intervention of medicine. They advocate the termination of suffering and the lawful foreshortening of the dying process. Secondly, although the patient is committing suicide, and the physician is an accomplice in such a suicide, both acts are morally justifiable to cut short the suffering of one who is dying.

It is important to be very clear about the precise moral reasoning by which advocates of voluntary euthanasia justify suicide and assisting a suicide. They make no moral distinction between those instances when a patient or a physician chooses to have life shortened by failing to accept or use life-prolonging techniques and those instances when a patient or a physician shortens life by employing a death-dealing chemical or instrument. They make no moral distinction between a drug given to kill pain, which also shortens life, and a substance given precisely to shorten life and for no other reason. Presumably these distinctions are not honored, because regardless of the stratagem employed—regardless of whether one is permitting to die or killing directly—the result is the same, the patient's life is shortened. Hence, it is maintained that, if you can justify one kind of act that shortens the life of the dying, you can justify any act that shortens the life of the dying when this act is seen to be willed by the one who is dying. Moral reasoning of this sort is strictly utilitarian; it focuses solely on the consequences of acts, not on their intent. . . .

Because of this loss of a merely descriptive term for a happy death, it is necessary to invent a term for a happy or good death—namely, benemortasia. The familiar derivatives for this new term are *bene* (good) and *mors* (death). . . . An ethic of benemortasia does not stand in opposition to the values of compassion and human freedom. It differs, however, from the ethic of euthanasia in its understanding of how these values are best realized. In particular, certain constraints upon human freedom are recognized and emphasized as enabling human beings to increase compassion and freedom rather than diminish them. . . .

Our ethic of benemortasia acknowledges the freedom of patients who are incurably ill to refuse interventions that prolong dying and the freedom of physicians to honor such wishes. However, these actions are not acts of suicide and assisting in suicide. In our ethic of benemortasia, suicide and assisting in suicide are unjustifiable acts of killing. Unlike the ethic of those who would legalize voluntary euthanasia, our ethic makes a moral distinction between acts that permit death and acts that cause death. . . . From the point of view of the dying person, when could his or her decisions be called a deliberate act to end life, the act we usually designate as suicide? Only, it seems to me, when the dying person commits an act that has the immediate intent of ending life and has no other purpose. That act may be to use, or ask the physician to use, a chemical or an instrument that has no other immediate effect than to end the dying person's life. If, for the sake of relieving pain, a dying person chooses drugs administered in potent doses, the intent of this act is not to shorten life, even though it has that effect. It is a choice as to how to live while dying. Similarly, if a patient chooses to forego medical interventions that would have the effect of prolonging his or her life without in any way promising release from death, this also is a choice as to what is the most meaningful way to spend the remainder of life, however short that may be. The choice to use drugs to relieve pain and the choice not to use medical measures that cannot promise a cure for one's dying are no different in principle from the choices we make throughout our lives as to how much we will rest, how hard we will work, how little and how much medical intervention we will seek or tolerate, and the like. For society or physicians to map out life styles for individuals with respect to such decisions is surely beyond anything that we find in Stoic, Jewish, or Christian ethics. Such intervention in the liberty of individuals is far beyond what is required in any society whose rules are intended to constrain people against harming others.

But human freedom should not be extended to include the taking of one's own life. Causing one's own death cannot generally be justified, even when one is dying. To see why this is so, we have to consider how causing one's death does violence to one's self and harms others.

The person who causes his or her own death repudiates the meaningfulness and worth of his or her own life. To decide to initiate an act that has as its primary purpose to end one's life is to decide that that life has no worth to anyone, especially to oneself. It is an act that ends all choices regarding what one's life and whatever is left of it is to symbolize.

Suicide is the ultimately effective way of shutting out all other people from one's life. Psychologists have observed how hostility for others can be expressed through taking one's own life. People who might want access to the dying one to make restitution, offer reparation, bestow last kindnesses, or clarify misunderstandings are cut off by such an act. Every kind of potentially and actually meaningful contact and relation among persons is irrevocably severed except by means of memories and whatever life beyond death may offer. Certainly for those who are left behind by death, there can remain many years of suffering occasioned by that death. The sequence of dying an inevitable death can be much better accepted than the decision on the part of a dying one that he or she has no worth to anyone. An act that presupposes that final declaration leaves tragic overtones for anyone who participated in even the smallest way in that person's dying.

But the problem is even greater. If in principle a person can take his or her own life whenever he or she no longer finds it meaningful, there is nothing in principle that prevents anyone from taking his or her life, no matter what the circumstances. For if the decision hinges on whether one regards his or her own life as meaningful, anyone can regard his or her own life as meaningless even under circumstances that would appear to be most fortunate and opportune for an abundant life.

What about those who would commit suicide or request euthanasia in order to cease being a "burden" on those who are providing care for them? If it is a choice to accept death by refusing non-curative care that prolongs dying, the freedom to embrace death or give one's life in this way is honored by our ethic of benemortasia. What is rejected is the freedom to cause death whether by suicide or by assisting in one.

How a person dies has a definite meaning for those to whom that person is related. In the first year of bereavement, the rate of death among bereaved relatives of those who die in hospitals is twice that of bereaved relatives of those who die at home; sudden deaths away from hospital and home increase the death rate of the bereaved even more.

The courage to be, as expressed in Christian and Jewish thought, is more than the overcoming of the fear of death, although it includes that Stoic dimension. It is the courage to accept one's own life as having worth no matter what life may bring, including the threat of death, because that life remains meaningful and is regarded as worthy by God, regardless of what that life may be like. . . . The courage to be as a part recognizes that one is not merely one's own, that one's life is a gift bestowed and protected by the human community and by the ultimate forces that make up the cycle of birth and death. In the cycle of birth and death, there may be suffering, as there is joy, but suffering does not render a life meaningless or worthless. Suffering people need the support of others; suffering people should not be encouraged to commit suicide by their community, or that community ceases to be a community.

This consideration brings us to a further difficulty with voluntary euthanasia and its legalization. Not only does euthanasia involve suicide, but also, if legalized, it sanctions assistance in suicide by physicians. Legislation like the Voluntary Euthanasia Act of 1969 makes it a duty of the medical profession to take someone else's life for him. Here the principle not to kill is even further eroded and violated by giving the physician the power and the encouragement to decide that someone else's life is no longer worth living. The whole notion that a physician can engage in euthanasia implies acceptance of the principle that another person's life is no longer meaningful enough to sustain, a principle that does not afford protection for the lives of any of the most defenseless, voiceless, or otherwise dependent members of a community. Everyone in a community is potentially a victim of such a principle, particularly among members of racial minorities, the very young, and the very old.

Those who would argue that these consequences of a policy of voluntary euthanasia cannot be predicted fail to see two things: that we have already had an opportunity to observe what happens when the principle that sanctions euthanasia is accepted by a society; and that regardless of what the consequences may be of such acts, the acts themselves are wrong in principle.

With respect to the first point, Leo Alexander's (1949) very careful analysis of medical practices and attitudes of German physicians before and during the reign of Nazism in Germany should serve as a definite warning against the consequences of making euthanasia a public policy. He notes that the outlook of German physicians that led to their cooperation in what became a policy of mass murders,

> started with the acceptance of that attitude, basic in the euthanasia movement, that there is such a thing as life not worthy to be lived. This attitude in its early stages concerned itself merely with the severely and chronically sick. Gradually the sphere of those to be included in this category was enlarged to include the socially unproductive, the racially unwanted, and finally all non-Germans. But it is important to realize that the infinitely small wedged-in lever from which this entire trend of mind received its impetus was the attitude toward the nonrehabilitable sick.

Those who reject out of hand any comparison of what happened in Nazi Germany with what we can expect here in the United States should consider current examples of medical practice in this nation. The treatment of mongoloids is a case in point. Now that the notion is gaining acceptance that a fetus diagnosed in the womb as mongoloid, can, at the discretion of a couple or the pregnant woman, be justifiably aborted, instances of infanticide in hospitals are being reported. At Johns Hopkins Hospital, for example, an allegedly mongoloid infant whose parents would not permit an operation that is generally successful in securing normal physical health and development, was ordered to have "nothing by mouth," condemning that infant to a death that took 15 days. . . .

Someone may argue that the mongoloid was permitted to die, not killed. But this is faulty reasoning. In the case of an infant whose future life and happiness could be reasonably assured through surgery, we are not dealing with someone who is dying and with intervention that has no curative effect. The fact that some physicians refer to this as a case of permitting to die is an ominous portent of the dangers inherent in accepting the principle that a physician or another party can decide for a patient that his or her life is not worth living. Equally ominous is the assumption that this principle, once accepted, can easily be limited to cases of patients for whom no curative intervention is known to exist. . . .

The hesitation to commit suicide and the ambivalence of the dying about their worth should give one pause before one signs a declaration that empowers a physician to decide that at some point one can no longer be trusted as competent to judge whether or not one wants to die. Physicians are also frail humans, and mistaken diagnoses, research interests, and sometimes errors of judgment that stem from a desire for organs, are part of the practice of medicine.

Comatose patients pose special problems for an ethic of benemortasia as they do for the advocates of voluntary euthanasia. Where patients are judged to be irreversibly comatose and where sustained efforts have been made to restore such persons to consciousness, no clear case can be made for permitting to die, even though it seems merciful to do so. It seems that the best we can do is to develop some rough social and medical consensus about a reasonable length of time for keeping "alive" a person's organ systems after "brain death" has been decided. Because of the pressures to do research and to transplant organs, it may also be necessary to employ special patient advocates who are not physicians and nurses. These patient advocates, trained in medical ethics, would function as ombudsmen.

In summary, even if the practice of euthanasia were to be confined to those who voluntarily request an end to their lives, no physician could in good conscience participate in such an act. To decide directly to cause the death of a patient is to abandon a cardinal principle of medical practice—namely, to do no harm to one's patient. The relief of suffering, which is surely a time-honored role for the physician, does not extend to an act that presupposes that the life of a patient who is suffering is not worthy to be lived. As we have argued, not even the patient who is dying can justifiably and unilaterally universalize the principle by which a dying life would be declared to be worthless.

Margaret Battin, "Euthanasia: The Way We Do It, The Way They Do It"
in *Journal of Pain and Symptom Management*, Vol. 6, No. 5, 1991

Euthanasia: The Way We Do It, The Way They Do It
Margaret Battin

INTRODUCTION

Because we tend to be rather myopic in our discussions of death and dying, especially about the issues of active euthanasia and assisted suicide, it is valuable to place the question of how we go about dying in an international context. We do not always see that our own cultural norms may be quite different from those of other nations, and that our background assumptions, and actual practices, differ dramatically. Thus, I would like to examine the perspectives on end-of-life dilemmas in three countries, the Netherlands, Germany, and the USA.

The Netherlands, Germany, and the United States are all advanced industrial democracies. They all have sophisticated medical establishments and life expectancies over 70 years of age; their populations are all characterized by an increasing proportion of older persons. They are all in what has been called the fourth stage of the epidemiologic transition[1]—that stage of societal development in which it is no longer the case that most people die of acute parasitic or infectious diseases. In this stage, most people do not die of diseases with rapid, unpredictable onsets and sharp fatality curves; rather, the majority of the population—as much as perhaps 70%–80%—dies of degenerative diseases, especially delayed degenerative diseases, that are characterized by late, slow onset and extended decline. Most people in highly industrialized countries die from cancer, atherosclerosis, heart disease (by no means always suddenly fatal), chronic obstructive pulmonary disease, liver, kidney or other organ disease, or degenerative neurological disorders. Thus, all three of these countries are alike in facing a common problem: how to deal with the characteristic new ways in which we die.

DEALING WITH DYING IN THE UNITED STATES

In the United States, we have come to recognize that the maximal extension of life-prolonging treatment in these late-life degenerative conditions is often inappropriate. Although we could keep the machines and tubes—the respirators, intravenous lines, feeding tubes—hooked up for extended periods, we recognize that this is inhumane, pointless, and financially impossible. Instead, as a society we have developed a number of mechanisms for dealing with these hopeless situations, all of which involve withholding or withdrawing various forms of treatment.

Some mechanisms for withholding or withdrawing treatment are exercised by the patient who is confronted by such a situation or who anticipates it; these include refusal of treatment, the patient-executed DNR order, the Living Will, and the Durable Power of Attorney. Others are mechanisms for decision by second parties about a patient who is no longer competent or never was competent. The latter are reflected in a long series of court cases, including *Quinlan, Saikewicz, Spring, Eichner, Barber, Bartling, Conroy, Brophy,* the trio *Farrell, Peter* and *Jobes,* and *Cruzan.* These are cases that attempt to delineate the precise circumstances under which it is appropriate to withhold or withdraw various forms of therapy, including respiratory support, chemotherapy, antibiotics in intercurrent infections, and artificial nutrition and hydration. Thus, during the past 15 years or so, roughly since *Quinlan* (1976), we have developed an impressive body of case law and state statute that protects, permits, and facilitates our characteristic American strategy of dealing with end-of-life situations. These cases provide a framework for withholding or withdrawing treatment when we believe there is no medical or moral point in going on. This is sometimes termed *passive euthanasia;* more often, it is simply called *allowing to die,* and is ubiquitous in the United States.

For example, a recent study by Miles and Gomez indicates that some 85% of deaths in the United States occur in health-care institutions, including hospitals, nursing homes, and other facilities, and of these, some 70% involve electively withholding some form of life-sustaining treatment.[2] A 1989 study cited in the *Journal of the American Medical Association* claims that 85%–90% of critical care professionals state that they are withholding and withdrawing life-sustaining treatments from patients who are "deemed to have irreversible disease and are terminally ill."[3] Still another study identified some 115 patients in two intensive-care units from whom care was withheld or withdrawn; 110 were already incompetent by the time the decision to limit care was made. The 89 who died while still in the intensive care unit accounted for 45% of all deaths there.[4] It is estimated that 1.3 million American deaths a year follow decisions to withhold life support;[5] this is a majority of the just over 2 million American deaths per year. Withholding and withdrawing treatment is the way we in the USA go about dealing with dying, and indeed "allowing to die" is the only legally protected alternative to maximal treatment recognized in the United States. We do not legally permit ourselves to actively cause death.

DEALING WITH DYING IN THE NETHERLANDS

In the Netherlands, voluntary active euthanasia is also an available response to end-of-life situations. Although active euthanasia remains prohibited by statutory law, it is protected by a series of lower and supreme court decisions and is widely regarded as legal, or, more precisely, *gedoeken,* legally "tolerated." These court decisions have the effect of protecting the physician who performs euthanasia from prosecution, provided the physician meets a rigorous set of guidelines.

These guidelines, variously stated, contain five central provisions:

1.   that the patient's request be voluntary;

2.   that the patient be undergoing intolerable suffering;

3.   that all alternatives acceptable to the patient for relieving the suffering have been tried;

4.   that the patient have full information;

5.   that the physician consult with a second physician whose judgment can be expected to be independent.

Of these criteria, it is the first which is central: euthanasia may be performed only at the voluntary request of the patient. This criterion is also understood to require that the patient's request be a stable, enduring, reflective one—not the product of a transitory impulse. Every attempt is to be made to rule out depression, psychopathology, pressures from family members, unrealistic fears, and other factors compromising voluntariness.

Putting an end to years of inflammatory discussion in which speculation about the frequency of euthanasia had ranged from 2,000 (close to correct) to 20,000 cases a year, a comprehensive study requested by the Dutch government was published in late 1991; an English version appeared in *The Lancet*.[6] Popularly known as the Remmelink Commission report, this study provided the first objective data about the incidence of euthanasia as well as a wider range of medical practices at the end of life: the withholding or withdrawal of treatment, the use of life-shortening doses of opiods for the control of pain, and direct termination, including active euthanasia, physician-assisted suicide, and life-ending procedures not termed euthanasia. This study was supplemented by a second empirical examination, focusing particularly carefully on the characteristics of patients and the nature of their euthanasia requests.[7]

About 130,000 people die in the Netherlands every year, and of these deaths, about 30% are acute and unexpected; 70% are predictable and foreseen, usually the result of degenerative illnesses comparatively late in life. Of the total deaths in the Netherlands, the Remmelink Commission's study found, about 17.5% involved decisions to withhold or withdraw treatment although continuing treatment would probably have prolonged life; another 17.5% involved the use of opiods to relieve pain but in dosages probably sufficient to shorten life. A total of 2.9% of all deaths involved euthanasia and related practices.

About 2,300 people, 1.8% of the total deaths in the Netherlands, died by euthanasia, understood as the termination of the life of the patient at the patient's explicit and persistent request. Another 400 people, 0.03% of the total, chose physician-assisted suicide. About 1,000 additional patients died as the result of "life-terminating procedures," not technically called euthanasia, in virtually all of which euthanasia had either been previously discussed with the patient or the patient had expressed in a previous phase of the disease a wish for euthanasia if his or her suffering became unbearable, or the patient was near death and clearly suffering grievously, yet verbal contact had become impossible.

Although euthanasia is thus not frequent—a small fraction of the total annual mortality— it is nevertheless a conspicuous option in terminal illness, well known to both physicians and the general public. There has been *very* widespread public discussion of the issues in euthanasia during the last several years, especially as the pros and cons of full legalization have been debated, and surveys of public opinion show that the public support for a liberal euthanasia policy has been growing: from 40% in 1966 to 81% in 1988.[8] Doctors too support this practice, and although there is a vocal opposition group, the opposition is in the clear minority. Some 54% of Dutch physicians said that they performed euthanasia or provide assistance in suicide, including 62% of *huisarts* or general practitioners, and an additional 34% said that although they had not actually done so, they could conceive of situations in which they would be prepared to do so. Thus, although many who had practiced euthanasia mentioned that they would be most reluctant to do so again and that "only in the face of unbearable suffering and with no alternatives would they be prepared to take such action,"[9] some 88% of Dutch physicians appear to accept the practice in some cases. As the Remmelink Commission commented, ". . . a large majority of physicians in the Netherlands see euthanasia as an accepted element of medical practice under certain circumstances."[10]

In general, pain alone is not the basis for euthanasia, since pain can, in most cases, be effectively treated. Rather, "intolerable suffering," among the criteria for euthanasia, is understood to mean suffering that is intolerable in the patient's (rather than the physician's) view, and can include a fear of or unwillingness to endure *entluisterung*, that gradual effacement and loss of personal identity that characterizes the end stages of many terminal illnesses. In a year, about 25,000 patients seek reassurance from their physicians that they will be granted euthanasia if their suffering becomes severe; there are about 9,000 explicit requests, and more than two-thirds of these are turned down, usually on the grounds that there is some other way of treating the patient's suffering, and in just 14% on the grounds of psychiatric illness.

In Holland, many hospitals now have protocols for the performance of euthanasia; these serve to ensure that the court-established guidelines have been met. However, euthanasia is often practiced in the patient's home, typically by the *huisarts* or general practitioner who is the patient's long-term family physician. Euthanasia is usually performed after aggressive hospital treatment has failed to arrest the patient's terminal illness; the patient has come home to die, and the family physician is prepared to ease this passing. Whether practiced at home or in the hospital, it is believed that euthanasia usually takes place in the presence of the family members, perhaps the visiting nurse, and often the patient's pastor or priest. Many doctors say that performing euthanasia is never easy, but that it is something they believe a doctor ought to do for his or her patient, when nothing else can help.

Thus, in Holland a patient facing the end of life has an option not openly practiced in the United States: to ask the physician to bring his or her life to an end. Although not everyone does so—indeed, about 97% of people who die in a given year do not—it is a choice widely understood as available.

FACING DEATH IN GERMANY

In part because of its very painful history of Nazism, Germany appears to believe that doctors should have no role in causing death. Although societal generalizations are always risky, it is fair, I think, to say that there is vigorous and nearly universal opposition in Germany to the notion of active euthanasia, Euthanasia is viewed as always wrong, and the Germans view the Dutch as stepping out on a dangerously slippery slope.

However, it is an artifact of German law that, whereas killing on request (including voluntary euthanasia) is prohibited, assisting suicide is not a violation of the law, provided the person is *tatherrschaftsfähig*, capable of exercising control over his or her actions, and also acting out of *freiverantwortliche Wille*, freely responsible choice. Responding to this situation, there has developed a private organization, the *Deutsche Gesellschaft fur Humanes Sterben* (DGHS), or German Society for Humane Dying, which provides support to its very extensive membership (over 50,000 persons) in choosing suicide as an alternative to terminal illness.

After a person has been a member of the DGHS for at least a year, and provided that he or she has not received medical or psychotherapeutic treatment for depression or other psychiatric illness during the last two years, he or she may request a copy of DGHS's booklet *Menschenwürdiges und selbstverantworliches Sterben*, or "Dignified and Responsible Death." This booklet provides a list of about ten drugs available by prescription in Germany, together with the specific dosages necessary for producing a certain, painless death. (The DGHS no longer officially recommends cyanide, though its president, Hans Henning Atrott, was recently charged with selling it.) DGHS recommends that the members approach a physician for a prescription for the drug desired, asking, for example, for a barbiturate to help with sleep, or chloroquine for protection against malaria on a trip to India. If necessary, the DGHS may also arrange for someone to obtain drugs from neighboring countries, including France, Italy, Spain, Portugal, and Greece, where they may be available without prescription. In unusual cases, the DGHS will also provide what it calls *Sterbebegleitung* or "accompaniment in dying," providing a companion to remain with the person during the often extended period that is required for the lethal drug to take full effect. However, the *Sterbebegleiter* is typically a layperson, not someone medically trained, and physicians play no role in assisting in these cases of suicide. To preclude suspicion by providing evidence of the person's intentions, the DGHS also provides a form—printed on a single sheet of distinctive pink paper—to be signed once when joining the organization, expressing the intention to determine the time of one's own death, and to be signed again at the time of the suicide and left beside the body.

Because assisting suicide is not illegal in Germany, provided the person is competent and in control of his or her own will, there is no legal risk for family members, *Sterbebegleiter*, or others in reporting information about the methods and effectiveness of suicide attempts, and the DGHS encourages its network of regional bureaus (five, in major cities throughout the country) to facilitate feedback. On this basis, it regularly updates and revises the drug information it provides. It claims some 2,000–3,000 suicides per year among its members.

To be sure, assisted suicide is not the only option open to the terminally ill patient in Germany, nor is there clear evidence concerning its frequency either within the DGHS or in nonreported cases outside it. There is increasing emphasis on help in dying that does not involve direct termination, and organizations like Ormega, offering hospice-style care and an extensive program of companionship, are attracting increasing attention. Furthermore, there has been recent scandal directed towards the founder and president of the DGHS, Hans Henning Atrott, accused in late 1991 of selling cyanide to an attorney hospitalized for mental illness; in May 1992 police raided his office, finding capsules of cyanide, barbiturates, and a large amount of cash. What the outcome of this event will be remains at this writing to be seen, though it is clear that the scandal focuses on Atrott's alleged profiteering and assisting a mentally ill person, rather than with the DGHS's regular practice of assisting competent terminally ill individuals in suicide. Furthermore, the DGHS is a conspicuous, widely known organization, and many Germans appear to be aware that assisted suicide is available even if they do not use the services of the DGHS.

OBJECTIONS TO THE THREE MODELS OF DYING

In response to the dilemmas raised by the new circumstances of death, in which the majority of the population in each of the advanced industrial nations dies of degenerative diseases after an extended period of terminal deterioration, different countries develop different practices. The United States legally permits only withholding and withdrawal of treatment, though of course active euthanasia and assisted suicide do occur. Holland also permits voluntary active euthanasia, and although Germany rejects euthanasia, it tolerates assisted suicide. But there are serious moral objections to be made to each of these practices, objections to be considered before resolving the issue of which practice our own culture ought to adopt.

OBJECTIONS TO THE GERMAN PRACTICE

German law does not prohibit assisting suicide, but postwar German culture discourages physicians from taking any active role in death. This gives rise to distinctive moral problems. For one thing, it appears that there is little professional help or review provided for patients' choices about suicide; because the patient makes this choice essentially outside the medical establishment, medical professionals are not in a position to detect or treat impaired judgment on the part of the patient, especially judgment impaired by depression. Similarly, if the patient must commit suicide assisted only by persons outside the medical profession, there are risks that the patient's diagnosis and prognosis are inadequately confirmed, that the means chosen for suicide will be unreliable or inappropriately used, that the means used for suicide will fall into the hands of other persons, and that the patient will fail to recognize or be able to resist intrafamilial pressures and manipulation. The DGHS policy for providing assistance requires that the patient be terminally ill and have been a member of the DGHS for at least one year in order to make use of its services, the latter requirement is intended to provide evidence of the stability of such a choice. However, these minimal requirements are hardly sufficient to answer the charge that suicide decisions, which are made for medical reasons but must be made without medical help, may be rendered under less than ideally informed and voluntary conditions.

OBJECTIONS TO THE DUTCH PRACTICE

The Dutch practice of physician-performed active voluntary euthanasia also raises a number of ethical issues, many of which have been discussed vigorously both in the Dutch press and in commentary on the Dutch practices from abroad. For one thing, it is sometimes said that the availability of physician-performed euthanasia creates a disincentive for providing good terminal care. I have seen no evidence that this is the case; on the contrary, Peter Admiraal, the anesthesiologist who is perhaps Holland's most vocal proponent of voluntary active euthanasia, insists that pain should rarely or never be the occasion for euthanasia, as pain (in contrast to suffering) is comparatively easily treated.[11] Instead, it is a refusal to endure the final stages of deterioration, both mental and physical, that motivates requests.

It is also sometimes said that active euthanasia violates the Hippocratic Oath. Indeed, it is true that the original Greek version of the Oath prohibits the physician from giving a deadly drug, even when asked for it; but the original version also prohibits performing surgery and taking fees for teaching medicine, nether of which prohibitions has survived into contemporary medical practice. Dutch physicians often say that they see performing euthanasia—where it is genuinely requested by the patient and nothing else can be done to relieve the patient's condition—as part of their duty to the patient, not as a violation of it.

The Dutch are also often said to be at risk of starting down the slippery slope, that is, that the practice of voluntary active euthanasia for patients who meet the criteria will erode into practicing less-than-voluntary euthanasia on patients whose problems are not irremediable, and perhaps by gradual degrees develop into terminating the lives of people who are elderly, chronically ill, handicapped, mentally retarded, or otherwise regarded as undesirable. This risk is often expressed in vivid claims of widespread fear and wholesale slaughter, claims that are repeated in the right-to-life press in both the Netherlands, and the USA, though there is no evidence for these claims. However, the Dutch are now beginning to agonize over the problems of the incompetent patient, the mentally ill patient, the newborn with serious deficits, and other patients who cannot make voluntary choices, though these are largely understood as issues about withholding or withdrawing treatment, not about direct termination.[12]

What is not often understood is that this new and acutely painful area of reflection for the Dutch—withholding and withdrawing treatment from incompetent patients—has already led in the United States to the development of a vast, highly developed body of law: namely that series of cases just cited, beginning with *Quinlan* and culminating in *Cruzan*. Americans have been discussing these issues for a long time, and have developed a broad set of practices that are regarded as routine in withholding and withdrawing treatment. The Dutch see Americans as much further out on the slippery slope than they are, because Americans have already become accustomed to second-party choices about other people. Issues involving second-party choices are painful to the Dutch in a way they are not to us precisely because *voluntariness* is so central in the Dutch understanding of choices about dying. Concomitantly, the Dutch see the Americans' squeamishness about first-party choices—voluntary euthanasia, assisted suicide—as evidence that we are not genuinely committed to recognizing *voluntary* choice after all. For this reason, many Dutch commentators believe that the Americans are at a much greater risk of sliding down the slippery slope into involuntary killing than they are. I fear, I must add, that they are right about this.

OBJECTIONS TO THE AMERICAN PRACTICE

There may be moral problems raised by the German and the Dutch practices, but there are also moral problems raised by the American practice of relying on withholding and withdrawal of treatment in end-of-life situations. The German, Dutch, and American practices all occur within similar conditions—in industrialized nations with highly developed medical systems, where a majority of the population dies of illnesses exhibiting characteristically extended downhill courses—but the issues raised by our own response to this situation may be even more disturbing than those of the Dutch or the Germans. We often assume that our approach is "safer" because it involves only letting someone die, not killing him or her; but it too raises very troubling questions.

The first of these issues is a function of the fact that withdrawing and especially withholding treatment are typically less conspicuous, less pronounced, less evident kinds of actions than direct killing, even though they can equally well lead to death. Decisions about nontreatment have an invisibility that decisions about directly causing death do not have, even though they may have the same result, and hence there is a much wider range of occasions in which such decisions can be made. One can decline to treat a patient in many different ways, at many different times—by not providing oxygen, by not instituting dialysis, by not correcting electrolyte imbalances, and so on—all of which will cause the patient's death; open medical killing also brings about death, but is a much more overt, conspicuous procedure. Consequently, letting die also invites many fewer protections. In contrast to the standard slippery slope argument which sees killing as riskier than letting die, the more realistic slippery slope argument warns that because our culture relies primarily on decisions about nontreatment, grave decisions about living or dying are not as open to scrutiny as they are under more direct life-terminating practices, and hence, are more open to abuse.

Second, and closely related, reliance on withholding and withdrawing treatment invites rationing in an extremely strong way, in part because of the comparative invisibility of these decisions. When a health care provider does not offer a specific sort of care, it is not always possible to discern the motivation; the line between believing that it would not provide benefit to the patient and that it would not provide benefit worth the investment of resources in the patient can be very thin. This is a particular problem where health care financing is highly decentralized, as in the United States, and where rationing decisions without benefit of principle are not always available for easy review.

Third, relying on withholding and withdrawal of treatment can often be cruel. It requires that the patient who is dying from one of the diseases that exhibits a characteristic extended, downhill course (as the majority of patients in the Netherlands, Germany and the U.S. do) must in effect wait to die until the absence of a certain treatment will cause death. For instance, the cancer patient who foregoes chemotherapy or surgery does not simply die from this choice; he or she continues to endure the downhill course of cancer until the tumor finally destroys some crucial bodily function or organ. The patient with amyotropic lateral sclerosis who decides in advance to decline respiratory support does not die at the time the choice is made, but continues to endure increasing paralysis until breathing is impaired and suffocation occurs. We often try to ameliorate these situations by administering pain medication or symptom control at the same time we are withholding treatment, but these are all ways of disguising the fact that we are letting the disease kill the patient rather than directly bringing about death. But the ways diseases kill people are far more cruel than the ways physicians kill patients when performing euthanasia or assisting in suicide.

THE PROBLEM: A CHOICE OF CULTURES

Thus we see three similar cultures and countries and three similar sets of circumstances, but three different basic practices in approaching death. All three of these practices generate moral problems; none of them, nor any others we might devise, is free of moral difficulty. But the question that faces us is this: which of these practices is best?

It is not possible to answer this question in a less-than-ideal world without some attention to the specific characteristics and deficiencies of the society in question. In asking which of these practices is best, we must ask which is best *for us*. That we currently employ one set of these practices rather than others does not prove that it is best for us; the question is, would practices developed in other cultures or those not yet widespread in any be better for our own culture than that which has developed here? Thus, it is necessary to consider the differences between our society and these European cultures that have real bearing on which model of approach to dying we ought to adopt.

First, notice that different cultures exhibit different degrees of closeness between physicians and patients—different patterns of contact and involvement. The German physician is sometimes said to be more distant and more authoritarian than the American physician; on the other hand, the Dutch physician is sometimes said to be closer to his or her patients than either the American or the German is. In the Netherlands, basic primary care is provided by the *huisarts*, the general practitioner or family physician, who typically lives in the neighborhood, makes house calls frequently, and maintains an office in his or her own home. The *huisarts* is usually the physician for other members of the patient's family, and will remain the family's physician throughout his or her practice. Thus, the patient for whom euthanasia becomes an issue—say, the terminal cancer patient who has been hospitalized in the past but who has returned home to die—will be cared for by the trusted family physician on a regular basis. Indeed, for a patient in severe distress, the physician, supported by the visiting nurse, may make house calls as often as once a day, twice a day, or more (after all, it is right in the neighborhood), and is in continuous contact with the family. In contrast, the traditional American institution of the family doctor who makes house calls is rapidly becoming a thing of the past, and although some patients who die at home have access to hospice services and house calls from their long-term physician, many have no such long-term care and receive most of it from staff at a clinic or housestaff rotating through the services of a hospital. The degree of continuing contact the patient can have with a familiar, trusted physician clearly influences the nature of his or her dying, and also plays a role in whether physician-performed active euthanasia, assisted suicide, and/or withholding and withdrawing treatment is appropriate.

Second, the United States has a much more volatile legal climate than either the Netherlands or Germany; our medical system is increasingly litigious, much more so than that of any other country in the world. Fears of malpractice action or criminal prosecution color much of what physicians do in managing the dying of their patients. We also tend to evolve public policy through court decisions, and to assume that the existence of a policy puts an end to any moral issue. A delicate legal and moral balance over the issues of euthanasia, as is the case in the Netherlands, would not be possible here.

Third, we in the United States have a very different financial climate in which to do our dying. Both the Netherlands and Germany, as well as every other industrialized nation except South Africa, have systems of national health insurance or national health care. Thus the patient is not directly responsible for the costs of treatment, and consequently the patient's choices about terminal care and/or euthanasia need not take personal financial considerations into account. Even for the patient who does have health insurance in the United States, many kinds of services are not covered, whereas the national health care or health insurance programs of many other countries variously provide many sorts of relevant services, including at-home physician care, home nursing care, home respite care, care in a nursing-home or other long-term facility, dietitian care, rehabilitation care, physical therapy, psychological counseling, and so on. The patient in the United States needs to attend to the financial aspects of dying in a way patients in many other countries do not, and in this country both the patient's choices and the recommendations of the physician are very often shaped by financial considerations.

There are many other differences between the USA on the one hand and the Netherlands and Germany, with their different models of dying, on the other. There are differences in degrees of paternalism in the medical establishment and in racism, sexism, and ageism in the general cultures, as well as awareness of a problematic historical past, especially Nazism. All of these and the previous factors influence the appropriateness or inappropriateness of practices such as active euthanasia and assisted suicide. For instance, the Netherlands' tradition of close physician/patient contact, its absence of malpractice-motivated medicine, and its provision of comprehensive health insurance, together with its comparative lack of racism and ageism and its experience in resistance to Nazism, suggest that this culture is able to permit the practice of voluntary active euthanasia, performed by physicians, without risking abuse. On the other hand, it is sometimes said that Germany still does not trust its physicians, remembering the example of Nazi experimentation, and given a comparatively authoritarian medical climate in which contact between physician and patient is quite distanced, the population could not be comfortable with the practice of active euthanasia. There, only a wholly patient-controlled response to terminal situations, as in non-physician-assisted suicide, is a reasonable and prudent practice.

But what about the United States? This is a country where (1) sustained contact with the personal physician is decreasing, (2) the risk of malpractice action is increasing, (3) much medical care is not insured, (4) many medical decisions are financial decisions as well, (5) racism is on the rise, and (6) the public is naive about direct contact with Nazism or similar totalitarian movements. Thus, the United States is in many respects an untrustworthy candidate for practicing active euthanasia. Given the pressures on individuals in an often atomized society, encouraging solo suicide, assisted if at all only by nonprofessionals, might well be open to considerable abuse too.

However, there are several additional differences between the United States and both Holland and Germany that seem relevant here.

So far, the differences cited between the U.S. and both the Netherlands and Germany are negative ones, one in which the U.S. falls far short. But there are positive differences as well, differences in which distinctive aspects of American culture are more favorable than those of Holland or Germany to the practice of euthanasia and assisted suicide. For example:

First, although the U.S. is indeed afflicted by a great deal of racism and sexism, it is also developing an increasingly strong tradition of independence in women. In many other countries, especially the Far East and the Islamic countries, the role of women still involves much greater disempowerment and expectations of subservience; in contrast, the U.S. is particularly advanced—though, of course, it has a long way to go. The U.S. may even be ahead of the Netherlands and perhaps Germany in this respect. Whatever the case, this issue is of particular importance with respect to euthanasia, especially among elderly persons, because it is women whose life expectancies are longer than those of men and hence are more likely to be confronted with late-life degenerative terminal conditions.

Second, American culture is more confrontational than many others, including Dutch culture. While the Netherlands prides itself rightly on a long tradition of rational discussion of public issues and on toleration of others' views and practices, the U.S. (and to some degree, also Germany) tends to develop highly partisan, moralizing oppositional groups. In general, this is a disadvantage; but in the case of euthanasia it may serve to alert a public to issues and possibilities it might not otherwise consider, and especially to the risks of abuse.

Third, though this may at first seem to be a trivial difference, it is Americans, who are particularly given to personal self-analysis. This tendency is evident not only in America's high rate of utilization of counseling services, including religious counseling, psychological counseling, and psychiatry, but is even more clearly evident in its popular culture: its diet of soap operas, situation comedies, and pop psychology books. It is here that the ordinary American absorbs models for analyzing his or her own personal relationships and individual psychological characteristics. While of course things are changing and our cultural tastes are widely exported, the fact remains that the ordinary American's cultural diet contains more in the way of both professional and do-it-yourself amateur psychology and self-analysis than anyone else's. This long tradition of self-analysis may put us in a better position for certain kinds of end-of-life practices than many other cultures—despite whatever other deficiencies we have, just because we live in a culture that encourages us to inspect our own motives, anticipate the impact of our actions on others and scrutinize our own relationships with others, including our physicians. This disposition is of importance in euthanasia contexts because euthanasia is the kind of fundamental choice about which one may have somewhat mixed motives, be subject to various interpersonal and situational pressures, and so on. If the voluntary character of these choices is to be protected, it may be a good thing to inhabit a culture in which self-inspection of one's own mental habits and motives is encouraged.

Finally, the U.S. is also characterized by a kind of "do-it-yourself" ethic, an ethic that does not rely on others to direct you or provide for you, but encourages individual initiative and responsibility. (To be sure this feature has been somewhat eclipsed in recent years, and is little in evidence in the series of court cases cited earlier, but it is still part, I think, of the American character.) This is coupled with a sort of resistance to authority that is sometime also said to be basic to the American temperament. If these things are the case, it would seem to suggest that Americans would seek a style of end-of-life practices which would emphasize these characteristics rather than others.

These, of course, are all mere conjectures about features of American culture which would have a positive effect on the practice of euthanasia, or assisted suicide. These are the features that one would want to reinforce, should these practices become general, in part to minimize the effects of the negative features. But, of course, these positive features will differ from one country and culture to another, just as negative features do. In each country, a different architecture of antecedent assumptions and cultural features develops around the issues of the end of life, and in each country the practice of euthanasia, if it is to be free from abuse at all, must be adapted to the culture in which it takes place.

What, then, is appropriate for our own cultural situation? Physician-performed euthanasia, though not in itself morally wrong, is morally jeopardized where the legal, time, and especially financial pressures on both patients and physicians are severe; thus, it is morally problematic in our culture in a way that it is not in the Netherlands. Solo suicide outside the institution of medicine (as in Germany) may be problematic in a culture (like the United States) that is increasingly alienated, offers deteriorating and uneven social services, is increasingly racist, and in other ways imposes unusual pressures on individuals despite opportunities for self-analysis. Reliance only on withholding and withdrawing treatment (as in the United States) can be, as we've seen, cruel, and its comparative invisibility invites erosion under cost containment and other pressures. These are the three principal alternatives we've considered; but none of them seems wholly suited to our actual situation for dealing with the new fact that most of us die of extended-decline, deteriorative diseases. However, permitting physicians to supply patients with the means for ending their own lives grants physicians some control over the circumstances in which this can happen—only, for example, when the prognosis is genuinely grim and the alternatives for symptom control are poor—but leaves the fundamental decision about whether to use these means to the patient alone. It is up to the patient then—the independent, confrontational self-analyzing, do-it-yourself, authority-resisting patient—and his or her advisors, including family, clergy, physician, other health-care providers, and a raft of pop-psychology books, to be clear about whether he or she really wants to use these means or not. Thus, the physician is involved, but not directly; and it is the patient's choice, but the patient is not alone in making it. We live in a quite imperfect world, but, of the alternatives for facing death—which we all eventually must—I think the practice of permitting physician-assisted suicide is the one most nearly suited to the current state of our own somewhat flawed society. This is a model not yet central in any of the three countries examined here—the Netherlands, Germany, or the United States—but it is the one I think suits us best.

Notes

1. Olshansky SJ. Ault AB. The fourth stage of the epidemiological transition: the age of delayed degenerative diseases. *Milbank Memorial Fund Quarterly/Health and Society* 1986;64:355–391.

2. Miles S. Gomez C. *Protocols for elective use of life-sustaining treatment.* New York: Springer-Verlag. 1988.

3. Sprung CL. Changing attitudes and practices in foregoing life-sustaining treatments. *JAMA* 1990; 263:2213.

4. Smedira NG et al. Withholding and withdrawal of life support from the critically ill. *N Engl J Med* 1990: 322:309–315.

5. *New York Times.* July 23, 1990, p. A13.

6. Paul J. van der Maas, Johannes J.M. vanDelden, Loes Pijnenborg, and Casper W. N. Looman, "Euthanasia and Other Medical Decisions Concerning the End Of Life." *The Lancet* 338 (Sept. 14, 1991): 669–674.

7. G. van der Wal, J .Th. M. van Eijk, H. J. J. Leenen, and C. Spreeuwenberg, "Euthanasie en hulp hij selfdoding door artsen in de thuissituatie. I. Diagnosen, leeftijd en geslacht van de patienten," *Nederlands Tijdschrift voor Geneesekunde* 135 (1991: 1593–1598: and II. "Lijden van de patienten," 1500–1603.

8. Else Borst-Eilers, paper delivered at the conference "Controversies in the Care of Dying Patients." University of Florida, Orlando, Feb. 14–16, 1991.

9. Van der Maas, p. 673.

10. Van der Maas, p. 671.

11. Admiraal P. *Euthanasia in a general hospital.* Address to the Eighth World Congress of the International Federation of Right-To-Die Societies, Maastricht. Holland. June 8, 1990.

12. Ten Have, H. "Coma: controversy and consensus."*Newsletter of the European Society for Philosophy of Medicine and Health Care* (May 1990) 8:19–20.

United States Supreme Court, 110 S.Ct. 2841 (1990).

Majority Opinion in *Cruzan v. Director, Missouri Department of Health*
Justice William H. Rehnquist

This case developed when the parents of Nancy Beth Cruzan—a woman existing in a persistent vegetative state subsequent to an automobile accident suffered at the age of twenty-five—sought authorization from a Missouri trial court to terminate their daughter's artificial nutrition and hydration. The trial court authorized termination of treatment, but the Supreme Court of Missouri reversed the decision of the trial court. The United States Supreme Court upheld the judgment of the Missouri Supreme Court.

Writing the majority opinion in a five-to-four decision, Justice Rehnquist acknowledges that a *competent* person has a constitutionally protected right to refuse lifesaving nutrition and hydration. However, in the case of an *incompetent* person, he argues, it is not unconstitutional for Missouri to insist that nutrition and hydration can be terminated only if there is "clear and convincing evidence" that termination of treatment is what the person would have wanted. Since this standard of proof has presumably not been satisfied in the case of Nancy Beth Cruzan, he concludes, the judgment of the Missouri Supreme Court is affirmed. (In subsequent developments, a Missouri court considered new evidence presented by Cruzan's parents and concluded that there was "clear and convincing evidence" that she would have chosen to terminate treatment. Nutrition and hydration were subsequently withheld and Nancy Cruzan died in December of 1990.)

Petitioner Nancy Beth Cruzan was rendered incompetent as a result of severe injuries sustained during an automobile accident. Co-petitioner Lester and Joyce Cruzan, Nancy's parents and co-guardians, sought a court order directing the withdrawal of their daughter's artificial feeding and hydration equipment after it became apparent that she had virtually no chance of recovering her cognitive faculties. The Supreme Court of Missouri held that because there was no clear and convincing evidence of Nancy's desire to have life-sustaining treatment withdrawn under such circumstances, her parents lacked authority to effectuate such a request. We . . . now affirm.

On the night of January 11, 1983, Nancy Cruzan lost control of her car as she traveled down Elm Road in Jasper County, Missouri. The vehicle overturned, and Cruzan was discovered lying face down in a ditch without detectable respiratory or cardiac function. Paramedics were able to restore her breathing and heartbeat at the accident site, and she was transported to a hospital in an unconscious state. An attending neurosurgeon diagnosed her as having sustained probable cerebral contusions compounded by significant anoxia (lack of oxygen). The Missouri trial court in this case found that permanent brain damage generally results after 6 minutes in an anoxia state; it was estimated that Cruzan was deprived of oxygen from 12 to 14 minutes. She remained in a coma for approximately three weeks and then progressed to an unconscious state in which she was able to orally ingest some nutrition. In order to ease feeding and further the recovery, surgeons implanted a gastrostomy feeding and hydration tube in Cruzan with the consent of her husband. Subsequent rehabilitative efforts proved unavailing. She now lies in a Missouri state hospital in what is commonly referred to as a persistent vegetative state: generally, a condition in which a person exhibits motor reflexes but evinces no indications of significant cognitive function.[1] The State of Missouri is bearing the cost of her care.

After it had become apparent that Nancy Cruzan had virtually no chance of regaining her mental faculties her parents asked hospital employees to terminate the artificial nutrition and hydration procedures. All agree that such a removal would cause her death. The employees refused to honor the request without court approval. The parents then sought and received authorization from the state trial court for termination. The court found that a person in Nancy's condition had a fundamental right under the State and Federal Constitutions to refuse or direct the withdrawal of "death prolonging procedures." The court also found that Nancy's expressed thoughts at age twenty-five in somewhat serious conversation with a housemate friend that if sick or injured she would not wish to continue her life unless she could live at least halfway normally suggests that given her present condition she would not wish to continue on with her nutrition and hydration."

The Supreme Court of Missouri reversed by a divided vote. The court recognized a right to refuse treatment embodied in the common-law doctrine of informed consent, but expressed skepticism about the application of that doctrine in the circumstances of this case. The court also declined to read a broad right of privacy into the State Constitution which would "support the right of a person to refuse medical treatment in every circumstance," and expressed doubt as to whether such a right existed under the United States Constitution. It then decided that the Missouri Living Will statute (1986) embodied a state policy strongly favoring the preservation of life. The court found that Cruzan's statements to her roommate regarding her desire to live or die under certain conditions were "unreliable for the purpose of determining her intent," "and insufficient to support the co-guardians claim to exercise substituted judgment on Nancy's behalf." It rejected the argument that Cruzan's parents were entitled to order the termination of her medical treatment, concluding that "no person can assume that choice for an incompetent in the absence of the formalities required under Missouri's Living Will statutes or the clear and convincing, inherently reliable evidence absent here." . . .

We granted certiorari to consider the question of whether Cruzan has a right under the United States Constitution which would require the hospital to withdraw life-sustaining treatment from her under these circumstances.

At common law, even the touching of one person by another without consent and without legal justification was a battery. Before the turn of the century, this Court observed that "[n]o right is held more sacred, or is more carefully guarded, by the common law, than the right of every individual to the possession and control of his own person, free from all restraint or interference of others, unless by clear and unquestionable authority of law." This notion of bodily integrity has been embodied in the requirement that informed consent is generally required for medical treatment. Justice Cardozo, while on the Court of Appeals of New York, aptly described this doctrine: "Every human being of adult years and sound mind has a right to determine what shall be done with his own body; and a surgeon who performs an operation without his patient's consent commits an assault, for which he is liable in damages." The informed consent doctrine has become firmly entrenched in American tort law.

The logical corollary of the doctrine of informed consent is that the patient generally possesses the right not to consent, that is, to refuse treatment. Until about 15 years ago and the seminal decision [of the New Jersey Supreme Court] in *In re Quinlan* (1976), the number of right-to-refuse-treatment decisions were relatively few. Most of the earlier cases involved patients who refused medical treatment forbidden by their religious beliefs, thus implicating First Amendment rights as well as common law rights of self-determination. More recently, however, with the advance of medical technology capable of sustaining life well past the point where natural forces would have brought certain death in earlier times, cases involving the right to refuse life-sustaining treatment burgeoned.

In the *Quinlan* case, young Karen Quinlan suffered severe brain damage as the result of anoxia, and entered a persistent vegetative state. Karen's father sought judicial approval to disconnect his daughter's respirator. The New Jersey Supreme Court granted the relief, holding that Karen had a right of privacy grounded in the Federal Constitution to terminate treatment. Recognizing that this right was not absolute, however, the court balanced it against asserted state interests. Noting that the State's interest "weakens and the individual's right to privacy grows as the degree of bodily invasion increases and the prognosis dims," the court concluded that the state interests had to give way in that case. The court also concluded that the "only practical way" to prevent the loss of Karen's privacy right due to her incompetence was to allow her guardian and family to decide "whether she would exercise it in these circumstances."

After *Quinlan*, however, most courts have based a right to refuse treatment either solely on the common law right to informed consent or on both the common law right and a constitutional privacy right. . . .

. . . State courts have available to them for decision a number of sources—state constitutions, statutes, and common law—which are not available to us. In this Court, the question is simply and starkly whether the United States Constitution prohibits Missouri from choosing the rule of decision which it did. This is the first case in which we have been squarely presented with the issue of whether the United States Constitution grants what is in common parlance referred to as a "right to die." We follow the judicious counsel . . . that in deciding a "question of such magnitude and importance . . . it is the [better] part of wisdom not to attempt, by any general statement, to cover every possible phase of the subject."

The Fourteenth Amendment provides that no State shall "deprive any person of life, liberty, or property, without due process of law." The principle that a competent person has a constitutionally protected liberty interest in refusing unwanted medical treatment may be inferred from our prior decisions. In *Jacobson* v. *Massachusetts* (1905), for instance, the Court balanced an individual's liberty interest in declining an unwanted smallpox vaccine against the State's interest in preventing disease. . . .

Just this Term, in the course of holding that a State's procedures for administering antipsychotic medication to prisoners were sufficient to satisfy due process concerns, we recognized that prisoners possess "a significant liberty interest in avoiding the unwanted administration of antipsychotic drugs under the Due Process Clause of the Fourteenth Amendment." Still other cases support the recognition of a general liberty interest in refusing medical treatment.

But determining that a person has a "liberty interest" under the Due Process Clause does not end the inquiry;[2]"whether respondent's constitutional rights have been violated must be determined by balancing his liberty interests against the relevant state interests."

Petitioners insist that under the general holdings of our cases, the forced administration of life-sustaining medical treatment, and even of artificially-delivered food and water essential to life, would implicate a competent person's liberty interest. Although we think the logic of the cases [referred to] above would embrace such a liberty interest, the dramatic consequences involved in refusal of such treatment would inform the inquiry as to whether the deprivation of that interest is constitutionally permissible. But for purposes of this case, we assume that the United States Constitution would grant a competent person a constitutionally protected right to refuse lifesaving hydration and nutrition.

Petitioners go on to assert that an incompetent person should possess the same right in this respect as is possessed by a competent person. . . .

The difficulty with petitioners' claim is that in a sense it begs the question: an incompetent person is not able to make an informed and voluntary choice to exercise a hypothetical right to refuse treatment or any other right. Such a "right" must be exercised for her, if at all, by some sort of surrogate. Here, Missouri has in effect recognized that under certain circumstances a surrogate may act for the patient in electing to have hydration and nutrition withdrawn in such a way as to cause death, but it has established a procedural safeguard to assure that the action of the surrogate conforms as best it may to the wishes expressed by the patient while competent. Missouri requires that evidence of the incompetent's wishes as to the withdrawal of treatment be proved by clear and convincing evidence. The question, then, is whether the United States Constitution forbids the establishment of this procedural requirement by the State. We hold that it does not.

Whether or not Missouri's clear and convincing evidence requirement comports with the United States Constitution depends in part on what interests the State may properly seek to protect in this situation. Missouri relies on its interest in the protection and preservation of human life, and there can be no gainsaying this interest. As a general matter, the States— indeed, all civilized nations—demonstrate their commitment to life by treating homicide as serious crime. Moreover, the majority of States in this country have laws imposing criminal penalties on one who assists another to commit suicide. We do not think a State is required to remain neutral in the face of an informed and voluntary decision by a physically-able adult to starve to death.

But in the context presented here, a State has more particular interests at stake. The choice between life and death is a deeply personal decision of obvious and overwhelming finality. We believe Missouri may legitimately seek to safeguard the personal element of this choice through the imposition of heightened evidentiary requirements. It cannot be disputed that the Due Process Clause protects an interest in life as well as an interest in refusing life-sustaining medical treatment. Not all incompetent patients will have loved ones available to serve as surrogate decisionmakers. And even where family members are present, "[t]here will, of course, be some unfortunate situations in which family members will not act to protect a patient." A State is entitled to guard against potential abuses in such situations. Similarly, a State is entitled to consider that a judicial proceeding to make a determination regarding an incompetent's wishes may very well not be an adversarial one, with the added guarantee of accurate factfinding that the adversary process brings with it. Finally, we think a State may properly decline to make judgments about the "quality" of life that a particular individual may enjoy, and simply assert an unqualified interest in the preservation of human life to be weighed against the constitutionally protected interests of the individual.

In our view, Missouri has permissibly sought to advance these interests through the adoption of a "clear and convincing" standard of proof to govern such proceedings. "The function of a standard of proof, as that concept is embodied in the Due Process Clause and in the realm of factfinding, is to 'instruct the factfinder concerning the degree of confidence our society thinks he should have in the correctness of factual conclusions for a particular type of adjudication.'" . . .

We think it self-evident that the interests at stake in the instant proceedings are more substantial, both on an individual and societal level, than those involved in a run-of-the-mine civil dispute. But not only does the standard of proof reflect the importance of a particular adjudication, it also serves as "a societal judgment about how the risk of error should be distributed between the litigants." The more stringent the burden of proof a party must bear, the more that party bears the risk of an erroneous decision. We believe that Missouri may permissibly place an increased risk of an erroneous decision on those seeking to terminate an incompetent individual's life-sustaining treatment. An erroneous decision not to terminate results in a maintenance of the status quo; the possibility of subsequent developments such as advancements in medical science, the discovery of new evidence regarding the patient's intent, changes in the law, or simply the unexpected death of the patient despite the administration of life-sustaining treatment, at least create the potential that a wrong decision will eventually be corrected or its impact mitigated. An erroneous decision to withdraw life-sustaining treatment, however, is not susceptible of correction. . . .

In sum, we conclude that a State may apply a clear and convincing evidence standard in proceedings where a guardian seeks to discontinue nutrition and hydration of a person diagnosed to be in a persistent vegetative state. . . .

The Supreme Court of Missouri held that in this case the testimony adduced at trial did not amount to clear and convincing proof of the patient's desire to have hydration and nutrition withdrawn. In so doing, it reversed a decision of the Missouri trial court which had found that the evidence "suggest[ed]" Nancy Cruzan would not have desired to continue such measures, but which had not adopted the standard of "clear and convincing evidence" enunciated by the Supreme Court. The testimony adduced at trial consisted primarily of Nancy Cruzan's statements made to a housemate about a year before her accident that she would not want to live should she face life as a "vegetable," and other observations to the same effect. The observations did not deal in terms with withdrawal of medical treatment or of hydration and nutrition. We cannot say that the Supreme Court of Missouri committed constitutional error in reaching the conclusion that it did.[3]

Petitioners alternatively contend that Missouri must accept the "substituted judgment" of close family members even in the absence of substantial proof that their views reflect the views of the patient. . . .

No doubt is engendered by anything in this record but that Nancy Cruzan's mother and father are loving and caring parents. If the State were required by the United States Constitution to repose a right of "substituted judgment" with anyone, the Cruzans would surely qualify. But we do not think the Due Process Clause requires the State to repose judgment on these matters with anyone but the patient herself. Close family members may have a strong feeling—a feeling not at all ignoble or unworthy, but not entirely disinterested, either—that they do not wish to witness the continuation of the life of a loved one which they regard as hopeless, meaningless, and even degrading. But there is no automatic assurance that the view of close family members will necessarily be the same as the patient's would have been had she been confronted with the prospect of her situation while competent. All of the reasons previously discussed for allowing Missouri to require clear and convincing evidence of the patient's wishes lead us to conclude that the State may choose to defer only to those wishes, rather than confide the decision to close family members.

The judgment of the Supreme Court of Missouri is *Affirmed*.

Notes

1. The State Supreme Court, adopting much of the trial court's findings, described Nancy Cruzan's medical condition as follows: ". . . In sum, Nancy is diagnosed as in a persistent vegetative state. She is not dead. She is not terminally ill. Medical experts testified that she could live another thirty years." . . .

2. Although many state courts have held that a right to refuse treatment is encompassed by a generalized constitutional right of privacy, we have never so held. We believe this issue is more properly analyzed in terms of a Fourteenth Amendment liberty interest. See *Bowers* v. *Hardwick* (1986).

3. The clear and convincing standard of proof has been variously defined in this context as "proof sufficient to persuade the trier of fact that the patient held a firm and settled commitment to the termination of life supports under the circumstances like those presented," and as evidence which "produces in the mind of the trier of fact a firm belief or conviction as to the truth of the allegations sought to be established, evidence so clear, direct and weighty and convincing as to enable [the factfinder] to come to a clear conviction, without hesitancy, of the truth of the precise facts in issue." . . .

Questions

1. If you were in a persistent vegetative state like Nancy Cruzan was, would you want artificial nutrition and hydration to be terminated?

2. If you were a citizen of Missouri, would you endorse a legislative proposal to recognize and honor the substituted judgment of close family members even in cases where there was no "clear and convincing evidence" that a now incompetent patient would have chosen to refuse life-sustaining treatment?

James Rachels, "Active and Passive Euthanasia" in *The New England Journal of Medicine*, Vol. 292, No. 2, January 9, 1975

Active and Passive Euthanasia
James Rachels

Rachels identifies the standard (conventional) view on the morality or euthanasia as the doctrine which permits passive euthanasia but rejects active euthanasia. He then argues that the conventional doctrine may be challenged for four reasons. First, active euthanasia is in many cases more humane than passive euthanasia. Second, the conventional doctrine leads to decisions concerning life and death on irrelevant grounds. Third, the doctrine rests on a distinction between killing and letting die that itself has no moral importance. Fourth, the most common arguments in favor of the doctrine are invalid.

The distinction between active and passive euthanasia is thought to be crucial for medical ethics. The idea is that it is permissible, at least in some cases, to withhold treatment and allow a patient to die, but it is never permissible to take any direct action designed to kill the patient. This doctrine seems to be accepted by most doctors, and it is endorsed in a statement adopted by the House of Delegates of the American Medical Association on December 4, 1973:

> The intentional termination of the life of one human being by another—mercy killing—is contrary to that for which the medical profession stands and is contrary to the policy of the American Medical Association.
>
> The cessation of the employment of extraordinary means to prolong the life of the body when there is irrefutable evidence that biological death is imminent is the decision of the patient and/or his immediate family. The advice and judgment of the physician should be freely available to the patient and/or his immediate family.

However, a strong case can be made against this doctrine. In what follows, I will set out some of the relevant arguments, and urge doctors to reconsider their views on this matter.

To begin with a familiar type of situation, a patient who is dying of incurable cancer of the throat is in terrible pain, which can no longer be satisfactorily alleviated. He is certain to die within a few days, even if present treatment is continued, but he does not want to go on living for those days since the pain is unbearable. So he asks the doctor for an end to it, and his family joins in the request.

Suppose the doctor agrees to withhold treatment, as the conventional doctrine says he may. The justification for his doing so is that the patient is in terrible agony, and since he is going to die anyway, it would be wrong to prolong his suffering needlessly. But now notice this. If one simply withholds treatment, it may take the patient longer to die, and so he may suffer more than he would if more direct action were taken and a lethal injection given. This fact provides strong reason for thinking that, once the initial decision not to prolong his agony has been made, active euthanasia is actually preferable to passive euthanasia, rather than the reverse. To say otherwise is to endorse the option that leads to more suffering rather than less, and is contrary to the humanitarian impulse that prompts the decision not to prolong his life in the first place.

Part of my point is that the process or being "allowed to die" can be relatively slow and painful, whereas being given a lethal injection is relatively quick and painless. Let me give a different sort of example. In the United States about one in 600 babies is born with Down's syndrome. Most of these babies are otherwise healthy—that is, with only the usual pediatric care, they will proceed to an otherwise normal infancy. Some, however, are born with congenital defects such as intestinal obstructions that require operations if they are to live. Sometimes, the parents and the doctor will decide not to operate, and let the infant die. Anthony Shaw describes what happens then:

> . . . When surgery is denied [the doctor] must try to keep the infant from suffering while natural forces sap the baby's life away. As a surgeon whose natural inclination is to use the scalpel to fight off death, standing by and watching a salvageable baby die is the most emotionally exhausting experience I know. It is easy in a conference, in a theoretical discussion, to decide that such infants should be allowed to die. It is altogether different to stand by in the nursery and watch as dehydration and infection wither a tiny being over hours and days. This is a terrible ordeal for me and the hospital staff—much more so than for the parents who never set foot in the nursery.[1]

I can understand why some people are opposed to all euthanasia, and insist that such infants must be allowed to live. I think I can also understand why other people favor destroying these babies quickly and painlessly. But why should anyone favor letting "dehydration and infection wither a tiny being over hours and days?" The doctrine that says that a baby may be allowed to dehydrate and wither, but may not be given an injection that would end its life without suffering, seems so patently cruel as to require no further refutation. The strong language is not intended to offend, but only to put the point in the clearest possible way.

My second argument is that the conventional doctrine leads to decisions concerning life and death made on irrelevant grounds.

Consider again the case of the infants with Down's syndrome who need operations for congenital defects unrelated to the syndrome to live. Sometimes, there is no operation, and the baby dies, but when there is no such defect, the baby lives on. Now, an operation such as that to remove an intestinal obstruction is not prohibitively difficult. The reason why such operations are not performed in these cases is, clearly, that the child has Down's syndrome and the parents and doctor judge that because of that fact it is better for the child to die.

But notice that this situation is absurd, no matter what view one takes of the lives and potentials of such babies. If the life of such an infant is worth preserving, what does it matter if it needs a simple operation? Or, if one thinks it better that such a baby should not live on, what difference does it make that it happens to have an unobstructed intestinal tract? In either case, the matter of life and death is being decided on irrelevant grounds. It is the Down's syndrome, and not the intestines, that is the issue. The matter should be decided, if at all, on that basis, and not be allowed to depend on the essentially irrelevant question of whether the intestinal tract is blocked.

What makes this situation possible, of course, is the idea that when there is an intestinal blockage, one can "let the baby die," but when there is no such defect there is nothing that can be done, for one must not "kill" it. The fact that this idea leads to such results as deciding life or death on irrelevant grounds is another good reason why the doctrine should be rejected.

One reason why so many people think that there is an important moral difference between active and passive euthanasia is that they think killing someone is morally worse than letting someone die. But is it? Is killing, in itself, worse than letting die? To investigate this issue, two cases may be considered that are exactly alike except that one involves killing whereas the other involves letting someone die. Then, it can be asked whether this difference makes any difference to the moral assessments. It is important that the cases be exactly alike, except for this one difference, since otherwise one cannot be confident that it is this difference and not some other that accounts for any variation in the assessments of the two cases. So, let us consider this pair of cases:

In the first, Smith stands to gain a large inheritance if anything should happen to his six-year-old cousin. One evening while the child is taking his bath, Smith sneaks into the bathroom and drowns the child, and then arranges things so that it will look like an accident.

In the second, Jones also stands to gain if anything should happen to his six-year-old. Like Smith, Jones sneaks in planning to drown the child in his bath. However, just as he enters the bathroom Jones sees the child slip and hit his head, and fall face down in the water. Jones is delighted; he stands by, ready to push the child's head back under if it is necessary, but it is not necessary. With only a little thrashing about the child drowns all by himself, "accidentally," as Jones watches and does nothing.

Now Smith killed the child, whereas Jones "merely" let the child die. That is the only difference between them. Did either man behave better, from a moral point of view? If the difference between killing and letting die were in itself a morally important matter, one should say that Jones's behavior was less reprehensible than Smith's. But does one really want to say that? I think not. In the first place, both men acted from the same motive, personal gain, and both had exactly the same end in view when they acted. It may be inferred from Smith's conduct that he is a bad man, although that judgment may be withdrawn or modified if certain further facts are learned about him—for example, that he is mentally deranged. But would not the very same thing be inferred about Jones from his conduct? And would not the same further considerations also be relevant to any modification of this judgment? Moreover, suppose Jones pleaded, in his own defense, "After all, I didn't do anything except just stand there and watch the child drown. I didn't kill him; I only let him die." Again, if letting die were in itself less bad than killing, this defense should have at least some weight. But it does not. Such a "defense" can only be regarded as a grotesque perversion of moral reasoning. Morally speaking, it is no defense at all.

Now, it may be pointed out, quite properly, that the cases of euthanasia with which doctors are concerned are not like this at all. They do not involve personal gain or the destruction of normally healthy children. Doctors are concerned only with cases in which the patient's life is of no further use to him, or in which the patient's life has become or will soon become a terrible burden. However, the point is the same in these cases: the bare difference between killing and letting die does not, in itself, make a moral difference. If a doctor lets a patient die, for humane reasons he is in the same moral position as if he had given the patient a lethal injection for humane reasons. If his decision was wrong—if, for example, the patient's illness was in fact curable—the decision would be equally regrettable no matter which method was used to carry it out. And if the doctor's decision was the right one, the method used is not in itself important.

The AMA policy statement isolates the crucial issue very well; the crucial issue is "the intentional termination of the life of one human being by another." But after identifying this issue, and forbidding "mercy killing," the statement goes on to deny that the cessation of treatment is the intentional termination of a life. This is where the mistake comes in, for what is the cessation of treatment, in these circumstances, if it is not "the intentional termination of the life of one human being by another?" Of course, it is exactly that, and if it were not, there would be no point to it.

Many people will find this judgment hard to accept. One reason, I think, is that it is very easy to conflate the question of whether killing is, in itself, worse than letting die, with the very different question of whether most actual cases of killing are more reprehensible than most actual cases of letting die. Most actual cases of killing are clearly terrible (think, for example, of all the murders reported in the newspapers), and one hears of such cases every day. On the other hand, one hardly ever hears of a case of letting die, except for the actions of doctors who are motivated by humanitarian reasons. So one learns to think of killing in a much worse light than of letting die. But this does not mean that there is something about killing that makes it in itself worse than letting die, for it is not the bare difference between killing and letting die that makes the difference in these cases. Rather, the other factors—the murderer's motive of personal gain, for example, contrasted with the doctor's humanitarian motivation—account for different reactions to the different cases.

I have argued that killing is not in itself any worse than letting die; if my contention is right, it follows that active euthanasia is not any worse than passive euthanasia, What arguments can be given on the other side? The most common, I believe, is the following:

"The important difference between active and passive euthanasia is that, in passive euthanasia, the doctor does not do anything to bring about the patient's death. The doctor does nothing, and the patient dies of whatever ills already afflict him. In active euthanasia, however, the doctor does something to bring about the patient's death: he kills him. The doctor who gives the patient with cancer a lethal injection has himself caused his patient's death; whereas if he merely ceases treatment, the cancer is the cause of the death."

A number of points need to be made here. The first is that it is not exactly correct to say that in passive euthanasia the doctor does nothing, for he does do one thing that is very important: he lets the patient die. "Letting someone die" is certainly different, in some respects, from other types of action—mainly in that it is a kind of action that one may perform by way of not performing certain other actions. For example, one may let a patient die by way of not giving medication, just as one may insult someone by way of not shaking his hand. But for any purpose of moral assessment, it is a type of action nonetheless. The decision to let a patient die is subject to moral appraisal in the same way that a decision to kill him would be subject to moral appraisal: it may be assessed as wise or unwise, compassionate or sadistic, right or wrong. If a doctor deliberately let a patient die who was suffering from a routinely curable illness, the doctor would certainly be to blame for what he had done, just as he would be to blame if he had needlessly killed the patient. Charges against him would then be appropriate. If so, it would be no defense at all for him to insist that he didn't "do anything." He would have done something very serious indeed, for he let his patient die.

Fixing the cause of death may be very important from a legal point of view, for it may determine whether criminal charges are brought against the doctor. But I do not think that this notion can be used to show a moral difference between active and passive euthanasia. The reason why it is considered bad to be the cause of someone's death is that death is regarded as a great evil—and so it is. However, if it has been decided that euthanasia—even passive euthanasia—is desirable in a given case, it has also been decided that in this instance death is no greater an evil than the patient's continued existence. And if this is true, the usual reason for not wanting to be the cause of someone's death simply does not apply.

Finally, doctors may think that all of this is only of academic interest—the sort of thing that philosophers may worry about but that has no practical bearing on their own work. After all, doctors must be concerned about the legal consequences of what they do, and active euthanasia is clearly forbidden by the law. But even so, doctors should also be concerned with the fact that the law is forcing upon them a moral doctrine that may well be indefensible, and has a considerable effect on their practices. Of course, most doctors are not now in the position of being coerced in this matter, for they do not regard themselves as merely going along with what the law requires. Rather, in statements such as the AMA policy statement that I have quoted, they are endorsing this doctrine as a central point of medical ethics. In that statement, active euthanasia is condemned not merely as illegal but as "contrary to that for which the medical profession stands," whereas passive euthanasia is approved. However, the preceding considerations suggest that there is really no moral difference between the two, considered in themselves (there may be important moral differences in some cases in their consequences, but, as I pointed out, these differences may make active euthanasia, and not passive euthanasia, the morally preferably option). So, whereas doctors may have to discriminate between active and passive euthanasia to satisfy the law, they should not do any more than that. In particular, they should not give the distinction any added authority and weight by writing it into official statements of medical ethics.

Notes

1.   A. Shaw: "Doctor, Do We Have a Choice?" *The New York Times Magazine*, Jan. 30, 1972, p. 54.

Questions

1. If you were a physician, what would you do when the parents of a baby with Down's syndrome and an intestinal obstruction decided against surgery? Would you let the baby slowly die from dehydration and starvation, would you take some active step to end the baby's life, or would you take the case to court to force the surgery? How would you justify your decision?

2. Can the conventional doctrine on active and passive euthanasia be defended against Rachel's arguments?

Euthanasia: Suggested Additional Readings

Beauchamp, Tom L.: "A Reply to Rachels on Active and Passive Euthanasia." In Tom L. Beauchamp and Seymour Perlin, eds., *Ethical Issues in Death and Dying*. Englewood Cliffs, N.J.: Prentice-Hall, 1978, pp. 246–258. Beauchamp suggests that rule-utilitarian considerations can provide a basis for defending the moral significance of the distinction between active and passive euthanasia.

"Cruzan: Clear and Convincing?" *Hastings Center Report,* vol. 20, September/October 1990, pp. 5–11. This set of six short articles provides critical reflections on the ruling of the United States Supreme Court in the *Cruzan* case.

Downing, A. B., ed.: *Euthanasia and the Right to Death: The Case for Voluntary Euthanasia.* New York: Humanities Press; London: Peter Owen, 1969. Two articles are especially notable in this collection of material on euthanasia. In "The Principle of Euthanasia," Antony Flew constructs "a general moral case for the establishment of a legal right" to voluntary (active) euthanasia. In a very well known article, "Euthanasia Legislation: Some Non-Religious Objections," Yale Kamisar argues against the legalization of voluntary (active) euthanasia.

Kohl, Marvin, ed.: *Beneficient Euthanasia.* Buffalo, N.Y.: Prometheus, 1975. This anthology includes a number of helpful articles on the moral aspects of euthanasia. Also included are articles that provide statements of various religious positions on euthanasia. Other articles address the medical and legal aspects of euthanasia.

Lynn, Joanne, ed.: *By No Extraordinary Means: The Choice to Forgo Life-Sustaining Food and Water.* Bloomington: Indiana University Press, 1986. This anthology provides a wide range of material on the issue of forgoing artificial nutrition and hydration.

May, William E., et al.: "Feeding and Hydrating the Permanently Unconscious and Other Vulnerable Persons." *Issues in Law and Medicine,* vol. 3, Winter 1987, pp. 203–217. A group of ten authors argues that it is morally wrong to withhold or withdraw artificial nutrition and hydration from the permanently unconscious or from those who are seriously debilitated but nondying.

"Mercy, Murder, and Morality: Perspectives on Euthanasia." *Hastings Center Report,* vol. 19, January/February 1989, special supplement, pp. 1–32. This supplement contains nine articles on various aspects of (active) euthanasia. Especially noteworthy is an article by Daniel Callahan, "Can We Return Death to Disease?" Callahan argues against the morality of active euthanasia and defends the coherence and importance of the distinction between killing and allowing to die.

President's Commission for the Study of Ethical Problems in Medicine and Biomedical and Behavioral Research. *Deciding to Forgo Life-Sustaining Treatment.* 1983. This valuable document provides a broad-based discussion of decision making regarding life-sustaining treatment.

Steinbock, Bonnie, ed.: *Killing and Letting Die.* Englewood Cliffs, N.J.: Prentice-Hall, 1980. This anthology provides a wealth of material on the killing–letting die distinction.

Trammell, Richard L.: "Euthanasia and the Law." *Journal of Social Philosophy,* vol. 9, January 1978, pp. 14–18. Trammel contends that the legalization of voluntary positive (i.e., active) euthanasia would probably not "result in overall positive utility for the class of people eligible to choose." He emphasizes the unwelcome pressures that would be created by legalization.

Weir, Robert F. *Selective Nontreatment of Handicapped Newborns: Moral Dilemmas in Neonatal Medicine.* New York: Oxford University Press, 1984. Weir surveys and critically analyzes a wide range of views (advanced by various pediatricians, attorneys, and ethicists) on the subject of selective nontreatment. He then presents and defends an overall policy for the guidance of decision making in this area.

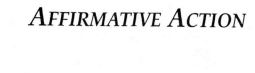

AFFIRMATIVE ACTION

Bernard Boxill, "The Color-Blind Principle" in *Blacks and Social Justice*, 1984

The Color-Blind Principle
Bernard Boxill

PLESSY

In 1892, Homer Plessy, an octoroon, was arrested in Louisiana for taking a seat in a train car reserved for whites. He was testing a state law which required the "white and colored races" to ride in "equal but separate" accommodations, and his case eventually reached the Supreme Court.

Part of Plessy's defense, though it must be considered mainly a snare for the opposition, was that he was "seven-eighths Caucasian and one-eighth African blood," and that the "mixture of colored blood was not discernible in him." The bulwark of his argument was, however, that he was "entitled to every right, privilege and immunity secured to citizens of the white race," and that the law violated the Fourteenth Amendment's prohibition against unequal protection of the laws.[1] Cannily, the court refused the snare. Perhaps it feared—and with reason—that the ancestry of too many white Louisianans held dark secrets. But it attacked boldly enough Plessy's main argument that the Louisiana law was unconstitutional. That argument, Justice Henry Billings Brown wrote for the majority, was unsound. "Its underlying fallacy," he averred, was its "assumption that the enforced separation of the two races stamps the colored race with a badge of inferiority." "If this be so," Brown concluded, "it is not by reason of anything found in the act, but solely because the colored race chooses to put that construction upon it."[2]

Only one judge dissented from the court majority—Justice John Marshall Harlan. It was the occasion on which he pronounced his famous maxim: "Our Constitution is color-blind." In opposition to Justice Brown, Justice Harlan found that the "separation of citizens on the basis of race [was a] badge of servitude . . . wholly inconsistent [with] equality before the law."[3]

Plessy's is the kind of case which makes the color-blind principle seem indubitably right as a basis for action and policy, and its contemporary opponents appear unprincipled, motivated by expediency, and opportunistic. This impression is only strengthened by a reading of Justice Brown's tortuously preposterous defense of the "equal but separate" doctrine. It should make every advocate of color-conscious policy wary of the power of arguments of expediency to beguile moral sense and subvert logic. Yet I argue that color-conscious policy can still be justified. The belief that it cannot is the result of a mistaken generalization from *Plessy*. There is no warrant for the idea that the color-blind principle should hold in some general and absolute way.

"I DIDN'T NOTICE" LIBERALS

In his book *Second Wind*, Bill Russell recalls how amazed he used to be by the behavior of what he called "I didn't notice" liberals. These were individuals who claimed not to notice people's color. If they mentioned someone Russell could not place, and Russell asked whether she was black or white, they would answer, "I didn't notice." "Sweet and innocent," Russell recalls, "sometimes a little proud."[4] Now, the kind of color-blindness the "I didn't notice" liberals claim to have may be a worthy ideal—Richard Wasserstrom, for example, argues that society should aim toward it—but it is absolutely different from the color-blind principle which functions as a basis for policy.[5] Thus, while Wasserstrom supports color-conscious policies to secure the ideal of people not noticing each others' color, the principle of color-blindness in the law opposes color-conscious policies and does not necessarily involve any hope that people will not notice each others' color. Its thesis is simple: that no *law* or *public policy* be designed to treat people differently because they are of a different color.

COLOR-BLIND AND COLOR-CONSCIOUS POLICIES

The essential thing about a color-conscious policy is that it is designed to treat people differently because of their race. But there are many different kinds of color-conscious policies. Some, for example the Jim Crow policies now in the main abolished, aim to subordinate blacks, while others, such as busing and preferential treatment, aim at elevating blacks.

Some color-conscious policies explicitly state that persons should be treated differently because of their race, for example the segregation laws at issue in *Plessy*; others make no mention of race, but are still designed so that blacks and whites are treated differently, for example, the "grandfather clauses" in voting laws that many states adopted at the turn of the century. To give one instance, in Louisiana this clause stated that those who had had the right to vote before or on 1 January 1867, or their lineal descendants, did not have to meet the educational, property, or tax requirements for voting. Since no blacks had had the right to vote by that time, this law worked effectively to keep blacks from voting while at the same time allowing many impoverished and illiterate whites to vote—yet it made no mention of race.

My object in this chapter is to demonstrate that the color-blind principle, which considers all color-conscious policies to be invalid, is mistaken. I do not deny that many color-conscious policies are wrong. Jim Crow was certainly wrong, and, for different reasons, proposals for black control of inner cities and inner city schools are probably wrong. But this is not because they are color-conscious, but for reasons which indicate that color-conscious policies like busing and affirmative action could be correct.

Advocates of the belief that the law should be color-blind often argue that this would be the best means to an ideal state in which people are color-blind. They appeal to the notion that, only if people notice each other's color can they discriminate on the basis of color and, with considerable plausibility, they argue that color-conscious laws and policies can only heighten people's awareness of each other's color, and exacerbate racial conflict. They maintain that only if the law, with all its weight and influence, sets the example of color-blindness, can there be a realistic hope that people will see through the superficial distinctions of color and become themselves color-blind.

But this argument is not the main thesis of the advocates of legal color-blindness. Generally, they eschew it because of its dependency on the empirical. Their favorite argument, one that is more direct and intuitively appealing, is simply that it is wicked, unfair, and unreasonable to penalize a person for what he cannot help being. Not only does this seem undeniably true, but it can be immediately applied to the issue of race. No one can help being white or being black, and so it seems to follow that it is wicked, unfair, and unreasonable to disqualify a person from any consideration just because he is white or black. This, the advocates of color-blindness declare, is what made Jim Crow law heinous, and it is what makes affirmative action just as heinous.

The force of this consideration is enhanced because it seems to account for one peculiar harmfulness of racial discrimination—its effect on self-respect and self-esteem. For racial discrimination makes some black people hate their color, and succeeds in doing so because color cannot be changed. Furthermore, a racially conscious society has made color seem an important part of the individual's very essence, and since color is immutable it is easily susceptible to this approach. As a result, the black individual may come, in the end, to hate even himself. Even religion is here a dubious consolation. For if God makes us black or white, to the religious black that by which he is marked may come to seem a curse by the Almighty, and he himself therefore essentially evil.

Of course, there are strategies that attempt to circumvent these effects of racial discrimination, but their weaknesses seem to confirm the need for color-blindness. For example, some black people concede that black is bad and ugly, but attempt to soften the effects of this concession by insisting that black is only "skin deep," we are all brothers beneath the skin, and the body, which is black and ugly, is no part of and does not sully the soul, which is the real self and is good. Thus, black people sometimes protested that although their skins were black, their souls were white, which is to say, good. There is truth to this feeling, in that nothing is more certain than that neither a black nor a white skin can make a person good or bad. Yet it is not a wholly successful approach to the problem of color. It requires that the black person believe that he is in some sense a ghost, which he can believe only if he is a lunatic. Another strategy is put forth by Black Nationalism. The black nationalist agrees with the racists' view that his color is an important and integral part of his self, but affirms, in opposition to the racists, that it has value. This strategy, which is exemplified by the slogans "black is beautiful" and "black and proud," has the obvious advantage of stimulating pride and self-confidence. Nevertheless, it is no panacea. For one thing, it has to contend with the powerful propaganda stating that black is *not* beautiful. And there is a more subtle problem. Since the black cannot choose *not* to be black, he cannot be altogether confident that he would choose to *be* black, nor, consequently, does he really place a special value in being black. Thus, some people, black and white, have expressed the suspicion that the slogan "black is beautiful" rings hollow, like the words of the man who protests too loudly that he loves the chains he cannot escape. In this respect the black who can pass as white has an advantage over the black who cannot. For, though he cannot choose not to be black, he can choose not to be *known* to be black.

THE RESPONSIBILITY CRITERION

A final argument in favor of legal color-blindness is related to, and further develops, the point that people do not choose to be, and cannot avoid being, black or white. This links the question of color-blindness to the protean idea of individual responsibility. Thus, William Frankena writes, that to use color as a fundamental basis for distributing "opportunities, offices, etc." to persons is "unjust in itself," because it is to distribute goods on the basis of a feature "which the individual has not done, and can do nothing about; we are treating people differently in ways that profoundly affect their lives because of differences for which they have no responsibility."[6] Since this argument requires that people be treated differently in ways which profoundly affect their lives only on the basis of features for which they are responsible, I call it the responsibility criterion.

The responsibility criterion also seems to make the principle of color-blindness follow from principles of equal opportunity. Joel Feinberg takes it to be equivalent to the claim that "properties can be the grounds of just discrimination between persons only if those persons had a fair opportunity to acquire or avoid them."[7] This implies that to discriminate between persons on the basis of a feature for which they can have no responsibility is to violate the principle of fair opportunity. But color (or sex) is a feature of persons for which they can have no responsibility.

The responsibility criterion may seem innocuous because, though, strictly interpreted it supports the case for color-blindness, loosely interpreted it leaves open the possibility that color-conscious policies are justifiable. Thus, Frankena himself allows that color could be an important basis of distribution of goods and offices if it served "as [a] reliable sign[s] of some Q, like ability or merit, which is more justly employed as a touchstone for the treatment of individuals."[8] This sounds like a reasonable compromise and is enough to support some arguments for color-conscious policies. For example, it could support the argument that black and white children should go to the same schools because being white is a reliable sign of being middle-class, and black children, who are often lower-class, learn better when their peers are middle-class. Similarly, it might support the argument that preferential hiring is compensation for the harm of being discriminated against on the basis of color, and that being black is a reliable sign of having been harmed by that discrimination.

But however loosely it is interpreted, the responsibility criterion cannot be adduced in support of all reasons behind color-conscious policies. It cannot, for example, sustain the following argument, sketched by Ronald Dworkin, for preferential admission of blacks to medical school. "If quick hands count as 'merit' in the case of a prospective surgeon this is because quick hands will enable him to serve the public better and for no other reason. If a black skin will, as a matter of regrettable fact, enable another doctor to do a different medical job better, then that black skin is by the same token "merit as well."[9] What is proposed here is not that a black skin is a justifiable basis of discrimination because it is a reliable sign of merit or some other factor Q. A closely related argument does make such a proposal, viz., that blacks should be preferentially admitted to medical school because being black is a reliable sign of a desire to serve the black community. But this is not the argument that Dworkin poses. In the example quoted above what he suggests is that being black is in *itself* merit, or, at least, something very like merit.

According to the responsibility criterion, we ought not to give A a job in surgery rather than B, if A is a better surgeon than B only because he was born with quicker hands. For if we do, we treat A and B "differently in ways that profoundly affect their lives because of differences for which they have no responsibility." This is the kind of result which puts egalitarianism in disrepute. It entails the idea that we might be required to let fumblers do surgery and in general give jobs and offices to incompetents, and this is surely intolerable. But, as I plan to show, true egalitarianism has no such consequences. They are the result of applying the responsibility criterion, not egalitarian principles. Indeed, egalitarianism must scout the responsibility criterion as false and confused.

Egalitarians should notice first, that, while it invalidates the merit-based theories of distribution that they oppose, it also invalidates the need-based theories of distribution they favor. For, if people are born with special talents for which they are not responsible, they are also born with special needs for which they are not responsible. Consequently, if the responsibility criterion forbids choosing A over B to do surgery because A is a better surgeon because he was born with quicker hands, it also forbids choosing C rather than D for remedial education because C needs it more than D only because he was born with a learning disability and D was not.

At this point there may be objections. First, that the responsibility criterion was intended to govern only the distribution of income, not jobs and offices—in Feinberg's discussion, for example, this is made explicit. Second, that it does not mean that people should not be treated differently because of differences, good or bad, which they cannot help, but rather that people should not get less just because they are born without the qualities their society prizes or finds useful. This seems to be implied in Frankena's claim that justice should make the "same proportionate contribution to the best life for everyone" and that this may require spending more on those who are "harder to help"—probably the untalented—than on others. Qualified in these ways, the responsibility criterion becomes more plausible. It no longer implies, for example, that fumblers should be allowed to practice surgery, or that the blind be treated just like the sighted. But with these qualifications it also becomes almost irrelevant to the color-blind issue. For that issue is not only about how income should be distributed. It is also about how jobs and offices should be distributed.

Most jobs and offices are distributed to people in order to produce goods and services to a larger public. To that end, the responsibility criterion is irrelevant. For example, the purpose of admitting people to medical schools and law schools is to provide the community with good medical and legal service. It does not matter whether those who provide them are responsible for having the skills by virtue of which they provide the goods, or whether the positions they occupy are "goods" to them. No just society makes a person a surgeon just because he is responsible for his skills or because making him a surgeon will be good for him. It makes him a surgeon because he will do good surgery.

Accordingly, it may be perfectly just to discriminate between persons on the basis of distinctions they are not responsible for having. It depends on whether or not the discrimination serves a worthy end. It may be permissible for the admissions policies of professional schools or give preference to those with higher scores, even if their scores are higher than others only because they have higher native ability (for which they cannot, of course, be considered responsible), if the object is to provide the community with good professional service. And, given the same object, if for some reason a black skin, whether or not it can be defined as merit, helps a black lawyer or doctor to provide good legal or medical service to black people who would otherwise not have access to it, or avail themselves of it, it is difficult to see how there can be a principled objection to admissions policies which prefer people with black skins—though, again, they are not responsible for the quality by virtue of which they are preferred.

JUSTICE AND THE RESPONSIBILITY CRITERION

A further point needs to be made in order to vindicate color-conscious policies. The principles of justice are distributive: Justice is concerned not only with increasing the total amount of a good a society enjoys, but also with how that good should be distributed among individuals. Generally, judicial principles dictate that people who are similar in ways deemed relevant to the issue of justice, such as in needs or rights, should get equal amounts of a good, and people who are dissimilar in these regards should get unequal amounts of the good. In terms of these principles certain laws and rules must be considered unjust which would not otherwise be thought unjust. Consider, for example, a policy for admitting persons to medical school which resulted in better and better medical service for white people, but worse and worse medical service for black people. This policy would be unjust, however, great the medical expertise—certainly a good—it produced, unless color is relevant to the receiving of good medical attention.

In a case like this, where it is not, the theoretical circumstance outlined by Dworkin, in which black skin might be considered a "merit," becomes viable. It is true, of course, that color is not, precisely, merit. But to insist on strict definition in this context is to cavil. The point is that if black clients tend to trust and confide more in black lawyers and doctors, then color—functioning as merit—enables a good to be produced and distributed according to some principle of justice.

If these considerations are sound, then the responsibility criterion thoroughly misconstrues the reasons for which racial discrimination is unjust. Racial discrimination against blacks is unjust. Racial discrimination against blacks is unjust because it does not enable goods to be produced and distributed according to principles of justice. It is not unjust because black people do not choose to be black, cannot *not* be black, or are not responsible for being black. This is completely irrelevant. For example, a policy denying university admission to people who parted their hair on the right side would be unjust because the way in which people part their hair is irrelevant to a just policy of school admission. It does not matter in the least, in relation to the nature and object of education, that they choose how they part their hair. Similarly, even if black people could choose to become white, or could all easily pass as white, a law school or medical school that excluded blacks because they were black would still act unjustly. Nothing would have changed.

The arguments in support of color-blindness tend to make the harmfulness of discrimination depend on the difficulty of avoiding it. This is misleading. It diverts attention from the potential harmfulness of discrimination that *can* be avoided and brings the specious responsibility criterion into play. Suppose again, for example, that a person is denied admission to law school because he parts his hair on the right side. Though he, far more easily than the black person, can avoid being unfairly discriminated *against*, he does not thereby more easily avoid being the object, indeed, in a deeper sense, the victim, of unfair discrimination. If he parts his hair on the left side he will presumably be admitted to law school. But then he will have knowingly complied with a foolish and unjust rule and this may well make him expedient and servile. Of course, he will not be harmed to the same extent and in the same way as the victim of racial discrimination. For example, he probably will not hate himself. Unlike color, the cause of his ill-treatment is too easily changed for him to conceive of it as essential to himself. Moreover, if he chooses to keep his hair parted on the right side and thus to forego law school, he *knows* that he is not going to law school because he freely chose to place a greater value on his integrity or on his taste in hairstyles than on a legal education.

He knows this because he knows he could have chosen to change his hairstyle. As I noted earlier, this opportunity for self-assertion, and thus for self-knowledge and self-confidence, is denied the black who is discriminated against on the basis of his color.

Nevertheless, as I stated earlier, the considerations that stem from applying the responsibility criterion to a judgment of racial discrimination are secondary to understanding its peculiar harmfulness. Suppose, for example, that a person is not admitted to medical school to train to be a surgeon because he was born without fingers. If all things he wants require that he have fingers, he may conceivably come to suffer the same self-hatred and self-doubt as the victim of racial discrimination. Yet his case is different, and if he attends to the difference, he will not suffer as the victim of racial discrimination suffers. The discrimination that excludes him from the practice of surgery is not denigrating his interests because they are his. It is a policy that takes into account a just object—the needs of others in the community for competent surgery. Allowing him to be a surgeon would rate other, equally important, interests below his. But racial discrimination excludes its victims from opportunities on the basis of a belief that their interests are ipso facto less important than the interests of whites. The man without fingers may regret not being born differently, but he cannot resent how he is treated. Though his ambitions may be thwarted, he himself is still treated as a moral equal. There is no attack on his self-respect. Racial discrimination, however, undermines its victims' self-respect through their awareness that they are considered morally inferior. The fact that racial discrimination, or any color-conscious policy, is difficult to avoid through personal choice merely adds to its basic harmfulness if it is in the first place unjust, but is not the *reason* for its being unjust.

It remains to consider Feinberg's claim that if people are discriminated for or against on the basis of factors for which they are not responsible the equal opportunity principle is contravened. This I concede. In particular, I concede that color-conscious policies giving preference to blacks place an insurmountable obstacle in the path of whites, and since such obstacles reduce opportunities, such policies may make opportunities unequal. But this gives no advantage to the advocates of color-blind policies. For giving preference to the competent has exactly the same implications as giving preference to blacks. It, too, places obstacles in the paths of some people, this time the untalented, and just as surely makes opportunities unequal. Consequently, an advocate of color-blindness cannot consistently oppose color-conscious policies on the grounds that they contravene equal opportunity and at the same time support talent-conscious policies. Nor, finally, does my concession raise any further difficulty with the issue of equal opportunity. As I argue later, equal opportunity is not a fundamental principle of justice, but is derived from its basic principles. Often these basic principles require that opportunities be made more equal. Invariably, however, these same principles require that the process of equalization stop before a condition of perfect equality of opportunity is reached.

To conclude, adopting a color-blind principle entails adopting a talent-blind principle, and since the latter is absurd, so also is the former. Or, in other words, differences in talent, and differences in color, are from the point of view of justice, on a par. Either, with equal propriety, can be the basis of a just discrimination. Consequently, the color-blind principle is not as simple, straightforward, or self-evident as many of its advocates seem to feel it is. Color-conscious policies can conceivably be just, just as talent-conscious policies can conceivably be—and often are—just. It depends on the circumstances.

Notes

1. Derrick A. Bell, Jr., ed., *Plessy v. Ferguson* in *Civil Rights: Leading Cases* (Boston: Little, Brown, 1980), 64–77.

2. Ibid., 71.

3. Ibid., 71–77.

4. Bill Russell and Taylor Brand, *Second Wind* (New York: Random House, 1979), 187.

5. Richard A. Wasserstrom, "Racism and Sexism," in Richard A. Wasserstrom, *Philosophy and Social Issues* (Notre Dame, Ind.: University of Notre Dame Press, 1980), 24, 25.

6. William Frankena, "Some Beliefs About Justice," in *Justice,* ed. Joel Feinberg and Hyman Gross (Encino, Calif.: Dickenson, 1977), 49.

7. Joel Feinberg, *Social Philosophy* (Englewood Cliffs, N.J.: Prentice-Hall, 1973), 49.

8. Frankena, "Some Beliefs About Justice," 49.

9. Ronald Dworkin, "Why Bakke Has No Case," *New York Review of Books,* 10 Nov. 1977, 14.

Lisa H. Newton, "Reverse Discrimination as Unjustified" in *Ethics*, Vol. 83, July 1973

Reverse Discrimination as Unjustified
Lisa H. Newton

I have heard it argued that "simple justice" requires that we favor women and blacks in employment and educational opportunities, since women and blacks were "unjustly" excluded from such opportunities for so many years in the not so distant past. It is a strange argument, an example of a possible implication of a true proposition advanced to dispute the proposition itself, like an octopus absentmindedly slicing off his head with a stray tentacle. A fatal confusion underlies this argument, a confusion fundamentally relevant to our understanding of the notion of the rule of law.

Two senses of justice and equality are involved in this confusion. The root notion of justice, progenitor of the other, is the one that Aristotle (*Nichomachean Ethics* 5. 6; *Politics* 1. 2; 3. 1) assumes to be the foundation and proper virtue of the political association. It is the condition which free men establish among themselves when they "share a common life in order that their association bring them self-sufficiency"—the regulation of their relationship by law, and the establishment, by law, of equality before the law. Rule of law is the name and pattern of this justice; its equality stands against the inequalities—of wealth, talent, etc.—otherwise obtaining among its participants, who by virtue of that equality are called "citizens." It is an achievement—complete, or, more frequently, partial—of certain people in certain concrete situations. It is fragile and easily disrupted by powerful individuals who discover that the blind equality of rule of law is inconvenient for their interests. Despite its obvious instability, Aristotle assumed that the establishment of justice in this sense, the creation of citizenship, was a permanent possibility for men and that the resultant association of citizens was the natural home of the species. At levels below the political association, this rule-governed equality is easily found; it is exemplified by any group of children agreeing together to play a game. At the level of the political association, the attainment of this justice is more difficult, simply because the stakes are so much higher for each participant. The equality of citizenship is not something that happens of its own accord, and without the expenditure of a fair amount of effort it will collapse into the rule of a powerful few over an apathetic many. But at least it has been achieved, at some times in some places; it is always worth trying to achieve, and eminently worth trying to maintain, wherever and to whatever degree it has been brought into being.

Aristotle's parochialism is notorious; he really did not imagine that persons other than Greeks could associate freely in justice, and the only form of association he had in mind was the Greek *polis*. With the decline of the *polis* and the shift in the center of political thought, his notion of justice underwent a sea change. To be exact, it ceased to represent a political type and became a moral ideal: the ideal of equality as we know it. This ideal demands that all men be included in citizenship—that one Law govern all equally, that all men regard all other men as fellow citizens, with the same guarantees, rights, and protections. Briefly, it demands that the circle of citizenship achieved by any group be extended to include the entire human race. Properly understood, its effect on our associations can be excellent: it congratulates us on our achievement of rule of law as a process of government but refuses to let us remain complacent until we have expanded the associations to include others within the ambit of the rules, as often and as far as possible. While one man is a slave, none of us may feel truly free. We are constantly prodded by this ideal to look for possible unjustifiable discrimination, for inequalities not absolutely required for the functioning of the society and advantageous to all. And after twenty centuries of pressure, not at all constant, from this ideal, it might be said that some progress has been made. To take the cases in point for this problem, we are now prepared to assert, as Aristotle would never have been, the equality of sexes and of persons of different colors. The ambit of American citizenship, once restricted to white males of property, has been extended to include all adult free men, then all adult males including ex-slaves, then all women. The process of acquisition of full citizenship was for these groups a sporadic trail of half-measures, even now not complete; the steps on the road to full equality are marked by legislation and judicial decisions which are only recently concluded and still often not enforced. But the fact that we can now discuss the possibility of favoring such groups in hiring shows that over the area that concerns us, at least, full equality is presupposed as a basis for discussion. To that extent they are full citizens, fully protected by the law of the land.

It is important for my argument that the moral ideal of equality be recognized as logically distinct from the condition (or virtue) of justice in the political sense. Justice in this sense exists *among* a citizenry, irrespective of the number of the populace included in that citizenry. Further, the moral ideal is parasitic upon the political virtue, for "equality" is unspecified—it means nothing until we are told in what respect that equality is to be realized. In a political context, "equality" is specified as "equal rights"—equal access to the public realm, public goods and offices, equal treatment under the law—in brief, the equality of citizenship. If citizenship is not a possibility, political equality is unintelligible. The ideal emerges as a generalization of the real condition and refers back to that condition for its content.

Now, if justice (Aristotle's justice in the political sense) is equal treatment under law for all citizens, what is injustice? Clearly, injustice is the violation of that equality, discriminating for or against a group of citizens, favoring them with special immunities and privileges or depriving them of those guaranteed to the others. When the southern employer refuses to hire blacks in white-collar jobs, when Wall Street will only hire women as secretaries with new titles, when Mississippi high schools routinely flunk all black boys above ninth grade, we have examples of injustice, and we work to restore the equality of the public realm by ensuring that equal opportunity will be provided in such cases in the future. But of course, when the employers and the schools *favor* women and blacks, the same injustice is done. Just as the previous discrimination did, this reverse discrimination violates the public equality which defines citizenship and destroys the rule of law for the areas in which these favors are granted.

To the extent that we adopt a program of discrimination, reverse or otherwise, justice in the political sense is destroyed, and none of us, specifically affected or not, is a citizen, a bearer of rights—we are all petitioners for favors. And to the same extent, the ideal of equality is undermined, for it has content only where justice obtains, and by destroying justice we render the ideal meaningless. It is, then, an ironic paradox, if not a contradiction in terms, to assert that the ideal of equality justifies the violation of justice; it is as if one should argue, with William Buckley, that an ideal of humanity can justify the destruction of the human race.

Logically, the conclusion is simple enough: all discrimination is wrong *prima facie* because it violates justice, and that goes for reverse discrimination too. No violation of justice among the citizens may be justified (may overcome the *prima facie* objection) by appeal to the ideal of equality, for that ideal is logically dependent upon the notion of justice. Reverse discrimination, then, which attempts no other justification than an appeal to equality, is wrong. But let us try to make the conclusion more plausible by suggesting some of the implications of the suggested practice of reverse discrimination in employment and education. My argument will be that the problems raised there are insoluble, not only in practice but in principle.

We may argue, if we like, about what "discrimination" consists of. Do I discriminate against blacks if I admit none to my school when none of the black applicants are qualified by the tests I always give? How far must I go to root out cultural bias from my application forms and tests before I can say that I have not discriminated against those of different cultures? Can I assume that women are not strong enough to be roughnecks on my oil rigs, or must I test them individually? But this controversy, the most popular and well-argued aspect of the issue, is not as fatal as two others which cannot be avoided: if we are regarding the blacks as a "minority" victimized by discrimination, what is a "minority"? And for any group—blacks, women, whatever—that has been discriminated against, what amount of reverse discrimination wipes out the initial discrimination? Let us grant as true that women and blacks were discriminated against, even where laws forbade such discrimination, and grant for the sake of argument that a history of discrimination must be wiped out by reverse discrimination. What follows?

First, are there other groups which have been discriminated against? For they should have the same right of restitution. What about American Indians, Chicanos, Appalachian Mountain whites, Puerto Ricans, Jews, Cajuns, and Orientals? And if these are to be included, the principle according to which we specify a "minority" is simply the criterion of "ethnic (sub) group," and we're stuck with every hyphenated American in the lower-middle class clamoring for special privileges for *his* group—and with equal justification. For be it noted, when we run down the Harvard roster, we find not only a scarcity of blacks (in comparison with the proportion of the population) but an even more striking scarcity of those second-, third-, and fourth-generation ethnics who make up the loudest voice of Middle America. Shouldn't they demand *their* share? And eventually, the WASPs will have to form their own lobby, for they too are a minority. The point is simply this: there is no "majority" in America who will not mind giving up just a bit of their rights to make room for a favored minority. There are only other minorities, each of which is discriminated against by the favoring. The initial injustice is then repeated dozens of times, and if each minority is granted the same right of restitution as the others, an entire area of rule governance is dissolved into a pushing and shoving match between self-interested groups. Each works to catch the public eye and political polarity by whatever means of advertising and power politics lend themselves to the effort, to capitalize as much as possible on temporary polarity until the restless mob picks another group to feel sorry for. Hardly an edifying spectacle, and in the long run no one can benefit: the pie is no larger—it's just that instead of setting up and enforcing rules for getting a piece, we've turned the contest into a free-for-all, requiring much more effort for no larger a reward. It would be in the interests of all the participants to reestablish an objective rule to govern the process, carefully enforced and the same for all.

Second, supposing that we do manage to agree in general that women and blacks (and all the others) have some right of restitution, some right to a privileged place in the structure of opportunities for a while, how will we know when that while is up? How much privilege is enough? When will the guilt be gone, the price paid, the balance restored? What recompense is right for centuries of exclusion? What criterion tells us when we are done? Our experience with the Civil Rights movement shows us that agreement on these terms cannot be presupposed: a process that appears to some to be going at a mad gallop into a black takeover appears to the rest of us to be at a standstill. Should a practice of reverse discrimination be adopted, we may safely predict that just as some of us begin to see "a satisfactory start toward righting the balance," others of us will see that we "have already gone too far in the other direction" and will suggest that the discrimination ought to be reversed again. And such disagreement is inevitable, for the point is that we could not *possibly* have any criteria for evaluating the kind of recompense we have in mind. The context presumed by any discussion of restitution is the context of rule of law: law sets the rights of men and simultaneously sets the method for remedying the violation of those rights. You may exact suffering from others and/or damage payments for yourself if and only if the others have violated your rights; the suffering you have endured is not sufficient reason for them to suffer. And remedial rights exist only where there is law: primary human rights are useful guides to legislation but cannot stand as reasons for awarding remedies for injuries sustained. But then, the context presupposed by any discussion of restitution is the context of preexistent full citizenship. No remedial rights could exist for the excluded; neither in law nor in logic does there exist a right to *sue* for a standing to sue.

From these two considerations, then, the difficulties with reverse discrimination become evident. Restitution for a disadvantaged group whose rights under the law have been violated is possible by legal means, but restitution for a disadvantaged group whose grievance is that there was no law to protect them simply is not. First, outside of the area of justice defined by the law, no sense can be made of "the group's rights," for no law recognizes that group or the individuals in it, *qua* members, as bearers of rights (hence *any* group can constitute itself as a disadvantaged minority in some sense and demand similar restitution). Second, outside of the area of protection of law, no sense can be made of the violation of rights (hence the amount of the recompense cannot be decided by any objective criterion). For both reasons, the practice of reverse discrimination undermines the foundation of the very ideal in whose name it is advocated; it destroys justice, law, equality, and citizenship itself, and replaces them with power struggles and popularity contests.

Cornel West, "Beyond Affirmative Action" in *Race Matters*, 1993

Beyond Affirmative Action
Cornel West

> Institutionalized rejection of *difference* is an absolute necessity in a profit economy which needs outsiders as surplus people. As members of such an economy, we have all been programmed to respond to the human differences between us with fear and loathing and to handle that difference in one of three ways: ignore it, and if that is not possible, copy it if we think it is dominant, or destroy it if we think it is subordinate. But we have no patterns for relating across our human differences as equals. As a result, those differences have been misnamed and misused in the service of separation and confusion.
>
> Audre Lorde, *Sister Outsider* (1984)

The fundamental crisis in black America is twofold: too much poverty and too little self-love. The urgent problem of black poverty is primarily due to the distribution of wealth, power, and income—a distribution influenced by the racial caste system that denied opportunities to most "qualified" black people until two decades ago.

The historic role of American progressives is to promote redistributive measures that enhance the standard of living and quality of life for the have-nots and have-too-littles. Affirmative action was one such redistributive measure that surfaced in the heat of battle in the 1960s among those fighting for racial equality. Like earlier *de facto* affirmative action measures in the American past—contracts, jobs, and loans to select immigrants granted by political machines; subsidies to certain farmers; FHA mortgage loans to specific home buyers; or GI Bill benefits to particular courageous Americans—recent efforts to broaden access to America's prosperity have been based upon preferential policies. Unfortunately, these policies always benefit middle-class Americans disproportionately. The political power of big business in big government circumscribes redistributive measures and thereby tilts these measures away from the have-nots and have-too-littles.

Every redistributive measure is a compromise with and concession from the caretakers of American prosperity—that is, big business and big government. Affirmative action was one such compromise and concession achieved after the protracted struggle of American progressives and liberals in the courts and in the streets. Visionary progressives always push for substantive redistributive measures that make opportunities available to the have-nots and have-too-littles, such as more federal support to small farmers, or more FHA mortgage loans to urban dwellers as well as suburban home buyers. Yet in the American political system, where the powers that be turn a skeptical eye toward any program aimed at economic redistribution, progressives must secure whatever redistributive measures they can, ensure their enforcement, then extend their benefits if possible.

If I had been old enough to join the fight for racial equality in the courts, the legislatures, and the board rooms in the 1960s (I *was* old enough to be in the streets), I would have favored—as I do now—a class-based affirmative action in principle. Yet in the heat of battle in American politics, a redistributive measure in principle with no power and pressure behind it means no redistributive measure at all. The prevailing discriminatory practices during the sixties, whose targets were working people, women, and people of color, were atrocious. Thus, an *enforceable* race-based—and later gender-based—affirmative action policy was the best possible compromise and concession.

Progressives should view affirmative action as neither a major solution to poverty nor a sufficient means to equality. We should see it as primarily playing a negative role—namely, to ensure that discriminatory practices against women and people of color are abated. Given the history of this country, it is a virtual certainty that without affirmative action racial and sexual discrimination would return with a vengeance. Even if affirmative action fails significantly to reduce black poverty or contributes to the persistence of racist perceptions in the workplace, without affirmative action black access to America's prosperity would be even more difficult to obtain and racism in the workplace would persist anyway.

This claim is not based on any cynicism toward my white fellow citizens; rather, it rests upon America's historically weak will toward racial justice and substantive redistributive measures. This is why an attack on affirmative action is an attack on redistributive efforts by progressives unless there is a real possibility of enacting and enforcing a more wide-reaching class-based affirmative action policy.

In American politics, progressives must not only cling to redistributive ideals, but must also fight for those policies that—out of compromise and concession—imperfectly conform to those ideals. Liberals who give only lip service to these ideals, trash the policies in the name of *realpolitik,* or reject the policies as they perceive a shift in the racial bellwether give up precious ground too easily. And they do so even as the sand is disappearing under our feet on such issues as regressive taxation, layoffs or takebacks from workers, and cutbacks in health and child care.

Affirmative action is not the most important issue for black progress in America, but it is part of a redistributive chain that must be strengthened if we are to confront and eliminate black poverty. If there were social democratic redistributive measures that wiped out black poverty, and if racial and sexual discrimination could be abated through the good will and meritorious judgments of those in power, affirmative action would be unnecessary. Although many of my liberal and progressive citizens view affirmative action as a redistributive measure whose time is over or whose life is no longer worth preserving, I question their view because of the persistence of discriminatory practices that increase black social misery, and the warranted suspicion that good will and fair judgment among the powerful does not loom as large toward women and people of color.

If the elimination of black poverty is a necessary condition of substantive black progress, then the affirmation of black humanity, especially among black people themselves, is a sufficient condition of such progress. Such affirmation speaks to the existential issues of what it means to be a degraded African (man, woman, gay, lesbian, child) in a racist society. How does one affirm oneself without reenacting negative black stereotypes or overreacting to white supremacist ideals?

The difficult and delicate quest for black identity is integral to any talk about racial equality. Yet it is not solely a political or economic matter. The quest for black identity involves self-respect and self-regard, realms inseparable from, yet not identical to, political power and economic status. The flagrant self-loathing among black middle-class professionals bears witness to this painful process. Unfortunately, black conservatives focus on the issue of self-respect as if it were the one key that would open all doors to black progress. They illustrate the fallacy of trying to open all doors with one key: they wind up closing their eyes to all doors except the one the key fits.

Progressives, for our part, must take seriously the quest for self-respect, even as we train our eye on the institutional causes of black social misery. The issues of black identity—both black self-love and self-contempt—sit alongside black poverty as realities to confront and transform. The uncritical acceptance of self-degrading ideals, that call into question black intelligence, possibility, and beauty not only compounds black social misery but also paralyzes black middle-class efforts to defend broad redistributive measures.

This paralysis takes two forms: black bourgeois preoccupation with white peer approval and black nationalist obsession with white racism.

The first form of paralysis tends to yield a navel-gazing posture that conflates the identity crisis of the black middle class with the state of siege raging in black working-poor and very poor communities. That unidimensional view obscures the need for redistributive measures that significantly affect the majority of blacks, who are working people on the edge of poverty.

The second form of paralysis precludes any meaningful coalition with white progressives because of an undeniable white racist legacy of the modern Western world. The anger this truth engenders impedes any effective way of responding to the crisis in black America. Broad redistributive measures require principled coalitions, including multiracial alliances. Without such measures, black America's sufferings deepen. White racism indeed contributes to this suffering. Yet an obsession with white racism often comes at the expense of more broadly based alliances to affect social change and borders on a tribal mentality. The more xenophobic versions of this viewpoint simply mirror the white supremacist ideals we are opposing and preclude any movement toward redistributive goals.

How one defines oneself influences what analytical weight one gives to black poverty. Any progressive discussion about the future of racial equality must speak to black poverty and black identity. My views on the necessity and limits of affirmative action in the present moment are informed by how substantive redistributive measures and human affirmative efforts can be best defended and expanded.

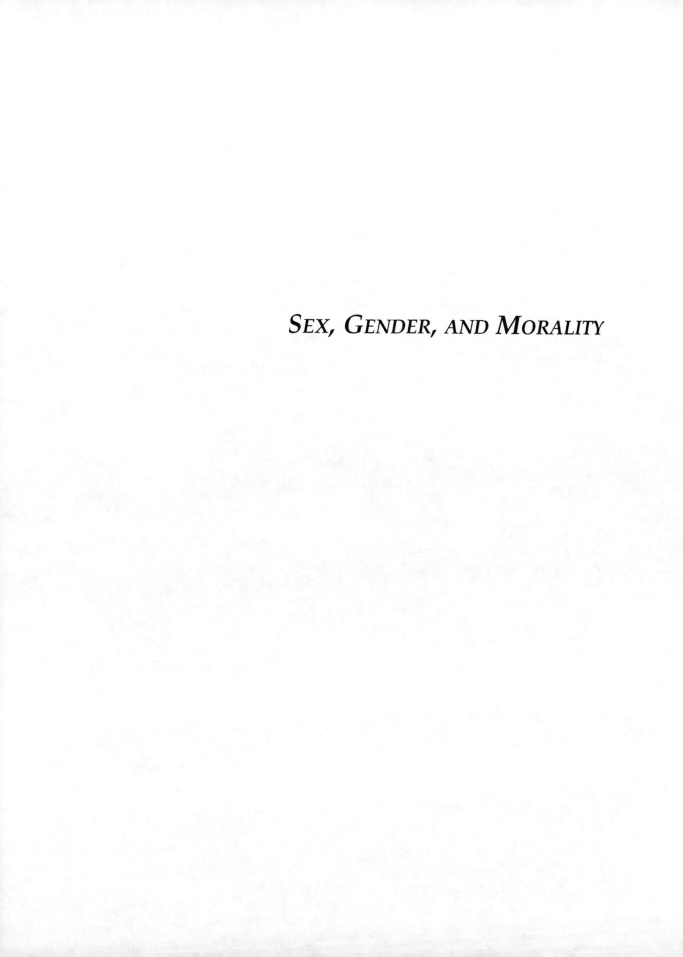

SEX, GENDER, AND MORALITY

Declaration on Sexual Ethics
The Vatican

1.   According to contemporary scientific research, the human person is so
profoundly affected by sexuality that it must be considered as one of the factors
which give to each individual's life the principal traits that distinguish it. In fact
it is from sex that the human person receives the characteristics which, on the
biological, psychological and spiritual levels, make that person a man or a
woman, and thereby largely condition his or her progress towards maturity and
insertion into society. Hence sexual matters, as is obvious to everyone, today
constitute a theme frequently and openly dealt with in books, reviews,
magazines, and other means of social communication.

In the present period, the corruption of morals has increased, and one of the most serious
indications of this corruption is the unbridled exaltation of sex. Moreover, through the means
of social communication and through public entertainment this corruption has reached the
point of invading the field of education and of infecting the general mentality.

In this context certain educators, teachers, and moralists have been able to contribute to a
better understanding and integration into life of the values proper to each of the sexes; on the
other hand there are those who have put forward concepts and modes of behavior which are
contrary to the true moral exigencies of the human person. Some members of the latter group
have even gone so far as to favor a licentious hedonism.

As a result, in the course of a few years, teachings, moral criteria, and modes of living
hitherto faithfully preserved have been very much unsettled, even among Christians. There
are many people today who, being confronted with so many widespread opinions opposed to
the teachings which they received from the Church, have come to wonder what they must still
hold as true.

2.   The Church cannot remain indifferent to this confusion of minds and relaxation
of morals. It is a question, in fact, of a matter which is of the utmost importance
both for the personal lives of Christians and for the social life of our time.[1]

The Bishops are daily led to note the growing difficulties experienced by the faithful in
obtaining knowledge of wholesome moral teaching, especially in sexual matters, and of the

growing difficulties experienced by pastors in expounding this teaching effectively. The Bishops know that by their pastoral charge they are called upon to meet the needs of their faithful in this very serious matter, and important documents dealing with it have already been published by some of them or by Episcopal Conferences. Nevertheless, since the erroneous opinions and resulting deviations are continuing to spread everywhere, the Sacred Congregation for the Doctrine of the Faith, by virtue of its function in the universal Church[2] and by a mandate of the Supreme Pontiff, has judged it necessary to publish the present Declaration.

3.   The people of our time are more and more convinced that the human person's dignity and vocation demand that they should discover, by the light of their own intelligence, the values innate in their nature, that they should ceaselessly develop these values and realize them in their lives, in order to achieve an ever greater development.

In moral matters man cannot make value judgments according to his personal whim: "In the depths of his conscience, man detects a law which he does not impose on himself, but which holds him to obedience. . . . For man has in his heart a law written by God. To obey it is the very dignity of man; according to it he will be judged."[3]

Moreover, through his revelation God has made known to us Christians his plan of salvation, and he has held up to us Christ, the Saviour and Sanctified, in his teaching and example, as the supreme and immutable law of life: "I am the light of the world; anyone who follows me will not be walking in the dark, he will have the light of life."[4]

Therefore, there can be no true promotion of man's dignity unless the essential order of his nature is respected. Of course, in the history of civilization many of the concrete conditions and needs of human life have changed and will continue to change. But all evolution of morals and every type of life must be kept within the limits imposed by the immutable principles based upon every human person's constitutive elements and essential relations—elements and relations which transcend historical contingency.

These fundamental principles, which can be grasped by reason, are contained in "the divine law—eternal, objective, and universal—whereby God orders, directs, and governs the entire universe and all the ways of the human community, by a plan conceived in wisdom and love. Man has been made by God to participate in this law, with the result that, under the gentle disposition of divine Providence, he can come to perceive ever increasingly the unchanging truth."[5] This divine law is accessible to our minds.

4.   Hence, those many people are in error who today assert that one can find neither in human nature nor in the revealed law any absolute and immutable norm to serve for particular actions other than the one which expresses itself in the general law of charity and respect for human dignity. As a proof of their assertion they put forward the view that so-called norms of the natural law or precepts of Sacred Scripture are to be regarded only as given expressions of a form of particular culture at a certain moment of history.

But in fact, divine Revelation and, in its own proper order, philosophical wisdom, emphasize the authentic exigencies of human nature. They thereby necessarily manifest the existence of immutable laws inscribed in the constitutive elements of human nature and which are revealed to be identical in all beings endowed with reason.

Furthermore, Christ instituted his Church as "the pillar and bulwark of truth."[6] With the Holy Spirit's assistance, she ceaselessly preserves and transmits without error the truths of the moral order, and she authentically interprets not only the revealed positive law but "also . . . those principles of the moral order which have their origin in human nature itself"[7] and which concern man's full development and sanctification. Now in fact the Church throughout her history has always considered a certain number of precepts of the natural law as having an absolute and immutable value, and in their transgression she has seen a contradiction of the teaching and spirit of the Gospel.

> 5. Since sexual ethics concern certain fundamental values of human and Christian life, this general teaching equally applies to sexual ethics. In this domain there exist principles and norms which the Church has always unhesitatingly transmitted as part of her teaching, however much the opinions and morals of the world may have been opposed to them. These principles and norms in no way owe their origin to a certain type of culture, but rather to knowledge of the divine law and of human nature. They therefore cannot be considered as having become out of date or doubtful under the pretext that a new cultural situation has arisen.

It is these principles which inspired the exhortations and directives given by the Second Vatican Council for an education and an organization of social life taking account of the equal dignity of man and woman while respecting their difference.[8]

Speaking of "the sexual nature of man and the human faculty of procreation," the Council noted that they "wonderfully exceed the dispositions of lower forms of life."[9] It then took particular care to expound the principles and criteria which concern human sexuality in marriage, and which are based upon the finality of the specific function of sexuality.

In this regard the Council declares that the moral goodness of the acts proper to conjugal life, acts which are ordered according to true human dignity, "does not depend solely on sincere intentions or on an evaluation of motives. It must be determined by objective standards. These, based on the nature of the human person and his acts, preserve the full sense of mutual self-giving and human procreation in the context of true love."[10]

These final words briefly sum up the Council's teaching—more fully expounded in an earlier part of the same Constitution[11]—on the finality of the sexual act and on the principal criterion of its morality: it is respect for its finality that ensures the moral goodness of this act.

This same principle, which the Church holds from divine Revelation and from her authentic interpretation of the natural law, is also the basis of her traditional doctrine, which states that the use of the sexual function has its true meaning and moral rectitude only in true marriage.[12]

> 6. It is not the purpose of the present declaration to deal with all the abuses of the sexual faculty, nor with all the elements involved in the practice of chastity. Its object is rather to repeat the Church's doctrine on certain particular points, in view of the urgent need to oppose serious errors and widespread aberrant modes of behavior.

> 7. Today there are many who vindicate the right to sexual union before marriage, at least in those cases where a firm intention to marry and an affection which is already in some way conjugal in the psychology of the subjects require this completion, which they judge to be connatural. This is especially the case when the celebration of the marriage is impeded by circumstances or when this intimate relationship seems necessary in order for love to be preserved.

This opinion is contrary to Christian doctrine, which states that every genital act must be within the framework of marriage. However firm the intention of those who practice such premature sexual relations may be, the fact remains that these relations cannot ensure, in sincerity and fidelity, the interpersonal relationship between a man and a woman, nor especially can they protect this relationship from whims and caprices. Now it is a stable union that Jesus willed, and he restored its original requirement, beginning with the sexual difference. "Have you not read that the creator from the beginning made them male and female and that he said: This is why a man must leave father and mother, and cling to his wife, and the two become one body? They are no longer two, therefore, but one body. So then, what God has united, man must not divide."[13] Saint Paul will be even more explicit when he shows that if unmarried people or widows cannot live chastely they have no other alternative than the stable union of marriage: ". . . it is better to marry than to be aflame with passion."[14] Through marriage, in fact, the love of married people is taken up into that love which Christ irrevocably has for the Church,[15] while dissolute sexual union[16] defiles the temple of the Holy Spirit which the Christian has become. Sexual union therefore is only legitimate if a definitive community of life has been established between the man and the woman.

This is what the Church has always understood and taught,[17] and she finds a profound agreement with her doctrine in men's reflection and in the lessons of history.

Experience teaches us that love must find its safeguard in the stability of marriage, if sexual intercourse is truly to respond to the requirements of its own finality and to those of human dignity. These requirements call for a conjugal contract sanctioned and guaranteed by society—a contract which establishes a state of life of capital importance both for the exclusive union of the man and the woman and for the good of their family and of the human community. Most often, in fact, pre-marital relations exclude the possibility of children. What is represented to be conjugal love is not able, as it absolutely should be, to develop into paternal and maternal love. Or, if it does happen to do so, this will be to the detriment of the children, who will be deprived of the stable environment in which they ought to develop in order to find in it the way and the means of their insertion into society as a whole.

The consent given by people who wish to be united in marriage must therefore be manifested externally and in a manner which makes it valid in the eyes of society. As far as the faithful are concerned, their consent to the setting up of a community of conjugal life must be expressed according to the laws of the Church. It is a consent which makes their marriage a Sacrament of Christ.

> 8.   At the present time there are those who, basing themselves on observations in the psychological order, have begun to judge indulgently, and even to excuse completely, homosexual relations between certain people. This they do in opposition to the constant teaching of the Magisterium and to the moral sense of the Christian people.

A distinction is drawn, and it seems with some reason, between homosexuals whose tendency comes from a false education, from habit, from bad example, or from other similar causes, and is transitory or at least not incurable; and homosexuals who are definitively such because of some kind of innate instinct or a pathological constitution judged to be incurable.

In regard to this second category of subjects, some people conclude that their tendency is so natural that it justifies in their case homosexual relations within a sincere communion of life and love analogous to marriage insofar as such homosexuals feel incapable of enduring a solitary life.

In the pastoral field, these homosexuals must certainly be treated with understanding and sustained in the hope of overcoming their personal difficulties and their inability to fit into society. Their culpability will be judged with prudence. But no pastoral method can be employed which would give moral justification to these acts on the grounds that they would be consonant with the condition of such people. For according to the objective moral order, homosexual relations are acts which lack an essential and indispensable finality. In Sacred Scripture they are condemned as a serious depravity and even presented as the sad consequence of rejecting God.[18] This judgment of Scripture does not of course permit us to conclude that all those who suffer from this anomaly are personally responsible for it, but it does attest to the fact that homosexual acts are intrinsically disordered and can in no case be approved.

9. The traditional Catholic doctrine that masturbation constitutes a grave moral disorder is often called into doubt or expressly denied today. It is said that psychology and sociology show that it is a normal phenomenon of sexual development, especially among the young. It is stated that there is real and serious fault only in the measure that the subject deliberately indulges in solitary pleasure closed in on self ("ipsation"), because in this case the act would indeed be radically opposed to the loving communion between persons of different sex which some hold is what is principally sought in the use of the sexual faculty.

This opinion is contradictory to the teaching and pastoral practice of the Catholic Church. Whatever the force of certain arguments of a biological and philosophical nature, which have sometimes been used by theologians, in fact both the Magisterium of the Church—in the course of a constant tradition—and the moral sense of the faithful have declared without hesitation that masturbation is an intrinsically and seriously disordered act.[19] The main reason is that, whatever the motive for acting in this way, the deliberate use of the sexual faculty outside normal conjugal relations essentially contradicts the finality of the faculty. For it lacks the sexual relationship called for by the moral order, namely the relationship which realizes "the full sense of mutual self-giving and human procreation in the context of true love."[20] All deliberate exercise of sexuality must be reserved to this regular relationship. Even if it cannot be proved that Scripture condemns this sin by name, the tradition of the Church has rightly understood it to be condemned in the New Testament when the latter speaks of "impurity," "unchasteness," and other vices contrary to chastity and continence.

Sociological surveys are able to show the frequency of this disorder according to the places, populations, or circumstances studied. In this way facts are discovered, but facts do not constitute a criterion for judging the moral value of human acts.[21] The frequency of the phenomenon in question is certainly to be linked with man's innate weakness following original sin; but it is also to be linked with the loss of a sense of God, with the corruption of morals engendered by the commercialization of vice, with the unrestrained licentiousness of so many public entertainments and publications, as well as with the neglect of modesty, which is the guardian of chastity.

On the subject of masturbation modern psychology provides much valid and useful information for formulating a more equitable judgment on moral responsibility and for orienting pastoral action. Psychology helps one to see how the immaturity of adolescence (which can sometimes persist after that age), psychological imbalance, or habit can influence behavior, diminishing the deliberate character of the act and bringing about a situation whereby subjectively there may not always be serious fault. But in general, the absence of serious responsibility must not be presumed; this would be to misunderstand people's moral capacity.

In the pastoral ministry, in order to form an adequate judgment in concrete cases, the habitual behavior of people will be considered in its totality, not only with regard to the individual's practice of charity and of justice but also with regard to the individual's care in observing the particular precepts of chastity. In particular, one will have to examine whether the individual is using the necessary means, both natural and supernatural, which Christian asceticism from its long experience recommends for overcoming the passions and progressing in virtue. . . .

Notes

1. See Vatican II, *Pastoral Constitution on the Church in the World of Today*, no 47: *Acta Apostolicae Sedis* 58 (1966) 1067 [*The Pope Speaks* XI, 289–290].

2. See the Apostolic Constitution *Regimini Ecclesiae universae* (August 15, 1967), no. 29: *AAS* 59 (1967) 897 [*TPS* XI, 268].

3. *Pastoral Constitution on the Church in the World of Today*, no. 16: *AAS* 58 (1966) 1037 [TPS XI, 268].

4. *Jn* 8, 12.

5. *Declaration of Religious Freedom*, no. 3: *AAS* 58 (1966) 931 [*TPS* XI, 86].

6. 1 Tm 3, 15.

7. *Declaration of Religious Freedom*, no. 14: AAS 58 (1966) 940 [TPS XI, 93]. See also Pius XI, Encyclical *Casti Connubii* (December 31, 1930); *AAS* 22 (1930) 579–580; Pius XII, Address of November 2, 1954 *AAS* 46 (1954) 671–672 [*TPS* I 380–381]; John XXIII, Encyclical *Mater et Magistra* (May 25, 1961), no. 239; *AAS* 53 (1961) 457 [TPS VII, 388]; Paul VI, Encyclical *Humanae Vitae* (July 25, 1968), no. 4: *AAS* 60 (1968) 483 [TPS XIII, 331–332].

8. See Vatican II, *Declaration on Christian Education*, nos. 1 and 8: *AAS* 58 (1966) 729–730. 734–736 [*TPS* XI, 201–202, 206–207]; *Pastoral Constitution on the Church in the World of Today*, nos. 29, 60, 67; *AAS* 598 (1966) 1048–1049, 1080–1081, 1088–1089 [*TPS* XI, 276–277, 299–300, 304–305.

9. *Pastoral Constitution on the Church in the World of Today*, no. 51: *AAS* 58 (1966) 1072 [*TPS* XI, 293].

10. *Loc cit.;* see also no. 49; *AAS* 58 (1966) 1069–1070 [*TPS* XI, 291–292].

11. See *Pastoral Constitution on the Church in the World of Today*, nos. 4950: *AAS* 58 (1966) 1069–1072 [*TPS* XI, 291–293].

12. The present Declaration does not review all the moral norms for the use of sex, since they have already been set forth in the encyclicals *Casti Connubii* and *Humanae Vitae*.

13. *Mt.* 19, 46.

14. *1 Cor* 7, 9.

15. See *Eph* 5, 2532.

16. Extramarital intercourse is expressly condemned in *1 Cor* 5, 1; 6, 9; 7, 2; 10, 8; *Eph* 5, 57; *I Tm* 1, 10; *Heb* 13, 4; there are explicit arguments given in *I Cor* 6, 12–20.

17. See Innocent IV, Letter *Sub Catholicae professione* (March 6, 1254) (DS 835); Pius II, Letter *Cum sicut accepimus* (November 14, 1459) (*DS* 1367); Decrees of the Holy Office on September 24, 1665 (*DS* 2045) and March 2, 1679 (*DS* 2148); Pius XI, Encyclical *Casti Connubii* (December 31, 1930): *AAS* 22 (1930) 538–539.

18. Rom 1:24–27: "In consequence, God delivered them up in their lusts to unclean practices; they engaged in the mutual degradation of their bodies, these men who exchanged the truth of God for a lie and worshipped and served the creature rather than the Creator—blessed be he forever, amen! God therefore delivered them to disgraceful passions. Their women exchanged natural intercourse for unnatural, and the men gave up natural intercourse with women, and burned with lust for one

another. Men did shameful things with men, and thus received in their own persons the penalty for their perversity" See also what St. Paul says of sodomy in *I Cor* 6, 9; *I Tm* I, 10.

19.   See Leo IX, Letter *Ad splendidum nitentes* (1054) (*DS* 687–688); Decree of the Holy Office on March 2, 1679 (*DS* 2149); Pius XII, Addresses of October 8, 1953: *AAS* 45 (1953) 677–678, and May 19, 1956: *AAS* (1956) 472473.

20.   *Pastoral Constitution on the Church in the World of Today*, no. 51: *AAS* 58 (1966) 1072 [*TPS* XI, 293].

21.   See Paul VI, Apostolic Exhortation *Quinque iam anni* (December 8, 1970): AAS 63 (1971) 102 [*TPS* XV, 329]: "If sociological surveys are useful for better discovering the thought patterns of the people of a particular place, the anxieties and needs for those to whom we proclaim the word of God, and also the oppositions made to it by modern reasoning through the widespread notion that outside science there exists no legitimate form of knowledge, still the conclusions drawn from such surveys could not of themselves constitute a determining criterion of truth."

Alison M. Jaggar, "Feminist Ethics: Some Issues for the Nineties" in *Journal of Social Philosophy, Vol. 20, Nos. 1–2, Spring/Fall, 1989*

Feminist Ethics: Some Issues for the Nineties
Alison M. Jaggar

Feminist approaches to ethics are distinguished by their explicit commitment to re-thinking ethics with a view to correcting whatever forms of male bias it may contain. Feminist ethics, as these approaches are often called collectively, seeks to identify and challenge all those ways, overt but more often and more perniciously covert, in which western ethics has excluded women or rationalized their subordination. Its goal is to offer both practical guides to action and theoretical understandings of the nature of morality that do not, overtly or covertly, subordinate the interests of any woman or group of women to the interests of any other individual or group.

While those who practice feminist ethics are united by a shared project, they diverge widely in their views as to how this project may be accomplished. These divergences result from a variety of philosophical differences, including differing conceptions of feminism itself, a perennially contested concept. The inevitability of such disagreement means that feminist ethics cannot be identified in terms of a specific range of topics, methods or orthodoxies. For example, it is a mistake, though one to which even some feminists occasionally have succumbed, to identify feminist ethics with any of the following: putting women's interests first; focusing exclusively on so-called women's issues; accepting women (or feminists) as moral experts or authorities; substituting "male" or (or "feminine") for "male" (or "masculine") values; or extrapolating directly from women's experience.

Even though my initial characterization of feminist ethics is quite loose, it does suggest certain minimum conditions of adequacy for any approach to ethics that purports to be feminist.

1. Within the present social context, in which women remain systematically subordinated, a feminist approach to ethics must offer a guide to action that will tend to subvert rather than reinforce this subordination. Thus, such an approach must be practical, transitional and nonutopian, an extension of politics rather than a retreat from it. It must be sensitive, for instance, to the symbolic meanings as well as the practical consequences of any actions that we take as gendered subjects in a male dominated society, and it must also provide the conceptual resources for identifying

and evaluating the varieties of resistance and struggle in which women, particularly, have tended to engage. It must recognize the often unnoticed ways in which women and other members of the underclass have refused co-operation and opposed domination, while acknowledging the inevitability of collusion and the impossibility of totally clean hands.

2. Since so much of women's struggle has been in the kitchen and the bedroom, as well as in the parliamentary chamber and on the factory floor, a second requirement for feminist ethics is that it should be equipped to handle moral issues in both the so-called public and private domains. It must be able to provide guidance on issues of intimate relations, such as affection and sexuality, which, until quite recently, were largely ignored by modern moral theory. In so doing, it cannot assume that moral concepts developed originally for application to the public realm, concepts such as impartiality or exploitation, are automatically applicable to the private realm. Similarly, an approach to ethics that is adequate for feminism must also provide appropriate guidance for activity in the public realm, for dealing with large numbers of people, including strangers.

3. Finally, feminists must take the moral experience of all women seriously, though not, of course, uncritically. Though what is feminist will often turn out to be very different from what is feminine, a basic respect for women's moral experience is necessary to acknowledging women's capacities as moralists and to countering traditional stereotypes of women as less than full moral agents, as childlike or "natural." Furthermore, as Okin [1987], among others, has argued, empirical claims about differences in the moral experience of women and men make it impossible to assume that any approach to ethics will be unanimously accepted if it fails to consult the moral experience of women. Additionally, it seems plausible to suppose that women's distinctive social experience may make them especially perceptive regarding the implications of domination, especially gender domination, and especially well equipped to detect the male bias that has been shown to pervade so much of male-authored western moral theory.

On the surface, at least, these conditions of adequacy for feminist ethics are quite minimal—although I believe that fulfilling them would have radical consequences for ethics. I think most feminist, and perhaps even many nonfeminist,* philosophers would be likely to find the general statement of these conditions relatively uncontroversial, but that inevitably there will be sharp disagreement over when the conditions have been met. Even feminists are likely to differ over, for instance, just what are women's interests and when they have been neglected, what is resistance to domination and which aspects of which women's moral experience are worth developing and in which directions.

I shall now go on to outline some of these differences as they have arisen in feminist discussions of five ethical and meta-ethical issues. These five certainly are not the only issues to confront feminist ethics; on the contrary, the domain of feminist ethics is identical with that of nonfeminist ethics—it is the whole domain of morality and moral theory. I have selected these five issues both because I believe they are especially pressing in the context of contemporary philosophical debate, and because I myself find them especially interesting. As will shortly become evident, the issues that I have selected are not independent of each other; they are unified at least by recurrent concern about questions of universality and particularity. Nevertheless, I shall separate the issues for purposes of exposition.

1.   EQUALITY AND DIFFERENCE

The central insight of contemporary feminism without doubt has been the recognition of gender as a sometimes contradictory but always pervasive system of social norms that regulates the activity of individuals according to their biological sex. Thus individuals whose sex is male are expected to conform to prevailing norms of masculinity, while female individuals are expected to conform to prevailing norms of femininity. In 1970, Shulamith Firestone began her classic *The Dialectic of Sex* with the words "Sex class is so deep as to be invisible" and, for the first decade of the contemporary women's movement, feminists devoted themselves to rendering "sex-class" or gender visible; to exploring (and denouncing) the depth and extent of gender regulation in the life of every individual. Norms of gender were shown to influence not only dress, occupation and sexuality, but also bodily comportment, patterns of speech, eating habits and intellectual, emotional, moral and even physical development—mostly in ways that, practically and/or symbolically, reinforced the domination of men over women.

The conceptual distinction between sex and gender enabled feminists to articulate a variety of important insights. These included recognizing that the superficially nondiscriminatory acceptance of exceptional, i.e., "masculine" women is not only compatible with but actually presupposes a devaluation of "the feminine." The sex/gender distinction also enabled feminists to separate critical reflection on cultural norms of masculinity from antagonism towards actual men.

Useful as the concept of gender has been to feminism, however, more recent feminist reflection has shown that it is neither as simple nor as unproblematic as it seemed when feminists first articulated it. Some feminists have challenged the initially sharp distinction between sex and gender, noting that, just as sex differences have influenced (though not ineluctably determined) the development of gender norms, so gender arrangements may well have influenced the biological evolution of certain secondary sexual characteristics and even of that defining criterion of sex, procreation itself. Other feminists have challenged the distinction between gender and other social categories such as race and class. Recognizing that feminist claims about "women" often had generalized illicitly from the experience of a relatively small group of middle-class white women, feminists in the last ten years have emphasized that gender is a variable rather than a constant, since norms of gender very not only between but also within cultures, along dimensions such as class, race, age, marital status, sexual preference and so on. Moreover, since every woman is a woman of some determinate age, race, class and marital status, gender is not even an independent variable; there is no concept of pure or abstract gender that can be isolated theoretically and studied independently of class, race, age or marital status. Neither, of course, can these other social categories be understood independently of gender.

Their increasingly sophisticated understandings of gender have complicated feminists' discussions of many moral and social issues. One of these is sexual equality. At the beginning of the contemporary women's movement, in the late 1960s, this seemed to be a relatively straightforward issue. The nineteenth century feminist preference for "separate spheres" for men and women had been replaced by demands for identity of legal rights for men and women or, as it came to be called, equality before the law. By the end of the 1960s, most feminists in the United States came to believe that the legal system should be sex-blind, that it should not differentiate in any way between women and men. This belief was expressed in the struggle for an Equal Rights Amendment to the U.S. Constitution, an amendment that, had it passed, would have made any sex-specific law unconstitutional.

By the late 1970s and early 1980s, however, it was becoming apparent that the assimilationist goal of strict equality before the law does not always benefit women, at least in the short term. One notorious example was "no fault" divorce settlements that divided family property equally between husband and wife but invariably left wives in a far worse economic situation than they did husbands. In one study, for instance, ex-husbands' standard of living was found to have risen by 42% a year after divorce, whereas ex-wives' standard of living declined by 73%. This huge discrepancy in the outcome of divorce resulted from a variety of factors, including the fact that women and men typically are differently situated in the job market, with women usually having much lower job qualifications and less work experience. In this sort of case, equality (construed as identity) in the treatment of the sexes appears to produce an outcome in which sexual inequality is increased.

The obvious alternative of seeking equality by providing women with special legal protection continues, however, to be as fraught with dangers for women as it was earlier in the century when the existence of protective legislation was used as an excuse for excluding women from many of the more prestigious and better paid occupations. For instance, mandating special leaves for disability on account of pregnancy or childbirth promotes the perception that women are less reliable workers than men; recognizing "pre-menstrual syndrome" or post-partum depression as periodically disabling conditions encourages the perception that women are less responsible than men; while attempts to protect women's sexuality through legislation restricting pornography or excluding women from employment in male institutions such as prisons, perpetuate the dangerous stereotypes that women are by nature the sexual prey of men. This cultural myth serves as an implicit legitimation for the prostitution, sexual harassment and rape of women, because it implies that such activities are in some sense natural. In all these cases, attempts to achieve equality between the sexes by responding to perceived differences between men and women seem likely to reinforce rather than reduce existing differences, even differences that are acknowledged to be social rather than biological in origin.

Furthermore, a "sex-responsive," as opposed to "sex-blind," conception of equality ignores differences between women, separating all women into a single homogenous category and possibly penalizing one group of women by forcing them to accept protection that another group genuinely may need.

Sooner or later, most feminist attempts to formulate an adequate conception of sexual equality run up against the recognition that the baseline for discussions of equality typically has been a male standard. In Catharine MacKinnon's inimitable words:

> Men's physiology defines most sports, their needs define auto and health insurance coverage, their socially designed biographies define workplace expectations and successful career patterns, their perspectives and concerns define quality in scholarship, their experiences and obsessions define merit, their objectivication of life defines art, their military service defines citizenship, their presence defines family, their inability to get along with each other—their wars and rulerships—defines history, their image defines god, and their genitals define sex. [MacKinnon 1987:36]

Having once reached this recognition, some feminist theorists have turned away from debating the pros and cons of what MacKinnon calls the "single" versus the "double standard" and begun speculating about the kinds of far-reaching social transformation that would make sex differences "costless." In discussions elaborating such notions as that of "equality as acceptance," feminists seem to be moving towards a radical construal of equality as similarity of individual outcome, equality of condition or effect, a conception quite at odds with traditional liberal understandings of equality as equality of procedure or opportunity.

While some feminists struggle to formulate a conception of sexual equality that is adequate for feminism, others have suggested that the enterprise is hopeless. For them, equality is an integral part of an "ethic of justice" that is characteristically masculine insofar as it obscures human difference by abstracting from the particularity and uniqueness of concrete people in their specific situations and seeks to resolve conflicting interests by applying an abstract rule rather than by responding directly to needs that are immediately perceived. Such feminists suggest that a discourse of responsibility or care may offer a more appropriate model for feminist ethics—even including feminist jurisprudence. Both of these suggestions remain to be worked out in detail.

The tangled debate over equality and difference provides an excellent illustration of one characteristic feature of contemporary feminist ethics, namely, its insistence that gender is often, if not invariable, a morally relevant difference between individuals. Given this insistence, the starting point of much feminist ethics may be different from that of modern moral theory: instead of assuming that all individuals should be treated alike until morally relevant grounds for difference in treatment can be identified, feminist theorists may shift the traditional burden of moral proof by assuming, until shown otherwise, that contemporary men and women are rarely "similarly situated." This leads into a related and equally crucial question for feminist ethics in the nineties, namely, how to characterize and evaluate impartiality.

2.   IMPARTIALITY

In the modern western tradition, impartiality typically has been recognized as a fundamental value, perhaps even a defining characteristic of morality, distinguishing true morality from tribalism. Impartiality is said to require weighing the interests of each individual equally, permitting differentiation only on the basis of differences that can be shown to be morally relevant. Impartiality thus is linked conceptually with equality and also with rationality and objectivity, insofar as bias often has been defined as the absence of impartiality.

In the last few years, the preeminence traditionally ascribed to impartiality has been challenged both by feminist and nonfeminist philosophers. Nonfeminists have charged that an instance on impartiality disregards our particular identities, constituted by reference to our particular projects and our unchosen relationships with others; and that it substitutes abstract "variables" for real human agents and patients. Williams [1973, 1981], for instance, has argued that the requirement of impartiality may undermine our personal integrity because it may require us to abandon projects that are central to our identity, and he also suggests that acting from duty may sometimes be less valuable than acting from an immediate emotional response to a particular other. MacIntyre [1981] and Sommers [1986] have argued that impartiality fails to respect tradition, customary expectations and unchosen encumbrances, and may require behavior that is morally repugnant.

While some of the moral intuitions that motivate the nonfeminist critics of impartiality certainly are shared by many feminists, other intuitions most likely are not. It is implausible to suppose, for instance, that most feminists would join Williams in applauding Gaugin's abandonment of his family in order to pursue his art, or that they would join Sommers in accepting without question the claims of customary morality on issues such as women's responsibilities. Instead, the feminist criticisms of impartiality tend to be both less individualistic and less conventionalist. They are quite varied in character.

Nell Noddings [1984] is one of the most extreme opponents of impartiality and her work has been influential with a number of feminists, even though the sub-title of her book makes it clear that she takes herself to be elaborating a feminine rather than a feminist approach to ethics. Noddings views the emotion of caring as the natural basis of morality, a view that would require impartiality to be expressed in universal caring. Noddings claims, however, that we are psychologically able to care only for particular others with whom we are in actual relationships, i.e., relationships that can be "completed" by the cared-for's acknowledgment of our caring. She concludes that pretensions to care for humanity at large are not only hypocritical but self defeating, undermining true caring for those with whom we are in actual relationship. Noddings' arguments, if valid, of course would apply indifferently to caring practiced either by men or by women, and so the distinctively feminist interest of Noddings' work might seem to reside solely in her obviously debatable claim that women are "better equipped for caring than men" (97) and therefore less likely to be impartial. As we have noted already, however, feminist ethics is not committed to reproducing the moral practice even of most women and so feminist (and nonfeminist) moral theorists need to evaluate critically all of Noddings' arguments against impartiality, independently of whether her claims about "feminine" morality can be empirically confirmed.

A different criticism of impartiality has been made by those feminist philosophers who assert that, while impartiality is associated historically with individualism, it paradoxically undermines respect for individuality because it treats individuals as morally interchangeable [Code 1988; Sherwin 1987]. Many, though certainly not all, feminists claim that women are less likely than men to commit this alleged moral error because they are more likely to appreciate the special characteristics of particular individuals; again, however, feminist estimates of the soundness or otherwise of Code's and Sherwin's argument must be independent of this empirical claim.

Finally, at least one feminist has extended the claim that women need special protection in the law by recommending that feminist ethics should promote a double standard of morality, limiting moral communities on the basis of gender or perhaps gender solidarity. Susan Sherwin writes that feminists feel a special responsibility to reduce the suffering of women in particular; thus, "(b)y acknowledging the relevance of differences among people as a basis for a difference in sympathy and concern, feminism denies the legitimacy of a central premise of traditional moral theories, namely that all persons should be seen as morally equivalent by us" [Sherwin 1987:26 . . .]. However, since women and even feminists are not homogenous groups, as we have seen, this kind of reasoning seems to push the suggested double standard towards becoming a multiple moral standard—which Enlightenment theorists might well interpret as the total abandonment of impartiality and thus of morality itself.

A variety of responses seems to be available to the foregoing criticisms of impartiality. One alternative is to argue that the criticisms are unwarranted, depending on misrepresentation, misunderstanding and caricature of the impartialist position. If this response can be sustained, it may be possible to show that there is no real conflict between "masculine" impartialism and "feminine" particularism, "masculine" justice and "feminine" care. Another alternative is to bite the bullet of direct moral confrontation, providing arguments to challenge the intuitions of those who criticize impartiality as requiring courses of action that are morally repugnant or politically dangerous. Yet a third alternative may be to reconceive the concept of impartiality and the considerations appropriate for determining our responsibilities toward various individuals and groups. Feminist ethics must find a way of choosing between those or other options and evaluating the proper place of impartiality in ethics for the nineties.

3.   MORAL SUBJECTIVITY

Related to the foregoing questions about impartiality are questions about how to conceptualize individuals, the subjects of moral theory. Feminists and nonfeminists alike have criticized the neo-Cartesian model of the moral self, a disembodied, separate, autonomous, unified, rational being, essentially similar to all other moral selves. Marx challenged the historicism of this model; Freud challenged its claims to rationality; contemporary communitarians, such as Sandel and MacIntyre, challenge the assumption that individuals are "unencumbered," arguing instead that we are all members of communities from which we may be able to distance ourselves to some extent but which nevertheless are deeply constitutive of our identities; postmodernists have deconstructed the model to reveal fractured rather than unitary identities.

The gender bias alleged to contaminate each of the traditions mentioned above means that feminists cannot appropriate uncritically existing critiques of the neo-Cartesian moral self. Nevertheless, in developing their own challenges to this model of the self, feminist theorists often have paralleled and/or built on some nonfeminist work. . . .

Given this burgeoning literature, it is evident that a central concern for feminist ethics in the nineties must be to develop ways of thinking about moral subjects that are sensitive both to their concreteness, inevitable particularity and unique specificity, expressed in part through their relations with specific historical communities, and to their intrinsic and common value, the ideal expressed in Enlightenment claims about common humanity, equality and impartiality.

4.   AUTONOMY

One aspect of this task is the rethinking of autonomy which, like impartiality (to which it is often conceptually connected), has been a continuing ideal of modern moral theory. (In addition, a closely related concept of autonomy has played a central role in the Cartesian epistemological tradition, which envisions the search for knowledge as a project of the solitary knower.) The core intuition of autonomy is that of independence or self legislation, the self as the ultimate authority in matters of morality or truth. In the Kantian tradition, where the ideal of autonomy is particularly prominent, moral autonomy has been elaborated in terms of disinterest, detachment from particular attachments and interests, and freedom from prejudice and self-deception [Hill 1987].

Contemporary feminists have had a mixed response to the modern ideal of moral autonomy. On the one hand, they have insisted that women are as autonomous in the moral and intellectual sense as men—as rational, as capable of a sense of justice, and so on; and they have also demanded political, social and economic autonomy for women through political representation, the abolition of sex discrimination and respect for women's choices on issues such as abortion. On the other hand, however, some feminists have questioned traditional interpretations of autonomy as masculine fantasies. For instance, they have explored some of the ways in which "choice" is socialized and "consent" manipulated. In addition, they have questioned the possibility of separating ourselves from particular attachments and still retaining our personal identity, and they have suggested that freeing ourselves from particular attachments might result in a cold, rigid, moralistic rather than a truly moral response [Noddings 1984]. Rather than guaranteeing a response that is purely moral, freeing ourselves from particular attachments might instead make us *incapable* of morality if an ineliminable part of morality consists in responding emotionally to particular others.

Feminist ethics in the nineties must find ways of conceptualizing moral agency, choice and consent that are compatible with the feminist recognition of the gradual process of moral development, the gendered social construction of the psyche, and the historical constraints on our options. This is one area in which some promising work by feminists exists already.

5.   MORAL EPISTEMOLOGY AND ANTI-EPISTEMOLOGY

Enlightenment moral theory characteristically assumed that morality was universal—that, if moral claims held, they were valid at all times and in all places. However, the modern abandonment of belief in a teleological and sacred universe rendered the justification of such claims constantly problematic, and much moral theory for the last three centuries has consisted in attempts to provide a rational grounding for morality. At the present time, both the continental European tradition, especially but not only in the form of post-modernism, and the Anglo-American tradition, especially but not only in the form of communitarianism, have developed powerful challenges to the very possibility of the view that morality consists in universally valid rules grounded in universal reason. The inevitable result of these skeptical challenges has been to reinforce normative and meta-ethical relativism.

Feminists are ambivalent about these challenges. On the one hand, many of the feminist criticisms of modern moral theory parallel the criticisms made by communitarianism and post-modernism. On the other hand, however, feminists are understandably concerned that their critique of male dominance should not be dismissed as just one point of view. It is therefore crucial for feminist ethics to develop some ways of justifying feminist moral claims. However, moral epistemology is an area in which feminists' critiques are better developed than their alternatives.

Feminist discussions of moral epistemology may be divided into two categories, each distinguished by a somewhat different view of the nature of morality. Feminists in the first category do not explicitly challenge the modern conception of morality as consisting primarily in an impartial system of rationally justified rules or principles, though few feminists would assert that it is possible to identify rules that are substantive, specific and hold in all circumstances. Those in the second category, by contrast, deny that morality is reducible to rules and emphasize the impossibility of justifying the claims of ethics by appeal to a universal, impartial reason. The contrast between these two groups of feminists is not as sharp as this initial characterization might suggest: for instance, both share several criticisms of existing decision procedures in ethics. But feminists in the former group are more hopeful of repairing those procedures, while feminists in the latter group seem ready to abandon them entirely.

Feminists in the latter group frequently claim to be reflecting on a moral experience that is distinctively feminine and for this reason they are often—incorrectly—taken to represent a feminist orthodoxy. They include authors such as Gilligan [1982], Noddings [1984], Baier [1987], Blum [1987], Ruddick [1989] and Walker [1989]. While there is considerable variation in the views of these authors, they all reject the view attributed to modern moral theorists that the right course of action can be discovered by consulting a list of moral rules, charging that undue emphasis on the epistemological importance of rules obscures the crucial role of moral insight, virtue and character is determining what should be done. A feminist twist is given to this essentially Aristotelian criticism when claims are made that excessive reliance on rules reflects a juridical-administrative interest that is characteristic of modern masculinity [Blum 1982] while contemporary women, by contrast, are alleged to be more likely to disregard conventionally accepted moral rules because such rules are insensitive to the specificities of particular situations [Gilligan 1982; Noddings 1984]. A morality of rule, therefore, is alleged to devalue the moral wisdom of women, as well as to give insufficient weight to such supposedly feminine virtues as kindness, generosity, helpfulness and sympathy.

Some feminists have claimed that "feminine" approaches to morality contrast with supposedly masculine rule-governed approaches in that they characteristically consist in immediate responses to particular others, responses based on supposedly natural feelings of empathy, care and compassion [Gilligan 1982; Noddings 1984] or loving attention [Murdoch 1970; Ruddick 1989]. However, apart from the difficulties of establishing that such a "particularist" approach to morality [Blum 1987] indeed is characteristically feminine, let alone feminist, attempts to develop a moral epistemology based on such responses face a variety of problems. First, they confront the familiar, though perhaps not insuperable, problems common to all moral epistemologies that take emotion as a guide to right action, namely, the frequent inconsistency, unavailability or plain inappropriateness of emotions. In other words, they face the danger of degenerating into a "do what feels good" kind of subjective relativism. In addition, it is not clear that even our emotional responses to others are not responses to them under some universal description and so in this sense general rather than particular—or, if indeed particular and therefore nonconceptual, then perhaps closer to animal than to distinctively human responses. It is further uncertain how these sorts of particular responses can guide our actions towards large numbers of people, most of whom we shall never meet. Finally, the feminist emphasis on the need for "contextual" reasoning opens up the obvious dangers of ad hocism, special pleading and partiality.

Not all feminists, of course, are committed to a particularist moral epistemology. Even some of those who take emotions as a proper guide to morality emphasize the intentionality of emotions and discuss the need for their moral education. Additionally, while most feminists criticize certain aspects of the decision procedures developed by modern moral theory, some believe it may be possible to revise and reappropriate some of these procedures. The main candidates for such revision are the methods developed by Rawls and Habermas, each of whom believes that an idealized situation of dialogue (which each describes differently) will both generate and justify morally valid principles. . . .

One possible alternative both to an unwelcome relativism and to what many feminists see as the pretensions of moral rationalism may be the development of a moral standpoint that is distinctively feminist. Sara Ruddick claims that such a standpoint can be found in maternal thinking [1989], but her work has been criticized by some feminists as ethnocentric and overvaluing motherhood. Even if the feminist standpoint were differently identified, however, problems would remain. Standpoint epistemology derives from Marx and, at least in its Lukacian version, it seems to require an objectivist distinction between appearance and reality that is quite alien to the social constructionist tendencies in much contemporary feminism.

The controversy in feminist moral epistemology currently is so sharp that Held [1948] has suggested abandoning the search for a "unified field theory" covering all domains of life activity. However, other authors have pointed to the danger that, if a supposedly feminine "ethic of care" were limited to the realm of personal life, as Kohlberg, for instance has suggested, it would be perceived as subordinate to the supposedly masculine "ethic of justice," just as, in contemporary society, the private is subordinate to the public.

CONCLUSION

Even such a limited survey as this should make it evident that feminist ethics, far from being a rigid orthodoxy, instead is a ferment of ideas and controversy, many of them echoing and deepening debates in nonfeminist* ethics. The centrality of the issues and the liveliness of the on-going discussions suggest that the nineties will be a fruitful period for feminist ethics—and thus for ethics generally.

References

Baier, Annette, "The Need for More Than Justice," *Science, Morality and Feminist Theory*, ed. Marsha Hanen and Kai Nielsen. Calgary: University of Calgary Press, 1987.

Blum, Lawrence, "Kant's and Hegel's Moral Rationalism: A Feminist Perspective," *Canadian Journal of Philosophy* 12:2 (June 1982).

Blum, Lawrence, "Particularity and Responsiveness," *The Emergence of Morality in Young Children*, eds. Jerome Kagan and Sharon Lamb. Chicago: University of Chicago Press, 1987.

Code, Lorraine, "Experience, Knowledge and Responsibility," *Feminist Perspectives in Philosophy*, eds. Morwenna Griffiths and Margaret Whitford. Bloomington and Indianapolis: Indiana University Press, 1988.

Gilligan, Carol, *In a Different Voice: Psychological Theory and Women's Development*. Cambridge, MA: Harvard University Press, 1982.

Held, Virginia, *Rights and Goods*. New York: The Free Press, 1984.

Hill, Thomas E., Jr., "The Importance of Autonomy," *Women and Moral Theory*, eds. Eva Feder Kittay and Diana T. Meyers, Totowa, NJ: Rowman and Littlefield, 1987.

MacIntyre, Alasdair, *After Virtue: A Study in Moral Theory*. London: Duckworth, 1981.

MacKinnon, Catherine A., *Feminism Unmodified: Discourses on Life and Law*. Cambridge, MA: Harvard University Press, 1987.

Murdoch, Iris, *The Sovereignty of Good*. London: Routledge & Kegan Paul, 1970.

Noddings, Nell, *Caring: A Feminine Approach to Ethics and Moral Education*. Berkeley: University of California Press, 1984.

Okin, Susan Moller, "Justice and Gender," *Philosophy and Public Affairs* 16:1 (Winter 1987).

Ruddick, Sara, *Maternal Thinking: Toward a Politics of Peace*. Boston: Beacon Press, 1989.

Sherwin, Susan, "A Feminist Approach to Ethics," *Resources for Feminist Research* 16:3, 1987. (Special issue on "Women and Philosophy.")

Sommers, Christina Hoff, "Filial Morality," *The Journal of Philosophy* 83:8 (August 1986).

Walker, Margaret, "Moral Understandings: Alternative 'Epistemology' for a Feminist Ethics," *Hypatia: A Journal of Feminist Philosophy* 4:2 (Summer 1989).

Williams, B., "Morality and Emotions," *Problems of the Self*. Cambridge: Cambridge University Press, 1973.

Williams, B., "Persons, Character and Morality," "Moral Luck," and "Utilitarianism and Moral Self Indulgence," *Moral Luck*. Cambridge: Cambridge University Press, 1981.

*"Nonfeminist" here refers to philosophers who do not make their feminist concerns explicit in their philosophical work; it is not intended to imply that such philosophers do not demonstrate feminist concern in other ways.

Catharine A. MacKinnon, "Sex and Violence" in *Feminism Unmodified: Discourses on Life and Law*, 1989

Sex and Violence
Catharine A. MacKinnon

I want to raise some questions about the concept of this panel's title, "Violence against Women," as a concept that may coopt us as we attempt to formulate our own truths. I want to speak specifically about four issues: rape, sexual harassment, pornography, and battery. I think one of the reasons we say that each of these issues is an example of violence against women is to reunify them. To say that aggression against women has this unity is to criticize the divisions that have been imposed on that aggression by the legal system. What I see to be the danger of the analysis, what makes it potentially cooptive, is formulating it—and it is formulated this way—these are issues of violence, *not sex:* rape is a crime of violence, not sexuality; sexual harassment is an abuse of power, not sexuality; pornography is violence against women, it is not erotic. Although battering is not categorized so explicitly, it is usually treated as though there is nothing sexual about a man beating up a woman so long as it is with his fist. I'd like to raise some questions about that as well.

I hear in the formulation that these issues are violence against women, not sex, that we are in the shadow of Freud, intimidated at being called repressive Victorians. We're saying we're *op*pressed and they say we're *re*pressed. That is, when we say we're against rape, the immediate response is, "Does that mean you're against sex?" "Are you attempting to impose neo-Victorian prudery on sexual expression?" This comes up with sexual harassment as well. When we say we're against sexual harassment, the first thing people want to know is "What's the difference between that and ordinary male-to-female sexual initiation?" That's a good question . . . The same is also true of criticizing pornography. "You can't be against erotica?" It's the latest version of the accusation that feminists are antimale. To distinguish ourselves from this, and in reaction to it, we call these abuses violence. The attempt is to avoid the critique—we're not against sex—and at the same time retain our criticism of these practices. So we rename as violent those abuses that have been seen to be sexual, without saying that we have a very different perspective on violence and on sexuality and their relationship. I also think a reason we call these experiences violence is to avoid being called lesbians, which for some reason is equated with being against sex. In order to avoid that, yet retain our opposition to sexual violation, we put this neutral, objective, abstract word *violence* on it all.

To me this is an attempt to have our own perspective on these outrages without owning up to having one. To have our point of view, but present it as *not* having a particular point of view. Our problem has been to label something as rape, as sexual harassment, as pornography in the face of a suspicion that it might be intercourse, it might be ordinary sexual initiation, it might be erotic. To say that these purportedly sexual events violate us, to be against them, we call them not sexual. But the attempt to be objective and neutral avoids owning up to the fact that women do have a specific point of view on these events. It avoids saying that from women's point of view, intercourse, sex roles, and eroticism can be and at times are violent to us as women.

My approach would claim our perspective; we are not attempting to be objective about it, we're attempting to represent the point of view of women. The point of view of men up to this time, called objective, has been to distinguish sharply between rape on the one hand and intercourse on the other; sexual harassment on the one hand and normal, ordinary sexual initiation on the other; pornography or obscenity on the one hand and eroticism on the other. The male point of view defines them by distinction. What women experience does not so clearly distinguish the normal, everyday things from those abuses from which they have been defined by distinction. Not just "Now we're going to take what *you* say is rape and call it violence"; "Now we're going to take what *you* say is sexual harassment and call it violence"; "Now we're going to take what *you* say is pornography and call it violence." We have a deeper critique of what has been done to women's sexuality and who controls access to it. What we are saying is that sexuality in exactly these normal forms often *does* violate us. So long as we say those things are abuses of violence, not sex, we fail to criticize what has been made of *sex*, what has been done to us *through* sex, because we leave the line between rape and intercourse, sexual harassment and sex roles, pornography and eroticism, right where it is.

I think it is useful to inquire how women and men (I don't use the term *persons*, I guess, because I haven't seen many lately) live through the meaning of their experience with these issues. When we ask whether rape, sexual harassment, and pornography are questions of violence or questions of sexuality, it helps to ask, to whom? What is the perspective of those who are involved, whose experience it is—to rape or to have been raped, to consume pornography or to be consumed through it. As to what these things *mean* socially, it is important whether they are about sexuality to women and men or whether they are instead about "violence"—or whether violence and sexuality can be distinguished in that way, as they are lived out.

The crime of rape—this is a legal and observed, not a subjective, individual, or feminist definition—is defined about penetration. That seems to me a very male point of view on what it means to be sexually violated. And it is exactly what heterosexuality as a social institution is fixated around, the penetration of the penis into the vagina. Rape is defined according to what men think violates women, and that is the same as what they think of as the *sine qua non* of sex. What women experience as degrading and defiling when we are raped includes as much that is distinctive to us as is our experience of sex. Someone once termed penetration a "peculiarly resented aspect" of rape—I don't know whether that meant it was peculiar that it was resented or that it was resented with heightened peculiarity. Women who have been raped often do resent having been penetrated. But that is not all there is to what was intrusive or expropriative of a woman's sexual wholeness.

I do think the crime of rape focuses more centrally on what men define as sexuality than on women's experience of our sexual being, hence its violation. A common experience of rape victims is to be unable to feel good about anything heterosexual thereafter—or anything sexual at all, or men at all. The minute they start to have sexual feelings or feel sexually touched by a man, or even a woman, they start to relive the rape. I had a client who came in with her husband. She was a rape victim, a woman we had represented as a witness. Her husband sat the whole time and sobbed. They couldn't have sex anymore because every time he started to touch her, she would flash to the rape scene and see his face change into the face of the man who had raped her. That, to me, is sexual. When a woman has been raped, and it is sex that she then cannot experience without connecting it to that, it was her sexuality that was violated.

Similarly, men who are in prison for rape think it's the dumbest thing that ever happened . . . It isn't just a miscarriage of justice; they were put in jail for something very little different from what most men do most of the time and call it sex. The only difference is they got caught. That view is nonremorseful and not rehabilitative. It may also be true. It seems to me we have here a convergence between the rapist's view of what he has done and the victim's perspective on what was done to her. That is, for both, their ordinary experiences of heterosexual intercourse and the act of rape have something in common. Now this gets us into intense trouble, because that's exactly how judges and juries see it who refuse to convict men accused of rape. A rape victim has to prove that it was not intercourse. She has to show that there was force and she resisted, because if there was sex, consent is inferred. Finders of fact look for "more force than usual during the preliminaries." Rape is defined by distinction from intercourse—not nonviolence, intercourse. They ask, does this event look more like fucking or like rape? But what is their standard for sex, and is this question asked from the *woman's point of view*? The level of force is not adjudicated at her point of violation; it is adjudicated at the standard of the normal level of force. Who sets this standard?

In the criminal law, we can't put everybody in jail who does an ordinary act, right? Crime is supposed to be deviant, not normal. Women continue not to report rape, and a reason is that they believe, and they are right, that the legal system will not see it from their point of view. We get very low conviction rates for rape. We also get many women who believe they have never been raped, although a lot of force was involved. They mean that they were not raped in a way that is legally provable. In other words, in all these situations, there was not *enough* violence against them to take it beyond the category of "sex"; they were not coerced enough. Maybe they were forced-fucked for years and put up with it, maybe they tried to get it over with, maybe they were coerced by something other than battery, something like economics, maybe even something like love.

What I am saying is that unless you make the point that there is much violence in intercourse, as a usual matter, none of that is changed. Also we continue to stigmatize the women who claim rape as having experienced a deviant violation and allow the rest of us to go through life feeling violated but thinking we've never been raped, when there were a great many times when we, too, have had sex and didn't want it. What this critique does that is different from the "violence, not sex" critique is ask a series of questions about normal, heterosexual intercourse and attempt to move the line between heterosexuality on the one hand—intercourse—and rape on the other, rather than allow it to stay where it is.

Having done that so extensively with rape, I can consider sexual harassment more briefly. The way the analysis of sexual harassment is sometimes expressed now (and it bothers me) is that it is an abuse of power, not sexuality. That does not allow us to pursue whether sexuality, as socially constructed in our society through gender roles, is *itself* a power structure. If you look at sexual harassment as power, not sex, what is power supposed to be? Power is employer/employee, not because courts are Marxist but because this is a recognized hierarchy.

Among men. Power is teacher/student, because courts recognize a hierarchy there. Power is on one side and sexuality on the other. Sexuality is ordinary affection, everyday flirtation. Only when ordinary, everyday affection and flirtation and "I was just trying to be friendly" come into the context of *another* hierarchy is it considered potentially an abuse of power. What is not considered to be a hierarchy is women and men—men on top and women on the bottom. That is not considered to be a question of power or social hierarchy, legally or politically. A feminist perspective suggests that it is.

When we have examples of coequal sexual harassment (within these other hierarchies), worker to worker on the same level, involving women and men, we have a lot of very interesting, difficult questions about sex discrimination, which is supposed to be about gender difference, but does not conceive of gender as a social hierarchy. I think that implicit in race discrimination cases for a brief moment of light was the notion that there is a social hierarchy between Blacks and whites. So that presumptively it's an exercise of power for a white person to do something egregious to a Black person or for a white institution to do something egregious systematically to many Black people. Situations of coequal power—among coworkers or students or teachers—are difficult to see as examples of sexual harassment unless you have a notion of male power. I think we lie to women when we call it not power when a woman is come onto by a man who is not her employer, not her teacher. What do we labor under, what do we feel, when a man—any man—comes and hits on us? I think we require women to feel fine about turning down male-initiated sex so long as the man doesn't have some *other* form of power over us. Whenever—every and any time—a woman feels conflicted and wonders what's wrong with her that she can't decline although she has no inclination, and she feels open to male accusations, whether they come from women or men, of "why didn't you just tell him to buzz off?" we have sold her out, not named her experience. We are taught that we exist for men. We should be flattered or at least act as if we are—be careful about a man's ego because you never know what he can do to you. To flat out say to him, "You?" or "I don't want to" is not *in* most women's sex-role learning. To say it is, is bravado. And that's because he's a man, not just because you never know what he can do to you because he's your boss (that's two things—he's a man and he's the boss) or your teacher or in some other hierarchy. It seems to me that we haven't talked very much about gender *as* a hierarchy, as a division of power, in the way that's expressed and acted out, primarily I think sexually. And therefore we haven't expanded the definition according to women's experience of sexuality, including our own sexual intimidation, of what things are sexual in this world. So men have also defined what can be called sexual about us. They say, "I was just trying to be affectionate, flirtatious and friendly," and we were just all felt up. We criticize the idea that rape comes down to her word against his—but it really *is* her perspective against his perspective, and the law has been written from *his* perspective. If he didn't mean to be sexual, it's not sexual. If he didn't see it as forced, it wasn't forced. Which is to say, only male sexual violations, that is, only male ideas of what sexually violates us as women are illegal. We buy into this when we say our sexual violations are abuses of power, not sex.

Just as rape is supposed to have nothing against intercourse, just as sexual harassment is supposed to have nothing against normal sexual initiation (men initiate, women consent— that's mutual?), the idea that pornography is violence against women, not sex, seems to distinguish artistic creation on the one hand from what is degrading to women on the other. It is candid and true but not enough to say of pornography, as Justice Stewart said, "I know it when I see it." *He* knows what he thinks it is when he sees it—but is that what *I* know? Is that the same "it"? Is he going to know what I know when I see it? I think pretty much not, given what's on the newsstand, given what is not considered hard-core pornography. Sometimes I think what is obscene is what does *not* turn on the Supreme Court—or what revolts them more. Which is uncommon, since revulsion is eroticized. We have to admit that pornography turns men on; it is therefore erotic. It is a lie to say that pornography is not erotic. When we say it is violence, not sex, we are saying, there is this degrading to women, over here, and this erotic, over there, without saying to whom. It is overwhelmingly disproportionately men to whom pornography is erotic. It is women, on the whole, to whom it is violent, among other things. And this is not just a matter of perspective, but a matter of reality.

Pornography turns primarily men on. Certainly they are getting something out of it. They pay incredible amounts of money for it; it's one of the largest industries in the country. If women got as much out of it as men do, we would buy it instead of cosmetics. It's a massive industry, cosmetics. We are poor but we have *some* money; we are some market. We spend our money to set ourselves up as the objects that emulate those images that are sold as erotic to men. What pornography says about us is that we enjoy degradation, that we are sexually turned on by being degraded. For me that obliterates the line, as a line at all, between pornography on one hand and erotica on the other, if what turns men on, what men find beautiful, is what degrades women. It is pervasively present in art, also, and advertising. But it is definitely present in eroticism, if that is what it is. It makes me think that women's sexuality as such is a stigma. We also sometimes have an experience of sexuality authentic somehow in all this. We are not allowed to have it; we are not allowed to talk about it; we are not allowed to speak of it or image it as from our own point of view. And, to the extent we try to assert that we are beings equal with men, we have to be either asexual or virgins.

To worry about cooptation is to realize that lies make bad politics. It is ironic that cooptation often results from an attempt to be "credible," to be strategically smart, to be "effective" on existing terms. Sometimes you become what you're fighting. Thinking about issues of sexual violation as issues of violence not sex could, if pursued legally, lead to opposing sexual harassment and pornography through morals legislation and obscenity laws. It is actually interesting that this theoretical stance has been widely embraced but these legal strategies have not been. Perhaps women realize that these legal approaches would not address the subordination of women to men, specifically and substantively. These approaches are legally as abstract as the "violence not sex" critique is politically abstract. They are both not enough and too much of the wrong thing. They deflect us from criticizing everyday behavior that is pervasive and normal and concrete and fuses sexuality with gender in violation and is not amenable to existing legal approaches. I think we need to think more radically in our legal work here.

Battering is called violence, rather than something sex-specific: this is done to women. I also think it is sexually done to women. Not only in where it is done—over half of the incidents are in the bedroom. Or the surrounding events—precipitating sexual jealously. But when violence against women is eroticized as it is in this culture, it is very difficult to say that there is a major distinction in the level of sex involved between being assaulted by a penis and being assaulted by a fist, especially when the perpetrator is a man. If women as gender female are defined as sexual beings, and violence is eroticized, then men violating women has a sexual component. I think men rape women because they get off on it in a way that fuses dominance with sexuality. (This is different in emphasis from what Susan Bronmiller says.) I think that when men sexually harass women it expresses male control over sexual access to us. It doesn't mean they all want to fuck us, they just want to hurt us, dominate us, and control us, and that *is* fucking us. They want to be able to have that and to be able to say when they can have it, to *know* that. That is in itself erotic. The idea that opposing battering is about saving the family is, similarly, abstracted, gender-neutral. There are gender-neutral formulations of all these issues: law and order as opposed to derepression, Victorian morality as opposed to permissiveness, obscenity as opposed to art and freedom of expression. Gender-neutral, objective formulations like these avoid asking *whose* expression, from whose point of view? Whose law and whose order? It's not just a question of who is free to express ourselves; it's not just that there is almost no, if any, self-respecting women's eroticism. The fact is that what we do see, what we are allowed to experience, even in our own suffering, even in what we are allowed to complain about, is overwhelmingly constructed from the male point of view. Laws against sexual violation express what men see and do when they engage in sex with women; laws against obscenity center on the display of women's bodies in ways that men are turned on by viewing. To me, it not only makes us cooptable to define such abuses in gender-neutral terms like violence; when we fail to assert that we are fighting for the affirmative definition and control of our own sexuality, of our own lives as women, and that these experiences violate *that,* we have already been bought.

Study Questions

1. Why does MacKinnon think women have placed specifically sexual violations against women under the generic genderless heading of "violence"? What are women protecting themselves against by doing this? What is lost in the process?

2. Why is there a fear of allowing sexuality into the discussion of rape, sexual harassment, pornography, and battery, according to MacKinnon?

3. Who has defined what rape is, and why it is wrong? What are the consequences of this?

4. Is MacKinnon saying or suggesting that all sex is inherently violent toward women?

5. What is the difference between pornography and erotica, according to MacKinnon?

Paul Cameron, "A Case Against Homosexuality" in *Human Life Review*, Vol. 4, 1978

A Case Against Homosexuality
Paul Cameron

In some segments of the mass media, the homosexuality issue takes on the appearance of a struggle between orange juice peddlers and bathhouse owners. At a different level individual rights vs. the interests of society provide the conflict. Some argue that adult homosexuals ought to be allowed to do what they want behind closed doors. Others, often seeing the issue in terms of rights, honesty, and overpopulation, seek to grant homosexuality equal status with heterosexuality. The school system of San Francisco, apparently resonating with the latter tack, is offering a course including "homosexual life-styles." Liberals attempt to shame as unenlightened all who oppose complete equality as vigorously as conservative Bible-thumpers threaten wrath from above.

No known human society has ever granted equal status to homo-and heterosexuality. What information do those who desire social equivalence for these two sexual orientations possess that assures them that this new venture in human and social organization is called for at this time? Have the cultures of the past practiced discrimination against homosexuality out of a mere prejudice, or was there substance to their bias? At the risk of seeming rather out of step with the academic community, no new information has surfaced that would lead me to discount the social policies of the past. On the contrary, the policies of the past in regard to homosexuality appear generally wise, and considerable discrimination against homosexuality and for heterosexuality, marriage and parenthood appears needful for the social good.

DISCRIMINATION

Discrimination is something all humans, and all human communities do. Individually we discriminate for certain things and against others, e.g., movies over T.V. Collectively we discriminate for and against selected: 1) acts (pleasantries, sharing vs. murder, robbery) 2) traits (generous, kind vs. whiny, hostile) and 3) life-styles (independent, productive vs. gambling, indolent). Prejudice is unwarranted discrimination. The issue is not whether discrimination should exist—for human society to exist, it must. The issues are always: 1) is discrimination called for? and 2) how much is necessary? Reasonable people can and do disagree on what ought to be discriminated for and against, to what degree, and even if discrimination is prejudicial rather than called for. But reasoned opinion *can* hold that homosexuality and homosexuals ought to be discriminated against. . . .

THE CASE AGAINST HOMOSEXUALITY/WISDOM OF THE AGES

No contemporary society accords homosexuality equivalent status with heterosexuality. No known society has accorded equivalent status in the past (Karlen, 1971). No current or ancient religion of any consequence has failed to teach discrimination against homosexuality. The Judeo-Christian tradition is no exception to this rule. The Old Testament made homosexuality a capital offense, and while the New Testament writers failed to invoke capital punishment for any offense, they did manage to consign homosexuals to eternal hell for the practice. Church fathers and traditions have stayed in line with this position until recently. To the degree that tradition and agreed-upon social policy ought to carry weight in our thinking about issues, the weight of tradition is preponderately on the side of discrimination. . . .

While one cannot carry the "wisdom of the ages" argument too far—just because all peoples up to a certain point in time believed something does not necessarily mean that it was so—yet it appears more than a little injudicious to cast it aside as merely "quaint." Probably no issue has occupied man's collective attentions more than successful living together. That such unanimity of opinion and practice should exist must give one pause. Certain such congruence "puts the ball in the changer's court." As in so many spheres of human endeavor, when we know that we can get on in a particular way, the burden of proof that we can get on as well or better by following a different custom falls upon those seeking the change. . . .

To date, those seeking change have not been flush with scientific evidence that homosexuality is not socially disruptive. On the contrary, the arguments that have been advanced have been little more than "people ought not to be discriminated against; homosexuals are people; ergo homosexuals ought not to be discriminated against" shouted larger and louder. No one to my knowledge has ever claimed that homosexuals were not people, and one would have to be a dunce to believe that being a person qualifies one, *ipso facto*, for nondiscrimination. Aside from this argument repeated in endless variations and *ad nauseam*, the evidence is simply not there.

HOMOSOCIALITY COUPLED WITH INCREASING SELF-CENTEREDNESS COULD LEAD TO WIDESPREAD HOMOSEXUALITY

. . . Jimmy Carter said: "I don't see homosexuality as a threat to the family" (*Washington Post*, June 19, 1977). His sentiments probably echo those of the educated class of our society. They trust that "only deviants" are really into homosexuality anyway, and, more importantly, that "mother nature" will come through in the last analysis. Biology, they assume, has a great deal to do with sexuality and sexual attraction, and millions of years of heterosexuality has firmly engraved itself on the genetic code.

Such thinking betrays a lack of appreciation of the enormous component of learning that goes into human sexuality. The point that anthropology has made over the past hundred years is the *tremendous diversity of human social organization*. . . .While the onset of the events of puberty vary relatively little from one society to another, the onset of copulation varies over a full quarter of life-span—from 5 or 6 years of age to mid-20s. . . . Many mammals practice sex for only a few days or weeks in the year, but man varies from untrammeled lust to studied virginity. While I have enumerated my reasons more fully elsewhere (Cameron, 1977), I believe that the most reasonable construal of the evidence to date suggests that *human sexuality is totally learned.* ...

Because human sexuality is totally learned, humans must be pointed in the "right" direction, and taught how and with whom to perform. And there's the rub. Homosexuality and heterosexuality do not start off on the same footing. *Au contraire,* one gets a number of important boosts in the scheme of things. In our society the development process is decidedly *tilted toward the adoption of homosexuality!*

Part of the homosexual tilt is the extreme homosociability of children starting around the age of 5. As everyone is aware, boys want to play with boys and girls with girls, and they do so with a vengeance. It's quite reasonable, on their part. First, boys' and girls' bodies are different and they are aware that their bodies-to-be will differ still more. In part because of this the games, sports and skills they practice differ. As if in anticipation of the differing roles they will have, their interests and proclivities differ. Even if they try, few girls can do as well as most boys at "boy things" and few boys can do as well as girls at "girl things." They almost inhabit different worlds. Not surprisingly for members of two different "races" poles apart psychologically, socially, and physically, they "stick to their own kind." ...

There are three other components that contribute to the homosexual tilt. First, on the average in our society, males are considerably more taken with sex than females are. In my 1975 survey of 818 persons on the east coast of the U.S., respondents were asked to rate the degree of pleasure they obtained from 22 activities including "being with one's family," "listening to music," "being out in nature," "housework," and "sexual activity." Between the late teens through middle age, sexual activity topped the male list as the "most pleasurable activity." It did manage to rank as high as fifth place for young adult women (aged 18 to 25), but, overall for the female life span, was outscored by almost everything including "housework" (which, incidentally, ranked dead last among males). ...

How well suited are "hot" males to "cool" females? Not very. One of (if not the) most common problems in marital counseling is sexual incompatibility. *Females pay sex as the price of love/companionship and males pay love for sex.* While this is rather too aphoristic to capture all that goes on in the male-female struggle, there is a great deal of truth to it. Even among homosexuals, the males probably out sex lesbians by a factor of 5 to 1 (see Tripp's sympathetic treatment for elaboration on this theme). Where is a male most apt to find his counterpart, among maledom or femaledom? If he wants hot, dripping sex, what better place to find it than with another of similar bent? If she wants tender companionship, which sex is apt to provide the partner? The answers are obvious.

The second part of the homosexual tilt derives from the fact that [the] *homosexual encounter offers better sex,* on the average, *than heterosexual sex.* If pleasure is what you are after, who better to fulfill you than a partner who has a body and predilections like yours? One of things that both the male homosexual and lesbian societies advertise is that "they satisfy." ... From a sexual standpoint, a female can offer a little extra orifice as compensation for her: ignorance, timidity, desire for companionship first, etc. Further, sex between members of a sex assures that there will be no pregnancy problems further down the line.

Another developmental boost for homosexuality comes from the self-servingness/ego-centricity of the young. Humans are born with, at best, rudimentary consciousness. Then, over time and experience, they learn to differentiate themselves from the environment. From about the age of 5 or 6 onward for the next decade or so for life, they are engrossed in themselves, in the service of themselves, their pleasures, their interests, their ways. Reciprocity of interaction is rendered begrudgingly, certainly, far from spontaneously. My research, involving the interviewing of over 8,000 respondents from the U.S. and five other nations, in which we asked persons to tell us: 1) whose interests they had just been thinking about serving—their own or another's or others' and 2) whether they had just been thinking about themselves, things, or other people, indicated that younger persons more frequently reported themselves in a self-serving attitude and thinking about themselves than adults did. In the U.S., adults of both sexes typically reported themselves in an other-serving attitude. But U.S. males "switched" from self-servingness to other-servingness around age 26 while for females the switch occurred in the middle teens. If one is after self-fulfillment, pleasure for self, which sexual orientation "fits" better? Homosexuality, obviously. One can have his homosociality and sex too. One can comfortably neglect the painful transformation from self-interest to other-interest. Me and mine to the fore.

Which kind of sexuality is the more compelling? The one that can say "come, sex my way and I will show you a life of complexity. Of children and responsibility. Of getting on with 'that other kind.' I will offer you poorer sex initially, and, who knows, perhaps you will just have to satisfy yourself with poorer sex permanently. But you will be able to 'glimpse immortality in your children' (Plato.)" Or "come, sex my way and I will give it to you straight and hot. Pleasures of the best quality, almost on demand, with persons with whom you already share a great deal, and I will enable you to share more. It will not be difficult, in fact, it will be fun. You will not have to change or adapt your personality style or your egocentric orientation. You'll fit right in immediately. None of this hemming and hawing—you'll get what you want when you want it. Motto? Pleasure—now. The future? Who knows, but the present is going to be a dilly." Which kind of sexuality is the more compelling? Does anyone doubt which way most youth would turn if equivalent social status attended homosexuality and heterosexuality? . . .

A CLUSTER OF UNDESIRABLE TRAITS IS DISPROPORTIONATELY ASSOCIATED WITH HOMOSEXUALITY

Though some may shriek that "my personality traits are my business," let us acknowledge that some traits are society's business. A person's traits can lead to actions which affect the collectivity. Megalomania often proves socially disruptive, and sometimes, as in the case of Hitler, leads to incredible human destruction. It is obviously in society's interest to encourage those social roles and traits that tend to social cohesion and betterment. Similarly, it is in the social interest to discourage those that tend to produce disruption and harm. . . .

It would be as silly to contend that each of the following traits is associated with each homosexual as to argue that none of these appear in heterosexuals (or even worse, that the obverse of these traits always accompanies heterosexuality). However, for social policy formulation, it is enough to demonstrate disproportionate "loading" of undesirable traits within a given subgroup or subculture to justify social discrimination.

THE EGOCENTRIC/SUPERCILIOUS/NARCISSISTIC/ SELF-ORIENTED/ HOSTILE COMPLEX

This cluster of traits appears to "go together" with homosexuality. . . . A person who, in part, seeks more of himself in his lover, is more apt to remain in the egocentric/self-centered orientation of youth. Such a person is more apt to gravitate toward those kinds of professions in which he can be a "star" and be noticed. . . .

The "star" lives for gratification of self. *My* way is his motto . . . The star need not accommodate himself to the needs of others to the same degree as most folk. If a current love is "not working out" he can be discarded and a more suitable one found. . . .

Superciliousness—an attitude of aloof, hostile disdain—is also consonant with the ego-centric person. If you will not realize his marvelous qualities and pay homage, he still has you one down. After all he treated you with contempt *first.* Even if you become hostile, his preceded yours. . . .

The greatest component of the childish "I want it my way" associated with homosexuality stems, in part, form the greater ease connected with homosexual attachments. Develop-mentally, both hetero- and homosexuals want things "their way." But the kinds of accommodations and adjustments necessary for successful heterosexuality assure participants that it won't be all their way. Just because so much of the time things don't work out perfectly in the face of such effort helps wean one from the coddled security of childhood. Parents and the rest of society work to "make the world nice" for children. Every childhood painting is worthy of note, as is every musical note. But adulthood is strewn with disappointments. Heterosexuality is a "maturing" sexual orientation. . . .

It appears to me that homosexuality leads to a shallower commitment to society and its betterment. Such shallowness comes about both because of a lack of children and the ease of sexual gratification. The *effort* involved in being heterosexual, the *effort* expended in being a parent—these are denied the homosexual. As he *has* less responsibility and commitment, so he *is* or becomes less responsible and committed. It is difficult to develop personality characteristics that fail to resonate with one's environment. While we are not totally creatures of our environment, it is far easier to "swim with the tide."

It is difficult to find anything like "hard" scientific evidence to substantiate the notion that homosexuals are on the average, less responsible/trustworthy than heterosexuals. The Weinberg and Williams sample of homosexuals was asked a question that bears upon the issue. Do you agree or disagree with the statement "most people can be trusted"? To a degree, since a person cannot know "most people" it appears reasonable to assume that he might project his own personality onto "most people" and/or assume that those people with whom he comes in contact are like "most people." While 77% of a reasonable representative sample of the U.S. population chose "agree," only 47% of the homosexuals ticked the same response. Because of the ambiguity of such items, I would not make too much of the difference. But it could suggest that homosexuals are less trustworthy.

HOMOSEXUALITY IS ASSOCIATED WITH PERSONAL LETHALITY

One of the most troubling traits associated with homosexuality is personal lethality. Extending back in time to classical Greece, a lethal theme shines through. In Greece, if historical sources are to be believed, companies of homosexual warriors were assembled because it was believed that they made better killers. The same pattern appears to be repeated in history. . . .

In our society the childless are more apt to suicide and childless couples are more apt to be involved in homicide. Further, both suicide and homicide accompany divorce and separation disproportionately frequently. Social cohesion needs to be developed and maintained for optimum personal and social health. . . .

HETEROSEXUALITY PROVIDES THE MOST DESIRABLE MODEL OF LOVE

Myths are created not only by storytellers but by people living within the myths. Almost all (95% or so) heterosexuals get married, and 75%–80% stay married to their original partner till death. To be sure, there are marriage "hogs" within the heterosexual camp who play serial monogamy and assure that a third of all marriages end in divorce. Further, about half of all married men and about a third of all married women admit to one or more infidelities over the duration of their marriage (probably the greater bulk of the "cheaters" come from the serial monogamy camp). While heterosexuality's colors are far from simon pure, the relationship heterosexuality spawns is among, if not *the*, most enduring of human bonds. . . .

Homosexuality offers no comparison in durability. While "slam, bam, thank you ma'am" occurs in heterosexuality, few heterosexuals could more than fantasize about what occurs in homosexual bathhouses or tearooms. As Weinberg and Williams note, the homosexual community typically features "sex for sex's sake." Their survey in which two thirds of their respondents chose to respond "no" to whether they had limited their ". . . sexual relationships primarily to (another)" is telling. Names and banter are typically neglected in bathhouses. . . .

When people are merely "getting their jollies," and fantasizing perfection while doing so, reduced communication is an asset. If you discover that your beautiful lover holds political views antithetical to your own, how can you really enjoy him/her? The "less known the better" is fantasy sex. Communicating, mutually knowledgeable people often have to "work it out" before attempts at sex can even occur. But while typically short on durability, some homosexual relationships are more lasting. The quality of even these is often questionably desirable. Part of the problem lies in the lack of commitment that follows lower effort in the homosexual pairing. Tripp, for instance, opines that part ". . . of the reason many homosexual relationships do not survive the first serious quarrel is that one or both partners simply find it much easier to remarket themselves than work out conflicts (p. 155)." In heterosexuality, no matter how similar the participants, there is always a considerable gap between them. To stay together takes great effort, and the expenditure of this effort prompts both personal and social commitment to the partner. . . .

Because the heterosexual partners are so dissimilar, accommodation and adjustment are their key strategies. Because mutually satisfying heterosexual sexing takes so long and so much effort, both participants have to "hang in there" long after "sane people" would have toddled off in frustration. *We become the way we act. The heterosexual relationship places a premium on "getting on" and thus provides a model to smooth countless other human interactions.* The homosexual model is a considerably less satisfactory one upon which to build a civilization. Note Tripp again (p. 167): ". . . the problems encountered in balancing heterosexual and homosexual relationships are strikingly different. The heterosexual blend tends to be rich in stimulating contrasts and short on support—so much so that popular marriage counseling literature incessantly hammers home the advice that couples should develop common interests and dissolve their conflicts by increasing their 'communication.' By comparison, homosexual relationships are overclose, fatigue-prone, and are often adjusted to such narrow, trigger-sensitive tolerances that a mere whisper of disrapport can jolt the partners into making repairs, or into conflict."

Our social system also features large components of delay of gratification. The heterosexual "carrot" is hard to get and requires a lot of input before successful outcome is achieved. The homosexual model is too immediate and influences people to expect instant results. . . .

In short, heterosexuality is effortful, durable, and demands delay of gratification. While any human relationship takes effort, homosexuality pales in comparison to heterosexuality one each count. . . .

From the prudent standpoint, homosexuality is an obstacle in the pursuit of happiness . . . .

Does homosexuality make being happy more difficult? In the Weinberg and Williams study, homosexuals were asked to respond "yes" or "no" to the statement "no one cares what happens to you." While a general population sample had chosen "yes" 23% of the time, 34% of homosexuals chose "yes." . . . Homosexuality, with its emphasis upon self-gratification, does little to generate others who care about you . . . *In the long run,* heterosexuality has a lot more to offer as a life-style than homosexuality. . . .

SUMMARY

In sum, there are a number of reasons why homosexuality is best treated as a deviant sexual mode. I do not believe that homosexuality ought to be placed on an even-keel with heterosexuality. Further, homosexuals ought not, in my opinion, to be permitted to openly ply their sexual orientation and retain influential positions in the social system. Thus teachers, or pastors who "come out," ought, in my opinion, to lose their claim to the roles they occupy.

References

Allport, G. W. *The Person in Psychology.* NY: Beacon, 1961.

Atkins, J. *Sex in Literature.* NY: Grove Press, 1970.

Bergler, E. *Homosexuality: Disease or Way of Life?* NY: Macmillan, 1956.

Bieber, I. *Homosexuality: A Psychoanalytic Study,* NY: Basic Books, 1962.

Cameron, P. "Immolations to the Juggernaut," *Linacre Quarterly,* 1977, 44, 64–74.

Cameron, P. *The Life-Cycle: Perspectives and Commentary.* NY: General Health, 1977.

Cameron, P. & Oeschger, D. "Homosexuality in the Mass Media as Indexed by Magazine Literature over the Past Half Century in the U.S." Paper presented at Eastern Psychological Association Convention, New York, April 4, 1975.

Davis, N. & Graubert J. *Heterosexual.* NY: Vantage Press, 1975.

Freud, S. "Three Contributions to Sexual Theory," *Nervous and Mental Disease Monograph Series,* 925, 7.

Gubrium, J. F. "Being Single in Old Age," International Journal of Aging and Human Development, 1975, 6, 2941.

Hunt, M. *Sexual Behavior in the 1970s.* Chicago: Playboy Press, 1974.

Karlen, A. *Sexuality and Homosexuality.* NY: Norton, 1971.

Kastenbaum, R. J. & Costa, P. T. "Psychological Perspectives on Death," *Annual Review of Psychology* 1977, 28, 225–49.

Maugham, S. *El Greco.* NY: Doubleday, 1950.

Sears, R. R. "Sources of Life Satisfactions of the Terman Gifted Man," *American Psychologist,* 1977, 32, 119–128.

Tripp, C. A. *The Homosexual Matrix,* NY: McGraw-Hill, 1975.

Weinberg, M. S. & Williams, C. J. *Male Homosexuals: Their Problems and Adaptations.* NY: Oxford University Press, 1974.

The Ick Factor: Homosexuality, Citizenship, and the Constitution
Michael Nava and Robert Dawidoff

A QUESTION OF TASTE

Homosexuality disqualifies an American for citizenship. Whatever rights someone may enjoy on account of other identities, attributes, accomplishments, and positions cannot ensure either the free exercise of individual liberty or equal protection of the laws if that person is known to be lesbian or gay. American society still automatically accepts homosexuality as a sufficient cause for deprivation of normal civil rights, and American culture promotes the prejudice that sustains this second-class citizenship. For instance, in September of 1993 a Virginia judge took a child away from his mother solely because she was a lesbian. Routinely exposed to official persecution, common violence, prejudicial treatment, and denied legal recourse, gay and lesbian Americans are only whimsically protected in life, liberty, and property, let alone the myriad understandings of happiness.

Consider what amounts to a national epidemic of gay-bashing. A 1987 Justice Department study reported that gays are the "most frequent victims" of hate crimes. More telling is the fact that 73 percent of these attacks were not reported to the police because, as another study concludes, 14 percent of the victims feared more harm from the police. In 1991, anti-gay harassment and violence increased 31 percent in five major cities, including New York, San Francisco, Chicago, Boston, and Minneapolis–St. Paul. A 1993 study found that 28 percent of lesbians and gay men surveyed were subject to antigay harassment or gay-bashed within a one-year period, the vast majority not reporting the incidents to authorities. Yet, despite such evidence of the sometimes lethal effects of hatred of lesbians and gay men, the anti-gay right continues to object even to classifying attacks on homosexuals as hate crimes.[1]. . . .

At times, the controversy surrounding the recognition of sexual orientation as a category of individual liberty makes it seem that what homosexual Americans are claiming differs in some fundamental way from what other groups of individuals who have claimed in their

310

movements for the recognition of their civil rights. Frequently, for instance, when gays talk about gay rights, heterosexuals hear talk about sex, not personal freedom. The claim that gays want "special rights" reflects the degree to which lesbians and gay men am seen as so out of the ordinary that their claims to ordinary rights seem special.

But in fact, gays want an end to their special status, their status as pariahs under the Constitution. In twenty-three states sodomy statutes criminalize certain sexual practices—specifically, oral and anal sex—that both homosexuals and heterosexuals engage in. In the 1986 decision *Bowers v. Hardwick*, the Supreme Court held, in effect, that these laws are valid when applied to homosexuals but not when applied to heterosexuals. It doesn't take a legal scholar to ask how these laws, which govern the most intimate behavior, can be an affront to the protected liberty interests of heterosexual people, and not also be an affront to the protected liberty of homosexual people? It was a question the Court declined, with startling animosity, to answer. Yet this refusal was itself an answer: The sexual behavior of homosexuals, the Court implied, is not constitutionally protected *because they are not heterosexuals,* even though the practices are identical. . . .

A patriotic American who happens to be lesbian or gay can only serve in the military by hiding the existence of a private life. The recent and thwarted attempt to lift the ban against gays and lesbians in the armed forces has not changed the message that has greeted returning homosexual soldiers in every American war: You can give your life for your country, but you can't live your life in your country. The line between private and public life overlaps for everybody, not just heterosexuals. The effort to compel gays to lie about their lives and deny their own human experience is itself a deprivation of liberty.

The constitutional status of homosexuals is inextricably bound up with the intense prejudice against them. The straight majority acquiesces in the constitutional disenfranchisement of the gay minority because lesbians and gays have sex with partners of the same sex and because that goes against the majority's grain. That, rather than any truth about homosexuals, has resulted in the common belief that gay rights are about sex. This struggle is not about sex. It is about privacy, individuality, and civil equality and the right of all Americans, not just gay and lesbian Americans, to be free. And, yes, that freedom must include the freedom to express one's own desire for sexual intimacy, homosexual or heterosexual.

The routine denial of civil rights to gays and lesbians reflects a powerful prejudice, one so pervasive and so connected to everything else in society that it is treacherously hard to isolate. Even when not activated into energetic hostility, this prejudice is deeply rooted in and continually reaffirmed by the rituals of family formation, child-rearing, and gender in our culture. One of the tragic ironies in the lives of lesbians and gay men is the degree to which they inevitably assimilate much of this prejudice against them. Another is how the prejudice against homosexuals thrives, even among the family and friends of gay people. (But it is also true that people who know someone who is lesbian or gay are less likely to oppose gay rights than people who claim not to know someone gay; indeed, a recent survey of American voters showed that 53 percent of respondents who know someone gay are inclined to be more favorable to gay rights than the 47 percent who think they do not know someone gay.[2]) . . . .

The decision to regard homosexuality as a species of alien behavior, and to punish it, makes a law of the majority's personal taste and habits. For most people, the "sin" of homosexuality is a question of taste. The question embarrasses people not because they can't imagine it, but because they can and do. The revulsion many men and women feel at the thought of sexual activity between people of their own sex remains a formidable obstacle on the path of gay rights. This revulsion, which we call the Ick Factor, equates distaste with immorality. It is a child's vision of life, in which the things one wants to do are natural, and the things one doesn't want to do are matters of morality: "I don't like it; it's bad." The undertone of the debate and the refusal to entertain a discussion about gay rights echoes the schoolyard din of "'Ick," "Yuck," and "Gross." Teenagers apparently react this way to scenes of gay affection in movies. Of course, teenagers react that way to all but a few things. Adults are supposed to leave this stage when they assume the responsibilities and privileges of citizenship.

We believe that adults can think about issues of sexual orientation without being threatened as if they were adolescents imprisoned in the metabolism of puberty. We think that adults can learn to treat lesbians and gay men with the calm and neighborly regard democracy requires to survive. The prejudice against homosexuality is not so much religious as visceral, but neither religious nor visceral feelings justify the denial of constitutional rights in our system of government. Discrimination against gays reflects an awkward and inevitably failed attempt to isolate some people on account of whom they love, a matter that is supremely and constitutionally their own business.

Prejudice requires an elaborate social support to thrive, and the formidably articulated system of reinforcing prejudice toward homosexuality remains the bulwark of legal discrimination against gays and lesbians. What it all boils down to, however, is neither elaborate nor particularly complicated. At the core of the alleged "unnaturalness" of homosexuality is how unnatural it would feel to someone for whom it would indeed be unnatural. This distaste—understandable, though not constitutionally privileged—lurks among even those who wish gays and lesbians well and indeed would sympathize with, if not champion, their claiming of their rights. What blocks gay equality is prejudice. What fuels the movement for gay equality is the conviction that this prejudice is not constitutionally protected, but that the individual rights of homosexual Americans are. . . .

WHAT'S AT STAKE

At stake in the movement for lesbian and gay equality are established constitutional protections of a species of individual liberty, called by the courts the right of privacy, and the more familiar guarantee of equal protection of the laws. The agitation for gay civil rights confronts the nation with the question of whether these rights will be subordinated to the religious and ideological views of a minority that blames gays and lesbians for what it dislikes and fears in society. Unquestionably, their attack on gays and lesbians amounts to an attack on individual freedom itself.

At its core, gay rights are an issue of individual liberty, the very individual liberty protected by the Constitution. . . .

[T]he price you must pay for the enjoyment of your own liberty is the recognition that other people, especially people with whom you may not like to identify, have an equal claim to the same liberty. America requires an allegiance to a stern principle of individual liberty. This is the reason gay rights matter to Americans generally and not just to lesbians and gay men.

. . . [T]he opponents of gay rights, like the opponents of every other historical struggle for civil rights, have to encroach on the liberty of the majority to prevent liberty from being extended to the minority. . . .

THE AMERICAN ROOTS OF GAY RIGHTS

Gay rights restates, as all great civil rights and liberties movements do, the essential grounds of American constitutional nationhood. . . .

In our system it is the individual who makes moral choices as well as material, sexual, and political ones. While the individual's choices in these matters are not unmediated by the community, they are not to be dictated by it. The moral history of this nation might well be seen as the assumption by more and more individuals of their fundamental rights and their insistence on their part of the social contract. That we are used to thinking of these rights as belonging to classes comes from convenience and legal habit. But the equal protection of the law extends through classes to the individual, and the rights belong to the individual, not the class.

. . . [T]he movement for gay rights relies on two broad principles, the first is the individual right of homosexuals to enjoy the privacy that is the precondition for the enjoyment of civil liberty. The second is the enjoyment by homosexuals as a class or group of equal protection of the laws, essentially that one's individual right to equal treatment under the law may not be violated because one belongs to the class of people whose sexual orientation is toward the same sex. The individual right to privacy is a supreme constitutional value; equal protection of the laws is an inescapable constitutional guarantee. Without privacy and without equal protection of the laws, one simply does not enjoy American citizenship. The deprivation of privacy and equal protection constitutes the central ground for the gay civil rights movement.

When we talk about the right of privacy, we are talking, as the Supreme Court did in a recent abortion case, about a right that exists "at the heart of liberty," the right "to define one's own concept of existence, of meaning, of the universe and the mystery of human life. Beliefs about these matters could not define the attributes of personhood were they formed under the compulsion of the state."[3] Gays and lesbians do not constitute an identifiable minority along the lines of ethnic, racial, or class minorities. Being gay cuts across all human lines; gays and lesbians exist in all strata of society and in each group within those strata. For this reason, their struggle for equal rights particularly calls on the underlying constitutional principle of individual liberty.

In addition, not only the status of being gay but also the process of self-discovery is particularly individual. The lesbian and gay population consists of women and men who have arrived, by very different paths, at the same self-knowledge. The feelings that prompt ordinary people to love members of their own gender against the grain of convention, and the decision to honor those feelings, are different for every person. The decision to accept one's homosexuality occurs in that interior space where a person's deepest truths reside: the core of personal liberty. It is exactly that part of the self to which neither government nor other people's religion has legitimate access. This argument is not about sexual practices or particular lifestyles. It hinges on whether gay and lesbian Americans are entitled to the same enjoyment as their fellow citizens of the freedom to make choices about how to live their lives without suffering discrimination in consequence. . . .

SEX, RACE, AND GAY RIGHTS

The gay and lesbian Americans' movement for civil equality raises constitutional principles as well as legal arguments, and it makes sense to consider the general problem of individual freedom in light of that movement. When we speak of equality under the law and of personal freedom, we are not—as even a majority of the Supreme Court appears to believe—talking about the right to have sex. People have always engaged in homosexual practices, with or without the sanction of family, church, and state. But sexual orientation goes beyond sex, because it involves not only the body but also the heart, mind, and soul. Sexual orientation involves the intimate associations—happily, including the sexual—that individuals form and that help give meaning and richness to life. The continuing categorical denial of basic civil rights to lesbian and gay Americans sends the message that their lives are less valuable than the lives of heterosexuals.

Sexual desire is natural. Sexual formation is social. To criminalize a kind of sexual desire, a society must articulate a common good that is rationally served by elevating some desires over others. It is possible, for instance, that a theocratic Christian fundamentalist state might criminalize homosexuality—along with adultery, nonmarital sexual relations of any sort, and all sexual practices but the missionary position—for reasons that make sense to its purpose as a regime dedicated to furthering its adherents' notions of divine revelation. The United States, however, is explicitly not such a regime, and it may not impose restrictions on individual freedom in order to serve the purposes of religious sects. The First Amendment protects religious freedom in the same way it protects individual freedom; such protection does not license the invasion of individual freedom even on God's business or permit the substitution of particular moralities for the individual, rational choices the Bill of Rights enshrines.

Criminalizing behavior is not sufficient to establish that a kind of behavior is in fact criminal. For example, intermarriage between whites and blacks was once criminalized in this country. Criminalizing such behavior served the recognized social purpose of racial hegemony, but it did not transform that behavior itself into something criminal, let alone unnatural. In a similar fashion, decriminalization of rape and violence directed by whites against blacks did not remove the criminal quality from such acts. The criminalization of the subject race in a racially defined society is an example of the kind of criminalization that homosexuals experience. To criminalize some people because their sexual orientation is in the minority is a crude tool of social policy—and, as it happens, that social policy serves no function in our society other than the preservation of a heterosexual privilege that does not appear to have had a beneficial effect on the social or moral common life.

Legal preference for heterosexual over homosexual orientation must be based on arguments about the human good in this society, not just on moralistic pronouncements. What reasons can be advanced for restricting individual sexual desire that apply to homosexual and not to heterosexual people? Stereotypical libels notwithstanding, gays do not commit sexual abuse more often than straights; the opposite is true, judging by rape statistics.[4] Family formation is not at risk because of gay and lesbian equality. In fact, if the goal of social policy is healthy family life, the equal recognition of families in which homosexual children and adults play a part will advance the purposes of those for whom strong families are the foundation of a good society. Lesbians and gay men do not prevent heterosexuals from forming families; and, as parents and children, lesbians and gays are equally capable of carrying on the social functions of families. . . .

Although there are many grounds for identity and community among homosexuals—even across the important divide between lesbians and gay men—the deepest ground of sharing arises from a common oppression that has created a common culture and a shared form of desire that no doubt contributes to some common values. There is no reason to believe that the millions of lesbians and gay men in fact share connections analogous to the obvious and compelling ones of race, religion, gender, and nationality, or that even the groups that do share such connections founded in homosexuality are in the majority. The common experience of being gay is deeply individual. You discover your sexual identity yourself, your closet is your own, your coming out is individual.

It may be that the key contribution of the gay and lesbian movement to the history of civil rights and civil liberties is its re-emphasis on the individual. Being gay is an individuality that cuts across all the other identities around which civil rights movements have formed. It presents a challenge by individuality to group identity and group allegiance. The only culture we can say for certain that American homosexuals share is the common American culture. Central to this culture is a professed belief in individual freedom, yours as well as mine. The drama of the gay civil rights movement is less its statement of group aims than its necessary return to the ground of the individual asserting personal rights to personal freedom for personal choice about the personal life. . . .

HOW GAY RIGHTS RESTATES INDIVIDUAL RIGHTS

Lesbians and gay men who have come out and begun to insist that their lives and their choices about how to live deserve parity with the lives and choices of heterosexuals symbolize the fears of many Americans that freedom is going too far. For some, homosexuality is a marker of moral and social decay; the emergence of the lesbian and gay rights movement suggests to them not freedom but license. Moreover, among the religious right and self-styled cultural conservatives, lesbians and gays occupy the place once held by Jews and Communists in the practice of paranoid politics. Right-wing and restrictionist activists speak as darkly of the "homosexual agenda" as anti-Semites used to talk of *The Protocols of the Elders of Zion*, pretending knowledge of what they fear to know. Reactionary religionists warn of gays converting unsuspecting heterosexuals in the same way anticommunists used to warn of femmes fatales dispatched from Moscow to seduce innocent American boys. The scapegoating of gays and lesbians has less to do with homosexuality than with powerful cultural anxieties about family and sexuality, which express themselves in a wave of anti-individualist rhetoric. . . .

The labeling of gays as sexually degenerate and unnatural is the same kind of labeling that has always been used to justify the denial of rights to individuals belonging to "minority" communities. It was less than forty years ago that a Virginia Supreme Court judge wrote in defense of the Old Dominion's miscegenation law: "[The] law which forbids their intermarriage and the social amalgamation which leads to the corruption of the races is as clearly divine as that which imparted to them their different natures."[5] Similarly, assertions of "natural law," warnings of corruption, and the invocation of the divine repeatedly find their way into arguments justifying discrimination against gays and lesbians. Such appeals are arguments against individual freedom because they deny the validity of personal experience when it is at odds with convention. Much of the fierce opposition to gay rights consists of this kind of denial. In effect, gay men and women are taught that their experience of themselves as decent, productive, loving humans is false, because homosexuality is unnatural and sinful. In this case, however, their own self-knowledge has helped gays and lesbians overcome the labels attached to their sexual natures. The process of coming out is harrowing, but it can leave in its wake an unshakable core of certainty of self.

Coming out is more than an acknowledgment, acceptance, or even announcement of one's sexual identity. It represents a continuing process founded on an act of compassion toward oneself—a compassion, alas, seldom shown by one's own family or friends, let alone society.

That act is the acceptance of one's fundamental worth, including, and not despite, one's homosexuality, in the face of social condemnation and likely persecution. Coming out is the process through which one arrives at one's values the hard way, testing them against what one knows to be true about oneself. Gay men and lesbians must think about family, morality, nature, choice, freedom, and responsibility in ways most people never have to. Truly to come out, a gay person must become one of those human beings who, as psychiatrist Alice Miller writes, "want to be true to themselves. Rejection, ostracism, loss of love, and name calling will not fail to affect them; they will suffer as a result and they will dread them, but once they have their authentic self they will not want to lose it. And when they sense something is being demanded of them to which their whole being says no, they cannot do it. They simply cannot."[6]

It bears repeating that what is sought by gays and lesbians is not new or special rights, but, rather, the extension rights guaranteed to all American citizens by the Constitution and identified by the Declaration of Independence as the purpose, not the gift, of government. Nor would the removal of legal disabilities suffered by gays and lesbians "promote" homosexuality, as is sometimes argued. Ending discrimination does no more than dismantle the props by which one group of citizens unfairly enjoys a superior status over another group of citizens.

We must also again emphasize that gays and lesbians do not seek the right to *be* homosexual. This "right" is not one within the authority of government to give. They are fighting for the right to secure the conditions under which they may lead ordinary, civilized lives. . . .

The movement for gay rights would have surprised the Founders, many of whom, after all, were slaveholders, and who limited the franchise to male property owners. But they wrote a binding set of laws that were meant to surprise them. Their own habits and prejudices were among the conventions that the Constitution was meant to trump. They believed in the progress of liberty, which they based on their conception of human beings as rational creatures. The issue of gay rights is often lost in a morass of prejudice, religious and secular, but prejudice can be overcome by reason and reflection. We believe that when bias is put to one side, reason reveals that the cause of gay rights is a matter of simple justice.

Notes

1. Hate crime statistics: *USA Today*, March 30, 1992; news release of the Anti-Violence Project of the Los Angeles Gay and Lesbian Community Services Center, March 11, 1993. For an example of how antigay extremists try to exclude gay-bashing from the category of hate crimes, see Marian Wallace, "Junior Scholastic Pushes Gay Agenda," in *Family Voice*, May 1993 (vol. 15, no. 5),p. 29.

2. *U.S. News and World Report*, July 5, 1993, p. 42.

3. *Casey v. Planned Parenthood of Southeastern Pennsylvania* (1992), 120 L.Ed.2d 674, 698.

4. Bureau of Justice Statistics, *Sourcebook of Criminal Justice Statistics*, (Washington, D.C.: Department of Justice, 1992), p. 266.

5. *Loving v. Virginia* (1966), 388 US 1. 3.

6. Alice Miller, *For Your Own Good: Hidden Cruelty in Child Rearing and the Roots of Violence* (New York: Farrar, Straus, Giroux, 1989), p. 85.

THE DEATH PENALTY

Stephen Nathanson, *An Eye for an Eye? The Morality of Punishing by Death*, 1987

An Eye for an Eye?
Stephen Nathanson

Suppose we . . . try to determine what people deserve from a strictly moral point of view. How shall we proceed?

The most usual suggestion is that we look at a person's actions because what someone deserves would appear to depend on what he or she does. A person's actions, it seems, provide not only a basis for a moral appraisal of the person but also a guide to how he should be treated. According to the *lex talionis* or principle of "an eye for an eye," we ought to treat people as they have treated others. What people deserve as recipients of rewards or punishments is determined by what they do as agents.

This is a powerful and attractive view, one that appears to be backed not only by moral common sense but also by tradition and philosophical thought. The most famous statement of philosophical support for this view comes from Immanuel Kant, who linked it directly with an argument for the death penalty. Discussing the problem of punishment, Kant writes,

> What kind and what degree of punishment does legal justice adopt as its principle and standard? None other than the principle of equality . . . the principle of not treating one side more favorably than the other. Accordingly, any undeserved evil that you inflict on someone else among the people is one that you do to yourself. If you vilify, you vilify yourself; if you steal from him, you steal from yourself; if you kill him, you kill yourself. Only the law of retribution (*jus talionis*) can determine exactly the kind and degree of punishment.[1]

Kant's view is attractive for a number of reasons. First, it accords with our belief that what a person deserves is related to what he does. Second, it appeals to a moral standard and does not seem to rely on any particular legal or political institutions. Third, it seems to provide a measure of appropriate punishment that can be used as a guide to creating laws and instituting punishments. It tells us that the punishment is to be identical with the crime. Whatever the criminal did to the victim is to be done in turn to the criminal.

In spite of the attractions of Kant's view, it is deeply flawed. When we see why, it will be clear that the whole "eye for an eye" perspective must be rejected.

PROBLEMS WITH THE EQUAL PUNISHMENT PRINCIPLE

There are two main problems with this view. First, appearances to the contrary, it does not actually provide a measure of moral desert. Second, it does not provide an adequate criterion for determining appropriate levels of punishment.

Let us begin with the second criticism, the claim that Kant's view fails to tell us how much punishment is appropriate for particular crimes. We can see this, first, by noting that for certain crimes, Kant's view recommends punishments that are not morally acceptable. Applied strictly, it would require that we rape rapists, torture torturers, and burn arsonists whose acts have led to deaths. In general, where a particular crime involves barbaric and inhuman treatment, Kant's principle tells us to act barbarically and inhumanly in return. So, in some cases, the principle generates unacceptable answers to the question of what constitutes appropriate punishment.

This is not its only defect. In many other cases, the principle tells us nothing at all about how to punish. While Kant thought it obvious how to apply his principle in the case of murder, his principle cannot serve as a general rule because it does not tell us how to punish many crimes. Using the Kantian version or the more common "eye for an eye" standard, what would we decide to do to embezzlers, spies, drunken drivers, airline hijackers, drug users, prostitutes, air polluters, or persons who practice medicine without a license? If one reflects on this question, it becomes clear that there is simply no answer to it. We could not in fact design a system of punishment simply on the basis of the "eye for an eye" principle.

In order to justify using the "eye for an eye" principle to answer our question about murder and the death penalty, we would first have to show that it worked for a whole range of cases, giving acceptable answers to questions about amounts of punishment. Then, having established it as a satisfactory general principle, we could apply it to the case of murder. It turns out, however, that when we try to apply the principle generally, we find that it either gives wrong answers or no answers at all. Indeed, I suspect that the principle of "an eye for an eye" is no longer even a principle. Instead, it is simply a metaphorical disguise for expressing belief in the death penalty. People who cite it do not take it seriously. They do not believe in a kidnapping for a kidnapping, a theft for a theft, and so on. Perhaps "an eye for an eye" once was a genuine principle, but now it is merely a slogan. Therefore, it gives us no guidance in deciding whether murderers deserve to die.

In reply to these objections, one might defend the principle by saying that it does not require that punishments be strictly identical with crimes. Rather, it requires only that a punishment produce an amount of suffering in the criminal which is equal to the amount suffered by the victim. Thus, we don't have to hijack airplanes belonging to airline hijackers, spy on spies, etc. We simply have to reproduce in them the harm done to others.

Unfortunately, this reply really does not solve the problem. It provides no answer to the first objection, since it would still require us to behave barbarically in our treatment of those who are guilty of barbaric crimes. Even if we do not reproduce their actions exactly, any action which caused equal suffering would itself be barbaric. Second, in trying to produce equal amounts of suffering, we run into many problems. Just how much suffering is produced by an airline hijacker or a spy? And how do we apply this principle to prostitutes or drug users, who may not produce any suffering at all? We have rough ideas about how serious various crimes are, but this may not correlate with any clear sense of just how much harm is done.

Furthermore, the same problem arises in determining how much suffering a particular punishment would produce for a particular criminal. People vary in their tolerance of pain and in the amount of unhappiness that a fine or a jail sentence would cause them. Recluses will be less disturbed by banishment than extroverts. Nature lovers will suffer more in prison than people who are indifferent to natural beauty. A literal application of the principle would require that we tailor punishments to individual sensitivities, yet this is at best impractical. To a large extent, the legal system must work with standardized and rather crude estimates of the negative impact that punishments have on people.

The move from calling for a punishment that is identical to the crime to favoring one that is equal in the harm done is no help to us or to the defense of the principle. "An eye for an eye" tells us neither what people deserve nor how we should treat them when they have done wrong.

PROPORTIONAL RETRIBUTIVISM

The view we have been considering can be called "equality retributivism," since it proposes that we repay criminals with punishments equal to their crimes. In the light of problems like those I have cited, some people have proposed a variation on this view, calling not for equal punishments but rather for punishments which are *proportional* to the crime. In defending such a view as a guide for setting criminal punishments, Andrew von Hirsch writes:

> If one asks how severely a wrongdoer deserves to be punished, a familiar principle comes to mind: Severity of punishment should be commensurate with the seriousness of the wrong. Only grave wrongs merit severe penalties; minor misdeeds deserve lenient punishments. Disproportionate penalties are undeserved—severe sanctions for minor wrongs or vice versa. This principle has variously been called a principle of "proportionality" or "just deserts"; we prefer to call it commensurate deserts.[2]

Like Kant, von Hirsch makes the punishment which a person deserves depend on that person's actions, but he departs from Kant in substituting proportionality for equality as the criterion for setting the amount of punishment.

In implementing a punishment system based on the proportionality view, one would first make a list of crimes, ranking them in order of seriousness. At one end would be quite trivial offenses like parking meter violations, while very serious crimes such as murder would occupy the other. In between, other crimes would be ranked according to their relative gravity. Then a corresponding scale of punishments would be constructed, and the two would be correlated. Punishments would be proportionate to crimes so long as we could say that the more serious the crime was, the higher on the punishment scale was the punishment administered.

This system does not have the defects of equality retributivism. It does not require that we treat those guilty of barbaric crimes barbarically. This is because we can set the upper limit of the punishment scale so as to exclude truly barbaric punishments. Second, unlike the equality principle, the proportionality view is genuinely general, providing a way of handling all crimes. Finally, it does justice to our ordinary belief that certain punishments are unjust because they are too severe or too lenient for the crime committed.

The proportionality principle does, I think, play a legitimate role in our thinking about punishments. Nonetheless, it is no help to death penalty advocates, because it does not require that murderers be executed. All that it requires is that if murder is the most serious crime, then murder should be punished by the most severe punishment on the scale. The principle does not tell us what this punishment should be, however, and it is quite compatible with the view that the most severe punishment should be a long prison term.

This failure of the theory to provide a basis for supporting the death penalty reveals an important gap in proportional retributivism. It shows that while the theory is general in scope, it does not yield any *specific* recommendations regarding punishment. It tells us, for example, that armed robbery should be punished more severely than embezzling and less severely than murder, but it does not tell us how much to punish any of these. This weakness is, in effect, conceded by von Hirsch, who admits that if we want to implement the "commensurate deserts" principle, we must supplement it with information about what level of punishment is needed to deter crimes.[3] In a later discussion of how to "anchor" the punishment system, he deals with this problem in more depth, but the factors he cites as relevant to making specific judgments (such as available prison space) have nothing to do with what people deserve. He also seems to suggest that a range of punishments may be appropriate for a particular crime. This runs counter to the death penalty supporter's sense that death alone is appropriate for some murderers.[4]

Neither of these retributive views, then, provides support for the death penalty. The equality principle fails because it is not in general true that the appropriate punishment for a crime is to do to the criminal what he has done to others. In some cases this is immoral, while in others it is impossible. The proportionality principle may be correct, but by itself it cannot determine specific punishments for specific crimes. Because of its flexibility and open-endedness, it is compatible with a great range of different punishments for murder.[5] . . .

THE SYMBOLISM OF ABOLISHING THE DEATH PENALTY

What is the symbolic message that we would convey by deciding to renounce the death penalty and to abolish its use?

I think that there are two primary messages. The first is the most frequently emphasized and is usually expressed in terms of the sanctity of human life, although I think we could better express it in terms of respect for human dignity. One way we express our respect for the dignity of human beings is by abstaining from depriving them of their lives, even if they have done terrible deeds. In defense of human well-being, we may punish people for their crimes, but we ought not to deprive them of everything, which is what the death penalty does.

If we take the life of a criminal, we convey the idea that by his deeds he has made himself worthless and totally without human value. I do not believe that we are in a position to affirm that of anyone. We may hate such a person and feel the deepest anger against him, but when he no longer poses a threat to anyone, we ought not to take his life.

But, one might ask, hasn't the murderer forfeited whatever rights he might have had to our respect? Hasn't he, by his deeds, given up any rights that he had to decent treatment? Aren't we morally free to kill him if we wish?

These questions express important doubts about the obligation to accord any respect to those who have acted so deplorably, but I do not think that they prove that any such forfeiture has occurred. Certainly, when people murder or commit other crimes, they do forfeit some of the rights that are possessed by the law-abiding. They lose a certain right to be left alone. It becomes permissible to bring them to trial and, if they are convicted, to impose an appropriate—even a dreadful—punishment on them.

Nonetheless, they do not forfeit all their rights. It does not follow from the vileness of their actions that we can do anything whatsoever to them. This is part of the moral meaning of the constitutional ban on cruel and unusual punishments. No matter how terrible a person's deeds, we may not punish him in a cruel and unusual way. We may not torture him, for example. His right not to be tortured has not been forfeited. Why do these limits hold? Because this person remains a human being, and we think that there is something in him that we must continue to respect in spite of his terrible acts.

One way of seeing why those who murder still deserve some consideration and respect is by reflecting again on the idea of what it is to *deserve* something. In most contexts, we think that what people deserve depends on what they have done, intended, or tried to do. It depends on features that are qualities of individuals. The best person for the job deserves to be hired. The person who worked especially hard deserves our gratitude. We can call the concept that applies in these cases *personal* desert.

There is another kind of desert, however, that belongs to people by virtue of their humanity itself and does not depend on their individual efforts or achievements. I will call this impersonal kind of desert *human* desert. We appeal to this concept when we think that everyone deserves a certain level of treatment no matter what their individual qualities are. When the signers of the Declaration of Independence affirmed that people had inalienable rights to "life, liberty, and the pursuit of happiness," they were appealing to such an idea. These rights do not have to be earned by people. They are possessed "naturally," and everyone is bound to respect them.

According to the view that I am defending, people do not lose all of their rights when they commit terrible crimes. They still deserve some level of decent treatment simply because they remain living, functioning human beings. This level of moral desert need not be earned, and it cannot be forfeited. This view may sound controversial, but in fact everyone who believes that cruel and unusual punishment should be forbidden implicitly agrees with it. That is, they agree that even after someone has committed a terrible crime, we do not have the right to do anything whatsoever to him.

What I am suggesting is that by renouncing the use of death as a punishment, we express and reaffirm our belief in the inalienable, unforfeitable core of human dignity.

Why is this a worthwhile message to convey? It is worth conveying because this belief is both important and precarious. Throughout history, people have found innumerable reasons to degrade the humanity of one another. They have found qualities in others that they hated or feared, and even when they were not threatened by these people, they have sought to harm them, deprive them of their liberty, or take their lives from them. They have often felt that they had good reasons to do these things, and they have invoked divine commands, racial purity, and state security to support their deeds.

These actions and attitudes are not relics of the past. They remain an awful feature of the contemporary world. By renouncing the death penalty, we show our determination to accord at least minimal respect even to those whom we believe to be personally vile or morally vicious. This is, perhaps, why we speak of the *sanctity* of human life rather than its value or worth. That which is sacred remains, in some sense, untouchable, and its value is not dependent on its worth or usefulness to us. Kant expressed this ideal of respect in the famous second version of the Categorical Imperative: "So act as to treat humanity, whether in thine own person or in that of any other, in every case as an end withal, never as a means only." . . .

[THE SECOND SYMBOLIC MESSAGE]

. . . When the state has a murderer in its power and could execute him but does not, this conveys the idea that even though this person has done wrong and even though we may be angry, outraged, and indignant with him, we will nonetheless control ourselves in a way that he did not. We will not kill him, even though we could do so and even though we are angry and indignant. We will exercise restraint, sanctioning killing only when it serves a protective function.

Why should we do this? Partly out of a respect for human dignity. But also because we want the state to set an example of proper behavior. We do not want to encourage people to resort to violence to settle conflicts when there are other ways available. We want to avoid the cycle of violence that can come from retaliation and counter-retaliation. Violence is a contagion that arouses hatred and anger, and if unchecked, it simply leads to still more violence. The state can convey the message that the contagion must be stopped, and the most effective principle for stopping it is the idea that only defensive violence is justifiable. Since the death penalty is not an instance of defensive violence, it ought to be renounced.

We show our respect for life best by restraining ourselves and allowing murderers to live, rather than by following a policy of a life for a life. Respect for life and restraint of violence are aspects of the same ideal. The renunciation of the death penalty would symbolize our support of that ideal.

Notes

1. Kant, *Metaphysical Elements of Justice*, translated by John Ladd (Indianapolis: Bobbs-Merrill, 1965), 101.

2. *Doing Justice* (New York: Hill & Wang, 1976), 66: reprinted in *Sentencing*, edited by H. Gross and A. von Hirsch (Oxford University Press, 1981), 243. For a more recent discussion and further defense by von Hirsch, see his *Past or Future Crimes* (New Brunswick, N.J.: Rutgers University Press, 1985).

3. Von Hirsch, *Doing Justice*, 93–94. My criticisms of proportional retributivism are not novel. For helpful discussions of the view, see Hugo Bedau, "Concessions to Retribution in Punishment," in *Justice and Punishment*, edited by J. Cederblom and W. Blizek (Cambridge, Mass.: Ballinger, 1977), and M. Golding, *Philosophy of Law* (Englewood Cliffs, N.J.: Prentice-Hall, 1975), 98.

4. See von Hirsch, *Past and Future Crimes*, ch. 8.

5. For more positive assessments of these theories, see Jeffrey Reiman, "Justice, Civilization, and the Death Penalty," *Philosophy and Public Affairs* 14 (1985):115–48; and Michael Davis, "How to Make the Punishment Fit the Crime," *Ethics* 93 (1983).

Questions

1. To what extent, if at all, should the principle of "an eye for an eye" be incorporated into our system of criminal justice?

2. Can a retributive rationale for retention of the death penalty be defended against the objections presented by Nathanson?

3. Does Nathanson's appeal to "the symbolism of abolishing the death penalty" provide a compelling argument for abolition? Could a retentionist develop a compelling argument based on the symbolism of *retaining* the death penalty?

United States Supreme Court, 428 U.S. 153 (1976).

Opinion in Gregg v. *Georgia*
Justices Potter Stewart, Lewis F. Powell, Jr., and John Paul Stevens

The State of Georgia reacted to the Court's decision in Furman v. Georgia (1972) by drafting a death penalty statute calculated to avoid the Court's objection to standardless discretion. Georgia's approach, in contrast to the approach of those states that made the death penalty mandatory for certain crimes, embodied an effort to specify standards that would guide a jury (or a judge) in deciding between the death penalty and life imprisonment. In this case, with only Justice Marshall and Justice Brennan dissenting, the Court upheld the constitutionality of imposing the death penalty for the crime of murder under the law of Georgia.

Justices Stewart, Powell, and Stevens initially consider the contention that the death penalty for the crime of murder is, under all circumstances, cruel and unusual punishment, thus unconstitutional. On their analysis, a punishment is cruel and unusual if it fails to accord with "evolving standards of decency." Moreover, even if a punishment does accord with contemporary values, it must still be judged cruel and unusual if it fails to accord with the "dignity of man," the "basic concept underlying the Eighth Amendment." They take this second stipulation to rule out "excessive" punishment, identified as (1) that which involves the unnecessary and wanton infliction of pain or (2) that which is grossly out of proportion to the severity of the crime. In light of these considerations, Justices Stewart, Powell, and Stevens argue that the imposition of the death penalty for the crime or murder does not invariably violate the Constitution. They contend that legislative developments since Furman have made clear that the death penalty is acceptable to contemporary society. Moreover, they contend, the death penalty is not invariably excessive: (1) It may properly be considered necessary to achieve two principal social purposes— retribution and deterrence. (2) When the death penalty is imposed for the crime of murder, it may properly be considered not disproportionate to the severity of the crime.

> *Turning their attention to the death sentence imposed under the law of Georgia in this case, Justices Stewart, Powell, and Stevens maintain that a carefully drafted statute, ensuring "that the sentencing authority is given adequate information and guidance," makes it possible to avoid imposing the death penalty in an arbitrary or capricious manner. The revised Georgia statutory system under which Gregg was sentenced to death, they conclude, does not violate the Constitution.*

The issue in this case is whether the imposition of the sentence of death for the crime of murder under the law of Georgia violates the Eighth and Fourteenth Amendments.

I

The petitioner, Troy Gregg, was charged with committing armed robbery and murder. In accordance with Georgia procedure in capital cases, the trial was in two stages, a guilt stage and a sentencing stage. . . .

. . . The jury found the petitioner guilty of two counts of armed robbery and two counts of murder.

At the penalty stage, which took place before the same jury, the trial judge instructed the jury that it could recommend either a death sentence or a life prison sentence on each count. . . . The jury returned verdicts of death on each count.

The Supreme Court of Georgia affirmed the convictions and the imposition of the death sentences for murder. . . . The death sentences imposed for armed robbery, however, were vacated on the grounds that the death penalty had rarely been imposed in Georgia for that offense. . . .

II

. . . The Georgia statute, as amended after our decision in *Furman v. Georgia* (1972), retains the death penalty for six categories of crime: murder, kidnapping for ransom or where the victim is harmed, armed robbery, rape, treason, and aircraft hijacking. . . .

III

We address initially the basic contention that the punishment of death for the crime of murder is, under all circumstances, "cruel and unusual" in violation of the Eighth and Fourteenth Amendments of the Constitution. In Part IV of this opinion, we will consider the sentence of death imposed under the Georgia statutes at issue in this case.

The Court on a number of occasions has both assumed and asserted the constitutionality of capital punishment. In several cases that assumption provided a necessary foundation for the decision, as the Court was asked to decide whether a particular method of carrying out a capital sentence would be allowed to stand under the Eighth Amendment. But until *Furman v. Georgia* (1972), the Court never confronted squarely the fundamental claim that the punishment of death always, regardless of the enormity or the offense or the procedure followed in imposing the sentence is cruel and unusual punishment in violation of the Constitution. Although this issue was presented and addressed in *Furman*, it was not resolved by the Court. Four Justices would have held that capital punishment is not unconstitutional *per se*; two Justices would have reached the opposite conclusion, and three Justices, while agreeing that the statutes then before the Court were invalid as applied, left open the question whether such punishment may ever be imposed. We now hold that the punishment of death does not invariably violate the Constitution.

A

The history of the prohibition of "cruel and unusual" punishment already has been reviewed at length. The phrase first appeared in the English Bill of Rights of 1689, which was drafted by Parliament at the accession of William and Mary. The English version appears to have been directed against punishments unauthorized by statute and beyond the jurisdiction of the sentencing court, as well as those disproportionate to the offense involved. The American draftsmen, who adopted the English phrasing in drafting the Eighth Amendment, were primarily concerned, however, with proscribing "tortures" and other "barbarous" methods of punishment.

In the earliest cases raising Eighth Amendment claims, the Court focused on particular methods of execution to determine whether they were too cruel to pass constitutional muster. The constitutionality of the sentence of death itself was not at issue, and the criterion used to evaluate the mode of execution was its similarity to "torture" and other "barbarous" methods. . . .

But the Court has not confined the prohibition embodied in the Eighth Amendment to "barbarous" methods that were generally outlawed in the 18th century. Instead, the Amendment has been interpreted in a flexible and dynamic manner. The Court early recognized that a "principle to be vital must be capable of wider application than the mischief which gave it birth." Thus the Clause forbidding "cruel and unusual" punishments "is not fastened to the obsolete but may acquire meaning as public opinion becomes enlightened by a humane justice." . . .

It is clear from the foregoing precedents that the Eighth Amendment has not been regarded as a static concept. As Mr. Chief Justice Warren said, in an oftquoted phrase, "[t]he Amendment must draw its meaning from the evolving standards of decency that mark the progress of a maturing society." Thus, an assessment of contemporary values concerning the infliction of a challenged sanction is relevant to the application of the Eighth Amendment. As we develop below more fully, this assessment does not call for a subjective judgment. It requires, rather, that we look to objective indicia that reflect the public attitude toward a given sanction.

But our cases also make clear that public perceptions of standards of decency with respect to criminal sanctions are not conclusive. A penalty also must accord with "the dignity of man," which is the "basic concept underlying the Eighth Amendment." This means, at least, that the punishment not be "excessive." When a form of punishment in the abstract (in this case, whether capital punishment may ever be imposed as a sanction for murder) rather than in the particular (the propriety of death as a penalty to be applied to a specific defendant for a specific crime) is under consideration, the inquiry into "excessiveness" has two aspects. First, the punishment must not involve the unnecessary and wanton infliction of pain. Second, the punishment must not be grossly out of proportion to the severity of the crime.

B

Of course, the requirements of the Eighth Amendment must be applied with an awareness of the limited role to be played by the courts. This does not mean that judges have no role to play, for the Eighth Amendment is a restraint upon the exercise of legislative power. . . .

But, while we have an obligation to insure that constitutional bounds are not overreached, we may not act as judges as we might as legislators. . . .

Therefore, in assessing a punishment selected by a democratically elected legislature against the constitutional measure, we presume its validity. We may not require the legislature to select the least severe penalty possible so long as the penalty selected is not cruelly inhumane or disproportionate to the crime involved. And a heavy burden rests on those who would attack the judgment of the representatives of the people.

This is true in part because the constitutional test is intertwined with in assessment of contemporary standards and the legislative judgment weighs heavily in ascertaining such standards. "[I]n a democratic society legislatures, not courts, are constituted to respond to the will and consequently the moral values, of the people."

The deference we owe to the decisions of the state legislatures under our federal system is enhanced where the specification of punishments is concerned, for "these are peculiarly questions of legislative policy." Caution is necessary lest this Court become, "under the aegis of the Cruel and Unusual Punishment Clause, the ultimate arbiter of the standards of criminal responsibility . . . throughout the country." A decision that a given punishment is impermissible under the Eighth Amendment cannot be reversed short of a constitutional amendment. The ability of the people to express their preference through the normal democratic processes. as well as through ballot referenda, is shut off. Revisions cannot be made in the light of further experience.

C

In the discussion to this point we have sought to identify the principles and considerations that guide a court in addressing an Eighth Amendment claim. We now consider specifically whether the sentence of death for the crime of murder is a *per se* violation of the Eighth and Fourteenth Amendments to the Constitution. We note first that history and precedent strongly support a negative answer to this question.

The imposition of the death penalty for the crime of murder has a long history of acceptance both in the United States and in England. . .

It is apparent from the text of the Constitution itself that the existence of capital punishment was accepted by the Framers. At the time the Eighth Amendment was ratified, capital punishment was a common sanction in every State. Indeed, the First Congress of the United States enacted legislation providing death as the penalty for specified crimes. . . .

For nearly two centuries, this Court, repeatedly and often expressly, has recognized that capital punishment is not invalid *per se*. . . .

Four years ago, the petitioners in *Furman* and its companion cases predicated their argument primarily upon the asserted proposition that standards of decency had evolved to the point where capital punishment no longer could be tolerated. The petitioners in those cases said, in effect, that the evolutionary process had come to an end, and that standards of decency required that the Eighth Amendment be construed finally as prohibiting capital punishment for any crime regardless of its depravity and impact on society. This view was accepted by two Justices. Three other Justices were unwilling to go so far; focusing on the procedures by which convicted defendants were selected for the death penalty rather than on the actual punishment inflicted, they joined in the conclusion that the statutes before the Court were constitutionally invalid.

The petitioners in the capital cases before the Court today renew the "standards of decency" argument, but developments during the four years since *Furman* have undercut substantially the assumptions upon which their argument rested. Despite the continuing debate, dating back to the 19th century, over the morality, and utility of capital punishment. it is now evident that a large proportion of American society continues to regard it as an appropriate and necessary criminal sanction.

The most marked indication of society's endorsement of the death penalty for murder is the legislative response to *Furman*. The legislatures of at least 35 States have enacted new statutes that provide for the death penalty for at least some crimes that result in the death of another person. And the Congress of the United States, in 1974, enacted a statute providing the death penalty for aircraft piracy that results in death. These recently adopted statutes have attempted to address the concerns expressed by the Court in *Furman* primarily (i) by specifying the factors to be weighed and the procedures to be followed in deciding when to impose a capital sentence, or (ii) by making the death penalty mandatory for specified crimes. But all of the post-*Furman* statutes make clear that capital punishment itself has not been rejected by the elected representatives of the people. . . .

The jury also is a significant and reliable objective index of contemporary values because it is so directly involved. The Court has said that "one of the most important functions any jury can perform in making . . . a selection [between life imprisonment and death for a defendant convicted in a capital case] is to maintain a link between contemporary community values and the penal system. It may be true that evolving standards have influenced juries in recent decades to be more discriminating in imposing the sentence of death. But the relative infrequency of jury verdicts imposing the death sentence does not indicate rejection of capital punishment *per se*. Rather, the reluctance of juries in many cases to impose the sentence may well reflect the humane feeling that this most irrevocable of sanctions should be reserved for a small number of extreme cases. Indeed, the actions of juries in many States since *Furman* are fully compatible with the legislative judgments, reflected in the new statutes, as to the continued utility and necessity of capital punishment in appropriate cases. At the close of 1974 at least 254 persons had been sentenced to death since *Furman*, and by the end of March, 1976, more than 460 persons were subject to death sentences.

As we have seen, however, the Eighth Amendment demands more than that a challenged punishment be acceptable to contemporary society. The Court also must ask whether it comports with the basic concept of human dignity at the core of the Amendment. Although we cannot "invalidate a category or penalties because we deem less severe penalties adequate to serve the ends of penology," the sanction imposed cannot be so totally without penological justification that it results in the gratuitous infliction of suffering.

The death penalty is said to serve two principal social purposes: retribution and deterrence of capital crimes by prospective offenders.[1]

In part, capital punishment is an expression of society's moral outrage at particularly offensive conduct. This function may be unappealing to many, but it is essential in an ordered society that asks its citizens to rely on legal processes rather than self-help to vindicate their wrongs.

> The instinct of retribution is part of the nature of man, and channeling that instinct in the administration of criminal justice serves an important purpose in promoting the stability of a society governed by law. When people begin to believe that organized society is unwilling or unable to impose upon criminal offenders the punishment they "deserve," then there are sown the seeds of anarchy—of self-help, vigilante justice, and lynch law. *Furman v. Georgia* (Stewart, J., concurring).

"Retribution is no longer the dominant objective of the criminal law," but neither is it a forbidden objective nor one inconsistent with our respect for the dignity of men. Indeed, the decision that capital punishment may be the appropriate sanction in extreme cases is an expression of the community's belief that certain crimes are themselves so grievous an affront to humanity that the only adequate response may be the penalty of death.

Statistical attempts to evaluate the worth of the death penalty is a deterrent to crimes by potential offenders have occasioned a great deal of debate. The results simply have been inconclusive. . . .

Although some of the studies suggest that the death penalty may not function as a significantly greater deterrent than lesser penalties, there is no convincing empirical evidence either supporting or refuting this view. We may nevertheless assume safely that there are murderers, such as those who act in passion, for whom the threat of death has little or no deterrent effect. But for many others, the death penalty undoubtedly is a significant deterrent. There are carefully contemplated murders, such as murder for hire, where the possible penalty of death may well enter into the cold calculus that precedes the decision to act. And there are some categories of murder, such as murder by a life prisoner, where other sanctions may not be adequate.

The value of capital punishment as a deterrent of crime is a complex factual issue, the resolution of which properly rests with the legislatures, which can evaluate the results of statistical studies in terms of their own local conditions and with a flexibility of approach that is not available to the courts. Indeed, many of the post-*Furman* statutes reflect just such a responsible effort to define those crimes and those criminals for which capital punishment is most probably an effective deterrent.

In sum, we cannot say that the judgment of the Georgia Legislature that capital punishment may be necessary in some cases is clearly wrong. Considerations of federalism, as well as respect for the ability of a legislature to evaluate, in terms of its particular State, the moral consensus concerning the death penalty and its social utility as a sanction, require us to conclude, in the absence of more convincing evidence, that the infliction of death as a punishment for murder is not without justification and thus is not unconstitutionally severe.

Finally, we must consider whether the punishment of death is disproportionate in relation to the crime for which it is imposed. There is no question that death as a punishment is unique in its severity and irrevocability. When a defendant's life is at stake, the Court has been particularly sensitive to insure that every safeguard is observed. But we are concerned here only with the imposition of capital punishment for the crime of murder, and when a life has been taken deliberately by the offender,[2] we cannot say that the punishment is invariably disproportionate to the crime. It is an extreme sanction, suitable to the most extreme of crimes.

We hold that the death penalty is not a form of punishment that may never be imposed, regardless of the circumstances of the offense, regardless of the character of the offender, and regardless of the procedure followed in reaching the decision to impose it.

IV

We now consider whether Georgia may impose the death penalty on the petitioner in this case.

A

While *Furman* did not hold that the infliction of the death penalty *per se* violated the Constitution's ban on cruel and unusual punishments, it did recognize that the penalty of death is different in kind from any other punishment imposed under our system of criminal justice. Because of the uniqueness of the death penalty. *Furman* held that it could not be imposed under sentencing procedures that created a substantial risk that it would be inflicted in an arbitrary and capricious manner. . . .

Furman mandates that where discretion is afforded a sentencing body on a matter so grave as the determination of whether a human life should be taken or spared, that discretion must be suitably directed and limited so as to minimize the risk of wholly arbitrary and capricious action.

It is certainly not a novel proposition that discretion in the area of sentencing be exercised in an informed manner. We have long recognized that "[f]or the determination of sentences, justice generally requires . . . that there be taken into account the circumstances of the offense together with the character and "propensities of the offender.". . .

Jury sentencing has been considered desirable in capital cases in order "to maintain a link between contemporary community values and the penal system—a link without which the determination of punishment could hardly reflect 'the evolving standards of decency that mark the progress of a maturing society.'" But it creates special problems. Much of the information that is relevant to the sentencing decision may have no relevance to the question of guilt, or may even be extremely prejudicial to a fair determination of that question. This problem, however, is scarcely insurmountable. Those who have studied the question suggest that a bifurcated procedure—one in which the question of sentence is not considered until the determination of guilt has been made—is the best answer. . . . When a human life is at stake and when the jury must have information prejudicial to the question of guilt but relevant to the question of penalty in order to impose a rational sentence, a bifurcated system is more likely to ensure elimination of the constitutional deficiencies identified in *Furman*.

But the provision of relevant information under fair procedural rules is not alone sufficient to guarantee that the information will be properly used in the imposition of punishment, especially if sentencing is performed by a jury. Since the members of a jury will have had little, if any, previous experience in sentencing, they are unlikely to be skilled in dealing with the information they are given. To the extent that this problem is inherent in jury sentencing, it may not be totally correctible. It seems clear, however, that the problem will be alleviated if the jury is given guidance regarding the factors about the crime and the defendant that the State, representing organized society, deems particularly relevant to the sentencing decision. . . .

While some have suggested that standards to guide a capital jury's sentencing deliberations are impossible to formulate, the fact is that such standards have been developed. When the drafters of the Model Penal Code faced this problem, they concluded "that it is within the realm of possibility to point to the main circumstances of aggravation and of mitigation that should be weighed *and weighed against each other* when they are presented in a concrete case.[3] While such standards are by necessity somewhat general, they do provide guidance to the sentencing authority and thereby reduce the likelihood that it will impose a sentence that fairly can be called capricious or arbitrary. Where the sentencing authority is required to specify the factors it relied upon in reaching its decision, the further safeguard of meaningful appellate review is available to ensure that death sentences are not imposed capriciously or in a freakish manner.

In summary, the concerns expressed in *Furman* that the penalty of death not be imposed in an arbitrary or capricious manner can be met by a carefully drafted statute that ensures that the sentencing authority is given adequate information and guidance. As a general proposition these concerns are best met by a system that provides for a bifurcated proceeding at which the sentencing authority is apprised of the information relevant to the imposition of sentence and provided with standards to guide its use of the information.

We do not intend to suggest that only the above-described procedures would be permissible under *Furman* or that any sentencing system constructed along these general lines would inevitably satisfy the concerns of *Furman*, for each distinct system must be examined on an individual basis. Rather, we have embarked upon this general exposition to make clear that it is possible to construct capital-sentencing systems, capable of meeting *Furman's* constitutional concerns.

B

We now turn to consideration of the constitutionality of Georgia's capital sentencing procedures. In the wake of *Furman* Georgia amended its capital punishment statute, but chose not to narrow the scope of its murder provisions. Thus, now as before *Furman* in Georgia "[a] person commits murder when he unlawfully and with malice aforethought, either express or implied, causes the death of another human being." All persons convicted of murder "shall be punished by death or by imprisonment for life."

Georgia did act, however, to narrow the class of murderers subject to capital punishment. by specifying 10 statutory aggravating circumstances, one of which must be found by the jury to exist beyond a reasonable doubt before a death sentence can ever be imposed. In addition, the jury is authorized to consider any other appropriate aggravating or mitigating circumstances. The jury is not required to find any mitigating circumstance in order to make a recommendation of mercy that is binding on the trial court, but it must find a *statutory* aggravating circumstance before recommending a sentence of death.

These procedures require the jury to consider the circumstances of the crime and the criminal before it recommends sentence. No longer can a Georgia jury do as Furman's jury did: reach a finding of the defendant's guilt and then, without guidance or direction, decide whether he should live or die. Instead, the jury's attention is directed to the specific circumstances of the crime: Was it committed in the course of another capital felony? Was it committed for money? Was it committed upon a peace officer or judicial officer? Was it committed in a particularly heinous way or in a manner that endangered the lives of many persons? In addition. the jury's attention is focused on the characteristics of the person who committed the crime: Does he have a record of prior convictions for capital offenses? Are there any special facts about this defendant that mitigate against imposing capital punishment (e.g., his youth, the extent of his cooperation with the police, his emotional state at the time of the crime). As a result, while some jury discretion still exists. "The discretion to be exercised is controlled by clear and objective standards so as to produce non-discriminatory application."

As an important additional safeguard against arbitrariness and caprice, the Georgia statutory scheme provides for automatic appeal of all death sentences to the State's Supreme Court. That court is required by statute to review each sentence of death and determine whether it was imposed under the influence of passion or prejudice, whether the evidence supports the jury's finding of a statutory aggravating circumstances and whether the sentence is disproportionate compared to those sentences imposed in similar cases.

In short, Georgia's new sentencing procedures require as a prerequisite to the imposition of the death penalty, specific jury findings as to the circumstances of the crime or the character of the defendant. Moreover, to guard further against a situation comparable to that presented in *Furman*, the Supreme Court of Georgia compares each death sentence with the sentences imposed on similarly situated defendants to ensure that the sentence of death in a particular case is not disproportionate. On their face these procedures seem to satisfy the concerns of *Furman*. No longer should there be "no meaningful basis for distinguishing the few cases in which [the death penalty] is imposed from the many cases in which it is not." . . .

V

The basic concern of *Furman* centered on those defendants who were being condemned to death capriciously and arbitrarily. Under the procedures before the Court in that case, sentencing authorities were not directed to give attention to the nature or circumstances of the crime committed or to the character or record of the defendant. Left unguided, juries imposed the death sentence in a way that could only be called freakish. The new Georgia sentencing procedures, by contrast, focus the jury's attention on the particularized nature of the crime and the particularized characteristics or the individual defendant. While the jury is permitted to consider any aggravating or mitigating circumstances, it must find and identify at least one statutory aggravating factor before it may impose a penalty of death. In this way the jury's discretion is channeled. No longer can a jury wantonly and freakishly impose the death sentence: it is always circumscribed by the legislative guidelines. In addition, the review function of the Supreme Court of Georgia affords additional assurance that the concerns that prompted our decision in *Furman* are not present to any significant degree in the Georgia procedure applied here.

For the reasons expressed in this opinion, we hold that the statutory system under which Gregg was sentenced to death (does not violate the Constitution. Accordingly, the judgment of the Georgia Supreme Court is affirmed.

Notes

1. Another purpose that has been discussed is the incapacitation of dangerous criminals and the consequent prevention of crimes that they may otherwise commit in the future.
2. We do not address here the question whether the taking of the criminal's life is a proportionate sanction where no victim has been deprived of life—for example, when capital punishment is imposed for rape, kidnapping, or armed robbery that does not result in the death of any human being.
3. The Model Penal Code proposes the following standards: "(3) Aggravating Circumstances.
   (a) The murder was committed by a convict under sentence of imprisonment.

(b) The defendant was previously convicted of another murder or of a felony involving the use or threat of violence to the person.

(c) At the time the murder was committed the defendant also committed another murder.

(d) The defendant knowingly created a great risk of death to many persons.

(e) The murder was committed while the defendant was engaged or was in an accomplice in the commission of, or attempt to commit, or flight after committing or attempting to commit robbery, rape or deviate sexual intercourse by force or threat or force, arson, burglary or kidnapping.

(f) The murder was committed for the purpose of avoiding or preventing a lawful arrest or effecting an escape from lawful custody.

(g) The murder was committed for pecuniary gain.

(h) The murder was especially heinous, atrocious or cruel, manifesting exceptional depravity.

4   Mitigating Circumstances.

(a) The defendant has no significant history of prior criminal activity.

(b) The murder was committed while the defendant was under the influence of extreme mental or emotional disturbance.

(c) The victim was a participant in the defendant's homicidal conduct or consented to the homicidal act.

(d) The murder was committed under circumstances which the defendant believed to provide a moral justification or extenuation for his conduct.

(e) The defendant was an accomplice in a murder committed by another person and his participation in the homicidal act was relatively minor.

(f) The defendant acted under duress or under the domination of another person.

(g) At the time of the murder, the capacity of the defendant to appreciate the criminality [wrongfulness] of his conduct or to conform his conduct to the requirements of law was impaired as a result of mental disease or defect or intoxication.

(h) The youth of the defendant at the time of the crime." ALI Model Penal Code 1210.6 (Proposed Official Draft 1962).

Questions

1. With regard to the imposition of the death penalty for the crime of murder, Justices Stewart, Powell, and Stevens write, "we cannot say that the punishment is invariably disproportionate to the crime." The Georgia statute under which Gregg was sentenced, however, retained the death penalty not only for the crime of murder but also for "kidnapping for ransom or where the victim is harmed armed robbery, rape, treason, and aircraft hijacking. In your view, is the death penalty a disproportionate punishment for such crimes?

2. In note 3, we find a set of proposed model standards for the guidance of a jury in deciding whether a murderer warrants the death penalty or some lesser penalty, typically life imprisonment. Is the proposed set of aggravating circumstances (those whose presence should incline a jury toward the death penalty) defensible and complete? Is the proposed set of mitigating circumstances (those whose presence should incline a jury away from the death penalty) defensible and complete?

United States Supreme Court, 428 U.S. 153 (1976).

Dissenting Opinion in Gregg v. Georgia
Justice Thurgood Marshall

Thurgood Marshall, associate justice of the United States Supreme Court, is the first black ever to be appointed to the Supreme Court. Much of his distinguished private career was given over to providing legal counsel for groups dedicated to the advancement of civil rights. Justice Marshall also served as United States circuit judge (1961–1965) and United States solicitor general (1965–1967), before his appointment in 1967 to the Supreme Court.

Justice Marshall reaffirms the conclusion be had reached in Furman v. Georgia *(1972): The death penalty is unconstitutional for two individually sufficient reasons. (1) It is excessive. (2) The American people, if fully informed, would consider it morally unacceptable. He insists that his conclusion in* Furman *his not been undercut by subsequent developments. Despite the fact that legislative activity since* Furman *would seem to indicate that the American people do not consider the death penalty morally unacceptable, Justice Marshall continues to maintain that the citizenry, if fully informed, would consider it morally unacceptable. At any rate, he maintains, the death penalty is unconstitutional because it is excessive, i.e., unnecessary to accomplish a legitimate legislative purpose. Neither deterrence nor retribution, the principal purposes asserted by Justices Stewart, Powell, and Stevens, can sustain the death penalty as nonexcessive in Justice Marshall's view. Since the available evidence does not show the death penalty to be a more effective deterrent than life imprisonment, he contends, the death penalty is not necessary to promote the goal of deterrence. Moreover, the death penalty is unnecessary to "further any legitimate notion of retribution." According to Justice Marshall, the notion that a murderer "deserves" death constitutes a denial or the wrongdoer's dignity and worth and thus is fundamentally at odds with the Eighth Amendment.*

In *Furman v. Georgia* (1972) (concurring opinion), I set forth at some length my views on the basic issue presented to the Court in [this case]. The death penalty, I concluded, is a cruel and unusual punishment prohibited by the Eighth and Fourteenth Amendments. That continues to be my view.

I have no intention of retracing the "long and tedious journey" that led to my conclusion in *Furman*. My sole purposes here are to consider the suggestion that my conclusion in *Furman* has been undercut by developments since then, and briefly to evaluate the basis for my Brethren's holding that the extinction of fire is a permissible form of punishment under the Cruel and Unusual Punishments Clause.

In *Furman* I concluded that the death penalty is constitutionally invalid for two reasons. First, the death penalty is excessive. And second, the American people, fully informed as to the purposes of the death penalty and its liabilities, would in my view reject it as morally unacceptable.

Since the decision in *Furman*, the legislatures of 35 States have enacted new statutes authorizing the imposition of the death sentence for certain crimes, and Congress has enacted a law providing the death penalty for air piracy resulting in death. I would be less than candid if I did not acknowledge that these developments have a significant bearing on a realistic assessment of the moral acceptability of the death penalty to the American people. But if the constitutionality (of the death penalty turns, as I have urged, on the opinion of an *informed* citizenry, then even the enactment of new death statutes cannot be viewed as conclusive. In *Furman*, I observed that the American people are largely unaware of the information critical to a judgment on the morality of the death penalty, and concluded that if they were better informed they would consider it shocking, unjust, and unacceptable. A recent study, conducted after the enactment of the post-*Furman* statutes, has confirmed that the American people know little about the death penalty, and that the opinions of an informed public would differ significantly from those of a public unaware of the consequences and effects of the death penalty.

Even assuming, however, that the post-*Furman* enactment of statutes authorizing the death penalty renders the prediction of the views of an informed citizenry an uncertain basis for a constitutional decision, the enactment of those statutes has no bearing whatsoever on the conclusion that the death penalty is unconstitutional because it is excessive. An excessive penalty is invalid under the Cruel and Unusual Punishments Clause "even though popular sentiment may favor" it. The inquiry here, then, is simply whether the death penalty is necessary to accomplish the legitimate legislative purposes in punishment, or whether a less severe penalty—life imprisonment—would do as well.

The two purposes that sustain the death penalty as nonexcessive in the Court's view are general deterrence and retribution. In *Furman*, I canvassed the relevant data on the deterrent effect of capital punishment. The state of knowledge at that point, after literally centuries of debate, was summarized as follows by a United Nations Committee:

> "It is generally agreed between the retentionists and abolitionists, whatever their opinions about the validity of comparative studies of deterrence, that the data which now exist show no correlation between the existence of capital punishment and lower rates of capital crime."

The available evidence, I concluded in *Furman*, was convincing that "capital punishment is not necessary as a deterrent to crime in our society." . . .

. . . The evidence I reviewed in *Furman* remains convincing, in my view, that "capital punishment is not necessary as a deterrent to crime in our society." The justification for the death penalty must be found elsewhere.

The other principal purpose said to be served by the death penalty is retribution. The notion that retribution can serve as a moral justification for the sanction of death finds credence in the opinion of my Brothers STEWART, POWELL, and STEVENS. . . . It is this notion that I find to be the most disturbing aspect of today's unfortunate [decision].

The concept of retribution is a multifaceted one, and any discussion of its role in the criminal law must be undertaken with caution. On one level, it can be said that the notion of retribution or reprobation is the basis of our insistence that only those who have broken the law be punished, and in this sense the notion is quite obviously central to a just system of criminal sanctions. But our recognition that retribution plays a crucial role in determining who may be punished by no means requires approval of retribution as a general justification for punishment. It is the question whether retribution can provide a moral justification for punishment—in particular, capital punishment—that we must consider.

My Brothers STEWART, POWELL, and STEVENS offer the following explanation of the retributive justification for capital punishment:

> The instinct for retribution is part of the nature of man, and channeling that instinct in the administration of criminal justice serves an important purpose in promoting the stability or a society governed by law. When people begin to believe that organized society is unwilling or unable to impose upon criminal offenders the punishment they "deserve," then there are sown the seeds of anarchy—of self-help, vigilante justice, and lynch law.

This statement is wholly inadequate to justify the death penalty. As my Brother BRENNAN stated in *Furman*, "[t]here is no evidence whatever that utilization of imprisonment rather than death encourages private blood feuds and other disorders." It simply defies belief to suggest that the death penalty is necessary to prevent the American people from taking the law into their own hands.

In a related vein, it may be suggested that the expression of moral outrage through the imposition of the death penalty serves to reinforce basic moral values—that it marks some crimes as particularly offensive and therefore to be avoided. The argument is akin to a deterrence argument, but differs in that it contemplates the individual's shrinking from antisocial conduct, not because he fears punishment, but because he has been told in the strongest possible way that the conduct is wrong. This contention, like the previous one, provides no support for the death penalty. It is inconceivable that any individual concerned about conforming his conduct to what society says is "right" would fail to realize that murder is "wrong" if the penalty were simply life imprisonment.

The foregoing contentions—that society's expression of moral outrage through the imposition of the death penalty pre-empts the citizenry from taking the law into its own hands and reinforces moral values—are not retributive in the purest sense. They are essentially utilitarian in that they portray the death penalty as valuable because of its beneficial results. These justifications for the death penalty are inadequate because the penalty is, quite clearly I think, not necessary to the accomplishment of those results.

There remains for consideration, however, what might he termed the purely retributive justification for the death penalty—that the death penalty is appropriate. not because of its beneficial effect on society, but because the taking of the murderer's life is itself morally good. Some of the language of the opinion of my Brothers STEWART, POWELL, and STEVENS . . . appears positively to embrace this notion of retribution for its own sake as a justification for capital punishment. They state:

> [T]he decision that capital punishment may be the appropriate sanction in extreme cases is an expression of the community's belief that certain crimes are themselves so grievous an affront to humanity that the only adequate response may be the penalty of death.

They then quote with approval from Lord Justice Denning's remarks before the British Royal Commission on Capital Punishment:

> The truth is that some crimes are so outrageous that society insists on adequate punishment, because the wrong-doer deserves it, irrespective of whether it is a deterrent or not.

Of course, it may be that these statements are intended as no more than observations as to the popular demands that it is thought must be responded to in order to prevent anarchy. But the implication of the statements appears to me to be quite different—namely, that society's judgment that the murderer "deserves" death must be respected not simply because the preservation of order requires it, but because it is appropriate that society make the judgment and carry it out. It is this latter notion, in particular, that I consider to be fundamentally at odds with the Eighth Amendment. The mere fact that the community demands the murderer's life in return for the evil he has done cannot sustain the death penalty, for as JUSTICES STEWART, POWELL, and STEVENS remind us, "the Eighth Amendment demands more than that a challenged punishment be acceptable to contemporary society." To be sustained under the Eighth Amendment, the death penalty must "compor[t] with the basic concept of human dignity at the core of the Amendment;" the objective in imposing it must be "[consistent] with our respect for the dignity of [other] men." Under these standards, the taking of life "because the wrongdoer deserves it" surely must fail, for such a punishment has as its very basis the total denial of the wrongdoer's dignity and worth.

The death penalty, unnecessary to promote the goal of deterrence or to further any legitimate notion of retribution, is an excessive penalty forbidden by the Eighth and Fourteenth Amendments. I respectfully dissent from the Court's judgment upholding the [sentence] of death imposed upon the [petitioner in this case].

Questions

1. Is Justice Marshall correct in claiming that the American people, *if fully informed* about the death penalty, would consider it morally unacceptable?

2. Is the death penalty, as Justice Marshall claims, "unnecessary to promote the goal of deterrence or to further any legitimate notion of retribution"?

Igor Primoratz, *Justifying Legal Punishment*, 1989

A Life for a Life
Igor Primoratz

Primoratz endorses a retributive rationale for the retention of the death penalty and defends this rationale against commonly made abolitionist arguments. He rejects the idea that the death penalty violates a murderer's right to life and insists that there is no contradiction involved in a system of criminal law that prohibits murder and yet allows the state to administer the death penalty. He also defends the retributive rationale against arguments claiming to show that the death penalty is in reality a disproportionate penalty for the crime of murder. Finally, Primoratz argues that neither the possibility of executing an innocent person nor the discriminatory application of the death penalty can provide a credible basis for abolition.

... According to the retributive theory, consequences of punishment, however important from the practical point of view, are irrelevant when it comes to its justification; *the* moral consideration is its justice. Punishment is morally justified insofar as it is meted out as retribution for the offense committed. When someone has committed an offense, he deserves to be punished: it is just, and consequently justified, that he be punished. The offense is the sole ground of the state's right and duty to punish. It is also the measure of legitimate punishment: the two ought to be proportionate. So the issue of capital punishment within the retributive approach comes down to the question, Is this punishment ever proportionate retribution for the offense committed, and thus deserved, just, and justified?

The classic representatives of retributivism believed that it was, and that it was the only proportionate and hence appropriate punishment, if the offense was *murder*—that is, criminal homicide perpetrated voluntarily and intentionally or in wanton disregard of human life. In other cases, the demand for proportionality between offense and punishment can be satisfied by fines or prison terms;[1] the crime of murder, however, is an exception in this respect, and calls for the literal interpretation of the *lex talionis*. The uniqueness of this crime has to do with the uniqueness of the value which has been deliberately or recklessly destroyed. We come across this idea as early as the original formulation of the retributive view—the biblical teaching on punishment: "You shall accept no ransom for the life of a murderer who is guilty of death; but he shall be put to death."[2] The rationale of this command—one that clearly distinguishes the biblical conception of the criminal law from contemporaneous criminal law systems in the Middle East—is that man was not only created by God, like every other creature, but also, alone among all the creatures, *in the image of God:*

> That man was made in the image of God . . . is expressive of the peculiar and supreme worth of man. Of all creatures, Genesis 1 relates, he alone possesses this attribute, bringing him into closer relation to God than all the rest and conferring upon him the highest value. . . . This view of the uniqueness and supremacy of human life . . . places life beyond the reach of other values. The idea that life may be measured in terms of money or other property . . . is excluded. Compensation of any kind is ruled out. The guilt of the murderer is infinite because the murdered life is invaluable; the kinsmen of the slain man are not competent to say when he has been paid for. An absolute wrong has been committed, a sin against God which is not subject to human discussion. . . . Because human life is invaluable, to take it entails the death penalty.[3]

This view that the value of human life is not commensurable with other values, and that consequently there is only one truly equivalent punishment for murder, namely death, does not necessarily presuppose a theistic outlook. It can be claimed that, simply because we have to be alive if we are to experience and realize any other value at all, there is nothing equivalent to the murderous destruction of a human life except the destruction of the life of the murderer. Any other retribution, no matter how severe, would still be less than what is proportionate, deserved, and just. As long as the murderer is alive, no matter how bad the conditions of his life may be, there are always at least *some* values he can experience and realize. This provides a plausible interpretation of what the classical representatives of retributivism as a philosophical theory of punishment, such as Kant and Hegel, had to say on the subject.[4]

It seems to me that this is essentially correct. With respect to the larger question of the justification of punishment in general, it is the retributive theory that gives the right answer. Accordingly, capital punishment ought to be retained where it obtains, and reintroduced in those jurisdictions that have abolished it, although we have no reason to believe that, as a means of deterrence, it is any better than a very long prison term. It ought to zbe retained, or reintroduced, for one simple reason: that justice be done in cases of murder, that murderers be punished according to their deserts.

There are a number of arguments that have been advanced against this rationale of capital punishment. . . .

[One] abolitionist argument . . . simply says that capital punishment is illegitimate because it violates the right to life, which is a fundamental, absolute, sacred right belonging to each and every human being, and therefore ought to be respected even in a murderer.[5]

If any rights are fundamental, the right to life is certainly one of them; but to claim that it is absolute, inviolable under any circumstances and for any reason, is a different matter. If an abolitionist wants to argue his case by asserting an absolute right to life, she will also have to deny moral legitimacy to taking human life in war, revolution, and self-defense. This kind of pacifism is a consistent but farfetched and hence implausible position.

I do not believe that the right to life (nor, for that matter, any other right) is absolute. I have no general theory of rights to fall back upon here; instead, let me pose a question. Would we take seriously the claim to an absolute, sacred, inviolable right to life—coming from the mouth of a *confessed murderer?* I submit that we would not, for the obvious reason that it is being put forward by the person who confessedly denied another human being this very right. But if the murderer cannot plausibly claim such a right for himself, neither can *anyone else* do that in his behalf. This suggests that there is an element of reciprocity in our general rights, such as the right to life or property. I can convincingly claim these rights only so long as I acknowledge and respect the same rights of others. If I violate the rights of others, I thereby lose the same rights. If I am a murderer, I have no *right* to live.

Some opponents of capital punishment claim that a criminal law system which includes this punishment is contradictory, in that it prohibits murder and at the same time provides for its perpetration: "It is one and the same legal regulation which prohibits the individual from murdering, while allowing the state to murder.... This is obviously a terrible irony, an abnormal and immoral logic, against which everything in us revolts."[6]

This seems to be one of the more popular arguments against the death penalty, but it is not a good one. If it were valid, it would prove too much. Exactly the same might be claimed or other kinds of punishment: of prison terms, that they are "contradictory" to the legal protection of liberty; of fines, that they are "contradictory" to the legal protection of property. Fortunately enough, it is not valid, for it begs the question at issue. In order to be able to talk of the state as "murdering" the person it executes, and to claim that there is "an abnormal and immoral logic" at work here, which thrives on a "contradiction," one has to use the word "murder" in the very same sense—that is, in the usual sense, which implies the idea of the *wrongful* taking the life of another—both when speaking of what the murderer has done to the victim and of what the state is doing to him by way of punishment. But this is precisely the question at issue: whether capital punishment *is* "murder," whether it is wrongful or morally justified and right.

The next two arguments attack the retributive rationale of capital punishment by questioning the claim that it is only this punishment that satisfies the demand for proportion between offense and punishment in the case of murder. The first points out that any two human lives are different in many important respects, such as age, health, physical and mental capability, so that it does not make much sense to consider them equally valuable. What if the murdered person was very old, practically at the very end of her natural life, while the murderer is young, with most of his life still ahead of him, for instance? Or if the victim was gravely and incurably ill, and thus doomed to live her life in suffering and hopelessness, without being able to experience almost anything that makes a human life worth living, while the murderer is in every respect capable of experiencing and enjoying things life has to offer? Or the other way round? Would not the death penalty in such cases amount either to taking a more valuable life as a punishment for destroying a less valuable one, or *vice versa*? Would it not be either too much, or too little, and in both cases disproportionate, and thus unjust and wrong, from the standpoint of the retributive theory itself?[7]

Any plausibility this argument might appear to have is the result of a conflation of differences between, and value of, human lives. No doubt, any two human lives are *different* in innumerable ways, but this does not entail that they are not *equally valuable*. I have no worked-out general theory of equality to refer to here, but I do not think that one is necessary in order to do away with this argument. The modern humanistic and democratic tradition in ethical, social, and political thought is based on the idea that all human beings finds its legal expression in the principle of equality of people under the law. If we are not willing to give up this principle, we have to stick to the assumption that, all differences notwithstanding, any two human lives, qua human lives, are equally valuable. If, on the other hand, we allow that, on the basis of such criteria as age, health, or mental or physical ability, it can be claimed that the life of one person is more or less valuable than the life of another, and we admit such claims in the sphere of law, including criminal law, we shall thereby give up the principle of equality of people under the law. In all consistency, we shall not be able to demand that property, physical and personal integrity, and all other rights and interests of individuals be given equal consideration in courts of law either—that is, we shall have to accept systematic discrimination between individuals on the basis of the same criteria across the whole field. I do not think any one would seriously contemplate an overhaul of the whole legal system along these lines.

The second argument having to do with the issue of proportionality between murder and capital punishment draws our attention to the fact that the law normally provides for a certain period of time to elapse between the passing of a death sentence and its execution. It is a period of several weeks or months; in some cases it extends to years. This period is bound to be one of constant mental anguish for the condemned. And thus, all things considered, what is inflicted on him is disproportionately hard and hence unjust. It would be proportionate and just only in the case of "a criminal who had warned his victim of the date at which he would inflict a horrible death on him and who, from that moment onward, had confined him at his mercy for months."[8]

The first thing to note about this argument is that it does not support a full-fledged abolitionist stand; if it were valid, it would not show that capital punishment is never proportionate and just, but only that it is very rarely so. Consequently, the conclusion would not be that it ought to be abolished outright, but only that it ought to be restricted to those cases that would satisfy the condition cited above. Such cases do happen, although, to be sure, not very often; the murder of Aldo Moro, for instance, was of this kind. But this is not the main point. The main point is that the argument actually does not hit at capital punishment itself, although it is presented with that aim in view. It hits at something else: a particular way of carrying out this punishment, which is widely adopted in our time. Some hundred years ago and more, in the Wild West, they frequently hanged the man convicted to die almost immediately after pronouncing the sentence. I am not arguing here that we should follow this example today; I mention this piece of historical fact only in order to show that the interval between sentencing someone to death and carrying out the sentence is not a part of capital punishment itself. However unpalatable we might find those Wild West hangings, whatever objections we might want to voice against the speed with which they followed the sentencing, surely we shall not deny them the description of "executions." So the implication of the argument is not that we ought to do away with capital punishment altogether, nor that we ought to restrict it to those cases of murder where the murderer had warned the victim weeks or months in advance of what he was going to do to her, but that we ought to reexamine the procedure of carrying out this kind of punishment. We ought to weigh the reasons for having this interval between the sentencing and executing, against the moral and human significance of the repercussions such an interval inevitably carries with it.

These reasons, in part, have to do with the possibility of miscarriages of justice and the need to rectify them. Thus we come to the argument against capital punishment which, historically, has been the most effective of all: many advances of the abolitionist movement have been connected with discoveries of cases of judicial errors. Judges and jurors are only human, and consequently some of their beliefs and decisions are bound to be mistaken. Some of their mistakes can be corrected upon discovery; but precisely those with most disastrous repercussions—those which result in innocent people being executed—can never be rectified. In all other cases of mistaken sentencing we can revoke the punishment, either completely or in part, or at least extend compensation. In addition, by exonerating the accused we give moral satisfaction. None of this is possible after an innocent person has been executed; capital punishment is essentially different from all other penalties by being completely irrevocable and irreparable.[9] Therefore, it ought to be abolished.

A part of my reply to this argument goes along the same lines as what I had to say on the previous one. It is not so far-reaching as abolitionists assume; for it would be quite implausible, even fanciful, to claim that there have never been cases of murder which left no room whatever for reasonable doubt as to the guilt and full responsibility of the accused. Such cases may not be more frequent than those others, but they do happen. Why not retain the death penalty at least for them?

Actually, this argument, just as the preceding one, does not speak out against capital punishment itself, but against the existing procedures for trying capital cases. Miscarriages of justice result in innocent people being sentenced to death and executed, even in the criminal-law systems in which greatest care is taken to ensure that it never comes to that. But this does not stem from the intrinsic nature of the institution of capital punishment; it results from deficiencies, limitations, and imperfections of the criminal law procedures in which this punishment is meted out. Errors of justice do not demonstrate the need to do away with capital punishment; they simply make it incumbent on us to do everything possible to improve even further procedures of meting it out.

To be sure, this conclusion will not find favor with a diehard abolitionist. "I shall ask for the abolition of Capital Punishment until I have the infallibility of human judgement demonstrated to me," that is, as long as there is even the slightest possibility that innocent people may be executed because of judicial errors, Lafayette said in his day.[10] Many an opponent of this kind of punishment will say the same today. The demand to do away with capital punishment altogether, so as to eliminate even the smallest chance of that ever happening—the chance which, admittedly, would remain even after everything humanly possible has been done to perfect the procedure, although then it would be very slight indeed—is actually a demand to give a privileged position to murderers as against all other offenders, big and small. For if we acted on this demand, we would bring about a situation in which proportionate penalties would be meted out for all offenses, except for murder. Murderers would not be receiving the only punishment truly proportionate to their crimes, the punishment of death, but some other, lighter, and thus disproportionate penalty. All other offenders would be punished according to their deserts, only murderers would be receiving less than they deserve. In all other cases justice would be done in full: only in cases of the gravest of offenses, the crime of murder, justice would not be carried out in full measure. It is a great and tragic miscarriage of justice when an innocent person is mistakenly sentenced to death and executed, but systematically giving murderers advantage over all other offenders would also be a grave injustice. Is the fact that, as long as capital punishment is retained. there is a possibility that over a number of years, or even decades, an injustice of the first kind may be committed, unintentionally and unconsciously, reason enough to abolish it altogether, and thus end up with a system of punishments in which injustices of the second kind are perpetrated daily, consciously, and inevitably?[11]

There is still another abolitionist argument that actually does not hit out against capital punishment itself, but against something else. Figures are sometimes quoted which show that this punishment is much more often meted out to the uneducated and poor than to the educated, rich, and influential people; in the United States, much more often to blacks than to whites. These figures are adduced as a proof of the inherent injustice of this kind of punishment. On account of them, it is claimed that capital punishment is not a way of doing justice by meting out deserved punishment to murderers, but rather a means of social discrimination and perpetuation of social injustice.

I shall not question these findings, which are quite convincing, and anyway, there is no need to do that in order to defend the institution of capital punishment. For there seems to be a certain amount of discrimination and injustice not only in sentencing people to death and executing them, but also in meting out other penalties. The social structure of the death rows in American prisons, for instance, does not seem to be basically different from the general social structure of American penitentiaries. If this argument were valid, it would call not only for abolition of the penalty of death, but for doing away with other penalties as well. But it is not valid; as Burton Leiser has pointed out,

> . . . this is not an argument, either against the death penalty or against any other form of punishment. It is an argument against the unjust and inequitable distribution of penalties. If the trials of wealthy men are less likely to result in convictions than those of poor men, then something must be done to reform the procedure in criminal courts. If those who have money and standing in the community are less likely to be charged with serious offenses than their less affluent fellow citizens, then there should be a major overhaul of the entire system of criminal justice . . . But the maldistribution of penalties is no argument against any particular form of penalty.[12]

Notes

1.   Cf. I. Primoratz, *Justifying Legal Punishment* (Atlantic Highlands, N.J.: Humanities Press, 1989), pp. 85–94.

2.   Numbers 35.31 (R.S.V.).

3.   M. Greenberg, "Some Postulates of Biblical Criminal Law," in J. Goldin (ed.), *The Jewish Expression* (New York: Bantam, 1970), pp. 25–26. (Post-biblical Jewish law evolved toward the virtual abolition of the death penalty, but that is of no concern here.)

4.   "There is no parallel between death and even the most miserable life, so that there is no equality of crime and retribution [in the case of murder] unless the perpetrator is judicially put to death" (I. Kant, "The Metaphysics of Morals," Kant's Political Writings, ed. H. Reiss, trans. H. B. Nisbet [Cambridge: Cambridge University Press, 1970], p. 156). "Since life is the full compass of a man's existence, the punishment [for murder] cannot simply consist in a 'value', for none is great enough, but can consist only in taking away a second life" (G. W. F. Hegel, Philosophy of Right, trans. T. M. Knox [Oxford: Oxford University Press, 19651, p. 247).

5.   For an example of this view, see L. N. Tolstoy, *Smertnaya kazn i hristianstvo* (Berlin: I. P. Ladizhnikov, n.d.), pp. 40–41.

6.   S. V. Vulovic, *Problem smrtne kazne* (Belgrade: Geca Kon, 1925), pp. 23–24.

7.   Cf. W. Blackstone, *Commentaries on the Laws of England*, 4th ed., ed. J. DeWitt Andrews (Chicago: Callaghan & Co., 1899). p. 1224.

8.   A. Camus, "Reflections on the Guillotine," *Resistance, Rebellion and Death*, trans. J. O'Brien (London: Hamish Hamilton, 1961), p. 143.

9.   For an interesting critical discussion of this point, see M. Davis, "Is the Death Penalty Irrevocable?," *Social Theory and Practice* 10 (1984).

10.   Quoted in E. R. Calvert, *Capital Punishment in the Twentieth Century* (London: G. P. Putnam's Sons, 1927), p. 132.

11.   For a criticism of this argument, see L. Sebba, "On Capital Punishment—A Comment," *Israel Law Review* 17 (1982), pp. 392–395.

12.   B. M. Leiser, *Liberty, Justice and Morals: Contemporary Value Conflicts* (New York: Macmillan, 1973), p. 225.

Questions

1. Would you endorse a retributive rationale for the retention of the death penalty? If so, would you say that all murderers deserve to die or just some? If just some deserve to die, which ones?

2. If blacks are more likely to receive the death penalty than whites, if the poor and uneducated are more likely to receive the death penalty than the affluent and educated, do these facts constitute a compelling argument for abolition of the death penalty?

ANIMAL RIGHTS

Tom Regan, "The Case for Animal Rights" in *In Defense of Animals*, 1985

The Case for Animal Rights
Tom Regan

I regard myself as an advocate of animal rights—as a part of the animal rights movement. That movement, as I conceive it, is committed to a number of goals, including:

- the total abolition of the use of animals in science;
- the total dissolution of commercial animal agriculture;
- the total elimination of commercial and sport hunting and trapping.

There are, I know, people who profess to believe in animal rights but do not avow these goals. Factory farming, they say, is wrong—it violates animals' rights—but traditional animal agriculture is all right. Toxicity tests of cosmetics on animals violates their rights, but important medical research—cancer research, for example—does not. The clubbing of baby seals is abhorrent, but not the harvesting of adult seals. I used to think I understood this reasoning. Not any more. You don't change unjust institutions by tidying them up.

What's wrong—fundamentally wrong—with the way animals are treated isn't the details that vary from case to case. It's the whole system. The forlornness of the veal calf is pathetic, heart wrenching; the pulsing pain of the chimp with electrodes planted deep in her brain is repulsive; the slow, tortuous death of the raccoon caught in the leg-hold trap is agonizing. But what is wrong isn't the pain, isn't the suffering, isn't the deprivation. These compound what's wrong. Sometimes—often—they make it much, much worse. But they are not the fundamental wrong.

The fundamental wrong is the system that allows us to view animals as our resources, here for us—to be eaten, or surgically manipulated, or exploited for sport or money. Once we accept this view of animals—as our resources—the rest is as predictable as it is regrettable. Why worry about their loneliness, their pain, their death? Since animals exist for us, to benefit us in one way or another, what harms them really doesn't matter—or matters only if it starts to bother us, makes us feel a trifle uneasy. . . .

In the case of animals in science, whether and how we abolish their use . . . are to a large extent political questions. People must change their beliefs before they change their habits.

Enough people, especially those elected to public office, must believe in change—must want it—before we will have laws that protect the rights of animals. This process of change is very complicated, very demanding, very exhausting, calling for the efforts of many hands in education, publicity, political organization and activity, down to the licking of envelopes and stamps. As a trained and practicing philosopher, the sort of contribution I can make is limited but, I like to think, important. The currency of philosophy is ideas—their meaning and rational foundation—not the nuts and bolts of the legislative process, say, or the mechanics of community organization. That's what I have been exploring over the past ten years or so in my essays and talks and, most recently, in my book, *The Case for Animal Rights.* I believe the major conclusions I reach in the book are true because they are supported by the weight of the best arguments. I believe the idea of animal rights has reason, not just emotion, on its side.

In the space I have at my disposal here I can only sketch, in the barest outline, some of the main features of the book. Its main themes—and we should not be surprised by this—involve asking and answering deep, foundational moral questions about what morality is, how it should be understood and what is the best moral theory, all considered. I hope I can convey something of the shape I think this theory takes. The attempt to do this will be (to use a word a friendly critic once used to describe my work) cerebral, perhaps too cerebral. But this is misleading. My feelings about how animals are sometimes treated run just as deep and just as strong as those of my more volatile compatriots. Philosophers do—to use the jargon of the day—have a right side to their brains. If it's the left side we contribute (or mainly should), that's because what talents we have reside there.

How to proceed? We begin by asking how the moral status of animals has been understood by thinkers who deny that animals have rights. Then we test the mettle of their ideas by seeing how well they stand up under the heat of fair criticism. If we start our thinking in this way, we soon find that some people believe that we have no duties directly to animals, that we owe nothing to them, that we can do nothing that wrongs them. Rather, we can do wrong acts that involve animals, and so we have duties regarding them, though none to them. Such views may be called indirect duty views. By way of illustration: suppose your neighbor kicks your dog. Then your neighbor has done something wrong. But not to your dog. The wrong that has been done is a wrong to you. After all, it is wrong to upset people, and your neighbor's kicking your dog upsets you. So you are the one who is wronged, not your dog. Or again: by kicking your dog your neighbor damages your property. And since it is wrong to damage another person's property, your neighbor has done something wrong—to you, of course, not to your dog. Your neighbor no more wrongs your dog than your car would be wronged if the windshield were smashed. Your neighbor's duties involving your dog are indirect duties to you. More generally, all of our duties regarding animals are indirect duties to one another—to humanity.

How could someone try to justify such a view? Someone might say that your dog doesn't feel anything and so isn't hurt by your neighbor's kick, doesn't care about the pain since none is felt, is as unaware of anything as is your windshield. Someone might say this, but no rational person will, since, among other considerations, such a view will commit anyone who holds it to the position that no human being feels pain either—that human beings also don't care about what happens to them. A second possibility is that though both humans and your dog are hurt when kicked, it is only human pain that matters. But, again, no rational person can believe this. Pain is pain wherever it occurs. If your neighbor's causing you pain is wrong because of the pain that is caused, we cannot rationally ignore or dismiss the moral relevance of the pain that your dog feels.

Philosophers who hold indirect duty views—and many still do—have come to understand that they must avoid the two defects just noted: that is, both the view that animals don't feel anything as well as the idea that only human pain can be morally relevant. Among such thinkers the sort of view now favored is one or other form of what is called contractarianism.

Here, very crudely, is the root idea: morality consists of a set of rules that individuals voluntarily agree to abide by, as we do when we sign a contract (hence the name contractarianism). Those who understand and accept the terms of the contract are covered directly; they have rights created and recognized by, and protected in, the contract. And these contractors can also have protection spelled out for others who, though they lack the ability to understand morality and so cannot sign the contract themselves, are loved or cherished by those who can. Thus young children, for example, are unable to sign contracts and lack rights. But they are protected by the contract nonetheless because of the sentimental interests of others, most notably their parents. So we have, then, duties involving these children, duties regarding them, but no duties to them. Our duties in their case are indirect duties to other human beings, usually their parents.

As for animals, since they cannot understand contracts, they obviously cannot sign; and since they cannot sign, they have no rights. Like children, however, some animals are the objects of the sentimental interest of others. You, for example, love your dog or cat. So those animals that enough people care about (companion animals, whales, baby seals, the American bald eagle), though they lack rights themselves, will be protected because of the sentimental interests of people. I have, then, according to the contractarianism, no duty directly to your dog or any other animal, not even the duty not to cause them pain or suffering; my duty not to hurt them is a duty I have to those people who care about what happens to them. As for other animals, where no or little sentimental interest is present—in the case of farm animals, for example, or laboratory rats—what duties we have grow weaker and weaker, perhaps to vanishing point. The pain and death they endure, though real, are not wrong if no one cares about them.

When it comes to the moral status of animals, contractarianism could be a hard view to refute if it were an adequate theoretical approach to the moral status of human beings. It is not adequate in this latter respect, however, which makes the question of its adequacy in the former case, regarding animals, utterly moot. For consider: morality, according to the (crude) contractarian position before us, consists of rules that people agree to abide by. What people? Well, enough to make a difference—enough, that is, collectively to have the power to enforce the rules that are drawn up in the contract. That is very well and good for the signatories but not so good for anyone who is not asked to sign. And there is nothing in contractarianism of the sort we are discussing that guarantees or requires that everyone will have a chance to participate equally in framing the rules of morality. The result is that this approach to ethics could sanction the most blatant forms of social, economic, moral and political injustice, ranging from a repressive caste system to systematic racial or sexual discrimination. Might, according to this theory, does make right. Let those who are the victims of injustice suffer as they will. It matters not so long as no one else—no contractor, or too few of them—cares about it. Such a theory takes one's moral breath away . . . as if, for example, there would be nothing wrong with apartheid in South Africa if few white South Africans were upset by it. A theory with so little to recommend it at the level of the ethics of our treatment of our fellow humans cannot have anything more to recommend it when it comes to the ethics of how we treat our fellow animals.

The version of contractarianism just examined is, as I have noted, a crude variety, and in fairness to those of a contractarian persuasion it must be noted that much more refined, subtle and ingenious varieties are possible. For example, John Rawls, in his *A Theory of Justice*, sets forth a version of contractarianism that forces contractors to ignore the accidental features of being a human being—for example, whether one is white or black, male or female, a genius or of modest intellect. Only by ignoring such features, Rawls believes, can we ensure that the principles of justice that contractors would agree upon are not based on bias or prejudice. Despite the improvement a view such as Rawl's represents over the cruder forms of contractarianism, it remains deficient: it systematically denies that we have direct duties to those human beings who do not have a sense of justice—young children, for instance, and many mentally retarded humans. And yet it seems reasonably certain that, were we to torture a young child or a retarded elder, we would be doing something that wronged him or her, not something that would be wrong if (and only if) other humans with a sense of justice were upset. And since this is true in the case of these humans, we cannot rationally deny the same in the case of animals.

Indirect duty views, then, including the best among them, fail to command our rational assent. Whatever ethical theory we should accept rationally, therefore, it must at least recognize that we have some duties directly to animals, just as we have some duties directly to each other. . . .

Some people think that the theory we are looking for is utilitarianism. A utilitarian accepts two moral principles. The first is that of equality: everyone's interests count, and similar interests must be counted as having similar weight or importance. White or black, American or Iranian, human or animal—everyone's pain or frustration matters, and matters just as much as the equivalent pain or frustration of anyone else. The second principle a utilitarian accepts is that of utility: do the act that will bring about the best balance between satisfaction and frustration for everyone affected by the outcome.

As a utilitarian, then, here is how I am to approach the task of deciding what I morally ought to do: I must ask who will be affected if I choose to do one thing rather than another, how much each individual will be affected, and where the best results are most likely to lie—which option, in other words, is most likely to bring about the best results, the best balance between satisfaction and frustration. That option, whatever it may be, is the one I ought to choose. That is where my moral duty lies.

The great appeal of utilitarianism rests with its uncompromising egalitarianism: everyone's interests count and count as much as the like interests of everyone else. The kind of odious discrimination that some forms of contractarianism can justify—discrimination based on race or sex, for example—seems disallowed in principle by utilitarianism, as is speciesism, systematic discrimination based on species membership.

The equality we find in utilitarianism, however, is not the sort an advocate of animal or human rights should have in mind. Utilitarianism has no room for the equal moral rights of different individuals because it has no room for their equal inherent value or worth. What has value for the utilitarian is the satisfaction of an individual's interests, not the individual whose interests they are. A universe in which you satisfy your desire for water, food and warmth is, other things being equal, better than a universe in which these desires are frustrated. And the same is true in the case of an animal with similar desires. But neither you nor the animal have any value in your own right. Only your feelings do.

Here is an analogy to help make the philosophical point clearer: a cup contains different liquids, sometimes sweet, sometimes bitter, sometimes a mix of the two. What has value are the liquids: the sweeter the better, the bitterer the worse. The cup, the container, has no value. It is what goes into it, not what they go into, that has value. For the utilitarian you and I are like the cup; we have no value as individuals and thus no equal value. What has value is what goes into us, what we serve as receptacles for; our feelings of satisfaction have positive value, our feelings of frustration negative value.

Serious problems arise for utilitarianism when we remind ourselves that it enjoins us to bring about the best consequences. What does this mean? It doesn't mean the best consequences for me alone, or for my family or friends, or any other person taken individually. No, what we must do is, roughly, as follows: we must add up (somehow!) the separate satisfactions and frustrations of everyone likely to be affected by our choice, the satisfactions in one column, the frustrations in the other. We must total each column for each of the options before us. That is what it means to say the theory is aggregative. And then we must choose that option which is most likely to bring about the best balance of totaled satisfactions over totaled frustrations. Whatever act would lead to this outcome is the one we ought morally to perform—it is where our moral duty lies. And that act quite clearly might not be the same one that would bring about the best results for me personally, or for my family or friends, or for a lab animal. The best aggregated consequences for everyone concerned are not necessarily the best for each individual.

That utilitarianism is an aggressive theory—different individuals' satisfactions or frustrations are added, or summed, or totaled—is the key objection to this theory. My Aunt Bea is old, inactive, a cranky, sour person, though not physically ill. She prefers to go on living. She is also rather rich. I could make a fortune if I could get my hands on her money, money she intends to give me in any event, after she dies, but which she refuses to give me now. In order to avoid a huge tax bite, I plan to donate a handsome sum of my profits to a local children's hospital. Many, many children will benefit from my generosity, and much joy will be brought to their parents, relatives and friends. If I don't get the money rather soon, all these ambitions will come to naught. The once-in-a-lifetime opportunity to make a real killing will be gone. Why, then, not kill my Aunt Bea? Oh, of course I might get caught. But I'm no fool and, besides, her doctor can be counted on to cooperate (he has an eye for the same investment and I happen to know a good deal about his shady past). The deed can be done . . . professionally, shall we say. There is very little chance of getting caught. And as for my conscience being guilt-ridden, I am a resourceful sort of fellow and will take more than sufficient comfort—as I lie on the beach at Acapulco—in contemplating the joy and health I have brought to so many others.

Suppose Aunt Bea is killed and the rest of the story comes out as told. Would I have done anything wrong? Anything immoral? One would have thought that I had. Not according to utilitarianism. Since what I have done has brought about the best balance between totaled satisfaction and frustration for all those affected by the outcome, my action is not wrong. Indeed, in killing Aunt Bea the physician and I did what duty required.

This same kind of argument can be repeated in all sorts of cases, illustrating, time after time, how the utilitarian's position leads to results that impartial people find morally callous. It is wrong to kill my Aunt Bea in the name of bringing about the best results for others. A good end does not justify an evil means. Any adequate moral theory will have to explain why this is so. Utilitarianism fails in this respect and so cannot be the theory we seek.

What to do? Where to begin anew? The place to begin, I think, is with the utilitarian's view of the value of the individual—or, rather, lack of value. In its place, suppose we consider that you and I, for example, do have value as individuals—what we'll call inherent value. To say we have such value is to say that we are something more than, something different from, mere receptacles. Moreover, to ensure that we do not pave the way for such injustices as slavery or sexual discrimination, we must believe that all who have inherent value have it equally, regardless of their sex, race, religion, birthplace and so on. Similarly to be discarded as irrelevant are one's talents or skills, intelligence and wealth, personality or pathology, whether one is loved and admired or despised and loathed. The genius and the retarded child, the prince and the pauper, the brain surgeon and the fruit vendor, Mother Teresa and the most unscrupulous used-car salesman—all have inherent value, all possess it equally, and all have an equal right to be treated with respect, to be treated in ways that do not reduce them to the status of things, as if they existed as resources for others. My value as an individual is independent of my usefulness to you. Yours is not dependent on your usefulness to me. For either of us to treat the other in ways that fail to show respect for the other's independent value is to act immorally, to violate the individual's rights.

Some of the rational virtues of this view—what I call the rights view—should be evident. Unlike (crude) contractarianism, for example, the rights view in principle denies the moral tolerability of any and all forms of racial, sexual or social discrimination; and unlike utilitarianism, this view in principle denies that we can justify good results by using evil means that violate an individual's rights—denies, for example, that it could be moral to kill my Aunt Bea to harvest beneficial consequences for others. That would be to sanction the disrespectful treatment of the individual in the name of the social good, something the rights view will not—categorically will not—ever allow.

The rights view, I believe, is rationally the most satisfactory moral theory. It surpasses all other theories in the degree to which it illuminates and explains the foundation of our duties to one another—the domain of human morality. On this score it has the best reasons, the best arguments, on its side. Of course, if it were possible to show that only human beings are included within its scope, then a person like myself, who believes in animal rights, would be obliged to look elsewhere.

But attempts to limit its scope to humans only can be shown to be rationally defective. Animals, it is true, lack many of the abilities humans possess. They can't read, do higher mathematics, build a bookcase or make baba ghanoush. Neither can many human beings, however, and yet we don't (and shouldn't) say that they (these humans) therefore have less inherent value, less of a right to be treated with respect, than do others. It is the similarities between those human beings who most clearly, most non-controversially have such value (the people reading this, for example), not our differences, that matter most. And the really crucial, the basic similarity is simply this: we are each of us the experiencing subject of a life, a conscious creature having an individual welfare that has importance to us whatever our usefulness to others. We want and prefer things, believe and feel things, recall and expect things. And all these dimensions of our life, including our pleasure and pain, our enjoyment and suffering, our satisfaction and frustration, our continued existence of our untimely death—all make a difference to the quality of our life as lived, as experienced, by us as individuals. As the same is true of those animals that concern us, . . . they too must be viewed as the experiencing subjects of a life, with inherent value of their own.

Some there are who resist the idea that animals have inherent value. "Only humans have such value," they profess. How might this narrow view be defended? Shall we say that only humans have the requisite intelligence, or autonomy, or reason? But there are many, many humans who fail to meet these standards and yet are reasonably viewed as having value above and beyond their usefulness to others. Shall we claim that only humans belong to the right species, the species Homo sapiens? But this is blatant speciesism. Will it be said, then, that all— and only—humans have immortal souls? Then our opponents have their work cut out for them. I am myself not ill-disposed to the proposition that there are immortal souls. Personally, I profoundly hope I have one. But I would not want to rest my position on a controversial ethical issue on the even more controversial question about who or what has an immortal soul. That is to dig one's hole deeper, not to climb out. Rationally, it is better to resolve moral issues without making more controversial assumptions than are needed. The question of who has inherent value is such a question, one that is resolved more rationally without the introduction of the idea of immortal souls than by its use.

Well, perhaps some will say that animals have some inherent value, only less than we have. Once again, however, attempts to defend this view can be shown to lack rational justification. What could be the basis of our having more inherent value than animals? Their lack of reason, or autonomy, or intellect? Only if we are willing to make the same judgment in the case of humans who are similarly deficient. But it is not true that such humans—the retarded child, for example, or the mentally deranged—have less inherent value than you or I. Neither, then, can we rationally sustain the view that animals, like them in being the experiencing subjects of a life, have less inherent value. All who have inherent value have it equally, whether they be human animals or not.

Inherent value, then, belongs equally to those who are the experiencing subjects of a life. Whether it belongs to others—to rocks and rivers, trees and glaciers, for example—we do not know and may never know. But neither do we need to know, if we are to make the case for animal rights. We do not need to know, for example, how many people are eligible to vote in the next presidential election before we can know whether I am. Similarly, we do not need to know how many individuals have inherent value before we can know that some do. When it comes to the case for animal rights, then, what we need to know is whether the animals that, in our culture, are routinely eaten, hunted and used in our laboratories, for example, are like us in being subjects of a life. And we do know this. We do know that many—literally, billions and billions—of these animals are the subjects of a life in the sense explained and so have inherent value if we do. And since, in order to arrive at the best theory of our duties to one another, we must recognize our equal inherent value as individuals, reason—not sentiment, not emotion—reason compels us to recognize the equal inherent value of these animals and, with this, their equal right to be treated with respect.

That, *very* roughly, is the shape and feel of the case for animal rights. Most of the details of the supporting argument are missing. They are to be found in the book to which I alluded earlier. Here, the details go begging, and I must, in closing, limit myself to four final points.

The first is how the theory that underlies the case for animal rights shows that the animal rights movement is a part of, not antagonistic to, the human rights movement. The theory that rationally grounds the rights of animals also grounds the rights of humans. Thus those involved in the animal rights movement are partners in the struggle to secure respect for human rights—the rights of women, for example, or minorities, or workers. The animal rights movement is cut from the same moral cloth as these.

Second, having set out the broad outlines of the rights view, I can now say why its implications for . . . science, among other fields, are both clear and uncompromising. In the case of the use of animals in science, the rights view is categorically abolitionist. Lab animals are not our tasters; we are not their kings. Because these animals are treated routinely, systematically as if their value were reducible to their usefulness to others, they are routinely, systematically treated with a lack of respect, and thus are their rights routinely, systematically violated. This is just as true when they are used in trivial, duplicative, unnecessary or unwise research as it is when they are used in studies that hold out real promise of human benefits. We can't justify harming or killing a human being (my Aunt Bea, for example) just for these sorts of reason. Neither can we do so even in the case of so lowly a creature as a laboratory rat. It is not just refinement or reduction that is called for, not just larger, cleaner cages, not just more generous use of anesthetic or the elimination of multiple surgery, not just tidying up the system. It is complete replacement. The best we can do when it comes to using animals in science is—not to use them. That is where our duty lies, according to the rights view. . . .

My last two points are about philosophy, my profession. It is, most obviously, no substitute for political action. The words I have written here and in other places by themselves don't change a thing. It is what we do with the thoughts that the words express—our acts, our deeds—that changes things. All that philosophy can do, and all I have attempted, is to offer a vision of what our deeds should aim at. And the why. But not the how.

Finally, I am reminded of my thoughtful critic, the one I mentioned earlier, who chastised me for being too cerebral. Well, cerebral I have been: indirect duty views, utilitarianism, contractarianism—hardly the stuff deep passions are made of. I am also reminded, however, of the image another friend once set before me—the image of the ballerina as expressive of disciplined passion. Long hours of sweat and toil, of loneliness and practice, of doubt and fatigue: those are the discipline of her craft. But the passion is there too, the fierce drive to excel, to speak through he body, to do it right, to pierce our minds. That is the image of philosophy I would leave with you, not "too cerebral" but disciplined passion. Of the discipline enough has been seen. As for the passion: there are times, and these not infrequent, when tears come to my eyes when I see, or read, or hear of the wretched plight of animals in the hands of humans. Their pain, their suffering, their loneliness, their innocence, their death. Anger. Rage. Pity. Sorrow. Disgust. The whole creation groans under the weight of the evil we humans visit upon these mute, powerless creatures. It is our hearts, not just our heads, that call for an end to it all, that demand of us that we overcome, for them, the habits and forces behind their systematic oppression. All great movements, it is written, go through three stages: ridicule, discussion, adoption. It is the realization of this third stage, adoption, that requires both our passion and our discipline, our hearts and our heads. The fate of animals is in our hands. God grant we are equal to the task.

Carl Cohen, "The Case for the Use of Animals in Biomedical Research" in *The New England Journal of Medicine*, Vol. 314, 1986

The Case for the Use of Animals in Biomedical Research
Carl Cohen

Using animals as research subjects in medical investigations is widely condemned on two grounds: first, because it wrongly violates the rights of animals,[1] and second, because it wrongly imposes on sentient creatures much avoidable suffering.[2] Neither of these arguments is sound. The first relies on a mistaken understanding of rights; the second relies on a mistaken calculation of consequences. Both deserve definitive dismissal.

WHY ANIMALS HAVE NO RIGHTS

A right, properly understood, is a claim, or potential claim, that one party may exercise against another. The target against whom such a claim may be registered can be a single person, a group, a community, or (perhaps) all humankind. The content of rights claims also varies greatly: repayment of loans, nondiscrimination by employers, noninterference by the state, and so on. To comprehend any genuine right fully, therefore, we must know who holds the right, against whom it is held, and to what it is a right.

Alternative sources of rights add complexity. Some rights are grounded in constitution and law (e.g., the right of an accused to trial by jury); some rights are moral but give no legal claims (e.g., my right to your keeping the promise you gave me); and some rights (e.g., against theft or assault) are rooted both in morals and in law.

The differing targets, contents, and sources of rights, and their inevitable conflict, together weave a tangled web. Notwithstanding all such complications, this much is clear about rights in general: they are in every case claims, or potential claims, within a community of moral agents. Rights arise, and can be intelligibly defended, only among beings who actually do, or can, make moral claims against one another. Whatever else rights may be, therefore, they are necessarily human; their possessors are persons, human beings.

The attributes of human beings from which this moral capability arises have been described variously by philosophers, both ancient and modern: the inner consciousness of a free will (Saint Augustine)[3]; the grasp, by human reason, of the binding character of moral law (Saint Thomas)[4]; the self-conscious participation of human beings in an objective ethical order (Hegel)[5]; human membership in an organic moral community (Bradley)[6]; the development of the human self through the consciousness of other moral selves (Mead)[7]; and the underivative, intuitive cognition of the rightness of an action (Prichard).[8] Most influential has been Immanuel Kant's emphasis on the universal human possession of a uniquely moral will and the autonomy its use entails.[9] Humans confront choices that are purely moral; humans—but certainly not dogs or mice—lay down moral laws, for others and for themselves. Human beings are self-legislative, morally *auto-nomous.*

Animals (that is, nonhuman animals, the ordinary sense of that word) lack this capacity for free moral judgment. They are not beings of a kind capable of exercising or responding to moral claims. Animals therefore have no rights, and they can have none. This is the core of the argument about the alleged rights of animals. The holders of rights must have the capacity to comprehend rules of duty, governing all including themselves. In applying such rules, the holders of rights must recognize possible conflicts between what is in their own interest and what is just. Only in a community of beings capable of self-restricting moral judgments can the concept of a right be correctly invoked.

Humans have such moral capacities. They are in this sense self-legislative, are members of communities governed by moral rules, and do possess rights. Animals do not have such moral capacities. They are not morally self-legislative, cannot possibly be members of a truly moral community, and therefore cannot possess rights. In conducting research on animal subjects, therefore, we do not violate their rights, because they have none to violate.

To animate life, even in its simplest forms, we give a certain natural reverence. But the possession of rights presupposes a moral status not attained by the vast majority of living things. We must not infer, therefore, that a live being has, simply in being alive, a "right" to its life. The assertion that all animals, only because they are alive and have interests, also possess the "right to life" is an abuse of that phrase, and wholly without warrant.

It does not follow from this, however, that we are morally free to do anything we please to animals. Certainly not. In our dealings with animals, as in our dealings with other human beings, we have obligations that do not arise from claims against us based on rights. Rights entail obligations, but many of the things one ought to do are in no way tied to another's entitlement. Rights and obligations are not reciprocals of one another, and it is a serious mistake to suppose that they are.

Illustrations are helpful. Obligations may arise from internal commitments made: physicians have obligations to their patients not grounded merely in their patients' rights. Teachers have such obligations to their students, shepherds to their dogs, and cowboys to their horses. Obligations may arise from differences of status: adults owe special care when playing with young children, and children owe special care when playing with young pets. Obligations may arise from special relationships: the payment of my son's college tuition is something to which he may have no right, although it may be my obligation to bear the burden if I reasonably can; my dog has no right to daily exercise and veterinary care, but I do have the obligation to provide these things for her. Obligations may arise from particular acts or circumstances: one may be obliged to another for a special kindness done, or obliged to put an animal out of its misery in view of its condition—although neither the human benefactor nor the dying animal may have had a claim of right.

Plainly, the grounds of our obligations to humans and to animals are manifold and cannot be formulated simply. Some hold that there is a general obligation to do no gratuitous harm to sentient creatures (the principle of nonmaleficence); some hold that there is a general obligation to do good to sentient creatures when that is reasonably within one's power (the principle of beneficence). In our dealings with animals, few will deny that we are at least obliged to act humanely—that is, to treat them with the decency and concern that we owe, as sensitive human beings, to other sentient creatures. To treat animals humanely, however, is not to treat them as humans or as the holders of rights.

A common objection, which deserves a response, may be paraphrased as follows:

> If having rights requires being able to make moral claims, to grasp and apply moral laws, then many humans—the brain-damaged, the comatose, the senile—who plainly lack those capacities must be without rights. But that is absurd. This proves [the critic concludes] that rights do not depend on the presence of moral capacities.[11]

This objection fails; it mistakenly treats an essential feature of humanity as though it were a screen for sorting humans. The capacity for moral judgment that distinguishes humans from animals is not a test to be administered to human beings one by one. Persons who are unable, because of some disability, to perform the full moral functions natural to human beings are certainly not for that reason ejected from the moral community. The issue is one of kind. Humans are of such a kind that they may be the subject of experiments only with their voluntary consent. The choices they make freely must be respected. Animals are of such a kind that it is impossible for them, in principle, to give or withhold voluntary consent or to make a moral choice. What humans retain when disabled, animals have never had.

A second objection, also often made, may be paraphrased as follows:

> Capacities will not succeed in distinguishing humans from the other animals. Animals also reason; animals also communicate with one another; animals also care passionately for their young; animals also exhibit desires and preferences.[12] Features of moral relevance—rationality, interdependence, and love—are not exhibited uniquely by human beings. Therefore [this critic concludes], there can be no solid moral distinction between humans and other animals.[13]

This criticism misses the central point. It is not the ability to communicate or to reason, or dependence on one another, or care for the young, or the exhibition of preference, or any such behavior that marks the critical divide. Analogies between human families and those of monkeys, or between human communities and those of wolves, and the like, are entirely beside the point. Patterns of conduct are not at issue. Animals do indeed exhibit remarkable behavior at times. Conditioning, fear, instinct, and intelligence all contribute to species survival. Membership in a community of moral agents nevertheless remains impossible for them. Actors subject to moral judgment must be capable of grasping the generality of an ethical premise in a practical syllogism. Humans act immorally often enough, but only they—never wolves or monkeys—can discern, by applying some moral rule to the facts of a case, that a given act ought or ought not to be performed. The moral restraints imposed by humans on themselves are thus highly abstract and are often in conflict with the self- interest of the agent. Communal behavior among animals, even when most intelligent and most endearing, does not approach autonomous morality in this fundamental sense.

Genuinely moral acts have an internal as well as an external dimension. Thus, in law, an act can be criminal only when the guilty deed, the actus reus, is done with a guilty mind, mens rea. No animal can ever commit a crime; bringing animals to criminal trial is the mark of primitive ignorance. The claims of moral right are similarly inapplicable to them. Does a lion have a right to eat a baby zebra? Does a baby zebra have a right not to be eaten? Such questions, mistakenly invoking the concept of right where it does not belong, do not make good sense. Those who condemn biomedical research because it violates "animal rights" commit the same blunder.

In Defense of "Speciesism"

Abandoning reliance on animal rights, some critics resort instead to animal sentience—their feelings of pain and distress. We ought to desist from the imposition of pain insofar as we can. Since all or nearly all experimentation on animals does impose pain and could be readily forgone, say these critics, it should be stopped. The ends sought may be worthy, but those ends do not justify imposing agonies on humans, and by animals the agonies are felt no less. The laboratory use of animals (these critics conclude) must therefore be ended—or at least very sharply curtailed.

Argument of this variety is essentially utilitarian, often expressly so;[14] it is based on the calculation of the net product, in pains and pleasures, resulting from experiments on animals. Jeremy Bentham, comparing horses and dogs with other sentient creatures, is thus commonly quoted: "The question is not, Can they reason? nor Can they talk? but, Can they suffer?"[15]

Animals certainly can suffer and surely ought not to be made to suffer needlessly. But in inferring, from these uncontroversial premises, that biomedical research causing animal distress is largely (or wholly) wrong, the critic commits two serious errors.

The first error is the assumption, often explicitly defended, that all sentient animals have equal moral standing. Between a dog and a human being, according to this view, there is no moral difference; hence the pains suffered by dogs must be weighed no differently from the pains suffered by humans. To deny such equality, according to this critic, is to give unjust preference to one species over another; it is "speciesism." The most influential statement of this moral equality of species was made by Peter Singer:

> The racist violates the principle of equality by giving greater weight to the interests of members of his own race when there is a clash between their interests and the interests of those of another race. The sexist violates the principle of equality by favoring the interests of his own sex. Similarly the speciesist allows the interests of his own species to override the greater interests of members of other species. The pattern is identical in each case.[16]

This argument is worse than unsound; it is atrocious. It draws an offensive moral conclusion from a deliberately devised verbal parallelism that is utterly specious. Racism has no rational ground whatever. Differing degrees of respect or concern for humans for no other reason than that they are members of different races is an injustice totally without foundation in the nature of the races themselves. Racists, even if acting on the basis of mistaken factual beliefs, do grave moral wrong precisely because there is no morally relevant distinction among the races. The supposition of such differences has led to outright horror. The same is true of the sexes, neither sex being entitled by right to greater respect or concern than the other. No dispute here.

Between species of animate life, however—between (for example) humans on the one hand and cats or rats on the other—the morally relevant differences are enormous, and almost universally appreciated. Humans engage in moral reflection; humans are morally autonomous; humans are members of moral communities, recognizing just claims against their own interest. Human beings do have rights; theirs is a moral status very different from that of cats or rats.

I am a speciesist. Speciesism is not merely plausible; it is essential for right conduct, because those who will not make the morally relevant distinctions among species are almost certain, in consequence, to misapprehend their true obligations. The analogy between speciesism and racism is insidious. Every sensitive moral judgment requires that the differing natures of the beings to whom obligations are owed be considered. If all forms of animate life—or vertebrate animal life?—must be treated equally, and if therefore in evaluating a research program the pains of a rodent count equally with the pains of a human, we are forced to conclude (1) that neither humans nor rodents possess rights, or (2) that rodents possess all the rights that humans possess. Both alternatives are absurd. Yet one or the other must be swallowed if the moral equality of all species is to be defended.

Humans owe to other humans a degree of moral regard that cannot be owed to animals. Some humans take on the obligation to support and heal others, both humans and animals, as a principal duty in their lives; the fulfillment of that duty may require the sacrifice of many animals. If biomedical investigators abandon the effective pursuit of their professional objectives because they are convinced that they may not do to animals what the service of humans requires, they will fail, objectively, to do their duty. Refusing to recognize the moral differences among species is a sure path to calamity. (The largest animal rights group in the country is People for the Ethical Treatment of Animals; its co-director, Ingrid Newkirk, calls research using animal subjects "fascism" and "supremacism." "Animal liberationists do not separate out the human animal," she says, "so there is no rational basis for saying that a human being has special rights. A rat is a pig is a dog is a boy. They're all mammals.")[17]

Those who claim to base their objection to the use of animals in biomedical research on their reckoning of the net pleasures and pains produced make a second error, equally grave. Even if it were true—as it is surely not—that the pains of all animate beings must be counted equally, a cogent utilitarian calculation requires that we weigh all the consequences of the use, and of the nonuse, of animals in laboratory research. Critics relying (however mistakenly) on animal rights may claim to ignore the beneficial results of such research, rights being trump cards to which interest and advantage must give way. But an argument that is explicitly framed in terms of interest and benefit for all over the long run must attend also to the disadvantageous consequences of not using animals in research, and to all the achievements attained and attainable only through their use. The sum of the benefits of their use is utterly beyond quantification. The elimination of horrible disease, the increase of longevity, the avoidance of great pain, the saving of lives, and the improvement of the quality of lives (for humans and for animals) achieved through research using animals is so incalculably great that the argument of these critics, systematically pursued, establishes not their conclusion but its reverse: to refrain from using animals in biomedical research is, on utilitarian grounds, morally wrong.

When balancing the pleasures and pains resulting from the use of animals in research, we must not fail to place on the scales the terrible pains that would have resulted, would be suffered now, and would long continue had animals not been used. Every disease eliminated, every vaccine developed, every method of pain relief devised, every surgical procedure invented, every prosthetic device implanted,—indeed, virtually every modern medical therapy—is due, in part or in whole, to experimentation using animals. Nor may we ignore, in the balancing process, the predictable gains in human (and animal) well-being that are probably achievable in the future but that will not be achieved if the decision is made now to desist from such research or to curtail it.

Medical investigators are seldom insensitive to the distress their work may cause animal subjects. Opponents of research using animals are frequently insensitive to the cruelty of the results of the restrictions they would impose.[18] Untold numbers of human beings—real persons, although not now identifiable—would suffer grievously as the consequence of this well-meaning but shortsighted tenderness. If the morally relevant differences between humans and animals are borne in mind, and if all relevant considerations are weighed, the calculation of long-term consequences must give overwhelming support for biomedical research using animals.

CONCLUDING REMARKS

Substitution

The humane treatment of animals requires that we desist from experimenting on them if we can accomplish the same result using alternative methods—*in vitro* experimentation, computer simulation, or others. Critics of some experiments using animals rightly make this point.

It would be a serious error to suppose, however, that alternative techniques could soon be used in most research now using live animal subjects. No other methods now on the horizon or perhaps ever to be available—can fully replace the testing of a drug, a procedure, or a vaccine, in live organisms. The flood of new medical possibilities being opened by the successes of recombinant DNA technology will turn to a trickle if testing on live animals is forbidden. When initial trials entail great risks, there may be no forward movement whatever without the use of live animal subjects. In seeking knowledge that may prove critical in later clinical applications, the unavailability of animals for inquiry may spell complete stymie. In the United States, federal regulations require the testing of new drugs and other products on animals, for efficacy and safety, before human beings are exposed to them.[19] We would not want it otherwise.

Every advance in medicine—every new drug, new operation, new therapy of any kind—must sooner or later be tried on a living being for the first time. That trial, controlled or uncontrolled, will be an experiment. The subject of that experiment, if it is not an animal, will be a human being. Prohibiting the use of live animals in biomedical research, therefore, or sharply restricting it, must result either in the blockage of much valuable research or in the replacement of animal subjects with human subjects. These are the consequences—unacceptable to most reasonable persons—of not using animals in research.

Reduction

Should we not at least reduce the use of animals in biomedical research? No, we should increase it, to avoid when feasible the use of humans as experimental subjects. Medical investigations putting human subjects at some risk are numerous and greatly varied. The risks run in such experiments are usually unavoidable, and (thanks to earlier experiments on animals) most such risks are minimal or moderate. But some experimental risks are substantial.

When an experimental protocol that entails substantial risk to humans comes before an institutional review board, what response is appropriate? The investigation, we may suppose, is promising and deserves support, so long as its human subjects are protected against unnecessary dangers. May not the investigators be fairly asked, Have you done all that you can to eliminate risk to humans by the extensive testing of that drug, that procedure, or that device on animals? To achieve maximal safety for humans we are right to require thorough experimentation on animal subjects before humans are involved.

Opportunities to increase human safety in this way are commonly missed; trials in which risks may be shifted from humans to animals are often not devised, sometimes not even considered. Why? For the investigator, the use of animals as subjects is often more expensive, in money and time, than the use of human subjects. Access to suitable human subjects is often quick and convenient, whereas access to appropriate animal subjects may be awkward, costly, and burdened with red tape. Physician-investigators have often had more experience working with human beings and know precisely where the needed pool of subjects is to be found and how they may be enlisted. Animals, and the procedures for their use, are often less familiar to these investigators. Moreover, the use of animals in place of humans is now more likely to be the target of zealous protests from without. The upshot is that humans are sometimes subjected to risks that animals could have borne, and should have borne, in their place. To maximize the protection of human subjects, I conclude, the wide and imaginative use of live animal subjects should be encouraged rather than discouraged. This enlargement in the use of animals is our obligation.

CONSISTENCY

Finally, inconsistency between the profession and the practice of many who oppose research using animals deserves comment. This frankly *ad hominem* observation aims chiefly to show that a coherent position rejecting the use of animals in medical research imposes costs so high as to be intolerable even to the critics themselves.

One cannot coherently object to the killing of animals in biomedical investigations while continuing to eat them. Anesthetics and thoughtful animal husbandry render the level of actual animal distress in the laboratory generally lower than that in the abattoir. So long as death and discomfort do not substantially differ in the two contexts, the consistent objector must not only refrain from all eating of animals but also protest as vehemently against others eating them as against others experimenting on them. No less vigorously must the critic object to the wearing of animal hides in coats and shoes, to employment in any industrial enterprise that uses animal parts, and to any commercial development that will cause death or distress to animals.

Killing animals to meet human needs for food, clothing, and shelter is judged entirely reasonable by most persons. The ubiquity of these uses and the virtual universality of moral support for them confront the opponent of research using animals with an inescapable difficulty. How can the many common uses of animals be judged morally worthy, while their use in scientific investigation is judged unworthy?

The number of animals used in research is but the tiniest fraction of the total used to satisfy assorted human appetites. That these appetites, often base and satisfiable in other ways, morally justify the far larger consumption of animals, whereas the quest for improved human health and understanding cannot justify the far smaller, is wholly implausible. Aside from the numbers of animals involved, the distinction in terms of worthiness of use, drawn with regard to any single animal, is not defensible. A given sheep is surely not more justifiably used to put lamb chops on the supermarket counter than to serve in testing a new contraceptive or a new prosthetic device. The needless killing of animals is wrong; if the common killing of them for our food or convenience is right, the less common but more humane uses of animals in the service of medical science are certainly not less right.

Scrupulous vegetarianism, in matters of food, clothing, shelter, commerce, and recreation, and in all other spheres, is the only fully coherent position the critic may adopt. At great human cost, the lives of fish and crustaceans must also be protected, with equal vigor, if speciesism has been forsworn. A very few consistent critics adopt this position. It is the reductio ad absurdum of the rejection of moral distinctions between animals and human beings.

Opposition to the use of animals in research is based on arguments of two different kinds— those relying on the alleged rights of animals and those relying on the consequences for animals. I have argued that arguments of both kinds must fail. We surely do have obligations to animals, but they have, and can have. no rights against us on which research can infringe In calculating the consequences of animal research, we must weigh all the long-term benefits of the results achieved—to animals and to humans—and in that calculation we must not assume the moral equality of all animate species.

Notes

1.   T. Regan, *The Case for Animal Rights* (Berkeley, CA: University of California Press, 1983).

2.   P. Singer, *Animal Liberation* (New York: Avon Books, 1977).

3.   Augustine (A.D. 397), *Confessions* (New York: Pocketbooks, 1957), bk. 7, pp. 104–126

4.   Aquinas (A.D. 1273), *Summa Theologica* (Philosophic Texts) (New York: Oxford University Press, 1960), pp. 353–366.

5.   G. W. F. Hegel (1821), *Philosophy of Right* (London: Oxford University Press, 1952), pp. 105–110.

6.   F. H. Bradley, "Why Should I Be Moral?" in *Ethical Theories*, ed. A. I. Melden (New York: Prentice Hall, 1950), pp. 345–359.

7.   G. H. Mead (1925), "The Genesis of the Self and Social Control" in *Selected Writings* ed. A. J. Reck (Indianapolis: Bobbs-Merrill, 1964), pp. 264–293.

8.   H. A. Prichard (1912), "Does Moral Philosophy Rest on a Mistake?" in *Readings in Ethical Theory*, ed. W. Sellars and J. Hospers (New York: Appleton-Century-Crofts, 1952), pp. 149–163.

9.   I. Kant (1785), *Fundamental Principles of the Metaphysic of Morals* (New York: Liberal Arts Press, 1949).

10. B. E. Rollin, *Animal Rights and Human Morality* (Buffalo, NY: Prometheus Books, 1981).

11. [See note I and] C. Hoff, "Immoral and Moral Uses of Animals," *New England Journal of Medicine* 302 (1980), 115–118.

12. [See note 11 and] D. Jamieson, "Killing Persons and Other Beings," in *Ethics and Animals*, ed. H. B. Miller and W. H. Williams (Clifton, NJ: Humana Press, 1983), pp. 135-146.

13. B. E. Rollin, *Animal Rights and Human Morality*.

14. P. Singer, "Ten Years of Animal Liberation," *New York Review of Books* 31 (1985), 46–52.

15. J. Bentham, *Introduction to the Principles of Morals and Legislation* (London: Athlone Press, 1970).

16. P. Singer, *Animal Liberation*.

17. K. McCabe, "Who Will Live, Who Will Die?" *Washingtonian*, August 1986, p. 115.

18. P. Singer, *Animal Liberation*.

19. U.S. Code of Federal Regulations, Title 21, Sect. 505(i). Food, Drug, and Cosmetic Regulations. U.S. Code of Federal Regulations, Title 16, Sect. 500.40-2. Consumer Product Regulations.

ENVIRONMENTAL ETHICS

David Keller, "Gleaning Lessons from Deep Ecology" in *Ethics and the Environment*, Vol. 2, 1997

Gleaning Lessons from Deep Ecology
David Keller

ABSTRACT: *By reflecting on deep ecology, several lessons can be culled for environmental philosophy in general. The deep ecology of Arne Naess, Bill Devall, and George Sessions is appropriately characterized as a theory founded on the principles of biocentric egalitarianism and metaphysical holism. After considering each of these principles in turn, and then in relation to each other, the lesson turns out to be that the ontological foundation for environmental ethics must be nonegalitarian and polycentric.*

By reflecting on Deep Ecology,[1] we can cull a few lessons for environmental philosophy in general. Our first task is to characterize the subject matter at hand, and Deep Ecology presents a problem right away, due to the eclectic diversity of its acolytes; connections have been made between Deep Ecology and ecological science,[2] Christianity, Eastern religions, ecological feminism, new age mysticism, the forewarnings of Aldo Leopold and Rachel Carson, the poetry of Robinson Jeffers, the philosophy of Baruch Spinoza and Martin Heidegger, and more.[3]

Regrettably, this wealth of perspective proves burdensome; it is hard to see what the unique "deep ecological" converging point is of all these various bodies of thought. As one commentator has put it, "Any one who attempts to reconcile Heidegger's with Leopold's contributions to deep ecology finds the going rugged" (Oelschlaeger 1991, 304).

To avoid the complications of trying to characterize Deep Ecology through a general survey of its advocates, it will be most efficacious to simply focus on the philosophy of the original deep ecologist, Arne Naess, and two well-known partisans, Bill Devall and George Sessions. Naess is a Norwegian philosopher and naturalist who coined the term in *The Shallow and the Deep, Long-Range Ecology Movement: A Summary* (1973), which has become a sort of manifesto for the Deep-Ecology movement. Though Naess conveys a humble, nonconfrontational, Gandhi-influenced demeanor, he lambastes Western civilization for arrogant human-centeredness and a related instrumentalization and subjugation of nonhuman nature by contrasting his new "deep" environmental ethic with "shallow" (or to put it less pejoratively, "reform") environmentalism. Shallow environmentalism is simply an extension of the anthropocentric Western paradigm, because the reasons for preserving wilderness or biodiversity are inevitably couched in terms of human welfare. Shallow environmentalism falls short of valuing nonhumans apart from their use-value. Deep Ecology, in contrast, asserts that all organisms have *intrinsic* value. In this way Deep Ecology is fundamentally nonanthropocentric.

There are two interrelated underpinnings of Deep Ecology's nonanthropocentrism. The first is the principle that all biota have *equal* intrinsic value. Naess, Devall, and Sessions use the phrases "biocentric equality," "biospherical egalitarianism," and "ecological egalitarianism" to express this principle (Naess 1973, 95; Devall and Sessions 1975, 67–69). The second is the principle that the biosphere does not consist of metaphysically discrete individuals, but ontologically-interconnected individuals comprising one unbroken whole. This is a principle of metaphysical holism, and is known through the process of "self-realization" (66–67). Therefore, we can characterize Deep Ecology as an *egalitarian* and *holistic* theory. To discover what lessons Deep Ecology has for environmental philosophy in general, let us consider each of these principles in turn, and then in relation to each other.

BIOCENTRIC EQUALITY

Biocentric equality is the view that all biota have equal intrinsic value, or, to put it another way, it denies differential valuation among living things. In this sense Deep Ecology is not merely nonanthropocentric, but *anti*-anthropocentric; in terms of moral considerability, human beings have absolutely no priority over nonhumans. Naess, Devall, and Sessions have all affirmed this way of thinking. In the words of Naess, "*the equal right to live and blossom* is an intuitively clear and obvious value axiom" (Naess 1973, 96). In the words of Devall and Sessions, "all organisms and entities in the ecosphere, as parts of the interrelated whole, are equal in intrinsic worth" (Devall and Sessions 1985, 67).

Obviously, the target of biocentric equality is Occidental anthropocentrism. In contrast to the extreme human-centeredness of mainstream Western thought, deep ecologists contend that organisms have equal intrinsic value, with the implication that no form of life (read: *Homo sapiens*) deserves more attention or carries more weight in situations of competing interests. Sessions is unequivocal in opposing any environmental philosophy which assigns differential intrinsic value to living things, on the grounds that value hierarchies adumbrate claims of moral priority. Quoting John Rodman, Sessions warns that any differential axiology merely reinstates a "pecking order in this moral barnyard" (Sessions and Devall, 1985, 236). In the case of Whiteheadian-inspired environmental ethics (for example, Frederick Ferré's "personalistic organicism" [Ferré 1996]), which confers all biota intrinsic—as well as extrinsic—value, yet distributes intrinsic value on the basis of the intensity and quality of sentience, Sessions argues:

> The point is not whether humans in fact do have the greatest degree of sentience on this planet (although dolphins and whales might provide a counterinstance), deep ecologists argue that the degree of sentience is *irrelevant* in terms of how humans relate to the rest of Nature. And so, contemporary Whiteheadian ecological ethics does not meet the deep ecology insistence on 'ecological egalitarianism in principle.' (Sessions 1979, 18)

Unfortunately, it is difficult to see how strident axiological egalitarianism can be of any use in situations of conflicting interests. If the only type of value relevant to moral dilemmas is equivalent, then on what basis are prescriptions to be made? In the end the principle of biocentric equality renders Deep Ecology impotent as an ethical theory, since the kind of value distinctions useful in evaluating moral situations is deliberately rebuffed. It must be pointed out that Naess and Sessions claim not to be interested in ethical theory, because they believe the psychological realization of metaphysical holism, which we will come to shortly, makes ethics superfluous. (Naess: "I'm not much interested in ethics or morals. I'm interested in how we experience the world . . ."; "The search . . . is not for environmental ethics but for ecological consciousness" [quoted in Fox 1990, 219 and 225]. Yet it is difficult to think Deep Ecology does not have a strong normative thrust! Unless some gradations of value are acknowledged, as in a Callicottian, Ferréan, or Rolstonian environmental ethic, the prospect for making normative judgments about environmental problems seems hopelessly bleak.

For this reason, not all people who claim to advocate deep ecology embrace biocentric equality. The Australian philosopher Warwick Fox has argued that the leveling axiology of orthodox Deep Ecology ought to be scrapped. Fox notes that if all organisms really are of equal intrinsic worth, the deep ecological doctrinaire might just as well eat veal as vegetables (Fox 1984, 198). In reality, Fox predicts, deep ecologists probably tend to be vegetarians, because—in Alan Watts's memorable words—"cows scream louder than carrots" (Fox 1984, 198). Orthodox Deep Ecology, Fox declares,

> does itself a disservice by employing a definition of anthropocentrism which is so overly exclusive that it condemns more or less *any* theory of value that attempts to guide 'realistic praxis' . . . Unless deep ecologists take up this challenge and employ a workable definition of anthropocentrism, they may well become known as the advocates of 'Procrustean Ethics' as they attempt to fit all organisms to the same dimensions of intrinsic value. (Fox 1984, 198–199)

Fox, of course, does not want to be known as a Procrustean Ethicist, and ends up arguing for a position which abandons biocentric equality and alternatively asserts that all biota *have* intrinsic value, but are not *equal* in intrinsic value.[4] Thus, although Fox has identified himself as a deep ecologist in the past, his deep ecology is certainly not orthodox Deep Ecology.[5] In fact, Fox's environmental philosophy is closer to Ferré than Sessions.

In a focused effort to avoid any vestige of a human-oriented value-system, Naess continues to resist any gradation or differentiation of intrinsic value among organisms. In response to Fox, Naess says that *some* intrinsic values *may* differ, but not the kind he talks about. He and Fox, says Naess, "probably do not speak about the same intrinsic view" (Naess 1984, 202). Naess reiterates his fundamental intuition that "living beings have a right, or an intrinsic or inherent value, or value in themselves, that is *the same* for all of them" (202).

For an environmental ethic to have any efficacy, it must make discriminations in value between biota. In Bryan Norton's words, "The 120,000th elk cannot be treated equally with one of the last California condors—not, at least, on a reasonable *environmental* ethic" (Norton 1991, 224). In short, the very possibility of environmental ethics is predicated on the possibility of a *nonegalitarian* value-theory.

EXPANSIONARY HOLISM

When Odysseus finally returns to Ithaka after his twenty-year absence, he finds his household filled by irreligious and dishonorable suitors, courting his wife Penélopê, and consuming his estate. With tactical skill (and the help of grey-eyed Athena), Odysseus slaughters all one hundred of them. Then his son Telémakhos and a faithful herdsman, before mutilating the infidel goat-herder, string up a rope and lynch twelve maids whose ignominy was sneaking off with suitors late at night. As Homer told:

> So now in turn each woman thrust her head
> into a noose and swung, yanked high in air,
> to perish there most piteously.
> Their feet danced for a little, but not long. (Fitzgerald 1963, 424)

This is the passage Aldo Leopold alludes to at the beginning of his most famous bit of writing, *The Land Ethic* (Leopold 1987, 201–226). His point in evoking Homer is not to appall us with thoughts of the young womens' horrible experience, but to point out that in antiquity the hanging was perfectly acceptable, while now repugnant to us. Moral considerability did not extend to the slaves; their place in the moral order is below Odysseus and the gods. As private property, they are of no intrinsic worth of their own but only extrinsic worth for Odysseus. Killing them for disrespecting the moral order of the cosmos was not merely acceptable, it was even laudable.

Leopold's original contribution to ecophilosophy was to argue that as moral considerability has expanded to include previously excluded groups (e.g., blacks and women), it should be further expanded to include the land (biosphere) as a whole. Entire ecosystems, Leopold hypothesized, have moral considerability. In making this claim Leopold is widely considered to be the founder of *holistic* (or ecosystemic) environmental philosophy.

Deep ecologists often cite Leopold as a major inspiration in their own thinking. For Devall and Sessions,

> Leopold's ideas are truly subversive and constitute a landmark in the development of the biocentric position. Conservationists have paid lip service to Leopold's outlook, but until recently, only a few other ecologists seem to have grasped the full impact of the radical nature of Leopold's ecological conscience. (Devall and Sessions 1985, 86)

Some deep ecologists (notably Devall, Sessions, and Fox) elaborate Leopold's holism by arguing for a breakdown of the ontological boundaries between self and other. This breakdown is achieved through the process of *self-realization*. As Fox says: "It is the idea that we can make no firm ontological divide in reality between the human and the non-human realms ... to the extent that we perceive boundaries, we fall short of deep ecological consciousness" (Fox 1984, 196). The ontological boundaries of the self are extended outward, including more and more of the lifeworld in the self. Thus, this particular formulation of metaphysical holism can be correctly thought of as "expansionary" holism. According to expansionary holism, there is in reality only one big Self, the life-world. (You might have heard someone say, "the Earth is my body.")

When ontological boundaries are overcome, one realizes nature's interests are one's own interests. Devall and Sessions believe that "if we harm the rest of Nature then we are harming ourselves. There are no boundaries and everything is interrelated" (Devall and Sessions 1985, 68). John Seed, an Australian environmental activist, nicely illustrates this attitude: "'I am protecting the rain forest' develops into 'I am part of the rain forest protecting myself.' I am that part of the rain forest recently emerged into thinking ... the change is a spiritual one, thinking like a mountain, sometimes referred to as 'deep ecology'" (quoted in Devall and Sessions 1985, 199). Since the rainforest is part of him, he has the moral obligation to look after its welfare. The rainforest's well-being is indistinguishable from his well-being, so its needs become Seed's needs.

As noble as these intentions are, the project of expanding the small egoistic self to the big ecological Self is founded on untenable assumptions. For example, in the case of activist Seed, Val Plumwood has pointed out that there is nothing to guarantee that the needs of the rainforest should become Seed's needs: why should not Seed's needs become the needs of the rainforest (Plumwood 1993, 178)? Or why should not the needs of unemployed loggers become the needs of Seed and the forest? Even while acknowledging the insights of scientific ecology, the unemployed logger is likely to prioritize the need to feed and cloth his children over the need for ecosystemic integrity and stability.

There are real conflicts of interest between constituent members of larger wholes, and expansionary holism does not adequately recognize the reality of these conflicts. In the political arena, the expansionary holist is forced into the uncomfortable position of implying that anyone in disagreement does not in fact *understand* what is for their own best interest. Instead of approaching a conflict with the mien "I realize your interests are different from my interests, so here we have a real conflict of interest that we need to resolve," the expansionary holist approaches the situation, tacitly or overtly, as: "I know what your real interests are, and here we have a conflict because you don't seem to understand what those interests are." I seriously doubt anyone concerned with ecological issues would want to convey this attitude, but in practical terms, this is what expansionary holism implies.

The upshot is that metaphysical holism, as conceived in the process of self-realization, is an inadequate model for adjudicating conflicts of interest.

Friction Between Biocentric Equality and Metaphysical Holism

Notwithstanding the intractable political problems posed by expansionary-type holism, holism is in fact totally inconsistent with biocentric equality. Sadly, there is no way to realize both ideals; the distribution of equal intrinsic value to all individual organisms is indefensible in light of real ecosystemic function. Innumerable and irresolvable conflicts exist between the ability of individuals to flourish to old age, and the integrity and stability of ecosystemic wholes. The welfare of the whole entails the premature death of individuals.

The problem of feral goats (*Capra hircus*) and feral pigs (*Sus scofa*) in the Galápagos and Hawaiian Archipelagos provides clear-cut examples. The Galápagos island of Pinta was free of introduced mammals until 1959, when a fisherman set loose three goats (one male and two females) for the purpose of providing fresh meat on future trips. By 1970 the goat population on Pinta was between five and ten thousand. In that short time the effects on native flora were astonishing: four species of endemic plants were no longer found on the island (*Alternanthera flavicoma, A. nudicaulis, Gossypium baradense,* and *Ipomoea habeliana*); five species (one endemic) were substantially reduced in abundance; six species of trees and shrubs (four endemic) were absent in the heavily populated southernmost reaches (Eckhardt 1972, 588). (On Española, ten species of plants have disappeared since the arrival of goats [588]). Feral pigs not only damage vegetation, they dig up and eat the eggs of tortoises (*Geochelone elephantopus*), marine and land iguanas (*Amblyrhynchus cristatus* and *Conolophus cristatus*), and Pacific green turtles (*Chelonia mydas agassizi* [Loope et al., 1988, 276]).

In 1971 an eradication program began on Pinta, and by 1977 about forty thousand goats had been killed (Hamann 1979, 219). The last goat was eliminated in 1986 (Loope et al., 1988, 275). The goats had caused severe damage to a thick peat layer on the northern slope, soil erosion, and the permanent disappearance of some plant species (Hamann 1979, 232). Overall, though, as a direct result of eliminating goats, the flora of Pinta is showing clear signs of rapid regeneration (234).

In Hawaii feral goats and pigs cause similar ecological damage. Feral pigs, which weigh two hundred pounds or more, push over entire trees in order to rip open and eat them (Burdick 1944, 55). This not only kills the trees and causes soil erosion but creates pools of standing water in which the malarial mosquito (*Culex quinquefasciatus*) breeds (Loope et al., 1988, 276). In order to head off further damage, eradication programs for feral mammals have also been instituted in Hawaii. The eradication of goats in Hawaii Volcanoes and Haleakela National Parks includes the building of fences, organized hunts with helicopters and dogs, and releasing radio-collared goats to help locate wild flocks (Stone and Keith 1987, 277–279). In Hawaii Volcanoes National Park, around seventy thousand goats were killed between 1970 and 1970 (Loope et al., 1988, 276). Pigs are also regularly hunted and killed (Stone and Keith 1987, 279–280; Burdick 1994, 55).

The point is that in both Galápagos and Hawaii, feral goats and pigs must be killed in order to ward off the extinction of other species, species which are necessary for the overall integrity and stability of those delicate tropical island ecosystems. (In North America hunting elk and deer is often cited as an ecologically beneficial practice, because it controls overpopulation in wolf-free ranges.) In an ecosystem the flourishing of some species is incompatible with the flourishing of other species, and the flourishing of all species is also incompatible with the health of the entire ecosystem. How is the egalitarian holist going to recognize the intrinsic value and right to flourish of individual *Capra hircus* and *Ipomoea habeliana*, or *Sus scrofa* and *Geochelone elephantopus*?

It is impossible. In the last analysis, the principle of biocentric equality is inconsistent with metaphysical holism. Regard for ecosystemic wholes requires treating individuals differently, since individuals of different species have unequal ecosystemic utility (or disutility). Value differs accordingly. The inclusion of both principles of biocentric equality and metaphysical holism in an ethical theory produces a discordant friction. One principle must be abandoned.

CONCLUSION

Any ethic—including an environmental one—presupposes an ontology of selfhood. Adjudication of moral interests depends upon metaphysical and axiological assumptions about which things are selves and how much value different types of selves have.

Accordingly, the mechanistic worldview which has dominated the Modern[6] period of Western culture is founded on the presupposition that only human beings are selves, and hence only human beings have moral value. All nonhumans are insensate automata—albeit extremely complex automata. On a larger scale, Nature is one superlative mega-machine. Johannes Kepler exemplified this attitude at the beginning of the seventeenth century when he wrote: "I am much occupied with the investigation of physical causes. My aim is to show that the celestial machine is to be likened not to a divine organism but rather to a clockwork" (quoted in Oelschlaeger 1991, 77). As Kepler, Bacon, Galileo, Harvey, Hobbes, Decartes, Newton, and others believed, all corporeal bodies operate predictably according to strict casual laws; all natural phenomena can be described in terms of inert matter in motion. Nature itself is devoid of any intrinsic value or purpose.

Deep ecologists are right to excoriate the Modern view of nature, since the practical outcome of Mechanism has been the instrumentalization of nature. Organisms are biomachines, and qua machines, the only value fauna, flora, fungi, protista, prokaryotae, and inanimate matter have is use-value for humankind. In other words, the nonhuman world has only instrumental value. The more natural resources are used by humans, the more value nature has—a Lockean notion[7] which has not surprisingly become the favorite mantra of the Wise Use Movement.[8] The importance of Deep Ecology, in my estimation, is the repudiation of the mechanical view of nature and the realization that nonhumans have value above and beyond use-value for humans.

In spite of Deep Ecology's noteworthy accomplishments, I hesitate to call myself a deep ecologist, in the orthodox sense I have outlined, for four overlapping reasons. First, in reaction against our culture's radical anthropocentrism, Deep Ecology goes too far the other way in denying *any* difference in value among biota. The result is that the possibility of all ethical decision making is precluded.

Second, while it is certain that we need ideals to aim at (even if there is no chance of achieving them), I think Deep Ecology's theme of holism (namely the expansionary holism of self-realization) is overly optimistic and ignores the reality of politics. In a synthesis of all individuals to one great ecological Self, multitudinous and disparate interests magically become unified. Unfortunately the path to this utopia is foggy and dark, because it's dubious *true* interests could ever be agreed upon. In situations where conflicts of interest arise, usually individuals or groups of individuals who claim to represent "the true interests of the whole" are ridiculed as egoists and self-servers by those with opposing claims. Expansionary holism is an inadequate model for politics, and politics is an integral part of environmental ethics.

However, that political and ecological wholes are comprised of discrete entities with incompatible and competing interests does not mean that there necessarily must be more than one ethical system. Ideally, one ethical system should handle the moral considerability of all concerned organisms. As several ecophilosophers have pointed out, to be coherent, environmental ethics must not be pluralistic.[9]

Third, in order to affirm the ontological interconnectedness of human and nonhuman organisms with each other and with the nonliving environment, it is not essential to embrace the thorough-going holism of self-realization. As Richard Sylvan notes in his caustic but brilliant critique of Deep Ecology, the recognition that individuals are not absolutely discrete but interconnected does not entail the conclusion that all relations are internal and in reality no individuals exist:

> . . . it is quite unnecessary to go the full metaphysical distance to extreme holism,
> to the shocker that there are no separate things in the world, no wilderness to traverse
> or for Muir to save. A much less drastic holism suffices for these purposes. (1985, 10)

Fourth, Deep Ecology suffers from its concomitant yet incompatible themes of equality and holism. If holism is to be genuinely affirmed, egalitarianism must be forsworn. This is one of the basic tenets of J. Baird Callicott's environmental philosophy. In his words, "The land ethic manifestly does not accord equal moral worth to each and every member of the biotic community" (Callicott 1980, 327).

To sum up, the contribution of Deep Ecology to environmental philosophy is the recognition that nonhumans have intrinsic value. But a workable environmental *ethic* can be founded on neither biocentric equality nor thoroughgoing holism. To have an ethic, we need an ontology which recognizes gradations of intrinsic value between different organisms (most pointedly, between humans and nonhumans). In addition, we need an ontology which recognizes that ecosystems are wholes comprised of interconnected individual organisms with often incompatible and competing interests. The lesson is that the ontological foundation for environmental ethics must be *nonegalitarian* and *polycentric*.

Notes

1. I will use capital letters to distinguish the specific environmental philosophy, Deep Ecology, from the generic use connoting any nonhuman-centered environmental philosophy.

2. On the connections between deep ecology and scientific ecology, see Golley 1987, 45–55.

3. For a sampling of these and other connections see Devall and Sessions 1985, Chapter 6.

4. This is because *richness of experience* differs. See Fox 1984, 198. On this point Fox agrees with Whiteheadian ("organismic") environmental ethics.

5. To mark the difference, Fox now calls his theory "transpersonal ecology," Vide *Toward a transpersonal ecology*. Alan Wittbecker (1986, 261–270) also defends a "deep ecological" position, but claims his deep ecology is "anthropometric." This ambiguity of the term "deep ecology" is the sort of difficulty that curses the strategy of trying to characterize its salient features through a general gloss of the literature.

6. *Modern* refers to the period of the Western tradition beginning with the Renaissance, continuing through the Enlightenment, and extending (roughly) to the present.

7. See Locke, "Of Property," in Morgan (ed.) 1992.

8. See Baum 1991 and Knox 1990.

9. See Ferré 1996 and Callicott 1990.

References

Baum, Dan. 1991. Wise guise. *Sierra* May/June:71–93.

Burdick, Alan, 1994. It's not the only alien invader. *New York Times Magazine* Nov. 15:55.

Callicott, J., Baird. 1990. The case against moral pluralism. *Environmental Ethics* 12(1):99–124.

_____. 1980. Animal liberation: A triangular affair. *Environmental Ethics* 2(4):311–338.

Devall, Bill and George Sessions. 1985. *Deep ecology: Living as if nature mattered.* Salt Lake City: Peregrine Smith.

Eckhardt, Robert. 1972. Introduced plants and animals in the Galápagos islands. *Bioscience* 22(10).

Ferré, Frederick. 1996. Persons in nature: Toward an applicable and unified environmental ethics. *Ethics and the Environment* 1(1):15–25.

Fitzgerald, Robert (trans.). 1963. *The odyssey.* Bk. 22. New York: Anchor.

Fox, Warwick. 1990. *Toward a transpersonal ecology: Developing new foundations for environmentalism.* Boston: Shambhala.

_____. 1984. Deep ecology: A new philosophy for our time? *The Ecologist* 14(5–6)198.

Golley, Frank. 1987. Deep ecology from the perspective of ecological science. *Environmental Ethics* 9(1):44–45.

Hamann, Ole. 1979. Regeneration of vegetation on Santa Fé and Pinta Islands, Galápagos, after the eradication of goats. *Biological Conservation* 15(3).

Knox, Margaret L. 1990. The wise use guys. *Buzzworm* 2(6):30–36.

Leopold, Aldo. 1987. *A sand county almanac and sketches here and there.* New York: Oxford University Press.

Loope, Lloyd et al. 1988. Comparative conservation biology of oceanic archipelagoes: Hawaii and the Galápagos. *Bioscience* 38(4).

Morgan, Michael (ed.). 1992. *Classics of moral and political theory.* Indianapolis: Hackett.

Naess, Arne. 1984. Intuition, intrinsic value and deep ecology. *The Ecologist* 14(5–6):202.

_____. 1973. The shallow and the deep, long-range ecology movement. *Inquiry* 16:95–100.

Norton, Bryan. 1991. *Toward unity among environmentalists.* New York: Oxford University Press.

Oelschlaeger, Max. 1991. *The idea of wilderness: From prehistory to the age of ecology.* New Haven: Yale University Press.

Plumwood, Val. 1993. *Feminism and the mastery of nature.* New York: Routledge.

Sessions, George. 1979. *Spinoza, perennial philosophy and deep ecology.* Unpublished manuscript, "Reminding"—i.e., "philosophy, where are you"? conference, Dominican College, San Raphael, CA.

Stone, C. P. and J. O. Keith. 1987. Control of feral ungulates and small mammals in Hawaii National Parks: Research and management strategies. *Control of mammal pests.* C. G. J. Richards and T. Y. Ku (eds.). New York: Taylor & Francis.

Sylvan, Richard. 1985. A critique of deep ecology. Part II. *Radical Philosophy* 41(Autumn):10.

Wittbecker, Alan. 1986. Deep anthropology: Ecology and human order. *Environmental Ethics* 8(3):261–270.

William F. Baxter, *People or Penguins: The Case for Optimal Pollution*, 1974

People or Penguins
William F. Baxter

I start with the modest proposition that, in dealing with pollution, or indeed with any problem, it is helpful to know what one is attempting to accomplish. Agreement on how and whether to pursue a particular objective, such as pollution control, is not possible unless some more general objective has been identified and stated with reasonable precision. We talk loosely of having clean air and clean water, of preserving our wilderness areas, and so forth. But none of these is a sufficiently generally objective: each is more accurately viewed as a means rather than as an end.

With regard to clean air, for example, one may ask, "how clean?" and "what does clean mean?" It is even reasonable to ask, "why have clean air?" Each of these questions is an implicit demand that a more general community goal be stated—a goal sufficiently general in its scope and enjoying sufficiently general assent among the community of actors that such "why" questions no longer seem admissible with respect to that goal.

If, for example, one states as a goal the proposition that "every person should be free to do whatever he wishes in contexts where his actions do not interfere with the interests of other human beings," the speaker is unlikely to be met with a response of "why"? The goal may be criticized as uncertain in its implications or difficult to implement, but it is so basic a tenet of our civilization—it reflects a cultural value so broadly shared, at least in the abstract—that the question "why" is seen as impertinent or imponderable or both.

I do not mean to suggest that everyone would agree with the "spheres of freedom" objective just stated. Still less do I mean to suggest that a society could subscribe to four or five such general objectives that would be adequate in their coverage to serve as testing criteria by which all other disagreements might be measured. One difficulty in the attempt to construct such a list is that each new goal added will conflict, in certain applications, with each prior goal listed; and thus each goal serves as a limited qualification on prior goals.

Without any expectation of obtaining unanimous consent to them, let me set forth four goals that I generally use as ultimate testing criteria in attempting to frame solutions to problems of human organization. My position regarding pollution stems from these four criteria. If the criteria appeal to you and any part of what appears hereafter does not, our disagreement will have a helpful focus: Which of us is correct, analytically, in supposing that his position on pollution would better serve these general goals? If the criteria do not seem acceptable to you, then it is to be expected that our more particular judgments will differ, and the task will then be yours to identify the basic set of criteria upon which your particular judgments rest.

My criteria are as follows:

1. The spheres of freedom criterion stated above.

2. Waste is a bad thing. The dominant feature of human existence is scarcity—our available resources, our aggregate labors, and our skill in employing both have always been, and will continue for some time to be, inadequate to yield to every man all the tangible and intangible satisfactions he would like to have. Hence, none of those resources, or labors, or skills, should be wasted—that is, employed so as to yield less than they might yield in human satisfactions.

3. Every human being should be regarded as an end rather than as a means to be used for the betterment of another. Each should be afforded dignity and regarded as having an absolute claim to an evenhanded application of such rules as the community may adopt for its governance.

4. Both the incentive and the opportunity to improve his share of satisfactions should be preserved to every individual. Preservation of incentive is dictated by the "no-waste" criterion and enjoins against the continuous, totally egalitarian redistribution of satisfactions, or wealth; but subject to that constraint, everyone should receive, by continuous redistribution if necessary, some minimal share of aggregate wealth so as to avoid a level of privation from which the opportunity to improve his situation become illusory.

The relationship of these highly general goals to the more specific environmental issues at hand may not be readily apparent, and I am not yet ready to demonstrate their pervasive implications. But let me give one indication of their implications. Recently scientists have informed us that use of DDT in food production is causing damage to the penguin population. For the present purposes let us accept that assertion as an indisputable scientific fact. The scientific fact is often asserted as if the correct implication—that we must stop agricultural use of DDT—followed from the mere statement of the fact of penguin damage. But plainly it does not follow if my criteria are employed.

My criteria are oriented to people, not penguins. Damage to penguins, or sugar pines, or geological marvels is, without more, simply irrelevant. One must go further, by my criteria, and say: Penguins are important because people enjoy seeing them walk about rocks; and furthermore, the well-being of people would be less impaired by halting use of DDT than by giving up penguins. In short, my observations about environmental problems will be people-oriented, as are my criteria. I have no interest in preserving penguins for their own sake.

It may be said by way of objection to this position, that it is very selfish of people to act as if each person represented one unit of importance and nothing else was of any importance. It is undeniably selfish. Nevertheless I think it is the only tenable starting place for analysis for several reasons. First, no other position corresponds to the way most people really think and act—i.e., corresponds to reality.

Second, this attitude does not portend any massive destructive of nonhuman flora and fauna, for people depend on them in many obvious ways, and they will be preserved because and to the degree that humans do depend on them.

Third, what is good for humans is, in many respects, good for penguins and pine trees—clean air for example. So that humans are, in these respects, surrogates for plant and animal life.

Fourth, I do not know how we could administer any other system. Our decisions are either private or collective. Insofar as Mr. Jones is free to act privately, he may give such preferences as he wishes to other forms of life: he may feed birds in winter and do with less himself, and he may even decline to resist an advancing polar bear on the ground that the bear's appetite is more important than those portions of himself that the bear may choose to eat. In short my basic premise does not rule out private altruism to competing life-forms. It does rule out, however, Mr. Jones' inclination to feed Mr. Smith to the bear, however hungry the bear, however despicable Mr. Smith.

Insofar as we act collectively on the other hand, only humans can be afforded an opportunity to participate in the collective decisions. Penguins cannot vote now and are unlikely subjects for the franchise—pine trees more unlikely still. Again each individual is free to cast his vote so as to benefit sugar pines if that is his inclination. But many of the more extreme assertions that one hears from some conservationists amount to tacit assertions that they are specifically appointed representatives of sugar pines, and hence that their preferences should be weighted more heavily than the preferences of other humans who do not enjoy equal rapport with "nature." The simplistic assertion that agricultural use of DDT must stop at once because it is harmful to penguins is of that type.

Fifth, if polar bears or pine trees or penguins, like men, are to be regarded as ends rather than means, if they are to count in our calculus of social organization, someone must tell me how much each one counts, and someone must tell me how these life-forms are to be permitted to express their preferences, for I do not know either answer. If the answer is that certain people are to hold their proxies, then I want to know how those proxyholders are to be selected: self-appointment does not seem workable to me.

Sixth, and by way of summary of all the foregoing, let me point out that the set of environmental issues under discussion—although they raise very complex technical questions of how to achieve any objective—ultimately raise a normative question: what ought we to do. Questions of ought are unique to the human mind and world—they are meaningless as applied to a nonhuman situation.

I reject the proposition that we ought to respect the "balance of nature" or to "preserve the environment" unless the reason for doing so, express or implied, is the benefit of man.

I reject the idea that there is a "right" or "morally correct" state of nature to which we should return. The word "nature" has no normative connotation. Was it "right" or "wrong" for the earth's crust to heave in contortion and create mountains and seas? Was it "right" for the first amphibian to crawl up out of the primordial ooze? Was it "wrong" for plants to reproduce themselves and alter the atmospheric composition in favor of oxygen? For animals to alter the atmosphere in favor of carbon dioxide both by breathing oxygen and eating plants? No answers can be given to these questions because they are meaningless questions.

All this may seem obvious to the point of being tedious, but much of the present controversy over environment and pollution rests on tacit normative assumptions about just such nonnormative phenomena: that it is "wrong" to impair penguins with DDT, but not to slaughter cattle for prime rib roasts. That it is wrong to kill stands of sugar pines with industrial fumes, but not to cut sugar pines and build housing for the poor. Every man is entitled to his own preferred definition of Walden Pond, but there is no definition that has any moral superiority over another, except by reference to the selfish needs of the human race.

From the fact that there is no normative definition of the natural state, it follows that there is no normative definition of clean air or pure water—hence no definition of polluted air—or of pollution—except by reference to the needs of man. The "right" composition of the atmosphere is one which has some dust in it and some lead in it and some hydrogen sulfide in it—just those amounts that attend a sensibly organized society thoughtfully and knowledgeably pursuing the greatest possible satisfaction for its human members.

The first and most fundamental step toward solution of our environmental problems is a clear recognition that our objective is not pure air or water but rather some optimal state of pollution. That step immediately suggests the question: How do we define and attain the level of pollution that will yield the maximum possible amount of human satisfaction?

Low levels of pollution contribute to human satisfaction but so do food and shelter and education and music. To attain ever lower levels of pollution, we must pay the cost of having less of these other things. I contrast that view of the cost of pollution control with the more popular statement that pollution control will "cost" very large numbers of dollars. The popular statement is true in some senses, false in others; sorting out the true and false senses is of some importance. The first step in that sorting process is to achieve a clear understanding of the difference between dollars and resources. Resources are the wealth of our nation; dollars are merely claim checks upon those resources. Resources are of vital importance; dollars are comparatively trivial.

Four categories of resources are sufficient for our purposes: At any given time a nation, or a planet if you prefer, has a stock of labor, of technological skill, of capital goods, and of natural resources (such as mineral deposits, timber, water, land, etc.). These resources can be used in various combinations to yield goods and services of all kinds—in some limited quantity. The quantity will be larger if they are combined efficiently, smaller if combined inefficiently. But in either event the resource stock is limited, the goods and services that they can be made to yield are limited; even the most efficient use of them will yield less than our population, in the aggregate, would like to have.

If one considers building a new dam, it is appropriate to say that it will be costly in the sense that it will require x hours of labor, y tons of steel and concrete, and z amount of capital goods. If these resources are devoted to the dam, then they cannot be used to build hospitals, fishing rods, schools, or electric can openers. That is the meaningful sense in which the dam is costly.

Quite apart from the very important question of how wisely we can combine our resources to produce goods and services, is the very different question of how they get distributed—who gets how many goods? Dollars constitute the claim checks which are distributed among people and which control their share of national output. Dollars are nearly valueless pieces of paper except to the extent that they do represent claim checks to some fraction of the output of goods and services. Viewed as claim checks, all the dollars outstanding during any period of time are worth, in the aggregate, the goods and services that are available to be claimed with them during that period—neither more nor less.

It is far easier to increase the supply of dollars than to increase the production of goods and services—printing dollars is easy. But printing more dollars doesn't help because each dollar then simply becomes a claim to fewer goods, i.e., becomes worth less.

The point is this: many people fall into error upon hearing the statement that the decision to build a dam, or to clean up a river, will cost $X million. It is regrettably easy to say: "It's only money. This is a wealthy country, and we have lots of money." But you cannot build a dam or clean a river with $X million—unless you also have a match, you can't even make a fire. One builds a dam or cleans a river by diverting labor and steel and trucks and factories from making one kind of goods to make another. The cost in dollars is merely a shorthand way of describing the extent of the diversion necessary. If we build a dam for $X million, then we must recognize that we will have $X million less housing and food and medical care and electric can openers as a result.

Similarly, the costs of controlling pollution are best expressed in terms of the other goods we will have to give up to do the job. This is not to say the job should not be done. Badly as we need more housing, more medical care, and more can openers, and more symphony orchestras, we could do with somewhat less of them, in my judgment at least, in exchange for somewhat cleaner air and rivers. But that is the nature of the trade-off, and analysis of the problem is advanced if the unpleasant reality is kept in mind. Once the trade-off relationship is clearly perceived, it is possible to state in a very general way what the optimal level of pollution is. I would state it as follows:

People enjoy watching penguins. They enjoy relatively clean air and smog-free vistas. Their health is improved by relatively clean water and air. Each of these benefits is a type of good or service. As a society we would be well advised to give up one washing machine if the resources that would have gone into that washing machine can yield greater human satisfaction when diverted into pollution control. We should give up one hospital if the resources thereby freed would yield more human satisfaction when devoted to elimination of noise in our cities. And so on, trade-off by trade-off, we should divert our productive capacities from the production of existing goods and services to the production of a cleaner, quieter, more pastoral nation up to—and no further than—the point at which we value more highly the next washing machine or hospital that we would have to do without than we value the next unit of environmental improvement that the diverted resources would create.

Now this proposition seems to me unassailable but so general and abstract as to be unhelpful—at least unadministerable in the form stated. It assumes we can measure in some way the incremental units of human satisfaction yielded by very different types of goods. The proposition must remain a pious abstraction until I can explain how this measurement process can occur. But I insist that the proposition stated describes the result for which we should be striving—and again, that it is always useful to know what your target is even if your weapons are too crude to score a bull's eye.

Karen J. Warren, "The Power and the Promise of Ecological Feminism" in *Environmental Ethics*, Vol. 12, No. 2, 1990

The Power and the Promise of Ecological Feminism
Karen J. Warren

INTRODUCTION

Ecological feminism (ecofeminism) has begun to receive a fair amount of attention lately as an alternative feminism and environmental ethic.[1] Since Francoise d'Eaubonne introduced the term *ecofeminism* in 1974 to bring attention to women's potential for bringing about an ecological revolution,[2] the term has been used in a variety of ways. As I use the term in this paper, ecological feminism is the position that there are important connections—historical, experiential, symbolic, theoretical—between the domination of women and the domination of nature, an understanding of which is critical to both feminism and environmental ethics. I argue that the promise and power of ecological feminism is that *it provides a distinctive framework both for reconcieving feminism and for developing an environmental ethic which take seriously connections between the domination of women and the domination of nature.* I do so by discussing the nature of a feminist ethic and the ways in which ecofeminism provides a feminist and environmental ethic. I conclude that any feminist theory *and* any environmental ethic which fails to take seriously the twin and interconnected dominations of women and nature is at best incomplete and at worst simply inadequate.

FEMINISM, ECOLOGICAL FEMINISM, AND CONCEPTUAL FRAMEWORKS

Whatever else it is, feminism is at least the movement to end sexist oppression. It involves the elimination of any and all factors that contribute to the continued and systematic domination or subordination of women. While feminists disagree about the nature of and solutions to the subordination of women, all feminists agree that sexist oppression exists, is wrong, and must be abolished.

A "feminist issue" is any issue that contributes in some way to understanding the oppression of women. Equal rights, comparable pay for comparable work, and food production are feminist issues wherever and whenever an understanding of them contributes to an understanding of the continued exploitation or subjugation of women. Carrying water and searching for firewood are feminist issues whenever and whenever women's primary responsibility for these tasks contributes to their lack of full participation in decision making, income producing, or high status positions engaged in by men. What counts as a feminist issue, then, depends largely on context, particularly the historical and material conditions of women's lives.

Environmental degradation and exploitation are feminist issues because an understanding of them contributes to an understanding of the oppression of women. In India, for example, both deforestation and reforestation through the introduction of a monoculture species tree (e.g., eucalyptus) intended for commercial production are feminist issues because the loss of indigenous forests and multiple species of trees has drastically affected rural Indian women's ability to maintain a subsistence household. Indigenous forests provide a variety of trees for food, fuel, fodder, household utensils, dyes, medicines, and income-generating uses, while monoculture-species forests do not.[3] Although I do not argue for this claim here, a look at the global impact of environmental degradation on women's lives suggests important respects in which environmental degradation is a feminist issue.

Feminist philosophers claim that some of the most important feminists issues are *conceptual* ones: these issues concern how one conceptualizes such mainstay philosophical notions as reason and rationality, ethics, and what it is to be human. Ecofeminists extend this feminist philosophical concern to nature. They argue that, ultimately, some of the most important connections between the domination of women and the domination of nature are conceptual. To see this, consider the nature of conceptual frameworks.

A *conceptual framework* is a set of *basic* beliefs, values, attitudes, and assumptions which shape and reflect how one views oneself and one's world. It is a socially constructed lens through which we perceive ourselves and others. It is affected by such factors as gender, race, class, age, affectional orientation, nationality, and religious background.

Some conceptual frameworks are oppressive. An *oppressive conceptual framework* is one that explains, justifies, and maintains relationships of domination and subordination. When an oppressive conceptual framework is *patriarchal,* it explains, justifies, and maintains the subordination of women by men.

I have argued elsewhere that there are three significant features of oppressive conceptual frameworks: (1) value-hierarchical thinking, i.e., "up-down" thinking which places higher value, status, or prestige on what is "up" rather than on what is "down"; (2) value dualisms, i.e., disjunctive pairs in which the disjuncts are seen as oppositional (rather than as complementary) and exclusive (rather than as inclusive), and which place higher value (status, prestige) on one disjunct rather than the other (e.g., dualisms which give higher value or status to that which has historically been identified as "mind," "reason," and "male" than to that which has historically been identified as "body," "emotion," and "female"); and (3) logic of domination, i.e., a structure of argumentation which leads to a justification of subordination.[4]

The third feature of oppressive conceptual frameworks is the most significant. A logic of domination is not *just* a logical structure. It also involves a substantive value system, since an ethical premise is needed to permit or sanction the "just" subordination of that which is subordinate. This justification typically is given on grounds of some alleged characteristic (e.g., rationality) which the dominant (e.g., men) have and the subordinate (e.g., women) lack.

Contrary to what many feminists and ecofeminists have said or suggested, there may be nothing *inherently* problematic about "hierarchical thinking" or even "value-hierarchical thinking" in contexts other than contexts of oppression. Hierarchical thinking is important in daily living for classifying data, comparing information, and organizing material. Taxonomies (e.g., plant taxonomies) and biological nomenclatures seem to require *some* form of "hierarchical thinking." Even "value-hierarchical thinking" may be quite acceptable in certain contexts. (The same may be said of "value dualisms" in non-oppressive contexts.) For example, suppose it is true that what is unique about humans is our conscious capacity to radically reshape our social environments (or "societies"), as Murray Bookchin suggests.[5] Then one could truthfully say that humans are better equipped to radically reshape their environments than are rocks or plants—a "value-hierarchical" way of speaking.

The problem is not simply *that* value-hierarchical thinking and value dualisms are used, but *the way* in which each has been used *in oppressive conceptual frameworks* to establish inferiority and to justify subordination.[6] It is the logic of domination, *coupled with* value-hierarchical thinking and value dualisms, which "justifies" subordination. What is explanatorily basic, then, about the nature of oppressive conceptual frameworks is the logic of domination.

For ecofeminism, that a logic of domination is explanatorily basic is important for at least three reasons. First, without a logic of domination, a description of similarities an differences would be just that—a description of similarities and differences would be just that—a description of similarities and differences. Consider the claim "Humans are different from plants and rocks in that humans can (and plants and rocks cannot) consciously and radically reshape the communities in which they live; humans are similar to plants and rocks in that they are both members of an ecological community." Even if humans are "better" than plants and rocks with respect to the conscious ability of humans to radically transform communities, one does not *thereby* get any *morally* relevant distinction between humans and nonhumans, or an argument for the domination of plants and rocks by humans. To get *those* conclusions one needs to add at least two powerful assumptions, viz., (A2) and (A4) in argument A below:

(A1) humans do, and plants and rocks do not, have the capacity to consciously and radically change the community in which they live.

(A2) Whatever has the capacity to consciously and radically change the community in which it lives is morally superior to whatever lacks this capacity.

(A3) Thus, humans are morally superior to plants and rocks.

(A4) For any X and Y, if X is morally superior to Y, then X is morally justified in subordinating Y.

(A5) Thus, humans are morally justified in subordinating plants and rocks.

Without the two assumptions that *humans are morally superior* to (at least some) nonhumans, (A2), and that *superiority justifies subordination,* (A4), all one has is some difference between humans and some nonhumans. This is true *even if* that difference is given in terms of superiority. Thus, it is the logic of domination, (A4), which is the bottom line in ecofeminist discussions of oppression.

Second, ecofeminists argue that, at least in Western societies, the oppressive conceptual framework which sanctions the twin dominations of women and nature is a patriarchal one characterized by all three features of an oppressive conceptual framework. Many ecofeminists claim that, historically, within at least the dominant Western culture, a patriarchal conceptual framework has sanctioned the following argument B:

(B1) Women are identified with nature and the realm of the physical; men are identified with the "human" and the realm of the mental.

(B2) Whatever is identified with nature and the realm of the physical is inferior to ("below") whatever is identified with the "human" and the realm of the mental; or, conversely, the latter is superior to ("above") the former.

(B3) Thus, women are inferior to ("below") men; or, conversely, men are superior to ("above") women.

(B4) For any X and Y, if X is superior to Y, then X is justified in subordinating Y.

(B5) Thus, men are justified in subordinating women.

If sound, argument B establishes *patriarchy*, i.e., the conclusion given at (B5) that the systematic domination of women by men is justified. But according to ecofeminists, (B5) is justified by just those three features of an oppressive conceptual framework identified earlier: value-hierarchical thinking, the assumption at (B2); value dualisms, the assumed dualism of the mental and the physical at (B1) and the assumed inferiority of the physical vis-a-vis the mental at (B2); and the logic of domination, the assumption at (B4), the same as the previous premise (A4). Hence, according to ecofeminists, insofar as an oppressive patriarchal conceptual framework has functioned historically (within at least dominant Western culture) to sanction the twin dominations of women and nature (argument B), both argument B and the patriarchal conceptual framework, from whence it comes, ought to be rejected.

Of course, the preceding does not identify which premises of B are false. What is the status of premises (B1) and (B2)? Most, if not all, feminists claim that (B1), and many ecofeminists claim that (B2), have been assumed or asserted within the dominant Western philosophical and intellectual tradition.[7] As such, these feminists assert, as a matter of historical fact, that the dominant Western philosophical tradition has assumed the truth of (B1) and (B2). Ecofeminists, however, either deny (B2) or do not affirm (B2). Furthermore, because some ecofeminists are anxious to deny any ahistorical identification of women with nature, some ecofeminists deny (B1) when (B1) is used to support anything other than a strictly historical claim about what has been asserted or assumed to be true within patriarchal culture—e.g., when (B1) is used to assert that women properly are identified with the realm of nature and the physical.[8] Thus, from an ecofeminist perspective, (B1) and (B2) are properly viewed as problematic though historically sanctioned claims: they are problematic precisely because of the way they have functioned historically in a patriarchal conceptual framework and culture to sanction the dominations of women and nature.

What *all* ecofeminists agree about, then, is the way in which *the logic of domination* has functioned historically within patriarchy to sustain and justify the twin dominations of women and nature.[9] Since *all* feminists (and not just ecofeminists) oppose patriarchy, the conclusion given at (B5), all feminists (including ecofeminists) must oppose at least the logic of domination, premise (B4), on which argument B rests—whatever the truth-value status of (B1) and (B2) *outside of* a patriarchal context.

That *all* feminists must oppose the logic of domination shows the breadth and depth of the ecofeminist critique of B: it is a critique not only of the three assumptions on which this argument for the domination of women and nature rests, viz., the assumptions at (B1), (B2), and (B4); it is also a critique of patriarchal conceptual frameworks generally, i.e., of those oppressive conceptual frameworks which put men "up" and women "down," allege some way in which women are morally inferior to men, and use that alleged difference to justify the subordination of women by men. Therefore, ecofeminism is necessary to *any* feminist critique of patriarchy, and, hence, necessary to feminism (a point I discuss again later).

Third, ecofeminism clarifies why the logic of domination, and any conceptual framework which gives rise to it, must be abolished in order both to make possible a meaningful notion of difference which does not breed domination and to prevent feminism from becoming a "support" movement based primarily on shared experiences. In contemporary society, there is no one "woman's voice," no *woman* (or *human*) *simpliciter*: every woman (or human) is a woman (or human) of some race, class, age, affectional orientation, marital status, regional or national background, and so forth. Because there are no "monolithic experiences" that all women share, feminism must be a "solidarity movement" based on shared beliefs and interests rather than a "unity in sameness" movement based on shared experiences and shared victimization.[10] In the words of Maria Lugones, "Unity—not to be confused with solidarity— is understood as conceptually tied to domination."[11]

Ecofeminists insist that the sort of logic of domination used to justify the domination of humans by gender, racial or ethnic, or class status is also used to justify the domination of nature. Because eliminating a logic of domination is part of a feminist critique—whether a critique of patriarchy, white supremacist culture, or imperialism—ecofeminists insist that *naturism* is properly viewed as an integral part of any feminist solidarity movement to end sexist oppression and the logic of domination which conceptually grounds it. . . .

An ecofeminist ethic involves a reconception of what it means to be human, and in what human ethical behavior consists. Ecofeminism denies abstract individualism. Humans are who we are in large part by virtue of the historical and social contexts and the relationships we are in, including our relationships with nonhuman nature. Relationships are not something extrinsic to who we are, not an "add on" feature of human nature; they play an essential role in shaping what it is to be human. Relationships of humans to the nonhuman environment are, in part, constitutive of what it is to be a human.

By making visible the interconnections among the dominations of women and nature, ecofeminism shows that both are feminist issues and that explicit acknowledgment of both is vital to any responsible environmental ethic. Feminism *must* embrace ecological feminism if it is to end the domination of women because the domination of women is tied conceptually and historically to the domination of nature.

A responsible environmental ethic also *must* embrace feminism. Otherwise, even the seemingly most revolutionary, liberational, and holistic ecological ethic will fail to take seriously the interconnected dominations of nature and women that are so much a part of the historical legacy and conceptual framework that sanctions the exploitation of nonhuman nature. Failure to make visible these interconnected, twin dominations results in an inaccurate account of how it is that nature has been and continues to be dominated and exploited and produces an environmental ethic that lacks the depth necessary to be truly *inclusive* of the realities of persons who at least in dominant Western culture have been intimately tied with that exploitation, viz., women. Whatever else can be said in favor of such holistic ethics, a failure to make visible ecofeminist insights into the common denominators of the twin oppressions of women and nature is to perpetuate, rather than overcome, the source of that oppression.

The last point deserves further attention. It may be objected that as long as the end result is "the same"—the development of an environmental ethic which does not emerge out of or reinforce an oppressive conceptual framework—it does not matter whether that ethic (or the ethic endorsed in getting there) is feminist or not. Hence, it simply is *not* the case that any adequate environmental ethic must be feminist. My argument, in contrast, has been that it *does* matter, and for three important reasons. First, there is the scholarly issue of accurately representing historical reality, and that, ecofeminists claim, requires acknowledging the historical feminization of nature and naturalization of women as part of the exploitation of nature. Second, . . . the conceptual connections between the domination of women and the domination of nature are located in an oppressive and, at least in Western societies, patriarchal conceptual framework characterized by a logic of domination. Thus, . . . the failure to notice the nature of this connection leaves at best an incomplete, inaccurate, and partial account of what is required of a conceptually adequate environmental ethic. An ethic which *does not* acknowledge this is simply *not* the same as one that does, whatever else the similarities between them. Third, the claim that, in contemporary culture, one can have an adequate environmental ethic which is *not* feminist assumes that, in contemporary culture, the label *feminist* does not add anything crucial to the nature or description of environmental ethics. I have shown that at least in contemporary culture this is false, for the word *feminist* currently helps to clarify just *how* the domination of nature is conceptually linked to patriarchy and, hence, how the liberation of nature, is conceptually linked to the termination of patriarchy. Thus, because it has critical bite in contemporary culture, it serves as an important reminder that in contemporary sex-gendered, raced, classed, and naturist culture, an unlabeled position functions as a privileged and "unmarked" position. That is, without the addition of the word *feminist*, one presents environmental ethics as if it has no bias, including male-gender bias, which is just what ecofeminists deny: failure to notice the connections between the twin oppressions of women and nature *is* male-gender bias.

One of the goals of feminism is the eradication of all oppressive sex-gender (and related race, class, age, affectional preference) categories and the creation of a world in which *difference does not breed domination*—say, the world of 4001. If in 4001 an "adequate environmental ethic" is a "feminist environmental ethic," the word *feminist* may then be redundant and unnecessary. However, this is *not* 4001, and in terms of the current historical and conceptual reality the dominations of nature and of women are intimately connected. failure to notice or make visible that connection in 1990 perpetuates the mistaken and privileged) view that "environmental ethics" is *not* a feminist issue, and that *feminist* adds nothing to environmental ethics.[12]

CONCLUSION

I have argued in this paper that ecofeminism provides a framework for a distinctively feminist and environmental ethic. Ecofeminism grows out of the felt and theorized about connections between the domination of women and the domination of nature. As a contextualist ethic, ecofeminism refocuses environmental ethics on what nature might mean, morally speaking, *for* humans, and on how the relational attitudes of humans to others—humans as well as nonhumans—sculpt both what it is to be human and the nature and ground of human responsibilities to the nonhuman environment. part of what this refocusing does is to take seriously the voices of women and other oppressed persons in the construction of that ethic. . . .

Notes

1. Explicit ecological feminist literature includes works from a variety of scholarly perspectives and sources. Some of these works are Leonie Caldecott and Stephanie Leland, eds., *Reclaim the Earth: Women Speak Out for Life on Earth* (London: The Women's Press, 1983); Jim Cheney, "Eco-Feminism and Deep Ecology," *Environmental Ethics* 9 (1987): 115–45; Andree Collard with Joyce Contrucci, *Rape of the Wild: Man's Violence against Animals and the Earth* (Bloomington: Indiana University Press, 1988); Katherine Davies, "Historical Associations: Women and the Natural World," *Women & Environments* 9, no. 2 (Spring 1987): 46; Sharon Doubiago, "Deeper than Deep Ecology: Men Must Become Feminist," in *The New Catalyst Quarterly,* no. 10 (Winter 1987/88): 10–11; Brian Easlea, *Science and Sexual Oppression: Patriarchy's Confrontation with Women and Nature* (London: Weidenfeld & Nicholson, 1981); Elizabeth Dodson Gray, *Green Paradise Lost* (Wellesley, Mass.: Roundtable Press, 1979); Susan Griffin, *Women and Nature: The Roaring Inside Her* (San Francisco: Harper and Row, 1978); Joan L. Griscom, "On Healing the Nature/History Split in Feminist Thought," in *Heresies #13: Feminism and Ecology* 4, no. 1 (1980): 49; Ynestra King, "The Ecology of Feminism and the Feminism of Ecology," in *Healing Our Wounds: The Power of Ecological Feminism,* ed. Judith Plant (Boston: New Society Publishers, 1989), pp. 1828, "The Eco-feminist Imperative" in *Reclaim the Earth,* ed. Caldecott and Leland (London: The Women's Press, 1983), p. 1216, "Feminism and the Revolt of Nature," in *Heresies #13: Feminism and Ecology* 4, no. 1 (1981): 216 and "What is Ecofeminism?" *The Nation,* 12 December 1987; Marti Kheel, "Animal Liberation Is a Feminist Issue," *The New Catalyst Quarterly,* no. 10 (Winter 198788): 89; Carolyn Merchant, *The Death of Nature: Women, Ecology and the Scientific Revolution* (San Francisco, Harper and Row, 1980); Patrick Murphy, ed., "Feminism Ecology, and the Future of the Humanities," special issue of *Studies in the Humanities* 15, no. 2 (December 1988); Abby Peterson and Carolyn Merchant, "Peace with the Earth: Women and the Environmental Movement in Sweden," *Women's Studies International Forum* 9, no. 56 (1986): 465–79; Judith Plant, "Searching for Common Ground: Ecofeminism and Bioregionalism," in *The New Catalyst Quarterly* no. 10 (Winter 1987/88): 67; Judith Plant, ed., *Healing Our Wounds: The Power of Ecological Feminism* (Boston: New Society Publishers, 1989); Val Plumwood, "Ecofeminism: An Overview and Discussion of Positions and Arguments," *Australasian Journal of Philosophy,* Supplement to vol. 64 (June 1986): 120–37; Rosemary Radford Ruether, *New Woman? New Earth: Sexist Ideologies & Human Liberation* (New York: Seabury Press, 1975); Kirkpatrick Sale, "Ecofeminism—A New Perspective," *The Nation,* 26 September 1987: 302–05; Ariel Kay Salleh, "Deeper than Deep Ecology: The Eco-Feminist Connection," *Environmental Ethics* 6 (1984): 33945, and "Epistemology and the Metaphors of Production: An Eco-Feminist Reading of Critical Theory," in *Studies in the Humanities* 15 (1988): 13039; Vandana Shiva, *Staying Alive: Women, Ecology and Development* (London: Zed Books, 1988); Charlene Spretnak, "Ecofeminism: Our Roots and Flowering," *The Elmswood Newsletter,* Winter Solstice 1988; Karen J. Warren, "Feminism and Ecology: Making Connections," *Environmental Ethics* 9 (1987): 321: "Toward an Ecofeminist Ethic," *Studies in the Humanities* 15 (1988): 140–156; Miriam Wyman, "Explorations of Ecofeminism," *Women & Environments* (Spring 1987): 67; Iris Young, "Feminism and Ecology" and "Women and Life on Earth: Eco-Feminism in the 80's" *Environmental Ethics* 5 (1983): 173–80; Michael Zimmerman, "Feminism, Deep Ecology, and Environmental Ethics," *Environmental Ethics* 9 (1987): 21–44.

2. Francoise d'Eauhonne, *Le Feminisme ou la Mort* (Paris: Pierre Horay, 1974), pp. 213–52.

3. I discuss this in my paper, "Toward an Ecofeminist Ethic."

4. The account offered here is a revision of the account given earlier in my paper "Feminism and Ecology: Making Connections." I have changed the account to be about "oppressive" rather than strictly "patriarchal" conceptual frameworks in order to leave open the possibility that there may be some patriarchal conceptual frameworks (e.g., in non-Western cultures) which are *not* properly characterized as based on value dualisms.

5. Murray Bookchin, "Social Ecology versus Deep Ecology," in *Green Perspectives: Newsletter of the Green Program Project*, no. 45 (Summer 1987): 9.

6. It may be that in contemporary Western society, which is so thoroughly structured by categories of gender, race, class, age, and affectional orientation, that there simply is no meaningful notion of "value-hierarchical thinking" which does not function in an oppressive context. For purposes of this paper, I leave that question open.

7. Many feminists who argue for the historical point that claims (B1) and (B2) have been asserted or assumed to be true within the dominant Western philosophical tradition do so by discussion of that tradition's conceptions of reason, rationality, and science. For a sampling of the sorts of claims made within that context, see "Reason, Rationality, and Gender," ed. Nancy Tuana and Karen J. Warren, a special issue of the American Philosophical Association's *Newsletter on Feminism and Philosophy* 88, no. 2 (March 1989): 1771. Ecofeminists who claim that (B2) has been assumed to be true within the dominant Western philosophical tradition include: Gray, *Green Paradise Lost*; Griffin, *Woman and Nature: The Roaring Inside Her*; Merchant, *The Death of Nature*; Ruether, *New Woman/New Earth*. For a discussion of some of these ecofeminist historical accounts, see Plumwood, "Ecofeminism." While I agree that the historical connections between the domination of women and the domination of nature is a crucial one, I do not argue for that claim here.

8. Ecofeminists who deny (B1) when (B1) is offered as anything other than a true, descriptive, historical claim about patriarchal culture often do so on grounds that an objectionable sort of biological determinism, or at least harmful female sex-gender stereotypes, underlie (B1). For a discussion of this "split" among those ecofeminists ("nature feminists") who assert and those ecofeminists ("social feminists") who deny (B1) as anything other than a true historical claim about how women are described in patriarchal culture, see Griscom, "On Healing the Nature/History Split."

9. I make no attempt here to defend the historically sanctioned truth of these premises.

10. See, e.g., Bell Hooks, *Feminist Theory: From Margin to Center* (Boston: South End Press, 1984), pp. 5152.

11. Maria Lugones, "Playfulness," "World-Travelling," and "Loving Perception," *Hypatia* 2. no. 2 (Summer 1987): 3.

12. I offer the same sort of reply to critics of ecofeminism such as Warwick Fox who suggest that for the sort of ecofeminism I defend, the word *feminist* does not add anything significant to environmental ethics and, consequently, that an ecofeminist like myself might as well call herself a deep ecologist. He asks: "Why doesn't she just call it [i.e. Warren's vision of a transformative feminism] deep ecology? Why specifically attach the label *feminist* to it . . . ?" (Warwick Fox, "The Deep Ecology-Ecofeminism Debate and Its Parallels," *Environmental Ethics* 11, no. 1 [1989]: 14, n. 22). Whatever the important similarities between deep ecology and ecofeminism (or, specifically, my version of ecofeminism)—and, indeed, there are many—it is precisely my point here that the word *feminist* does add something significant to the conception of environmental ethics, and that any environmental ethic (including deep ecology) that fails to make explicit the different kinds of interconnections among the domination of nature and the domination of women will be, from a feminist (and ecofeminist) perspective such as mine, inadequate.

Part Three

LITERARY TREATMENTS

A.J. Cronin, *Adventures in Two Worlds*, 1952

"Doctor, I can't . . . I won't have a child."
A. J. Cronin

"Doctor, I can't . . . I won't have a child."

It was four o'clock in the afternoon, the hour of my "best" consultations, and the woman who spoke so vehemently was tall, distinguished, and handsome, fashionably dressed in a dark grey costume, with an expensive diamond clip in her smart black hat.

I had just examined her, and now, having dried my hands methodically, I put away the towel and turned toward her. "It's a little late to make that decision now. You should have thought of it two months ago. You are exactly nine weeks pregnant. Your baby will be born toward the middle of July

"I won't have it. . . . You've got to help me, Doctor. You simply must."

How often had I heard these words before. I had heard them from frightened little shopgirls in trouble; from a shamed spinster, aged thirty-five, who told me in a trembling voice, exactly like the heroine of the old-time melodrama, that she had been "betrayed"; from a famous film actress defiantly resolved that her career should not be ruined; above all had I heard them from selfish and neurotic wives, afraid of the pangs of childbirth, afraid of losing their figure, their health, their life, afraid—most specious pretext of all—of "losing their husband's love."

This case was somewhat different. I knew my patient, Beatrice Glendenning, socially; knew also her husband, Henry, and her two grown-up sons. They were wealthy people, with a town house in Knightsbridge and a large estate in Hampshire, where the pheasant shooting was excellent and where, indeed, I had spent several pleasant weekends.

"You understand . . . , it isn't just money, Doctor . . . I must get out of this business, and to do so I'll give anything." She looked me full in the face.

There was no mistaking her meaning. Indeed, that same offer, indescribable in its implications, had been made to me before, though perhaps never so blatantly. It had been made by a young French modiste, estranged from her husband, who had compromised herself with another man and who, slim, elegant, and bewitching, with affected tears in her beautiful eyes, leaned forward and tried to take my hands in hers.

Doctors are only human, they have the same difficulty in repressing their instincts as other men. Yet, if not for moral reasons, from motives of sheer common sense, I had never lost my head. Once a doctor embarks upon a career as abortionist he is irretrievably lost.

There were, however, many such illicit practitioners in the vicinity, both men and women, plying their perilous undercover trade at exorbitant rates, until one day, inevitably, the death of some wretched girl brought them exposure, ruin, and a long term of imprisonment. Perhaps desperation blinded such patients as came to me, yet it always struck me as amazing how few of them were conscious of the infinite danger involved in illegal abortion. Under the best hospital conditions the operation holds a definite risk. Performed hastily in some backstairs room with a septic instrument by some brutal or unskilled practitioner, the result almost inevitably is severe hemorrhage, followed by infection and acute peritonitis.

There were others, too, among these women who believed it was within my power to relieve them of their incubus by such a simple expedient as an ergot pill or a mixture of jalap and senna. Others, too, who confessed to having tried the weirdest expedients, from boiling-hot baths to such eccentric gymnastics as descending the stairs backward, in a crouching position. Poor creatures, some were almost comic in their distress, and there were among them many who needed sympathy and comfort. This they got from me, with much good advice, but nothing more.

Beatrice Glendenning, however, was neither comic nor ignorant, but a strong-minded, intelligent woman of the world who moved with considerable éclat in the best society.

My only possible attitude was not to take her seriously. So I reasoned mildly:

"I daresay, it's rather inconvenient . . . , with these two grown-up sons of yours. And it'll spoil your London season. But Henry will be pleased."

"Don't be a fool, Doctor. Henry isn't the father."

Although I had half expected this, it silenced me.

During these country weekends I had met the inevitable family intimate, a close friend of Henry's, who went fishing and shooting with him, a sporting type, one of these "good fellows," whom I had disliked on sight and who obviously was on confidential terms with Henry's wife.

"Well," I said at last, "it's a bad business. But there's nothing I can do about it."

"You won't help me?"

"I can't."

There was a pause. The blood had risen to her cheeks and her eyes flashed fire at me. She drew on her gloves, took up her bag. A rejected woman is an enemy for life.

"Very well, Doctor, there's no more to be said."

"Just one thing before you go. . . . Don't put yourself in the hands of a quack. You may regret it."

She gave no sign of having heard, but swept out of the room without another word.

The interview left me not only with a bad taste in my mouth, but in a thoroughly bad mood. I felt that I had lost an excellent patient, an agreeable hostess, and the half dozen brace of admirable pheasants which I had come to regard as my annual autumnal perquisite. I never expected to see Mrs. Glendenning again. How wrong I was—how little I knew of that invincible woman's character!

About ten days later the telephone rang. It was Henry Glendenning himself. Beatrice, he told me, had a frightful cold, an attack of influenza, in fact. Would I be a dear chap and pop round to Knightsbridge as soon as convenient? Pleased by this *rapprochement,* I arrived within the hour at the Glendenning town house and was shown directly to Beatrice's room.

Attended by a nurse, a heavily built, middle-aged woman with a face like a trap, the patient was in bed. She appeared, at first sight, rather more ill than I had expected—fearfully blanched, with bloodless lips and every indication of a raging fever. Puzzled, I drew back the sheet . . ., and then the truth burst upon me. The thing had been done—botched and bungled— she was thoroughly septic and had been hemorrhaging for at least twelve hours.

"I have everything ready for you, Doctor." The nurse was addressing me in a toneless voice, proffering a container of swabs and gauze.

I drew back in cold fury. I wanted, there and then, to walk out of the room. But how could I? She was in extremis. I must do something for this damned woman, and at once. I was fairly trapped.

I began to work on her. My methods, I fear, were not especially merciful, but she offered no protest, suffered the severest pangs without a word. At last the bleeding was under control. I prepared to go.

All this time, as she lay there, Mrs. Glendenning's eyes had never left my face. And now, with an effort, she spoke:

"It's influenza, Doctor. Henry knows it's influenza. I shall expect you this evening."

Downstairs, in the library, Henry had a glass of sherry ready for me, concerned, naturally, about his wife, whom he adored, yet hospitable, as always. He was in stature quite a small man, shy and rather ineffectual in manner, who had inherited a fortune from his father and spent much of it in making others happy. As I gazed at his open, kindly face, all that I had meant to say died upon my tongue. I could not tell him. I could not.

"Nasty thing, this influenza, Doctor."

I took a quick breath.

"Yes, Henry."

"Quite a severe attack she has, too."

"I'm afraid so."

"You'll see her through, Doctor."

A pause.

"Yes, Henry. I'll see her through."

I called again that evening. I called twice a day for the next ten days. It was a thoroughly unpleasant case, demanding constant surgical attention. I suppose I did my part in maintaining the deception. But the real miracles of strategy were performed by Beatrice and the nurse. For Henry Glendenning, who lived all that time in the same house, who slept every night in the bedroom adjoining the sickroom, *never for a moment suspected the true state of affairs.* The thing sounds incredible, but it is true.

At the end of that month, I made my final visit. Mrs. Glendenning was up, reclining on the drawingroom sofa, looking ethereal and soulful in a rose-coloured tea gown with pure white lace at cuff and collar. Flowers were everywhere. Henry, delighted, still adoring, was dancing attendance. Tea was brought, served by a trim maid—the grim-visaged nurse had long since departed.

Toying with a slice of teacake, Beatrice gazed at me with wide and wistful eyes.

"Henry is taking me to Madeira next week, Doctor. He feels I need the change."

"You do indeed, darling."

"Thank you, sweetheart."

Oh God, the duplicity, the perfidy of woman . . . the calm, deep, premediated, and infernal cunning!

"We'll be alone together for the first week," she concluded sweetly. "A second honeymoon. Then we expect George to join us. We're both very fond of George."

Her eyes sought mine, held it, and did not for an instant falter.

"More tea, Doctor, dear? You must come and shoot with us when we get back."

When I rose to go, Henry saw me to the door, shook my hand warmly.

"Thank you for all you've done, Doctor." And he added, "Confoundedly nasty thing, that influenza."

I walked all the way home across Kensington Gardens, gritting my teeth and muttering, "That creature, oh that damned, that most damnable creature!"

But in September I got my half-dozen brace of pheasants. They were nice, tender birds!

Gwendolyn Brooks, *Blacks*, 1987

The Mother
Gwendolyn Brooks

Abortions will not let you forget.
You remember the children you got that you did not get,
The damp small pulps with a little or with no hair,
The singers and workers that never handled the air,
You will never neglect or beat
Them, or silence or buy with a sweet,
You will never wind up the sucking-thumb
Or scuttle off ghosts that come.
You will never leave them, controlling your luscious sigh,
Return for a snack of them, with gobbling mother-eye.

I have heard in the voices of the wind the voice of my dim killed children.
I have contracted, I have cased
My dim dears at the breasts they could never suck.
I have said, Sweets, if I sinned, if I seized
Your luck
And your lives from your unfinished reach,
If I stole your births and your names,
Your straight baby tears and your games,
Your stilted or lovely loves, your tumults, your marriages, aches, and your
    deaths,

If I poisoned the beginnings of your breaths,
Believe that even in my deliberateness I was not deliberate.
Though why should I whine,
Whine that the crime was other than mine?—
Since anyhow you are dead.
Or rather, or instead,
You were never made.

But that too, I am afraid,
Is faulty: oh, what shall I say, how is the truth to be said?
You were born, you had body, you died.
It is just that you never giggled or planned or cried.

Believe me, I loved you all.
Believe me, I knew you, though faintly, and I loved, I loved you,
All.

Linda Gordon, "The Prohibition on Birth Control" in *Woman's Right, Woman's Body: A Social History of Birth Control in America,* Second Edition, 1952

The Prohibition on Birth Control
Linda Gordon

Although birth control is very old, the birth-control movement is young, with less than two centuries behind it. In the nineteenth century, when the movement began, birth control had become immoral and illegal with legal dangers so great that propaganda on the subject was written and distributed anonymously. Birth-control advocates were sentenced to jail terms for violation of obscenity laws. A campaign for freedom of speech and freedom of the press, therefore, became part of the modern birth-control movement. To understand these struggles we must first understand something about the nature and sources of censoring ideology.

Birth control* has always been socially regulated in some way. This is because birth control has consequences for two social issues crucial to overall social development: sexual activity and population size. Birth control bears, too, on a third social phenomenon: the role of women. Women's status cannot be correlated to a one-on-one basis with any particular system of regulation. But if the connections between social patterns of sexual activity and female activity are complex, they are nonetheless close. Systems of sexual control change as women's status changes; they both reflect and affect each other. There has been an especially strong causal connection between the subjection of women and the prohibition on birth control: the latter has been a means of enforcing the former. . . .

The prohibition of birth control required constant reinforcement because some women have always wished to limit and space their pregnancies, a motive at times overwhelming their understanding of the need for large families. Legal prohibitions and sanctions could suppress birth-control propaganda but could not stop birth-control use. Private practices could more effectively be altered by convincing the individuals themselves that birth control was immoral, and in this task religious ideologies played the major role. The religious

---

* It bears repeating that birth control, in this book, means any kind of action taken to prevent having children, including not only abortion and infanticide but also periodic or even sustained sexual abstinence if it is done with that intent. Contraception, by contrast, will be used to refer to specific devices or chemicals or medicines used to prevent conception

tradition dominant in the United States has been the Judeo-Christian tradition, and thus our focus here.

The ancient Jews had a somewhat mixed attitude toward birth control, which reflected, no doubt their nomadic origins. One method—*coitus interruptus,* or withdrawal—was condemned by the Talmud on the basis of a passage from Genesis:

> And Er, Judah's first-born was wicked in the sight of the Lord; and the Lord slew him. And Judah said unto Onan: "Go in unto they brother's wife, and perform the duty of a husband's brother unto her, and raise up seed to thy brother!" And Onan knew that the seed would not be his; and it came to pass, whenever he went in unto his brother's wife, that he used to spill it on the ground, lest he should give seed to his brother. And the thing which he did was evil in the sight of the Lord; and He slew him also.[1]

From the sin of Onan came the word "onanism," later applied by Christian theologians to both masturbation and all nonprocreative intercourse. The Talmudic tradition, however, interpreted it much more narrowly. Some scholars argue for a literal reading of the passage, in which Onan's crime consists specifically in refusing to perform the required levitate marriage* and impregnate his brother's wife. Most Talmudists hold that the passage forbade any form of "unnatural intercourse," their descriptions of that process mostly referring to ejaculation outside the vagina.[2] Contraception that did not interfere with "correct" heterosexual intercourse was, however, permitted in some cases in ancient Jewish law, and the Talmud itself prescribed two methods: a potion called the Cup of Roots** and a vaginal sponge.[3] Drinking the Cup of Roots was permitted to women and forbidden to men, because the responsibility for propagation was laid on men but not on women.[4] Thus ironically, in male supremacist law, women because of their very insignificance became free to practice birth control.

The permissibility of contraception in ancient Jewish law is part of a relatively relaxed attitude toward sexuality. For the ancient Jews, sexual abstinence was never a virtue. Marriage was not a necessary evil, but a *mitzvah,* a religious duty; and within marriage the husband had the duty not only to procreate but also to give his wife sexual satisfaction. At times when conception would be either impossible (as with a sterile woman) or dangerous, the Jewish husband nevertheless had the obligation to continue having sexual relations with his wife.[5] Indeed, the Talmud is somewhat egalitarian on sexual matters, treating men and women as having equal sexual needs, in contrast to its male-supremacist assumptions in most other areas. This may be connected to the fact that population expansion was neither a religious priority nor an economic necessity for the ancient Jews, since the sexual suppression of women had been partly a means of enforcing frequent motherhood upon them.

In contrast to the Jews, the Christians gradually evolved a total condemnation of birth control, a condemnation integral to the over-all Catholic attitude toward sexuality and women. The general hostility to women, sex, and birth control did not appear immediately, however. The Christianity of Jesus, in terms of the status of women in his historical period, was, to a revolutionary extent, pro-woman. Never before had a religion argued the universal equality of human beings. Jesus' respectful behavior toward women was often astonishing to contemporary others. Even the notorious anti-woman declarations of the Pauline tradition

---

* Custom by which the brother or next of kin to a deceased man was bound to marry the widow.

** According to the Talmud, the Cup of Roots was made of Alexandrian gum, liquid alum, and garden crocus, pulverized together.

("Let a woman learn in silence and with submissiveness. I permit no woman to teach . . .", "and Adam was not deceived, but the woman was deceived . . . ," and so forth) are much worse as they have been used, out of context, by misogynistic churchmen; Paul himself was preoccupied with order and the good image of his new religion, and his pronouncements against women were conventional at worst.[6]

The early Christians developed an ascetic ideal that rejected sexual pleasure as the most evil of many evil pleasures, but at first it was not exclusively directed at the suppression of women. The Christian ascetics sought righteousness through mortifying themselves, not women. St. Paul's ideal was celibacy. When this was impracticable— "It is better to marry than to burn,"* after all—there was no condemnation of sexual enjoyment within marriage.

> Let the husband render to his wife what is due to her, and likewise the wife to her husband. . . . You must not refuse each other, except perhaps by consent, for a time, that you give yourselves to prayer, and return together again lest Satan tempt you because you lack self-control. But this I say by way of concession, not commandment.[7]

The Church Fathers developed these antisexual attitudes in new directions. In the first place, they had to be concerned with reproduction and with increasing the number of Christians. Paul had been able to recommend celibacy freely, since he expected the second coming imminently; Augustine, four centuries later, was more skeptical about the Messiah's imminent arrival and wanted to strengthen his religion. He distinguished for the first time in the Christian tradition between lust and procreation in order to condemn the former entirely, for married and unmarried people alike. Sexual intercourse, according to Augustinian thought, was inherently evil and could be justified only if procreation was its intent. The sexual drive itself was evil, laid as a burden upon man as a result of the Fall. Augustine's image of hell was "the burning of lust."[8] The pleasure of sex created a constant temptation to indulge in it for the wrong reasons. Best, perhaps, would have been to try to make the necessary procreative intercourse as pleasureless as possible. Couples that used an "evil appliance" to prevent propagation were not worthy of the name man and wife, were no longer covered by the license of matrimony, so to speak; they were in mortal sin. Augustine specifically condemned the "rhythm method" to avoid conception.[9]

In the thirteenth century Thomas Aquinas dogmatized and codified the idea that even within marriage sexual intercourse was justifiable only for procreation. Every act of intercourse was a sin unless performed with a reproductive intent.[10] That point of view was reaffirmed by Pope Pius XI in 1930 in the encyclical *Casti connubii*: the goods of marriage, it said, are offspring, fidelity, and sacrament, and offspring is the primary one.[11] . . .

Although individual women did use birth control despite this powerful prohibition, there was never an organized challenge to the ideology of motherhood until industrialization created a new economic system that did not require a high birthrate.

Several factors have made a lower birthrate economically advantageous in the more developed parts of the world in the last five centuries. They include improved diet and sanitation and thus a decline in the death rate, particularly the infant-mortality rate. Even before medical progress, however, mainly a nineteenth- and twentieth-century phenomenon, social changes made smaller families more desirable. A money economy, high costs of living for city dwellers, and the decreasing relative economic contribution that children could make

---

* That is, to burn with passion.

reversed the traditional family economy and made children cost more than they could contribute. Some social groups were affected by these changes before others, perhaps the earliest being professionals who had to live on salaries (in contrast to those who lived on the land, which could absorb children's labor power) and to cope with the high cost of education if their children were to inherit their status.[12] Gradually urbanization produced a decline in the birthrate among all classes. . . .

Greater public approval of birth control during the Renaissance was produced not by a smaller family ideal but by a higher valuation of extramarital sex. For this very reason the impact of the Renaissance in changing sexual values was probably confined to men of wealth and power. But since that group produced a significant literature about its new values, there is some evidence already (and undoubtedly much more to be found) about birth-control use. Pierre de Brantôme (1540–1614), a French courtier, chronicler, and abbé, in describing the sexual promiscuity of court life, wrote: "There are some who have no desire to receive the seed, like the noble lady who said to her lover, 'Do what you will, and give me delight, but on your life have a care to let no drop reach me.' Then the other must watch out for the right moment."[13] What is new in such expressions is not technique—withdrawal is as old as sexual intercourse itself, no doubt—but the proudly hedonistic attitude behind it. There were also new technological developments, however, as the rediscovery of pagan medical technology brought Arab and Persian contraceptive recipes to the attention of the educated.

During the Renaissance the men of new wealth—the bourgeoisie—tried to assimilate and even directly emulate the style of the aristocracy in the consumption of luxury goods and sexual pleasure. But as capitalists consolidated their economic dominance, most of them ceased imitating the nobility in favor of establishing new social standards more useful to their economic and political enterprises. These new social standards flowed from the need to develop and reinforce an individual character structure compatible with the new patterns of work and achievement possible under capitalism. Success in business came from willingness to take risks and to accept relative deprivation in the present in return for the hopes of long-range profits. The work of capitalist commerce and industry required discipline, the ability to resist temptations for immediate gratification a mentality that valued saving and reinvestment, and competitiveness. Bourgeois culture honored the personalities that exemplified these so-called virtues.

These changes were far more profound than those of the Renaissance, for they were produced by an economic revolution that affected nearly the whole Western world and were carried within a mass ideological revolution—the Reformation. Through it new sexual values reached even the artisans and peasants not yet directly influenced by the capitalist mode of production. New Protestant religions supported the new values even among those who did not desert the Catholic Church, by breaking up the hegemony of certain Catholic traditions uncomfortable for capitalism, such as the ban on usury, the hierarchical integration of the Church with the aristocracy, and the monastic ideal. By abolishing confession and making the individual directly responsible to God, Protestantism helped create a new human character structure in which morality and sin were internalized values, enforced by the individual upon himself, a character structure capable of self-denial without external compulsion. . . .

If the confinement of sexuality within the family was more stringent during these early stages of capitalism, it was because the family was economically and socially more important than ever. As long as private property has existed, sex and reproduction have been controlled so as to regularize inheritance procedures. But in agricultural society, the family was less isolated from the larger community than it became under conditions of commerce and industry. For some time, historians accepted the generalization that in preindustrial Europe and America, the extended family was the dominant form—that is, that married children continued to live in the homes of one of their parental families, thus bringing children, grandchildren, cousins, aunts, and uncles under one roof. More recent empirical studies suggest that the nuclear family—only mother, father, and children under one roof—dominated even in many peasant communities. To measure family closeness only in terms of who lives under one roof is misleading; relationships of visiting, borrowing, sharing work, and giving emotional and financial support did not depend on living in one house.

Puritan attitudes toward birth control were more relaxed than those of the Catholic tradition. Whereas Luther held to an absolute opposition to birth control,[14] Calvin placed less emphasis on the childbearing duty of women than Luther had and taught that procreation was not the primary purpose of marriage.[15] The later Protestant tradition did not include the constant attacks on these "unnatural practices" found in the Catholic Church. The reasons for the lack of vigilance against birth control are double: first, this was the period in which some communities of people developed, for the first time, an economic interest in smaller families; and second, the potential of birth control to promote sexual license was checked by more rigid enforcement of sexual chastity itself.

The process of industrialization that began in the eighteenth century set in motion several other social changes that ultimately weakened the Puritan family and sexual norm. Their immediate effect, however, was not to loosen the bonds on women and on human sexual expression but to secularize them and to apply them much more tightly to women than to men. The new cultural form of sexual repression is often called Victorian prudery, and it was the form of sexual repression that the birth-control campaigners had to contend with. . . .

As industrial production drew men out of their homes in socialized workplaces, the economic basis of family unity began to dissolve. In most working-class families, husbands and wives were separated for the greater part of their lives, so their attention was focused on rather different problems and they developed different skills and found different comrades. When women worked in factories, their jobs were almost always sexually segregated. All adult workers became individual employees, each with her or his separate wages. Wives became functionally independent of their husbands while remaining financially dependent. Furthermore, as industry began to produce outside the home what women had once manufactured for themselves, women's work at home became increasingly degraded to mere cleaning, repairing, consuming, and child-raising functions.[16]

Precisely because male authority was being weakened, the stability of the traditional family required the imposition of a repressive ideology. For women as for workers, internalized discipline was needed to supplement economic necessity. Victorian prudery was closely connected to the doctrine of a separate sphere of concerns for women. This notion that women were profoundly different from men—an idea newly emphasized after the late eighteenth century—was simultaneously a description of a new reality: a male-imposed doctrine to keep women from escaping from their homes and a women's adaptation to their new situation.

Because the rationale for Victorian prudery was the great difference between the sexes, its essential definition was the double standard. Seen as a system, Victorian sexual norms did not impose self-denial and chastity on all, but exclusively on women. Meanwhile men created the greatest prostitution industry in history. It is true, of course, that Victorian moralists continued some of the Puritan hostility to play, to spontaneous, unpredictable indulgence in pleasureful activity. Work had to be the first, and often the only, activity of most days; sex was reserved for bedtime, the hours of fatigue. Unlike their Puritan forebears, Victorian moralists argued that sex should be indulged in only for purposes of procreation. In response, men of all classes often patronized brothels rather than seek love with their wives. Sexual matters were slandered as dirty, immoral, and undignified and virtually removed from respectable discussion.

The very essence of Victorian respectability was hypocrisy. This hypocrisy accurately reflected the social function of prudery: an attempt to create in both working-class people and women of all classes a repression convenient for the new capitalist ruling class. (This attempt was complex as it required granting to working-class men some of the privileges of bourgeois men and to upper-class women some of the privileges of their husbands and fathers.) As it affected birth control, prudery was an obstacle partly because it defined any discussion of sexual matters as obscene. But as a system of sexual politics, prudery sought to hamper women's efforts to transcend their home-and-marriage prisons by keeping the burdens of motherhood upon them.

Thus Victorian prudery produced not only a prohibition on sexual discussion but also a cult of "motherhood." This romanticization of motherhood, like prudery itself, had many contributing factors. Partly it was a response of men and women alike to the decreasing permanence of families. New relations of production weakened ties between family members and undermined fathers' authority by making individuals economically independent. Simultaneously relationships outside the family for wage laborers and other big-city dwellers became less permanent and reliable, unlike the community patterns of mutual dependency that had prevailed in precapitalist society. All relationships, familial and otherwise, were increasingly composed of dependencies that were primarily psychological rather than material.* Furthermore, improved transportation and economic incentives to geographical mobility undermined close relationships with neighbors.

All these changes spelled greater freedom for individuals, especially those who had previously been subordinated to a master, such as children, unmarried women, apprentices. But these changes also carried the potential for loneliness and disorientation among individuals, and a resultant instability for the society as a whole which was quite alarming to many nineteenth-century working people, especially those who had recently migrated from non-industrial areas.

The disintegration of the economic basis of family life in no way ended its necessity as a social institution. On the one hand, the family remained, at least throughout the nineteenth and first half of the twentieth centuries, the primary means of the socialization of children into adults with personalities appropriate to the demands of industrial capitalism . . . . On the other hand, the family was called upon to absorb the heavy strains that the economy placed upon individuals. . . .

Both these familial functions contributed to an intensification of the cult of motherhood, that is, the extension of motherliness to the very definition of femininity. In one function, maternal virtues justified and idealized the restriction of sex within marriage, In another

---

* None of this should be taken to imply that family and community interdependencies vanished quickly or entirely. Many industrial workers to the present day continue to use patterns of sharing and mutual support which may be said to have originated in preindustrial communities but are now used in a fully proletarian manner to adapt to industrial conditions. My argument is only that a tendency toward increased individual independence was noticed and remarked upon by many people in the nineteenth century.

function, the maternal tenderings of wives were now expected to extend beyond their children to their husbands, to turn their homes into soothing, comforting, challengeless escapes* for men returning from exhausting workdays of cut-throat competition and constant vigilance to buy cheap and sell dear, or of grinding physical labor and rigid external control. . . .

In justifying this further specialization of the sexes in the division of labor, nineteenth-century ideologists offered the view that the two sexes were not only different in all things but nearly opposite. It became unfashionable among the educated to say outright that women were inferior. (By contrast a forthright male-supremacist line had dominated most discussions of the sexes, both religious and secular, before the nineteenth century.) Victorian ideology about women included the pretense that the spheres of men and women were separate but equal. This belief, in turn, was part of a larger ideological system in which women, although considered inferior in intellectual, artistic, and physical potential, were told that they were morally superior and that their greater holiness came from their innate capacity for motherliness. Such a division of qualities was convenient for a ruling class that got its profits and achievements by means of which even its own religion disapproved. Only the female half of the population was really expected to act on Christian morality. . . .

The theory of the oppositeness of the sexes was particularly marked in matters of sex. Sex drive became exclusively a part of the masculine sphere of things, and some theories even denied that sex drives existed in women. Female chastity was no longer merely a man's right but now also a woman's destiny, as a naturally asexual being; men were asked merely to moderate the extremes of their powerful sexual urge. Although purity was raised to first place among women's desired virtues, a significant number of working-class women were sacrificed in a different way to the maintenance of male supremacy and the sexual character structure that industrial capitalism created. Prostitutes were available to men of all classes, providing a sop to working-class men similar in function to wives themselves.

The motherhood ideology also defined the extent that sexuality was allowable for women: the only justifiable purpose of sexual intercourse for "respectable" women was reproduction.** The choice for women became motherhood or prostitution, as the sexual standards became so rigid that all sexual activity outside of motherhood became identified with (and often in fact led to) prostitution. Supporting this view was the new theory that women had no sex drive (in contrast to the male view of women that had dominated for most of human history—that women had powerful lusts, and in equal contrast to the Puritan view which considered it an obligation of comparable difficulty for both sexes to control their sexual urges). This myth was accommodated to the cult of motherhood through emphasis on the virtue of purity for mothers, and literally identified with motherhood through the idea that the female analog to the male sex drive was the maternal instinct. The chastity and passionlessness of women was expected to prevail within marriage just as outside it. The desire for maternity was presumably the only selfish reason that women submitted, literally,

---

* By contrast with the typical workplace-home of the seventeenth century, crowded, hectic, and noisy.

** Respectable" had originally meant nor working with one's hands, which required, among other things, being able to keep servants Thus originally working-class people were nor "respectable" by definition, in the European usage of the term. In the United Stares, and in Europe in the nineteenth century, there emerged a new concept of respectability which included those of the working class who had adopted the social and moral standards of the bourgeoisie such as refraining from drunkenness and requiring female virginity until marriage.

to sexual intercourse; beyond the immediate desire for children their motivation should be to please their husbands.

In the nineteenth century this strange sexual morality was being defined not only by the clergy and the political philosophers, as in previous centuries, but also by the medical profession, a new and powerful source of control over women's lives. Many doctors wrote manuals of sexual conduct aimed at women. These doctors were far from unanimous in their views on female sexuality, and some argued merely for moderation of sexual appetites and practices. Even their moderation, however, served a repressive function: writing prescriptive manuals, attempting to establish moral norms for sexual behavior in as well as outside of marriage, most of the moderates as well as the extremists emphasized the debilitating effects of sexual indulgence, defined normal sexual intercourse as that leading most directly to male orgasm, and opposed contraception.

A more complex matter is the degree of success of the ideologues in making their proposed norms work in practice. After years of assuming that the ministers' and doctors' prescriptions were women's reality, a few historians have lately looked for and found evidence that women's minds and bodies were not mere clay in the hands of their moral censors but remained resistant to this indoctrination. Middle and upper-middle-class women, the main audience for the prudish sex manuals, in small samples of letters, diaries, and at least one survey by a feminist gynecologist, said that they often enjoyed sex and experienced orgasm.[17] Furthermore, the mask of prudery stimulated hypocrisy, and many men and women behaved and felt differently in private than in public, no doubt. Still, we know from our own experiences how helpless people can be, even in their own minds, against the norms of beauty, love, and propriety. The euphemistic avoidance of direct discussion of sexual matters made sex appear a dirty fact of life, unavoidable but unpleasant, like excretion. The moral guides urged excluding sex from consciousness as well as from behavior. Women were told that their purity of mind and body would determine not only their fate in the hereafter but also their marriage-ability on earth. Prudery was not merely an ideological system, for the sanctions on women who deviated were material and, often, permanent, such as spinsterhood, desertion, economic ruin, disease, and death. Physical though its basis may be, the sexual drive is susceptible to great variation and control from psychological pressures; and the anxieties attached to sex may well have produced many women who did not experience sexual drive, at least not in a form recognizable to them. Thus, however many individuals were able to resist it, Victorian sexual ideology produced, among the middle classes at least, many other women hostile to and fearful of sex.

The repression of female sexuality may have been accomplished through physical as well as psychological changes. Women learned to hate their own bodies. Many women never undressed, even when alone, and bathed under their shifts. When they submitted sexually to their husbands, they remained clothed; for many women sexual intercourse was reduced to such a quick act of penetration that they never had time to become aroused. People never exposed to sexual stimulation may indeed have had truncated, undeveloped sexual drives. Ill health also contributed to lessening sexual energy. Lack of exercise and confinement indoors made women even of the privileged classes physically weak; terrible working and living conditions made working- class women unhealthy in other, more serious ways. Among fashionable women, heavy corseting may have caused serious and permanent internal damage. The approach to pregnancy ("confinement" it was called and confinement it was, for a pregnant woman was considered indecent in "respectable" circles and was expected not to appear in public) prohibited exercise and weakened muscles, thus making pregnancy and parturition possibly more painful than earlier in history, and canceling out improvements gained through better sanitation and health care. Nothing can be more effective than the fear of painful and dangerous pregnancies and childbirths in depressing sexual interest.

Beyond these obstacles to sexual development, Victorian constraints on women created particular practical problems for birth control. The most effective traditional forms of birth control under women's control required handling one's genitals. The task of inserting a vaginal pessary may have been beyond the emotional capabilities of many nineteenth-century women. Prudery also interfered with the communication of traditional birth-control remedies from one generation to the next. And even the limited ingenuity and basic common sense required for developing home-remedy birth-control techniques may have been blocked by deep psychological fears of thinking about sexual matters.

The factors making birth control immoral were intensifying for the first three quarters of the nineteenth century. Although the rights of women were in many respects greater by the nineteenth century than they had been before in the Western world, the prohibition on birth control and on any open discussion of sexual matters had never been more severe. In 1873 in the United States, birth control was legally prohibited for the first time by the "Comstock law," which forbade the sending of obscene matter through the U.S. mail. Religious and political leaders denounced sexual immorality increasingly after mid-century. The greater sexual repression was primarily a response to growing rebellion against the Victorian sexual system. That rebellion, as we shall see, was closely connected to the feminist movement that arose in the 1840s—and the two rebellions had common causes. The two rebellions were related as the two forms of repression—the repression of sex and the subjugation of women-were related. . . .

Notes

1. Genesis, 38: 7–10.

2. Norman Himes, *Medical History of Contraception* ([1936] New York: Gamut Press, 1963), pp. 71–73; David M. Feldman, *Birth Control in Jewish Law* (New York: New York University Press, 1968), Chapter 8.

3. Feldman, *Birth Control*, pp. 169–70. Recipe and indications for the Cup of Roots are given in *the Babylonian Talmud, Tractate Shabbath*, trans. 1. Epstein (London: Soncino Press, 1938), 109b–111a, 11, pp. 532–39.

4. Feldman, *Birth Control*, Chapter 3 passim, p. 53 particularly. This is discussed in the *Babylonian Talmud, Seder Nashim, Tractate Yebamoth*, trans. Israel W. Slotki (London: Soncino Press, 1936), 65b–66a, 1, pp. 436–40.

5. Feldman, *Birth Control*. pp. 297–98 and passim.

6. Mary Daly, *The Church and the Second Sex* ([1968] New York: Harper Torchbooks, 1975), pp. 79–82.

7. Quoted in John J. Noonan, Jr., *Contraception: A History of Its Treatment by Catholic Theologians and Canonists* (Cambridge: Harvard University Press, 1965), p. 42.

8. Quoted in Demosthenes Savramis, *The Satanizing of Woman*, trans. Martin Ebon (Garden City, New York: Doubleday, 1974), p. 51.

9. Ibid., Chapter 7; Glanville Williams, *The Sanctity of Life and the Criminal Law* (New York: Knopf, 1957), pp, 51–57.

10. Savramis, *Satanizing of Woman*, Chapter 7; Williams, *Sanctity of Life*, p. 55; Noonan, *Contraception*, pp. 240 ff.

11. Noonan, Contraception, p. 426.

12. Joseph Ambrose Banks, *Prosperity and Parenthood: A Study of Family Planning among the Victorian Middle Classes* (London: Routledge & Kegan Paul, 1954).

13.   Quoted in Himes, *Medical History of Contraception*, p. 90.

14.   Noonan, *Contraception*, p. 353.

15.   Vern Bullough, *The Subordinate Sex* (Urbana: University of Illinois Press, 1973), p. 199.

16.   There have been no overall studies of the rise of industrial capitalism from the perspective of women, but my interpretation has been influenced by Alice Clark, *The Working Life of Women in the 17th Century* (London: Routledge, 1919).

17.   For the findings of the survey and on the medical opposition to Victorian prudish extremism, see Carl N. Degler, "What Ought to Be and What Was: Women's Sexuality in the Nineteenth Century," *American Historical Review,* Winter 1974, pp. 1467–90. For other evidence of women's resistance to prudery, see Chapter 5.

Economic Justice for All: A Pastoral Message
The National Conference of Catholic Bishops

Issues of social importance have often been the impetus for the Roman Catholic Church to submit statements declaring its views on these issues. After much study and worldwide deliberation, a message is released to the Church and to the world, as was the case in this pastoral letter. The bishops' economic message in its entirety is lengthy. Significant points have been excerpted that apply to the moral and social responsibilities of business. The reading begins with the Introduction and uses portions of chapters one and four. The original numbering of the bishops has been retained.

PRINCIPAL THEMES OF THE PASTORAL LETTER

12. The pastoral letter is not a blueprint for the American economy. It does not embrace any particular theory of how the economy works, nor does it attempt to resolve the disputes between different schools of economic thought. Instead, our letter turns to Scripture and to the social teachings of the Church. There, we discover what our economic life must serve, what standards it must meet. Let us examine some of these basic moral principles.

13. *Every economic decision and institution must be judged in light of whether it protects or undermines the dignity of the human person. The pastoral letter begins with the human person.* We believe the person is sacred—the clearest reflection of God among us. Human dignity comes from God, not from nationality, race, sex, economic status, or any human accomplishment. We judge any economic system by what it does *for* and *to* people and by how it permits all to *participate* in it. The economy should serve people, not the other way around.

14. *Human dignity can be realized and protected only in community.* In our teaching, the human person is not only sacred but also social. How we organize our society—in economics and politics, in law and policy—directly affects human dignity and the capacity of individuals to grow in community. The obligation to "love our neighbor" has an individual dimension, but it also requires a broader social commitment to the common good. We have many partial ways to measure and debate the health of our

of our economy: Gross National Product, per capita income, stock market prices, and so forth. The Christian vision of economic life looks beyond them all and asks, Does economic life enhance or threaten our life together as a community?

15. *All people have a right to participate in the economic life of society.* Basic justice demands that people be assured a minimum level of participation in the economy. It is wrong for a person or group to be excluded unfairly or to be unable to participate or contribute to the economy. For example, people who are both able and willing, but cannot get a job are deprived of the participation that is so vital to human development. For, it is through employment that most individuals and families meet their material needs, exercise their talents, and have an opportunity to contribute to the larger community. Such participation has a special significance in our tradition because we believe that it is a means by which we join in carrying forward God's creative activity.

16. *All members of society have a special obligation to the poor and vulnerable.* From the Scriptures and church teaching, we learn that the justice of a society is tested by the treatment of the poor. The justice that was the sign of God's covenant with Israel was measured by how the poor and unprotected—the widow, the orphan, and the stranger—were treated. The kingdom that Jesus proclaimed in his word and ministry excludes no one. Throughout Israel's history and in early Christianity, the poor are agents of God's transforming power. "The Spirit of the Lord is upon me, therefore he has anointed me. He has sent me to bring glad tidings to the poor" (Lk 4:18). This was Jesus' first public utterance. Jesus takes the side of those most in need. In the Last Judgment, so dramatically described in St. Matthew's Gospel, we are told that we will be judged according to how we respond to the hungry, the thirsty, the naked, the stranger. As followers of Christ, we are challenged to make a fundamental "option for the poor"—to speak for the voiceless, to defend the defenseless, to assess life styles, policies, and social institutions in terms of their impact on the poor. This "option for the poor" does not mean pitting one group against another, but rather, strengthening the whole community by assisting those who are most vulnerable. As Christians, we are called to respond to the needs of *all* our brothers and sisters, but those with the greatest needs require the greatest response.

17. *Human rights are the minimum conditions for life in community.* In Catholic teaching, human rights include not only civil and political rights but also economic rights. As Pope John XXIII declared, "all people have a right to life, food, clothing, shelter, rest, medical care, education, and employment." This means that when people are without a chance to earn a living, and must go hungry and homeless, they are being denied basic rights. Society must ensure that these rights are protected. In this way, we will ensure that the minimum conditions of economic justice are met for all our sisters and brothers.

18. *Society as a whole, acting through public and private institutions, has the moral responsibility to enhance human dignity and protect human rights.* In addition to the clear responsibility of private institutions, government has an essential responsibility in this area. This does not mean that government has the primary or exclusive role, but it does have a positive moral responsibility in safeguarding human rights and ensuring that the minimum conditions of human dignity are met for all. In a democracy, government is a means by which we can act together to protect what is important to us and to promote our common values.

19. These six moral principles are not the only ones presented in the pastoral letter, but they give an overview of the moral vision that we are trying to share. This vision of economic life cannot exist in a vacuum; it must be translated into concrete measures. Our pastoral letter spells out some specific applications of Catholic moral principles. We call for a new national commitment to full employment. We say it is a social and moral scandal that one of every seven Americans is poor, and we call for concerted efforts to eradicate poverty. The fulfillment of the basic needs of the poor is of the highest priority. We urge that all economic policies be evaluated in light of their impact on the life and stability of the family. We support measures to halt the loss of family farms and to resist the growing concentration in the ownership of agricultural resources. We specify ways in which the United States can do far more to relieve the plight of poor nations and assist in their development. We also reaffirm church teaching on the rights of workers, collective bargaining, private property, subsidiary, and equal opportunity. . . .

Chapter I
The Church and the Future of the U.S. Economy

B. Urgent Problems of Today

10. The preeminent role of the United States in an increasingly interdependent global economy is a central sign of our times.[6] The United States is still the world's economic giant. Decisions made here have immediate effects in other countries; decisions made abroad have immediate consequences for steelworkers in Pittsburgh, oil company employees in Houston, and farmers in Iowa. U.S. economic growth is vitally dependent on resources from other countries and on their purchases of our goods and services. Many jobs in U.S. industry and agriculture depend on our ability to export manufactured goods and food.

11. In some industries the mobility of capital and technology makes wages the main variable in the cost of production. Overseas competitors with the same technology but with wage rates as low as one-tenth of ours put enormous pressure on U.S. firms to cut wages, relocate abroad, or close. U.S. workers and their communities should not be expected to bear these burdens alone.

12. All people on this globe share a common ecological environment that is under increasing pressure. Depletion of soil, water, and other natural resources endangers the future. Pollution of air and water threatens the delicate balance of the biosphere on which future generations will depend.[7] The resources of the earth have been created by God for the benefit of all, and we who are alive today hold them in trust. This is a challenge to develop a new ecological ethic that will help shape a future that is both just and sustainable.

13. In short, nations separated by geography, culture, and ideology are linked in a complex commercial, financial, technological, and environmental network. These links have two direct consequences. First, they create hope for a new form of community among all peoples, one built on dignity, solidarity, and justice. Second, this rising global awareness calls for greater attention to the stark inequities across countries in the standards of living and control of resources. We must not look at the

welfare of U.S. citizens as the only good to be sought. Nor may we overlook the disparities of power in the relationships between this nation and the developing countries. The United States is the major supplier of food to other countries, a major source of arms sales to developing nations, and a powerful influence in multilateral institutions such as the International Monetary Fund, the World Bank, and the United Nations. What Americans see as a growing interdependence is regarded by many in the less developed countries as a pattern of domination and dependence.

14. Within this larger international setting, there are also a number of challenges to the domestic economy that call for creativity and courage. The promise of the "American dream"—freedom for all persons to develop their God-given talents to the full—remains unfulfilled for millions in the United States today.

15. Several areas of U.S. economic life demand special attention. Unemployment is the most basic. Despite the large number of new jobs the U.S. economy has generated in the past decade, approximately 8 million people seeking work in this country are unable to find it, and many more are so discouraged they have stopped looking.[8] Over the past two decades the nation has come to tolerate an increasing level of unemployment. The 6 to 7 percent rate deemed acceptable today would have been intolerable twenty years ago. Among the unemployed are a disproportionate number of blacks, Hispanics, young people, or women who are the sole support of their families.[9] Some cities and states have many more unemployed persons than others as a result of economic forces that have little to do with people's desire to work. Unemployment is a tragedy no matter whom it strikes, but the tragedy is compounded by the unequal and unfair way it is distributed in our society.

16. Harsh poverty plagues our country despite its great wealth. More than 33 million Americans are poor, by any reasonable standard another 20 to 30 million are needy. Poverty is increasing in the United States, not decreasing.[10] For a people who believe in "progress," this should be cause for alarm. These burdens fall most heavily on blacks, Hispanics, and Native Americans. Even more disturbing is the large increase in the number of women and children living in poverty. Today children are the largest single group among the poor. This tragic fact seriously threatens the nation's future. That so many people are poor in a nation as rich as ours is a social and moral scandal that we cannot ignore.

17. Many working people and middle-class Americans live dangerously close to poverty. A rising number of families must rely on the wages of two or even three members just to get by. From 1968 to 1978 nearly a quarter of the U.S. population was in poverty part of the time and received welfare benefits in at least one year.[11] The loss of a job, illness, or the breakup of a marriage may be all it takes to push people into poverty.

18. The lack of a mutually supportive relation between family life and economic life is one of the most serious problems facing the United States today.[12] The economic and cultural strength of the nation is directly linked to the stability and health of its families.[13] When families thrive, spouses contribute to the common good through their work at home, in the community, and in their jobs; and children develop a sense of their own worth and of their responsibility to serve others. When families are weak or break down entirely, the dignity of parents and children is threatened. High cultural and economic costs are inflicted on society at large.

19. The precarious economic situation of so many people and so many families calls for examination of U.S. economic arrangements. Christian conviction and the American

promise of liberty and justice for all give the poor and the vulnerable a special claim on the nation's concern. They also challenge all members of the Church to help build a more just society.

20. The investment of human creativity and material resources in the production of the weapons of war makes these economic problems even more difficult to solve. Defense Department expenditures in the United States are almost $300 billion per year. The rivalry and mutual fear between superpowers divert into projects that threaten death, minds and money that could better human life. Developing countries engage in arms races they can ill afford, often with the encouragement of the superpowers. Some of the poorest countries of the world use scarce resources to buy planes, guns, and other weapons when they lack the food, education, and health care their people need. Defense policies must be evaluated and assessed in light of their real contribution to freedom, justice, and peace for the citizens of our own and other nations. We have developed a perspective on these multiple moral concerns in our 1983 pastoral letter, *The Challenge of Peace: God's Promise and Our Response.*[14] When weapons or strategies make questionable contributions to security, peace, and justice and will also be very expensive, spending priorities should be redirected to more pressing social needs.[15]

21. Many other social and economic challenges require careful analysis: the movement of many industries from the Snowbelt to the Sunbelt, the federal deficit and interest rates, corporate mergers and takeovers, the effects of n technologies such as robotics and information systems in U.S. industry, immigration policy, growing international traffic in drugs, and the trade imbalance. All of these issues do not provide a complete portrait of the economy. Rather they are symptoms of more fundamental currents shaping U.S. economic life today: the struggle to find meaning and value in human work, efforts to support individual freedom in the context of renewed social cooperation, the urgent need to create equitable forms of global interdependence in a world now marked by extreme inequality. These deeper currents are cultural and moral in content. They show that the long-range challenges facing the nation call for sustained reflection on the values that guide economic choices and are embodied in economic institutions. Such explicit reflection on the ethical content of economic choices and policies must become an integral part of the way Christians relate religious belief to the realities of everyday life. In this way, "split between the faith which many profess and their daily lives,"[16] which Vatican II counted among the more serious errors of the modern age, will begin to be bridged. . . .

Chapter IV
A New American Experiment:
Partnership for the Public Good

295. For over two hundred years the United States has been engaged in a bold experiment in democracy. The founders of the nation set out to establish justice, promote the general welfare, and secure the blessings of liberty for themselves and their posterity. Those who live in this land today are the beneficiaries of this great venture. Our review of some of the most pressing problems in economic life today shows, however, that this undertaking is not yet complete. Justice for all remains an aspiration; a fair share in the general welfare is denied to many. In addition to the particular policy

recommendations made above, a long-term and more fundamental response is needed. This will call for an imaginative vision of the future that can help shape economic arrangements in creative new ways. We now want to propose some elements of such a vision and several innovations in economic structures that can contribute to making this vision a reality.

296. Completing the unfinished business of the American experiment will call for new forms of cooperation and partnership among those whose daily work is the source of the prosperity and justice of the nation. The United States prides itself on both its competitive sense of initiative and its spirit of teamwork. Today a greater spirit of partnership and teamwork is needed; competition alone will not do the job. It has too many negative consequences for family life, the economically vulnerable, and the environment. Only a renewed commitment by all to the common good can deal creatively with the realities of international interdependence and economic dislocations in the domestic economy. The virtues of good citizenship require a lively sense of participation in the commonwealth and of having obligations as well as rights within it.[1] The nation's economic health depends on strengthening these virtues among all its people, and on the development of institutional arrangements supportive of these virtues.[2]

297. The nation's founders took daring steps to create structures of participation, mutual accountability, and widely distributed power to ensure the political rights and freedoms of all. We believe that similar steps are needed today to expand economic participation, broaden the sharing of economic power, and make economic decisions more accountable to the common good. As noted above, the principle of subsidiary states that the pursuit of economic justice must occur on all levels of society. It makes demands on communities as small as the family, as large as the global society and on all levels in between. There are a number of ways to enhance the cooperative participation of these many groups in the task of creating this future. Since there is no single innovation that will solve all problems, we recommend careful experimentation with several possibilities that hold considerable hope for increasing partnership and strengthening mutual responsibility for economic justice.

A. COOPERATION WITHIN FIRMS AND INDUSTRIES

298. A new experiment in bringing democratic ideals to economic life calls for serious exploration of ways to develop new patterns of partnership among those working in individual firms and industries.[3] Every business, from the smallest to the largest, including farms and ranches, depends on many different persons and groups for its success: workers, managers, owners or shareholders, suppliers, customers, creditors, the local community, and the wider society. Each makes a contribution to the enterprise, and each has a stake in its growth or decline. Present structures of accountability, however, do not acknowledge all these contributions or protect these stakes. A major challenge in today's economy is the development of new institutional mechanisms for accountability that also preserve the flexibility needed to respond quickly to a rapidly changing business environment.[4]

299. New forms of partnership between workers and managers are one means for developing greater participation and accountability within firms.[5] Recent experience has shown that both labor and management suffer when the adversarial relationship

between them becomes extreme. As Pope Leo XIII stated, "Each needs the other completely: capital cannot do without labor, nor labor without capital."[6] The organization of firms should reflect and enhance this mutual partnership. In particular, the development of work patterns for men and women that are more supportive of family life will benefit both employees and the enterprises they work for.

300. Workers in firms and on farms are especially in need of stronger institutional protection, for their jobs and livelihood are particularly vulnerable to the decisions of others in today's highly competitive labor market. Several arrangements are gaining increasing support in the United States: profit sharing by the workers in a firm enabling employees to become company stockholders; granting employees greater partici-pation in determining the conditions of work; cooperative ownership of the firm by all who work within it; and programs for enabling a much larger number of Americans, regardless of their employment status, to become shareholders in successful corporations. Initiatives of this sort can enhance productivity, increase the profitability of firms, provide greater job security and work satisfaction for employees, and reduce adversarial relations.[7] In our 1919 Program of Social Reconstruction, we observed "the full possibilities of increased production will not be realized so long as the majority of workers remain mere wage earners. The majority must somehow become owners, at least in part, of the instruments of production."[8] We believe this judgment remains generally valid today.

301. None of these approaches provides a panacea, and all have certain drawbacks. Nevertheless we believe that continued research and experimentation with these approaches will be of benefit. Catholic social teaching has endorsed on many occasions innovative methods for increasing worker participation within firms.[9] The appropriateness of these methods will depend on the circumstances of the company or industry in question and on their effectiveness in actually increasing a genuinely cooperative approach to shaping decisions. The most highly publicized examples of such efforts have been in large firms facing serious financial crises. If increased participation and collaboration can help a firm avoid collapse, why should it not give added strength to healthy businesses? Cooperative ownership is particularly worthy of consideration in new entrepreneurial enterprises.[10]

302. Partnerships between labor and management are possible only when both groups possess real freedom and power to influence decisions. This means that unions ought to continue to play an important role in moving toward greater economic participation within firms and industries. Workers rightly reject calls for less adversarial relations when they are a smokescreen for demands that labor make all the concessions. For partnership to be genuine it must be a two-way street, with creative initiative and a willingness to cooperate on all sides.

303. When companies are considering plant closures or the movement of capital, it is patently unjust to deny workers any role in shaping the outcome of these difficult choices.[11] In the heavy manufacturing sector today, technological change and international competition can be the occasion of painful decisions leading to the loss of jobs or wage reductions. While such decisions may sometimes be necessary, a collaborative and mutually accountable model of industrial organization would mean that workers not be expected to carry all the burdens of an economy in transition. Management and investors must also accept their share of sacrifices, especially when

management is thinking of closing a plant or transferring capital to a seemingly more lucrative or competitive activity. The capital at the disposal of management is in part the product of the labor of those who have toiled in the company over the years, including currently employed workers.[12] As a minimum, workers have a right to be informed in advance when such decisions are under consideration, a right to negotiate with management about possible alternatives, and a right to fair compensation and assistance with retraining and relocation expenses should these be necessary. Since even these minimal rights are jeopardized without collective negotiation, industrial cooperation requires a strong role for labor unions in our changing economy.

304. Labor unions themselves are challenged by the present economic environment to seek new ways of doing business. The purpose of unions is not simply to defend the existing wages and prerogatives of the fraction of workers who belong to them, but also to enable workers to make positive and creative contributions to the firm, the community, and the larger society in an organized and cooperative way.[13] Such contributions call for experiments with new directions in the U.S. labor movement.

305. The parts played by managers and shareholders in U.S. corporations also need careful examination. In U.S. law, the primary responsibility of managers is to exercise prudent business judgment in the interest of a profitable return to investors. But morally this legal responsibility may be exercised only within the bounds of justice to employees, customers, suppliers, and the local community. Corporate mergers and hostile takeovers may bring greater benefits to shareholders, but they often lead to decreased concern for the well-being of local communities and make towns and cities more vulnerable to decisions made from afar.

306. Most shareholders today exercise relatively little power in corporate governance.[14] Although shareholders can and should vote on the selection of corporate directors and on investment questions and other policy matters, it appears that return on investment is the governing criterion in the relation between them and management. We do not believe this is an adequate rationale for shareholder decisions. The question of how to relate the rights and responsibilities of shareholders to those of the other people and communities affected by corporate decisions is complex and insufficiently understood. We, therefore, urge serious, long-term research and experimentation in this area. More effective ways of dealing with these questions are essential to enable firms to serve the common good.

B. Local and Regional Cooperation

307. The context within which U.S. firms do business has direct influence on their ability to contribute to the common good. Companies and indeed whole industries are not sole masters of their own fate. Increased cooperative efforts are needed to make local, regional, national, and international conditions more supportive of the pursuit of economic justice.

308. In the principle of subsidiarity, Catholic social teaching has long stressed the importance of small- and intermediate-sized communities or institutions in exercising moral responsibility. These mediating structures link the individual to society as a whole in a way that gives people greater freedom and power to act.[15] Such groups include families, neighborhoods, church congregations, community organizations, civic and business associations, public interest and advocacy groups, community development corporations, and many other bodies. All these groups can play a crucial

role in generating creative partnerships for the pursuit of the public good on the local and regional level.

309. The value of partnership is illustrated by considering how new jobs are created. The development of new businesses to serve the local community is key to revitalizing areas hit hard by unemployment.[16] The cities and regions in greatest needs of these new jobs face serious obstacles in attracting enterprises that can provide them. Lack of financial resources, limited entrepreneurial skill, blighted and unsafe environments, and a deteriorating infrastructure create a vicious cycle that makes new investment in these areas more risky and therefore less likely.

310. Breaking out of this cycle will require a cooperative approach that draws on all the resources of the community.[17] Community development corporations can keep efforts focused on assisting those most in need. Existing business, labor, financial, and academic institutions can provide expertise in partnership with innovative entrepreneurs. New cooperative structures of local ownership will give the community or region an added stake in businesses and even more importantly give these businesses a greater stake in the community.[18] Government on the local, state, and national levels must play a significant role, especially through tax structures that encourage investment in hard hit areas and through funding aimed at conservation and basic infrastructure needs. Initiatives like these can contribute to a multilevel response to the needs of the community.

311. The Church itself can work as an effective partner on the local and regional level. First-hand knowledge of community needs and commitment to the protection of the dignity of all should put Church leaders in the forefront of efforts to encourage a community-wide cooperative strategy. Because churches include members from many different parts of the community, they can often serve as mediator between groups who might otherwise regard each other with suspicion. We urge local church groups to work creatively and in partnership with other private and public groups in responding to local and regional problems.

C. Partnership in the Development of National Policies

312. The causes of our national economic problems and their possible solutions are the subject of vigorous debate today. The discussion often turns on the role the national government has played in creating these problems and could play in remedying them. We want to point to several considerations that could help build new forms of effective citizenship and cooperation in shaping the economic life of our country.

313. First, while economic freedom and personal initiative are deservedly esteemed in our society, we have increasingly come to recognize the inescapably social and political nature of the economy. The market is always embedded in a specific social and political context. The tax system affects consumption, saving, and investment. National monetary policy, domestic and defense programs, protection of the environment and worker safety, and regulation of international trade all shape the economy as a whole. These policies influence domestic investment, unemployment rates, foreign exchange, and the health of the entire world economy.

314. The principle of subsidiarity calls for government intervention when small or intermediate groups in society are unable or unwilling to take the steps needed to promote basic justice. Pope John XXIII observed that the growth of more complex

relations of interdependence among citizens has led to an increased role for government in modern societies.[19] This role is to work in *partnership with* the many other groups in society, helping them fulfill their tasks and responsibilities more effectively, not replacing or destroying them. The challenge of today is to move beyond abstract disputes about whether more or less government intervention is needed, to consideration of creative ways of enabling government and private groups to work together effectively.

315.   It is in this light that we understand Pope John Paul II's recommendation that "society make provision for overall planning" in the economic domain.[20] Planning must occur on various levels, with the government ensuring that basic justice is protected and also protecting the rights and freedoms of all other agents. In the Pope's words:

> In the final analysis this overall concern weighs on the shoulders of the state, but it cannot mean onesided centralization by the public authorities. Instead what is in question is a just and rational coordination within the framework of which the initiative of individuals, free groups, and local work centers and complexes must be safeguarded.[21]

316.   We are well aware that the mere mention of economic planning is likely to produce a strong negative reaction in U.S. society. It conjures up images of centralized planning boards, command economies, inefficient bureaucracies, and mountains of government paperwork. It is also clear that the meaning of "planning" is open to a wide variety of interpretations and takes very different forms in various nations.[22] The Pope's words should not be construed as an endorsement of a highly centralized form of economic planning, much less a totalitarian one. His call for a " just and rational coordination" of the endeavors of the many economic actors is a call to seek creative new partnership and forms of participation in shaping national policies.

317.   There are already many forms of economic planning going on within the U.S. economy today. Individuals and families plan for their economic future. Management and labor unions regularly develop both long- and short-term plans. Towns, cities, and regions frequently have planning agencies concerned with their social and economic future. When state legislatures and the U.S. Congress vote on budgets or on almost any other bill that comes before them, they are engaged in a form of public planning. Catholic social teaching does not propose a single model for political and economic life by which these levels are to be institutionally related to each other. It does insist that reasonable coordination among the different parts of the body politic is an essential condition for achieving justice. This is a moral precondition of good citizenship that applies to both individual and institutional actors. In its absence no political structure can guarantee justice in society or the economy. Effective decisions in these matters will demand greater cooperation among all citizens. To encourage our fellow citizens to consider more carefully the appropriate balance of private and local initiative with national economic policy, we make several recommendations.

318,   *First, in an advanced industrial economy like ours, all parts of society, including government, must cooperate in forming national economic policies.* Taxation, monetary policy, high levels of government spending, and many other forms of governmental regulation are here to stay. A modern economy without governmental interventions of the sort we have alluded to is inconceivable. These interventions, however, should help, not replace, the contributions of other economic actors and institutions and should direct them to the common good. The development of effective new forms of partnership between private and public agencies will be difficult in a situation as immensely complex its that of the United States in which various aspects of national policy seem to contradict one another.[23] On the theoretical level, achieving greater coordination will make demands on those with the technical competence to analyze the relationship among different parts of the economy. More practically, it will require the various subgroups within our society to sharpen their concern for the common good and moderate their efforts to protect their own short-term interests.

319. *Second, the impact of national economic policies on the poor and the vulnerable is the primary criterion for judging their moral value.* Throughout this letter we have stressed the special place of the poor and the vulnerable in any ethical analysis of the U.S. economy. National economic policies that contribute to building a true commonwealth should reflect this by standing firmly for the rights of those who fall through the cracks of our economy: the poor, the unemployed, the homeless, the displaced. Being a citizen of this land means sharing in the responsibility for shaping and implementing such policies.

320 *Third, the serious distortion of national economic priorities produced by massive national spending on defense must be remedied.* Clear-sighted consideration of the role of government shows that government and the economy are already closely intertwined through military research and defense contracts. Defense-related industries make up a major part of the U.S. economy and have intimate links with both the military and civilian government, they often depart from the competitive model of free-market capitalism. Moreover, the dedication of so much of the national budget to military purposes has been disastrous for the poor and vulnerable members of our own and other nations, The nation's spending priorities need to be revised in the interests of both justice and peace.[24]

321. We recognize that these proposals do not provide a detailed agenda. We are also aware that there is a tension between setting the goals for coherent policies and actually arriving at them by democratic means . But if we can increase the level of commitment to the common good and the virtues of citizenship in our nation, the ability to achieve these goals will greatly increase. It is these fundamental moral concerns that lead us as bishops to join the debate on national priorities.

D. Cooperation at the International Level

322. If our country is to guide its international economic relationships by policies that serve human dignity and justice, we must expand our understanding of the moral responsibility of citizens to serve the common good of the entire planet. Cooperation is not limited to the local, regional, or national level. Economic policy can no longer be governed by national goals alone. The fact that the "social question has become worldwide"[25] challenges us to broaden our horizons and enhance our collaboration and sense of solidarity on the global level. The cause of democracy is closely tied to the cause of economic justice. The unfinished business of the American experiment includes the formation of new international partnerships, especially with the developing countries, based on mutual respect, cooperation, and a dedication to fundamental justice.

323. The principle of subsidiary calls for government to intervene in the economy when basic justice requires greater social coordination and regulation of economic actors

and institutions. In global economic relations, however, no international institution provides this sort of coordination and regulation. The, U.N. system, including the World Bank, the International Monetary Fund, and the General Agreement on Tariffs and Trade, does not possess the requisite authority. Pope John XXIII called this institutional weakness a "structural defect" in the organization of the human community. The structures of world order, including economic ones, "no longer correspond to the objective requirements of the universal common good."[26]

324. Locked together in a world of limited material resources and a growing array of common problems, we help or hurt one another by the economic policies we choose. All the economic agents in our society, therefore, must consciously and deliberately attend to the good of the whole human family. We must all work to increase the effectiveness of international agencies in addressing global problems that-cannot be handled through the actions of individual countries. In particular we repeat our plea made in *The Challenge of Peace* urging "that the United States adopt a stronger supportive leadership role with respect to the United Nations."[27] In the years following World War II, the United States took the lead in establishing multilateral bodies to deal with postwar economic problems. Unfortunately, in recent years this country has taken steps that have weakened rather than strengthened multilateral approaches. This is a shortsighted policy and should be reversed if the long-term interests of an interdependent globe are to be served.[28] In devising more effective arrangements for pursuing international economic justice, the overriding problem is how to get from where we are to where we ought to be. Progress toward that goal demands positive and often difficult action by corporations, banks, labor unions, governments, and other major actors on the international stage. But whatever the difficulty, the need to give priority to alleviating poverty in developing countries is undeniable; and the cost of continued inaction can be counted in human lives lost or stunted, talents wasted, opportunities foregone, misery and suffering prolonged, and injustice condoned.

325. Self-restraint and self-criticism by all parties are necessary first steps toward strengthening the international structures to protect the common good. Otherwise, growing interdependence will lead to conflict and increased economic threats to human dignity. This is an important long-term challenge to the economic future of this country and its place in the emerging world economic community.

Notes

Chapter I

1. Vatican Council 11, *The Pastoral Constitution on the Church in the Modern World*. 33. [Note: This pastoral letter frequently refers to documents of the Second Vatican Council, papal encyclicals, and other official teachings of the Roman Catholic Church. Most of these texts have been published by the United States Catholic Conference Office of Publishing and Pro motion Services; many are available in collections, though no single collection is comprehensive. See Selected Bibliography.

2. *Pastoral Constitution*, 1.

3. See ibid., 10, 42, 43; Congregation for the Doctrine of the Faith, *Instruction on Christian Freedom and Liberation*. (Washington, D.C.: USCC Office of Publishing and Promotion Services, 1986), 34–36.

4. See Pope John Paul II, *On Human Work* (1981), 14; and Pope Paul VI, *Octogesima Adveniens* (1971), 35. See also Arthur Okun, *Equality and Efficiency: The Big Tradeoff* (Washington, D.C.: The Brookings Institution, 1975), ch. 1; Michael Walter, *Spheres of Justice: A Defense of Pluralism and Equality* (New York: Basic Books, 1983), ch. 4; Jon P. Gunnemann, "Capitalism and Commutative Justice," paper presented the 1985 meeting of the Society of Christian Ethics.

5. Abraham Lincoln, Address at Dedication of National Cemetery at Gettysburg, November 9, 1863.

6. Pope John XXIII, *Peace on Earth* (1963), 130-131

7. Synod of Bishops, *Justice in the World* (1971), 8; Pope John Paul II, *Redeemer of Man* (1979), 15.

8. U.S. Department of Labor, Bureau of Labor Statistics, *The Employment Situation: August* 1985 (September 1985), Table A-l.

9. Ibid.

10. U.S. Bureau of the Census, Current Population Reports, Series P-60, 145 *Money, Income, and Povertyt Status of Families and Persons in the United States: 1983* (Washington, D.C.: U.S. Government Printing Office 1984), 20.

11. Greg H. Duncan, *Years of Poverty, Years of Plenty: The Changing Economic Fortunes of American Workers and Their Families* (Ann Arbor, Mich.: Institute for Social Research, University of Michigan, 1984).

12. See Pope John Paul II, *Familiaris Consortio* (1981), 46.

13. *Pastoral Constitution*, 47.

14. National Conference of Catholic Bishops, *The Challenge of Peace: God's Promise and Our Response* (Washington, D.C.: USCC Office of Publishing and Promotion Services, 1983).

15. Cardinal Joseph L. Bernardin and Cardinal John J. O'Connor, Testimony before the House Foreign Relations Committee, June 26, 1984, *Origins* 14:10 (August 10, 1984): 157.

16. *Pastoral Constitution*, 43.

17. See, for example, Peter Berger, Brigitte Berger, and Hansfried Kellner, *The Homeless Mind: Modernization and Consciousness* (New York: Vintage, 1974).

18. For a recent study of the importance and difficulty of achieving such a common language and vision see Robert N. Bellah, Richard Madsen, William M. Sullivan, Ann Swindler, and Stephen M. Tipton, *Habits of the Heart: Individualism and Commitment in American* Life (Berkeley, Calif.: University of California Press, 1985). See also Martin E. Marty, *The Public Church* (New York: Crossroads, 1981).

19. Pope John Paul XXIII, *Mater et Magistra* (1961), 219; *Pastoral Constitution*, 40.

20. Congregation for the Doctrine of the Faith, *Instruction on Certain Aspects of the Theology of Liberation* (Washington, D.C.: USCC Office of Publishing and Promotion Services, 1984); Pope Paul VI, *Octogesima Adveniens* (1971), 42.

21. *Octogesima Adveniens*, 4.

22. Administrative Committee of the National Catholic War Council, *Program of Social Reconstnstruction*, February 12, 1919. Other notable statements on the economy by our predecessors are *The Present Crisis*, April 25, 1933; *Statement on Church and Social Order*, February 4, 1940; *The Economy: Human Dimensions*, November 20, 1975. These and numerous other statements of the U.S. Catholic episcopate can be found in Hugh J. Nolan, ed., *Pastoral Letters of the United States Catholic Bishops*, 4 vols. (Washington, D.C.: USCC Office of Publishing and Promotion Services, 1984).

Chapter IV

1. *Octogesima Adveniens*, 24.

2. For different analyses along these lines with quite different starting points see Martin Carnoy, Derek Shearer, and Russell Rumberger, *A New Social Contract* (New York: Harper and Row, 1983); Amatai Elzioni, *An Immodest Agenda: Reconstructing America before the Twenty-First Century* (New York:

McGraw. Hill, 1983); Charles E. Lindblon, *Politics and Markets* (New York: Basic Books, 1977), esp. 346–348; George C. Lodge, *The New American Ideology* (New York: Alfred A. Knopf, 1975); Douglas Sturm, "Corporations, Constitutions, and Covenants," *Journal of the American Academy of Religion, 41* (1973); 331–55; Lester Thurow, *The Zero-Sum Society* (New York: Basic Books, 1980), esp. ch. 1; Roberto Mangabeira Unger, *Knowledge and Politics* (New York: Free Press, 1975); George F. Will, *Statecraft as Soulcraft: What Government Does* (New York: Simon and Schuster, 1982), esp. ch. 6.

3. *Pastoral Constitution*, 68. See *Mater et Magistra*, 75–77.

4. Charles W. Powers provided a helpful discussion of these matters in a paper presented at a conference on the first draft of this pastoral letter sponsored by the Harvard University Divinity School and the Institute for Policy Studies, Cambridge, Massachusetts, March, 29–31,1985.

5. See John Paul 11, "The Role of Business in a Changing Workplace," 3, *Origins* 15 (February 6. 1986): 567.

6. *Rerum Novarum*, 28. For an analysis of the relevant papal teachings on institutions of collaboration and partnership, see John Cronin, *Catholic Social Principles: The Social Teaching of the Catholic Church Applied to American Economic Life* (Milwaukee: Bruce, 1950), ch. VII; Oswald von Nell-Breuning, *Reorganization of Social Economy: The Social Encyclical Developed and Explained*, trans. J. R. Kirwan (Chicago: Regnery, 1961), ch. XIX.

7. Michael Conte, Arnold S. Tannenbaum, and Donna McCulloch, *Employee Ownership*, Research Report Series, Institute for Social Research (Ann Arbor, Mich.: University of Michigan, 1981); Robert A. Dahl, *A Preface to Economic Democracy* (Berkeley: University of California Press, 1985); Harvard Business School, "The Mondragon Cooperative Movement," case study prepared by David P. Ellerman (Cambridge, Mass.: Harvard Business School, n.d.); Robert Jackall and Henry M. Levin, eds., *Worker Cooperatives in America* (Berkeley: University of California Press, 1984); Derek Jones and Jan Svejnar, eds., *Participatory and Self-Managed Firms: Evaluating Economic Performance (Lexington, Mass.: D. C. Heath, 1982); Irving H. Siegel and Edgar Weinberg, *Labor-Management Cooperation: The American Experience* (Kalamazoo, Mich.: W. E. Upjohn Institute for Employment Research, 1982); Stuart M. Speiser, "Broadened Capital Ownership—The Solution to Major Domestic and International Problems," *Journal of Post Keynesian Economics* VIII (1985); 426–434; Jaroslav Vanek, ed., *Self-Management: Economic Liberation of Man* (London: Penguin, 1975); Martin L. Weitzman, *The Share Economy* (Cambridge, Mass.: Harvard University Press, 1984).

8. *Program of Social Reconstruction in Justice in the Marketplace, 381.*

9. *Mater et Magistra*, 32, 77, 85–103; *On Human Work*, 14.

10. For examples of worker-owned and operated enterprises supported by the Campaign for Human Development's revolving loan fund see CHD's *Annual Report* (Washington, D.C.: USCC).

11. *Quadragesimo Anno* states the basic norm on which this conclusion is based: "It is wholly false to ascribe to property alone or to labor alone whatever has been obtained through the combined effort of both, and it is wholly unjust for either, denying the efficacy of the other, to arrogate to itself whatever has been produced" (53).

12. *On Human Work*, 12.

13. Ibid., 20. This point was well made by John Cronin twenty-five years ago: "Even if most injustice and exploitation were removed, unions would still have a legitimate place. They are the normal voice of labor, necessary to organize social life for the common good. There is positive need for such organization today, quite independently of any social evils which may prevail. Order and harmony do not happen; they are the fruit of conscious and organized effort. While we may hope that the abuses which occasioned the rise of unions may disappear, it does not thereby follow that unions will have lost their function. On the contrary, they will be freed from unpleasant, even though temporarily necessary, tasks and able to devote all their efforts to a better organization of social life" *Catholic Social Principles*, 418. See also AFL-CIO Committee on the Evolution of Work, *The Future of Work* (Washington, D.C.: AFL-CIO, 1983).

14. For a classic discussion of the relative power of managers and shareholders see A. A. Berle and Gardiner C. Means, *The Modern Corporation and Private Property* (New York: Macmillan, *1932*).

15. Peter L. Berger and Richard John Neuhaus, *To Empower People: The Role of Mediating Structures in Public Policy* (Washington, D.C.: American Enterprise Institute, *1977*).

16. United States Small Business Administration, *1978 Annual Report* (Washington, D.C.: Government Printing Office, *1979*).

17. For recent discussion from a variety of perspectives see: Robert Friedman and William Schweke, eds., *Expanding the Opportunity to Produce: Revitalizing the American Economy through New Enterprise Development: A Policy Reader* (Washington, D.C.: Corporation for New Enterprise Development, 1981); Jack A. Meyer, ed., *Meeting Human Needs: Toward a New Public Philosophy* (Washington, D.C.: American Enterprise Institute, *1982*); Committee for Economic Development, *Jobs for the Hard-to-Employ: New Directions for a Public-Private Partnership* (New York: Committee for Economic Development, *1978*); Gar Alperovitz and Jeff Faux, *Rebuilding America: A Blueprint for the New Economy* (New York: Pantheon Books, *1984*).

18. Christopher Mackin, *Strategies for Local Ownership and Control: A Policy Analysis* (Somerville, Mass.: Industrial Cooperative Association, 1983).

19. *Mater et Magistra*, 59, 62.

20. *On Human Work*, 18.

21. Ibid.

22. For examples and analysis of different meanings of economic planning see Naomi Caiden and Aaron Wildavsky, *Planning and Budgeting in Poor Countries* (New York: Wiley, *1974*); Robert Dahl and Charles E. Lindblom, *Politics, Economics and Welfare: Planning and Politico-Economic Systems Resolved into Basic Social Processes* (Chicago: University of Chicago Press, 1976); Stephen S. Cohen, *Modern Capitalist Planning : The French Model* (Berkeley, University of California Press, *1977*); Albert Waterston, *Development Planning: Lessons of Experience* (Baltimore: Johns Hopkins Press, *1965*); *Rebuilding America*, chs. 14, 15.

23. For example, many students of recent policy point out that monetary policy on the one hand and fiscal policies governing taxation and government expenditures on the other have been at odds with each other, with larger public deficits and high interest rates the outcome. See Alice M. Rivlin, ed., *Economic Choices 1984* (Washington, D.C.: The Brookings Institution 1984), esp. ch. 2.

24. *The Challenge of Peace*, 270–271.

25. *On the Development of Peoples*, 3.

26. *Peace on Earth*, 134–135.

27. *The Challenge of Peace*, 268.

28. See Robert 0. Keohane and Joseph S. Nye, Jr., "Two Cheers for Multilateralism," *Foreign Policy* 60 (Fall 1985): 148–167.

Howard Fast, *Time and the Riddle*, 1975

The Cold, Cold Box
Howard Fast

As always, the annual meeting of the Board of Directors convened at nine o'clock in the morning, on the 10th of December. Nine o'clock in the morning was a sensible and reasonable hour to begin a day's work, and long ago, the 10th of December had been chosen as a guarantee against the seduction of words. Every one of the directors would have to be home for the Christmas holiday—or its equivalent—and therefore the agenda was timed for precisely two weeks and not an hour more.

In the beginning, this had caused many late sessions, sometimes two or three days when the directors met the clock round, with no break for sleep or rest. But in time, as things fell into the proper place and orderly management replaced improvisation, each day's meeting was able to adjourn by four o'clock in the afternoon—and there were even years when the general meeting finished its work a day or two early.

By now, the meeting of the Board of Directors was very matter-of-fact and routine. The big clock on the wall of the charming and spacious meeting room was just sounding nine, its voice low and musical, as the last of the directors found their seats. They nodded pleasantly to each other, and if they were seated close to old friends, they exchanged greetings. They were completely relaxed, neither tense nor uneasy at the thought of the long meeting that lay ahead of them.

There were exactly three hundred of these directors, and they sat in a comfortable circle of many tiers of seats—in a room not unlike a small amphitheatre. Two aisles cut through to a center circle or stage about twenty feet in diameter, and there a podium was placed which allowed the speaker to turn in any direction as he spoke. Since the number of three hundred was an arbitrary one, agreed upon after a good deal of trial and error, and maintained as an excellent working size, half the seats in the meeting room were always empty. There was some talk now and then of redesigning the meeting room, but nobody ever got down to doing it and by now the empty seats were a normal part of the decor.

The membership of the Board was about equally divided between men and women. No one could serve under the age of thirty, but retirement was a matter of personal decision, and a reasonable number of members were over seventy. Two thirds of them were in their fifties. Since the Board was responsible for an international management, it was only natural that all nations and races should be represented—black men and white men and brown men and yellow men, and all the shadings and gradations in between. Like the United Nations—they were too modest to make such a comparison themselves—they had a number of official languages (and a system of simultaneous translation), though English was most frequently used.

As a matter of fact, the Chairman of the Board who had been born in Indo-China, opened this meeting in English, which he spoke very well and with ease, and after he had welcomed them and announced the total attendance—all members present—he said:

"At the beginning of our annual meeting—and this is an established procedure, I may say—we deal with a moral and legal point, the question of Mr. Steve Kovac. We undertake this before the reading of the agenda, for we have felt that this question of Mr. Kovac is not a matter of agenda or business, but of conscience. Of our conscience, I must add, and not without humility; for Mr. Kovac is the only secret of this meeting. All else that the Board discusses, votes upon and decides or rejects, will be made public, as you know. But of Mr. Steve Kovac the world knows nothing; and each year in the past, our decision has been that the world should continue to know nothing about Mr. Kovac. Each year in the past, Mr. Kovac has been the object of a cruel and criminal action by the members of this Board. Each year in the past, it has been our decision to repeat this crime."

To these words, most of the members of the Board did not react at all—but here and there young men and women showed their surprise, bewilderment and unease, either by expressions on their faces or by low protestations of disbelief. The members of the Board were not insensitive people.

"This year, as in the past, we make this question of Mr. Kovac our first piece of business—because we cannot go onto our other business until it is decided. As in the past, we will decide whether to engage in a criminal conspiracy or not."

A young woman, a new member of the board, her face flushed and angry, rose and asked the chairman if he would yield for a question. He replied that he would.

"Am I to understand that you are serious, Mr. Chairman, or is this some sophomoric prank for the edification of new members?"

"This board is not used to such descriptive terms as sophomoric, as you should know, Mrs. Ramu," he answered mildly. "I am quite serious."

The young woman sat down. She bit her lower lip and stared at her lap. A young man arose.

"Yes, Mr. Steffanson?" the chairman said pleasantly.

The young man sat down again. The older members were gravely attentive, thoughtful without impatience.

"I do not intend to choke off any discussion, and I will gladly yield to any questions," said the Chairman, "but perhaps a little more about this troublesome matter first. There are two reasons why we consider this problem each year. Firstly, because the kind of crime we have committed in the past is hardly anything to grow indifferent to; we need to be reminded; premeditated crime is a deadly threat to basic decency, and God help us if we should ever become complacent! Secondly, each year, there are new members on this board, and it is necessary that they should hear all of the facts in the case of Mr. Kovac. This year, we have seven new members. I address myself to them, but not only to them. I include all of my fellow members of this Board."

Steve Kovac (the President of the Board began) was born in Pittsburgh in the year 1913. He was one of eleven children, four of whom survived to adulthood. This was not too unusual in those days of poverty, ignorance and primitive medicine.

John Kovac, Steve Kovac's father, was a steelworker. When Steve Kovac was six years old, there was a long strike—an attempt on the part of the steelworkers to increase their wages. I am sure you are all familiar with the method of the strike, and therefore I will not elaborate.

During this strike, Steve Kovac's mother died; a year later, John Kovac fell into a vat of molten steel. The mother died of tuberculosis, a disease then incurable. The father's body was dissolved in the molten steel. I mention these things in terms of their very deep and lasting effect on the mind and character of Steve Kovac. Orphaned at the age of seven, he grew up like an animal in the jungle. Placed in a county home for orphan children, he was marked as a bad and intractable boy, beaten daily, deprived of food, punished in every way the ignorance and insensitivity of the authorities could devise. After two years of this, he ran away.

This is a very brief background to the childhood of a most remarkable man, a man of brilliance and strong character, a man of high inventive genius and grim determination. Unfortunately, the mind and personality of this man had been scarred and traumatized beyond redemption. A psychiatric analysis of this process has been prepared, and each of you will find a copy in your portfolio. It also itemizes the trials and suffering of Steve Kovac between the ages of nine and twenty—the years during which he fought to survive and to grow to adulthood.

It also gives a great many details of this time of his life—details I cannot go into. You must understand that while the question before us is related to this background, there are many other features I will deal with.

At this point, the Chairman of the Board paused to take a drink of water and to glance through his notes. The younger members of the Board glanced hurriedly at the psychiatric report; the older members remained contemplative, absorbed in their own thoughts. As many times as they had been through this, somehow it was never dull.

At the age of twenty (the Chairman resumed) Steve Kovac was working in a steel mill outside of Pittsburgh. He was friendly then with a man named Emery. This man, Emery, was alone, without family or means of support. A former coal miner, he suffered from a disease of the lungs, common to his trade. All he had in the world was a five thousand dollar insurance policy. Steve Kovac agreed to support him, and in return he made Kovac the beneficiary of the insurance policy. In those days, insurance policies were frequently the only means with which a family could survive the death of the breadwinner.

Four months later, Emery died. Years afterward, it was rumored that Kovac had hastened his death, but there is no evidence for the rumor. The five thousand dollars became the basis for Steve Kovac's subsequent fortune. Twenty-five years later, the net worth of Steve Kovac was almost three billion dollars. As an individual, he was possibly the wealthiest man in the United States of America. He was a tycoon in the steel and aluminum industries, and he controlled chemical plants, copper mines, railroads, oil refineries and dozens of associated industries. He was then forty-six years old. The year was 1959.

The story of his climb to power and wealth is unique for the generations he lived through. He was a strong, powerful, handsome man—tortured within himself, driven by an insatiable lust to revenge himself, and his father and mother too, for the poverty and suffering of his childhood. Given the traumatic factors of his childhood, his cravings for power turned psychopathic and paranoid, and he built this structure of power securely. He owned newspapers as well as airlines, television stations and publishing houses, and much more than he owned, he controlled. Thereby, he was able to keep himself out of the public eye. In any year of the fifties, you can find no more than an occasional passing reference to him in the press.

How an individual achieved this in a time of the public corporation and the "corporation man" is a singular tale of drive and ambition. Steve Kovac was ambitious, ruthless, merciless and utterly without compassion or pity. His policy was to destroy what stood in his way, if he could; if he could not, he bent it to his will in one way or another. He wrecked lives and fortunes. He framed and entrapped his competitors; he used violence when he had to—when he could not buy or bribe what he wanted. He corrupted individuals and bribed parliaments and bought governments. He erected a structure of power and wealth and control that reached out to every corner of the globe.

And then, in his forty-sixth year, at the height of his wealth and power, he discovered that he had cancer.

The chairman of the Board paused to allow the impact of the words to settle and tell. He took another drink of water. He arranged the papers in front of him.

"At this time," he said. "I propose to read to you a short extract from the diary of Dr. Jacob Frederick. I think that most of you are familiar with the work of Dr. Frederick. In any case, you know that he was elected a member of our Board. Naturally, that was a long time ago. I need only mention that Dr. Frederick was one of the many wise and patient pioneers in the work of cancer research—not only a great physician, but a great scientist. The first entry I propose to read is dated January 12, 1959."

I had an unusual visitor today (the Chairman of the Board read), Steve Kovac, the industrial tycoon. I had heard rumors to the effect of the wealth and power of this man. In himself, he is a striking individual, tall, muscular, handsome, with a broad strong face and a great mane of prematurely-white hair. He has blue eyes, a ruddy complexion, and appears to be in the prime of life and health. Of course, he is not. I examined him thoroughly. There is no hope for the man.

"Doctor," he said to me, "I want the truth. I know it already. You are not the first physician I have seen. But I also want it from you, plainly and bluntly."

I would have told him in any case. He is not the kind of a man you can lie to easily. "Very well," I said to him, "you have cancer. There is no cure for your cancer. You are going to die."

"How long?"

"We can't say. Perhaps a year."

"And if I undergo operative procedure?"

"That could prolong your life—perhaps a year or two longer if the operation is successful. But it will mean pain and incapacity."

"And there is no cure?" His surface was calm, his voice controlled; he must have labored for years to achieve that kind of surface calm and control; but underneath, I could see a very frightened and desperate man.

"None as yet."

"And the quacks and diet men and the rest—they promise cures?"

"It's easy to promise," I said. "But there isn't any cure."

"Doc," he said to me, "I don't want to die and I don't intend to die. I have worked twenty-five years to be where I am now. The tree is planted, I'm going to eat the fruit. I am young and strong—and the best years of my life are ahead of me."

When Kovac talked like that, he was convincing, even to me. It is his quality not simply to demand life, but to take. He denies the inevitable. But the fact remained.

"I can't help you, Mr. Kovac," I told him.

"But you're going to help me," he said calmly, "I came to you because you know more about cancer than any man in the world. Or so I am told."

"You have been misinformed," I said shortly. "No man knows more than anyone else. Such knowledge and work is a collective thing."

"I believe in men, not mobs. I believe you. Therefore, I am ready to pay you a fee of one million dollars if you can make it possible for me to beat this thing and live a full life span." He then reached into his coat for his wallet and took out a certified check for one million dollars. "It is yours—if I live."

I told him to return the following day—that is tomorrow. And now I have been sitting here for hours, thinking of what one million dollars would mean to my work, my hopes—indeed, through them, to all people. I have been thinking with desperation and with small result. Only one thought occurs to me. It is fantastic, but then Steve Kovac is a fantastic man.

Again, the Chairman of the Board paused and looked inquiringly at some of the younger members. They had been listening with what appeared hypnotic concentration. There were no questions and no comments.

"Then I will continue with the diary of Dr. Frederick," the Chairman said.

January 13, (the Chairman said). Steve Kovac returned at 2:00, as we had arranged. He greeted me with a confident smile.

"Doc, if you are ready to sell, I am ready to buy."

"And you really believe that you can buy life?"

"I can buy anything. It's a question of price."

"Can you buy the future?" I asked him. "Because that is where the cure for cancer lies. Do you want to buy it?"

"I'll buy it because you have decided to sell," he said flatly. "I know who I am dealing with. Make your offer, Dr. Frederick."

I made it, as fantastic as it was. I told him about my experiments with the effects of intense cold upon cancer cells. I explained that though, as yet, the experiments had not produced any cure, I had made enormous strides in the intense and speedy application of extreme cold—or, to put it more scientifically, my success in removing heat from living objects, I detailed my experiments—how I had begun with frogs and snakes, freezing them, and then removing the cold and resuming the life process at a later date; how I had experimented with mice, cats, dogs—and most recently monkeys.

He followed me and anticipated me. "How do you restore life?" he wanted to know.

"I don't restore it. The life never dies. In the absence of heat, what might be called the ripening or aging process of life is suspended, but the life remains. Time and motion are closely related; and under intense cold, motion slows and theoretically could cease—all motion, even within the atomic structure. When the motion ceases, time ceases."

"Is it painful?"

"As far as I know, it isn't. The transition is too quick."

"I'd like to see an experiment."

I told him that I had in my laboratory a spider monkey that had been frozen seven weeks ago. My assistants could attest to that. He went into the laboratory with me and watched as we successfully restored the monkey. Seemingly, it was none the worse.

"And the mind?" he asked me.

I shrugged. "I don't know. I have never attempted it with a human being."

"But you think it would work?"

"I am almost certain that it would work. I would need better and larger equipment. With some money to spend, I can improve the process—well, considerably."

He nodded and took the certified check out of his wallet. "Here is your retainer—apart from what you have to spend. Buy whatever you need, and charge it to me. Spend whatever you have to spend and buy the best. No ceiling, no limit. And when I wake up, after a cure has been discovered, there will be a second million to add to your fee. I am not a generous man, but neither am I niggardly when I buy what I want. When will you be ready?"

"Considering the prognosis of your disease," I said, "we should not delay more than five weeks. I will be ready then. Will you?"

Steve Kovac nodded. "I will be ready. There are a good many technical and legal details to work out. I have many large interests, as you may know, and this is a journey of uncertain duration. I will also take care of your own legal responsibilities."

Then he left, and it was done—possibly the strangest agreement ever entered into by a doctor and his patient. I try to think of only one thing—that I now have a million dollars to put into my work and research.

The Chairman of the Board wore pince-nez, and now he paused to wipe them. He cleared his throat, rearranged the papers on the podium once again, and explained.

You see, the plan was a simple one and a sensible one too. Since Mr. Kovac's condition could not be cured, here was a means of preserving his life and arresting the disease until science had found a cure. Timidity was never one of Mr. Kovac's qualities. He analyzed the situation, faced it, and accepted the only possible escape offered to him. So he went about placing his affairs in such order as to guarantee the success and prosperity of his enterprise while he slept—and also their return to his bidding and ownership when he awoke.

In other words, he formed a single holding company for all of his many interests. He gathered together a Board of Directors to manage that holding company in his absence, making himself president in absentia with a substitute president to preside while he was gone. He made a set of qualifying bylaws, that no president could hold office for more than two years, that the Board was to be enlarged each year and a number of other details, each of them aimed at the single goal of retaining all power to himself. And because he was not dead, but merely absent, he created a unique situation, one unprecedented in the history of finance.

This holding company was exempted from all the traditional brakes and tolls placed upon previous companies through the mechanism of death. Until Mr. Kovac resumed, the holding company was immortal. Naturally, Dr. Frederick was placed upon the Board of Directors.

In other words (the Chairman of the Board concluded) that is how this Board of Directors came into being.

He allowed himself his first smile then. "Are there any questions at this point?" he asked mildly.

A new member from Japan rose and wanted to know why, if this was the case, the whole world should be told otherwise?

We thought it best (said the President). Just as we, on this Board, have great powers for progress and construction, so do we have no inconsiderable powers of concealment and alteration. The people of the United States and the United Kingdom might have accepted the knowledge that Steve Kovac brought this Board of Directors into being, but certainly in the Soviet Union and China, such knowledge might have been most disconcerting and destructive. Remember that once we had established an open trade area in the Soviet Union and had brought three of her leading government people onto our Board of Directors, our situation changed radically. We were enabled then, through a seizure of all fuel supplies on earth, to prevent the imminent outbreak of World War 111.

At that point, neither the extent of our holdings nor the amount of our profits could be further concealed. I say we (the Chairman deferred modestly) but of course it was our predecessors who faced these problems. Our cash balance was larger than that of the United States Treasury, our industrial potential greater than that of any major power. Believe me, without planned intent or purpose, this Board of Directors suddenly found itself the dominant force on earth. At that point, it became desperately necessary for us to explain what we represented.

A new member from Australia rose and asked, "How long was that, Mr. Chairman, if I may inquire, after the visit of Mr. Kovac to Dr. Frederick?"

The Chairman nodded. "It was the year Dr. Frederick died—twenty-two years after the treatment began. By then, five types of cancer had already surrendered their secret to science. But there was not yet any cure for Mr. Kovac's disease."

"And all the time, the treatment had remained secret?"

"All the time," the Chairman nodded.

You see (he went on), at that time, the Board felt that the people of Earth had reached a moment of crisis and decision. A moment, I say, for the power was only momentarily in the hands of this Board. We had no armies, navies or air-fleets—all we had were a major portion of the tools of production. We knew we had not prevented war but simply staved it off. This was a Board of Directors for management, not for power, and any day the installations and plants we owned and controlled could have been torn from our grasp. That was when our very thoughtful and wise predecessors decided to embark on a vast, global propaganda campaign to convince the world that we represented a secret Parliament of the wisest and best forces of mankind—that we were in effect a Board of Directors for the complex of mankind.

And in this, we succeeded, for the television stations, the newspapers, the radio, the film and the theatre—all these were ours. And in that brief, fortunate moment, we launched our attack. We used the weapons of Steve Kovac—let us be honest and admit that. We acted as he would have acted, but out of different motives entirely.

We bought and bribed and framed. We infiltrated the parliaments of all mankind. We bought the military commanders. We dissolved the armies and navies in the name of super-weapons, and then we destroyed the super-weapons in the name of mankind. Where leaders could not be bought or bribed, we brought them into our Board. And above all, we bought control—control of every manufacturing, farming or mining unit of any consequence upon the face of the earth.

It took the Board of Directors twenty-nine years more to accomplish this; and at the end of that twenty-nine years our earth was a single complex of production for use and happiness—and if I may say so, for mankind. A semblance of national structure remained, but it was even then as ritualistic and limited as any commonwealth among the old states of the United States. Wars, armies, navies, atom bombs—all of these were only ugly memories. The era of reason and sanity began, the era of production for use and life under the single legal code of man. Thus, we have become creatures of law, equal under the law, and abiding by the law. This Board of Directors was never a government, nor is it now. It is what it proposes to be, a group management for the holding company.

Only today, the holding company and the means of mankind are inseparable. Thereby, our very great responsibility.

The Chairman of the Board wiped his face and took a few more sips of water. A new member from the United States rose and said, "But Mr. Chairman, the cure for all types of cancer was discovered sixty-two years ago."

"So it was," the Chairman agreed.

"Then, Steve Kovac—"The new member paused. She was a beautiful, sensitive woman in her middle thirties, a physicist of note and talent, and also an accomplished musician.

"You see, my dear," the Chairman said, lapsing into a most informal mode of address, pardonable only because of his years and dignity, "it faced us. When we make a law for mankind and submit to it, we must honor it. Sixty-two years ago, Steve Kovac owned the world and all its wealth and industry, a dictator beyond the dream of any dictator, a tyrant above all tyrants, a king and an emperor to dwarf all other kings and emperors—"

As he spoke, two of the older members left the meeting room. Minutes later, they returned, wheeling into the room and up to the podium a rectangular object, five feet high, seven feet long and three feet wide, the whole of it covered with a white cloth. They left it there and returned to their seats.

"—yes, he owned the world. Think of it—for the first time in history, a just peace governed the nations of mankind. Cities were being rebuilt, deserts turned into gardens, jungles cleared, poverty and crime a thing of the past. Man was standing erect, flexing his muscles, reaching out to the planets and the stars—and all of this belonged to a single savage, merciless, despotic paranoid, Steve Kovac. Then, as now, my dear associates, this Board of Directors was faced with the problem of the man to whom we owed our existence, the man who all unwittingly unified mankind and ushered in the new age of man—yes, the man who gave us the right and authority to hold and manage, the man whose property we manage. Then as now, we were faced with Steve Kovac!"

Almost theatrical in his conclusion and gestures, the Chairman of the Board stepped down from the podium and with one motion swept the cloth aside. The entire Board fixed their eyes on the cabinet where, under a glass cover, in a cold beyond all concept of cold, a man lay sleeping in what was neither life nor death, but a subjective pause in the passage of time. He was a handsome man, big and broad, ruddy of face and with a fine mane of white hair. He seemed to sleep lightly, expectantly, confidently—as if he were dreaming hungrily but pleasantly of what he would awaken to.

"Steve Kovac," the President said. "So he sleeps from year to year, no difference, no changes. So he appeared to our predecessors sixty-two years ago, when they first had the means to cure him and the obligation to awaken him. They committed the first of sixty-two crimes; they took no action in the face of a promise, a duty, a legality and an almost sacred obligation. Can we understand them? Can we forgive them? Can we forgive the board that voted this same decision again and again? Above all, can we forgive ourselves if we stain our honor, break the law, and ignore our own inheritance of an obligation?

"I am not here to argue the question. It is never argued. The facts are presented, and then we vote. Therefore, will all those in favor of awakening Mr. Kovac raise their right hands?"

The President of the Board waited. Long moments became minutes, but no hands were raised. The two older members covered the cold, cold box and wheeled it out. The Chairman of the Board took a sip of water, and announced.

"We will now have the reading of the agenda."

Henrik Ibsen, *An Enemy of the People*, (adapted by Arthur Miller) 1951, 1979

An Enemy of the People
Henrik Ibsen

This excerpt is from Act One of An Enemy of the People. *In this play, Dr. Stockmann has discovered that the town bath' a major income for the community, is contaminated. He has convinced some townspeople, including the press, that persons coming to the baths for health reasons are actually being poisoned. His brother, the mayor, does not want the baths closed and convinces the town that Dr. Stockmann is actually an enemy of the people.*

Dr. Stockmann, *goes to dining room and looks in:*

Catherine! Oh, you're home already, Petra!

Petra, *coming in:*   I just got back from school.

Mrs. Stockmann, *entering:*   Hasn't he been here yet?

Dr. Stockmann: Peter? No, but I just had a long chat with Hovstad. He's really fascinated with my discovery, and you know, it has more implications than I thought at first. Do you know what I have backing me up?

Mrs. Stockmann: What in heaven's name have you got backing you up?

Dr. Stockmann: The solid majority.

Mrs. Stockmann: Is that good?

Dr. Stockmann: Good? It's wonderful. You can't imagine the feeling, Catherine, to know that your own town feels like a brother to you. I have never felt so at home in this town since I was a boy. *A noise is heard.*

Mrs. Stockmann: That must be the front door.

Dr. Stockmann: Oh, it's Peter then. Come in.

Peter Stockmann, *entering from the hall:*   Good morning!

Dr. Stockmann: It's nice to see you, Peter.

Mrs. Stockmann: Good morning. How are you today?

Peter Stockmann: Well, so so. *To Dr. Stockmann:* I received your thesis about the condition of the springs yesterday.

431

Dr. Stockmann: I got your note. Did you read it?

Peter Stockmann: I read it.

Dr. Stockmann: Well, what do you have to say? *Peter Stockmann clears his throat and glances at the women.*

Mrs. Stockmann: Come on, Petra. *She and Petra leave the room at the left.*

Peter Stockmann, *after a moment:* Thomas, was it really necessary to go into this investigation behind my back?

Dr. Stockmann: Yes. Until I was convinced myself, there was no point in—

Peter Stockmann: And now you are convinced?

Dr. Stockmann: Well, certainly. Aren't you too, Peter? *Pause.* The University chemists corroborated . . .

Peter Stockmann: You intend to present this document to the Board of Directors, officially, as the medical officer of the springs?

Dr. Stockmann: Of course, something's got to be done, and quick.

Peter Stockmann: You always use such strong expressions, Thomas. Among other things in your report you say that we *guarantee* our guests and visitors a permanent case of poisoning.

Dr. Stockmann: But, Peter, how can you describe it any other way? Imagine! Poisoned internally and externally!

Peter Stockmann: So you merrily conclude that we must build a waste-disposal plant—and reconstruct a brand-new water system from the bottom up!

Dr. Stockmann: Well, do you know some other way out? I don't.

Peter Stockmann: I took a little walk over to the city engineer this morning and in the course of conversation I sort of jokingly mentioned these changes—as something we might consider for the future, you know.

Dr. Stockmann: The future won't be soon enough, Peter.

Peter Stockmann: The engineer kind of smiled at my extravagance and gave me a few facts. I don't suppose you have taken the trouble to consider what your proposed changes would cost?

Dr. Stockmann: No, I never thought of that.

Peter Stockmann: Naturally. Your little project would come to at least three hundred thousand crowns.

Dr. Stockmann, *astonished:*   That expensive!

Peter Stockmann: Oh, don't look so upset—it's only money. The worst thing is that it would take some two years.

Dr. Stockmann: Two years?

Peter Stockmann: At the least. And what do you propose we do about the springs in the meantime? Shut them up, no doubt! Because we would have to, you know. As soon as the rumor gets around that the water is dangerous, we won't have a visitor left. So that's the picture, Thomas. You have it in your power literally to ruin your own town.

Dr. Stockmann: Now look, Peter! I don't want to ruin anything.

Peter Stockmann: Kirsten Springs are the blood supply of this town, Thomas—the only future we've got here. Now will you stop and think?

Dr. Stockmann: Good God! Well, what do you think we ought to do?

Peter Stockmann: Your report has not convinced me that the conditions are as dangerous as you try to make them.

Dr. Stockmann: Now listen; they are even worse than the report makes them out to be. Remember, summer is coming, and the warm weather!

Peter Stockmann: I think you're exaggerating. A capable physician ought to know what precautions to take.

Dr. Stockmann: And what then?

Peter Stockmann: The existing water supply for the springs is a fact, Thomas, and has got to be treated as a fact. If you are reasonable and act with discretion, the directors of the Institute will be inclined to take under consideration any means to make possible improvements, reasonably and without financial sacrifices.

Dr. Stockmann: Peter, do you imagine that I would ever agree to such trickery?

Peter Stockmann: Trickery?

Dr. Stockmann: Yes, a trick, a fraud, a lie! A treachery, a downright crime, against the public and against the whole community!

Peter Stockmann: I said before that I am not convinced that there is any actual danger.

Dr. Stockmann: Oh, you aren't? Anything else is impossible! My report is an absolute fact. The only trouble is that you and your administration were the ones who insisted that the water supply be built where it is, and now you're afraid to admit the blunder you committed. Damn it! Don't you think I can see through it all?

Peter Stockmann: All right, let's suppose that's true. Maybe I do care a little about my reputation. I will say I do it for the good of the town—without moral authority there can be no government. And that is why, Thomas, it is my duty to prevent your report from reaching the Board. Some time later I will bring up the matter for discussion. In the meantime, nor a single word is to reach the public.

Dr. Stockmann: Oh, my dear Peter, do you imagine you can prevent that!

Peter Stockmann: It will be prevented.

Dr. Stockmann: It can't be. There are too many people who already know about it.

Peter Stockmann, *angered:* Who? It can't possibly be those people from the *Daily Messenger* who—

Dr. Stockmann: Exactly. The liberal, free, and independent press will stand up and do its duty!

Peter Stockmann: You are an unbelievably irresponsible man, Thomas! Can't you imagine what consequences that is going to have for you?

Dr. Stockmann: For me?

Peter Stockmann: Yes, for you and your family.

Dr. Stockmann: What the hell are you saying now!

Peter Stockmann: I believe I have the right to think of myself as a helpful brother, Thomas.

Dr. Stockmann: You have been, and I thank you deeply for it.

Peter Stockmann: Don't mention it. I often couldn't help myself. I had hoped that by improving your finances I would be able to keep you from running completely hog wild.

Dr. Stockmann: You mean it was only for your own sake?

Peter Stockmann: Partly, yes. What do you imagine people think of an official whose closest relatives get themselves into trouble time and time again?

Dr. Stockmann: And that's what I have done?

Peter Stockmann: You do it without knowing it. You're like a man with an automatic brain— as soon as an idea breaks into your head, no matter how idiotic it may be, you get up like a sleepwalker and start writing a pamphlet about it.

Dr. Stockmann: Peter, don't you think it's a citizen's duty to share a new idea with the public?

Peter Stockmann: The public doesn't need new ideas— the public is much better off with old ideas.

Dr. Stockmann: You're not even embarrassed to say that?

Peter Stockmann: Now look, I'm going to lay this out once and for all. You're always barking about authority. If a man gives you an order he's persecuting you. Nothing is important enough to respect once you decide to revolt against your superiors. All right then, I give up. I'm not going to try to change you any more. I told you the stakes you are playing for here, and now I am going to give you an order. And I warn you, you had better obey it if you value your career.

Dr. Stockmann: What kind of an order?

Peter Srockmann: You are going to deny these rumors officially.

Dr. Stockmann: How?

Peter Stockmann: You simply say that you went into the examination of the water more thoroughly and you find that you overestimated the danger.

Dr. Stockmann: I see.

Peter Stockmann: And that you have complete confidence that whatever improvements are needed, management will certainly take care of them.

Dr. Stockmann, *after a pause:*   My convictions come from the condition of the water. My convictions will change when the water changes, and for no other reason.

Peter Stockmann: What are you talking about convictions? You're an official, you keep your convictions to yourself!

Dr. Stockmann: To myself?

Peter Stockmann: As an official, I said. God knows, as a private person that's something else, but as a subordinate employee of the Institute, you have no right to express any convictions or personal opinions about anything connected with policy.

Dr. Stockmann: Now you listen to me. I am a doctor and a scientist—

Peter Stockmann: This has nothing to do with science!

Dr. Stockmann: Peter, I have the right to express my opinion on anything in the world!

Peter Stockmann: Not about the Institute—that I forbid.

Dr. Stockmann: You forbid!

Peter Stockmann: I forbid you as your superior, and when I give orders you obey.

Dr. Stockmann: Peter, if you weren't my brother—

Petra, *throwing the door at the left open:*   Father! You aren't going to stand for this! *She enters.*

Mrs. Stockmann, *coming in after her:*   Petra, Petra!

Peter Stockmann: What have you two been doing, eavesdropping?

Mrs. Stockmann: You were talking so loud we couldn't help . . .

Petra: Yes, I was eavesdropping!

Peter Stockmann: That makes me very happy.

Dr. Stockmann, *approaching his brother:*   You said something to me about forbidding—

Peter Stockmann: You forced me to.

Dr Stockmann: So you want me to spit in my own face officially—is that it?

Peter Stockmann: Why must you always be so colorful?

Dr. Stockmann: And if I don't obey?

Peter Stockmann: Then we will publish our own statement, to calm the public.

Dr. Stockmann: Good enough! And I will write against you. I will stick to what I said, and I will prove that I am right and that you are wrong, and what will you do then?

Peter Stockmann: Then I simply won't be able to prevent your dismissal.

Dr. Stockmann: What!

Petra: Father!

Peter Stockmann: Dismissed from the Institute is what I said. If you want to make war on Kirsten Springs, you have no right to be on the Board of Directors.

Dr. Stockmann, *after a pause:* You'd dare to do that?

Peter Stockmann: Oh, no, you're the daring man.

Petra: Uncle, this is a rotten way to treat a man like Father!

Mrs. Stockmann: Will you be quiet, Petra!

Peter Stockmann: So young and you've got opinions already—but that's natural. *To Mrs. Stockmann:* Catherine dear, you're probably the only sane person in this house. Knock some sense into his head, will you? Make him realize what he's driving his whole family into.

Dr. Stockmann: My family concerns nobody but myself.

Peter Stockmann: His family and his own town.

Dr. Stockmann: I'm going to show you who loves his town. The people are going to get the full stink of this corruption, Peter, and then we will see who loves his town!

Peter Stockmann: You love your town when you blindly, spitefully, stubbornly go ahead trying to cut off our most important industry?

Dr. Stockmann: That source is poisoned, man. We are getting fat by peddling filth and corruption to innocent people!

Peter Stockmann: I think this has gone beyond opinions and convictions, Thomas. A man who can throw that kind of insinuation around is nothing but a traitor to society! . . .

Glossary

Altruism The promotion of the good of others; as a moral principle, to consider the consequences of action for everyone except oneself.

Aretaic Ethics The theory, first proposed by Aristotle, that the basis of ethical judgment is character; focuses on the character and dispositions of the moral agent rather than on actions and duties.

Categorical Imperative Commands actions that are necessary in themselves, without reference to other ends. In Kant's nonconsequentialism, moral duties represent the injunctions of reason that command actions categorically.

Civil Disobedience Nonviolent resistance to the law aimed at changing those laws deemed unjust.

Consequentialism Sometimes known as *teleological ethics;* the view that the correctness (rightness or wrongness) of moral conduct is judged in terms of its results (or consequences); *altruism, ethical egoism,* and *utilitarianism* are consequentialist ethical theories.

Cultural Relativism The descriptive thesis (sometimes known as "diversity thesis") that different cultures have different moral rules.

Divine Command Theory A theory holding that moral terms are defined in terms of God's commands or that moral duties are logically dependent on God's commands.

Ethical Absolutism The view that there is only one answer to every moral problem; a completely absolutist ethic is made up of absolute principles that provide an answer for every possible situation in life. It is diametrically opposed to *ethical relativism* and *ethical objectivism,* which hold that moral principles, while objective, may be overridden in certain situation.

Ethical Egoism A normative theory holding that we ought to act according to self-interest; our own success and happiness should be of primary and ultimate worth and all other values should flow from this.

Ethical Hedonism The theory that pleasure is the only intrinsic positive value and that pain is the only thing with negative intrinsic value; all other values are derived from these two.

Ethical Objectivism The view that moral principles have objective validity whether or not people recognize them as such; differs from ethical relativism and also ethical absolutism, in that moral principles may be overridden in certain situations.

Ethical Relativism The theory that the validity of moral judgments depends on subjective or cultural acceptance. It is opposed to *moral absolutism* and *moral objectivism.*

Ethical Skepticism The theory that we cannot know whether there is any moral truth.

Ethical Subjectivism The theory that moral values are expressions of human emotions, feelings, wishes, or desires, and that they have no objective referent in the world.

Ethics The systematic attempt to understand moral concepts and to justify moral principles and theories.

Ethnocentrism The belief of a group or a people that their ways (values, race, religion, language, culture) are superior to all others.

Feminist Ethics According to Hestor Eisenstein, a woman-centered analysis of morality that presupposes the centrality, normality, and value of women's experience and women's culture.

Formula of the End in Itself Kant's first expression of the Categorical Imperative as respect for persons: Act so that you treat humanity, whether in your own person or in that of another, always as an end and never as a means only.

Formula of Universal Law Kant's expression of the Categorical Imperative in *Fundamental Principles of the Metaphysics of Morals* (1785): Act only according to that maxim by which you can at the same time will that it should become a universal law.

Intellectualism The view that God's law is the expression of God's intellect, whose object is truth; therefore, the moral law is rational and the intellect superior to the will; opposed to *voluntarism.*

Metaethics A theoretical study that inquires into logical, semantic, and epistemological issues in ethics. Metaethics is contrasted with *normative ethics,* which constructs moral theories based on moral principles.

Morals Principles or rules of conduct that govern (or ought to govern) an individual or society.

Moral Skepticism The view that we cannot know whether there are valid moral principles.

Natural Law Theory The view, held by Saint Thomas Aquinas, that nature is a system of God's universal prescriptions for humankind; right and wrong can be determined by rational examination of nature and the consultation of conscience.

Nonconsequentialism Ethical theories, such as Kant's that deny the *consequentialist* claim that the intrinsic good and evil of consequences are the sole criteria of rightness and wrongness; sometimes called *deontological ethics.*

Psychological Egoism A descriptive theory about human motivation stating as fact that every person always acts to satisfy his or her self-interest.

Relativism See *cultural relativism* and *ethical relativism.*

Social Contract Theory The name given to a group of related and overlapping concepts and traditions in political theory and ethics that view the origin of collective society as based on an agreement; according to Thomas Hobbes, individuals agree to limit their autonomy in exchange for the peace and security that government provides. Without such an agreement, the precollective *state of nature* prevails.

State of Nature The condition of humanity without (or before) government. Hobbes portrays it as anarchy, with a continual war of all against all.

Utilitarianism A normative *consequentialist* ethical theory (originally espoused by Jeremy Bentham and John Stuart Mill) that holds right action to be that which maximizes utility, bringing about good consequences for all concerned--sometimes popularized as "the greatest good for the greatest number." *Act utilitarianism* holds that the right act in a given situation is that which results in the best consequences, whereas *rule utilitarianism* holds that the right act is that conforming to the set of rules that will in turn result in the best consequences.

Voluntarism The view that moral law is binding simply because it is God's will. (In the example of Abraham, if God asked Abraham to sacrifice his son, then the very request makes it right; there is no independent standard of judgment for morality outside of God's will.)